Experience without Qualities

Boredom and Modernity

Experience without Qualities

BOREDOM AND MODERNITY

Elizabeth S. Goodstein

Stanford University Press
Stanford, California
2005

Stanford University Press
Stanford, California
© 2005 by the Board of Trustees of the
Leland Stanford Junior University
Printed in the United States of America

Assistance for the publication of this work was
provided by Emory University

Library of Congress Cataloging-in-Publication Data

Goodstein, Elizabeth S.
  Experience without qualities : boredom and modernity / Elizabeth S.
Goodstein.
      p.   cm.
  Includes bibliographical references and index.
  ISBN 0-8047 5860-4 (paperback : alk. paper)
  1. Boredom.   I. Title.

bf575.b67g66   2005
128.4—dc22   2004010794

Original printing 2005

Last figure below indicates year of this printing:
    14   13   12   11   10   09   08   07   06   05

Designed and typeset at Stanford University Press in 10/13 Minion

In memory of

ARTHUR QUINN

rhetorician extraordinaire,

teacher,

friend

Acknowledgments

This book was first imagined more than a decade ago, in a café in Tübingen, on the way from Paris to Florence. Not, as this description might seem to imply, during a bored hour whiled away in the provinces but rather during the first of the many, many conversations that have accompanied this project from beginning to end. I am grateful to all of those whose interest and support have helped sustain me and my work through the intervening years—years not of boredom but of movement and transformation.

Thanks, first of all, to friends old and new whose love, encouragement, and solidarity have helped make it all possible: Misty Bastian, Purushottama Bilimoria, Jonathan Burt, Rajiv Chandra, Erik Doxtader, Eliza Garrison, Joshua Getz, Gabrielle Goodstein, Leslie Graham, Deana Guadagno, Volker Hagemann, Susan Katrin, Gerd Kimmerle, Ulla Konnertz, Christina Kopp-Oberstebrink, Herbert Kopp-Oberstebrink, Kim Loudermilk, Ron Malenbaum, Carla Mays, Judith Miller, Susanne Nabi, Margrit Nash, Melissa Ptacek, Rebecca Ratcliffe, Judy Rohrer, Ken Saint John, Rachel Saltz, Dirk Schumann, Sandra Simonson, Sheila Tefft, Pedro Vasquez, Katrin Volger-Schumann, Jochen Wagner. Special thanks to my parents, May and Bernard Goodstein, and to my brother Sam Goodstein for his steadfast faith in me.

I am indebted to the institutions that have generously provided material support without which the research and writing of this book would have been unthinkable: thanks to the Townsend Center and the Center for German and European Studies at the University of California at Berkeley, to King's College at Cambridge University, to Emory College and the Ford Foundation Crossing Borders/Vernacular Modernities Initiative at Emory University, and to the Alexander von Humboldt Foundation of the Federal Republic of Germany. Emory College and the Graduate School of Arts and Sciences at Emory University graciously helped offset printing costs.

Invitations from the Unofficial Knowledge Group at King's College, the Centre for Language and Cultural Theory at University of Southampton, the

Deutsches Haus at New York University, the Institut für Kulturwissen-schaften at the University of Leipzig, and the Vernacular Modernities Pro-gram at Emory provided occasions for important feedback at various phases of the project. Many thanks go to those who took "the boredom class" at Deep Springs College and the University of Rochester and to my students at Emory for asking the right questions. I am especially grateful to my col-leagues in the Graduate Institute of the Liberal Arts for making it such a con-genial environment for interdisciplinary work and to office manager Kendall Simpson for all his practical help.

Thanks, finally, to the colleagues who have been my teachers, readers, and mentors: to Martin Jay, who directed the dissertation that became the past life of this book, and to Wolf Lepenies, for his gracious reception of both author and critique; to Judith Butler, Marshall Duke, Charles Elder, Gerry Feldman, Tom Flynn, Gene Gendlin, Willfried Geßner, Felipe Gutterriez, Kimberley Healey, Jane Iwamura, Dieter Jähnig, Peter Jansen, Tony Kaes, Ivan Karp, Bruce Knauft, Klaus Köhnke, John Michael Krois, Cris Leven-duski, Valérie Loichot, Laurent Mayali, Patrick O'Connor, Robert Paul, Jean Pedersen, Walt Reed, Eric Santner, Elaine Tennant, Jeff Walker, Janet Wolff. I owe a singular debt of gratitude to David Tracy, whose intellectual gener-osity and warm encouragement of my fledging efforts as an undergraduate set me on the path that would eventually lead to *Experience without Qualities*; to Jay Bernstein, who understood what the boredom project was about be-fore I could say it clearly and whose thoughtful readings have done so much to make this book what it has become; to Patrice Petro, whose incisive re-sponse to the penultimate version of the text sharpened my sense of what still needed to be said; and to Arthur Quinn, whose faith in me helped make this work possible in the first place.

From our very first conversation, I knew that with Art I had found an in-tellectual home. With his rich wild mind and his rhetorician's gift for holding multiple perspectives in view at once, he listened in a way that showed me where to look. Patiently, vibrantly, Art helped me to think and rethink the story I was telling—and along the way taught me a great deal about teaching. It is a profound sorrow that he is not able to see the final product of all those hours of conversation. And so, with thanks for the wisdom, integrity, and humor that continue to help and sustain me in more ways than I can say, I dedicate this book to his memory.

Contents

In earlier times, one had an easier conscience about being a person than one does today. People were like stalks of grain; they were probably moved back and forth more violently by God, hail, fire, pestilence and war than today, but in their entirety, citywise or regionwise, as a field, and one could be responsible for the clearly delimited amount of personal movement that was left over for the individual stalk. Today, on the other hand, responsibility has its center of gravity not in people but in the connections among things. . . . A world of qualities without a man has arisen, of experiences without the person who experiences them, and it almost looks as though ideally a person won't experience anything at all privately and that the friendly gravity of personal responsibility is to dissolve into a system of formulas of possible meanings. Probably the dissolution of the anthropocentric point of view . . . has finally arrived at the "I" itself, for the belief that the most important thing about experience is that one experiences it or of action that one does it, is beginning to strike most people as naïve.

Robert Musil, *The Man without Qualities*

Introduction: The Rhetoric of Boredom

Experience

L'ennui . . . c'est la jouissance vue de rives du désire
Roland Barthes[1]

It is an experience without qualities, this quotidian crisis of meaning, an infuriating, demoralizing, despairing confrontation with . . . with "the boring"? But others are not bored. Only my desire, or its failure, is revealed: Boredom isolates, individuates, even as it blurs the world gray. A confrontation with nothing, then, or Nothing, or something like it. Perhaps just a name for what cannot be named, an encounter with the limits of language. An experience without qualities, with the deficits of the self masquerading as the poverty of the world. In boredom there is no distinguishing in here from out there, for the world in its failure to engage collapses into an extension of the bored subject who empties out in the vain search for an interest, a pleasure, a meaning. Self and world collapse in a nihilistic affirmation that nothing means, nothing pleases, nothing matters.

Boredom is first of all this tangle of word and experience: a subject in crisis, a vacuous world, interchangeable losses. Yet 'boredom' names a stalemate recognizable even by those lucky ones whose desires do not collapse into meaninglessness. In a time when the drives to novelty and innovation, speed and progress that have always defined modernity have become the foundation of a process of continuously accelerating transformation, boredom haunts the Western world. It appears as both cause and effect of this universal process—both as the disaffection with the old that drives the search for change and as the malaise produced by living under a permanent speedup. A symptom, then, of modernity, this experience without qualities, an ad-

---

[1]"Ennui . . . is ecstasy glimpsed from the banks of desire." *Le Plaisir du Texte*, 43. Unless otherwise noted, translations from French and German are my own.

aptation at once visceral and intellectual to life in a world where nothing stays put, to an era in which the idea of transcendent meaning seems hopelessly old-fashioned.

Boredom, psychoanalysis tells us, is a defense. A refusal to feel that protects a self threatened by its own fear or desire or need for what it seems to eschew. A means of stabilizing subjective existence without confronting the gaps between imagination and reality that render defense against feeling necessary. "Ecstasy glimpsed from the banks of desire" and simultaneously the "warm gray muffle lined with glowing silk" in which, according to Walter Benjamin, "we wrap ourselves when we dream."[2] Therapy, which aims to help the subject enter the river of desire or, in Benjamin's remarkable phrase, to turn out the lining of time, can make do with this definition of boredom as a subjective defense. Indeed, in any particular case of boredom, the diagnosis of affective resistance may be relevant. However, if we want to know not why so-and-so is bored or even what boredom does for people in general but why, to cite Benjamin again, "in the [eighteen-]forties boredom began to be felt on an epidemic scale" (165), a different model of interpretation is called for.

How did this experience without qualities infect entire populations? Benjamin is by no means alone in speaking of boredom as a disease afflicting modern subjects, and the "epidemic" has hardly abated since 1844, when Flaubert asked his friend Louis de Cormenin whether he knew "that modern boredom which gnaws at a man's entrails and makes of an intelligent being a walking shadow, a thinking phantom."[3] Surely the melange of pride and anxiety with which Flaubert represents this uncanny experience is an agency of transmission—for to admit that one does not suffer in this way, to write Flaubert that he is alone with his ennui, would doubtless be to turn oneself into the object of boredom. But can we really speak of a lineage that extends from the twenty-three year old budding novelist through figures such as Rimbaud, Breton, Hofmannsthal, and George to more contemporary avatars of cool such as James Dean, Lou Reed, Kurt Cobain? If boredom is a disease, then it is one in which contagion can be spread without direct contact—for the bored subject is generally found alone among unfeeling others (Emma in

---

[2] The locus classicus of the psychoanalytic approach is Otto Fenichel's 1934 "Zur Psychologie der Langeweile," which calls it "a state of instinctual tension with repressed aims" (271). Wanch expands on this idea in an essay that synthesizes the literature on "Boredom in Psychoanalytic Perspective"; Stern discusses therapeutic issues surrounding boredom from a more contemporary point of view. See Adam Phillips for an intriguing reading of boredom from an object relations perspective. Benjamin citations are from *Das Passagen-Werk*, 160.

[3] Letter of July 6 1844, *Correspondance* I, 208–9.

the provinces, Updike's suburbanites). And yet boredom is not simply a defense, a form of affective resistance, against such companions. As the dreamer's comforting muffle, ennui transmutes despair at the foreclosure of desire, at the experience of oneself as "thinking phantom," into a stable configuration of the self. The boredom that spreads throughout European society in the course of the nineteenth century is thus less a new feeling than a new way of feeling—or more precisely, a form of reflective distance that becomes a new attitude toward experience altogether.

If we may trust the Oxford English Dictionary, boredom was literally non-existent until the late eighteenth century—that is, it came into being as Enlightenment was giving way to Industrial Revolution. While its continental cousins "ennui" and "Langeweile" are older, they were not used synonymously, that is, in the modern sense that combines an existential and a temporal connotation, until about the same time. This linguistic convergence reflects experiential transformations that were transnational in nature, for modernization literally altered the quality of human being in time.[4] In the course of the nineteenth century, even as the temporal rhythms of everyday life were being revolutionized by technological and economic developments, a new, secular interpretation of human temporality was gaining ground. Faith in a coming redemption and in a divinely ordered eternity was increasingly being displaced by enlightened belief in human progress toward an earthly paradise; religious vocabularies of reflection on subjective existence were being eclipsed by a radically different language grounded in bodily materiality. The nineteenth-century discourse on boredom registers this epochal transformation in the rhetoric of reflection on human existence. In it, the impact of modernization on subjective experience was articulated, existential questions linked to a peculiarly modern experience of empty, meaningless time. As a discursively articulated phenomenon, then, boredom is at once objective and subjective, emotion and intellectualization—not just a response to the modern world but also an historically constituted strategy for coping with its discontents.

Boredom epitomizes the dilemma of the autonomous modern subject, for whom enlightenment has also meant fragmentation—for whom modernization and scientific progress have caused, in Max Weber's term, the "disenchantment" of the world such that history and religion can no longer anchor identity in the fabric of collective meaning. If rationality is the sus-

---

[4]Without asserting that the different words refer to a single experience (an implausible claim even within a single linguistic or national context), I shall therefore speak of 'the discourse on boredom' as a whole and will use the English term to refer to the phenomenon in general when the particular linguistic context is not essential.

taining myth of modernity, boredom, as an everyday experience of universalized skepticism, constitutes its existential reality. An heir to Enlightenment, the bored subject rejects the everyday world yet finds in it (negative)
metaphysical significance: the experience of boredom fosters a nihilistic dynamic that makes such disaffection seem a timeless feature of the human
condition. But the moment of critical distance that inheres in boredom as a
form of skepticism is undermined when it is universalized and naturalized in
this way. Lived as a pseudo-religious revelation of the ultimate meaninglessness of existence, such ennui obscures its own historical specificity as a
symptom of the particular losses that plague modern subjects. In thereby effacing the historicity of the crisis of meaning with which it is associated,
boredom exemplifies the deterioration of Enlightenment into mythology.

"Modern boredom" undeniably resembles, echoes, and resonates with
older forms of malaise—melancholy, acedia, *horror loci*, *taedium vitae*—
stretching back to antiquity. However, it can be identified with none of
them. The experience of malaise cannot simply be abstracted from the language in which it is expressed, for what appears as immediacy is in fact construction. Each of these forms of discontent is embedded in an historically
and culturally specific way of understanding and interpreting human experience—in what I call a *rhetoric of reflection*. Thus the language of melancholy
implies a deviance from the ideal of a homeostatic balance of humors in the
body, that of acedia a loss of spiritual connection to the divine. And the
boredom that is at once the bane of modern subjects and a homeopathic
strategy for stabilizing identity in a world of constant transformation instantiates a recognizably and specifically modern way of thinking about human
existence.

The experience without qualities is the plague of the enlightened subject,
whose skeptical distance from the certainties of faith, tradition, sensation
renders the immediacy of quotidian meaning hollow or inaccessible. If boredom gains sway over the language in which the human aspiration to meaning
is formulated—and thus appears "epidemic"—in modernity, then because
the rhetoric of reflection that gives rise to this negative configuration of self
and world has been naturalized. It is in the terms of this rhetoric, in relation
to a vision of human being as embodied, mortal, and defined by individual
rational autonomy, that so much that is historically and culturally specific in
modernity comes to be experienced as though it were proper to human existence as such.

The point, then, is not simply that boredom is an historically specific experience. Its pervasiveness in modern Western society has a larger significance, for it is the index of an historic paradigm shift in the rhetoric of re-

flection on subjective experience since the Enlightenment. While traditional vocabularies of reflection rendered subjective malaise meaningful by situating it in relation to religious or cultural metanarratives about human being, the language of boredom is secular, materialist, and resigned to the loss of meaning. The apparent reflective stability of the bored subject inheres in this resignation. But perhaps this stability is an illusion rather more like Vladmir's waiting for Godot, simultaneously "bored to death" and terrified lest the impoverished world suddenly vanish and leave him "alone once more, in the midst of nothingness!"[5] Stranded thus on the banks of desire, resigned to the loss of meaning and fearing worse, the modern subject brandishes boredom like an article of faith.

How, then, to interpret an experience through which the very possibility of meaning comes into question, in which the loneliness of the godforsaken subject is expressed as fate? To grasp the significance of boredom, I shall argue, it is necessary to think the relation between boredom as an experience of subjective crisis and boredom as an empirically conditioned social phenomenon. On one hand, to explicate the nihilistic dynamic of the experience not ontologically but historically, and on the other, to grasp its pervasiveness not sociologically but philosophically. It is necessary, in a word, to attend to the rhetoric of reflection, to the way of thinking about subjective experience boredom exemplifies. Even in its most quotidian manifestations, I contend, boredom embodies a specifically modern crisis of meaning. Developing a conception of the experience that reflects its historicity can therefore illuminate the human significance of the modernization process—and reveal how the dilemmas of modern subjectivity are imbricated with the vast cultural transformations of the West during the past two hundred years.

Historically speaking, it is the widespread assumption that boredom is a universal feature of the human condition that bears explanation, for in it, time is lived in a fashion proper to the modern world. On one hand, boredom is made possible by a form of human existence keyed to the precision of what Georg Simmel called the "supersubjective temporal schema" of clock time. And on the other, it depends on the modern conception of history as progress—it is internally linked to the ideal of human life itself as a process of incessant change and improvement. In boredom, both of these ways of experiencing time appear problematic—and interconnected. The moment lived as meaningless eternity undermines faith in the optimistic trajectory of the historical whole just as boredom with history—or with one's own life— as a series of senseless repetitions causes each moment to appear as a mean-

---

[5] Samuel Beckett, 52.

ingless eternity. As Charles Baudelaire described this nihilistic dynamic, by which boredom fosters the lived conviction that it is an ahistorical feature of the human condition: "Under the heavy flakes of snowy years / Ennui, the fruit of dismal incuriosity, / Takes on the proportions of immortality."[6]

My seemingly paradoxical claim, then, is that it is precisely *as an experience of modernity* that boredom appears timeless, the existential crisis associated with it universal.[7] While some people surely have always had moments of despairing conviction that the universe is darkly meaningless, the boredom that we know as occasioning such a sense of futility cannot simply be identified as a universal feature of the human condition. It is not only that as a post-Enlightenment entry into the vocabulary of subjective experience, modern boredom differs from its precursors in significant ways. To call an experience "modern" is to make philosophical as well as historical claims. In this case, it is to assert both that the relation between self and world found in boredom occurs in modernity and that it is an experience *of* modernity, a mode in which the historical particularity of the perception and the perceiving subject is revealed.[8]

However, boredom is an experience of modernity, of modern temporality, in which the conditions of possibility of experience become the conditions of its disappearance. The nihilistic dynamic through which boredom is lived as a timeless feature of the human condition expresses the paradoxical-

[6]"Rien n'égale en longueur les boiteuses journées / Quand sous les lourds flocons des neigeuses années / L'ennui, fruit de la morne incuriosité, / Prend les proportions de l'immortalité."

[7]While in this study I shall not attempt to extend my historical claims for boredom to colonial or post-colonial contexts, antecdotal evidence indicates that the structures of experience with which I am concerned appear at the "periphery" as well as the "center" of the modernization process. Thus my focus on the European origin of the discourse on boredom should not be read as imputing an "occidental" character to the experience itself. Indeed, on my understanding, insofar as boredom is a function of a modernized temporality, the shift from traditional to mechanical time (as integrated, of course, in the processes of industrialization and in the associated rationalization of everyday life) will itself tend to produce boredom as a symptom of "modern subjectivity." And since modernization in the colonial or post-colonial context is always also a process of discursive occupation and resignification of subjective experience, insofar as the agent of modernization speaks the language of boredom, we can expect very similar configurations of self-understanding to arise in colonial and post-colonial contexts. On the role of melancholy and boredom in nineteenth-century *colonizer* discourse, see Nina Berman, *Orientalismus, Kolonialismus und Moderne : zum Bild des Orients in der deutschsprachigen Kultur um 1900*.

[8]I am not claiming, of course, that the person who is bored *recognizes* the historicity of his or her experience. While one might propose, in a neo-Hegelian fashion, that the experience of boredom is in the fullest sense an experience of modernity only for those who know it as such, the absence of a reflective recognition *that* the experience is historically specific does not constitute counter-evidence for my more limited contention. The demonstration that boredom is a modern experience in both senses—historically limited to modernity and expressive of the modernity of the person experiencing it—depends on other sorts of evidence.

ity of the modern conception of temporality. The methodological challenge in theorizing boredom is, then, how to grasp the historical particularity of a mode of experience that effaces its own historicity. Before discussing the strategy through which I propose to overcome the reflective impasse that characterizes the experience without qualities, it will be helpful to pause to reflect more broadly upon the modernity boredom exemplifies.

In recent years, the assumptions embedded in the concept of modernity have come to seem increasingly problematic. The notion that Western standards and experiences ought to provide a model for the rest of the world is no longer taken for granted. Historians, anthropologists, and cultural theorists of all stripes have emphasized the significance of local and national differences in the construction of the modern in different contexts, even within the so-called developed world. Nonetheless, discussions of modernity and modernization still tend to focus on historical transformations that are the stuff of metanarratives. On secularization, the separation of spheres, the rise of industrial production, on the emergence of nation-states and of the political institutions of representative citizenship that correspond to them. What Jean-François Lyotard famously dubbed the "obsolescence of the meta-narrative apparatus of legitimation"[9] notwithstanding, such categories and the theoretical suppositions embedded in them continue to shape a great deal of what goes on in the social sciences. Indeed, in the very globalized world that seems, to many, to exemplify this "post-modern" circumstance, such assumptions—most notably the notion that there are intrinsic relations between political and economic modernization—continue to have very real effects.

All of this attests to the enduring importance of teleological narratives that are bound up, seemingly inseparably, with the topoi of modernity and modernization. The ubiquity of these topoi both reflects and reinforces a way of thinking about history and human identity that has proved remarkably resilient since the Enlightenment. Indeed, the power of this paradigm is such that doubts about whether the technological, scientific, and social transformations associated with modernization constitute "progress" do not necessarily call the conceptual framework into question. Much of the most exciting work done in cultural and social history in the past generation has been directed toward opening up these categories—emphasizing the limits of secularization, rationalization, and democratization to rewrite the story of modernity in more ambiguous terms. But to underline the importance of the modern forms of consumption that emerged alongside modern forms of

[9] Lyotard 1984, xxiv.

production or to call attention to the ways in which the historical evolution toward modern democratic nation-states is linked to a politics of the spectacle is not, in itself, to transcend the historical paradigm inherited from the Enlightenment.

There is, however, another sense of "modernity"—the modernity not of politics but of art, not of the historical epoch but of subjective experience. In this sense Charles Baudelaire, who is often, too generously, credited with coining the term "modernité,"[10] declared: "Almost all our originality comes from the stamp which *time* imprints on our impressions."[11] Modernity, he wrote, is "the ephemeral [*transitoire*], the fugitive, the contingent, the half of art whose other half is the eternal and immutable" (695/12). To posit the interest of modernity in this sense is quite a different matter from endorsing an evolutionary view of history since, as Baudelaire has it, "every old master has had his own modernity" (695/12). Here what is at stake in "modernity" is the historical particularity of aesthetic forms and of the modes of perception that correspond to them. It is manifest historically not in a progression but rather in a succession of different forms of art and life that embody the striving after the ever-new.

Of course, the idea that human existence is defined by such a striving for novelty is itself, historically speaking, a modern notion. The emphasis on the individual, the particular, the unique that for Baudelaire was the quintessence of modern art, is nearly as modern, historically speaking, as the Enlightenment stress on rationality. His modernité resonates with the historicist notion that human cultural existence consists of a succession of fundamentally different constellations—a conception that has its origins in romanticism. In Baudelaire's case, this romantic idea does not lead, as for Herder or Hegel, to an evolutionary model of history. Instead, it is bound to a peculiarly modernist anti-historicism that elevates beauty over truth, feeling over reason, experience over abstract knowledge. If rationality is the measure of modernity in the socio-political sense, here it is aesthetic judgment.

What is at stake in the embrace of modernity not as idea but as experi-

---

[10]In fact the source seems to be Chateaubriand's *Memoires*. See Jauss, "Literarische Tradition und gegenwärtiges Bewußtsein der Modernität" in *Literaturgeschichte als Provokation.*

[11]"Le Peintre de la vie moderne," was first published in Figaro in 1863. It is reproduced in Charles Baudelaire, *Œuvres completes* [OC] II, 683–724. English in *The Painter of Modern Life and Other Essays*, 1–41. The remark cited is on 696 in the French and 14 in the English text. Subsequent parenthetical citations give the French and then the English page numbers; I follow Mayne with modifications.

ence—what is at stake in aesthetic modernism—is by no means simply originality and novelty. It is the ability to give form to the new: to turn the transience of lived experience into the permanence of artistic form. If the first sense of modernity has its origins in Enlightenment ideas about science, the genealogy of the second may be traced to the seventeenth century *querelle des anciens et modernes*. Thus Baudelaire rejects the practice of imposing a "despotic form of perfection borrowed from the repertory of classical ideas" (696/14) upon the subjects to be represented and declares that "for any 'modernity' to be worthy of becoming 'antiquity,' it is necessary for the mysterious beauty which human life accidentally puts into it to be distilled from it" (695/13). The modern artist "makes it his business to extract [*dégager*] from fashion whatever element it may contain of poetry within history, to distil the eternal from the transitory" (694/12).[12] Baudelaire is on the side of the moderns, but what is at stake for him is the very thing that led Aristotle to assert (*Poetics* 9, 1451b) that poetry is "more philosophical" than history—the fact that it speaks of things in general rather than as particulars, that art is concerned with the universal and the timeless rather than with the flux of socio-cultural and historical life.

According to Walter Benjamin, Baudelaire "experienced the old claim [*Anspruch*] to immortality as his entitlement [*Anspruch*] one day to be read as an ancient author."[13] As Benjamin stresses, this wish came true with astonishing rapidity, for the world changed so quickly that "the distant future, the *époches lointaines*" of which the poet wrote arrived only a few decades after his death. Writing in the nineteen-thirties, Benjamin reflected: "Indeed Paris still stands; and the great tendencies of social development are still the same. But the more they have remained stable, the more fragile everything became that had stood under the sign of the 'truly new' in the experience of them. The modern has not in the least remained the same; and the ancient that is supposed to be contained in it yields in reality the image of the antiquated" (89). Benjamin's great, unfinished attempt to excavate the interior history of modernity in the *Passagen-Werk* has taught us much about this historical dynamic, by which the sociocultural dimension of modernity continuously destroys, undermines, and leaves behind the very novelty of experience and ipso facto of artistic creation that it calls forth. In a world dominated by modernity in the first sense, there can be no antiquity, but only ob-

---

[12]Or, more literally: "extract [*dégager*] from fashion whatever element it may contain of the poetic within the historical, to distil the eternal from the transitory" (694/12).

[13]*Charles Baudelaire: Ein Lyriker im Zeitalter des Hochkapitalismus*, 80.

solescence. On this view, what makes Baudelaire a modern classic is his success at grasping this transformation of the momentary into the outmoded as a permanent feature of modern life.

In 1905, less than forty years after Baudelaire's death, a thinker whose influence on Benjamin should not be underestimated, Georg Simmel, linked the increasing importance of fashion in contemporary culture both to "the specifically 'impatient' tempo of modern life" and to the fact that "the great, lasting, unquestioned convictions are more and more losing their force."[14] Modern experience is conditioned by the continuous destruction of the historical, cultural, spiritual and aesthetic contexts that give human life meaning—by what Benjamin called the eclipse of *Erfahrung* in favor of punctual *Erlebnisse*. In modernity, experience is defined, so to speak, by its own disappearance. As a consequence, in the words of Robert Musil, "A world of qualities without a man has arisen, of experiences without the person who experiences them. . . . Probably the dissolution of the anthropocentric point of view . . . has finally arrived at the "I" itself, for the belief that the most important thing about experience is that one experiences it or of action that one does it, is beginning to strike most people as naïve."[15]

In boredom, the disappearance of experience is manifested in precisely such alienation from one's own doing and being: it is a quotidian crisis of subjectivity. By attending to both the socio-historical and the linguistic construction of this experience without qualities, I bring social scientific perspectives on the constitution of subjective experience into conversation with aesthetic and cultural understandings of what makes subjective experience modern. The object is to mediate between humanistic and social scientific rhetorics in a fashion that neither reduces questions of meaning to sociological epiphenomena nor treats them in abstraction from the historical and material contexts in which they arise. My strategy for articulating these modes of interpretation is contained, in a nutshell, in the claim that the experience without qualities is a symptom of the *democratization of skepticism in modernity*. This formulation points to dimensions of modern experience that neither Weber's 'disenchantment of the world' nor Nietzsche's 'nihilism' capture: 'democratization' for the positive or at least potentially positive dimension of the loss of epistemic and cultural frameworks in modernity and 'skepticism' for the incomplete way in which religious and other metanarratives have actually been overcome.

Although the questions of meaning associated with boredom are not new,

---

[14]*Georg Simmel Gesamtausgabe* [GSG], vol. 14, 197–98.
[15]*Gesammelte Werke*, vol. I, 150.

I argue that the pervasiveness of the experience beginning in the nineteenth century is an index of the way traditional understandings of the significance of human existence had been undermined—an index of the democratization of skepticism in the broadest sense. On my reading, it is the way the language of boredom figures a relationship between subjective malaise and the materially palpable transformations of modern culture that led to its extremely rapid diffusion in the course of the nineteenth century. By turning the material effects of modernization into ciphers for the problem of meaning, the experience became a lived metaphor for the dilemmas that plague modern subjects. In other words, that in the mid-nineteenth century boredom "began to be felt on an epidemic scale" is a consequence of the diffusion of a new metaphorics, a new, skeptical idiom of reflection on subjective experience. Historically speaking, the ubiquity of such boredom is thus a sign of how deep and widespread epistemological and ethical problems remain in the purportedly rationalized and secularized landscape of modernity.

As I have already argued, this experience of subjective malaise—or more precisely, this way of talking about subjective malaise—embodies a specifically modern rhetoric of reflection on subjective experience. The difficulties in grasping boredom as an historically specific experience are grounded in structural features of that historically evolving rhetoric—features that, as I shall show in the next section, also map onto the disciplinary division of "modernity" into aesthetic and socio-political dimensions.

Discourse

Sans la faim des choses spirituelles on s'en ennuie . . .
Pascal[16]

From its beginnings in the Enlightenment, the modern discourse on boredom reflected a wide range of understandings of the experience, many of which still persist. Depending on the context, boredom is held to be merely subjective or to be a response to an objective reality; considered a spontaneous feeling or a cultivated mental attitude; diagnosed as a nervous illness or explained as an emotional response to the world; treated as ethical problem or dismissed as a physiological reflex. As this sampling of possible interpretations indicates, the discourse on boredom is deeply imbricated with fundamental questions regarding the nature of subjectivity. But how is this fact to be understood? Certainly the discourse on boredom has been shaped by the secular modern rhetoric of reflection on subjective experience.

[16]"Without the hunger for spiritual things one is bored" (*Pensées*, 378).

Conversely, however, the ambiguity of the experience itself, in which now self, now world seems decisive, seemingly destined 'boredom' to play a pivotal role in shaping that rhetoric.

While boredom appears to be a private experience of primarily subjective significance, its very pervasiveness marks it as a socially meaningful phenomenon. When boredom is approached from distinct, disciplinarily located perspectives, it tends to be defined in ways that divide along the lines of this ambiguity—roughly speaking into philosophical and sociological accounts of the experience. The scholarly discourse on boredom thus maps onto an existing division of labor within intellectual endeavor: matters of the heart and mind to the humanists, material conditions to the (social) scientists. Not only, qua experience, does boredom transcend such a division; as it was constituted historically, the language of boredom figured the effects of the material transformations taking place in the modern world on subjective experience. Examining how and why that discourse developed as it did in the course of the nineteenth century can therefore illuminate what is at stake in the contemporary bifurcation of reflection into abstractly philosophical and reductively sociological accounts of subjective experience.

As Nietzsche remarked, only that can be defined which has no history. Thus a universal definition of boredom could only be achieved at the cost of abstracting this highly ambiguous and eminently historical phenomenon from the very experiential context that gives the question of its meaning such significance. What is called for is, rather, a genealogy of the experience, an account that aims to discern in the vicissitudes of the discourse on boredom the traces of modernity's impact on subjective experience. By analyzing that discourse and interpreting the significance of its historical evolution, this study aims to elucidate the role "boredom" came to play within the wider discourse on the subjective effects of modernization. Rather than abstracting the experience from its historical context, this approach encompasses the real ambiguities and contradictions that characterize the discourse on boredom in a way that has methodological implications for the human sciences in general, since genuinely historical inquiry into the constitution of modern subjectivity needs to be grounded in the sociological and philosophical complexities of particular cultural phenomena.

As we have already noted, boredom is a peculiarly self-sufficient form of malaise, a misery in which existential despair is entirely compatible with subjective self-satisfaction. Rather than treating the nihilistic dynamic of the experience either as a metaphysical sign or as a sociological symptom, my genealogical approach to the discourse on the experience thus foregrounds the relations between the ambiguity of boredom and the organization of the categorial divisions that characterize the discourse surrounding it. Unlike its foes and advocates in either analytical camp, I am not concerned to demonstrate the importance of boredom per se. Its interest, on my reading, lies in what the discourse on boredom reveals about the way the language of reflection on subjective experience has changed over time. My argument therefore focuses on the historical vicissitudes of the experience—on the way the evolution of the discourse on boredom maps onto structural transformations in the post-Enlightenment discourse of reflection on subjective experience as such. Insofar as the genealogy of boredom illuminates the fundamental features of that modern rhetoric of experience, this study provides a model for experientially grounded, historical inquiry into the discursive constitution of modern subjectivity. Of particular interest is the way the historical development of the discourse on boredom illustrates the relations between subjective crisis and the paradigm shift toward the material explanation of malaise in modernity—relations to which the pervasiveness of the discourse on boredom itself attests.

Such an inquiry into the cultural significance of boredom is inherently inter- and indeed metadisciplinary. Interdisciplinary, because it integrates the seemingly incompatible results of previous studies, which have interpreted the experience from within particular hermeneutic horizons. Metadisciplinary, or to invoke a more old-fashioned idiom, *rhetorical*, because conceptualizing boredom as an historical phenomenon entails reflecting on the relationship between language and experience revealed by the historical development of the discourse. From this broader perspective, the emergence and evolution of that discourse as well as the contradictions and ambiguities within it prove to be symptomatic of more global transformations within the Western rhetoric of reflection on subjective experience in modernity, transformations that have also given rise to our familiar disciplinary divisions. To put the point more concretely: demonstrating that the language of boredom was forged in order to articulate the material and subjective effects of modernization does more than prove that boredom is of both socio-cultural and philosophical interest. It also indicates that the aporia encountered in reflection upon the significance of boredom—the interpretive impasse evident in the disciplinary bifurcation of such reflection—is of historical and philosophical importance. In tracing the development of the discourse on boredom through which that aporia came into being, therefore, my hope is not simply to illustrate the importance of attention to language in examining the historical and cultural construction of subjective experience. By simultaneously providing an interpretation of the significance of that development, I also aim to set out a method of rhetorical analysis that integrates empirical material and philosophical reflection in a truly interdisciplinary fashion.

Part I, "The Rhetoric of Experience," proceeds immanently from discussions of particular, disciplinarily located interpretations of subjective malaise to articulate general features of the discourse on boredom. I argue that it is as a distinctively modern form of malaise that boredom is so deeply ambiguous and show that the questions it raises concerning subjectivity must be analyzed historically. By closely examining the arguments of paradigmatic proponents of the philosophical and empirical approaches to the experience that dominate the secondary literature on boredom, Chapters 1 and 2 demonstrate that neither mode of conceptualizing boredom can achieve the requisite methodological distance to do so. On the one hand, the philosophical rhetoric of experience, which emphasizes the epistemic and ethical implications of the experience of boredom for the sufferer, universalizes the existential dilemmas of the isolated individual subject and abstracts them from their socio-cultural and historical context. On the other, the social scientific rhetoric of experience, which focuses on what boredom reveals about the effects of cultural and historical circumstances upon human beings, treats the subjective and philosophical significance of the experience as epiphenomenal. That is, both branches of the contemporary discourse of reflection on the experience treat the connection between concrete historical circumstances and the philosophical problems associated with boredom as accidental. This methodological convergence attests to the grounding of these diametrically opposed hermeneutics in a common modern rhetoric of reflection on subjective experience.

Within the discourse of reflection on boredom as a whole, then, the dichotomy between materialist and idealist rhetorics anchors complementary, equally ahistorical modes of interpreting a form of malaise that is pervasive only in modernity. Or to put the same point from a different angle: the modern rhetoric of reflection in which the discourse on boredom as a whole is grounded is characterized by an ahistorical understanding of subjective experience. Philosophical and social scientific approaches are constitutive elements of the modern discourse on subjective malaise. Insofar as both abstract boredom from its discursive context, neither can give an adequate account of the rhetoric of reflection on subjective experience in which both explanatory paradigms are embedded—an analysis that would be necessary to develop a conception of boredom that did justice to the mediating character of the experience itself.

Like the apparently ahistorical character of boredom, this failure of historical self-reflection is of great historical interest, for the development of the discourse on boredom illustrates a logical dilemma at the heart of the modern rhetoric of reflection on subjective experience. Taken together, Chapters 1 and 2 show that within the terms of that rhetoric, it is not possible to develop an historically grounded, self-reflexive concept of the experience, since both materialist and idealist approaches to boredom sunder problems of meaning from their historical context. The genealogical endeavor must therefore address the constraints on moving beyond this bifurcation in the rhetoric of reflection.

To do justice to the historical specificity of the experience, I argue, it is necessary to synthesize the strengths of both philosophical and empirical approaches. Literary texts therefore play a crucial role, for in representing boredom, they depict its sociological and philosophical significance as intertwined. Indeed, as Chapter 3 demonstrates, it was literary language that first identified boredom as a specifically modern malaise, as an experience that linked material circumstances and questions of meaning. If the experience that comes to language in boredom is, historically speaking, the consequence of the social transformations we think of as constituting "modernity"—rationalization, secularization, industrialization, urbanization—the language in which that experience takes place is in the first instance a literary language.

This language, this discourse, this metaphorics, figures historically specific experiences of subjective malaise and dislocation in universal, timeless terms—but in a disenchanted and irreligious idiom. Thus what is a very modern discourse on subjective experience, one rooted in a peculiarly modern experience of temporality, tended, and tends, to obscure the historical specificity of that malaise by making it seem universal. Chapter 3 demonstrates that what is at stake in focusing on boredom is the question of the status of the language in which reflection on subjective malaise takes place in modernity. My claim is that the evolution of the discourse on boredom both mirrors and illuminates the transformation—the modernization—of the rhetoric of reflection on subjective experience since the Enlightenment. Examining the linguistic and cultural vicissitudes of the metaphorics of boredom can therefore cast light on the relations between what are often thought of as opposed understandings of modernity and modern life.

The same sociological conditions that helped diffuse the language of boredom throughout society in the course of the nineteenth century also encouraged the development of a disenchanted, materialist and ultimately a medicalized vision of subjective malaise. Ironically, literary 'boredom' (like its cousins, 'ennui' and 'Langeweile') came to seem hackneyed, less an experience that revealed something about modern subjectivity than a fashionable stance for those who wished neither to engage with material reality nor to confront philosophical questions seriously. As a consequence, even as the experience of boredom grew ubiquitous, the metaphorics of boredom lost the power of figuring the relation between questions of meaning and the material effects of modernization. Notably, by the early twentieth century, the topos itself was giving way to a preoccupation with the evacuation of the language of reflection on subjective experience altogether in the modern world. Since this capacity for mediation is what makes boredom a key site for reflection on the relations between the two senses of modernity, the fact that the evolution of the discourse on boredom undermines the power of this language to figure reflection on the full complexity of modern experience is highly significant.

The resulting bifurcation within the rhetoric of reflection on boredom has more than a local or incidental significance, for it reflects the aporetic relation between scientific and humanistic modes of self-understanding that is a fundamental feature of modern thought. Indeed, it is noteworthy that the discourse on boredom should have undergone this development at all, since its original power stemmed from its ability to mediate between the registers kept separate by such disciplinary divisions. Pointing on the one hand toward traditional religious vocabularies of reflection and on the other toward physiological accounts of human experience, the language of boredom was secularized without being mechanistic. The discourse on boredom initially articulated a relationship between the questions of meaning associated with the experience and the social transformations which were underway in the period. However, the pressures that led to the larger split in the rhetoric of reflection on subjective experience soon fractured the rhetoric of boredom as well, so that it no longer seemed to be a single sort of experience which articulated the spiritual and material effects of modernization.

As a materialist interpretation of human existence took root in the course of the nineteenth century, the discourse on boredom fragmented. While empirical—sociological, physiological, psychological—interpretations traced the phenomenon back to the effects of modernization and urbanization on the human organism, interest in the experience of meaninglessness associated with boredom fell to older models of explanation—philosophical, moral, religious accounts of human malaise. If today these modes appear complementary—modernity and tradition, materialism and idealism paradigmatic poles of the modern rhetoric of reflection on subjective experience—then perhaps because we have begun to move beyond the discourse which, in opposing positivist science to substantive tradition, shaped the crisis of modern subjectivity that culminated in the previous fin-de-siècle. However, precisely in the absence of plausible metanarratives, the task of grasping the problems of meaning associated with boredom in their historical specificity remains. In defining the experience to suit their models, humanists and scientists alike disregard how the *experience* of boredom mediates subjective and objective, ideal and material. If its lived ambiguity renders boredom a paradigmatically modern experience, the persisting fragmentation of the discourse of reflection on subjective experience obscures boredom's historicity.

In Part I, I argue that to theorize boredom adequately, it is necessary to develop a strategy for historical reflection on the modern rhetoric of reflection as a whole. Chapters 1 and 2 show that the limits of the opposed approaches that dominate the scholarly literature on boredom are anchored in complementary rhetorics of experience, each of which makes it impossible to grasp the experience in an historically adequate fashion. Chapter 3 looks closely at the historical development of the discourse on boredom as a paradigmatically modern experience and thereby illustrates how problems of meaning and the response to concrete historical circumstances were intertwined in that nineteenth-century discourse. Shifting the emphasis from experience to discourse, from the literality to the metaphorics of boredom, makes it possible to interpret the significance of the evolution of the language of reflection on subjective malaise—and ipso facto the modern experience of temporality and desire—in this period. The bifurcated rhetoric of experience reflected in the approaches to boredom considered in the first two chapters is itself the product of a particular historical development.

Having established this historical perspective on the modern rhetoric of reflection on subjective experience, in Part II, "The Rhetoric of Reflection," I take up two more sophisticated attempts to conceptualize boredom. Neither Georg Simmel (Chapter 4) nor Martin Heidegger (Chapter 5) can be accused of disregarding the historicity of subjective experience. Nonetheless, the difficulties encountered in Chapters 1 and 2 return: as a consequence of the historical development of the discourse on boredom, the sociological and philosophical modes of reflection seem virtually to concern different experiences. Only from the genealogical perspective that recognizes the discourse in which both are embedded as the common ground of interpretation do Simmel's 'Blasiertheit' and Heidegger's 'Langeweile' converge. Seen in this light, I argue, their very different phenomenologies of subjective malaise in modernity underline the need to focus on the language in which that malaise is formulated—language that is itself shot through with historical particularity. The sixth and final chapter then reads Robert Musil's *Man without*

Qualities as an attempt to forge a new language of reflection on subjective experience that could heal the aporetic division between materialist and idealist rhetorics of experience and thereby overcome the evacuation of the language of reflection on subjective experience in modernity that is registered in the historical vicissitudes of the discourse on boredom. Before turning to this chapter-by-chapter investigation of the rhetoric of the discourse on boredom, however, it will be helpful to consider the historiographical implications of placing the experience without qualities at the center of an investigation of modernity—of interpreting modernity as a process that democratizes skepticism.

History

> Since boredom advances and boredom is the root of all evil, no wonder, then, that the world goes backwards, that evil spreads.
>
> Søren Kierkegaard[17]

Boredom, which arose in the age of Enlightenment and was democratized in the period of industrial revolution, is a disenchanted, secularized form of human discontent. Its pervasiveness is an index of the decline of traditional understandings of temporality and desire and in particular of religious understandings of human suffering. However, since this radically individualizing experience is lived as though it pertains to the self alone, the bored subject, for whom the experience of empty, meaningless time "takes on the proportions of immortality" cannot perceive that this experience is peculiar to modernity. The historicity of boredom is visible only from a position outside the nihilistic dynamic of the experience—a position that permits reflection on the discursive regime in which this peculiar experience came to be. We have noted that the discourse on boredom links questions of meaning to material effects of modernization. But how, exactly, were the ethical and philosophical effects associated with the experience related to the socio-historical context in which it began to flourish?

As a form of subjective malaise proper to modernity,[18] boredom is first of all an urban phenomenon. Contemporary proclamations about the idiocy of

---

[17]*Either/Or I*, 259.

[18]I will not be able to demonstrate this thesis fully until Chapter 3, when I turn explicitly to the discursive formation of the experience; my concern here is simply to provide the reader with a sense of the relationship between modern boredom and its historical circumstances that can render my position plausible. Having established this pre-understanding of the experience, in Chapter 1 I shall examine an alternative interpretation of boredom as a timeless phenomenon which simply has become more prevalent in modernity, in detail.

rural life notwithstanding, boredom with provincial existence is a secondary phenomenon: Madame Bovary's heart belonged to Paris. The experience emerged not out of surfeit with the rhythmic repetitions of life in pre-industrialized society but in response to the superabundance of stimulation, the superfluity of possibilities for personal achievement, the sheer excess of transformation, offered by the modern city. Insofar as boredom is an experience of temporality, it is worth noting that, at least for the working class, it was in the metropolis that the rational order of clock and calendar first eclipsed the natural rhythms of sun and season.

In the nineteenth-century metropolis, everything that had seemed the stable stuff of personal identity was up for grabs. Urbanization was driven by industrialization, both of which fostered new social formations and un-moored people from the strictures of traditional society. Urban anonymity brought both freedoms and terrors. The industrial reorganization of labor produced new forms of leisure and new "occupations" to fill these free hours; crowds flooded the streets and filled cafés, parks, and popular theaters in the evenings and on Sundays. As consumer society and its culture of mass entertainments took form, a newly heterogeneous public began to emerge. Shop-assistants and clerks, domestics and factory-workers, often isolated émigrés whose families were still in the countryside, shared public spaces with aristocrats, well-established bourgeois, and the members of a growing new industrial middle class. However, physical proximity and even shared diversions were by no means equivalent to democratization.[19] Political up-heavals proliferated, particularly on the continent, and what was perceived (particularly but by no means exclusively by the ruling classes) as a discon-certing breakdown of traditional social structures, especially of class- and gender-based behavioral norms, seemed to intensify as the century pro-gressed.

The same dissolution of long-established certitudes was evident in the spiritual realm as well. While nineteenth-century Europeans could by no means be called irreligious, the Christian worldview had begun to forfeit its hegemony. The publication of *The Origin of Species* in 1859 was just one in a series of powerful scientific affronts to traditional ways of thinking about human existence. Even as modern technological and especially medical ad-vances improved the safety and increased the comfort of everyday life, the

---

[19]See Siegfried Kracauer's intriguing 1926 attempt to revive Kant's notion that the public is the bearer of enlightenment by articulating the critical potential of the notion of an "homogenous cosmopolitan public" for theorizing contemporary visual culture in his "Kult der Zerstreuung" (Cult of Distraction).

social and religious narratives that had once situated individual existence in relation to larger wholes seemed to fall away. The rise of industrial capitalism exacerbated this process both by undermining the concrete social formations through which those narratives had been supported and perpetuated and by promoting the triumph of utilitarianism and mercantile values—in Max Weber's language, the rationalization process promoted formal over substantive traditional standards. While modernization may not be simply equated with secularization, nineteenth-century European life displayed an undeniable trend to replace the spiritual with the material, the qualitative with the quantitative.

From the outset, the discourse on boredom had comprised both idealist and materialist interpretations of the phenomena to which it referred. On one hand, boredom was regarded as having ethical and epistemological implications. While the authors of popular advice books treated it as a moral failure, a rejection of the legitimate demands of worldly existence, thinkers such as Kierkegaard and Schopenhauer applauded the distancing effect of boredom as an entrée into metaphysical reflection. In this ethical and philosophical register, the discourse on boredom was thoroughly bourgeois, as were both those who regarded it as a gaffe and those who applauded it as existential rebellion. However, in a different but no less significant register, the discourse was emphatically class-less. Here boredom was described not as a subjective intellectual or moral attitude but as a psycho-physiological response to the realities of modern life. This curious form of disenchantment was consistently linked to the material transformations of life in the industrialized world—to standardization, to train travel, to new forms of labor. Thus as a sociological phenomenon, boredom spread among the lower classes in the course of the nineteenth century, and by early in the twentieth, the philosophical dilemmas associated with the experience had also been thoroughly democratized.

Within the larger discourse on subjective experience in modernity, the material transformations with which boredom was linked were themselves often regarded in moral terms, as in the topos that grounded a subjective experience of meaninglessness in the anonymity of the modern metropolis. "Idealist" and "materialist" interpretations of boredom were thus quite compatible and initially functioned less as contrasting visions of the meaning of an experience than as complementary aspects of a single language of reflection on the subjective significance of modern developments. The rhetoric of the discourse on boredom, in other words, linked socio-historical transformations to questions of meaning by representing the ambiguity of this experience as exemplary for the contemporary experience of self. And since that discourse posited an interrelationship between material conditions and psychic effects in modernity, it implicitly raised the question of the ethical status of the transformations that had rendered the experience of boredom so widespread.[20]

The new prevalence of boredom may thus be read as an index of the *democratization of skepticism* in modernity. As the certitudes of the past dissolved in the tumult of modern developments, questions that had once been reserved for the upper classes were spreading throughout society. One manifestation of what Nietzsche called the 'death of god' was a significant transformation in the rhetoric of reflection on subjective experience. In the course of the nineteenth century, older religious vocabularies, with their focus on the immortal fate of the individual soul, were gradually displaced by new languages grounded in the social and natural sciences. People were redefined as citizens within a state and bodies within a physical world. As medicine modernized, the mixture of ethical evaluation and material description that had characterized discussion of malaise under the traditional doctrine of the four humors yielded to a materialist vocabulary of nervous effects inspired by the newly harnessed phenomenon of electricity and the laws of thermodynamics. While boredom's illustrious predecessors, melancholy and acedia, resonated with traditions extending into antiquity, the emergent language built upon a new, secular vision of a body constituted by fluctuations

---

[20]That it often did so in gendered ways will be apparent throughout. Martina Kessel's investigation of the discourse on boredom in the German context, which focuses on the relations between gender, boredom, temporality, and the construction of modern identities, complements this study with an empirically nuanced account of the gendering of what I call the modern rhetoric of experience. As Kessel's work underlines, the valorization of male and devaluation of female boredom is a basic, politically and culturally highly significant, feature of the discourse on boredom as a whole. Such splitting is hardly confined to the male/female opposition, though—differential evaluations of boredom are also mapped onto class, racial, and national difference, depending on the context.

However, my object is not these mappings themselves but the conceptual structure of the modern discourse on subjective experience as a whole through which such differential interpretations of the significance of boredom are distributed. As I shall argue in detail in Chapter 1, efforts to base such distinctions on a purportedly empirical difference between "types" of boredom are doomed to fail: there is no essential difference between "female" and "male" or "aristocratic" and "working class" boredom. The work of Kessel, Petro, and Spacks has demonstrated how crucial it is to inquire into the ideological function of such attributions and oppositions within the discourse on boredom. While my own emphasis lies rather on the conceptual slippage within modern modes of reflection on experience that is evident in the ways these divergent meanings of boredom come to be associated with gender, class, and race positions, the implication here, too, is that the discursive function of such strategies is to obscure gaps and contradictions in the hegemonic (post-)Enlightenment vision of human existence.

of abstract force, "nervous energy." As I show in Chapter 3, the language of boredom integrated older, religious motifs with this new energeticist idiom. Compatible with both materialist and idealist interpretations of experience, the language of boredom thus facilitated the modernization of the rhetoric of malaise.

However, while it was tied up with the very changes that made boredom a mass phenomenon, the wholesale shift to a materialist vision of human being would obscure the power of the discourse on boredom to articulate the relations between the process of modernization and the questions of meaning associated with contemporary forms of subjective malaise. As the explanatory paradigm implicit in the project of Enlightenment came to fruition in scientific and technological progress, sociology, psychology, and physiology were displacing religion, philosophy, and ethics. Within these newer disciplines, the language of boredom was deployed to describe a malaise understood to be medical or perhaps social rather than metaphysical or moral in origin. Thus the shift to a materialist vocabulary is registered in the global development of the discourse on boredom itself.

In the eighteenth century boredom had been characterized in ethical terms—the failure of interest was a condemnable fault, a sign of inadequate self-discipline or ethical wherewithal. By the end of the nineteenth century, boredom was likely to be regarded as the consequence of nervous exhaustion induced by the pace of modern life. The evolution of the rhetoric of reflection on subjective experience that I call the *medicalization of malaise* affected even those, like the Decadents, who still saw in the victim of ennui a Baudelairean heroism in the face of modern life. By the early twentieth century, the problems of meaning associated with the experience would be explained by appeals to the physiological dimension. And today, in a world thoroughly transformed by psychoanalysis—the scientific language of a renegade neurologist—to speak of the soul, or even of interiority, is to mark oneself as a relic.

From a materialist point of view, a philosophico-religious interpretation of boredom such as Kierkegaard's was sheerly anachronistic. However, as Kierkegaard's reception history attests, this untimeliness by no means led to the wholesale elimination of such nominally pre-scientific ways of thinking about boredom. On the contrary, idealist visions of the experience flourished alongside and in opposition to their materialist rivals. In this respect, the development of the discourse on boredom exemplifies a global cultural trend in nineteenth- and early twentieth-century European cultural history. The newly ascendant scientific world-view fell short of actually achieving that universality to which it laid claim, for the positivistic reduction of questions of meaning to epiphenoma of the physical world was neither entirely satisfying nor entirely successful, and religious and philosophical perspectives on human existence continued to prosper, generally more or less unmediated with their scientific rivals.

Within this branch of the discourse on boredom, the sociological and medical accounts that were gaining currency were found inadequate insofar as they psychologized the philosophical issues associated with the experience. However, those who wanted to emphasize the reflective significance of boredom did not necessarily oppose explaining others' experiences in this way. One began to distinguish between two different sorts of experiences—in English quite explicitly between (mundane) boredom and (existential) ennui—and to contend that the latter was inaccessible to materialist analysis. As I shall argue in detail in Chapter 1, this distinction is rhetorical rather than genuinely experiential: boredom as it is lived points rather to a continuum of possibilities extending between these two poles. Nonetheless, the corresponding division between materialist explanations of boredom and interpretations that focus on its subjective significance continues to structure our thinking about the experience today, as does the related assumption that the boredom of the factory worker is different in kind from the poet's. In this way too, the historical development of the discourse on boredom, in which philosophical and spiritual language has been reserved for elite sufferers and the boredom of the masses consigned to study by sociologists and psychologists, has obscured how all forms of boredom involve problems of meaning grounded in the concrete circumstances of modern life.

If we tend to think of boredom in ahistorical terms, then not simply on account of the nihilistic dynamic internal to the experience. The secularized discourse on subjective discontent that has flourished since the nineteenth century has also played a key role. While older idealist vocabularies retain cultural prestige, our everyday idiom is materialist; if the language of boredom remains ambiguous, to speak of stress, depression, hyperactivity, attention deficit disorder, and so on, is to locate subjective malaise firmly in the body. Surely it would be too optimistic to conclude from the fact that religiously tinged existential interpretations of boredom continue to retain their force even today, in the age of Prozac, that human malaise cannot be entirely medicalized. Perhaps it is only a matter of time: the laments about the emptiness, the meaninglessness of modern existence associated with the experience of boredom may be nothing more than residual elements of a form of human consciousness long since doomed to extinction. However, the pervasiveness of such anachronisms at least indicates that it is an error to identify the modernization process with secularization and an inevitable and univocal triumph of rationalistic thought. That radically unscientific interpretations of human malaise persist despite the galloping successes of the neurological paradigm attests to significant gaps in its explanatory power—gaps which must be erased, forgotten, to produce a truly secularized form of human self-understanding.

Modern work and modern leisure alike are tinged with an urgent need to escape the boredom they themselves foster, a need that the contemporary discourse on boredom simultaneously registers and disavows.[21] The experience of boredom renders the limitations of rationalized self-understanding visible: the impossibility of reducing questions of meaning to material calculations, the incommensurability of desire and world. Thus it is not simply that the existential dimension of the experience cannot (yet) be explained in purely physiological terms; the prevalence of boredom as a sociological phenomenon is a symptom of the discontents of modern life and is often experienced as such. Even when its most mundane symptoms are medicalized as 'attention deficit,' then, boredom's ambiguity remains significant. Although the hegemonic (materialist) discourse on subjective experience tends to erase the traces of its philosophical dimension, boredom's doubling under the aegis of ennui is symptomatic of the persistence of other understandings of the significance of human malaise. Indeed, the very tenacity of the language of boredom points to the limits of the hegemonic understanding of human subjectivity even as the rhetoric of boredom both as experience and as discourse tends to occlude the possibility of reflection on its historical significance.

In the problem of boredom—understood both as experience and as discourse—a set of questions about the nature and meaning of subjective experience take a modern form. Linked on the one hand to the larger discursive transformations of cultural modernization and on the other to the older languages of reflection on subjective malaise of which it is the heir, boredom challenges us to develop modes of reflection that link philosophical reflection and historical analysis. The impediments to thinking boredom's historicity reflect our own implication in the aporia that constitutes this paradigmatically modern form of subjective malaise.

Viewed as a whole, the discourse on boredom exemplifies the tensions between materialist and idealist explanation basic to the modern rhetoric of reflection on subjective experience. No amount of scientific progress has

---

[21]For a subtle discussion of the potentialities embedded in the ambiguities of modernity that emphasizes boredom's theoretical and historical significance for feminist theories of visual culture, see Patrice Petro, *Aftershocks of the New: Feminism and Film History*.

been able to dispel these tensions, for they are grounded in a conflict between paradigms of human self-understanding that rationalist explanations of the human heart exacerbate rather than soothe. The discourse on boredom therefore provides a particularly clear illustration of the aporetic structure of the modern discourse on subjective experience as a whole. In a world where the very nature of human existence is radically uncertain, it is not boredom alone that appears both as sociological epiphenomenon and as eternal feature of the human condition, as physiological symptom and as philosophical revelation. The difficulty in defining boredom—and hence, a fortiori, of recognizing its genuine manifestations—marks an instability in the language of experience that neither empirical study nor philosophical inquiry can truly remedy. Attempts at rationalization always produce a residue of unanswered, possibly unanswerable questions. The language of boredom can express both resignation to the existence of such questions and psychic suffering in the face of their persistence.

All of these forms of ambiguity helped to facilitate the remarkable democratization of this way of talking about subjective malaise in the course of the nineteenth century. The discourse on boredom can therefore function as a lens to examine the global transformation in modes of reflection upon subjective experience that accompanied secularization, urbanization, and rationalization—to examine how cultural modernization facilitated the democratization of skepticism. Through the language of boredom, religious and philosophical questions about human existence were reformulated in a modern, disenchanted idiom. The phenomenon is thereby discursively linked to a wide range of political and cultural transformations—most importantly to a new, rationalized understanding of temporality that emerged in the aftermath of the Enlightenment.

I argue that the historical vicissitudes of the discourse on boredom—both its diffusion and its internal evolution in the course of the nineteenth century—register a global paradigm shift in the rhetoric of reflection on subjective experience in urbanizing, industrializing Europe. As I show in Part I, historical narratives that depend on either idealist or materialist conceptions of what boredom is cannot establish a perspective for reflection on the significance of this discourse, for in it the nature and even the possibility of experience in modernity is called into question. Rather than beginning from such a decontextualized conception and constructing a narrative that accounts for the way 'boredom' seems to change in meaning over time, I therefore build a narrative around those discursive shifts, one that foregrounds both the constructedness and the ambiguity of the phenomenon itself. The story I tell integrates an historical analysis of the effects of cultural modernization on subjective experience with philosophical reflection about the relationship between the seemingly incompatible idioms that constitute the languages of reflection on this peculiarly modern malaise.

This approach casts a new light on the reciprocal limitations of the philosophical and sociological-anthropological accounts of boredom. Neither mode of reflection can do justice to the ambiguity of the experience, I contend, because the interpretive paradigms that underlie these models themselves constitute that ambiguity. The fact that the idioms of socio-historical causation and moral-epistemological significance seem to be incommensurable presents a serious obstacle to gaining conceptual purchase on the phenomenon of boredom. The point argued in Chapters 1 and 2 is not simply that the language in which critical analysis is couched inflects what can be said about boredom—but rather that this aporia is part of what constitutes the phenomenon itself. Chapter 3 therefore foregrounds boredom's ambiguity even as it situates these languages in relation to a larger discursive development underway in the course of the nineteenth century. Boredom itself is neither simply a sociological epiphenomenon nor purely a philosophical problem, yet from the beginning reflection on the experience tends to be couched in terms of one pole or the other. Although the *language of boredom* mediates between the ideal and the material, as it develops historically, the *discourse on boredom* thus establishes the foundation of the conceptual aporia laid out in Chapters 1 and 2.

In writing the history of this development in a way that foregrounds the global paradigm shift in the rhetoric of reflection on subjective experience in this period, I conceptualize modernization as a process that democratizes skepticism. This approach helps articulate the discursive role of boredom in accounts of contemporary socio-political transformations with its philosophical significance for individual subjects. By integrating social scientific and philosophical accounts of the phenomenon, it establishes a perspective for reflection on the significance of these approaches. I demonstrate that as the discourse on the experience evolves, it makes visible the very paradigm shift in the interpretation of subjective malaise on which the disjunction between humanistic and natural-scientific modes of explanation depends. Thus my interpretation of the discourse on boredom as a symptom of the democratization of skepticism in modernity has general methodological implications for the project of integrating historical and philosophical perspectives in the analysis of modern subjectivity.

While the phenomenon of boredom is by no means the only possible point of departure for such analysis, it is a crucial one. The vocabulary in which problems of meaning can be expressed has been impoverished, I argue, as a consequence of the very development toward materialist modes of reflection through which boredom came to seem a universal, ahistorical feature of the human condition. The prevalence of boredom in modernity therefore indicates a fundamental problem for thinking. There is, so to speak, disenchantment all the way down. If what Walter Benjamin called the "growing atrophy of experience"[22] in modern life provides the conditions of possibility for boredom, the simultaneous triumph of a materialist rhetoric of reflection on subjective experience occludes critical reflection on those conditions. As we have seen, affirmations of boredom's philosophical significance do not, in themselves, point the way beyond this dilemma. On the contrary: they tend to reinscribe the process by which boredom comes to seem inevitable, reifying the nihilistic dynamic that leads the bored subject to universalize the experience into a negative revelation of the horrible truth about the human condition. Such a way of viewing the world not only feeds the ennui that brought it into being; it elevates boredom to mythic, ahistorical status.

The interpretation of boredom as negative revelation appears, of course, in the thinking of philosophers such as Kierkegaard or Schopenhauer. What is less obvious, however, is that the same fundamentally nihilistic vision of human existence underlies the social scientific discourse on subjective experience in modernity as well. Here boredom and, more generally, the subjective perception of meaninglessness, is explained as the consequence of a socio-cultural context in which the collective norms that are necessary to make individual life significant fail to integrate subjects into a social whole. As we shall see, "anomic" phenomena include not only boredom and melancholy but also 'deviant' behavior more generally—anything that eludes or disrupts culturally normative expectations of how people should think and act comes to be labeled in this way. What masquerades as descriptive is in fact deeply normative. Foucault's critique of social science, which accepts the materialist metaphysics that underlie such theorizing, does not go far enough. To regard social life as a source of purposes for individual human beings is nothing short of nihilistic—as the fact that such a vision of society can be used to advocate either conformity (Durkheim) or innovation (Merton) confirms. From the point of view epitomized by Pareto's notion that human beings have a generic "besoin de faire quelche chose," culture is necessary because human life is not, in itself, meaningfully part of the world.

[22]Walter Benjamin, "Über einige Motive bei Baudelaire" in *Charles Baudelaire: Ein Lyriker im Zeitalter des Hochkapitalismus*, 107.

While such a notion of purpose is arguably incoherent, its widespread, if implicit, acceptance makes it difficult to achieve conceptual purchase on the phenomenon of boredom. Like the philosophical view of boredom as a negative revelation, the modern social scientific discourse on the experience fails to achieve a reflective perspective on the historical significance of boredom; both seem to reinscribe the nihilistic dynamic by which bored subjects universalize their malaise into totalizing visions of the meaninglessness of existence itself. An adequate approach to boredom must therefore establish a perspective for reflection upon that dynamic, one that links the "atrophy of experience" to larger historical developments. My contention is that shifting the emphasis from experience to discourse and examining the historical evolution of the rhetoric of reflection on boredom is the crucial first step. From a rhetorical perspective, the experiential conditions of possibility for boredom are grounded in the cultural process by which skepticism is democratized, and the evacuation of the language of reflection on subjective experience in modernity appears as an historically constituted phenomenon rather than as the revelation of an ontological or anthropological truth about the human condition.

This study takes as its point of departure a paradoxical fact: the boredom that "began to be felt on an epidemic scale" in the mid-nineteenth century is understood as an ahistorical feature of human existence. In the experience without qualities, the evacuation of the language of reflection on subjective experience in modernity takes the form of a disappearance of experience that is lived as a nihilistic revelation of the senselessness of existence itself. To the extent that such an atrophy of experience characterizes the modern world more generally, the difficulties involved in achieving an adequate reflective perspective on boredom exemplify more general difficulties in grasping the historical specificity of modern experience and modern subjectivity, and the strategies of reflection developed here have broader application.

In the first instance, *Experience without Qualities* aims to develop a fuller account of the complicated relationship between the discourse on boredom and historical reality than either sociological reduction or philosophical universalization of the experience allow. It is not simply a matter of showing how the discourse on boredom makes the disappearance of experience that is the condition of possibility of this experience without qualities appear as an ahistorical universal. To address the historical and philosophical significance of that discourse, it is necessary to move beyond such an implicit condemnation of boredom as false consciousness. Describing the conceptual transformations of the rhetoric of reflection exemplified by the discourse on boredom also involves accounting for why this new metaphorics for describing subjective experience took hold when it did. My rhetorical approach, which directs attention to the historical constitution of the language of reflection, therefore opens up a new perspective on questions about the constitution of subjective experience that have largely been treated in ahistorical terms. The global paradigm shift toward disenchanted, materialist modes of rhetoric on subjective experience evident in the evolution of the discourse on boredom should, I argue, be understood in the context of the larger historical development I call the democratization of skepticism in modernity. On this reading, not only is the experience of boredom constitutively dependent on historical transformations that render the disenchanted modern vision of self and world possible; the emergence and evolution of the discourse on boredom in the nineteenth century reflects a fundamental paradigm shift in the understanding of history and the meaning of historical experience in modernity. This paradigm shift, which both constitutes modern subjectivity and occludes the historical specificity of the problems of meaning that plague modern subjects, is the ultimate object of this study.

PART I

The Rhetoric of Experience

CHAPTER 1

Ennui in Western Literature:
Boredom as Existential Malaise

———◆———

Langeweile haben wir, wenn wir nicht wissen, worauf wir warten.
Walter Benjamin[1]

Boredom and History

From a philosophical perspective, the assertion that boredom must be understood as a modern phenomenon may appear problematic. After all, *taedium vitae* plagued Romans in the imperial era, acedia threatened the desert fathers, and at least since the Greeks, melancholia has been a perennial theme in art and literature. Is 'boredom' not just the latest name for a venerable, perhaps universal experience of disaffection with life? Because this objection must be taken seriously, I shall begin by engaging Reinhard Kuhn's ambitious attempt to understand such existential malaise, by whatever name, as an ubiquitous feature of the human condition. My reading of his *The Demon of Noontide: Ennui in Western Literature* will demonstrate that although a coherent and in many ways compelling intellectual history of boredom can be written from the perspective of such a philosophical universalism, such a narrative depends on presumptions about human existence that are themselves fundamentally modern. That is to say: it fails to satisfy its own claim to establish a perspective for reflection outside the historically constituted discourse on boredom—it is, rather, part of that—modern—discourse. And since the limitations of Kuhn's account are a function of the philosophical rhetoric of experience he invokes, any attempt to understand subjective malaise in such ahistorical terms will be open to the same objections.

Kuhn's *The Demon of Noontide: Ennui in Western Literature* is a remarkable book and a landmark in the literature on boredom. Conceived by its author as at once an exhaustive survey of the permutations of the topos of

[1]"We are bored when we don't know what we are waiting for" (*Das Passagen-Werk*, vol. I, 161).

ennui in Western literature and a contribution to the spiritual history of
humanity, it examines works in a half-dozen languages, ranging from Greek
tragedies to the twentieth-century nouveau roman. For Kuhn, ennui is at
once transhistorical plague—"in various guises . . . an ever-present phenomenon" (375)—and wellspring of human creativity—a product of the "monumental struggle against the power of nothingness" in which "man defines
himself and asserts his humanity" (378). Western literature is, as he sees it,
the document of this struggle.

The Demon of Noontide is indeed a testament to the power of the literary
tradition in shaping inherited ideas about subjective suffering, and Kuhn's
vision of the relation between historical experience and literary representation remains widespread even now—albeit couched in a different vocabulary. A close reading of the interpretation of the Western literary tradition
through which Kuhn argues that boredom in its various guises has "contributed to the formation of the human spirit" (3) will therefore illuminate more
general issues. In treating ennui as at once a "universal problem" (4) and an
object of intellectual history that has changed significantly over time, I argue,
his account exposes a tension basic to the philosophical rhetoric of reflection
on subjective malaise. The limitations of Kuhn's account thus demonstrate
that boredom cannot be adequately understood in abstraction from its historical context and cultural conditions of possibility.[2]

From a rhetorical perspective, what is at stake in universalist claims about
boredom is the status of the language of reflection on subjective experience:
to narrate the history of boredom is to interpret the significance of changes
in the representation of subjective malaise over time. Read in this light, what
Kuhn advances as the history of a putatively timeless experience can suggest
the outlines of an alternative account, one that analyzes the historical development of the rhetoric of reflection on subjective malaise registered in the

---

[2]Although Kuhn's is by far the most comprehensive work of its kind, there are a number of
other studies that take an understanding of boredom as a universal philosophical problem as their
point of departure. The mode in which this universality is formulated varies with larger intellectual fashions. Thus Vladmir Jankélévitch (1963) situates ennui in relation to angst, treating it as a
mode of temporality, Michèle Huguet (1984) treats it as a psychosocial symptom, Alfred Bellebaum (1990) and Norbert Jonard (1998) focus on explaining its evolving cultural significance, and
Friedhelm Decher (2000) pragmatically advocates strategies for coming to terms with boredom as
a constitutive feature of the human condition. Aside from Kuhn's, the most comprehensive study
is Madeleine Bouchez' 1973 reader, which traces the idea of ennui through Western literature for
students preparing for their exams. Her perspective, like his, is strongly influenced by existentialism. Two other, less far-reaching, studies that also share this philosophical point of departure are
worth noting. Frantz Antoine Leconte examines *La Tradition de L'Ennui Splénétique en France de
Christine De Pisan à Baudelaire* and Guy Sagnes focuses on the representation of ennui in French
literature between 1848 and 1884.

literary discourse on boredom. In conversation with Kuhn's universalist history of ennui, I begin to develop such an alternative account—one centered not on an ahistorical vision of human being finding expression in different vocabularies but on discursive continuities and rhetorical transformations within the historical field of reflection on subjective experience. I hope thereby both to do justice to Kuhn's work and to demonstrate how his universal history of ennui begs the question it sets out to prove.

Shifting the frame of interpretation from the experience to the rhetoric of boredom makes it possible to account for the curious convergence of timelessness and historicity that constitutes modern boredom without falling into the logical difficulties that issue from *The Demon of Noontide*'s idealism. My contention is that the boredom that arises, as Walter Benjamin put it, "when we don't know what we are waiting for," reflects a peculiarly modern conception of desire and identity. Unlike melancholy, acedia, or *taedium vitae*, such malaise is anchored in a linear vision of historical time that has its origins in Enlightenment thought. In the final analysis, the failure of the philosophical rhetoric of reflection to establish a point of view outside the historically constituted discourse on boredom may itself be traced to the same source—to the historical particularity of the vision of subjectivity and truth embedded in its purportedly universal perspective on subjective malaise.

Narrating Malaise: History and the Rhetoric of Reflection

On Kuhn's reading, the symptoms of ennui existed "as disparate elements" even in pagan antiquity: "the seeds of the modern plague" were present from the very beginning of Western thought in the form of melancholy, *horror loci, fastidium* and "the vague sorrow of some of the Greek and Latin poets" (375–76). However, he writes, it was "with the inception of Christianity that, under the name of acedia, ennui began to occupy a central position in man's intellectual and spiritual concerns" (376).[3] It did so in particular through the agency of the "desert fathers" who, beginning in the third century, retreated into the Near Eastern deserts to pursue Christian principles through "a life of solitude, fasting, and self-inflicted punishment" (40). While the Psalmist had alluded to the "demon of noontide" of Kuhn's title, it was these anchorites who formulated the catalogues of sins in which acedia (literally, lacking care or interest) would soon become central.[4] On Kuhn's

---

[3] Other writers have made more of the pagan and Jewish background to this transformation. See Morton Bloomfield, *The Seven Deadly Sins*.

[4] On acedia, see Wenzel's classic study. For a comparison of acedia with similar concepts in the Jewish, Hindu, and Buddhist visionary traditions, see Raposa 16ff.

reading, in the development of the concept of ennui, the two most important ancient influences on "medieval and Renaissance thought and literature" converged: the Christian conception of the seven deadly sins and "the division of the formative influences on man into the four humors" (19). Before proceeding with my résumé of Kuhn's universal history of ennui, according to which the "disparate elements" of Christian and pagan traditions are gradually consolidated into a single syndrome, let us consider the same development from a rhetorical perspective.

The hermits' battles against spiritual perils led not only to the foundation of the first monasteries but also to the establishment of a language of reflection that would remain remarkably stable for nearly a thousand years. St. Thomas Aquinas's codification of the concept of acedia in the *Summa theologica* (1267–73) then paved the way for future developments within the Christian rhetoric of reflection on subjective experience. Aquinas, who "follow[ed] the earlier tradition in listing among the 'daughters' of acedia idleness, drowsiness, uneasiness of the mind, restlessness of the body, curiosity, loquacity, and despair" (Raposa, 25), provided the definition of acedia as a "sorrow for the divine good" which Petrarch, Pascal, and Kierkegaard (to name a few key figures) would agree in recognizing as the source of human suffering par excellence. However, alongside Aquinas's definition of acedia as the refusal of the joy (*guadium*) which has its source in divine love, Christian thought also harbored a less spiritual understanding of acedia as sloth—an interpretation that came to predominate in medieval depictions of the seven deadly sins and which thus had a very significant history of effects. Since lethargy and lassitude were traditionally associated with an excess of black bile, the emphasis on the material manifestations of acedia prefigured its subsequent assimilation to melancholia.[5] This rapprochement between medical and religious interpretations of subjective malaise would be decisive for later developments.

In Blaise Pascal's *Pensées* (1670), ennui achieves perhaps its first apotheosis. What was once a capital sin is identified as a fundamental human disposition. This step—the mirror image of the poetic assimilation of melancholy to acedia evident nearly a century earlier in Shakespeare—was consonant with the Christian tradition and thus legitimate for a thinker such as Pascal. However, the rhetorical consequences of equating the melancholic temperament with a propensity to the sort of spiritual suffering traditionally as-

---

[5]This identification begins with Cassian (360–435) but is not yet dominant even in his conception. See Raposa (23), who refers to Wenzel (22) possibly redating when sloth became a dominant notion. I am in general agreement with Kuhn that little changes from Cassian to Thomas.

sociated with acedia were considerable. As Kuhn puts it, Pascal's "ennui," while linked to the Christian tradition, "is also the prototype of the 'mal du siècle' of the romantics" (113). That is to say, Pascal's ideas paved the way for a de-Christianization of acedia. This discursive evolution, not completed until the nineteenth century, was a crucial step in the secularization of the rhetoric of reflection on human malaise. In particular, this assimilation of melancholy and acedia was essential to the constitution of the modern concept of ennui that forms Kuhn's point of departure.

In contrast to my account of the pre-history of ennui, which interprets the apparent convergence between melancholy and acedia in the modern concept in terms of discursive transformations in Western culture, Kuhn treats history as testimony. For him, texts give readers direct, mimetic access to the experiences they describe. Furthermore, he sees no difficulty in drawing historical inferences on the basis of the testimony of a few canonical authors. Thus, having concluded on the basis of a reading of Cassian "that the early Christian state of sin and the modern pathological condition of ennui are in some essential respects identical" (53), he sets out to trace the subsequent historical development toward what he acknowledges as a specifically modern experience of boredom. Let us return to that account.

"In the Middle Ages began the secularization of ennui and its appearance in popular literature" (376). In particular, Kuhn argues, the "symptoms" of ennui—longing, surfeit, melancholy, laments of exile—reached a wider audience through the troubadours. However, the crucial step was yet to come. "The transformation of one of the mortal sins into the affliction of ennui was accomplished by Petrarch. During the Renaissance, which he ushered in, an overweening lust for life typified by Rabelais had as its counterpart a deep despondency that can be found even in Montaigne" (376). Petrarch (1304–74)—"perhaps," according to Kuhn, "the first modern man" (68)—suffered from "a condition that is an amalgam between medieval acedia and modern ennui," a restlessness, lassitude, and indifference that both hearkened back to the Roman experiences of *horror loci* and *taedium vitae* and anticipated the romantic *voluptas dolendi*.[6]

If Petrarch modernized acedia, then, according to Kuhn, Albrecht Dürer ("one of the first modern artists" (75)) did the same for melancholia. His account draws on Klibansky, Panofsky, and Saxl's monumental *Saturn and*

---

[6]It is worth noting that Kuhn's concept of "the Renaissance" is a product of the mid-nineteenth century, traceable in particular to Michelet and Burckhardt. This "attempt to capture the transition from the middle ages to modernity epochally . . . is problematic in a number of ways" (See Mittelstraß, *Enzyklopedie*, "Renaissance").

Melancholy, in which Albrecht Dürer's 1514 *Melencholia I* is used to illuminate the vicissitudes of the concept of melancholy from antiquity through
the Renaissance. Kuhn follows their argument that via Marsilio Ficino's
(1433–1499) neo-Platonist interpretation, the (pseudo-)Aristotelian account
of melancholy as the mark of "all great men" (*Problems* XXX, i) became the
foundation of the modern notion of genius.[7] For Kuhn, Dürer's *Melencholia*

---

[7]According to the ancient medical doctrine of the four humours, black bile was the corporeal
cause of an emotional state, melancholy, that was ambiguously understood as an illness or as a
temperamental predisposition. Klibansky et al. argue that the melding of this medical notion of
melancholy with Plato's conception of *mania* in the pseudo-Aristotelian text (which they attribute
to Aristotle's student and successor, Theophrastus, 18) laid the groundwork for that metaphorical
psychology of creativity. This locus classicus of melancholy merits a brief excursus.

Taking as its point of departure the remarkable question: "Why have all those who became
great men, whether by philosophizing or in politics, poetry (*poiêsin*), or the arts (*technas*) clearly
been melancholics?" (953a 10; translations from Aristotle are mine), *Problem* XXX, i argues that
because black gall is character-forming (*êthopoios*), "all melancholics are superior persons, not on
account of disease but by nature" (955a 30ff). This superiority depends on the "anomalous capacity" of black bile to heat and cool that renders the melancholics themselves "anomalous" (*anôma-
loi* 955a 30). While the melancholic character is in itself unstable, prone to ecstasies (*manikois*) and
prophetic inspiration (954a 35), but also to strong depressions (*athumiai*) or anxieties (*phoboi*)
(954b 30), there are also "more practically wise" (*phronismôteroi*) melancholics who are "less eccentric and superior to others in many respects, whether through education, art or political capacity" (954b 2). "Either through this anomaly being well balanced and somehow fortunate . . . or
through the opposite, on account of an excess of bile, all melancholics are superior" to other people (955a 35).

The opening passage of Aristotle's *Metaphysics* provides a clue as to what sort of superiority
this "ethopoietic" quality might entail. It states that because of an inborn love of knowledge, human beings take delight in the senses, and especially the sense of sight, which "most of all the
senses makes us know and reveals many distinctions" (980a 25). The apprehension of difference
and sameness is the basis of all experience. "Through memory experience comes to human beings, for many memories of the same thing finally produce the capacity for a single experience"
(980b 25). Through experience, in turn, both art and science become possible, for experience enables human beings to coordinate their perceptions into systematic modes of action (arts) and is a
necessary (though not sufficient) condition of that insight into the fundamental principles of a
given realm of reality which constitutes the foundation of a science.

Aristotle's notion of practical wisdom, developed in the *Nichomachean Ethics*, links the noetic
virtue of the senses, their ability to bring to light differences between things, with excellence in the
various forms of human endeavor listed at the beginning of Problem XXX, i. "Just as in the body,
sight is the good, so in the soul, intelligence [*nous*]" (1096b 28). *Phronesis* (practical wisdom) enables people to perceive relevant distinctions in situations of action; it develops through practice.
Similarly, character is formed through habitual action: experience is ethopoietic. Practical wisdom
for Aristotle is not simply cleverness, for in the full sense it depends upon ethical virtue, upon a
right conception of the ends that orient action. As the image of the eye of the soul indicates, practical wisdom mediates between the ethical and intellectual virtues. In fact, in the chapter on natural virtue, Aristotle uses the term *nous* to refer to perfected practical wisdom. This usage encompasses both the philosophical meaning of the term—*nous* as the faculty which perceives ultimate
particulars (1043b 1)—and the more general idea of "mind" or "sense," which encompasses an
ethical dimension. As in Platonic thought, virtue and wisdom are connected through the faculty

is a paradigmatically modern vision of artistic melancholy as the "Muse who, while herself paralyzed and as if suffocating in a pall of lethargy, inspires the Renaissance artist, that rival of God in creation" (76). In the sixteenth century, according to Kuhn, this vision of melancholy was exported to England and popularized under the name of spleen—"a fashionable illness" though only "in exceptional cases . . . a fruitful one" (376).[8]

The story Kuhn tells depends on a highly contentious reading of early modern thinkers as areligious. This assumption vexes his global narrative, since he clearly sees that a genuinely secularized vision of ennui, in which the dimensions of acedia and melancholy were integrated into a syndrome with a wide variety of manifestations, would not emerge until the eighteenth century. The difficulty can be detected in the sequence of chapter titles: "The Black Gall" of antiquity, "The Demon of Noontide" of early and medieval Christianity, and "The Nameless Woe" of the early modern period are succeeded by "The Dispossessed Monarch." While the previous titles refer to historically and culturally specific forms of malaise, the topos of the mon-

---

of nous; philosophizing may be the best life for human beings, but it cannot be entirely separated from politics.

It is now possible to grasp the relation put forward in *Problem XXX, i* between the anomalous potentiality of the melancholic temperament and melancholics' excellence in all realms of human endeavor. The link between experience, understood as the source of practical wisdom, and sense perception, through which experience comes to be, clarifies how such an instability can be the source of diverse forms of superiority. The anomalous nature of black bile, that which renders it ethopoietic, appears to be a sort of natural flexibility that serves to enrich experience. The melancholic perceives a greater range of differences in the world, has, in the terms of the *Metaphysics*, more experiences, and thus has the potential for excellence in the realms of art and science and in philosophy. Such sensitivity can overwhelm the melancholics' rational capacity and lead to rash actions. But the same "anomalous capacity" also underlies the overwhelming superiority of the practically wise melancholic, in whom the instability of character has been modulated into a salutary flexibility via a regimen that inculcates a reliable sense of the genuine ends of human activity (viz., *hoi men pros paideian, hoi de pros technas, hoi de pros politeian*).

Problem XXX, i not only foreshadows the notion of creativity that came to be associated with melancholic genius; if the links I have drawn to Aristotle's own thought are plausible, its vision of melancholy places philosophical eros on a continuum with the general human love for knowledge evinced by the senses in a way that suggests the potential for a democratization of that conception of genius. However, the melancholic of *Problem XXX, i* cannot simply be identified with the modern subjects who invoke the same language. On the ancient conception, melancholy is constitutive of the embodied person in a way that encloses an implicit link to larger orders of meaning: its very anomalousness connects the melancholic to both cosmos and polis. Modern melancholy refers, rather, to a lack of such links. And as we shall see, the language of boredom belongs to a skeptical subject for whom that lack has become constitutive—for whom experience itself has become a problem.

[8]The ambiguous figure of the suffering artist—charlatan, laughingstock, idol—would have a significant history of effects, as would the term spleen which, along with the epithet "English melancholy" were soon reimported to the continent.

arch provides a rhetorical common ground between what Kuhn sees as two distinct conceptions of ennui—Pascal's religious boredom ("an amalgam of acedia and 'black bile' . . . exacerbated by the concept of exile," 127) and the malaise of court life. According to Kuhn, in the seventeenth century the "distinction between superficial and profound ennui was transformed into one between religious and secular ennui; on the one hand there was the metaphysical void of Pascal and the Jansenists of Port Royal, and on the other, the empty boredom of La Rochefoucauld and the courtiers at Versailles" (376–77).

My contention is that this "dichotomy" is better viewed as a set of variations within a common discourse on subjective experience. For courtiers and Pascal alike, 'ennui' related to diversion and repetition within an established framework of meaning. In the seventeenth century, both earthly and divine Kings remained stable points of reference, and as Kuhn himself acknowledges, "La Rochefoucauld could use 'ennui' both to designate his deep spiritual distress and to complain of the trivial nuisances of court life" (6). For Pascal (1623–62) all human activities were ultimately the consequence of being unable "to remain tranquil, alone in a room" (205, cited in Kuhn, 109) and confront the void of ennui with a leap of faith; he saw all human activities as "diversions," distractions "that help us reach death imperceptibly" (217). La Rochefoucauld (1613–80), world-weary lamenter of the ennui of enforced social activity, surely would have agreed. If the ennui of the latter rarely sounds an explicitly spiritual note,[9] he is no less an explorer of the self than his Jansenist contemporary. Both struggled with the dissolution of the will and the limits of rationality. In their writings, a new language of subjective lamentation was beginning to emerge, a language in which the discourse on melancholy blends with a conception of ennui as a universal experience.

For Pascal and La Rochefoucauld alike, boredom is a fundamental feature of the human condition. However, their writings are not for that reason evidence for the truth of that vision of subjective experience. Both "secular" and "religious" forms of ennui belong to the philosophical discourse on subjective malaise that can be traced up to Kuhn's own existentialist interpretation. But such historical continuity does not in itself constitute proof of the ontological claims embedded in the discourse. On the contrary, it is precisely the historical depth and pervasiveness of the discourse on boredom that makes it difficult to establish an adequate perspective for reflection on the

---

[9] Kuhn cites what he regards as evidence for La Rochefoucauld's awareness of a "deeper form" of boredom, "Extreme ennui serves to dissipate ennui" (121). ("L'extrême ennui sert à nous désennuyer," 'Maximes Posthumes N. 532,' in La Rochefoucauld, 483.)

nature of the experience or experiences in question. If we do not posit the universality of ennui, then what is striking is not the continuity but the differences over time—and the fact that very different languages of reflection on subjective malaise converge in modernity.

Ennui and Enlightenment

For Kuhn, Pascal's abyss yawned on into the age of Enlightenment. Once again, his interpretation is based on an entirely decontextualized vision of the literary tradition of reflection on subjective experience. "The tragedy of eighteenth-century France is that the intellectuals accepted the Pascalian premise that the basis of the human condition is ennui, without being able to come to terms with it. Like Pascal, they rejected the alternatives of contemplation and distraction, but the tools they thought to have discovered, sensualism and rationalism, made it impossible for them to accept the Pascalian solution of faith" (139–40). They struggled to make do with reason alone, and, he declares, "Their efforts collapsed as dramatically as the social structure about them, and for the same reasons" (140). On Kuhn's reading, ennui is virtually omnipresent among Enlightenment thinkers. He contrasts Voltaire, who "devoted his whole life to the hopeless attempt to fend off ennui," becoming with his "gossamer" creations "the first esthetician of ennui," with Rousseau, "the explorer of the void over which Voltaire danced" (152). For Kuhn, Voltaire's voracious engagement with the world and Rousseau's withdrawal into self-absorbed reverie represent the alternatives before which the Enlightenment, having undermined the possibility of faith in God, placed Western man. "Ennui, as a general phenomenon of the Age of Enlightenment, going beyond literature and penetrating into every crevice of life, made the birth of [Goethe's] Werther and [Chateaubriand's] René not only possible but inevitable" (165).

Kuhn's narrative associating Enlightenment, the death of God, and widespread malaise was already a commonplace during the nineteenth century. There is no question that the discourse on boredom spread to ever wider sectors of society beginning in the late eighteenth century, but since this fact is open to other sorts of explanation as well, it is crucial to ask in what sense romanticism can be seen as the inevitable outgrowth of Enlightenment. We shall return to these issues in Chapter 3. Now, however, it will be helpful to strengthen Kuhn's position. In presenting ennui as the *causa finalis* of the transformation, he elides the historical events that intervened. By reading Hegel's account of the Enlightenment and the French Revolution as elements of a philosophical-historical myth about the origins of modern subjectivity, I propose to fill that lacuna in a fashion that, while consonant with Kuhn's idealist premises, points to the need for a more historically differentiated account of skepticism.

I have been arguing that Kuhn's decontextualized treatment of individual thinkers underestimates the power of the hegemonic religious discourse on subjective experience; he writes as though sheer doubt were enough to undermine its hold. A more complex vision of the relationship between epistemological skepticism and faith lies at the heart of Hegel's account of the emergence of modern subjectivity. In "The Battle of Enlightenment with Superstition," Hegel writes, "Enlightenment has an irresistible power over belief because it asserts itself on the basis of moments which are to be found in the consciousness of belief itself."[10] For Hegel, "Enlightenment" is "pure insight" gone into the world; it bears the legacy both of "skepticism" and of "theoretical and practical idealism," as "modes in which consciousness behaves negatively" vis-à-vis being (400). In Enlightenment, consciousness turns upon itself, negating belief: it "sees in the absolute essence nothing but the *être suprême*, or emptiness [*das Leere*]" (416).[11] However, according to Hegel, this negation, in which the fundamental "usefulness" of religion is revealed, is not independent of its religious other. It merely takes up the "principles" that define faith and "brings its own thoughts together for the believing consciousness" (417). By demonstrating that genuine interiority can only be realized in thought, Enlightenment robs faith of all content—and thereby inherits the negation of the world through which religious consciousness had defined and sustained itself. Thus "The Truth of Enlightenment," a new form of human consciousness, emerges: "absolute freedom" for which "all reality is only spiritual; the world . . . purely his will, and this is the general will" (432). For Hegel, the striving after subjective freedom advocated by mainstream Enlightenment thought culminated in the totalitarian fantasy of the proto-romantic Rousseau—and ultimately in the new religion of the state to which his thought helped give birth.

From the perspective of *The Phenomenology of Spirit*, all history is necessarily *Geistesgeschichte*—the story of the human spirit. Kuhn seems to share this conviction, yet he treats sociopolitical transformations as a mere backdrop to the permutations of ennui as expressed in significant literature. Hegel's approach points the way toward a more historically grounded and conceptually richer account of the relationship between language and experience that unfolds in the discourse on boredom. For him, the great philosophical

[10]*Die Phänomenologie des Geistes*, 422; subsequent references in text.
[11]Hegel alludes, of course, to the theological innovations of the French Revolution.

themes of the eighteenth century—the struggle between materialism and idealism, between the delights of this world and of the other, between subjective freedom and collective existence—come to a head in the French revolution. In his reading of that complex of events in the section of the *Phenomenology* entitled "Absolute Freedom and the Terror," the topoi of emptiness, repetition, and meaningless death which run through the discourse on boredom are situated in relation to the enlightened consciousness that knows itself as an absolutely free, rational being.

For Hegel, the very synthesis of skepticism, idealism, and absolute universality that had led to the victory of rational insight over the superstition of the past renders the "absolutely free" form of human consciousness peculiarly ruthless in pursuit of a democratic utopia. In the aftermath of the Enlightenment, the social order of the ancien régime, which had stabilized subjective identity in relation to faith in the next world, lost its meaning; qua rational being, Hegel writes, the individual is identical with the universal, "his goal the general goal, his work the general work" (433). But since absolute freedom is incompatible with representation, it is incapable of "positive work or deed . . . it is only the *fury* of disappearance" (435–36). After destroying all inherited forms of social organization in the revolution, the enlightened subject is left with nothing but "this knowledge of itself as an absolutely free and pure individual self" (436). Such a self cannot express its particularity without coming into opposition to the collective as such and thus negating its freedom.

Since "absolute freedom" consists in the identity between individual and collective, the same problem exists for the society as a whole. What Hegel, following Rousseau, calls the general will can only express itself via "the negation of the individual . . . The only work and deed of general freedom is thus death, and a death that has no inner extension and completion; for what is negated is the unfulfilled point of the absolutely free self; it is thus the coldest, most banal death, with no more significance than splitting a head of cabbage or a drink of water" (436). For Hegel, the guillotine is thus the birthplace of modern subjectivity: the link between absolute freedom and radically meaningless, mechanical death delineates the direction of post-Enlightenment thought. This new concept of death gives rise to an entirely new experience of boredom as the expression of the modern subject's genuine aloneness in a world without a divine referent—this death, as existentialism would confirm, is the Janus face of absolute freedom.

To make these claims comprehensible, it is necessary to follow Hegel's description of the experience of absolute freedom a few steps further. From the perspective of the *Phenomenology*, the dreadful culmination of the revolution is the fulfillment of subjective freedom as such. Through the Terror, he writes, "self-consciousness experiences what it *is*"—the power to destroy "all difference and all subsistence of difference in itself . . . The *terror* of death is the vision of its negative essence" (437). To think is to negate the world; for Hegel, such negation is the life of the human spirit, through which that which transcends physical existence comes into being. Human identity, as he put it in the Preface to the *Phenomenology*, inheres in "the monstrous power of the negative; it is the energy of thought, of the pure I" (36). People may attempt to return to a past where this truth was still obscured, for example by electing Napoleon Emperor or by restoring the monarchy. However, there is really no turning back. Belief and Enlightenment alike have been destroyed along with everything else "in the losses which the self experiences in absolute freedom" (439).

For Hegel, the global significance of the French Revolution turns on the new concept of death which has emerged, for in this concept death itself has revealed its historicity and thus its location within, rather than beyond, subjectivity. The death which is the work of the general will is a "meaningless death, the pure terror of the negative" but at the same time, since the individual subject is identical with that will, a death which is its own essence. Thus, Hegel writes, "meaningless death, the unfulfilled negativity of the self, is reversed in its inner concept into absolute positivity" (440). It is necessary, henceforth, actively to construct a world in which human existence can be made meaningful—to act historically. The only alternative is the "cycle of necessity" (438) in which history recommences and the lessons of absolute freedom are learned and forgotten, again and again, ad infinitum. For Hegel, who himself is reputed to have danced around a "freedom-tree" in his youth, the Terror revealed the truth of the French revolution: that without some form of substantial—that is to say, cultural, historical connection—to other people, the subjective consequence of freedom is utter nihilism. It is just this nihilism—and the vision of meaningless death that is its pendant—which I contend underlies the modern forms of boredom toward which Kuhn orients his study.

Hegel's reading of the significance of the French Revolution for the formation of modern subjectivity provides a philosophical framework for understanding an historic transformation that I shall discuss in detail in Chapter 3. The discourse on boredom developed in the nineteenth century reflected a new way of thinking about subjectivity itself—a mode of self-understanding in which human temporality was redefined as a consequence of the historical and cultural transformations that began in the Enlightenment. These larger shifts, I shall show, underlay the paradigm shift visible in the discourse of reflection on subjective malaise beginning in the late eighteenth century. In the plaints of ennui and melancholy that would become known as the *mal du siècle*, an experience began to take shape that was significantly closer to the radically godless experience of modern boredom than to acedia or melancholy.

Although Kuhn recognizes that the writers of the late eighteenth and early nineteenth century were describing significantly different experiences than their predecessors, he continues to read their works through the lens of his assumption that "ennui" is an ahistorical feature of the human condition. For him, the two godfathers of the modern malaise, Goethe's Werther and Chateaubriand's René, instantiate "a universal human trait, a dissatisfaction with reality that produces a certain longing after something beyond the mortal condition." Ennui is the "background of unfulfilled aspirations" that is a consequence of the longing that, "at least in life, is condemned to remain unsatisfied" (168). If neither Werther nor René comes to terms with this "nostalgia for the divine" (217), then, Kuhn contends, because both were too "egocentric," their thoughts "revolving constantly around the nothingness of their inner selves" (217).

In construing ennui as an effect of the inherent insufficiency of earthly existence in the face of the human longing for transcendence, Kuhn misses the historical particularity of the experiences described by Chateaubriand and Goethe. A rather different reading emerges if we take Hegel's narrative about the significance of the French Revolution to heart. From this point of view, the subjectivity at stake in each case was necessarily quite differently configured. *The Sufferings of Young Werther* (1774) ended in poetic self-destruction as an act of protest against a world in which individual worth was determined by social standing. Werther's melancholic longings and his suicide belong firmly to the pre-revolutionary period. The lassitude, hysteria, and fatigued will of *René* (1802) come from another world, one in which the meaninglessness of death has been universalized. Kuhn understands this historical change in moralistic terms: "The spiritual wasteland that René's goalless passions create is a reflection of the ruins left behind by the ethical and moral collapse that accompanied the French Revolution." While Hegel saw in the Terror a triumph of abstract reason and thus a revelation of the negativity of subjectivity with historic implications, Kuhn's more Hobbesian interpretation takes the part of the *ancient regime*: Chateaubriand's self-indulgent protagonist is "the product of the age of terror made possible by the unbridling of passions" (198) in the Revolution. However, Kuhn is not himself able to advocate a return to faith. The sociopolitical transformations of this historic conjuncture are, on his account, little more than means by

which eternal features of an essentially unchanging human condition are revealed. The veil of religion has been stripped away, and the meaninglessness
of human existence revealed.

It is as though history has come to an end in ennui's revelation of the
negativity of the self. From this point on Kuhn's narrative is little more than
a catalog of literary works that "illustrate the variety of guises under which
ennui appears" (221). By the end of the nineteenth century—in which "there
is such diversity of expression that it becomes increasingly difficult to discern
a pattern in the development of the concept"—ennui is on his view absolute,
having been "transformed into a negation that becomes an affirmation"
(329). In this world, he continues, "nothingness is the ultimate hope" (329).
The modern subject is face to face with the insignificance of human existence, with the meaninglessness of death in a world where no substantial
meaning can persist. Accordingly, Kuhn writes, "in the twentieth century
ennui is not one theme among others; it is the dominant theme . . . [E]ven
those literary works in which the spirit of ontological affirmation triumphs
contain the germs of the malady" (331). In the end, Kuhn's ahistorical vision
of the experience undermines his historical framework. All the contemporary permutations of ennui prove only that there is really nothing new under
the sun: "All the variations upon this theme are exaggerated versions of past
experiences" (373). "Twentieth-century literature depicts the triumph of the
demon of noontide over a despairing world" (374). For those who cannot
find consolation in religion, the only hope lies in a rediscovery of the positive
dimensions of ennui—in its link to the creative process in which the
"monumental struggle against the power of nothingness" bears fruit in an assertion of "humanity" (378).[12]

Ennui, Literature, and the Making of Western Man

Reinhard Kuhn's interpretation of ennui takes a common intuition as its
point of departure: Boredom seems by its very nature to be a universal and
all-pervasive experience, a fundamental way in which human beings relate to
the world. However, his own narrative indicates that the experience of ennui
that is so omnipresent a feature of modern life is a relatively new phenomenon, one rooted in the transformations of historical life that began in the late
eighteenth century. The tension between these perspectives is by no means
exclusive to Kuhn; it inheres in the idea of boredom as it took shape histori-

---

[12] In his recent *Boredom and the Religious Imagination,* Michael Raposa links these dimensions
in a Peircean reading of boredom as a sign that there is "something 'more' revealed at the very
heart of things" and thus as an invitation to creative "Musement."

cally. As the experience of boredom achieved Benjamin's "epidemic" proportions, so did its interpretation as a universal feature of the human condition. In rhetorical terms: a particular way of thinking about subjective malaise was becoming pervasive according to which boredom appears as both sign and product of the meaninglessness of life. As Kuhn's catalog of ennui in nineteenth-century literature (221–329) attests, quotations in which boredom is decried as an all-pervasive feature of the human condition could be multiplied *ad nauseum*. While there were those who emphasized the play of historical and socio-cultural factors in the spread of this sense of meaninglessness, Kuhn follows an even more considerable tradition of philosophical and idealist interpretation of boredom, according to which it was an idea that spread, a logical structure of experience playing itself out in history.

Kuhn's ahistorical and areligious conception of boredom, then, belongs to a new rhetoric of reflection on subjective experience that came into being in the aftermath of Enlightenment. The tension in the nineteenth-century discourse on boredom between awareness of the historical particularity of this experience of universalized skepticism and an insistence upon the omnipresence and universality of such meaninglessness reflects the ambiguous position of the emergent language of boredom between secular and religious understandings of the self. Kuhn's elaborate strategy for interpreting ennui as a universal feature of the human condition while acknowledging the fact that the experience is pervasive only in modernity is thus worth examining closely. In the Introduction to the narrative through which, as we have seen, he links the vicissitudes of ennui to the progress of Western civilization as such, Kuhn thoroughly and straightforwardly addresses difficulties often glossed over by other thinkers who share his intuition that boredom is, in the first instance, not a social but an intellectual and spiritual phenomenon—in the broadest sense, an idea. Kuhn not only addresses the problem of conceptualizing boredom as both timeless and historical; he also clearly delimits what he views as philosophically significant boredom from more quotidian varieties—those which he contends cannot be understood as manifestations of such an idea about human existence.

On Kuhn's view, the experience of ennui can be defined ahistorically, for not its name but rather its nature remains constant over time. That is to say, it is the philosophical—ideal—content, what the subject confronts in the experience, that makes boredom so important. *The Demon of Noontide* begins: "There are certain ideas that are far more than abstract intellectual concepts, ideas that through their dynamism have contributed to the formation of the human spirit. They do not merely reflect what already exists; as creative forces they in fact help mold the human mind and shape reality" (3). To support this idealist premise, Kuhn invokes Alfred Fouillée's conception of the *idée-force*, an idea that "does not reflect a reality" independent of itself but rather "becomes one of the factors of reality."[13] Fouillée, a proponent of a philosophy of experience based on a synthesis of evolutionary thought with idealist philosophy, understood ideas as fonts of energy and change through which spiritual realities were transmuted into material effects. According to Fouillée:

> One has not enumerated all the causes and forces in nature when one has enumerated all movements. There may be and there are other activities than those that are purely mechanical: these are the psychic activities. The ideas are at once the expression of their activities and the movements through which they reveal themselves externally. They are the intermediaries between the world of motion and the moral world. For true evolutionism, ideas are far from being inert but are conscious forms of action . . . Thinking is a manifestation of mental energy, not of mental inertia. (Fouillée 1890, xciii)[14]

In invoking Fouillée's concept of *idées-forces*, Kuhn does more than signal his opposition to materialist explanations of social phenomena. Like Fouillée, he sees a world full of such intermediaries between the material and the moral—a world of ideas such as "love, hate, charity, envy, pride and jealousy, to name just a few." And, Kuhn contends, careful studies of these concepts "and their transformation throughout the ages . . . have contributed much to our understanding of man as he is today" (3).[15] "The idea of boredom or ennui," he writes, has been "crucial in the formation of Western man"—the experience is "certainly a universal problem"—and yet no study exists for boredom comparable to those of other key ideas (3–4). He proposes "partially to fill this gap by investigating ennui in its various manifestations in Western literature" (4).

By focusing on literature, *The Demon of Noontide* places the problem of representing what is simultaneously an emotional phenomenon and a reflective concept at the center of theoretical reflection on boredom. For Kuhn, "ennui" is both a literary theme and an existential experience that

---

[13] Alfred Fouillée, *Morale des idées-forces*, cited in Kuhn, 3. Fouillée, an opponent of Durkheimian sociology and a social conservative, "saw societies as systems of idea-forces." These ideas, he believed, played "a causal role in the social process, partly through an inherent tendency to achieve their own realization" (Ringer, *Fields of Knowledge,* 253–54). Alfred Fouillée first developed his theory of *idées-forces* in his 1865 *Théorie des Ideés de Platon*, in relation to the notion of moral freedom (*liberté moral*) (Guyau, 3).

[14] Fouillée developed his concept in a philosophical trilogy, *L'evolutionnisme des Idées-forces* (1890), *La psychologie des Idées-forces* (1893), and *La morale des Idées-forces* (1907).

[15] Prominent among the examples he names are Denis de Rougemont's *Love in the Western World* and Erich Auerbach's *Mimesis*.

produces a "desire to express in writing [one's] state of mind" (4). To trace the history of its representation is therefore to illuminate human existence itself. *The Demon of Noontide* is, then, simultaneously a survey of the "history of boredom" from a transhistorical point of view, an argument that ennui is a universal feature of human existence, and a philosophical interpretation of the significance of the material it surveys. As we have already noted, there is a fundamental tension within Kuhn's project—one that may be traced to the humanist tradition in which he situates his work. With the ambiguous notion of an "idea-force," Kuhn attempts to save a fundamentally ahistorical understanding of subjective experience and its "universal" problems without suppressing the recognition that human existence has been transformed throughout Western history.

Kuhn does not want his study to be construed as instrumentalizing literature. Thus Fouillée's concept of *idées-forces* allows him to distinguish his approach to ennui in *The Demon of Noontide* from one which would treat literature as a mere "vehicle for ideas":

> If the critic is primarily interested in philosophical concepts, linguistic paradigms, political ideas, or sociological phenomena, he is perfectly justified in using literature as a mirror of man's problems and of his attempts to come to terms with them (although he may find that the reflection is often a distorted one). But for the critic who is concerned first and foremost with the nature of literature as such and only indirectly with what it might reveal about man, the 'history of ideas' approach may easily lead to the disappearance of the very essence of the body of works under analysis. (5)

In contrast to the sort of history in which ideas are treated as signs of something beyond themselves, genuinely humanistic study is concerned with "the human spirit" and its development in the world of ideas—not with "man" and his prosaic concerns but with art and literature. Fouillée's notion of an *idée-force* allows Kuhn to pose his problem in formal, literary-theoretical terms—ennui is "not only a subject of certain works of art but also a part of their temporal fabric and spatial structure"—and at the same time contend that the import of his study extends beyond the realm of literary study per se. For Kuhn, "ennui is not just an idea about which authors have written," but a form of experiencing time and space that is expressed as a formal feature of texts that thematize the experience (5).

Qua *idée-force*, ennui is part of the overarching historical and cultural process in which, on Kuhn's view, human self-consciousness develops. The "common and constant element" among ennui's "various permutations," he writes, is its nature as a "negative force" that induces efforts of self-assertive transcendence. Through this negativity, ennui fosters the human struggle "to fill the void which it hollows out. It is the state that, if it does not render sterile, precedes and makes possible creation in the realms of the practical, the spiritual, and the aesthetic" (378). Showing how the Western literary tradition bears witness to the vicissitudes of the encounter with nothingness, of the human struggle to create meaning, will therefore demonstrate the philosophical power of literary criticism. Because Kuhn understands textual representations of experience as privileged "expressions" of fundamental human problems and literature as the realm in which "man" confronts the eternal questions of human existence, the canon seems to him to represent the proper domain for a study of the *idées-forces* that have been "crucial in the formation of western man." In particular, he claims that his study of ennui "can provide insights into the nature of the creative act itself" (4) because literary representation is the paradigmatic mode through which this *idée-force* so essential to the development of the human spirit has been realized. Indeed, since the study of literature is tantamount to engagement with the fundamental problems of human existence, the "psycho-literary" concept of ennui "can be used as a critical tool for new and deeper interpretations of man's actions and of the expression that he gives to them through works of art" (378). Kuhn's vision of ennui as an idea-force effaces the distinction between experience and its representation: literary history illuminates human existence as such.

For Kuhn, literature is thus far more than a "vehicle for ideas": it is a cultural phenomenon that both embodies and facilitates philosophical self-reflection. When he claims that "most victims of boredom" share "the desire to express in writing their state of mind" (4), he is asserting not that all literature is biographical but that literature is per se shaped by the human attempt to come to terms with existential dilemmas. Literature does not simply "mirror man's problems and his attempts to come to terms with them" (5); it is a privileged site for reflection on the meaning of human experience. Kuhn's study of the topos of ennui in Western literature can therefore double as an investigation of the universal development of the human spirit. The purportedly existential link between ennui and writing allows him to integrate his philosophical ambitions and his concern with the "essence" of literary works, his idealism and his formalism. Since ennui is part of the formal structure of literary works (essential, for example, to the way Thomas Mann represents time in *Zauberberg*), a study of the representation of ennui illuminates the problem of existence itself. Great literature, by definition, fulfills a basic human desire to express the enigmas of subjective experience. Thus Kuhn can call his "literary topography of ennui" an "attempt to chart what Donne called 'the strict map of our misery'"; a meditative literary history of the sort he offers constitutes a distinctive contribution to the process of collective self-reflection that forms the Western cultural tradition (13). Of course, such project is aimed at a very particular audience: only from the perspective of an elite community of literary consumers who see no difficulty in identifying "the human spirit" with "Western man" and creativity with writing can it appear unproblematic that only canonically regarded great books enter into consideration in a study of the "universal problem" of ennui.

But how, exactly, is this idea of ennui to be related to the experience as it is lived or represented in literature? Many different qualities, Kuhn writes, characterize the state of ennui. It has both mental and physical symptoms— among them estrangement, inertia of the will, "the obsession with death, the lack of involvement, monotony, immobility, and . . . distortion of the sense of time" (13). Nonetheless, "by reducing [ennui's] multitudinous characteristics to their essential common factor" (13), he writes, it is possible to arrive at a working definition of the topic that accounts for the importance of the idea in Western civilization. The Introduction to the *Demon of Noontide* culminates in a definition of ennui:

> the state of emptiness that the soul feels when it is deprived of interest in action, life, and the world (be it this world or another), a condition that is the immediate consequence of the encounter with nothingness, and has as an immediate effect a disaffection with reality. (13)

For Kuhn and his implied reader, "man's" propensity to ennui—to the "loss of interest in action, life, and the world" as a result of the encounter with ever-proximate nothingness—delineates a fundamental feature of the human condition. Although it may have gone under different names at different times, this experience, in which the meaninglessness of ordinary engagement with the world is revealed, raises metaphysical issues about action and human identity itself. Just as ennui itself leads ineluctably to philosophical self-reflection, Kuhn's project of tracing the development of the idea of ennui through its literary manifestations should thus issue in insights into the human condition itself.

The discursive specificity of Kuhn's argumentative appeal notwithstanding, his notion that such philosophically significant experiences of boredom are a universal feature of the human condition and the idealist vision of intellectual history with which this interpretation is correlated are proper to a much larger philosophical tradition of reflection on boredom. Though it may be tempting to dismiss out of hand an approach that begins by positing a soul in search of meaning and encountering nothingness, perhaps what jars in Kuhn's definition is simply his unfashionable language. Just as he has numerous predecessors, a similarly ahistorical approach to the theorization of the experience might sound far more up-to-date. One might, for example, reformulate the point of Kuhn's study as follows: Working through the most diverse texts, exhibiting by its very appearance that even those who understood themselves to live in a meaningful world created by a benevolent God suffered from the epistemic dilemmas that have become so pervasive in modernity, 'ennui' manifests the perpetual undermining of the subject through the encounter with the groundlessness of Being. In it, one might claim, a metaphysical dilemma inseparable from human self-reflection becomes palpable; what we call 'ennui' is endemic to any language that tries to express or represent the experience of desire and thus constitutes a foundational problem of subjectivity.

Couched in a less dated vocabulary, the notion that ennui is a fundamentally philosophical experience appears rather more plausible. Kuhn's existentialist vocabulary and reverence for canonical writers obscures the continuity of his contribution to the history of "the human spirit" with the more contemporary search for perennial metaphysical dilemmas in intertextual frameworks. It is by no means necessary to accept Kuhn's idiosyncratic ontology to share his belief that, since genuine philosophical reflection occurs in a realm of thought separate from ordinary life, metaphysically significant ennui can be abstracted from the historical context in which it transpires.

It is Kuhn's formalist invocation of a philosophical rhetoric of experience rather than his idealist vision of literary endeavor per se which leads him to make such large claims for boredom. Thus in treating the philosophical issues associated with the idea of ennui as historically invariable dilemmas of the human condition, Kuhn evades the crucial hermeneutic issue of the place of the literary tradition(s) he analyzes within the larger, historically evolving discourse on subjective experience. Any approach that treats boredom as an idea or concept, even one that embodies far more sophisticated views about language, will remain open to the same objections. By examining the arguments through which Kuhn establishes a supposedly phenomenological distinction between ennui and garden-variety boredom, I will demonstrate that the philosophical rhetoric of reflection he invokes makes it impossible to pose the problem of the significance of boredom in a theoretically adequately fashion. The notion that epistemologically interesting boredom can be defined in ahistorical terms is grounded in a rhetoric of experience that begs the question of how problems of meaning arise in human life.

The Philosophical Rhetoric of Experience

Kuhn's argument appeals to a purportedly experiential distinction between two registers of boredom, between trivial annoyances or pains and profound spiritual suffering; he limits his study to the latter "particular form, which, to distinguish it from the more general concept, we shall call 'ennui'" (5).[16] On his view, though both sorts of boredom are perennial features of human existence, only the second, metaphysical dis-ease, is an idea with transhistorical significance—as attested by its role in the great literary works of the Western tradition that form the focus of his study. As we have seen, although he recognizes historical distinctions between ancient acedia, renaissance melancholy, and modern boredom, Kuhn conceives of all these forms of malaise—religious and secular, pre- and post-industrial alike—as manifestations of 'ennui.' By distinguishing existential alienation by whatever name from the more ordinary forms of disaffection also classed as boredom, Kuhn establishes a crucial foundation for his claim that only cases of what he designates as 'ennui' play a role in the development of "the human spirit." However, his argument is universalist in a very particular, elitist sense; to be convinced, the reader must share Kuhn's fundamental assumptions about literature and culture. In the absence of such common ground, his argument actually underlines the difficulty of distinguishing ordinary boredom from its philosophically significant variants. Indeed, I shall show that the argumentative strategy by which Kuhn arrives at the definition quoted earlier begs the question of whether there is a genuine distinction between boredom and ennui—that is, one independent of his very particular understanding of culture.

Kuhn arrives at his ahistorical definition of ennui via a neo-Aristotelian "saving of the phenomena" that does not directly depend upon privileging literature. Beginning from the assumption that "ennui" can be distinguished from "the more general concept" of boredom (5), he "enumerates the various forms of boredom that for our purposes do not fall under the heading of ennui" (6). On Kuhn's view, "because they are peripheral to our central problem, neither '*désoeuvrement*,' psychosomatic boredom, monotony, nor anomie falls within the domain of this study" (9). After dismissing these other kinds of boredom through an argument to which we shall return in a moment, he provides two portraits of concert-goers suffering from the form

[16]This distinction, embedded both in the Italian *noia* and the French *ennui*, may also, according to Kuhn, be found in their etymological precursors.

of boredom which *does* interest him.[17] He then abstracts from his descriptions of their experiences "the principal characteristics of ennui." These four "main attributes" provide a sort of structural framework for the psychological symptoms, such as "obsession with death" and "distortion of the sense of time," that accompany the experience.

These characteristics are in effect the attributes of boredom as *idée-force*. First, although ennui's "origins are always to be found in the soul, its manifestations are both spiritual and physical." "Second, the state of ennui is entirely independent of any external circumstances." Third, "it is also independent of our will." Finally, "this condition is usually characterized by the phenomenon of estrangement. In the state of ennui the world is emptied of its significance" (12). From these highly abstract qualities, Kuhn distills his "working definition of the topic" for the study upon which he is embarking. "By reducing [ennui's] multitudinous characteristics to their essential common factor," he arrives at the definition of ennui that we have already cited:

> the state of emptiness that the soul feels when it is deprived of interest in action, life, and the world (be it this world or another), a condition that is the immediate consequence of the encounter with nothingness, and has as an immediate effect a disaffection with reality. (13)

Since genuine ennui is the existential crisis of an isolated consciousness, the question of which factors brought about such a crisis of self that the world seems absolutely "emptied of its significance" is irrelevant. Kuhn's use of the passive voice in his definition obscures questions of causality; even the question of whether the sufferer understands the experience in religious terms is bracketed. Since the historical vicissitudes of the *idée-force* must be understood in relation to the predicament of human existence itself, it is "the encounter with nothingness" as such that occasions all philosophically interesting boredom.

Kuhn's claim that his study can be universal in its significance, although particular in its literary scope, thus depends upon a conception of ennui that excludes historically contingent forms of boredom *in principle*. No matter how great the estrangement or suffering associated with ordinary forms of boredom, experiences that cannot be understood in abstraction from their cultural milieus as pure "states of mind" do not, on Kuhn's understanding, bear any necessary relation to the metaphysical experience that is the wellspring of human creativity. However, unlike many thinkers who share his assumption that metaphysically significant ennui is categorically different from

---

[17]These portraits describe the experiences of Gide's *Gérard* and a fictive "music-lover" of his own devising.

quotidian forms of malaise, Kuhn does not simply presume the existence of an existentially basic form of boredom.

In the introduction to *The Demon of Noontide*, he describes forms of boredom that cannot be extricated from their worldly conditions in an attempt to show that "external circumstances" and "the will" *must* be irrelevant to the aetiology of an experience that reflects the sufferer's ontological susceptibility to existential crisis. Although Kuhn concedes that "the other types of boredom are often confused with ennui because they can never be completely divorced from it" (9), these descriptions function to establish a quasi-empirical distinction between the "encounter with nothingness" and the more prosaic forms of malaise that populate the wider discursive field of "boredom." Through a close examination of Kuhn's descriptions of what he calls the "peripheral forms" of the experience and the criteria he uses to evaluate their significance, I shall show that his conceptual and methodological claim that ennui is radically different from "ordinary" boredom is bound up with elitist presuppositions about what forms of human experience are philosophically significant. The purportedly experiential distinction upon which Kuhn's philosophical claims for ennui depend rests on an unacknowledged discursive foundation: The difference between ennui and quotidian boredom is perceptible to those who understand themselves and represent their experiences of meaning and meaninglessness in terms shaped by the canonical literary tradition.

Housewife, Worker, Native: Boredom as Mimesis

> Or as, when an underground train, in the tube, stops
>   too long between stations
> And the conversation rises and slowly fades into silence
> And you see behind every face the mental emptiness deepen
> Leaving only the growing terror of nothing to think about . . .
>
> T. S. Eliot, *Four Quartets*

Kuhn's claims for his literary study of boredom depend on an assumption that genuine reflection upon the meaning of human existence is the province of the leisured few for whom the "encounter with nothingness" is a philosophical one. Because the sheer prevalence of boredom seems to call this presumption into question, Kuhn must establish a bounded "domain" by which other people's malaise is excluded from philosophical consideration. In the introduction, he explains why "désœuvrement," psychosomatic boredom, monotony, and anomie all fall outside the realm of his study. As I shall show, however, it is Kuhn's descriptions—i.e., the way in which the four other "kinds" of boredom are represented—rather than any substantial difference between the experiences that justifies their exclusion from the realm of ennui.

Each of these "peripheral" forms of boredom is defined metonymically, through its instantiation in a "typical" bearer of the experience. The forms of boredom identified with the figures of the housewife, the worker, and the 'native' are then excluded from his study on the grounds that they are fundamentally different from that negative, yet transcendental experience of the human condition known as "ennui." However, Kuhn's own arguments in favor of these exclusions illustrate that the difference between ennui and such "peripheral" forms of boredom appears phenomenologically verifiable only from a culturally specific perspective. Read against the grain, the strategies Kuhn uses to marginalize the four other "kinds" of boredom illuminate the blind spots of that perspective and thereby clarify what is at stake in defining boredom in terms of a philosophical rhetoric of experience.

The first of the peripheral forms of boredom is an experience Kuhn regards as "hardly worth serious study." "Désœuvrement" is a result of involuntary idleness; it ends, he writes, "when the conditions that make for this frame of mind cease, as they always do" (6). Although Kuhn describes this form of boredom with an example taken from Flaubert's *The Sentimental Education*, his decisive examples are drawn not from literature but from the cultural commonplaces of 1976. "Frédéric's boredom [in the lecture-hall] is similar in quality if not in kind to that so often felt by a very different type of person, namely, by the housewife standing in line at the supermarket who taps her heels as she wonders whether her turn will ever come. The commuter sitting in the subway train" and staring out the window waiting for his station is in "exactly the same state" (6).

Kuhn's confidence that he can define the quality of others' experience is quite striking. Because he is appealing to commonplaces shared with his audience—presumably his readers know boredom in the lecture hall, likely they are also commuters with wives who do the shopping—Kuhn can unselfconsciously claim the clairvoyance of an omniscient narrator while disavowing that the narrative in which these figures are placed is of his own devising. While he quickly pronounces the transiency of this malaise—"the cure for 'désœuvrement' is its termination, which the passage of time inevitably brings" (7)—from a different perspective, one might imagine that such "types of persons" suffer from something other than the frustration of idle waiting. Indeed, Kuhn can only pronounce the housewife's boredom different in kind from Frédéric's because he assumes that, having made her purchases, she will be satisfied.

Kuhn's own account of the second "peripheral form" of boredom suggests that this conclusion may have been wishful thinking on his part.

> A somewhat different case is illustrated by the typical portrait of the suburbanite. She is tired of the magazine that she is reading or the television show that she is watching and mixes another cocktail for herself. Or perhaps she telephones an equally bored friend and they talk for hours about nothing, or perhaps she drifts into an affair that means as little to her as the television show or the magazine article. Despite its banality such a case presents infinitely more serious problems that the preceding ones . . . [because] this is a condition that has no foreseeable or inevitable end but death. It could be called a case of extended or timeless 'désœuvrement.' It is a problem for the psychologist, and the victim of this malady is a prospective patient for the psychiatrist. (7)

There is much to recommend this portrait of a latter-day Emma Bovary as a depiction of someone suffering from ennui. However, Kuhn underplays the crisis of meaning implicit in his description. Categorizing the suburbanite's experience as "a primarily medical problem," he places her suffering outside the purview of his study.

By defining this paradoxical, terminally banal condition as a consequence of "forced inactivity of the mind" (7), Kuhn tacitly acknowledges that *désœuvrement*, at least in this extended or "timeless" form, is proximate to ennui and must be taken seriously. However, because he is working with a commonplace whose inner life is by definition transparent, he can dismiss "the suburbanite's" experience from the realm of philosophical significance, this time as a merely psychological malady. For him, this is not a "typical portrait" of someone permanently condemned to an existence without meaning or hope. While Kuhn recognizes that things are not so simple as they seemed in line at the grocery store, his analysis of the "housewife's" dilemma emphasizes not her estrangement but the dimension of frustrated desire. According to him, the suburbanite's boredom results from a permanent inability to reach her "true goals" or to find satisfactory substitutes. Kuhn thus distinguishes her malaise from the metaphysical experience of ennui which has its origins "in the soul." In this case, forced mental "inactivity" has its origins in the suburbanite's neurotic personality. Since her boredom, unlike genuine ennui, is 'psychological,' it is curable. By finding a means of realizing the unarticulated desire that underlies her condition, the suburbanite could, theoretically, cease seeking mere distraction and bring her long *désœuvrement* to an end. In terms of Kuhn's criteria, her condition depends both on external circumstances and upon her will; good therapy should be capable of alleviating her estrangement.

From a perspective that does not find the suffering of "the typical suburbanite" to be quite so transparently psychosomatic, it is difficult to see why such "timeless *désœuvrement*" is not ennui.[18] The distinction Kuhn draws in the case of this example between psychologically and metaphysically engendered forms of boredom seems tendentious—it is never explicitly defended, and since the argument succeeds only if the audience can share Kuhn's certainty that he knows what the "typical suburbanite" is feeling, it begs the question about whether external circumstances are relevant to authentic ennui.[19] The attributes of independence of external circumstances and of the will of the sufferer are supposed to capture, respectively, the indiscriminate way ennui comes upon one (as when it overwhelms what should be a satisfying experience of attending a concert) and the inability of the sufferer to *decide* to escape boredom or undertake any effective strategies for combating it (in Kuhn's description of genuine ennui, the concert-goer's excruciating attempts to engage with music that fails to move him). For Kuhn the housewife is so inseparable from her life of involuntary mental inactivity that it seems self-evident that her experience must modulate between the poles of satisfaction and disaffection with her vapid pastimes. The possibility that, in becoming conscious of this circumstance, she could be gripped by a genuine existential malaise evidently does not to occur to him.

A cruel irony is at work. Kuhn's analysis of the "housewife's" psychological malaise illustrates that he views her very existence as meaningless; it is based in falsely oriented or entirely disoriented desire. Nonetheless, he finds her condition "banal" and pronounces her suffering psychosomatic. Her misery, because dependent on external circumstances, is vacuous, yet it is her lack of will that causes the situation to continue. Thus "the suburbanite" is on the one hand blamed as the cause of the condition to which she is condemned and on the other excoriated as incapable of genuine ennui because of her imbrication in the circumstances which constitute that condition. Her boredom is not sufficiently separable from her social identity to achieve existential status. But she is not alone: this mimetic model also underlies the exclusion of two male figures from the high cultural wasteland.

The third "type of boredom" from which Kuhn distinguishes genuine ennui is that which "accompanies the performance of routine and meaningless

---

[18] In her recent *Langeweile: Zum Umgang mit Zeit und Gefühlen in Deutschland vom späten 18. bis zum frühen 20. Jahrhundert*, Martina Kessel demonstrates that the discourse on boredom is highly gendered. As in Kuhn's example, feminine boredom tended historically to be construed as a psychological or moral problem—something that a proper education in renunciation would ideally prevent—while masculine boredom was not only acknowledged as legitimate but often valorized.

[19] Consider, by contrast, Betty Friedan's account of "the problem that has no name," Friedan 14–18 and passim in the chapter of the same title.

labor" (7–8). As a product of the industrial revolution, the experience of "monotony" is, he argues, of sociological rather than philosophical significance. Once again, Kuhn elucidates the experience by appealing to a contemporary commonplace: "This sort of deadening boredom has become identified with the worker who every morning and every evening punches the time-clock and who in between these two events mechanically performs the same routine task" (8). While sociologists have rightly turned their attention to this problem, he optimistically remarks, it "has already almost been solved for them by another industrial revolution. Automation is tending more and more to abolish this type of work" (8). Ironically, on his view, this advance has exacerbated the sociological problem of working-class boredom. "As the working week becomes progressively shorter, the worker has more time on his hands than he knows what to do with" (8).

From an historical perspective, both the suburban housewife's "timeless *désœuvrement*" and the worker's experience of monotony are linked to what I call the democratization of leisure in modernity—both are effects of the disoccupation produced by labor-saving devices. Since both of these forms of boredom are precipitated by external circumstances that can in principle be overcome, on Kuhn's definition both fail to qualify as genuine ennui. However, he distinguishes these explicitly modern forms of boredom in a fashion that bears closer consideration. For Kuhn, the worker lacks precisely that negative self-understanding that distinguished the bourgeois housewife, and different outside experts are brought in to treat his boredom. In the first instance, working-class boredom is the province of "sociologists and human relations engineers" (8). Unfortunately, Kuhn laments, like the housewives' psychiatrists, they propose distractions rather than developing cures.

> In their attempt (seconded vigorously by the amusement industries) to find ever more means of 'killing time,' they negate all the positive qualities of leisure and all the potentiality inherent in such a condition. . . . Perhaps it would be more sensible of them to search for means of making the members of this new 'leisure class' aware of their aspirations, rather than to offer them cheap and inadequate substitutes that cheat them of their true possibilities. (8)

For Kuhn, the worker's boredom reflects the external circumstance of meaninglessly monotonous activities, but like the suburbanite he is incapable of reflection on that vacuity. Both experience a form of leisure devoid of self-reflection. As the slippage between transient and timeless, endemic *désœuvrement* in Kuhn's portrait of the suburbanite already illustrated, consumption is inadequate for relieving boredom: because consumer culture provides false satisfactions, it fosters rather than alleviates the desire for meaning.

"The worker," like "the suburbanite," is ignorant of his own authentic self; his will to self-transcendence must first be awakened. But while the housewife's "timeless *désœuvrement*" expresses an inchoate awareness of the frustrated desire which is the profounder cause of her discontent, on Kuhn's reading, the worker's experience of "monotony" simply mirrors the external circumstance of a monotonous existence; he instantiates a form of boredom devoid even of that rudimentary level of self-consciousness that rendered the housewife's tedium accessible to therapy. Thus, although in the case of the bourgeois housewife, a therapeutic refusal to offer distractions may be enough to cause her to identify her "true goals" and desires, the worker, who is new to leisure, must be educated in its possibilities. For this reason, Kuhn views "monotony" not as a psychological but as a social problem.

Although Kuhn's plea for developing the working classes' consciousness of the genuine possibilities of their new-found leisure seems anti-elitist, his argument in fact begs the question of whether working-class boredom, like that of suburban housewives, is ontologically distinct from the metaphysical malady that is the object of his study. Kuhn's treatment of these examples illustrates that the distinction between ennui and quotidian forms of boredom is rhetorical rather than perceptual. In claiming that these "peripheral" forms of boredom can be alleviated by psycho-social interventions, Kuhn excludes the housewife and the worker from the realm of ennui proper on the basis of an idealist vision of culture in which leisure maintains its traditional significance as the necessary condition for theoretical reflection. For him, philosophically interesting boredom is a result of the confrontation with the void that is the thinker's privilege; it is not an historical but an existential phenomenon. But as Kuhn's own examples suggest, this perspective occludes the subjective effects of modern democratized leisure. To realize the gesture he makes toward including "the worker" in the project of culture would entail abandoning his philosophical rhetoric of experience and with it the hierarchical model that places the wellsprings of genuine human creativity beyond the reach of those whose boredom is linked to specific historical conditions.

A critical reading of Kuhn's own analysis thus leads to the question of whether the distinction between ennui and its "peripheral forms" can really be maintained. Although the description of the worker's dilemma begins with the time-clock and the externalities of labor, it seems to end with an internal crisis, with a persistent experience of time—which "it is not possible to kill"—dooming the efforts of supposed experts to distract a soul thrown back upon itself. As in the case of the bored suburbanite, it is Kuhn's narrative placement of the worker's experience which entails that the estrangement he experiences when meaningless work slides into meaningless leisure is not authentic ennui. For each of these figures, one could imagine another narrative in which the emptiness of time and the apparent meaninglessness of their existence produced an experience of boredom with the philosophical significance Kuhn denies them.

If Kuhn's claims are read in historical context, his purported ability to distinguish ennui from quotidian boredom on empirical grounds appears as an ideological maneuver that effectively excludes women and the working class from the realm of cultural production and philosophical reflection. Indeed, his interpretation of the malaise proper to these figures is symptomatic of the crisis induced in the self-proclaimed representatives of the highest values of Western civilization by the democratization of leisure in modernity. The bourgeois housewife and the increasingly irrelevant manual worker are metonymic for two forms of the chronic *désœuvrement* that characterizes the modern world—a world in which leisure is no longer a privileged realm of elite self-cultivation. Kuhn's "typical portrait of the bored suburbanite" symbolizes the crisis brought on by women's recognition of their inability to realize their "true goals" while subordinated to the institution of the bourgeois family that defines their identity by restricting it to the ahistorical private sphere. His disaffected worker is a metonym for the masses whose disintegrating social function no longer provides them with a stable identity that allows them to accept the order of society, masses whose forms of diversion seem to the mandarins to threaten the very foundation of Western culture.

Kuhn clearly recognizes the pervasiveness of various forms of boredom in modernity as a phenomenon of historical significance. However, by consigning concrete work on the problem to the social engineers and psychotherapists who are materialist modernity's high priests, he clings to the subjectivistic understanding of ennui that makes his study a contribution to the timeless project of culture: understanding "man" as such. What is at stake in his philosophical approach to boredom becomes fully apparent in his treatment of "anomie" as the fourth "peripheral form" of boredom. Here Kuhn individualistically redefines the sociological notion that modernity is characterized by a collective sense of meaninglessness and then projects that sense outside of Western society itself.

In the sociological literature, "anomie" generally describes the spiritual malaise prevalent in the context of modern, urban existence. Strikingly, though, Kuhn locates the experience in a radically foreign, "primitive" realm. Citing Marcel Mauss, he defines "this fatal despondency of a person who lacks the exertion to live" as a result of exclusion from the larger community as a consequence of ritual transgressions. He gives as his example "the afflicted Polynesian" who dies as a result of "'anomie,' the total loss of the will to live" (9). While Durkheim's concept referred to anomie as "a state of social disequilibrium in which the hierarchy of values disintegrates and 'all regulation is lacking,'"[20] Kuhn uses the term to describe not society but the individual, not the worldly conditions but the subjective state they produce. This idiosyncratic redefinition of anomie as a form of boredom dependent on external circumstances excludes the phenomenon from the realm of philosophical significance. As in the case of *désœuvrement* and monotony, Kuhn reduces anomie to a subjective phenomenon and thereby begs the question of whether philosophically interesting boredom can be understood independently of its historical enabling conditions.

Most importantly, the highly questionable rhetorical strategy of placing anomie outside the realm of Western civilization and treating it as the consequence of an exotic and backward intolerance for a "warrior" who incurs "some infraction of the social customs" allows Kuhn to evade the question of how this experience, considered more broadly, might be linked to the others he has discussed. Like the grand malaise of the disoccupied workers, the experience of anomie seems to describe the same "timeless *désœuvrement*" that, as we have already seen, resembles ennui so closely as to be virtually indistinguishable. Once again, Kuhn achieves closure by relegating concern for this problem to experts in the relevant field. Although the "symptoms" of anomie "are not far removed from those manifested in the state of acute boredom, it represents a case study for anthropologists" (9). Kuhn's procedure is blatantly ideological. By defining "anomie" as the experience of a figure emphatically foreign, whose alienation is a result of a well-functioning social system, he prevents this concept from becoming a way of linking the previous forms of boredom in an historical analysis that emphasizes their common cultural origins.

If 'anomie' were defined in the conventional fashion, as a phenomenon characteristic of modern societies—not as a timeless "deadly melancholy" but as an historically located experience of meaninglessness—it would not appear as a "peripheral form" of boredom capable of being relegated to the margins of a study of the "confrontation with negativity" in the canonical texts of Western literature. On the contrary, anomie—socio-historical disequilibrium and the absence of value hierarchies—might, instead, appear to be the enabling condition of "ennui" and of the "peripheral forms" of bore-

[20] As described by H. Stuart Hughes, *Consciousness and Society*, 282–83. On Durkheim, see pages 69–71.

dom alike. As a consequence, the experiences that Kuhn admits resemble genuine ennui both in their phenomenology and in their effects could no longer be legitimately relegated to philosophical insignificance on the grounds that they are not sufficiently independent of their historical circumstances.

If anomie is a basic characteristic of modern societies, then "timeless *désœuvrement*" is its consequence, and the distinctions between the ennui of the intellectual and that boredom which results from enforced leisure or monotonous labor must be drawn in concrete historical and cultural, rather than philosophical, terms. Viewed from an historical perspective that does not endorse the elitist presumption of the bearers of high culture that their "ennui" is distinct from and superior to the quotidian boredom of people immersed in ordinary existence, the experiences Kuhn discusses appear on a continuum. Insofar as the philosophical claims he makes for the significance of ennui can be salvaged, they will have to be extended to the "peripheral forms" of boredom as well.

I have argued that because Kuhn's "phenomenology" depends on an appeal to a very particular reader's intuitive sense of the distinction between the "metaphysical malady" of ennui and ordinary boredom—a sense his demonstrations confirm rather than prove—his examples must be read against the grain. By his own account, the quotidian forms of boredom seem to have "both spiritual and physical" manifestations such that the world seems "emptied of significance" to their sufferers. They do fail to fulfill the other two requirements of being entirely independent of external circumstances or of the will of the sufferer. But does this dependence on either subjective or objective conditions really disqualify them as authentic experiences of existential distress? As we have noted, although Kuhn claims to derive his definition from descriptions of genuine cases of ennui, this derivation comes only after he has eliminated the "peripheral forms" of boredom from his study. In a word, he can define ennui ahistorically because he has excluded ennui's poor cousins from the realm of metaphysical suffering by metonymically instantiating these other forms of boredom in figures whose identity is, for himself as well as for his audience, incompatible with the sort of experience of meaninglessness associated with the ennui discourse in Western literature. The assumption that a timeless form of ennui as an intellectual and spiritual phenomenon can be experientially distinguished from more ordinary boredom appears to depend on historical and cultural tenets that are by no means innocent.[21] If the peripheral

---

[21] It should be emphasized that what I am calling the "philosophical" understanding of boredom is by no means limited to philosophers and literary theorists but constitutes one of the basic

forms of boredom, too, have philosophical significance, it will be necessary to turn the question around, to ask about the significance of defining boredom in ahistorical terms.

The claim that metaphysically significant boredom cannot be abstracted from its historical and cultural context has wide-ranging implications. The elimination of the distinction between boredom and ennui not only calls Kuhn's larger claims for the philosophical achievements of his literary study into question; it undermines the idealist foundations of the philosophical rhetoric of reflection on boredom as a whole. If the question of what boredom *is* cannot be legitimately separated from the question of how it comes about, intellectual history and phenomenological reflection upon individual experience are insufficient means of inquiry into its significance. If boredom in all its forms indeed constitutes a modern "plague" of sorts, we must pose its prevalence as an historical problem. Rather than seeking the Platonic essence of the experience, we must ask what the discourse on boredom signifies; rather than identifying acedia and melancholy as primitive forms of ennui, we must find a more complex way of articulating the relations between the modern experience and its historical antecedents. Chapter 2 begins this task by addressing the sociological perspectives on anomie, melancholy, and boredom.

---

ways in which the discourse of reflection on boredom operates. The conviction that there is an experientially tangible difference between boredom and ennui is a feature of that discourse that may even be shared by those who generally espouse a more "sociological" view of the problem of boredom.

CHAPTER 2

The Normalization of Anomie:
Boredom as Sociological Symptom

Müßiggang ist aller Laster Anfang. Was die Leute nicht Alles aus
Langeweile treiben! Sie studieren aus Langeweile, sie beten aus
Langeweile, sie verlieben, verheiraten und vermehren sich aus
Langeweile und sterben endlich aus Langeweile, und—alles mit
den wichtigsten Gesichtern, ohne zu merken, warum.

Georg Büchner[1]

Boredom and Culture

In his 1969 *Melancholy and Society*, Wolf Lepenies interprets melancholy
and boredom in a mode diametrically opposed to Reinhard Kuhn's. For him,
ennui is not an idea that has shaped Western culture, but a symptom of what
Norbert Elias called the civilizing process (*Prozeß der Zivilizations*); subjective malaise is the consequence not of a metaphysical "encounter with nothingness" but of the frustrated impulses to act that follow from socially imposed constraints on bodily spontaneity. Melancholy and ennui indeed give
rise to reflection—and to literature—but they do so as part and parcel of an
"affective economy" (*Affekthaushalt*) shaped by the demands of civilized life
on individual existence.[2] For Lepenies, the notion that such phenomena
could be meaningful in themselves is illusory, for subjective experience is
always historically and culturally constructed.

From Lepenies' perspective, the question is not what melancholy *is* but

---

[1] "Idleness is the root of all evil. What people don't do on account of boredom! They study out
of boredom, they pray out of boredom, they fall in love, marry, and reproduce out of boredom
and finally die out of boredom, and—all with the most solemn countenances, without noticing
why" (*Leonce und Lena* [1836], I, 1).

[2] Insofar as his emphasis lies on the sociological constellations in which the experiences arise,
Lepenies does not lay much weight on the distinctions between melancholy, boredom, and ennui.
While I shall argue later in the chapter that his historical material suggests the need for a more
rigorous delineation of the differences between these experiences, in the first half, I follow his usage in order to demonstrate the analytic advantages of viewing the discourse of reflection on subjective malaise as a whole.

"what it signifies when someone claims to be [melancholy]."[3] For Kuhn, of course, these questions were as inseparable as the experience and its representation: the perennially renewed "encounter with nothingness" attested in the literary tradition was itself the proof of ennui's philosophical significance. In posing the problem of the significance of subjective malaise in sociological terms, Lepenies avoids the conceptual tangles that follow from such an idealist understanding of experience. As he acknowledges, *Melancholy and Society* is in the first instance "a collection of cases" (VII) that illustrate how the social function fulfilled by attributions of melancholy and boredom differs according to historical context and political circumstances. He does not, like Kuhn, assimilate historically distinct experiences to one another in a universal history of malaise. That is not to say, however, that Lepenies does not venture any broader claims about the significance of the experiences he examines. On the contrary, *Melancholy and Society* sets out to illuminate the relationship between action and reflection at the most general socio-anthropological level. Melancholy, Lepenies argues, is a symptom of "resignation" to "action-inhibition"; the attribution of this state to oneself or to others is part of a striving for "legitimation" under conditions when meaningful action seems impossible. From his point of view, then, the melancholy associated since antiquity with thinkers and artists signifies their (political or social) impotence.

Like Kuhn's abstraction of ennui from its worldly conditions, the reduction of the reflective experiences associated with subjective malaise to sociological epiphenomena must be taken with a grain of salt. Nonetheless, this sweeping gesture makes *Melancholy and Society* a particularly instructive model on which to measure the strengths and weaknesses of the rhetoric of experience it instantiates. Like Kuhn's idealism, Lepenies' materialism is paradigmatic. While the former consigns anomie to the margins and emphasizes the individual subject's confrontation with nothingness as the essence of an experience at once ideal and real, the latter understands such ennui as the by-product of anomic social circumstances. From Lepenies' point of view, Kuhn's "encounter with nothingness" has a sociologically specifiable form. Human beings, he thinks, have a fundamental "besoin de faire quelque chose," a need to act meaningfully. In the absence of an intersubjective and relatively stable framework of means and ends, this sense of purpose cannot be realized, and people become prone to malaise. It is when they disregard the sociological conditions that give rise to their subjective states that the inability to act

[3] My citations follow the 1998 edition of *Melancholie and Gesellschaft*, which includes a new introduction to a work that was originally Lepenies' dissertation. All translations are my own, but for the reader's convenience, in my parenthetical references to the text, the first number refers to the original German, the second to the published translation. The passage just cited: 7/1.

meaningfully can appear as a fundamental dilemma of human existence, as a Kuhnian "idea" independent of external circumstances and the will.

To ask what melancholy signifies is to recall the experience from this realm of abstract universals. For the author of *Melancholy and Society*, subjective interiority is a construct—and the apprehension of supposedly universal features of the human condition with which it is associated, an illusion with an intelligible social function. What can be known, Lepenies contends, are the social parameters within which problems of meaning come into being: melancholics are disenfranchised agents whose preoccupation with philosophical dilemmas functions as a mode of self-legitimation. With literary texts and historical material serving as an empirical foundation, *Melancholy and Society* integrates distinct social scientific traditions in an illuminating interpretation of subjective experiences often considered accessible only to introspection. Using Robert Merton's influential theory of anomie as a bridge, it brings Norbert Elias's long-range theory of the civilizing process into conversation with the conceptual strategies of structuralism, interpreting melancholy and boredom in terms of their relation to the abstract parameters of social order and disorder.

In its emphasis on the social significance of emotional configurations, Lepenies' argument registers the broader twentieth-century paradigm shift from subject to structure—a rhetorical and conceptual transformation that has been of enormous consequence for representing and interpreting subjective experience in modernity.[4] However, his materialist account of malaise fails to establish an adequate perspective for reflection on the historical specificity of the experiences it thematizes because it is part of the discourse in which those experiences are constructed. As in the case of Kuhn's idealist approach to ennui, it is necessary to read against the grain to uncover the historical and discursive specificity behind this purported universality.

In the first half of this chapter, I situate Lepenies' approach within the context of the larger social scientific discourse on subjective malaise and show that the historiographical tenets of *Melancholy and Society* are surprisingly close to Kuhn's. While he makes constant reference to historical sources, for Lepenies melancholy is not, qua sociological object, an historical phenomenon: he regards these sources as case studies that exemplify "social constellations of power and affective tendencies" (80/59). Like Kuhn, then, he places historical material in the service of an ahistorical understanding of human ex-

---

[4]Indeed, the influence of social scientific modes of thought has been so powerful that even though *Melancholy and Society* antedates *The Demon of Noontide*, Kuhn's interpretations sometimes sound like naïve relics of a lost culture.

perience. However, *Melancholy and Society*'s purportedly context-independent, structuralist analysis of subjective malaise as sociological phenomenon is based upon theories—Merton's structural-functionalism and Elias's reflexive sociology—formulated to interpret the impact of modernization on subjective experience. Furthermore, the concept of anomie that forms his point of departure has its origins in the preoccupation of nineteenth-century social thought with the discontents of the modern socio-political order. As in my discussion of *The Demon of Noontide*, reading against the grain serves constructive ends. Situating Lepenies' argumentative strategy within its historical and discursive context both helps to clarify the ways in which *Melancholy and Society* is paradigmatic for the social scientific discourse of reflection on subjective malaise and reveals the distinctiveness of his accomplishment.

In conversation with Lepenies' interpretation of the significance of changes in the representation of subjective malaise over time, I continue, in the second half of the chapter, to develop my rhetorical analysis of the historically evolving discourse of reflection on subjective malaise. I argue that Lepenies' central historical examples—the ennui that plagued aristocrats in pre-Revolutionary France, the melancholy of the German bourgeoisie in the eighteenth century, the disdainful interiority of nineteenth-century philosophers and novelists—mark decisive moments in the historical evolution of the discourse of reflection on subjective experience in post-Enlightenment Europe. His aspiration to use particular cases to illuminate the relations between social structures and affective states in general notwithstanding, on my reading, *Melancholy and Society* attests to the theoretical importance of the historically evolving discourse of reflection on subjective malaise for understanding the cultural significance of modernization.

Anomie and Deviance: Subjective Malaise as an Object of Social Science

> Eine konfliktlose Gesellschaft mag als Gipfel der Rationalität erscheinen, aber sie ist zugleich auch eine Gesellschaft der Grabesstille, der äußersten Gefühlskälte und höchsten Langeweile—eine Gesellschaft überdies ohne jede Dynamik.
> Norbert Elias[5]

Lepenies, writing for an audience of sociologists, begins *Melancholy and Society in medias res* by extrapolating a functionalist framework for inter-

[5]"A society without conflict may appear as the pinnacle of rationality, but it is at the same time a society still as the grave, a society of the most extreme affective coldness and the greatest boredom—and in addition a society without any dynamics" (*Studien über die Deutschen*, 384).

preting the social genesis of subjective malaise from Robert K. Merton's "Social Structure and Anomie." This essay, which had already been reproduced in successive editions of Merton's highly influential standard work, *Social Theory and Social Structure,* for a generation, incorporates a groundbreaking approach to the "sociology of deviance" that Lepenies sees as offering a fundamental orientation for his own study.[6] By abstracting sociological topoi from Merton's theory of anomie, Lepenies develops the theoretical framework that he then uses to analyze the relationship between malaise and social structure in historically specific instances. Both to make his highly specialized and technical arguments easier to follow and to illuminate broader features of the larger social scientific discourse on subjective malaise in which those arguments are situated, I shall begin by setting out the intellectual context with which Lepenies assumes his audience is familiar.

Merton's topic had a venerable history in social scientific reflection on modern life. According to the Oxford English Dictionary, 'anomie,' the ancient Greek term for lawlessness, first appears in English in seventeenth-century theological sources with a now archaic connotation of "disregard of divine law." The modern sense of the term is traced to Émile Durkheim (1858–1917), for whom the phenomenon was proper to modernity. On Durkheim's view, society has the moral function of regulating and limiting the passions (necessary because "our sensibility is in itself an insatiable and bottomless abyss") and of determining the appropriate rewards for different contributions to the whole "in the name of the common interest."[7] As a consequence of capitalism and secularization, Durkheim argued, both desire and identity had come unmoored from their social frameworks, isolating individuals and depriving their lives of meaning.[8] Modern prosperity stimulates the appetites; traditional modes of restraint no longer function. "One thirsts for novelties, unknown ecstasies, nameless sensations, but as soon as they are known, they lose their savor" (285/256). In a world ruled by the ideology of

---

[6]Lepenies used the revised edition of 1957, to which Merton had added a chapter called "Continuities in the Theory of Social Structure and Anomie." In it, Merton wrote, he had "trie(d) to consolidate empirical and theoretical analyses" published after his original study of anomie by refining and specifying his own approach (*Preface* to the revised edition; Merton, 1968, xi).] Unless otherwise noted, all of my references to Merton refer to the 1968 edition of *Social Theory and Social Structure*, to which Merton added only an expanded introduction.

[7]See *Le Suicide*, chapter V. I follow the 1951 English translation of this 1897 text with modifications. The first number in the citations refers to the original French, the second to the translation. Here: 273/246 and 275/249. Subsequent references in text.

[8]The process of cultural modernization, he argued, thus gave rise to the two related, "morbid" forms of suicide (428/373), the egotistical (characterized by a "state of depression and apathy produced by an exaggerated individuation"[406/ 356]) and the anomic (frequent only "where industrial and commercial activity are very great" [409/358]).

industrial progress, "the longing for infinity is daily represented as a mark of moral distinction, whereas it can only appear within unruly consciences which elevate to a rule the lack of rule from which they suffer" (287/257). 'Anomie' names this lack of integrative collective norms. It describes the moral circumstance of a world in which science has supplanted religion, in which family and community no longer exercise their socializing force on the individual, and in which unlimited and hence unrealizable desires give rise to malaise.

The concept of anomie embodies a tension between Durkheim's commitment to the objective analysis of "social facts" and his desire to construct a scientific morality for the secular world. On the one hand, he considered anomie a normal condition in modern (i.e. high capitalist) society and always emphasized that the sociologist must view phenomena associated with it, such as crime and suicide, objectively, as unavoidable realities. On the other hand, however, Durkheim regarded the absence of collective norms as a sign of illness in the social body, as a pathology that should be combated through the development of corporative group bonds.[9] It is in this context that the sociological notion of "deviance" must be understood.

Merton's 1938 article, "Social Structure and Anomie," became a classic of sociological thought by translating Durkheim's concept into the idiom of American structural-functionalism. Eschewing grand narratives about secularization and modernization in favor of a more sober focus on contemporary American society, Merton extended Durkheim's scientific attitude toward the normality of "deviant" phenomena. He thereby developed a sociological perspective on anomie that presents its social criticism in a less sweeping, yet arguably even more devastating fashion. For Durkheim, the integration of individuals into the collective was the standard for societal "health"; in "integrated" societies, the social world was constituted as a meaningful totality, a life sphere imbued with significance. Merton functionalizes this notion. For him, 'integration' describes a state of society that is not inherently better or more desirable than a less highly integrated one. He emphasizes "mid-range" phenomena, focusing on how anomie arises from the disintegration of action in specific social contexts. For Merton, then, 'anomie' no longer bears the ethical weight that had blurred the scientific objectivity in Durkheim's use of the term. The term simply describes the functional result of a certain failure of cohesion in a society, a phenomenon that may be studied in its genesis and effects by the sociologist, who prescribes no remedies.

---

[9] Like Max Weber, Durkheim did not hold out hope that religious institutions or family bonds could effect such a regeneration.

Merton regarded himself as a "transatlantic Durkheimian" whose engagement with the work of his French predecessor had "laid the groundwork for what would become [his] own mode of structural and functional analysis."[10] However, while Durkheimian sociology takes as its starting point the notion that social mechanisms had withered in modern society, giving rise to disintegration and anomie, Merton shies away from such global analysis, with its implicit assumption that scientific diagnosis should issue in prescriptions for change. Rejecting Durkheimian organicism, Merton produces an account of modern anomie in which the lack of collective norms no longer appears as a pathological expression of modern society's nihilistic tendency. For him, the functional analysis of social structures is an end in itself. The scientific study of society should aim not to discover the means of healing the ills of modernity but simply to analyze social reality as it is, without presuming that even anomie is inherently undesirable.

While the earliest period of American sociology tended to ignore the sweeping questions about society that had preoccupied the European sociologists of the previous generation, the economic crises of the twenties and the rise of fascism in the thirties had underlined the need for richer theoretical models. Merton's "transatlantic Durkheimianism" played a key role in the development of American sociology, for it articulated the concerns of the European social thinkers with a focus on practical social problems. Merton's 1938 essay reflects the concerns of a sociological community preoccupied by the question of how to theorize social change in a non-ideological fashion. It considers the attitudes and values associated with anomie "from the standpoint of how the social structure promotes or inhibits their appearance in specified types of situations" (186, n. 3). Since it is "only because behavior is typically oriented toward the basic values of the society that we may speak of a human aggregate as comprising a society" (195), Merton asserts, "conformity" to the established order of things is, sociologically speaking, individuals' normal mode of adaptation. "Anomie" results from the spread of "deviance" from this norm: when non-conforming behavior becomes normal, societies grow unstable. Anomie is on this view the predictable result of modes of social organization that facilitate dysfunctional, non-conforming behavior by normalizing deviance.

---

[10]In autobiographical reflections in "A Life of Learning," Merton relates how, as a graduate student, he was asked by his mentor, Pitirim Sorokin, to write a review article on recent French sociology, which led to an invitation to review Durkheim's *Division of Labor in Society* when it was published in English. "The intensive work on those two papers resulted in my becoming a transatlantic Durkheimian and laid the groundwork for what would become my own mode of structural and functional analysis" (Merton 1994, 12).

Merton's "Social Structure and Anomie" establishes a strategy for discussing the relationship between ideology, social order, and subjective experience in abstraction from metanarratives about modernization—a strategy that Lepenies sets out to extend. Rather than beginning as Durkheim did from the "social facts," the structuration of the whole society, Merton argues inductively from the parameters of individual behavior. In his terms, it is when too many people lose their orientation toward using socially legitimated means to collectively recognized ends that anomie ensues. By bracketing reflection on the historical context in which such a situation comes to be, Merton's functional analysis extends Durkheim's concept to establish a non-normative perspective for the sociological analysis of "deviant" behavior. While Durkheim saw individual behavior as virtually epiphenomenal to social realities—for him psychological explanations were both beyond sociology's range and irrelevant to the scientific explanation of action—Merton takes a less stringent line. The emphasis on mid-range structures allows him to show that social orders can operate in such a way that the "normal" response may be "dysfunctional" from the point of view of a society as a whole. His functionalist understanding of anomie thus extends the notion of scientific objectivity into a realm where Durkheim himself fell into a moralizing attitude.

Merton's analysis of how "conformity" (the mode of behavior associated with societies integrated in Durkheim's sense) dissolves into the "ritualism" and "retreatism" of anomic social circumstances provides the foundation for *Melancholy and Society*'s attempt to illuminate the relations between subjective malaise, order, and structures of social power as such. Merton explains deviance from conformity as a symptom of "dissociation" between the "frame of aspiration reference" formed through the "pattern of cultural goals" valorized in a society on the one hand and the "institutional" or "regulatory" norms that constitute the legitimate, socially recognized means to those ends on the other. This is the sociological language in which things fall apart. Using social "integration" and individual "conformity" as descriptive rather than normative terms, Merton offers a definition of anomie as a "breakdown in the cultural structure" that arises when large numbers of individuals are for structural reasons unable to realize the very desires that define them as members of their societies. Although such a model is not normative, it is nonetheless predictive: a social structure, Merton writes, that "strains the cultural values, making action in accord with them readily possible for those occupying certain statuses within the society and difficult or impossible for others" produces a tendency to formlessness (216–17).[11]

---

[11] As we have noted, Merton takes contemporary American society as his exemplary case. The

Nonetheless, "Social Structure and Anomie" incorporates a relatively optimistic vision of the historical process: while the state of anomie may be inevitable in modernity, for Merton it is not simply an absence of social regulation with pathological results such as suicide but also a liminal collective situation in which possibilities for "innovation" are multiplied. This account of anomie implicitly embraces the democratizing tendency that accompanies the dissolution of inherited social structures. *Melancholy and Society* thus takes as its point of departure a vision of modern anomie quite remote from its fin-de-siècle European origins. Indeed, as we have just seen, far from lamenting the loss of traditional values, Merton regards their persistence in unlivable forms as the cause of social malaise! While Durkheim saw in anomie the theoretical challenge to create a new, scientific morality of the social, his American disciple emphasizes how the dissolution of traditional practices fosters the innovative behavior through which social praxis produces new cultural goals.

Lepenies' study extends Merton's strategy for explaining affective and ethical human responses sociologically by examining melancholy and boredom as phenomena of dissociation between collectively valorized ends and agents' resources for achieving them. He builds upon the analysis of 'retreatism' in "Social Structure and Anomie." 'Retreatism' is, according to Merton, that mode of role adaptation in which individuals reject both "culturally acclaimed ends" and "institutional means." Those who adapt by retreating are, in his words, "*in* the society but not *of* it . . . Not sharing the common frame of values, they can be included as members of the *society* (in distinction from the *population*) only in a fictional sense" (207). Paradoxically, Merton observes, individuals prone to retreatism (among whom he includes psychotics, pariahs, vagrants, and drug addicts [207]) have "thoroughly assimilated" and "imbued with affect and high value" *both* the culture's goals and the dominant institutional practices. Unable to "innovate" by incorporating new and thus illegitimate means to achieve those goals, yet equally unable to renounce the ideal of success as defined by the culture, such people withdraw from the world of social conformity. "Defeatism, quietism, and resignation are manifested in escape mechanisms which ultimately lead [them] to 'es-

---

fact that certain groups in the society are systematically excluded from achieving the monetary success which is a key feature of the American Dream, he argues, produces a significant tendency to anomie. When legitimate means and hard work cannot achieve the culturally valorized and promised ends, he claims, both the means and the ends may become devalued. Ironically, American society's high degree of integration in the orientation toward common values, when combined with a relative lack of insistence that success come through legitimate means, breeds anomie.

cape' from the requirements of the society" (207).[12] As Lepenies notes, Merton wrote that acedia and melancholy were traditional names for the "syndrome of retreatism," though he did not elaborate on this insight.[13] *Melancholy and Society* uses historical and literary sources to extend Merton's model, interpreting melancholy and boredom as consequences of what Lepenies calls the "loss of cultural self-evidence [kultureller Selbstverständlichkeiten]" (13/6)and the inability to act that follows upon that loss.

Building upon this sociological foundation, *Melancholy and Society* refigures the anomie problematic anthropologically. Abandoning the concept of role adaptations, which is linked to modern social systems, and drawing upon Norbert Elias' theory of the civilizing process to illuminate the process by which "deviant" modes of adaptation are normalized, Lepenies argues that the framework Merton introduced in "Social Structure and Anomie" can be made even more general. While Merton speaks of cultural values and institutionalized norms, Lepenies moves to an even higher level of abstraction, speaking instead of 'order' and 'disorder,' 'arbitrariness' and 'bindingness.' Arguing that melancholy and boredom are anthropological signs of specific sorts of social conditions, he develops a materialist critique of theories that portray subjective malaise in philosophical terms. As a consequence, Lepenies' conceptualization of melancholy and boredom issues in a profound empirical challenge to the idealist interpretation of subjective malaise as a universal feature of the human condition.

Lepenies' first step is to extend Merton's functionalist account of anomie as a systemic consequence of certain social structures. He builds upon a suggestion from Merton himself that a sequential connection between the various 'deviant' social roles could be developed. Indeed, Lepenies argues, Merton's distinctions between "types of adaptation according to acceptance or rejection of cultural goals and the institutionalized means of attaining them"

---

[12]It is worth comparing Merton's account of the etiology of retreatism with a psychoanalytic description of the genesis of melancholia. Freud's melancholic cannot renounce the desire for an object which is not attainable in reality; this leads to a sort of self-consumption as the ego is overwhelmed by the image of the lost object. The melancholic finds both narcissistic and masochistic satisfaction through cherishing the lost object as a permanent part of the self. Merton's 'retreatism' also arises from desire frustrated in the pursuit of an unattainable object—from "continued failure" to achieve satisfaction because legitimate means are ineffective and "internalized prohibitions" block access to illegitimate ones. Crucially, this process must occur *"while the supreme value of the success goal has not yet been renounced"* (207, Italics in original). As a result, no other goal takes the place of the unattainable object of desire; retreatism results in the elimination of conflict in such a way that "the individual is asocialized" (208).

[13]The syndrome is mentioned in a passage is from the essay added to *Social Theory and Social Structure* in 1957, "Continuities in the Theory of Social Structure and Anomie" (243) quoted in Lepenies 12/5.

(10/3) should be placed on a continuum. Read in this way, he claims, the description of the movement from 'conformity' to 'ritualism' to 'retreatism' could form the basis of "a much further reaching and theoretically better grounded" account of the relationship between melancholy and social structure than Merton himself had attempted (14/7). From a more global, "anthropologically fixed" perspective, Lepenies writes, "the sequence of deviant behavior Merton outlines [i.e. the movement from 'conformity' to 'innovation' or 'ritualism,' 'retreatism,' and 'rebellion,' EG] can be described as a growing loss of those things which are taken to be self-evident in a culture, a loss which is accompanied by an increasing fear of action" (13/6). When culturally validated goals cease to provide a meaningful framework for action, the social fabric fragments.

Like so many accounts of the impacts of modernization, Merton's "Social Structure and Anomie" does seem to imply a sort of negative teleology—one that begins in conformity and moves through a sequence of ever more chaotic states to culminate in social disintegration. As the shared ends for action that integrate relatively undifferentiated societies disappear, social bonds loosen. If 'innovation' fails, it is followed by 'ritualism,' melancholic 'retreatism' and even 'rebellion.' Collective life becomes colored by a pervasive sense of indifference that is the subjective reflection of anomie. Distancing himself from the sociological tradition that explains such effects in terms of the modernization process, Lepenies characterizes anomic phenomena from an agent-centered point of view that does not depend on an historical metanarrative. However, in his effort to establish a scientific account of the relationship between melancholy and social structure per se, Lepenies develops a structuralist framework not unlike Durkheim's—one in which the parameter of order is an ambiguously normative term.

If, as Vilfredo Pareto contended and he believes, there is a basic human "besoin de faire quelque chose," then according to Lepenies, this need to act gives rise to a "pragmatic, in the deeper sense anthropological" requirement that societies provide people with purposes (13/6).[14] In the absence of stable frameworks for action that integrate individuals into larger social wholes, the

---

[14]Lepenies adopts this assumption from his *Doktorvater* Dieter Claessens, whom he thanks in the Introduction to the original German edition for inspiring *Melancholy and Society* (Lepenies 1969, 11; not reproduced in the second edition or the English version). Claessens is also the source of the terminology upon which Lepenies builds his analysis. See "Rationalität, revidiert," in which Claessens presents his "revision" of the sociological concept of modern "rationality." Using Elias' analyses of the civilizing process and Georg Simmel's sociology of modernity, Claessens connects the "loss of that which is taken to be self-evident in a culture [*kulturelle Selbstverständlichkeiten*]" to the process of modernization. In a passage Lepenies cites, Claessens contends that "arbitrariness" (*Beliebigkeit*) constitutes the specificum of modern rationality (Claessens 118).

phenomena Merton classes as leading to anomie necessarily begin to prevail. Without such shared and "binding" ends, a sense of "arbitrariness," of the "indifference" of values, gains the upper hand. When systemic disparities arise between agents' goals and their chances of achieving them, social ideals are undermined; unable to participate meaningfully in a framework of socially recognized ends, yet unable to cease aspiring to those ends, people 'retreat' into reflection. Thus "arbitrariness" in the social world deprives individuals of the capacity for acting meaningfully; without a common foundation of shared values, they become anxious, melancholic, and prone to boredom.

Melancholy and Society uses this model of the relations between individual existence and social structure to describe melancholy and ennui as affective manifestations of frustrated agency.

> boredom signifies the condition of a disburdening [i.e. from action: *Entlastung*-EG] mandated contrary to one's will. Melancholy is the reaction against a situation of disburdening without the chance of doing anything with it: disburdening can only be a resource when the category of the future is still open. (183/140)

Situating the affective phenomena associated with modern anomie in relation to the structural transformations that accompany social change as such enables Lepenies to analyze sources that invoke these reflective categories in terms of a transhistorical account of the pathologies of social order.[15]

On Lepenies' view, sociology must turn to anthropological categories because it can neither appeal to a priori features of subjective experience nor presume that such features do not exist. His strategy is thus a response to the dilemma formulated by Georg Simmel in a diary entry: "There probably is an absolutely necessary and valid a priori—only we can never know what it is. The criterion by which we could recognize it would have to possess the very absoluteness to which it is supposed to lead us."[16] To move from Merton's schema to a more general theoretical framework for inquiry into "the sociological conditions and relations of various understandings of melan-

[15] For an account of "pathologies of the social" as motivating the project of critical social theory, see Honneth.

[16] Simmel 1923, cited in Lepenies, 41/28. In fact, Lepenies implicitly offers his approach to sociology as a model for the human sciences in general. A few years later, in *Soziologische Anthropologie*, he argues explicitly that, insofar as they self-reflexively turn "the principles of scientific critique on their own praxis of organization, teaching, and research," all the human sciences are "necessarily directed toward a nexus of sociology, historiography, and (biological and ethnological) anthropology" (40). In Lepenies' later work, the historical reflection that I am arguing is uncomfortably subordinated to structuralist analysis in *Melancholie und Gesellschaft* comes into its own. See particularly *Die Drei Kulturen: Soziologie zwischen Literatur und Wissenschaft* and *Sainte-Beuve: auf der Schwelle zur Moderne*.

choly" (15/8), then, Lepenies needs analytic concepts that are formally determined and anthropologically grounded. He contends that a structuralist orientation for developing such concepts is implicit in Merton's account of how the dissociation between collectively valorized ends and individually accessible means makes society a breeding ground of "anomie" and "deviant" behavior.

"Social Structure and Anomie," Lepenies argues, was only nominally linked to the description of contemporary American society that provided its ostensible object. Viewed structurally, he claims, Merton's analysis depends only on a notion of a "stable society and conforming behavior devoid of all [historical] content" (16/8). Merton's working concept of a generalized social order is "empty" in the way that Lepenies claims is "a prerequisite for the development of analytic concepts" in sociology.

> Taking this [lack of content] as a standard of measurement, the parameter on which Merton appears to base his description is not any particular society . . . but the concept of *order*. Order, stripped of framing content, refers to the state of a society which continues to exist and to 'function' because its members behave *in such a way that* it functions. (16/8)

In effect, Lepenies reads between the lines to discover and rejuvenate Merton's "transatlantic Durkheimianism." His structuralist approach makes explicit the methodological presumption he shares with both Merton and Durkheim: "The concept of order signifies the parameter for every description of society" (16/8). As a sociological topos, the functional concept of order operates at a different level than practical arguments about the value of particular orders as concrete modes of social organization. "Society and phenomena of parts of society are not *evaluated* against that concept of order—for no universally accepted value exists—but rather *measured*, because in the concept of order, a *standard [Maß]* is provided" (16/8–9).

It is not simply that 'deviant' responses may be evaluated in a non-normative fashion using this concept of order as a standard. Expanding on Merton, Lepenies uses historical case analyses to show that melancholy and boredom stand in a complex, dialectical relation to social order as such—for it is social order that, anthropologically speaking, both produces and alleviates subjective malaise. (Thus an increase in order can result in the disintegration of the relation between social ends and agents' means for action: the emergence of bureaucratic modes of organization rationalizes society as a whole, yet makes individuals' experience seem more arbitrary.) If melancholy and boredom are understood as normal, anthropologically founded responses to situations in which social orders inhibit agents from acting meaningfully, Lepenies argues, both utopian ambitions to eliminate subjective malaise altogether and philosophical resignation to its inevitability must be taken with a grain of salt.

In abstracting Merton's theory of the genesis of anomie from its historical context as part of the sociological discourse on modernization, *Melancholy and Society* extends the Durkheimian project of producing a non-normative, scientific description of social processes in which agents lose their cultural moorings. Viewed from an anthropological perspective, 'ritualism' and 'retreatism' themselves embody the collective process of loss of self-evidence. In theory, at least, the category of 'loss' sheds its subjective, affective tenor and becomes part of an objective sociological analysis. Indeed, for Lepenies, the notion of a progressive loss of cultural self-evidence does not necessarily signal decline. Melancholy and boredom are constituent elements of a cultural process that the sociological discourse on anomie has always been attempting to describe, and—like Merton and unlike Durkheim—Lepenies does not assume that the disintegrative process that follows on rationalization is necessarily bad for society.

Elaborating on the functionalist understanding of social order that underlies Merton's account, Lepenies claims for his own approach a scientifically grounded objectivity which avoids the error of assuming that the process of de-naturalization of cultural goals is exclusive to modern societies. *Melancholy and Society* is concerned with the relation of affect to more basic cultural processes. Thus while his invocation of the "loss of cultural self-evidence" makes him sound like a gloomy cultural critic lamenting the inevitable fruits of historical change, Lepenies' argument actually turns the tables on cultural pessimism. From the point of view of his anthropological sociology, cultural critique is symptomatic of an intelligentsia robbed of worldly efficacy, for the melancholic attitudes it expresses are signs of an unfulfilled need for meaningful activity. As we shall see, though, Lepenies overstates the conclusions that may be drawn from the existence of empirical relations between subjective malaise and breakdowns of social structure. The conceptual apparatus he elaborates presupposes a reductive account of the significance of subjective experience that construes reflection upon questions of meaning as a function of a need for social "legitimation"—and thereby begs the very question it set out to answer. But even if we reject Lepenies' Mannheimian notion that social critique can be explained as a reflex of the critic's sociological position (as he implies in his discussion of Arnold Gehlen), *Melancholy and Society* makes a compelling practical case for the need to consider in each case how invocations of melancholy and boredom function to legitimate subjects excluded from the centers of power.

History, Structure, and Subjective Malaise

> Durch die Interdependenz größere Menschengruppen von-
> einander und durch die Aussonderung der physischen Gewalttat
> innerhalb ihrer stellt sich eine Gesellschaftsapparatur her, in der
> sich dauernd die Zwänge der Menschen aufeinander in Selbst-
> zwänge umsetzen . . . manchmal geht die Gewöhnung an eine
> Affektdämpfung so weit—beständige Gefühle der Langeweile
> oder Einsamkeitsempfindungen sind Beispiele dafür—das dem
> Einzelnen eine furchtlose Äußerung der verwandelten Affekte,
> eine geradlinige Befriedigung der zurückgedrängten Triebe in
> keiner Form mehr möglich ist.
>
> Norbert Elias[17]

For Reinhard Kuhn, the significance of ennui lies in the questions of meaning it raises for the subject. For Lepenies, the question is, rather, what it signifies about particular social circumstances when subjects invoke the vocabulary of subjective malaise. Since "ennui does not appear as a 'fundamental condition' [*Grundbefindlichkeit*] of human existence independent of social structure" (57/40), Lepenies organizes his argument around the sociological investigation of historically distinct constellations of melancholy and boredom such as the aristocratic ennui of the seventeenth-century French salons, the Werther syndrome, and the *mal du siècle*. By focusing on the causal nexus surrounding concrete instances of melancholy and boredom, Lepenies moves beyond Kuhn's idealized and subjectivist account of why such phenomena arise in the first place. But since the object of his analysis is to elucidate a structuralist argument about "social constellations of power and affective tendencies" (80/59) in general, his historical sources become decontextualized 'cases' that serve to elaborate a transhistorical account of the relation between melancholy and social structure.

While the sociological topoi he uses to explicate the anthropology of melancholy are derived from Merton's structural-functionalist account of anomie, Lepenies draws upon Norbert Elias' theory of the civilizing process to illuminate the socio-historical genesis of the affective configurations he interprets. In particular, he uses Elias's notion of "action-inhibition" (*Handlungshemmung*) to explain the subjective consequences of the disintegration

---

[17]"Through the interdependence of larger groups of humans on one another and through the exclusion of acts of physical violence from within them, a social apparatus comes into being in which the constraints [*Zwänge*] of people on one another are transformed into self-constraints [*Selbstzwänge*] . . . sometimes—as in the case of constant feelings of boredom or sensations of loneliness—the accommodation to a dampening of affect goes so far that a fearless expression of the transformed affects, a direct satisfaction of the drives that have been pushed out of the way, is no longer possible in any form." *Der Prozeß der Zivilisation*, vol. 2, 342–43.

of inherited norms. The notion of *Handlungshemmung* has its origin in Elias' sociological expansion of a Freudian concept: the "civilizing process" is that development through which threats of violence from the natural world and from other human beings are brought under ever greater levels of social control. For Elias, action-inhibition is thus a subjective effect of the rationalization process; the concept refers both to the high level of socially imposed restrictions on behavior and to the intensity of self-control required of individuals in modern societies. However, Lepenies emphasizes the relation between *Handlungshemmung* and social order as such. In adopting this term, then, he disregards its original context in a narrative about cultural modernization; treating history as but the illustration of structure, he focuses on what he takes to be Elias' scientific description of the sociological genesis of affective phenomena.

In *Melancholy and Society*, "action-inhibition" forms the structural link between objective frustration and the subjective phenomena of melancholy and boredom; it is the sociological counterpart of the frustrated anthropological need to do something meaningful. According to Lepenies, societies may inhibit action either through surfeit or deficit of order. In either case, agents are compelled to think too much, which propels them from ritualistic behavior into retreatism and melancholy. From an anthropological perspective, Lepenies writes, "reflection means nothing more than the compulsion (and opportunity) for the human being to turn back on himself when he is relieved of the pressure to act" (199/153). Whether actors feel that their actions are without personal meaning (for example, due to an excess of bureaucratic order) or without social significance (due, for example, to a perception that the world is so arbitrary that justice no longer exists), action-inhibition leads on this account to melancholic retreatism. Lepenies contends that such responses arise among groups or classes who are in economic circumstances that free them for reflection while disempowering them politically—circumstances, that is, of action-inhibition in the sociological sense. On his view, the loss of purpose (expressed in Merton's schema as the transition to "ritualism") provokes "fear of action" and eventually causes the deterioration of the desire for action itself (Merton's "retreatism"); thus melancholy and ennui are a consequence of a lack of meaningful connection to the collective world of human endeavor.

Über den Prozeß der Zivilisation (English: *The History of Manners*) also suggests Lepenies' historical case studies. In that work, Norbert Elias identifies courtly life and more generally the development of elite mores as key sites for theorizing the subjective effects of cultural modernization. In line with his structuralist transformation of Eliasian concepts, Lepenies treats his historical examples in abstraction from that narrative context. A brief sketch of two of his cases will make evident why this approach is problematic. At the same time, it will indicate how the methodological innovations of *Melancholy and Society* suggest a new way of formulating the social scientific perspective on subjective malaise that can make a substantial contribution to the historical interpretation of modernization.

Lepenies directs his attention first to the seventeenth-century French salon, which he argues must be understood sociologically as an "attempt to establish a new system of order to dispel the boredom" provoked among the aristocracy by the consolidation of absolutist rule (52/36). Although boredom was an inevitable result of enforced inactivity in courtly society, etiquette required that it be concealed or dispersed through useless yet intricately absorbing pastimes. In the salon, by contrast, the aristocracy could escape the repressive atmosphere of the court. There, though the fundamental disoccupation imposed by the system of social order still prevailed, the resulting malaise could be expressed publicly.

For Lepenies, what is "sociologically interesting" in seventeenth-century salon culture and its particular historical constellation of aristocratic boredom and melancholy is the way it institutionalizes the "behavioral mechanisms that crystallized out after the failure of the Fronde" (54/38), a failed attempt by members of the nobility to reassert feudal prerogatives in 1648, during Louis XIV's minority. According to Lepenies, this revolt against what Elias called the primary system of order, the "mechanism of kingship" that concentrated the power of decision-making in a single person, ended by paving the way for the consolidation of royal authority and hence the emergence of the modern French state. Having rebelled against the new order of things without "any vision of the future" (53/37) they hoped to achieve, the aristocrats were quickly defeated but then pardoned and thereby forced to reconcile themselves to absolutist rule. On Lepenies' interpretation, the consequence was a significant change in the mechanisms for maintaining social order. Louis XIV surmised that the uprising had taken place because his predecessor had failed to provide sufficient social satisfactions to compensate the nobles for their loss of real political power. The Sun King therefore developed court etiquette into an extremely elaborate repertoire of rituals and honors that consolidated his absolute sovereignty, maintaining order among the aristocracy by providing secondary occupations proportionate to the primary *dèsoeuvrement* they now endured. This strategy not only kept the nobility busy and close at hand; it diverted the boredom of their enforced political impotence into the pursuit of tangible social achievements.

According to Lepenies, courtly etiquette constituted a second system of "formal power" that compensated for "what the aristocracy was denied in reality." "Boredom," he continues, "named that dissatisfaction with the second system of order that ultimately developed into an attack on the primary, real system for the distribution of power" (54/38). Since the intricate rules of etiquette only made the court more oppressive, they exacerbated the nobility's need to escape the King's vigilance, even if they had renounced the hope of overthrowing his power. Thus, Lepenies argues, the need to give direct expression to boredom and frustration gave rise to an institution from which the King was explicitly excluded—one that later evolved to play an important role in the French revolution. In the salons, Lepenies claims, the nobles could share the melancholy produced by the defeat of the Fronde, which had spelled a definitive end to aristocratic hopes of regaining the power which the monarch had arrogated to himself. Here the boredom banned from the court could be freely expressed, and dissatisfaction with the social rituals that had replaced feudal prerogatives intensified the melancholic atmosphere in which the nobility mourned their loss of real power.

Thus according to Lepenies, for the aristocrats of the Fronde, boredom was a common fate: this "melancholy of a closed culture" (74/53) expressed the situation of the *honnête homme* banned from the life of action. Their ennui was caused by the perfected mechanism of kingship—a "consequence of the established and enduring order" and "permanent control over affects" required in the aftermath of historic defeat (61/43). Under such circumstances, Lepenies writes, there is nothing to do but "respectably kill the time with which one can't do anything more because there is nothing more to do" (56/40). In their shared resignation to the inevitability of absolutist rule, then, the denizens of the salon cultivated their ennui. However, salon culture retained the court as referent both in the structures of feeling that unified it and in the ideals of behavior that regulated it.

> Ennui dominated the court but was brought under control by etiquette; it resided in the salon and was "processed" [*verarbeitet*] collectively—an expression that is to be taken literally. The literary production of the salon is processed boredom. (69/50)

As part of a "closed culture" this "world-oriented" (74/54) ennui operated as a mark of distinction for the nobility. Thus salon culture promoted a literature of reflection that remained profoundly social in its orientation—represented paradigmatically, for Lepenies, by La Rochefoucauld's letters and *Maximes*. In this literature, "ennui" names the aristocratic dilemma in the socio-historical context of the absolutist court.

Lepenies contrasts the worldliness of aristocratic ennui and melancholy under the Sun King with the "escapism" of the German bourgeoisie in the period before its economic ascendancy. In eighteenth-century German society, Lepenies argues, the vocabulary of boredom and melancholy became linked to an ideal of interiority and sentimental self-cultivation that located "a source of self-worth within enforced inactivity and powerlessness" (90/66). The bourgeois discourse on subjective malaise valorized solitude in poetic longings for unity with nature, elaborating an ideal of spiritual superiority that was explicitly un-worldly. If the French aristocracy's refined melancholy had expressed collective solidarity, the German bourgeoisie cultivated private emotions for the sake of individual distinction. Thus while the melancholy of the salons embodied a politics of resignation that openly expressed dissatisfaction with the world of the absolutist court, the melancholy of the eighteenth-century bourgeoisie invoked a rhetoric of interiority that disavowed the importance of worldly things altogether.

Following Elias, Lepenies argues that the vocabulary of subjective experience—flight from the world, sentimentality, sensitivity, the cult of genius, originality, and inner freedom, etc.—established in eighteenth-century bourgeois German literature must be understood sociologically, in relation to the very exclusion from temporal power that the rhetoric of interiority seems to disdain. During the eighteenth century, "Under the pressure of economic developments, the stability of absolutism entered into flux" (82/60), and order was reestablished via the creation of a bureaucratic apparatus in which state power was distributed. In France, those rich enough to attain such positions were granted a noble status, but in Germany the bourgeoisie remained consigned to "subaltern positions" (83/60) since the aristocracy took over the bureaucracy itself. Thus while the French middle class gained a considerable degree of power as the absolutist monarchy modernized, the German middle class was marginalized politically until the nineteenth century. It was in this context, on Lepenies' view, that the German bourgeoisie legitimated its powerlessness through the cultivation of "spiritual" values.[18] As Elias puts it, in Germany members of the bourgeoisie were allowed at most "to think and poetize [*dichten*] independently, but not to act independently. In this situation writing becomes the most important outlet. There their new sense of self and their vague dissatisfaction with things as they are finds a

---

[18] See Fritz Ringer's study, *The German Mandarins*, for a more differentiated account of this position. More recent scholarship has called into question the assumptions that underlie this view of the German bourgeoisie. According to David Blackbourn, "The enlightened German public of the late eighteenth century was not wrapped up in its own, apolitical world . . . enlightened ideas had larger political implications" (Blackbourn 1998, 43).

more or less covert expression."[19] On this view, the ideals of the Enlightenment functioned in Germany as a substitute for action; the melancholic cultivation of interiority rendered the individual subject universal without engagement in the public sphere.[20]

While incorporating a Marxian perspective that explains the melancholy
of the German bourgeoisie as the "mystification of real impotence," Lepenies
interprets the "tendency [to melancholy] ... which became decisive for the
development of Germany" in the terms of anthropological sociology.[21] "Subjective" experiences, he argues, must be understood in the context of what
Elias called the "Affekthaushalt" of the community: there is a "connection
between enforced political abstinence and the restructuring of the 'economy
of affects'" (78/57). As we have underlined, on Elias's account, action-
inhibition is a consequence of the "civilizing process" as an historical phenomenon: changes in power relations beginning with courtly society lead on
the one hand to the progressive "pacification of spaces" in the collective
world and on the other to increasing control over affect in the individual
psyche. Lepenies' strategy of abstracting this concept from its metanarrative
context is problematic.

Like Merton's theory of anomie, Elias' conceptual apparatus is bound up
with an attempt to construct a non-normative account of the significance of
historical change. His background narrative is an alternative to the tragic vision of modernization as a process of disenchantment: Elias interprets the
emergence of individuation, and therefore modern subjectivity, as an aspect
of objective historical development. In emphasizing the general relations
between malaise, action-inhibition, and social order, Lepenies skirts the
question of the relation between his historical cases and the original narrative
context of a "civilizing process" in which modern subjectivity emerges.
Nonetheless, his historical analyses amount to a synthesis of Elias' conception with Merton's emphasis on the innovative potential of "deviance." He

[19] Elias, 21. This passage is partially cited in Lepenies (77/56).

[20] See Habermas 1965. See also James van Horn Melton's recent attempt to rethink *The Rise of the Public in Enlightenment Europe.*

[21] 76/55. The English translation exaggerates the extent to which Lepenies' characterization of Marxist analyses can be identified with his own position. In the original, his invocation of Marx and Engels appears to be more a gesture of conformity to what he saw as the scholastic of the time (see Lepenies 1997). Substantively, his argument depends upon the (not necessarily Marxist) trope of German exceptionalism and with it a tradition of German historiography that has been called into question by more differentiated accounts of the development of modern capitalism in the years since *Melancholy and Society* was published. See Blackbourn and Eley. Terry Pinckard's *German Philosophy 1760–1860: The Legacy of Idealism* offers a vivid history of philosophical devel-opments in the period that underlines the vital links between socio-political transformations and the focus on subjectivity on Kantian and post-Kantian thought.

argues that while aristocratic ennui was backward-looking, a painful reminder of the nobility's loss of corporate power in relation to the modern state, bourgeois melancholy points toward the future: that in it, the position of retreatism is transformed into the basis for a new, modern understanding of agency based on individual achievement. *Melancholy and Society* thereby casts light on the historical process through which ever greater individuation has been achieved—the evolution from exterior constraint to interiorized compulsion that for Elias defines the civilizing process as a whole.

On my reading, it is with respect to the interpretation of the transformations associated with the modernization process, which he does not thematize at all, that Lepenies' study has its most interesting implications. The point holds not only for his appropriations of Merton and Elias. Lepenies explicitly "disregards … the further implications" of Dieter Claessens' "Rationalität Revidiert" [Rationality Revised] (175/133), while adopting the latter's contention that an increase in "rationality" brings an increase in "arbitrariness"—in the "indifference" of values—and thereby threatens to undermine the viability of collectively recognized ends that form the anthropological foundation of action. As Claessens, following Georg Simmel, argues, such an increase in arbitrariness is a fundamental characteristic of the modern world. Lepenies implicitly accepts Claessens' notion that modernization and particularly modern technology have increased the sway of "arbitrariness" in human life. It is this "loss of that which is taken to be self-evident in a culture [*kulturelle Selbstverständlichkeiten*]" that renders the basic need to act meaningfully unfulfilled. Lepenies' sociological analysis of the relationship between subjective malaise and social order has implications for the historiography of modernity.

As we have seen, Lepenies extends Merton's theory of anomie into a global interpretation of the relation between subjective malaise and social structure by explaining melancholic retreat into reflection as a function of action-inhibition. By abstracting from the particularities of subjective response to the "loss of cultural self-evidence" and focusing on the increase in perceived arbitrariness that accompanies social change, *Melancholy and Society* correlates subjective malaise with the objective parameter of a loss of social order. Such an analysis can do justice neither to the reflective complexity nor to the historical specificity of the experiences of subjective discontent that arise in relation to the perceived arbitrariness of life in a highly rationalized world. There is a tension between Lepenies' structuralism and his historical analyses that simply cannot be resolved by an appeal to the anthropological hypothesis of a basic human need to do something meaningful. His sociological categories, which supposedly serve as an objective standard for

interpreting divergent instances of melancholy and boredom, bypass a crucial dimension of the experiences themselves. Reflection is not reducible to
the inhibition of action, even if we grant that the latter is genuinely its sociological precondition.

By situating the theoretical approach of *Melancholy and Society* historically, I have underlined the ways in which Lepenies' account of the sociological origins of subjective malaise is part of an ongoing social scientific discourse about the subjective effects of modernization. Read in this context,
his concrete analyses suggest that historical variations in the discourse on
subjective malaise can help in understanding the cultural transformations associated with the emergence of modern Western society. To focus on the
discourse of reflection on subjective experience in this way is consonant with
the broader contemporary historiographical shift from social structure to
cultural particularity. However, in emphasizing the importance of the theoretical framework that forms the background to Lepenies' analysis, I also underline the need to sustain the conversation with social scientific methods
that has been so productive for social history. Particularly when the nexus of
rationality and arbitrariness is emphasized, Lepenies' account of the vicissitudes of boredom and melancholy since the eighteenth century suggests a
new perspective for talking about modernization. That subjective malaise has
become so prevalent in modernity is indeed related to the absence of traditional, collective understandings of what is culturally "self-evident," for the
process of rationalization—understood both as modernization and as Enlightenment—far from humanizing the world, has normalized anomie.

Melancholy and Society demonstrates that the assumption that ennui has
an ahistorical, philosophical significance reflects a universalizing tendency of
bourgeois self-understanding to disavow the importance of its own historical
standpoint. On the other hand, Lepenies' interpretation of the discourse on
interiority as a function of the malaise that arises when individuals are systematically marginalized by the social systems in which they must act reduces the problems of meaning expressed in that discourse to sociological
epiphenomena. If Kuhn abstracted ennui from its worldly conditions, Lepenies' structural analysis occludes the way it expresses an implicit critique of
the world that occasioned it. Neither is able to establish an adequate perspective for reflection on the historical specificity of modern experiences of
subjective malaise, for the diametrically opposed hermeneutic approaches
they exemplify are equally constitutive of the discourse of reflection in which
melancholy and boredom are constructed as apparently ahistorical features
of the human condition.

An adequate approach to the general problem of anomie and "the loss of cultural self-evidence" in modernity therefore requires historical reflection on the formation of the *discourse* on subjective malaise in which both "idealist" and "materialist" understandings of subjective experience play a part. The genealogy of the modern discourse on boredom developed in Chapter 3 will bring the sociological understanding of boredom and melancholy as collective phenomena into conversation with the philosophical perspective underlying Kuhn's history of the idea of ennui. The remainder of this chapter will continue to set out the historical foundations for this rhetorical approach to the interpretation of subjective malaise. My argument builds upon Lepenies' insistence that the significance of emotional structures varies historically, drawing upon his case histories to extend an argument I began to make in Chapter 1—that qualitatively new experiences of malaise emerged in the aftermath of the French Revolution. From an historical perspective, the sociological analysis of melancholy and boredom constitutes a crucial step in theorizing the constitution of modern subjectivity. My contention is that, read against the grain, *Melancholy and Society* outlines the spread of a new rhetoric of reflection on subjective malaise since the eighteenth century—and thereby illustrates that the establishment of melancholy and boredom as endemic to subjectivity is a fundamental feature of cultural modernization.

Work, Leisure, and Modern Subjectivity

> Alle Instinkte, welche sich nicht nach Aussen entladen, *wenden sich nach Innen*—dies ist das, was ich die *Verinnerlichung* des Menschen nenne: damit wächst erst das an den Menschen heran, was man später seine "Seele" nennt.
>
> Friedrich Nietzsche[22]

For Lepenies, "History serves as an aid for hypothesis formation" (65/47); the analysis of particular examples serves the project of making a conceptual contribution to sociological methodology. As I have already suggested, though, his cases point the way toward a more historically differentiated account of what the discourse on melancholy and boredom signifies. Resituated in their cultural context, the examples he considers document historic developments in human self-understanding since the Enlightenment, developments that I argue are linked to the emergence of an identifiably modern rhetoric of reflection on subjective malaise.

---

[22]"All instincts that do not discharge themselves outwardly *turn inward*—this is what I call the *interiorizing* [*Verinnerlichung*] of the human being: through it, what one later called his 'soul' first grew attached to the human being." *Genealogy of Morals* II, 16; Nietzsche, *Sämtliche Werke* 5, 322.

The implications of Lepenies' arguments are obscured by the reductive rhetoric he invokes. Although *Melancholy and Society* links boredom and melancholy both thematically and structurally to questions of meaning, for Lepenies subjective malaise and the reflective phenomena associated with it have a purely sociological explanation. As a "psychic state," he writes, melancholy appears "when resignation has taken on the character of final validity [*End'gültigkeit'*]" (214/164)—when what once seemed culturally self-evident and therefore oriented action has disappeared. Under such circumstances, according to Lepenies, "a need for legitimation arises, at least if a state of apathy has not already been reached" in which only reflection, but no action, is possible any longer (214/164). Indeed, on his view, "The question of meaning is always also the question of legitimation—for to recognize something as meaningful is at the same time to legitimize it" (225/173). Thus from the point of view of his anthropological sociology, the legitimation function played by the bourgeois discourse on melancholic interiority explains the rhetoric of Enlightenment universalism.

> The disburdened aristocracy documented its boredom. The bourgeoisie combated it—this offered the possibility of concealing their action-inhibition and finding in reflection, in an introspective turn to the self, that legitimation which the aristocrat . . . never needed to seek. If the nobility turned to pure pastimes, which not only may have been meaningless but indeed had to be so in order for them not to be considered work, the bourgeoisie developed an ethics that was directed against the nobility and invoked 'humanity.'

Within the bourgeois rhetoric of interiority, Lepenies continues, "the question of meaning [*Sinnfrage*]" is posed "not so much to ground one's own position as to undermine" the aristocratic one (203–4/156–57). As I have already argued, his reductive approach to questions of meaning must be treated skeptically. However, in pointing to this constellation, Lepenies identifies a moment of great importance in the development of the modern rhetoric of reflection on subjective experience.

From within the Western European feudal order, legitimation had been unnecessary. Questions of meaning were situated firmly in a Christian context shared by all social estates. Inherited forms of "self-evidence" dictated the occupations of rich and poor alike—the parameters of action were largely fixed, for peasants as for aristocrats. What one did was an expression of who one was. But well before the French Revolution, this stable system of reference in relation to which identity and community existed had begun to dissolve. The rise of the bourgeoisie was itself a symptom of this global 'loss of cultural self-evidence,' as was the ideology of individualism they opposed to the traditional, corporatist notion of social order. This strategy of differentiation based on the cultivation of the self paved the way for the Nietzsche-an revaluation of values that brought this world definitively to an end.

According to Lepenies, as Germany industrialized, the bourgeoisie abandoned its melancholic penchant for reflection and with it the indirect, disavowed competition with the nobility. The cult of interiority underwent an historic transformation as, "in secularized form," the Pietist "valuation of one's own powerless position" came to define the "bourgeois ethic" (200/154). On Lepenies' view, "Sentimentality and melancholic reflection on one's own ego and emotions [*Gemüt*] would surely have remained relatively inconsequential if the economic importance of the bourgeoisie had not gradually increased" (204/157). As it happened, these tendencies gave rise to a work ethic that proved a more effective means of self-legitimation than the cultivation of melancholy, which, as Lepenies wryly notes, "in its action-inhibiting form did not exactly offer a good psychological foundation for the striving for economic success" (204/157). His argument, which has its point of departure in Elias' distinction between aristocratic self-definition based on ideal modes of *behavior* [*Verhalten*] and that of the German-speaking intelligentsia which, excluded from "political activity," found "its whole legitimation ... in its scientific or cultural *accomplishment* [*Leistung*]" (Vol I, 8–9; cited in Lepenies, 77/56) also resonates with Weber's account of modernization: the ethos of worldly productivity that animated capitalism eventually outgrew the metaphysical trappings of its youth.

The novelty of the bourgeois embrace of work cannot be over-emphasized. This distinctive means of "self-legitimation" literally transformed the way in which the question of the meaning of human life could be posed. Lepenies cites from Friedrich Nietzsche's aphorism on "Leisure and Idleness" (*Muße und Müßiggang*) in the *Gay Science*: "Soon we could be so far that one would be unable to give in to the appeal of the *vita contemplativa* ... without self-hatred and a bad conscience. —Well! Once upon a time it was the other way around: labor had the bad conscience on its side."[23] In adopting the work ethic, the bourgeoisie definitively rejected the aristocratic ideal that identified the cultivation of leisure as the means to the highest ends, thus forsaking their melancholic attachment to values which were sublimated versions of aristocratic ones. If the first phase of bourgeois development was characterized by the cult of interiority and its counterpart, the worship of nature, in the next phase, the rhetoric of individual self-cultivation appears as the ideology of modernization.

---

[23] *Sämtliche Werke* 3, 557; cited in Lepenies 204/157. See also Arendt's discussion of these issues in *The Human Condition*.

Lepenies rightly argues that the bourgeois celebration of interiority cannot be understood in immanent terms. However, in light of recent work on
the German Enlightenment, it is necessary to go beyond his emphasis on its
putatively compensatory function—without, however, falling back into the
sort of reductive ideology critique Lepenies was resisting. My contention is
that the rhetoric of interiority should be understood as a response to the beginnings of the democratization of leisure in modernity—a process that, as I
shall argue in Chapter 3, is linked to the emergence of a new understanding
of time and temporality. The vicissitudes of this vocabulary, which soon
spread throughout society, are therefore a crucial locus for examining the
cultural significance of modernization.

It will be helpful to consider a key witness to this transformation, the
philosopher Immanuel Kant (1724–1804). Within bourgeois Enlightenment
culture, boredom and melancholy increasingly appeared as ethical failures.
In contrast to the aristocratic embrace of a leisured way of life, the bourgeoisie had begun to pursue an ideal of individual accomplishment in which the
cultivation of emotion came to be seen as a distraction. Popular weeklies and
moral handbooks directed at the middle classes emphasized the importance
of practical occupations with the goal of worldly achievement.[24] According to
Kant, "to feel one's life, to enjoy oneself, is nothing other than to feel oneself

---

[24]Spacks discusses the English discourse on boredom as a moral phenomenon. In *Langeweile:
Zum Umgang mit Zeit und Gefühlen in Deutschland vom späten 18. bis zum frühen 20. Jahrhundert*,
Martina Kessel demonstrates that the changing attitude toward boredom in post-Enlightenment
German bourgeois culture maps onto the consolidation of modern conceptions of subjectivity
and gender relations. In the second half of the nineteenth century, she argues, the Enlightenment
ideal of a balanced and self-controlled male subject defined by "the harmonious connection between head, heart, and body" (331) gives way to a vision of a rational subject oriented toward
worldly accomplishments. Particularly after 1848, the cosmopolitan ideal of a "virtuoso of life"
(*Lebenskünstler*) yields to an ideal that subordinates individual interests to those of society as a
whole. According to Kessel, under the earlier model, masculine boredom signifies a failure to differentiate interests and accomplishments sufficiently or arises as a consequence of excessive control over affect. However, the shift from "experience to expectation as a life-structuring category
characteristic of the *Sattelzeit*" (332) meant it was now men unable to realize their worldly ambitions who were in danger of boredom. Although the same sources attest that bourgeois ideals of
femininity kept boredom a permanent danger for women, since they were expected to accept their
enforced leisure, their boredom was regarded as a sign of moral failure. Kessel traces the gendered
differences mapped in the discourse on boredom to the ambiguities of what Carol Pateman labeled "the sexual contract": although modern society depends on a constitutive, gendered division
between public and private spheres, the masculine realm was treated as synonymous with the
whole—the state and politics defined as public, economic and social activity as private (159–60).
The ascendance of the rational ideal of masculinity intensified the polarization of the sexes—and
the demands upon women to control and channel their feelings in the service of masculine accomplishment.

continually driven to go beyond the present state."[25] Weber's 'Protestant ethic' and Foucault's 'technologies of the self' converge in Kant's advice for dealing with the ever-present threat of subjective malaise within this worldly horizon.

Kant regards the fact that human beings could attain "satisfaction (*acquiescentia*) during life . . . neither from a moral . . . nor from a pragmatic point of view" as providential, since such satisfaction would spell the end of desire and hence death (§ 58; BA 175). Paradoxically, though, this tension between human aspirations and the possibilities of worldly existence is also the source of the danger of boredom. "The only certain means of becoming happy with life and thereby also satisfied with life is to fill out the time with progressively ordered occupations that have a great purpose in mind as their consequence (*vitam extendere factis* [to extend life through actions])" (ibid.). Life, on Kant's view, is to be cultivated rather than enjoyed, for it is the possession of laudable purposes that renders it valuable (§ 63; BA 182–83). In the pursuit of pleasure, Kant writes, a "principal maxim" (*Hauptmaxime*) is therefore necessary: "To portion it out to oneself [*es sich so zuzumessen*] so that one can always still increase it; for to become sated with pleasure brings about that repulsive state that makes life itself a burden to the spoiled person and consumes women under the name of the vapors (§ 60; BA 179). At this point, Kant breaks into exhortation: "Young person! Learn to love work; deny yourself pleasures not for the sake of renunciation but, so far as possible, to keep them in prospect." Through this "sacrifice," he avers, "you will assure yourself of a capital of satisfaction that is independent of accidents or natural laws" (§60; BA 179). The bourgeois attitude toward enjoyment could not be more clearly expressed. While the aristocracy, "sated with pleasure," succumbed to *taedium vitae*, the rising class would preserve its appreciation of life by cultivating interiority and focusing desire on the future.[26]

Kant's anthropology attests that the democratization of leisure which began with the rise of the bourgeoisie had occasioned a profound paradigm shift in the understanding of subjective malaise. If work was a positive value, the boredom and melancholy associated with leisure came to be regarded as marks of decadence. Since Aristotle, melancholy had been regarded as the province of artists and thinkers. Although the related claim to spiritual dis-

---

[25] Immanuel Kant, *Anthropologie in Pragmatischer Hinsicht*, §58; BA 173, subsequent citations in text.

[26] For a more complete account of my reading of Kant and the significance of his way of thinking about temporality for the construction of modern subjectivity, see my "Getrennte Liebe."

tinction would be invoked again by the romantics, the elitist conception of leisure on which that claim depends was gradually eclipsed in the course of the nineteenth century, along with the depredation of work that had accompanied it. In fact, among bourgeois artists, creative activity, too, would come to be regarded as work—for example by Flaubert, whose ambivalent relationship to the literary market in which he was embedded may be taken as paradigmatic. Unfortunately, as the correspondence of that virtuoso of boredom attests, following Kant's advice to create a "capital of satisfaction" by renouncing pleasures in the pursuit of "progressively ordered occupations" did not really eliminate subjective malaise. Indeed, despite the rampant productivity and activity, boredom and melancholy spread. As leisure, along with everything else, was further democratized, by the end of the nineteenth century the working classes, too, were struggling with boredom. While this development conforms to the Eliasian conception of an action-inhibiting civilizing process that fosters individuation through increasing social requirements for control over affect, a sociological description cannot do justice to the reflective complexity of the experiences concerned.

As Kant's emphasis on the cultivation of the self suggests, the reinterpretation of the ends of human existence that valorized work over leisure brought with it a fundamental shift in the rhetoric of reflection on subjective experience. Lepenies' account of the changing social function of invocations of melancholy and boredom points the way toward an historically articulated analysis of this transformation. According to him, both bourgeois and aristocratic melancholy were the consequence of enforced inactivity. However, while the French aristocrats were not thereby robbed of their status—in the salon "the same behavioral ideals prevailed" as at court, and aristocratic "melancholy was an emotional state of the group, not of the individual" (180/137)—the German bourgeois cultivation of interiority was a means of disavowing the fact of being banned from the community of effective actors. What was nominally the "same" experience thus had quite a different significance in the latter case. The distinction, to put it in Nietzschean terms, was that the legitimation function enfolded into supposedly subjective bourgeois melancholy produced a rhetoric of reflection colored by *ressentiment* rather than by noble resignation to the unhappy order of the world.

According to Nietzsche, subjectivity in the modern sense emerges out of such *ressentiment*, for the cultivation of interiority creates a new form of inherent value that compensates the disadvantaged "slave" for the inaccessible inborn value proper to the noble. On this analysis, sociological function must be distinguished from historical significance: though the bourgeois elevation of the individual was reactive, it led to a productive negation of aristocratic values in the resignification of work. From a Nietzschean point of view, the bourgeois emphasis on subjectivity that Lepenies interpreted as a reaction to a lack of worldly power must therefore be seen as an historically significant step in the transformation of Christian ideas in post-Enlightenment thought. That the preoccupation with "the question of meaning" functions sociologically to legitimate bourgeois disoccupation is less significant than the fact that answers to that question began to be sought in this world rather than another. Subjective malaise and the phenomena of reflection that accompany it are not simply reactive responses to the inhibition of action in traditional society. They are the heralds of a new and productive "depth" of the self that has ceased to find its truth in God.[27]

From a rhetorical perspective, it is not, as Lepenies implies, the new class position of the melancholic but rather the new consciousness of individuality developed in the Enlightenment that is decisive for the fact that by the early nineteenth century, "melancholy and boredom appear definitively [*endgültig*] as categories of the individual" (141/108). The shift from the "worldly" melancholy of the aristocracy to the melancholic interiority of the bourgeois self reflects a truly historic transformation in the discourse of reflection on subjective malaise. While affective phenomena always have worldly conditions of possibility, the discursive triumph of individualism occluded the importance of the historical and collective context of subjective experience. The modern rhetoric of reflection on subjective malaise is radically individualist. As Lepenies puts it, "in the nineteenth century there are only melancholics; melancholy no longer exists" (180/138). What had once characterized an entire social group was henceforth a pathology of the individual self.

The idealist understanding of subjective malaise considered in Chapter 1 emerges as a consequence of this development. From a rhetorical perspective that focuses on evolution of the language of reflection on subjective experience, Lepenies' sociological insights can thus be retained even if they must be situated historically rather than anthropologically. Through the "reduction" of socially structured experience to "categories of the individual," he writes, "it becomes possible to grasp boredom and melancholy as 'existentials' which are 'in the human being' and therefore supposedly inaccessible to a merely 'external' sociological approach" (141–42/108). Kierkegaard's attempt to salvage Christianity via an existential interpretation of subjective malaise is paradigmatic for the philosophical turn taken by such interiority in the

---

[27] For Nietzsche, the "priestly form of existence," with its denial of the body, was the original point of departure for this transformation. Through it, "the human soul first gained depth in a higher sense ..." (SW 5, 266). See my discussion of Simmel's interpretation of Nietzsche in Chapter 4.

nineteenth century; he was, by his own proclamation, "a genius in a small town."[28] If for La Rochefoucauld "knowing how to be bored" constituted a form of worldly wisdom, a century later the ennui of *ressentiment* had routed the melancholy of resignation. But the individualized understanding of malaise that had emerged foreclosed reflection on its own historicity.

The Modern Rhetoric of Reflection on Subjective Malaise

> Die fortwährende Umwälzung der Produktion, die ununter-
> brochene Erschütterung aller gesellschaftlichen Zustände, die
> ewige Unsicherheit und Bewegung zeichnet die Bourgeoisepoche
> vor allen anderen aus. Alle festen eingerosteten Verhältnisse mit
> ihrem Gefolge von altehrwürdigen Vorstellungen und Anschau-
> ungen werden aufgelöst, alle neugebildeten veralten, ehe sie
> verknöchern können. Alles Ständische und Stehende verdampft,
> alles Heilige wird entweiht, und die Menschen sind endlich ge-
> zwungen, ihre Lebensstellung, ihre gegenseitigen Beziehungen
> mit nüchternen Augen anzusehen.
>   Marx and Engels[29]

The *mal du siècle* is but one of many names for the spiritual malaise that began to plague the French and German bourgeois intelligentsia in the nineteenth century. As their more practical class comrades proceeded rapaciously toward empires abroad and commercial success at home, inventing, transforming, and creating a new world while actively destroying the old, they suffered from neurasthenia and hysteria, worried about fatigue, decadence and decline. Since these phenomena are extremely widespread, Lepenies' *bon mot* that "in the nineteenth century there are only melancholics; melancholy no longer exists" (180/138) bears further reflection. While he refers simply to the disappearance of melancholy as a class-wide affective phenomenon, his remark has a deeper significance when placed in the context of the historically developing discourse of reflection on subjective malaise.

From the point of view of the "civilizing process," the sociological migration of the problem of action-inhibition to the individual registers a process of interiorization, a deepening of the self, characteristic of modernity. This

---

[28] *The Point of View for My Work as an Author*, 100; cited in Lepenies, 89/118. See also my discussion of Kierkegaard in Chapter 3, pp. 156–60.

[29] "Constant revolutionizing of production, uninterrupted disturbance of all social conditions, everlasting uncertainty and agitation distinguish the bourgeois epoch from all earlier ones. All fixed, fast-frozen relations, with their train of ancient and venerable prejudices and opinions, are swept away, all new-formed ones become antiquated before they can ossify. All that is solid melts into air, all that is holy is profaned, and man is at last compelled to face with sober senses, his real conditions of life, and his relations with his kind" (*The Communist Manifesto*, Tucker 476).

change is linked, I contend, to an epochal discursive transformation. 'Melancholy' implies a longing for a (lost) state of wholeness—whether for worldly power, as in the case of the aristocrats of the Fronde, or for an end to the metaphysical solitude lamented in German literature beginning in the eighteenth century. Melancholy is an experience, furthermore, tied up with the traditional vision of leisure that had been rendered obsolete by the new valorization of work and individual achievement. Thus the rebellious sons of the bourgeoisie proclaimed their pseudo-aristocratic *ennui* in the face of the dominant vision of human life in which enjoyment was hoarded, in which one was supposed to live only from 'interest' and never for pleasure. However, because these self-professed melancholics were dependent upon capital of a less ethereal sort, they were obliged to resign themselves to the dreadful state of the world ruled by the money-grubbing sorts they disdained. The leisure they enjoyed was dependent on a commitment to productive labor they abhorred. The discourse on subjective malaise that took shape in the nineteenth century thus defined a form of identity shaped by a crisis of desire and meaning with quite precise sociological preconditions, conditions that rendered melancholy in the traditional sense obsolete. It was, in a word, the ennui of *ressentiment.*

Abstracting from the historical context of the post-Enlightenment discourse of reflection on subjective experience, Lepenies grasps the change in terms of structural transformations in the relationship between melancholy and society. During the nineteenth century, he argues, the legitimation strategy associated with a defense of the claims of interiority against the corrupt world came to characterize the stance of the outsider to bourgeois modernity. When the bourgeoisie as a class overcame its impotence vis-à-vis the aristocracy through their revolutionary resignification of work, he writes,

> it became possible to claim melancholy for the individual. The "Werthersickness" of the eighteenth century symbolizes the state of consciousness of a whole class; the *mal du siècle* is a label only for isolated melancholics. Here begins the development that leads from melancholy to spleen and from the melancholic to the dandy—to bourgeois literature with aristocratic manners. (204/157)

If the eighteenth-century bourgeoisie had turned melancholic interiority into a sign of spiritual distinction by disavowing its worldly conditions, the nineteenth-century outsiders claimed that their abhorrence for the modern world made them spiritually superior to the rest of their class. According to Lepenies, the combination of an "aristocratic worship of the boredom that documents exceptionality" with an "originally bourgeois tendency to reflection" produces a literary attitude "particularly disdained by the bourgeoisie" both for its dependence on "aristocratic behavioral models" and for its "allegiance to principles that the bourgeoisie had thrown overboard long ago" (206/158). Just as the bourgeoisie as a whole had used melancholic interiority as a mark of distinction that differentiated them from the bored and blasé aristocracy, these skeptical subjects defined themselves by flaunting their boredom with the world of work and industry built up by their bourgeois fathers.

While the melancholic aristocrats of the Fronde could long, however ineffectually, for "restoration," for the sons of the bourgeoisie there was no turning back to a pre-modern world. Though contemptuous of the strivings for scientific and technical progress that characterized the hegemonic vision of human purpose, as I shall show in Chapter 3, they, too, were ultimately rationalists who ended by importing Enlightenment values into modern art and literature. They were creatures of the modern city, for whom retreat into sentimental communion with nature was a thing of the past. If the melancholy of their romantic grandfathers was filled with longing, theirs was a boredom that easily modulated into despair; rejecting the worldly success of their fathers, these proto-bohemians defiantly proclaimed their realistic resignation to a meaningless existence as a hollow self. At the same time, as Lepenies rightly emphasizes, such "eccentric-aesthetic" suffering fulfilled a legitimation function: for the nineteenth-century dandies, an attitude of ennui was an aesthetic affirmation of the impotence of the subject in the face of the arbitrariness of modern existence. With it, the rebellious sons of the bourgeoisie appropriated for themselves the prerogatives of aristocratic distance from the world. Thus, via the "eccentric" individuality of the bourgeois critics of the bourgeoisie, the rhetoric of ressentiment that characterized the original bourgeois retreat into the self migrated into the writings of the nineteenth-century critics of modernity.

Ironically, the very transformation that marginalized melancholy as a social phenomenon and confined it to the realm of eccentrics and bohemians guaranteed its importance for the future. According to Lepenies, although "melancholy is a bourgeois form of behavior which the bourgeoisie has abandoned since capitalism" ascended (206/158), because of the cultural function of the *Bildungsbürger*, the tradition of melancholic reflection would be extended whenever—whether in literature, sociology, or philosophy—a critique of modern life was proffered. Beginning in the nineteenth century, resignation to the loss of meaning, the decline of civilization, the dissolution of morals, and so on were proclaimed in countless permutations by bourgeois critics of modernity. The lamentations of Kierkegaard, Schopenhauer, Nietzsche et al., despite their internal differences, all attempt to come to

terms with the same contradictions that led their artistic counterparts to pro-
claim their boredom with it all. As the link Lepenies demonstrates between
melancholy and order implies, the social context of bourgeois melancholy
can illuminate the nihilistic dynamic in which attempts at critique oscillate
between utopian fantasies of total revolution and despairing acceptance of
the status quo.

In drawing attention to the bourgeois origins of the relation between
subject and historical world that corresponds to the interpretation of boredom and melancholy as individual, ahistorical experiences, *Melancholy and
Society* establishes a sociological perspective for criticizing philosophical uni-
versalizations of ennui such as Reinhard Kuhn's. However, the mere demonstration that a form of experience is historically specific does not constitute
an interpretation of that experience. Because he equates reflective distance
with impotence, Lepenies does not raise further questions about the significance of the affective tendencies of the *Bildungsbürgertum*, the modern intellectual class whose *raison d'être*, so to speak, was reflection. His sociological account reduces the subject of boredom and melancholy to the subject-
position of bored and melancholic retreatism and thereby misses the critical
potential of the experiences themselves. Nonetheless, here too Lepenies' own
analysis indicates a direction in which it is possible to go further.

The dominant modern rhetoric of interiority entails that boredom and
melancholy are grasped as problems of the self. Both the internal dynamic of
the experiences and the language in which they are expressed seem to mili-
tate against a recognition of their historical significance. To recognize in
them historical effects of the normalization of anomie that has resulted from
the social transformations of modernity is, therefore, to gain a perspective
for critical reflection on the world that evokes such responses. The most significant implications of Lepenies' study thus become visible through a focus
not on the anthropological universals he identifies but rather on how the answer to the question of "what it signifies when someone claims to be" melancholy or bored varies over time.

To underline, as I have, that *Melancholy and Society* traces a major shift in
the rhetoric of reflection on subjective malaise since the Enlightenment is
not to assimilate Lepenies, contrary to his own self-understanding, to "conceptual history" (*Begriffsgeschichte*) (7/1). My claim, rather, is that by documenting the centrality of discourses on melancholy and boredom for interpreting the subjective significance of the process of modernization, Lepenies'
study points to the need for a synthesis of the concerns of intellectual, cultural, and social history in reflecting on modernity and modernization. Since
the seventeenth century, Lepenies shows, the discourse on subjective malaise

has grown increasingly "worldless," thereby underpinning an understanding of subjective experience that effaces its own historicity. Thus although, as I have emphasized, his analyses themselves focus on "the sociological conditions and connections between various understandings of melancholy" (15/8), his study nonetheless has implications for the historical question of how the experiences of melancholy and boredom came to appear to be timeless features of the human condition. As the discourse of reflection on subjective experience evolved, the "worldless" forms of malaise associated with the emergence of modern subjectivity were democratized. From a rhetorical point of view, the way the experience of boredom individualizes and effaces subjective awareness of its historical specificity is a sign of its modernity.

In the course of the eighteenth and early nineteenth century, an aristocratic, worldly mode of resignation yielded to bourgeois withdrawal into the "interior"—literally, of the home and, figuratively, of the self. Through this discursive shift from public mourning to private suffering, from collective to individual forms of malaise, itself born along by a revolutionary resignification of temporality, a modern conception of subjectivity came into being. The new discourse of reflection on subjective malaise, the language of interiority in which the modern conception of boredom has its place, bears within itself the scars of historical struggle. The melancholic longing for wholeness that animates romantic literature is already forsaken in what Friedrich Schiller christened the "sentimental" consciousness of the modern artist who knows that "naïve" unity with nature is ineffably lost. The interiority of the cultivated self becomes the only refuge in a world "fragmented" by the emergence of modern modes of social organization.[30] The romantic exploration of the depths of the self could not restore what had disappeared from the disenchanted real world, and in the course of the nineteenth century, subjective malaise grew ever less worldly, ever more overshadowed by renunciation in the face of metaphysical loss. As all that was solid melted into air in the ever-busy hands of the bourgeoisie, the modern experience of boredom as a radically isolating "encounter with nothingness" became possible.

In other words, the democratization of leisure that conditions the emergence of modern subjectivity was accompanied by a *democratization of skepti-*

---

[30] See See Schiller, *Über naïve und sentimentalische Dichtung*; the reference to fragmentation is in the sixth of the letters *Über die aesthetische Erziehung des Menschen*. In contrast to the polis, the "mechanical life" of modern society entails that "state and church, laws and mores are torn apart." As a consequence, "eternally fettered to a single small fragment of the whole, the human being develops only as fragment," 323.

cism. Among the fruits of bourgeois industry were the processes of industrialization and urbanization that transformed the sociological conditions of everyday life. As people moved from the intimacy and inter-generational continuity of rural and village life into the anonymity of urban populations, the traditional parameters of identity and community were undermined with such rapidity and thoroughness that it is not too much to speak of a collective "loss of cultural self-evidence." As the bourgeois reinterpretation of the ends of human existence via a revaluation of labor and worldly accomplishment gained sway, so did a pragmatic and rationalistic attitude toward questions of meaning. "Modernity" was valorized; scientific progress converged with social transformations, and traditional modes of thinking came to seem outdated on a hitherto unheard-of scale. Religious institutions began to lose their sway over the mass of the population. With the rise of modern technology and the successes of science—in themselves transformations that democratized leisure—the skeptical attitudes of the Enlightenment were also popularized.

The corollary to this process was a democratization of boredom. As the conditions of mass leisure emerged, an initially elitist discourse of subjective disaffection gradually took hold in popular culture, so that by the early twentieth century the experience of ennui had become truly universal. While a century earlier, melancholy had been cultivated as a sign of spiritual distinction, this modern boredom signified, if anything, the lack of an inner life, the failure to find meaning in anything at all. Such boredom was the reflex of a culture in which time had become money, for from the outset the democratization of leisure was allied with the marketing of pastimes. True, the bourgeois condemnation of ennui as a moral failure—the Enlightenment's secularized formulation of the religious proscription against the sin of acedia—persists in the contemporary world where eighty-hour work weeks are a status symbol. Nonetheless, the very frenzy of the "successful" attests to the ultimate inefficacy of activity as such in alleviating subjective malaise. The democratization of leisure has bred a culture of frenetic amusement, one in which Kracauer's 1920 remark that "The form of free-time busy-ness necessarily corresponds to the form of business"[31] is truer than ever. The contemporary terror of boredom, which testifies to its apparent inevitability, is saturated with the post-romantic resignation to a world in which neither work nor leisure can bring happiness to subjects who no longer hope for divine restitution in the next.

---

[31]"Der Form des Betriebs entspricht mit Notwendigkeit die des 'Betriebs.'" From "Kult der Zerstreuung" (I quote Thomas Y. Levin's translation (325); the original is in *Das Ornament der Masse*, 314).

Modern boredom, which masquerades as a universal feature of the human condition, is a democratized form of the disaffection that plagued the nineteenth-century outsiders, ineffectual protestors against an order ineluctably on the rise. As I shall show in Chapter 3, Baudelaire's poetry of urban despair excavated the foundations of the youthful malaise that has been discovered and rediscovered in every generation since. In it, the modern subject's nihilistic vacillation between desires for total renewal (and their accompanying political expressions) and bitter acceptance of an inhuman order (and the flight into the self) is represented as a product of ennui, that "delicate monster" who "would happily destroy the earth and swallow the world in a yawn." In the very movement by which it effaces its own historicity, such ennui also raises profound questions about the meaning of existence and the significance of action. Its nihilistic dynamic captures the fundamental dilemma of the modern subject, for whom the loss of cultural self-evidence has inaugurated both the radical transcendence of absolute freedom and the radical immanence of a lonely and meaningless death.

Despite its philosophical limitations, *Melancholy and Society* indicates that there is a way to retrieve the questions raised by Kuhn without idealizing such ennui into an ahistorical feature of the human condition. The question of "what it means when someone claims to be bored" must be posed in relation to the social-cultural matrix in which both the ontological possibility and the ethical significance of action are located. Recognizing the rhetoric of experience embedded in the discourse on boredom as a subjective effect of the modernization process is the first step. However, it is also necessary to reflect from a philosophical perspective on the language of boredom as a modern mode of interpreting experience. Chapter 3 will focus not on boredom as an experience but on the significance of the discourse on boredom that symbolically links the material effects of modernization to the crisis of modern subjectivity. The experience of boredom is not only a literal effect of modernization, a product of the rationalization of the lifeworld, but also a figure for the dilemma of the modern subject unable to find a meaningful grounding for action in a world robbed of all metaphysical anchors. By examining the historicity of the rhetoric of reflection that universalizes the experience of boredom into a natural and inevitable feature of human existence, I will demonstrate how the discourse on boredom can be read as an important locus for philosophical and historical reflection on the subjective effects of cultural modernization.

CHAPTER 3

Boredom and the Modernization of Subjectivity

⸻ ◆ ◆ ◆ ⸻

> Durch die moderne Zeit . . . geht ein Gefühl von Spannung, Er-
> wartung, ungelöstem Drängen—als sollte die Hauptsache erst
> kommen, das Definitive, der eigentliche Sinn und Centralpunkt
> des Lebens und der Dinge.
>
> Georg Simmel[1]

Introduction: Boredom and the Rhetoric of Experience

In the mid-nineteenth century, as industrialization and urbanization
transformed the European landscape, the problem of boredom emerged as a
mass phenomenon. Recurring in a variety of critical, descriptive, and aesthe-
ticizing discourses on the subjective effects of modernization, 'boredom'
constitutes a crucial term in the vocabularies with which writers, artists, and
scientists, social reformers, politicians, and historians manifested their ambivalent fascination with the way in which the psychic landscape of human
experience, too, was being transformed. The discourse on boredom in which
these languages of reflection converge mingles accents of gloom with bound-
less optimism—boredom appears on one hand as a response to fatigue, decay, depletion, and on the other, as a spur to freedom, innovation, renewal.
Depending on the context, boredom may be identified with inchoate, melancholic attachment to the past or splenetic rejection of an unsatisfactory
present; viewed positively as a source of that restless and productive discontent which fuels the motor of progress; or used analytically as an explanation
of the frenetic embrace of new sources of diversion which characterized the
period. The discourse on boredom thus epitomizes the modern rhetoric of
reflection on subjective experience as it took shape in this period—a rhetoric
wrought with ambivalence toward the effects of modernization, in which the

---

[1]"The modern era . . . is permeated by a feeling of tension, expectation, unresolved longing—
as though the definitive thing, the genuine meaning and central point of life and of things were
yet to come" (GSG 5, 189).

celebration of human triumphs in the form of scientific and technological advances was paired with growing malaise in the face of the rationalization of the world wrought by those changes.[2]

I contend that the evolution of the discourse on boredom traces the constitution of a new rhetoric of experience—a modern idiom of self-understanding—as it develops through the nineteenth century. On one hand, the discourse spreads as religious and moral frameworks of human self-understanding are displaced by disenchanted scientific thinking. On the other, however, the language of boredom remains ambiguous, continuing to resonate with those older frameworks even as it epitomizes the process by which materialist interpretations of subjective malaise become culturally dominant. The resulting constitutive ambiguity of boredom gives rise to difficulties of interpretation. Although 'boredom' belongs to the rhetoric of enlightened skepticism, it names an experience of malaise in the face of the disenchanted world. Within the discourse on boredom, a modern rhetoric of experience mingles with traditional modes of reflection on subjective discontent. My argument, which emphasizes the role of skeptical attitudes in the evolution and diffusion of this language, links the ambiguity of the discourse on boredom to a fundamental transformation in modern Europe in the way the human relation to history was understood.

This chapter discusses an array of nineteenth-century participants in the discourse on boredom, underlining the imbrication of 'idealist' and 'materialist' modes of reflection on subjective experience in romantic and post-romantic thought. It shows that while the discourse on boredom spreads as a function of an increasingly hegemonic, disenchanted understanding of subjective malaise, as a language of reflection, it continues to raise problems of meaning. This circumstance has methodological consequences. It implies that the task of describing the discursive operations of modern modes of reflection must be distinguished from that of criticizing their constitutive impulses and metaphors. That is, a philosophically reflexive mode of rhetorical analysis is called for, one that can transcend the rhetoric of experience which forms its point of departure without losing touch

---

[2]In using the term 'modernization,' I do not endorse the claim that there is any inherent teleology involved, for example one that would connect technological or industrial development and political liberalization. My object is not to define a putatively extra-discursive historical process but to examine how the discourse on boredom fits into the larger discourse on modern life and modern identity in which the notion of 'modernization' is invoked. On the use of the term in its social scientific sense in historical contexts, see Wehler 1975. My approach has affinities with Robert Pippin's project, insofar as we are both concerned to develop resources for the philosophically oriented analysis of cultural change.

with the historical specificity of the constellation of experience and language it examines.

Chapters 1 and 2 laid out the complementary strengths and limitations of philosophical-humanistic and social-scientific modes of reflection on boredom, using historical examples as illustrations. Each approach, I showed, envisions subjective malaise in a different way and thereby generates a different sort of narrative about the ascendance and evolution of the discourse on boredom in modernity. Because the language of boredom reflects the impact of social and cultural transformations underway in this period on the modes in which subjective experience itself is understood, I argued that neither focusing on the socio-historical determinants of boredom nor emphasizing its philosophical significance can provide an adequate account of the experience.

To grasp why the language of boredom becomes so pervasive in modernity, I contend, it is necessary to synthesize the strengths of the two approaches—to reflect simultaneously on boredom's socio-historical conditions of possibility and on its philosophical significance as the exemplar of a specifically modern language of reflection on subjective experience. To do so means unpacking claims that have become our commonplaces—that experience does not exist outside of language, that subjectivity is constituted in culture. Indeed, simultaneous attention to both the linguistic and the historical construction of boredom is required, for it is not as experience "in itself" but rather as part of a broader cultural discourse that boredom articulates problems of meaning with the material effects of modernization.

This chapter attempts, therefore, to develop strategies for thinking the relationship between subjective experience and cultural modernization by combining historical and philosophical reflection on boredom as a phenomenon in which the profound contradictions of progress are lived. The analysis developed here attempts to meet the need for an historiographical approach that can reflect the genuine ambiguity of reason and rationality in modern life. In the last two hundred years, epistemic relativism, profound reservations about 'progress,' and awareness of the operations of unconscious and ideological motivations have become ubiquitous. That is to say, doubt, self-doubt, and deeply felt unfreedom seem to have become constitutive elements of modern identity. In the words of Robert Musil, "in earlier times, one had an easier conscience about being a person than one does today" when it seems that "the dissolution of the anthropocentric point of view" as a consequence of centuries of scientific progress "has finally arrived at the "I" itself." The discourse on boredom, I argue, is an index of this diffusion of skepticism into subjectivity itself.

The distinction established in the first two chapters between the rhetoric of reflection on boredom and the discourse on the experience itself thus forms the point of departure for a mode of historical analysis that reflects on boredom both as experiential phenomenon and as discursive construction. Concentrating on the historical specificity of the nineteenth-century phenomenon of boredom and foregrounding the evolution of the discourse on that phenomenon, it asks about the significance of the way this idiom of reflection on subjective experience changes over time. This form of rhetorical analysis thereby moves beyond the question of what boredom *is* that guided the analyses considered in the first two chapters. Focusing not on the experience itself but on the way the category of boredom is historically and linguistically constructed and on how what it is said to be changes over time, it asks what the discourse on boredom *signifies*—and thereby inquires into the meaning of boredom's cultural status.

This chapter begins by considering how the broad post-Enlightenment paradigm shift from an idealist to a materialist rhetoric of subjective experience appears in the etymology of ennui. Far from providing access to an understanding of boredom "as such," this evidence powerfully demonstrates that the experience cannot be understood in abstraction from its linguistic expressions and their historically evolving significations. 'Ennui,' it shows, refers to a form of emptiness that is open to multiple, mutually contradictory interpretations. Although the experience remains, in this sense, ambiguous, etymological reference works nonetheless register a significant evolution in the course of the nineteenth century. They attest that as materialist interpretations of subjective experience gained sway in European culture, boredom increasingly came to be understood as a psychological or physiological rather than a spiritual phenomenon. The democratization of skepticism went hand in hand with a medicalization of malaise.

The following sections focus on interpreting the changes in the rhetoric of reflection on subjective experience that are visible in this etymological evidence. Examining the discursive shift toward materialist explanation and situating it in historical context, I argue that political and industrial-scientific revolution provided the experiential conditions of possibility for modern boredom. Thus while invocations of ennui initially fell in the category of romantic and idealistic reactions to the attendant historic changes, as the language of boredom spread and evolved, it rapidly came into the force field of materialist modes of reflection. The historical evidence underlines why the discourse on boredom cannot be understood simply as a reflex of the material and political cultural transformations known as the modernization process. As a language of reflection, it is a way of interpreting subjective experience. To account for the stunning spread of boredom in the course of the nineteenth century, it is therefore necessary to consider the phenomenon from a rhetorical perspective as well: to attend to the fact that it is in the first instance the *language* of boredom, a new way of talking about subjective experience, that spreads in this period.

The concept of discourse is ambiguous, encompassing both theoretically articulated and everyday ways of talking about experience. I shall use 'the discourse on boredom' in both these ways: to refer to a whole family of experiences that I contend register the psychic and perceptual impacts of modernization—not only to *ennui* and *Langeweile,* but also to tedium, fatigue, and blaséness—and also to mean the contemporary language of reflection on subjective malaise in which such experiences and perceptions play a central role. The discussion of etymology in the first section will lay the groundwork for an examination of the evolution of the discourse on boredom in this broader sense in the course of the nineteenth century. Drawing on evidence from a wide range of fields, I shall show how the evolution of the discourse on boredom maps onto an historic paradigm shift in the rhetoric of reflection on subjective experience in this period—and thereby leads to questions about the constitution and operation of this new language of reflection that are not purely historical.

Chapter 3 thus addresses in a systematic way questions that already arose in Chapters 1 and 2. What does it mean for an entirely new metaphorics of malaise to gain sway? What made this way of talking about subjective experience powerful enough to displace older idioms of reflection in all echelons of society? I approach these issues by situating the discursive development attested by the etymological evidence in the larger interpretive context of the democratization of skepticism in modernity. I argue that, on one hand, the evolution of the discourse on boredom must be understood in relation to the emergence of the modern materialist paradigm of reflection on subjective experience, a shift that can only partially be explained in terms of sociological categories like 'rationalization' and 'secularization.' On the other, I show that the ambiguity that opens boredom to both idealist and materialist interpretations remains integral to the experience even as the language of boredom fosters a materialization and medicalization of the terms in which subjective malaise is understood. This combination, which allows boredom to mediate between traditional and modern modes of self-understanding, helps to explain the prominence of talk about ennui in nineteenth-century European culture.

The first half of the chapter demonstrates that while the burgeoning *phenomenon* of boredom may be regarded as a symptom of modernity's discontents, the *language* of boredom functions as a locus of reflection upon the relations between subjective experience and historical reality—and thereby enables timeless questions about the meaning of human existence to be reformulated in a modern idiom. The nihilistic dynamic of the experience cannot be taken at face value; it is necessary to reformulate the question of what boredom signifies in figurative terms. Having examined the discourse on boredom as historical phenomenon, I turn in the second half of the chapter to discussions of literary works by Charles Baudelaire and Gustave Flaubert, whose representations of boredom did so much to establish the centrality of the experience without qualities for modern subjectivity.

I argue that Baudelaire's poetry depicts the alchemy by which ancient and modern vocabularies of reflection come together in the discourse on boredom. As the source and setting of new and terrible experiences that overwhelm the lyric subject, modern Paris is the crucible in which this linguistic process takes place. Here the boredom in which that subject both registers and rebels against the destruction of everything that had once rendered life meaningful becomes the foundation of a modern poetics of subjective experience—a way of writing in which description and critique converge. Published in the same year as the *Fleurs du mal*, Flaubert's *Madame Bovary* examines boredom as it appears in the provinces. Emma Bovary is a romantic subject *manqué* whose ennui with her meaningless life leads only to false and destructive palliatives. As such, she comes to epitomize the modern subject whose malaise, at once significant and superficial, stands as a metaphor for all that is lacking in modern life. However, Madame Bovary is both the subject and the object of ennui—at once the tragic heroine and the pathetic scapegoat burdened with Flaubert's own contempt for the bourgeois existence that defined his world. Through this ambiguity, the literary representation of her ennui exceeds the straightforward mimesis of historical reality. Indeed, because Flaubert's critical impulse quavers on the edge of nihilistic affirmation of boredom's inevitability, his readers may be tempted to disregard the historical dimension of the experience being represented.

In these texts, 'ennui' is not analyzed but anatomized through embodiment in literary figures. Here, where boredom and the bored subject exist only as representations, the operation of the metaphorics that links problems of meaning to their historical context are made visible. The problem of defining the true nature of boredom thus falls away, for as we have seen, that problem is a manifestation of attempts to explain what boredom *is* from the outside. Flaubert and Baudelaire show how the historical and philosophical significance of boredom are imbricated. However, because their texts imaginatively enact the nihilistic dynamic of the experience, neither is able to achieve an adequate reflective perspective on boredom. In them, 'ennui' is both the historical fate of the modern subject and an effect of language, a genuine form of suffering and a sham substitute for religious longing. These representations of ennui thus reveal both the strengths and the limitations of the modern rhetoric of experience that governs the discourse on boredom as a whole. Even as their texts forge a metaphorics of boredom that links subjective experience to cultural modernization, they demonstrate how, lived from the inside, the modern language of reflection must obscure its own historicity. The discussion of Flaubert and Baudelaire therefore provides a point of departure for the reformulation of the problem of boredom undertaken in Part II, 'The Rhetoric of Reflection.'

Defining Boredom: Etymology and the Modernization of Reflection on Subjective Malaise

For the historian, there are no banal things
Siegfried Gideon[3]

The word 'boredom' was unknown before the mid-nineteenth century; its etymology remains uncertain. In the sense of "the state of being bored; tedium, ennui," the earliest citations in *The Oxford English Dictionary* are to Charles Dickens (*Bleak House*, 1852) and George Eliot (*Daniel Deronda*, 1876). While the word 'bore' was used as both substantive and verb starting in the second half of the eighteenth century,[4] its etymology is equally unclear. As in the case of the now more familiar 'boredom,' the definition of the substantive sense of 'bore' invokes the French: "The malady of *ennui*, supposed to be specifically 'French,' as 'the spleen' was supposed to be English: a fit of ennui or sulks; a dull time." As the editor implies, one ought not to take the association of forms of malaise with national character too seriously. If for the British it was 'French ennui,' the French spoke of 'la maladie anglais,' and 'spleen' can be traced to a much older way of thinking about character as a function of the balance of humors in the body. The phenomenon is international. That 'boredom' emerged, as it were, out of nowhere precisely at this juncture makes it appropriate to use the English term to signify the Europe-wide discourse.

This usage is suggested as well by the fact that 'boredom' refers both to a temporal elongation and to an existential state. That is, the English term sig-

---

[3] Cited in Patrice Petro's fascinating "After Shock / Between Boredom and History."
[4] The earliest citations are to the Earl of March and G. Williams, 1766, for the nominal and Earl Carlisle, 1768, for the verbal uses.

nifies from the beginning both the paradigmatically German sense of boredom as unpleasantly extended time and the paradigmatically French or Italian sense of boredom as existential or spiritual suffering. Although these nationally distinct accents remain, around the turn of the nineteenth century, a new international idiom for describing subjective malaise was emerging, and the meanings of 'Langeweile' and 'ennui' tended to converge. Since the term 'boredom' embodies this convergence of temporal and existential connotations, I shall use it to signify the broader European discourse on subjective malaise in which questions of meaning are related to a distinctly modern experience of empty, meaningless time. This usage underlines that the focus is not on the vicissitudes of the words themselves but on the way that discourse figures the relationship between subjective experience and the materially palpable transformations of modern culture.

On account of its etymological singularity, 'boredom' can appropriately be used to refer to the new discourse on subjective malaise that develops in Europe in this period as a conceptual whole. However, for historical reasons, in examining the perceptual and discursive transformations that constituted that discourse, I shall focus on the French case. It is in the Paris that Walter Benjamin famously called the "Capital of the Nineteenth Century," at the epicenter of the social and political upheavals that, beginning in 1789, transformed the face of Europe, that this new language for expressing subjective disaffection most visibly takes shape.

As we have noted, 'boredom' entered the English language just after 1848—that is, after the final wave of revolutionary emanations from Paris had done their part toward consolidating the new bourgeois order on the continent. The second half of the nineteenth century was a time of enormous cultural change. The lived qualities of time and space were literally being transformed by urbanization and industrialization; the transport revolution and the newspaper explosion shrunk the lived world of the mass of people. Even as the profound social consequences of the industrial and political revolutions began to make themselves felt, the experience of empty, meaningless time found its classical formulations in French bourgeois literature. Not only, in contrast to the aristocratic privilege associated with 'ennui' in ancien régime writers from La Rochefoucauld to Chateaubriand, did the works of Stendhal, Baudelaire and Flaubert register the process of boredom's democratizing spread to the middle classes. In writings by contemporary French historians, psychologists, philosophers, and sociologists, the prevalence of 'ennui' among an even broader social spectrum is grasped as a significant social problem and a spiritual symptom of the material and political transformations wrought by modernization.

Furthermore, the French case vividly illustrates the cultural and philosophical significance of the evolution of the discourse on boredom. During the nineteenth century, amidst the upheavals of urbanization and industrialization, even as state and society modernized, a new language of reflection on subjective experience emerged, a language in which the philosophical materialism of the Enlightenment mingles with the technological materialism of the second industrial revolution. In literature, in philosophy, in the sciences, a new, secular understanding of human existence was on the ascendant. The discourse on boredom that flourished, paradoxically, as the pace of change accelerated is both symptom and product of this disenchantment. It belongs to a world in which social thought cultivates statistics, in which medicine and psychology speak not of the soul but of the body. In this milieu, the world of Comte and Durkheim, Taine and Renan, Fourier and Marx, a new, materialist vision of human existence radically transformed the vocabulary of subjective malaise. This chapter traces how the discourse on 'ennui'—an experience conceived of as both a physiological or psychological response and as a cipher for the loss of meaning in an increasingly godless world—registers this transformation. First, however, we must examine how the global paradigm shift toward disenchanted modes of reflection on subjective experience is inscribed in the history of the word for a phenomenon at once spiritual and visceral.

The word 'ennui' entered the French language in the first half of the twelfth century in the *chansons*. It initially signified a "tristesse profonde, chagrin, dègoût"—a form of moral pain particularly associated with the loss of a loved one. In the seventeenth century it took on additional associations with spiritual malaise as a "lassitude d'esprit, manque de goût, de plaisir" in general.[5] The entry in the philosophes' eighteenth-century *Encyclopédie* classifies 'ennui' as a term of moral philosophy but denies that it can be defined.[6] Neither grief (*chagrin*) nor sorrow (*tristesse*), ennui is "a privation of all pleasure" in which "a malaise or aversion [*dégoût*]" fills the soul. As such, according to the encyclopedist, it is "the most dangerous enemy of our being and the tomb of the passions."[7] In this enlightened interpretation of ennui,

[5] That is, it was initially a "profound sadness, grief, aversion" and later signified "spiritual lassitude, lack of inclination, of pleasure" more broadly. The latter usage is particularly associated with Pascal. "Ennui," *Le Tresor de la Langue francaise: Dictionnaire de la Langue du XIX et du XXe Siècle* (1979).

[6] "Ennui," *Encyclopédie, ou Dictionnaire-Raisonné des Sciences, des Arts et des Métiers*, XII, ed. Denis Diderot, 467–69. This article was written by M. le Chevalier de Jaucourt. See Jonard for a discussion of influences on Jaucourt's way of thinking, which he argues include Locke, Du Bos, Condillac, Helvétius and Holbach (chapter 5 passim).

[7] "L'ennui est le plus dangereux ennemi de notre être, & le tombeau des passions."

the experience is elevated and generalized even as it is disenchanted and materialized. Severing ideas of loss and sorrow from the definition in this way would turn out to be a decisive rhetorical step toward rendering the problems of meaning associated with the experience accessible to practical interventions.

Up until the eighteenth century, 'ennui' had belonged to the aristocratic milieu. The semantic shift registered in the *Encyclopédie* article attests that in the Enlightenment, 'ennui' was beginning to undergo a process of democratization. This process, which we shall trace throughout this chapter, had momentous consequences. Few people, the encyclopedist writes, are blessed by Providence with a temperament that frees them from the danger of ennui; most will therefore have recourse to "the pleasures of the commonality of men [*aux plaisirs du commun des hommes*]." If one is to avoid falling prey to the pains that inevitably follow on giving oneself over in this way to the passions, the encyclopedist advises, "it is necessary to be devoted from youth to studies and occupations that demand a great deal of meditation" and to form "the habit of putting one's ideas in order and thinking over what one reads."[8] It is most important "to avoid inaction and idleness [*l'inaction et l'oisivité*]." Indeed, "work of all sorts is the true remedy for this evil," this being true, he emphasizes, "as much for the most powerful monarch as for the poorest laborer." The *Encylopédie*'s emphasis on the need [*besoin*] of the soul to "be occupied [*d'être occupée*]" and on work as a cure for ennui marks a fundamental departure from traditional understandings of subjective malaise—a departure characteristic of enlightened thought.[9] The resemblance to the venerable monastic remedy for acedia is misleading; for enlightened thinkers, the prescription to work was based in a materialist psychology that saw the soul's occupations as ends in themselves rather than as means to a transcendent end. In modernity, even as the problem of ennui is democratized, the notion of spiritual suffering is subordinated to an individualized and mechanistic understanding of human existence.

The experience of spiritual lassitude known as ennui remained open, however, to other, less materialist, interpretations. In the seventeenth cen-

[8]"... il faut encore s'être adonné dès la jeunesse à des études & à des occupations dont les travaux demandent beaucoup de méditation; il faut que l'esprit ait contracté l'habitude de mettre en ordre ses idées, & de penser sur ce qu'il lit ..."

[9]Grounded in Lockean psychology, this idea can be found *expressis verbis* in Holbach, who links it to what will become a recurring topos in the nineteenth century: boredom as a symptom of cultural decadence. While ennui reigns in the wealthy and civilized world, he writes, in a "savage nation, everyone works and no one has either the time or the means to be bored" (cited in Jonard, 64).

tury, Blaise Pascal had linked ennui to the problem of desire—to pride, to habit, to the need for pleasure.[10] His interpretation assimilated ennui to the sin of acedia: one does not become tired (*s'ennuie*), he wrote, with eating and sleeping every day, since the desire for these are renewed. However, "sans la faim des choses spirituelles on s'en ennuie . . ."—without the hunger for spiritual things, one is bored (378). On Pascal's interpretation, because it is caused by a lack of desire for the things of the spirit, ennui is a manifestation of pride for which the subject is culpable. In proto-romantic figures such as Rousseau, these religious resonances of ennui were reconfigured, and the secular understanding of boredom as a form of subjective spiritual distinction began to emerge.[11]

By the late eighteenth century, the word was attaining its current range of meaning, in which an experience of elongated time is linked to questions of meaning. As we have noted, it was also around the turn of the nineteenth century that the German 'Langeweile' underwent the diametrically opposed development—in which an existential sense became conjoined to the original temporal meaning of boredom as a 'lange Weile,' a 'long time.'[12] This sense of ennui as an experience that distinguishes the sufferer, underlining his or her individuality, persists. However, even before the beginning of the

---

[10]Pascal, *Pensées*, 56–57.

[11]This sense of ennui may be viewed as an elaboration on the original sense of the pains of love lost, as in *La Nouvelle Heloise* (Part 3, Letter 6). Another precursor of the romantics, the Marquise du Deffand (1697–1780), was famous for her inveterate ennui; in her case, the word is synonymous with the ancient *taedium vitae*. An oft-professed hatred of life and profound metaphysical pessimism drove this worldly and educated woman to devote her existence to the pursuit of distractions and to the production of a vast correspondence that documents her long despair. One might speculate that her conviction that "there is but a single misfortune in life, which is having been born" is missing a qualifier: "woman." At any rate, even meeting the love of her life (in 1766!) did not put an end to her suffering.

[12]Ludwig Völker's erudite study, *Langeweile: Untersuchungen zur Vorgeschichte eines Literarischen Motivs,* documents this development. According to him, before the eighteenth century, there were distinct registers of meaning within German usage—the courtly sense of *Langeweile* as *Überdruß,* which, like the French *ennui* on which it was modeled, often assimilated the experience to melancholy, and the temporal sense. Völker writes that the first person to bring the "cultivation of a modern feeling for life" (176) into the expression by combining the two registers of meaning was Goethe. However, this synthesis was still an exception to contemporary usage, and Goethe himself most often used the French *ennui* instead. Although Völker shares many of Kuhn's idealist premises—that modern boredom realizes potentials existent since antiquity, that there is an experiential distinction between the temporal experience of *désœuvrement* and existential boredom, that literary representations of subjectivity become historical forces—his discussion of the relationship between *Langeweile*, acedia, melancholy, *taedium vitae*, and ennui provides a succinct treatment of the philological background to the emergence of the modern discourse on boredom. See especially "Bezüge zur europaischen Geistes- und Ideengeschichte," Völker, 121–46.

twentieth century, boredom had become suspect. Was ennui simply a pose adopted by would-be aristocrats of the spirit in search of some way of distinguishing themselves from others? The problem of the genuineness of boredom echoes in the debates we have already examined over what boredom really is.

It is important to emphasize that our interest lies not in the history of the word—or of the experience—as such, but rather in the way etymology attests to significant discursive transformations taking place in modernizing Europe. The secular notion of ennui belongs to a new language of reflection, one that registers the epochal changes in human self-understanding associated with what I am calling the democratization of skepticism in modernity. The French etymological sources that provide testimony about the evolving significance of the experience of boredom thus also serve more broadly as indices of the emerging modern discourse of reflection on subjective malaise in this period. They make tangible how the modern, "scientific" rhetoric of experience, with its emphasis on materialist explanation at both individual and collective levels, gained sway without entirely eradicating a still-resonant religious understanding of human suffering.

My contention is that the mingling of existential and temporal senses in the discourse on boredom is symptomatic of ambiguities basic to the post-Enlightenment vision of human existence. On one hand, in the course of the nineteenth century, the traditional understanding of ennui as a malaise of longing is psychologized. Boredom becomes an experience of time understood as a Newtonian, mechanical process—time, to put it in Bergsonian terms, without the lived experience of *durée*. On the other hand, even as 'ennui' is devalued into a cliché for hopeless romantic strivings for meaning, the discourse on the experience continues to bear vestiges of the religious horizon that had formerly framed mundane existence in the glow of eternity. The empty time of nineteenth-and early twentieth-century boredom is, often quite explicitly, a time emptied of the divine presence. Both of these lines of development lead to the fundamental dubiousness about strivings for meaning that renders the bored subject prone to suspicions of inauthenticity.

The 1979 edition of *Tresor de la langue francaise. Dictionnaire de la langue du XIXe et du XXe siècle (1789–1960)* distinguishes the traditional conception of ennui as an "abattement causé par ... profonde douleur" from the contemporary understanding of it as a "sentiment de lassitude."[13] It is this mod-

---

[13]That is, ennui as "despondency caused by ... profound suffering" yielded to ennui as a "sentiment of lassitude." (I leave a secondary modern sense cognate with the English "annoyance" out of consideration.)

ern understanding of ennui as a feeling of lassitude, which according to the lexicographer may be associated with subjective experiences either of spiritual emptiness or of physical exhaustion, that concerns us. On the one hand, 'ennui' may refer to a "sentiment de lassitude . . . coincïdant avec une impression plus ou moins profonde de vide, d'inutilité qui ronge l'âme sans cause précise ou qui est inspiré par des considérations de caractère métaphysique ou moral."[14] On the other, the word may refer to a feeling more accessible to medical science than the perception of a philosophical abyss—to a "sentiment de fatigue, de découragement provoqué par l'inaction ou le manque total d'intérêt de quel qu'un ou de quelche chose."[15] The first of these modern senses of the word remains close to the Pascalian usage that associates the pain of lack with the mortal sin of acedia. The second definition, by contrast, moves decisively toward the secular. Indeed, as a consequence of inactivity and withdrawal from the world, the state of disaffection described as a feeling of fatigue corresponds quite closely to the sociological account of ennui we encountered in Chapter 2.

The historical dictionary's distinction between spiritual and physical senses of lassitude registers the tension between idealist and materialist interpretations of subjective malaise that bifurcates the modern discourse on ennui. It thus provides a useful framework for reflection upon the ambiguous status of boredom, which appears now a subjective, now an objective ailment, in nineteenth-century France. Contemporary reference works tended to collapse the 'idealist' and 'materialist' senses of lassitude distinguished by the *Trésor*. However, the emphasis fell differently depending on the perspective of the writer. Two important nineteenth-century dictionaries may be taken as representative of these poles of the emergent European discourse on boredom. Both distinguish the traditional definition of ennui (i.e. the usage of the term still current in French classicism) as a pain caused by the death or loss of a loved one, by exile or similar misfortunes, from a more 'modern' sense. We shall examine the latter definitions closely, for despite their apparent opposition, they make visible a paradigm shift in the interpretation of subjective malaise in the nineteenth century.

Emile Littré's 1860 *Dictionnaire de la langue française* defines the philo-

---

[14]A "sentiment of lassitude . . . coincident with a more or less profound impression of emptiness, of uselessness that scourges the soul without a precise cause or which is inspired by considerations of a metaphysical or moral character." The editors remark that in this sense ennui is associated with *abattement*, *langeur*, *mélancolie*, and *tristesse*; the entry provides references not only to *Madame Bovary* but also to Emma's beloved Chateaubriand.

[15]A "sentiment of fatigue, of discouragement provoked by inaction or the total lack of interest of someone or something."

sophical dimension of ennui as an effect of its material determinants: ennui is a "sorte de vide qui se fait sentir à l'âme privée d'action ou d'intérêt aux cho-ses."[16] The 1874 edition of Bescherelle's *Dictionnaire Nationale ou Dictionnaire Universel de la langue française,* on the other hand, reverses the order of expla-nation. Ennui is an "état de dècouragement et de langeur, sorte d'atonie mo-rale, dans laquelle notre âme ne prenant et ne pouvant prendre aucun intérêt ni aux choses du dehors ni à ses operations intérieures, èprouve un malaise, un dégout qui lui parait insupportable."[17] Here it is the soul's despondency and "moral slackness" that produces the malaise in which disinterest in self and world alike renders existence repugnant. While Littré identified the state of being deprived of action and interest as the cause of the spiritual effects, Bescherelle saw disaffection with self and world as effects of a spiritual cause.

The *Tresor*'s distinction between spiritual lassitude and fatigue serves the objective of producing an historically accurate classification of usages. The task of contemporary dictionaries was quite different. To define the meaning of 'ennui' itself, Littré and Bescherelle were obliged to specify the relation between these distinct semantic domains. Taken together, the two defini-tions tell us a great deal about the discourse on boredom—about the ways this vocabulary of reflection was used. To judge from these contemporary accounts, 'ennui' named an experience in which fatigue, disinterest, and the problem of meaning intermingled, an experience that could justly be defined either as a form of emptiness or as a state of languorous despondency. Fur-thermore, their basic (idealist or materialist) explanatory paradigms notwith-standing, both contemporary definitions of ennui attest to the discursive transformation that accompanies the movement from romanticism to posi-tivism, from a metaphysical interpretation of subjective malaise to a materi-alist model centered on the notion of nervous fatigue. Both dictionaries reg-ister an evolution away from religious or spiritual interpretations toward dis-enchanted, scientific accounts of subjective malaise.

This point becomes clearer if we stop to reflect on a seeming peculiarity. Only Littré's more materialistic definition identifies ennui as a "species of emptiness," while Bescherelle's language indicates a psychological (rather than spiritual) interpretation of the experience. Located firmly within the context of materialist explanation, Littré's "sorte de vide" resonates but dis-

---

[16] A "species of emptiness that impresses itself on the soul deprived of action or of interest in things."

[17] A "state of discouragement and languor, a species of moral atony in which our soul, not taking or unable to take any interest either in things outside it or in its interior operations, experi-ences a malaise, a disgust that seems unbearable."

tantly with the Psalmist's melancholy lament that God has hidden his face. This boredom is, so to speak, a secular emptiness, one that results from a lack of engagement with the world that can be understood in prosaic, non-metaphysical terms. If read symptomatically, in relation to the global evolution of the discourse on subjective experience in the nineteenth century, Littré's "void" may be said to register the absence of God. Overtly, however, it refers to a new experience of time as a series of empty, inherently meaningless moments; ennui results if the subject does not fill time, if "the soul is deprived of action or of interest in things."[18] Even more tellingly, despite its emphasis on the non-material causes of subjective malaise, Bescherelle's definition also attests to the dominance of a secularized vocabulary of reflection. The "sorte de atonie morale" said to cause the subject's disaffection resonates far more with the modern psychological idiom than with the religious antecedents of ennui in the language of sin.

Juxtaposing Littré's and Bescherelle's definitions of ennui reveals a shared impetus to explain subjective experience without reference to God and to substitute psychological for philosophical categories. This rationalizing tendency, which, as we have already seen, may be traced to the Enlightenment, is carried to an even greater extreme in another contemporary work. In M-N. Bouillet's *Dictionnaire Universel des Sciences, des Lettres et des Arts* (1864), the mode of explanation is less psychological than physiological. Bouillet gives no entry at all for 'ennui.' Instead, he offers a number of interrelated references in which the metaphysical and moral dimension of subjective malaise is subjected to a medicalizing interpretation. Although the category that would eventually come to prevail, *neurasthenie*, does not yet appear in the *Dictionnaire Universel* (according to the *Grande Larousse de la langue française*, that term first entered French in 1888),[19] a network of references lead from the traditional (but emphatically un-French) category of spleen to the modern *maladies* of *hypochondrie, consumption,* and *nevrose.*

[18]Further evidence for this link between Littré's understanding of boredom and the problem of time may be found in his remark that in the "elevated style" the word "applies to all sorts of suffering of the soul" but the "langue ordinaire" uses "ennui" simply to "designate that which makes time appear long." The dichotomy discussed in Chapter 1 between quotidian boredom (*désœuvrement*) and existentially significant ennui may thus be taken to have been lexically well established by the mid-nineteenth-century. (The same dichotomy is reflected in the German, where the opposition to *Kurzweile* as a description of the subjective experience of time persists alongside the more existential sense of *Langeweile* into the twentieth century.)

[19]Presumably as a consequence of the reception of George Beard's 1880 *A Practical Treatise on Nervous Exhaustion (Neurasthenia)*. Shorter traces the entry of Beard's ideas into French psychiatry to Charcot (Shorter 1992, 221).

Bouillet's definition of spleen bears quoting in full, for it illustrates a highly significant conceptual and discursive shift in this period—what I call the medicalization of malaise.

> Mot employé en francais pour désigner une sorte d'hypocondrie, qui consiste en un état de consomption engendré par la mélancolie et charactérisé par la tristesse du malade, le dégoût de la vie, une grande apathie, de l'indifference pour toute chose. Cette maladie, qui et plus commune en Angleterre que partout ailleurs, entraîne souvent la mort et porte au suicide. Son nom vient de ce qu'on a longtemps placé dans la rate la bile noire (mélancolie), qui, disait-on, déterminait par son action sur le cerveau les accidents de tristesse qui constituent le spleen.[20]

In this "scientific" definition of spleen, the historical connection to the temperament named for the predominance of black bile, the Greek *melan-kole*, is subordinated to a contemporary vision of romantic malaise with its symptoms of sickly sorrow, distaste for life, apathy, and universal indifference. Unlike Littré and Bescherelle, Bouillet eschews all reference to states of the soul. On his medical interpretation of subjective malaise, the moral and psychological phenomena that others used to define the state of ennui are of interest only as symptoms of a physiological condition. Indeed, under the entry for what Bouillet designates as the more generic malady, hypochondria, the characteristics of the melancholic as defined in the (pseudo-)Aristotelian Problem XXX are reconceptualized as the basis for nervous illness.[21]

The reversal effected by Bouillet's definitions is emblematic of the more general transformation in the discourse on subjective malaise during this period. While the humoral model defined the melancholic temperament, with its inherent lability, as prone to agitation, but also to greatness, Bouillet identifies hypochondria as a problematic, albeit rarely serious, mental ailment. He contends that is mostly a masculine complaint, one that plagues those with "grandes facultées intellectuelles, mais irritables, impressionnables."[22] In redefining spleen as a species of hypochondria, he undercuts the

---

[20]"Word employed in French to designate a species of hypochondria that consists in a state of consumption engendered by melancholy and characterized by the patient's sadness, a distaste for life, a great apathy, and by indifference to everything. This illness, which is more common in England than everywhere else, frequently leads to death and inclines to suicide. Its name comes from the fact the spleen was long held to be the location of black bile (melancholy), which, one said, determined by its action in the brain the incidents of sadness that constitute *spleen*."

[21]On the origins of the modern idea of nervous illness, see Janet Oppenheim, *"Shattered Nerves": Doctors, Patients, and Depression in Victorian England.*

[22]"Those with great intellectual faculties but who are irritable, impressionable." The examples given under *hypochondrie* attest that Bouillet's conception of nervous illness maps onto the semantic field of "ennui": hypochondria arises among those "épuisés par les travaux de l'esprit, par des passions vive, ou chez les riches blasés."

potential for interpreting the experience philosophically, i.e., conceptualizing its manifestations in terms of their inherent significance. While the temperament determined by black bile, melancholia, was traditionally understood as the cause, rather than the consequence, of both intellectual superiority and extreme sensitivity, Bouillet inverts the traditional order of explanation, thereby reducing the qualities of character associated with melancholy to symptoms of a nervous disease.

The omission of 'ennui' from the *Dictionnaire Universel* is no oversight. It signals Bouillet's allegiance to a modern, scientific approach to subjective suffering, one that evacuates it of problems of meaning. He does, however, implicitly concede that there are limits to the conceptual model that defines malaise as the psychic manifestation of a physiological circumstance. Bouillet acknowledges that the "English malady" of spleen may lead to suicide, and his claim that hypochondria in general is not so dangerous is qualified by an exception for "l'éspece de anèantissement intellectuel dont elle frappe le malade."[23] The sort of "intellectual annihilation" associated with nervous illness can, of course, have drastic effects on a human life. This remark thus indicates an uneasy awareness that the metaphysical and moral symptoms associated with forms of "hypochondria" may not be reducible to their physiological causes.[24] Nonetheless, as the definitions cited indicate, Bouillet's omission of 'ennui' from his *Dictionnaire Universel* marks a reinscription of subjective malaise into a medical order of signification that undermines the sorts of reflective vocabulary through which it was traditionally approached.[25] It is not simply that, as Michel Foucault demonstrated, the abandonment of the traditional humoral model, with its logic of homologies between individual and cosmos, and its replacement by a modern, subject-centered medical paradigm played a crucial role in the emergence of the modern human sciences. The medicalization of malaise evident here played a significant role in the consolidation of a new mode of understanding the very nature of subjective experience itself—a modern rhetoric of reflection that appeared to render older idioms of self-understanding incoherent.

If the efforts of Littré and Bescherelle to negotiate idealist and materialist perspectives on boredom registered the more general discursive evolution

---

[23]"The species of intellectual annihilation with which it strikes the patient."

[24]As we saw in Chapter 1, the same awareness inflects Reinhard Kuhn's dismissal of the "suburbanite's" suffering from the realm of genuine ennui. Even as he consigned her "psychological" ailment to the psychotherapists, Kuhn was forced to acknowledge that hers "is a condition that has no foreseeable or inevitable end but death" (Kuhn, 7).

[25]This development has been radicalized in our own time as psychotherapy—itself arguably an ersatz for pastoral care—is replaced by antidepressants.

toward a disenchanted account of subjective malaise, Bouillet's *Dictionnaire Universel* directly reflects the epochal transformation in the rhetoric of reflection on subjective experience. The humoral model had subordinated individual affect to supra-individual realities, ultimately explaining the permutations of malaise and malady in relation to the cosmic factors that were the final cause of temperaments. As Bouillet's inverted etiology of splenetic disorder attests, the modern focus on the individual as the locus of experience reversed the order of explanation. If the traditional teaching of the temperaments had identified characteristic modes of response to the world to classify people into orders of being, now medical categories came to name disorders of the individual that must be traced to deviations from a putatively normal adaptation of subjects to the world.

Experiences of malaise were now located in the body through a new kind of medical terminology that severed the implicit link to the problem of meaning. The vocabulary of all our lexicographers—not only *fatigue* but also *vide*, *atonie*, *action*, *langeur*, and *lassitude*—attests to the same fundamentally mechanistic vision of human existence. It is the vision that would become the foundation of an understanding of subjective malaise as a consequence of an unfulfilled anthropological "besoin de faire quelche chose." From Bouillet's thoroughly disenchanted point of view, the conflict between idealist and materialist accounts reflected in the more conventional dictionaries was simply irrelevant: *Ennui* fell outside the realm of scientific explanation altogether. The category of "soul," whether as mover or moved, was as extraneous to his psychiatric explanations of phenomena once associated with ennui as it would be to Durkheim's sociological account of anomie a few years later.

Of course, as countless works by Bouillet's contemporaries attest, boredom had by no means disappeared. And despite the ascendant tendency to explain subjective malaise in materialist terms, it continued to be grasped as a spiritual problem. Linked equally to melancholy, fatigue, and despair, the nineteenth-century conception of ennui combined the older religious and secular senses of painful absence with a modern, materialist vocabulary. Invoking boredom thus became a means of articulating subjective disenchantment with an experience of temporality basic to modern existence. The laments quickly became clichéed: the rise of bourgeois society and the demise of God had conspired to empty time; standardized and rationalized into a bad infinity of fragmentary moments, time could only be filled by work or killed by distractions. Surrounded by the thoughtless bustle of money-making and progress, the literati bemoaned their ennui as the scourge of the sensitive soul in a reified world.

There were many like Bouillet who regarded such complaints as symptoms of nervous illness. However, as Bescherelle and Littré's diametrically opposed explanations of the emptiness and lassitude associated with ennui attest, the significance of the subjective effects registered in the discourse on boredom remained highly ambiguous. Both paradigms of explanation seem plausible: if the state of being deprived of action and interest in the world can be understood as the cause of the spiritual symptoms, so too can disaffection with self and world be understood as effects of a spiritual cause. In its bifurcation into materialist and idealist modes of interpretation, the discourse on boredom epitomizes the conflicted rhetoric of reflection on subjective experience that emerged in this period. In the terms of that rhetoric, the discontents of modernization seem equally accessible to diametrically opposed interpretive models. As the etymological evidence indicates, however, subjective experience was in fact increasingly being understood in materialist terms.

We turn next to the historical context in which the expansion of the discourse on boredom attested by the etymological evidence took place. I argue that the democratization of boredom, like the evolution toward a materialist conception of subjective experience with which it was associated, must be seen in the context of the momentous transformations of human political and practical life known as the double or dual revolution.[26] Initially, my focus will be not on the construction and interpretation of the experience of boredom as such but on its historico-philosophical conditions of possibility. As this line of argument will demonstrate, the substantial historical significance of boredom cannot be explained in abstraction from the rhetoric of reflection on subjective experience in which it is embedded. My rhetorical investigation of the discourse on boredom should thus not be confused with the sort of empirical inquiry into the causes of the phenomenon that run up against the explanatory aporiai illustrated by the etymological dictionaries. Taking the existence of such aporiai as a starting point, this approach relates the phenomenon of boredom to the modern rhetoric of reflection on subjective experience that was evolving as a consequence of the historical transformations underway in this period. My purpose is not to adjudicate between idealist and materialist, philosophical and sociological interpretations of boredom but to develop a philosophical interpretation of the historical transformations of the discourse on subjective malaise in this period.

---

[26]The language of a "dual revolution" is Eric Hobsbawm's; Hans-Ulrich Wehler speaks of *Doppelrevolution. Deutsche Gesellschaftsgeschichte*, vol. 2: *Von der Reform Ära bis zur industriellen und politischen 'Deutschen Doppelrevolution' 1815–1845/49*, 3–4. In *Modernisierungstheorie und Geschichte*, he uses the term "europäisch-atlantische 'Doppelrevolution,'" an Atlantic-European double revolution.

By stepping outside the rhetoric of experience that bifurcates the material from the ideal, the "objective" from the "subjective" malaise of the modern subject, I argue, it becomes possible to ground the hermeneutic conflict between these understandings in the operations of the larger discourse of reflection on the subjective effects of modernization. In other words, rather than asking what boredom *is* that it can be understood in such contradictory ways, it is necessary to bracket the judgments about the experience and ask instead what the *discourse* on boredom *signifies*.[27] That 'boredom' continues to provoke philosophical and religious interpretations even as the materialist explanatory paradigm becomes dominant indicates that the *experience* of boredom names something that calls the philosophical assumptions that anchor the modern rhetoric of reflection on subjective experience into question. As the etymological evidence attests, materialist explanations of subjective malaise have their limits: as an experience of emptiness, lassitude, and indifference, ennui raises questions that cannot be dismissed as effects of psychological or physiological causes. The discourse on boredom is symptomatic, finally, of phenomena that cannot be explained in terms of the individual subject. In examining the historical context in which this new language of reflection on subjective malaise developed, I shall argue that by turning the material effects of modernization into ciphers for the problem of meaning, the experience of boredom becomes a lived metaphor for the dilemmas that plague modern subjects. Its pervasiveness is thus an index of how deep and widespread epistemological and ethical problems remain in the purportedly secularized modern world.

Boredom, Romanticism, and the Temporality of Progress

> Le romantisme n'est précisément ni dans le choix des sujets ni
> dans la vérité exacte, mais dans la manière de sentir.
> Baudelaire, Salon de 1846[28]

It would be difficult to overestimate the profundity of the changes that followed upon what Eric Hobsbawm has called the "dual revolution." 1789 and its aftermath had reshaped the political landscape not just of France, but

---

[27]This formulation underlines the difference between my approach and Lepenies'. He presents his structuralist analysis of social order and its pathological tendency to frustrate basic human needs as a response to the question of what 'melancholy' signifies. I contend that the question of what the *discourse* on boredom signifies cannot be answered via a structuralist analysis of any sort, for this is an historical question that must in principle remain open to the emergence of new interpretations.

[28]OC II, 420. "Romanticism lies strictly speaking neither in the choice of subjects nor in the precise truth but in the way of feeling."

of Europe. In the course of the nineteenth century, the less rapid, but equally radical spread of industrial revolution across the Channel would likewise transform human life in ways unimaginable even a generation before. In both politics and industry, change had taken on a qualitatively new aspect, one that seemed, at least to that substantial minority in a position to benefit from it, to promise the fulfillment of hallowed dreams.

In the past, governing had been the unquestioned prerogative of a tiny class. The French revolution gave shape to an enduring vision of political self-determination and democratic government—the very real limits to its realization in the period notwithstanding. Events in the late eighteenth century also taught that inherited economic wisdom had reached its limit. The self-sustaining quality of industrial production and the seemingly unlimited potential for growth and technological innovation that went along with it spelled the advent of a new age in which the world would grow perceptibly smaller.[29] Although the immediate profits of both of these revolutions accrued to the bourgeoisie, the qualitative transformations associated with them inevitably made themselves felt in a far wider sphere.

The spread of boredom in the nineteenth century must be understood in relation to the changes brought by the dual revolution. As we shall see, the phenomenon was widely viewed as a consequence of disappointed political aspirations in the generation whose members, in the words of the poet and politician Alphonse de Lamartine, wanted "to act and to fatigue themselves in turn." However, boredom was also represented as a bodily (physiological and/or psychological) response to the epiphenomena of industrialization— the monotonous landscape of the railway journey, the numbing repetition of factory labor, the unnatural, hollow rhythms of unfamiliar urban life. If the democratization of boredom is placed, as it must be, in the context of the spread of the Enlightenment vision of rational progress, it illuminates the way the relationship between industrialization and political modernity was lived. Although boredom is associated with powerlessness and with an inability to act, its ascendancy comes in a world more thoroughly made by human beings than any before it. It is as though this experience without qualities, arising again and again as people confronted industrial innovations, made visible the contradiction between political impotence and a new and profound control over external nature.

Nineteenth-century boredom thus reflects not only the material but also the ideological transformations associated with the dual revolution. When

---

[29]See Hobsbawm (28) regarding the economic "take-off into self-sustained growth" in the 1780's.

the phenomenon is understood in historical context, the fact that the discourse on boredom flourishes in the midst of the upheavals of political and industrial modernization no longer appears paradoxical. The experience of boredom registers the fundamental transformation in attitude toward change that distinguishes traditional from modern Western societies. During the nineteenth century, the Enlightenment vision of rational progress, according to which scientific improvements went hand-in-hand with moral and social advances, came of age. Secular visions of progress found their prophets—Saint-Simon, Fourier, Marx and Engels—who rewrote eschatological expectations under the sign of science, arguing that history's ineluctable advance would heal all social ills. However, as Hans Blumenberg has argued, the notion of a "secularization" of religious narratives cannot do justice to the transformation in ways of thinking that accompanies the emergence of the modern.[30] The multivalent relationship between boredom and the dual revolution attests to the thoroughgoing reinterpretation and refiguration of individual and collective experience underway in this period—to the emergence of what I call a new rhetoric of reflection on subjective experience.

The concept of progress redefined history itself. In *Vergangene Zukunft* [*Futures Past*], Reinhart Koselleck shows that the modern "semantics of historical time" delimited a new form of futurity marked on the one hand by its "unknownness" and on the other by its ever-increasing proximity to the present. The profound significance of the modern notion of progress follows from the convergence of these factors. The idea of progress meant that action was oriented toward an uncertain, yet imminent future—and thus that in contrast to the world of tradition, past experience no longer provided a reliable orientation for human life. "Time accelerated in itself, i.e. our history," he writes, "abbreviates the dimensions of experience [*Erfahrungsräume*], robs them of their continuity and brings ever new unknown elements into play such that, on account of these unknowns, even the present withdraws into inexperienceablity [*Unerfahrbarkeit*]."[31] My contention is that the global change in the understanding of historicity Koselleck identifies—a change inextricably linked to both the political and the industrial dimensions of the dual revolution—provides the horizon of individual experience that constitutes the condition of possibility for modern boredom. Indeed, 'boredom'

---

[30] For Blumenberg, the discourse of secularization must be examined as a strategy of self-legitimation. See *The Legitimacy of the Modern Age*. What is at stake here is not an attempt to reconstruct the intentions of contemporary thinkers but a venture in interpreting the historical significance of their innovations.

[31] *Vergangene Zukunft*, 34.

refers to the "inexperienceability" of the present in the face of historical acceleration into the unknown.

Koselleck is writing not of individual but of historical time under the sign
of progress. However, in the course of the nineteenth century, the disappearance of experience that he describes as making itself felt "even before the
French revolution" becomes ever more tangible as a subjective phenomenon. Because individual, embodied existence remains embedded in the sort
of cyclical rhythms that collective historical understanding has superseded, a
cleft opens between subjective and objective temporalities. Here, in its purest
form, is the space of fragmentation, of alienation. Bergson's concept of *durée*
(1896) is but the most prominent attempt to capture the loss that threatens
the subject if all time is understood in terms of fragmented, isolated moments linked together in infinite linear progression toward an unknown future.[32]

Koselleck's reflections on the semantics of modern historical time illuminate why boredom, in which the empty, monotonous temporality of linear
progress invades the interiority of the subject, is an experience without
qualities. In boredom, the "abbreviation" or even disappearance of immediate experience in the all-encompassing anticipation of the future becomes
tangible. This connection suggests, furthermore, that the ambiguities of the
discourse on boredom are a function of its relation to a particularly modern
experience of time. If the temporal horizon of modern experience—which, it
must be recalled, is both product and symptom of the dual revolution—is
kept in mind, the very multiplicity and indeterminacy of the discourse on
the experience without qualities underlines the significance of the problem
of boredom in modernity.

As I have already shown, the modern concept of boredom, in which
questions of meaning converge with a peculiarly modern experience of temporality, emerges in the late eighteenth century. The transnational discourse
on the experience, which defines it now as metaphysical or moral emptiness
and futility, now as a sociological-psychological symptom of modernization,
confirms that in boredom the fragmentation and alienation associated with
progress are negotiated. Thus the associations noted earlier between boredom and industrialization on the one hand and boredom and modern politics on the other must also be seen in relation to the *imaginative horizon of
modern historicity*. Talk of boredom arises whenever technological advances
seem to eclipse human agency—for example, by mechanizing the workplace

---

[32]See Bergson, *Matière et mémoire*.

or transforming leisure into passive consumption—but also, as Lamartine's famous proclamation, "La France s'ennui," indicates, whenever the promise of political emancipation is frustrated. In both cases, boredom marks the discrepancy between the actual and the imagined—the subjective cost of the limits to realizing the Enlightenment vision of infinite rational progress. If the significance of the "semantics of historical time" inaugurated in the eighteenth century is kept in mind, it is clear that the intimate association between boredom and modernization is not coincidental but genealogical. Boredom is coeval with the peculiarly modern experience of temporality that finds its absolute expression, as Georg Simmel would put it, in "the universal diffusion of pocket watches."[33] In boredom, the subject both registers and rebels against the regulation of lived, subjective time by the inhuman demands of technologized progress.

For all of these reasons, 'boredom'—signifying a malaise at once temporal and existential—becomes a key term in responses by contemporaries to the political and social upheavals of the dual revolution. It is conceived both as a symptom of modernization and as a category within which the subjective significance of modernization is reflected. The relationship between these two dimensions is decisive. As the etymological evidence attests, the nineteenth-century discourse on boredom registers epochal transformations in the way subjective experience itself is understood. It is not simply that religious and humoral explanations of subjective experience are being eclipsed by newer, more secular and materialistic interpretive frameworks. With the rise of modern science, the traditional emphasis on explicitly or implicitly collective interpretations of experience yields to an ever greater focus on the individual, embodied self. Moral evaluations yield to methods of measuring and calculating utility. Psychological and medical accounts of human existence undermine theology's privileged status. The discourse on boredom in which all of these developments converge registers a paradigm shift in the rhetoric of reflection on subjective experience.

This paradigm shift, which begins in the Enlightenment and culminates in the secularized and medicalized vision of subjective malaise still predominant today, goes by the enigmatic name of *romanticism*. To be sure, both the rationalist origin and the scientist end of the process by which the new vision of human existence took hold seem to belie this connection. However, to put my seemingly paradoxical point in Hegelian terms: as a form of self-assertion, romantic rebellion against the subjugation of existence to reason was doomed, for this very rebellion confirmed the modern subject's dialecti-

---

[33] In "Die Großstädte und das Geistesleben," GSG 7, 119 ; see Chapter 4.

cal dependency upon a vision of history as progress. The legacy of romantic attempts to reenchant history was an invigoration of the ideology of histori cal progress under the sign of a quasi-eschatological inevitability. To assert that romanticism presided over the attendant modernization of subjectivity is not to deny that its advocacy of the irrational and uncontrollable in humanity and nature has had enduring cultural effects. The point is that these effects are inseparable from the consolidation of the very model of human self-understanding against which the romantics rebelled. Just as, in the case of nationalism, romantic attempts to reinvigorate traditions and create new myths fell to the service of the modernizing nation-state, romantic insights into human psychology helped to create the medical apparatus through which the subjects of that state were regulated and judged.

In the literature on romanticism, there is widespread agreement with M. H. Abrams' assertion that "Romantic thought and literature represented a decisive turn in Western culture. The writers of that age, in reinterpreting their cultural inheritance, developed new modes of organizing experience, new ways of seeing the outer world, and a new set of relations of the individual to himself, to nature, to history, and to his fellow men."[34] Nonetheless, the dubiousness of speaking in the singular of 'romanticism,' given the complex, wide-ranging, and often internally contradictory phenomena associated with it, is all too evident.[35] My suggestion that we should regard 'romanticism' as the name of that "decisive turn in Western culture"—of the modern paradigm shift in the rhetoric of reflection on subjective experience—does not, however, oversimplify it in this way.

As we shall see, attending to the vicissitudes of this language of reflection in fact helps to capture the sense of romanticism as a transformative moment in cultural and intellectual history while circumventing vexing questions about national differences, about the relationship between romantic "movements" in politics and art, and about how influence is to be understood. From a rhetorical perspective, it is evident that the historical and philosophical significance of romanticism cannot be understood in abstraction from the discursive transformations with which it is associated—the new modes of writing and speaking about experience, identity, and history to

---

[34]*Natural Supernaturalism*, 14.

[35]In his concise account of the etymology and conceptual history of romanticism, Gerhart Hoffmeister notes that "the three most important West-European nations [i.e. England, France, and Germany—EG] all participated in the history of the word [*Wortgeschichte*]." He also remarks that the imprecision which results from the fact that a popular notion of romanticism ("romantic love, romantic landscape, etc.") has always coexisted with the technical use of the term cannot be eliminated by fiat (4).

which it gave rise. Focusing on the discourse on subjective experience in which multifarious aspects of romantic culture were embedded thus provides a methodological alternative to the idealism exemplified by nebulous concepts such as "the spirit of the age" or "the romantic mind."[36]

Romanticism indeed gave rise to new "modes of organizing experience," a new imaginative idiom or, in my terms, to a new rhetoric of reflection. The romantics helped create the modern conception of subjectivity—not only through what Abrams characterizes as an admirable (68) attempt to "save the overview of human history and destiny, the experiential paradigms, and the cardinal values of their religious heritage, by reconstituting them in a way that would make them intellectually acceptable, as well as emotionally pertinent" (66) for the post-Enlightenment era, but also through their embrace of what H. G. Schenk calls "the eruption of the irrational" in this period and the consequent elevation of feeling over intellect in romantic thought. In the new, romantic vision of subjective self-cultivation, Enlightenment ideas about human power took root in a new vision of history. Individuals became the subjects of history, their increase in happiness the measure of progress conceived as a secular path to salvation. Thus romanticism contributed to an historical reinterpretation of human destiny that elevated the individual, yet simultaneously placed qualitatively new burdens upon a subject now regarded as responsible for integrating self and world.[37]

As the evolution of the discourse on subjective malaise in this period illustrates, romantic strategies for reinfusing the world with meaning were

---

[36] See H. G. Schenk, *The Mind of the European Romantics*. The notion of a modern rhetoric of reflection proposed here also differs significantly from Paul de Man's conception of a "rhetoric of temporality." On de Man's reading, figuration subsumes historical reality: "The dialectical relationship between subject and object is no longer the central statement of romantic thought, but this dialectic is now located entirely in the temporal relationships that exist within a system of allegorical signs. It becomes a conflict between a conception of the self seen in its authentically temporal predicament and a defensive strategy that tries to hide from this negative self-knowledge" (de Man, 1983, 208). My contention is that figuration is embodied, historical, intersubjective, and performative. The forms in which the modern (romantic) subject lives its "authentically temporal predicament," whether or not they inevitably give rise to delusion and self-deception, cannot be understood without reference to history—that is to say, to that extra-individual reality that shapes the "dialectical relationship between subject and object." These arguments about temporality will developed further in my discussion of Martin Heidegger in Chapter 5.

[37] In Terry Pinkard's terms, modern people were faced with a new question: what it means to "live one's 'own' life." His nuanced history of the philosophical vicissitudes of attempts in Kantian and post-Kantian thought to come to terms with the burden of such freedom illuminates the political dimension of what I am calling the democratization of skepticism: the relations between this new conception of subjectivity and the challenges of establishing and maintaining normative authority in modern society.

fated to have the opposite effect. In the discourse on boredom that took shape in response to the dual revolution, subjective malaise was implicated in the new conception of history associated with the romantic vision of modernity. It is not just that boredom as we know it is made possible by an understanding of temporality based on the assumption of historical progress. In the mid-century discourse on this experience without qualities, the weight of human responsibility for producing and guiding that progress comes into awareness. The ambivalent desire for a rapidly impending future gives rise to an idiom of reflection in which the moral burden of time that must be used and not wasted becomes palpable. Just as Enlightenment rationalism had called forth the romantic reaction, the intensity of romantic desire for meaning produced as its dialectical consequence a skepticism about the possibilities of action. Such skepticism was inconsolable in the very measure of the hopes it had renounced.

The evolution of the discourse on boredom in the nineteenth century illustrates quite clearly how the romantic cultivation of the heart paved the way for the historic triumph of the head. The first romantic generation was inspired by the French Revolution, which seemed to herald a new era of subjective freedom and national self-determination. As Wordsworth put it in "The Prelude" (Book XI, l. 108):

> Bliss was it in that dawn to be alive
> But to be young was very heaven!

Humanity was recreating itself; history was being made rather than suffered. However, with the Napoleonic wars, disenchantment quickly set in. Romantic exultation over revolutionary possibilities for radical redefinition gave way to an equally romantic longing for tradition and ritual. In France, the restoration of 1830 coincided with the rise of a second romantic generation for whom the plague of ennui was already more social than political, more psychological than theological in origin. As René's "vague des désirs" and the "Wertherkrankheit" grew into the "mal du siècle," complaints of subjective disaffection grew more frequent, more prevalent, and, most importantly, underwent a qualitative transformation. By mid-century, as the etymological evidence attests, a medicalized understanding of subjective malaise was redefining the emptiness associated with ennui in secular, psychological terms.

To interpret 'romanticism' as the name for the paradigm shift in the ways of thinking and speaking about subjective experience that was the dialectical consequence of enlightenment suggests a new way of talking about the subjective significance of modernization registered in this redefinition of malaise. For the romantics, 'ennui' signified a melancholic longing for a unity with nature that humanity had lost and not yet recreated in a new and higher form. The discrepancy between imagination and reality exacerbated romantic suffering. However, in the course of the nineteenth century, that discrepancy came to seem insurmountable. At the bloody height of the French Revolution, Friedrich Schiller had evoked the pernicious effects of a one-sided progress in unsurpassed form. In modernity, he wrote, each individual labored only on a "fragment" of the social and historical whole. Under such conditions, the human being "never develops the harmony of his being, and instead of expressing the humanity of his nature, he becomes a mere copy of his business, his science."[38] As urbanization, industrialization, and specialization proceeded apace, hopes faded that the fragmentation so powerfully described by Schiller could ever be overcome. In less than a hundred years, the idea that historical progress was the enemy of individuality had become a commonplace. By the end of the nineteenth century, the romantic vision of history seemed hopelessly outmoded.

During the period between 1789 and 1848, the romantic notion that the sources of subjective discontent could be overcome—that, whether through a new social order or a new mythology, a healing transformation of the world was imminent—lost its power to produce conviction. The language of progress was firmly in the hands of the party of order. Particularly after the upheavals of 1848, the expressions of melancholic longing for a reintegration of the individual into a larger whole that had reached their apogee in the second romantic generation give way to a discourse on boredom that, whether philosophically, cynically, or despairingly, expresses profound resignation to the fallen state of the modern human being and to the corruption and unhappiness of modern society. Baudelaire and Flaubert are the acknowledged masters of the post-romantic discourse on boredom in which all of these developments are reflected. Their literary "anatomies" depict the struggles of the modern subject whose addiction to change distorts the foundations of desire, for whom existence is finally palpable only in the form of the disappearance of experience known as ennui. Before turning to them, however, it is necessary to place the changing interpretation of subjective malaise in historical context. We begin with two very different contemporaries—a conservative doctor and a liberal poet-politician—who invoke the language of ennui in a way that bears witness to the significance of the passing of the paradigm of romantic melancholy that had dominated subjective expressions of discontent with modern life during the first half of the nineteenth century.

---

[38] *Über die Aesthetische Erziehung des Menschen* (Sixth letter): 323.

The Doctor and the Poet: Romanticism, Skepticism, and the Medicalization of Malaise

> L'ennui ne naît pas de l'uniformité; car la vie des hommes simples
> est très-uniforme, et les hommes simples ne connoissent pas l'ennui.
>
> Senancour[39]

In 1850, Alexandre Brierre de Boismont published "De L'Ennui (Taedium Vitae)" in *Les Annales Médico-psychologiques*. Because his arguments were enormously influential, this essay, which is nominally an analysis of the testimonials of 237 contemporaries who committed suicide out of "distaste for life," is worth examining closely.[40] In it, I shall argue, the prominent doctor and alienist modernizes the venerable topos of ennui as a disease of civilization. Brierre's approach thus embodies and reflects upon the cultural legacy of romanticism even as it contributes to the emergence of a modern, disenchanted discourse on subjective malaise.

Without mentioning the philosopher by name, Brierre starts by invoking Rousseau's ideas in a way that suggests his own complex relation to romanticism. The essay begins: "The man who thinks is a depraved animal." However, he continues, "it would have been more natural to say, an animal who is bored" (545). For Brierre, subjective malaise is no purely medical problem. In what follows, he therefore brings his medical authority to bear against the purely materialist interpretation of malaise, contending that even when it leads to suicide, ennui should not be considered a species of madness. Indeed, he criticizes the very notion that ennui could be classified as a disease as "the consequence of a system that excessively generalizes insanity" (573). For Brierre, ennui is, rather, a "maladie morale" that "depends more on social than individual causes: it is the symptom of a civilization aged and blasé, of epochs of decadence and religious and political indifference, of universal analysis" (561–62). The causes of modern *taedium vitae*, he argues, must be located firmly in the post-Enlightenment historical context.

Brierre positions himself as a moralist. His account of how nervous over-

---

[39] "Ennui is not born of uniformity, for the life of simple people is very uniform, and simple people do not know ennui" (*Rêveries*, IV, 184).

[40] Brierre's study of suicides examined a total of 4,595 cases. It was the basis of his 1856 magnum opus, *Du suicide et de la folie suicide, considérés dans leurs rapports avec la médecine, la statistique, et la philosophie*, in which the original essay was reproduced without significant modifications. According to Brierre, the motivation for suicide had "no other source" than ennui (under which he includes invocations of "rêverie, découragement, mélancholie, désespérance") for 99 of the 237 for whom it was a factor at all. (Statistics: Brierre, 1850, 562. Subsequent citations are from this version.)

stimulation, uncertainty, and worldly frustrations drove his informants to take their lives links subjective malaise to the ascendance of skepticism in modernity. "De L'Ennui" places these dangers of an age of "universal analysis" in an explicitly theological perspective. God, according to Brierre, "is not content with thought because it soon vanishes into reverie and because reverie has always inspired distaste for work and induced suicide" (556). As a moral malady, ennui differs from "spiritual disorders brought about by insanity" in that it can be overcome by those who have a resolute will to control their thoughts and actions (553). Given his allegiance to a religious and moral vision of ennui, it is ironic that, as I shall show, Brierre's wide-ranging meditation on ennui and suicide modernizes the topic, transforming it in ways that would culminate in the fin-de-siècle discourse on nervous "degeneration" in modern urban society.

In the first part of the essay, Brierre surveys the historical antecedents of modern boredom. Here the doctor's cases are writers and literary figures—the cast of characters familiar from Reinhard Kuhn's similar narrative about the spread of the 'plague' of ennui and its culmination in post-revolutionary Europe. Goethe's Werther typifies for him the "ardent and exalted" youth who has been infected by "the spirit of doubt," that is, "the spirit of the eighteenth century, of skepticism" (556). Attacks on religious faith and sensualist doctrines have left their evil mark on Werther's character. In his "idle melancholy," he "disdains true work"; according to Brierre, he lacks that "respect for the will of God, that taste for order [*la règle*] that makes life simple and sweet because . . . he does not have the simple and stable faith of his fathers" (556–57).

Brierre sees Werther as more than a representative figure. Not only did Goethe's hero himself succumb to the tender "sensibility" that results from indolence and excessive reverie. Invoking Madame de Staël, Brierre asserts that Werther bequeathed this "fatal disposition of the spirit to a generation of dreamers in whom it would produce the most unfortunate results" (558). As a consequence of this insidious skepticism, on Brierre's view, traditional ways of life have been abandoned, the divine commandment to work abrogated: a generation has been lost to unproductive reverie. To illustrate these dire consequences, he invokes the example of another literary figure—Chateaubriand's René, for whom matters are even worse. Religious education has been to no avail. "Doubt is at the base of his soul"; a hopeless yet infinite desire inflames his imagination. The "horrors" witnessed during the revolution (which "toppled the two central pillars of France, religion and royalty") have kindled in him, as in his entire generation "a distaste for life." Hope and belief are equally annihilated: "Despair, skepticism, vengeance reign" (558). Such is Brierre's literary genealogy of the modern penchant for suicidal ennui that is his topic.

Brierre appears to be telling a story in which the ennui of romantic figures reflects and fosters the pernicious individualism that has its origin in the loss of faith. However, his diagnosis is couched in psychological rather than theological terms. For him, skepticism is a pragmatic problem: the aimless reverie of romantic heroes is symptomatic, he avers, of societies in which "the purpose of activity [*la but d'activité*] has been lost" (560). Insofar as it turns on an ahistorical notion of a loss of telos, Brierre's mode of analyzing ennui represents a significant departure from the interpretive tradition to which, at first blush, he seems to belong. To regard ennui as the result of a socially conditioned, yet abstract purposelessness is quite unlike defining it in theological terms as the philosophical "consequence of the encounter with nothingness." For Brierre, rather than disclosing metaphysical truths about human existence, boredom reveals the nature of the human "animal."

The abstract conception of purposelessness that underlies this account marks a significant development in the rhetoric of reflection on subjective malaise. The view of purposive action as *morally* necessary for human flourishing paves the way for a conception of action as a *physiological* requirement for human thriving. To say that ennui arises because "the purpose of activity is lost" is not far from regarding a "need to do something" as an anthropological constant. In Brierre's essay, ennui is on its way to the functional definition as "action-inhibition" we have already encountered in the twentieth-century sociological discourse on boredom.

The doctor's fundamentally disenchanted view of modern malaise comes into relief when, in the second half of "De L'Ennui," he turns to the suicides' testimonials. Even if it does encourage "the abuse of reverie and the predominance of thought over action" which foster despair with life (584), romantic literature turns out to be a symptom rather than a cause. The modern world as a whole is responsible for the epidemic of malaise that leads to so many suicides. "In this age," Brierre proclaims, "it is by no means necessary to be crazy to have your heart gnawed by ennui and by distaste for life. When no one is sure of the morrow, when reputation, property, fortune have nothing stable about them, when conservatives and socialists begin all of their writings with the phrase: *we are marching toward the unknown,* when one looks about oneself and discovers nothing but ruins, not a single institution standing . . ." (566), people's lack of tranquility and even a general "premonition of impending evil" can come as no surprise. Nor can the fact that, fleeing that evil, "populations plunge into the pursuit of pleasure" as though echoing the ancient cry: "'Let us drink and eat, for tomorrow we shall die'" (566).

Brierre's characterization of his time as one in which conservatives and socialists alike declare that humanity is "marching toward the unknown" is worth emphasizing. His remarks confirm the link I have drawn between ennui and an understanding of history that, as Koselleck puts it, "abbreviates the dimensions of experience" into punctuality through an emphasis on the "unknownness" of the future and its menacing "proximity to the present." To Brierre, the temporal structure that provides the horizon of modern boredom appears as the source of moral decay. His remarks imply that the ideology of progress undermines the very foundations of purposive action by turning change into an end in itself. Thus ennui and selfish egoism flourish in the modern world, unchecked by faith in God or respect for the traditional social order. Paradoxically, however, "De L'Ennui" links this global indictment of modern skepticism to a quite disenchanted account of the genesis of subjective malaise.

As the founder of a successful private sanitorium fashionably located near the Pantheon,[41] Brierre personified nineteenth-century medical authority. "De L'Ennui," in a representative melange of moralizing and questionable physiology, elaborates upon the relationship between the pursuit of pleasure, nervous excitability, and life-threatening ennui in contemporary life. "It is," Brierre intones, "an epoch in which distaste for life appears everywhere linked to the modifications undergone by the sexual organs" (566). Puberty, particularly for those inclined to reverie, brings preoccupation with unattainable desires. "Their sensibility is over-excited . . . The imagination never ceases to enlarge the obstacles and perils . . . . They live in a world of chimerae, and in their eyes, everything takes on enormous dimensions. This state is common especially among tender souls, with nervous, impressionable organizations" (566–67). Artists and women are on Brierre's view particularly susceptible. However, the nervous irritability that feeds the moral malady is not limited to them, nor is sexuality its only possible source. According to Brierre, his suicides' testimonials demonstrate that "all human distresses may engender ennui and the distaste for life" (570).[42] Furthermore, this extreme, suicidal form of malaise appears in every social group—besides "genuine bohemians, not valuing life at all and abandoning it as soon as they can no longer satisfy their base appetites" (576), his sample included "workers without ability, without education, lazy with pleasure . . . discontented with their lot" (576) and "young people who cannot bear the least impediment without abandoning

---

[41]"In the rue Neuve-Sainte-Geneviève" (Shorter, 123).

[42]His table includes, besides illness and poverty, domestic and other troubles, love, vanity, fear, and jealousy (563).

themselves entirely to rages of frustration" (576–77). In "De L'Ennui," Brierre paints a grim picture of a society without cohesion, in which everything stimulates unrealizable demands for immediate gratification and subjective suffering has reached truly epidemic proportions.

There is a tension at the heart of Brierre's view of ennui as moral malady. As we have seen, he depicts it as a universal phenomenon grounded in human nature. "Our limitless and insatiable desires, our continual pursuit of pleasure, our discomforts, our anxieties, our aversions, in a word our ennui which is at the bottom of everything, are nothing but the aspirations of finitude towards the sovereign master" (583). But this religious vision of boredom as "a protest against the fall" vies with his proto-sociological observation that ennui in fact "exercises its ravages principally in epochs of general indifference, doubt, and individualism" (583). The doctor's uneasy synthesis of these views, expressed in his conviction that people bear a certain responsibility for falling prey to the "moral malady" of the modern era, captures a tension that exists within the discourse on boredom as a whole. Indeed, the much-vaunted influence of Brierre's writings on ennui[43] may be attributed to his success at negotiating the seeming contradiction between idealist and materialist interpretations of the experience—between an old-fashioned, philosophico-religious understanding of ennui as a universal feature of the human condition, and the emergent modern, psychologizing and medicalizing approach to subjective malaise. His success at this balancing act is epitomized by his advice for coping with the problem of ennui in modern life.

Brierre sets out, but does not elaborate, his metaphysical vision of ennui as a phenomenon proper to finite beings, declaring that he must respect the limits set by "the spirit of this [medical] journal" (583) and consider how to treat the symptoms of the moral malady he has diagnosed. As we have seen, his diagnosis is couched in a materialist idiom: typical features of modern life—nervous stimulation, cultivated oversensitivity, debauchery, excess of all kinds, including "frivolous reading" (577)—can lead to a state of the soul in which the slightest frustration can lead to threats of suicide. Brierre appears to prescribe the most traditional of cures. Taking a page from St. John Chrysosthomos, he suggests three remedies: "Do not love the sadness that is born of ennui"; "have a family"; and "exercise a profession" (583–84). The last is particularly important. Although Brierre avers that a true cure for ennui can only be brought about by "unanimous efforts" on the part of the whole society "to reanimate religious faith" (584) and thereby render the ends of action

---

[43]According to Kuhn, this essay had "a profound impact on Baudelaire [who mentions Brierre's book in the Fusées (ix; OC I, 656)—EG] and many of his contemporaries" (Kuhn, 64).

commensurate with the infinite desire proper to fallen beings, his final word is in accord with Kant's maxim: the constant pursuit of a "great purpose" in action may save the individual by rendering day-to-day life meaningful.

Despite appearances and arguably contrary to his own self-understanding, Brierre's prescription for alleviating ennui is diametrically opposed to the venerable recommendation of manual labor as a remedy for acedia. In modernity, work is no longer a means to a religious end. As a substitute for faith in divine purpose, the commitment to work has become an end in itself.[44] Brierre's essay thus both reflects upon and embodies the dialectic through which romantic rebellion against reason facilitates the ultimate triumph of the Enlightenment's materialist conception of human existence. His argument turns, as we have seen, on a critique of romanticism, which he argues has helped turn life-threatening ennui into a societal plague by fostering the ascendance of reverie over purposive activity. On his reading, such reverie is shot through with skepticism and subjectivism; that is, the distaste of the romantics for the rationalism of the eighteenth century notwithstanding, their malaise is quite clearly the legacy of the Enlightenment. However, the same must be said for Brierre's own attempt to alleviate the ravages of skepticism through his threefold strategy for avoiding potentially life-threatening disaffection.

As the doctor concedes, ennui is not simply a romantic affectation—it is an experience entirely to be expected in a world that has turned "marching toward the unknown" into a way of life. The notion that faith might be "reanimated" in modernity is therefore just as romantic—or just as enlightened—as romanticism itself. Like the romantics, Brierre laments the loss of immediacy that plagues modern society while recognizing it as the condition of modern subjectivity. In recommending that, in the absence of the requisite cultural transformation, people should cultivate their own gardens, he indeed suggests a way to move beyond romantic ennui. However, this solution requires accepting precisely what the romantics refused to accept—that it is impossible to humanize progress, to imbue modern life with a purpose capable of compensating for the loss of religious faith. To embrace a stoic devotion to profession and family is to concede that there is no escape from the all-embracing skepticism that is the legacy of Enlightenment. Ennui is a symptom of that skepticism, one that Brierre acknowledges as an established feature of modern society. Far from proposing a cure for the moral malady of the age, the doctor is counseling resignation. His provisional cure is tantamount to surrender to the ideology of progress, which feeds boredom by

[44]Kierkegaard would argue, following Pascal, that such forms of occupation were mere distractions and hence means of concealing rather than curing ennui. See Raposa's discussion, 51–52.

pretending to allay it. If devotion to the mundane ends of everyday existence alleviates ennui, then by occluding, rather than by satisfying, the longing for a more meaningful existence that made romantics of an entire generation.

With its ambiguous relationship to Enlightenment, Brierre's essay not only illustrates how the tensions between idealist and materialist conceptions of subjective experience play out in the nineteenth-century discourse on ennui. In its mode of argumentation as much as in its overt claims, "De L'Ennui" also epitomizes the historic shift in the rhetoric of reflection through which victory would fall to the materialist vision of human existence. The role of romanticism in this paradigm shift is illustrated perfectly by Brierre's essay. As we have seen, although he shares the romantic hope that faith might be rekindled in modernity, he incisively indicts romanticism as the fruit of insidious skepticism. His own argument illustrates how ineffectual such hope already seemed in the face of the social and technological transformations of the mid-nineteenth century.

In the end, his pontificating against the Enlightenment and his religious vision of ennui notwithstanding, the author of *Du suicide et de la folie suicide, considérés dans leurs rapports avec la médecine, la statistique, et la philosophie* extends the legacy of the eighteenth century. Brierre approaches the problem of ennui via precisely the sort of empirical research that was leading, as the etymological evidence assessed at the outset of this chapter attests, to the eclipse of idealist categories of reflection. His emphasis on the value of work is thoroughly in line with ascendant bourgeois values; the stress he lays on nervous fatigue is prescient. And it is but a short step from the statistical categorization of suicides according to motivation to Durkheim's radical statistical undermining of subjective motivation as an explanatory category.[45] Thus while he diagnoses ennui as the consequence of a culture-wide crisis of (historical) meaning, Brierre concedes that he can only practice a "medicine of symptoms" (583)—one that leaves the ultimate causes of subjective suffering untouched. This is, in effect, a capitulation to skepticism, for Brierre's prescription against ennui is also the prescription of his era: embrace a generalized purposefulness that renders the search for meaning a practical, rather than a spiritual task.

Brierre de Boismont's "De L'Ennui" epitomizes the discursive transformations which, in the course of the nineteenth century, changed the interpretation of subjective malaise so profoundly. Like the etymologies we have

[45]Brierre's analytic breakdown of the motivating forms of "distaste with life" attests to the contemporary transition from traditional moral categories (love, vanity, fear, and jealousy) to more modern objective descriptions (despair, weakening of forces, poverty, troubles) in accounting for suicides.

considered, his argument moves from an idealist to a materialist conception of emptiness. Even as he insists that ennui should not be considered a form of nervous illness, Brierre blames its prevalence on the decaying social order and the stresses of life in a world self-consciously "marching toward the unknown." "De L'Ennui" cannot finally sustain the moral and philosophical vision of ennui he initially proposes. At the same time, however, the essay illustrates how profoundly political, ethical, and epistemological concerns are imbricated in the medicalized discourse on the subjective effects of modernization that takes shape in the nineteenth century. It powerfully demonstrates how ennui, as at once a moral, a psychological, and a philosophical problem, is implicated in all of these registers.

Both the medicalization of malaise and the reinterpretation of ennui's moral significance in sociological terms evident in Brierre de Boismont's analysis of ennui as *maladie morale* register a larger development. By mid-century, the global transformation in the rhetoric of reflection that I call the democratization of skepticism in modernity was well under way. The same ambiguous relationship between the discourse on boredom and the project of Enlightenment is thus evident in the political sphere as well. Romanticism is the medium through which a materialist interpretation of subjective malaise comes to dominate not just the psychological but also the political representation of human experience in the age of industrial and political revolution.

From its beginnings, romanticism had an ambivalent relationship both to the ideal of progress and to the social transformations associated with the dual revolution. Although the vision of cultural renewal through emancipation from the past associated with the French Revolution inspired romantics throughout Europe, the movement had always encompassed politically conservative, religious, and anti-modern (irrationalist, mythologizing) tendencies as well. The latter tendencies were reinforced by the fates of the revolution itself, for the Terror and the emergence of a modern politics of charisma sorely disappointed democratic aspirations. Moreover, in the course of the nineteenth century, progress took a shape quite foreign to the vision of political and moral renewal that had motivated many early romantic thinkers. Thus as urbanization and industrialization transformed the face of Europe in the post-Napoleonic period, the critique of modernity linked to the more inner-directed strands of romantic thought grew sharper. Romanticism came to be identified with a nostalgic and irrationalist anti-capitalism, and figures like the Vicomte de Chateaubriand or the Abbé de Lammenais sought respite from the uncertainty of skepticism in the arms of the Church. Well before 1848, when Louis-Napoleon rose to power, many once-democratic romantics were embracing the principle of a powerful state as the only means of realizing the humanism to which they clung.

Both as proponents and opponents of the ideal of historical progress, the second generation of romantics contributed to the emerging discourse on boredom as a national or political problem.[46] Whether or not romantic literature can be held responsible for the spread of boredom itself, figures such as René, Oberman, and Manfred found vast audiences.[47] The *language* of romantic malaise grew familiar—and popular.[48] Although the political significance of the experience of ennui, like that of romanticism itself, remained ambiguous, the emergence of the notion of a *mal du siècle* in the period around 1830 was decisive. By mid-century, this romantic conception of a malaise at once individual and collective, subjective and historical, had achieved significant resonance. It is thus no accident that commentators from Brierre to Benjamin have envisaged ennui as a plague or metaphysical infection. Boredom was indeed "contagious," insofar as a concatenation of factors rendered this new metaphorics ever more irresistible.

Boredom spread as a function of the democratization of skeptical habits of thought. That democratization, it must be emphasized, should not be conceived as an intentional or even a cohesive process—it was, rather, the sum of a wide range of changes in the ways people were thinking about themselves and the world in which they lived, changes that were both the cause and consequence of the cultural transformations known as modernization. As we have seen, Enlightenment and romanticism alike helped to reconfigure the rhetoric of reflection on subjective experience to center on individual, embodied existence. However, the romantic idea of progress as a striving for wholeness and reunification with nature rapidly lost ground. Another notion of individual fulfillment was on the ascendant, one that was not only compatible with fragmentation but that in fact fostered it.

One of the cultural consequences of this new way of thinking was a secularization and in particular a medicalization of subjective malaise—indeed, there was talk not just of a *mal* but of a *maladie du siècle*. Religious ways of thinking about experience did not, of course, become obsolete overnight. However, as Brierre's essay illustrates, the discursive transformation underway in this period affected the language even of the sworn foes of skepticism. Even as he attempted to hold fast to a vision of ennui as a moral malady, the

[46]We have already noted that even the etymological discussion had echoes of nationalism, with the British and French accusing one another of being the source of the problem.

[47]Kuhn, taking a page from Musset, christens them the "Children of the Century" (Ch 7, 221–77).

[48]A circumstance thematized by Flaubert in *Madame Bovary*, to which we shall return.

doctor could prescribe only secular remedies. Similarly, the romantics' embrace of the metaphorics of disease attests to their unwitting role in fostering the disenchantment to which they were consciously opposed. As the discourse on boredom as a disease of modern times entered the political realm, the same shift toward a materialist rhetoric of reflection evident in Brierre's analysis of ennui as a modern moral malady makes itself felt. We turn next to a prototypical example of the way this disenchanted language of medicalized malaise becomes politically significant. Like "De L'Ennui," it illustrates the imbrication of romanticism and Enlightenment in fostering the democratization of skeptical modes of thought in modernity.

The political career of the erstwhile romantic poet Alphonse de Lamartine (1790–1869) exemplifies the internal conflicts and ambiguities of political romanticism. A member of the provincial nobility committed to the principles of 1789, Lamartine began by situating himself as a pragmatic supporter of Louis-Philippe despite his residual allegiance to the deposed Bourbons, under whom he had served as a diplomat. Escaping from his perennial ennui into parliamentary politics, he became a champion of the "social question" and an advocate of a politics of morality. Lamartine stood for a romantic ideal of realizing revolutionary principles via moral transformation, for a revolution of the heart through good government. For him, the principles of 1789 were ultimately grounded in Christian values, and a characteristically romantic mixture of politics and religion colored his thought throughout his career.[49] As the years passed, his advocacy of law and order in the service of liberal ideals came into increasing contradiction with his critical stance toward a government that was abandoning the masses to misery and suffering while the bourgeoisie increased in wealth and strength. By 1843, despite his opposition to socialism, Lamartine was aligning himself with the left opposition to the regime and speaking as a populist supporter of democracy, which he called "the holy and divine ideology of the French Revolution."[50] In 1848, his support would be crucial in the proclamation of the Second Republic, and he served briefly as head of the provisional government after the fall of Louis-Philippe.

Since throughout his life Lamartine complained of being plagued by ennui, it is fitting that the romantic poet-politician is remembered as having introduced into politics the image of France itself suffering from immobility and boredom. On January 10, 1839, Lamartine made a speech in the Chamber

---

[49]Lamartine's *profession du foi, Des Destinées de la Poésie,* was published in 1834. Part apologia for his entry into politics, part political treatise on the historic task of the July Revolution, Lamartine's essay presented the blueprint for his romantic politics of moralization.

[50]Cited in Fortescue, 115.

of Deputies in which he condemned the parliamentary wrangling that was undermining the "harmony of powers" he regarded as the "vital condition" of representative government.[51] Since 1830, he declared, the government had entirely lacked ideas and, unable to derive sufficient "vital energy" from "a dead past," was allowing France to stultify.

> [Y]ou have allowed the country to be deficient in action. You must not imagine, sirs, that because we are fatigued from the great movements which have stirred the century and ourselves, everybody is fatigued like us and fears the slightest movement. The generations that mature behind us—they are not weary; they want to act and to fatigue themselves in turn. What action have you given them? Is France a nation that is bored? [bravos from the left]
>   And take heed—the ennui of peoples may easily become convulsion and ruin![52]

The poet metaleptically identifies the nation with its youth, which is figured as a romantic subject condemned by the exigencies of contemporary existence to inactivity and therefore to ennui. Significantly, Lamartine translates the national moral crisis expressed in boredom into ergonomic terms: ennui is the fate of a population deprived of outlets for creative expression. If France is bored, then because the obstinate conservatism of the bourgeois monarchy, which refuses change, expansion, *mouvement* in general, results in an insalubrious damming-up of national energy. To forestall more revolutionary upheaval, Lamartine thought, the government should facilitate moral and social progress to fulfill the promise of 1789. While the first revolution had achieved "political reform," that of "1830 must accomplish reform in the society itself; the organization, the moralization, the constitution of rights, of interests, of work, in the most numerous class!" Thus, he proclaimed, "the mission of a new government in the nineteenth century" is to accomplish these changes "legislatively, by the gradual, reasoned, entirely religious and entirely political application of the grand principles of democracy and fraternity that have descended from Christianity" (148–49).

His subjective convictions notwithstanding, the poet is clearly situating political romanticism as the agency of secularization. Indeed, Lamartine's much-quoted romantic accusation against the powers that be epitomizes the discursive transformation we have been tracing. His image of a bored nation whose political aspirations are tantamount to physiological needs attests how

---

[51]"sur La Discusssion de L' Adresse en Réponse a M. Thiers," cited in Alphonse de Lamartine, *La France Parlementaire (1834–1851): Oeuvres Oratoires et Écrits Politiques*, 144. Subsequent citations in text refer to this speech.

[52]Ibid., 148. In 1968, Viansson-Ponté once again cried out "la France, s'ennuie"—but probably, according to Xavier de la Fournièr, without knowing of the historical precedent.

fundamentally the enlightened perspective on human existence had recon-figured the language of reflection on subjective experience, even for a thinker as idealistic as Lamartine. In his imagery, the relationship between romanti-cism and the contemporary paradigm shift in ways of understanding human existence becomes visible. As in the case of Brierre de Boismont, the historic evolution toward secular and materialist modes of explanation inflects the language of one who is consciously opposed to the developments such changes represent.

Lamartine's concern with the energy levels of the French populace is the political correlate of Brierre's reflections on nervous overstimulation. Even as it transposes the trope of romantic youth onto the nation as a whole, his speech extends the materialist vision of subjective malaise onto the political field. "Health" and "strength," Lamartine proclaims, are to be found in the unity of thought and action (148–49). Both aristocrats endorse the bourgeois notion that ennui can be cured by activity; both, despite their fundamentally Christian outlooks, contribute to the rise of a secular language of reflection on subjective experience. For both, ennui is the consequence of purposeless-ness, and the substantive ends that might once have filled that void seem to have dissolved. Just as the doctor prescribes the "constant pursuit of a pur-pose of action" as a psychological prophylactic against the personal perils of ennui, the politician advises legislative engagement to preserve the nation from the political consequences of mass ennui. The incipient nihilism of these proposed remedies is evident. Within the thinking of both these very different observers of the *mal du siècle*, action threatens to become an end in itself, a mere palliative for a malaise whose pervasiveness appears to be a stubborn fact of modern life.

Power, Knowledge, and Fatigue: The Materialist Rhetoric of Reflection on Subjective Experience

> Skepsis nämlich ist der geistigste Ausdruck einer gewissen viel-fachen physiologischen Beschaffenheit, welche man in gemeiner Sprache Nervenschwäche und Kränklichkeit nennt.
>
> Friedrich Nietzsche[53]

Both the etymology and discursive history of 'ennui,' I have argued, attest that a paradigm shift took place in the rhetoric of reflection on subjective experience in the course of the nineteenth century. By examining the discur-

---

[53]"For skepticism is the most spiritual expression of a certain multifarious physiological con-dition, which in ordinary language one calls weak nerves and sickliness," *Beyond Good and Evil*, section 208; *Sämtliche Werke* 5, 138.

sive field in which this experience was historically and linguistically constituted, we can begin to explain why this new way of talking about subjective
malaise took hold so rapidly and so profoundly. In the trans-national discourse on boredom, the connections between new ways of thinking about
what it means to be a person and the cultural changes I am calling the democratization of skepticism became visible. As the examples just discussed
suggest, this modern language of reflection on subjective discontent articulates the medicalization of malaise with a new sort of politics—one in which
modern ways of thinking about human existence literally remake collective
life. In the discourse on boredom, the thoroughgoing effect of Enlightenment even on its opponents became visible. As participants in that discourse,
both Brierre and Lamartine were, so to speak, materialists despite themselves: they had adopted a metaphorics that deeply affected the ways they
could conceive of subjective experience, one that ultimately dictated an historically very particular way of thinking about the ends of action. To achieve
reflective purchase on the paradigm shift in human self-understanding embedded in that metaphorics, it will be helpful to take a broader look at the
contemporary discourse of reflection on subjective experience.

   Doing so, I should underline, it is not simply a matter of adducing more
historical evidence for the spread of boredom. My argument that the democratization of the language of boredom is linked to a paradigm shift in the
rhetoric of reflection on subjective experience raises historiographical issues.
If the historical significance of the discourse on boredom lies in the constraints that this modern metaphorics places on reflection and self-reflection,
what does it mean to take this discourse as the object of analysis? How does
rhetorical analysis engage the historical particularity of the discourse on
boredom? How can it move, rigorously and legitimately, from that particularity to a consideration of the paradigm shift in the way subjective experience is understood? That is, questions about the constitution of boredom as
an historical object lead directly to critical reflection on methodology. Situating the metaphorics of boredom in the larger field of post-Enlightenment
reflection on subjective experience therefore provides an occasion for critically examining the disclosive and reflective capacities of Michel Foucault's
model of discourse analysis and differentiating it from my own rhetorical
approach to the historico-philosophical field in which the modern discourse
of reflection on subjective experience took shape.

   By way of introduction, let us turn back briefly to Lamartine's speech.
The features that I have construed as historical evidence for a paradigm shift
toward a materialist language of reflection on subjective experience also illustrate some of Foucault's most fundamental ideas about modern politics.

Lamartine's rhetoric, in which historical action takes on a quasi-medicinal role and politics is reduced to the necessity of exercising human faculties, augurs historic changes. In the latter part of the nineteenth century, particularly after the humiliating defeat by Prussia in 1871, anxieties about the declining population of France would reach the level of a national obsession.[54] Such anxieties were often figured in terms of an alleged depletion or decline in the national energy supply. In this discursive context, ennui becomes assimilated to fatigue, which, whether attributed to the working class or to the exhausted fecundity of the upper classes, is grasped as a national problem. Lamartine's association of boredom with inactivity and his notions about national "health" and "exhaustion" foreshadow this crucial development in the discourse on the subjective effects of modernization; his depiction of the fatigue and weariness that followed on the "great movements" of the revolutionary era as threatening to overshadow and thwart the energies of youth was prescient. The poet-politician's commitment to the ideals of 1789 notwithstanding, the object of his concern is the French nation conceived as a biological population in danger of atrophy through disoccupation.

Lamartine's reply to Thiers thus registers the trend toward physiological explanation that defines the perspective which Foucault christened "biopower."[55] In modern society, Foucault claims, political power underwent a fundamental transformation. No longer content simply to rule over subjected bodies, it "assigned itself the task of administering life" and developed two entirely new sets of techniques for exercising domination. The first, "centered on the body as a machine," attempted to control and integrate its capacities through "the procedures of power that characterized the *disciplines*: an *anatomo-politics of the human* body." The second focused on "the species body" and was deployed through "*regulatory controls: a biopolitics of the population*" (139; his emphases). Taken together, the "explosion of numerous and diverse techniques for achieving the subjugation of bodies and the control of populations" defines, according to Foucault, "the beginning of an era of 'bio-power'" (140) that was crucial for the development of modern capitalism. For him, the decisive accomplishment of the age of Enlightenment was to effect this "entry of life into history," that is, "into the order of knowledge and power, into the sphere of political techniques" (142). Since "a power whose task is to take charge of life needs continuous regulatory and corrective mechanisms," he argues, in modernity the traditional juridical ac-

[54]See Robert A. Nye *Crime, Madness, and Politics in Modern France: The Medical Concept of National Decline.*

[55]Michel Foucault, *The History of Sexuality, Volume I*, 140–41. Subsequent citations in this paragraph are also to Hurley's translation of this text.

tion of the law is displaced in favor of a "normalizing society," in which the effects of power on the subject are omnipresent yet indirect (144).

Foucault's bio-power paradigm links the ascendance of the idea of societies as biologically defined populations to the consolidation of social scientific forms of "power/knowledge" in the period after the French Revolution. Inspired by him, social and cultural historians have detailed how such scientific formations displaced moral and religious discourses about problems such as nervous illness, alcoholism, poverty, and prostitution in the nineteenth century.[56] It was not simply that these and other similar phenomena became objects of science. The vision of the nation as a population of bodies in need of regulation fostered the notion that what had once been viewed as moral maladies were diseases of the social; the accompanying political shift was the collective counterpart of the medicalization of malaise. Furthermore, as morality lost its anchor in religious belief, the power of the regulatory model increased. The nineteenth century is full of experimental efforts by zealous members of the middle class to heal their inferiors through various modalities of reform—efforts in which Foucault has taught us to see more or less covert attempts to develop new strategies for controlling undesirable behavior.

Foucault draws a strong connection between the regulatory model and the creation of modern forms of self-understanding. To take a paradigmatic example, he argues in *Discipline and Punish* that in the shift from corporal punishment to the incarceration of transgressors, the control and subjection of bodies effected an internalization of discipline—a subjectivation [*assujettissement*] of the individual. Taking a page from Nietzsche, Foucault describes the modern "soul" as "the prison of the body."[57] It is "the element in which are articulated the effects of a certain type of power and the reference of a certain type of knowledge, the machinery by which the power relations give rise to a possible corpus of knowledge, and knowledge extends and reinforces the effects of this power" (29). The last point is crucial: according to Foucault, the normative and productive dimensions of this modern form of "power/knowledge" are inseparably intertwined in modern subjectivity. The varieties of disciplining control over the body and its movements are the means by which "the fabrication of the disciplinary individual" (308) is achieved.

As we have seen, physiological language plays a crucial part in the evolu-

---

[56] Recent works include Ute Daniel, *Compendium Kulturgeschichte: Theorien, Praxis, Schlüsselwörter* and Hunt and Bonnell, *Beyond the Cultural Turn: New Directions in the Study of Society and Culture*. See also Lynn Hunt's collection, *The New Cultural History*, Barrows' discussion of crowd theory, Nye's work on criminology, and Corbin. For a recent defense of "old" social history, see Hans-Ulrich Wehler, *Die Herausforderung der Kulturgeschichte*.

[57] *Discipline and Punish*, 30. Subsequent citations in this paragraph are also to Sheridan's rendering.

tion toward a rationalized and disenchanted discourse on subjective malaise. Foucault's ideas about the relations between the emergent "bio-power" paradigm and modern subjectivity should, therefore, help to illuminate the historical development of the discourse on boredom in the nineteenth century. On the surface, his account seems to fit the facts. The experience of boredom can be read as an effect of normalizing forms of power, a by-product of the continuous regulation and self-policing that together constitute "the disciplinary individual." Furthermore, as boredom or the threat of it spread to larger populations, it came to be seen in physical rather than metaphysical or moral terms; indeed, under the aegis of fatigue, ennui became the object of science. However, as we have already seen, this paradigm shift toward materialist explanation remains incomplete, suggesting that there are limits to the explanatory power of Foucault's bio-power model in the case of the discourse on boredom. Examining a cultural history of scientific attempts to regulate fatigue and thereby overcome the physiological limits to progress—attempts that seem to conform to his account—will disclose a perspective that has significant implications for Foucault's method of conceptualizing modern subjectivity.

Writing at the intersection of intellectual and cultural history opened up by Foucault's ideas, Anson Rabinbach has examined the efforts that began at the end of the nineteenth century to develop a "science of work." In *The Human Motor: Energy, Fatigue, and the Origins of Modernity*, he uncovers the progressive origins of what would become known as Taylorization or rationalization. A wide-ranging study guided in Benjaminian fashion by the ambiguous utopian dream-image of the "human motor," of a "body without fatigue," Rabinbach's book examines the explosion of medical and scientific studies of fatigue after 1860.[58] In these studies, "fatigue"—a concept developed to analyze how much "stress" metals and other industrial substances could bear without succumbing to materially dangerous "exhaustion"—was extended both literally and metaphorically for the purposes of measuring and regulating the human capacity for labor. The scientific discourse on fatigue thus carried the disenchantment of subjective experience well beyond medicalization, taking the development we have been tracing to its logical conclusion by quantifying and operationalizing the will. Indeed, it created a way of thinking about human activity that dispensed with even an abstract notion of subjective purpose.

[58] Before this date, according to Rabinbach, "almost no" such studies are recorded. By the end of the nineteenth century, more than a hundred had been published on "muscle fatigue" alone, "as well as numerous studies of "nervous exhaustion," "brain exhaustion," "asthenia," and "spinal exhaustion" (20).

By elucidating the links between scientific progress, industrialization, and the rhetorical movement from 'soul' to 'nerves,' *The Human Motor* provides some of the cultural background for the evolution toward a rationalized and secularized discourse on subjective malaise we have been tracing in other sources. It also illustrates how, as the morally inflected discourse of idle selves yields to the "scientific" language of fatigued nerves, the modern, materialist rhetoric of reflection on subjective experience becomes anchored in the sciences that took bodies and populations as their objects.[59] The discourse on fatigue epitomizes the tendency to conceive of the subjective effects of modernization not in historical or political but in physiological and sociological terms. Rabinbach's book thus elucidates the significance of the paradigm shift we have been examining, attesting to the role such attempts to measure and manage subjective disaffection played in the development of modern capitalism. It also underlines the links between those attempts and the pessimistic and materialist philosophies that gained so many adherents during this period. With the new paradigm of the social body taking hold, the connection between politics and morality was being reimagined in terms of vitality and degeneration; individual malaise was medicalized, but it was also regarded as a symptom of cultural dysfunction that called for new forms of social engineering.

The science of work extended the notion of labor power in the name of making workers' lives better. According to Rabinbach, its creators, who wanted to reform and improve capitalism, reasoned that "if fatigue, the endemic disorder of industrial society, could be analyzed and overcome, the last obstacle to progress would be eliminated" (2). Through studies of fatigue, they hoped to muster objective evidence against excessively long workdays and dangerous, stressful industrial environments—and thereby to persuade the captains of industry that they could actually increase productivity by attending to the workers' bodily limitations. As Rabinbach shows, this populationist discourse was extraordinarily flexible. By the end of the century, he writes, the vision of "maximum productive output and mini-

---

[59]See Shorter, *From Paralysis to Fatigue*, for evidence of this transformation in the context of a rather different argument about the discourse on subjective suffering. The language of nerves was not new. However, as Janet Oppenheim has argued, although the attribution of mental distress to nervous disorders can be traced back beyond the eighteenth century "through the Elizabethan age to ancient medicine and philosophy," the Victorian emphasis on nerves was "different in kind . . . because it was substantially more informed about the nervous system itself" (14–15). My concern is not with the details of this shift, which have been amply documented by Oppenheim and others, but with its philosophical significance for understanding modernity. My contention is that the dominance of a metaphorics centered on nerves marks a significant shift in human self-understanding in the post-Enlightenment period.

mum exhaustion as the *summum bonum* of modern society" (23) was shared
by bourgeois industrialists, the labor movement, and scientific would-be reformers of capitalism alike. However, by then the humanist agenda of the
science of work had been supplanted by a technocratic focus on maximizing
the efficient deployment of the human body in industry through innovations
such as the assembly line. From our perspective, the passage from the science
of work to Taylorism reveals the socio-political significance of the abstract
conception of purpose associated with the paradigm shift toward materialist
explanation.

As Lamartine's speech illustrates, the discourse on fatigue was by no
means limited to those concerned with laboring bodies. The quantification
of will exemplified by the science of work also proved amenable to wide
metaphoric extensions. If "energy" was necessary for progress, as Rabinbach
shows, fatigue (often going by the name of neurasthenia) became a "pathology of the will." This pathology was open to divergent interpretations—it
could be read in terms of a "natural conservatism of the body's forces" or in
relation to the metaphysical notion that progress depended on reserves of
energy, of will (171). In other words, exhaustion could be blamed on the
weak individual unable to keep up with the demands of modernity upon the
body or, as in the case of pessimistic philosophers of culture and their
epigones, the incidence of nervous illness could be viewed as an inevitable
consequence of modern civilization itself.[60] Later in the chapter, we will examine Émile Tardieu's influential *L'Ennui*, a prominent and indeed paradigmatic example of the metaphorically extended discourse on fatigue
common in the second half of the nineteenth century. At this point, however, we need to consider the relation between Rabinbach's study and the
conceptual implications of the bio-power paradigm more closely.

In the introduction to *The Human Motor*, Rabinbach notes that Foucault

---

[60]In his extremely influential 1892 treatise, *Degeneration*, Max Nordau asserts that the
"murderous suddenness" of progress is physically overwhelming the West (40). He cites an array
of statistics that "indicate in what measure the sum of work of civilized humanity has increased
during the half-century" and show how "positive and unambiguous symptoms of exhaustion" are
affecting modern psyches (40). His evidence ranges from "new nervous diseases" to "the great increase in consumption of narcotics and stimulants" to signs of more rapid aging in "the present
generation" (41). According to Nordau, the great upheavals of the nineteenth century, and especially the profound and traumatic reversal of national fortune in 1870–71, made matters even
worse in France, so that "hysteria and neurasthenia are much more frequent in France . . . than
anywhere else." As a consequence, it was there "that the morbid exhaustion of which we have
spoken became for the first time sufficiently distinct to consciousness to allow a special name to
be coined for it, namely, the designation of fin-de-siècle" (43). On the relationship of modernization to stimulants and narcotics, see Wolfgang Schivelbusch, *Das Paradies, der Geschmack und die
Vernunft: Eine Geschichte der Genußmittel.*

draws powerful connections between the progress of scientific knowledge and the extension of "the normative power of knowledge over the self and the institutions that encompass it" (17). However, he contends that the "tension that exists between intention and outcome" is more significant than Foucault's model acknowledges (17). His study of the science of work is to illustrate the importance of this ambiguity. As we have already noted, Rabinbach goes on to show that within the scientific community working on fatigue, the "tendency to generate and extend social scientific systems of control" coexisted with a progressive "commitment to humanitarian reform and moral responsibility" (17). By using discourse analysis to link scientific developments to cultural transformations, he aims to construct a less totalizing narrative about the "origins of modernity," one that emphasizes "the ambiguity of the term *discourse* . . . to evoke the tension that characterizes the relations between knowledge and power, relations that are neither entirely fixed nor predictable" (18). This narrative thus brings into the writing of social and intellectual history the perspective associated with the Frankfurt School (16)—that there is a "dialectic of Enlightenment" on account of which, in the words of Siegfried Kracauer, technology and instrumental reason come to dominate human existence under capitalism because "it rationalizes not too much but rather *too little*."[61]

Rabinbach's account centers on the cultural consequences of scientific innovations. He argues that "fatigue became the permanent nemesis of an industrializing Europe" as a consequence of developments in nineteenth-century physics (4). The thermodynamic conception of "energy" as the universal and transmutable force underlying all natural phenomena and the associated specter of entropy, he writes, "radically transformed" the way labor was understood. Moral perspectives were eclipsed. "In the energetic image of labor the intellectual, purposeful, or *teleological*, side is incidental"; significantly, he argues, 'work' became what "all motors, animate or inanimate" (4) do. These developments culminated, on Rabinbach's reading, in a "productivist metaphysic in which the concept of energy, united with matter, was the basis of all reality and the source of all productive power—a materialist idealism" (4). As Rabinbach shows, this "transcendental materialism" was at once the ideology of capitalist industrial expansion and the inspiration for visions of new Edens: a modern way of thinking rent with contradictions.

But can such tensions or contradictions within the discourse on fatigue—be they a function of the complexity of individual agency or expressions of the historical cunning of reason itself—really suffice to refute Foucault's

---

[61] The phrase occurs in "The Mass Ornament" (Kracauer 1995, 81).

dark account of the relation between rationalization and subjection? After all, Rabinbach's own research provides ample evidence that, despite the progressive aspirations of many involved, the science of work indeed contributed to the "fabrication of the disciplinary individual" through the scientific investigation, surveillance, and regulation of working bodies. The issue is not empirical but historiographical. What is at stake is whether Foucault's narrative about the relationship between modern science and modern forms of identity is the best way of accounting for the complexity of the changes in human life unleashed by the dual revolution. On my reading, *The Human Motor* has significant implications for how to assess the value of that narrative, though these are not necessarily connected with tensions or contradictions within the empirical evidence per se.

Rabinbach's brief remarks on Foucault's approach and his claim that the history of the science of work points to dimensions neglected in the latter's Weberian interpretation of the origins of social modernity occur in the introduction to his book. He goes on to state his preference for Foucault's "early model of discourse as an epistemological category" over the later "reductive position that different forms of knowledge are simply an 'endlessly repeated form of domination'" (18).[62] However, he does not actually discuss the later Foucault's ideas on power/knowledge in the body of the text at all.[63] This is unfortunate, for Rabinbach's richly nuanced cultural history of the scientific ideas and practices associated with the mechanist reconceptualization of the human body in the nineteenth century suggests an important critical perspective on Foucauldian discourse analysis. Indeed, it seems to imply that Foucault's description of modern subjectivity as an effect of the "microphysics of power" is itself a form of "transcendental materialism."

To unfold these implications, a philosophical detour will be necessary. It is important to bear in mind that, as Rabinbach notes (17), Foucault's suspicion of reason can be traced to Nietzsche.[64] My contention is that insofar as Foucault's mode of interpreting modernity rests on a Nietzschean commitment to describing historical developments as manifestations of the will to power, the claims he makes for the bio-power paradigm are not empirically

---

[62] Rabinbach, 18; Foucault used this phrase in "Nietzsche, Genealogy, History" (in Foucault, *Language, Counter-memory, Praxis*, 150).

[63] Rabinbach's only reference to Foucault outside the introduction cites his first book, *Madness and Civilization*, on the significance of sloth (27).

[64] Insofar as Nietzsche saw cultural fatigue—"decadence"—and progress as intertwined, Rabinbach regards him as a typical representative of his time. See Rabinbach's discussion of Nietzsche and the contemporary discourse on fatigue (19–20).

but rather metaphysically grounded. And while metaphysical positions cannot be empirically falsified, their foundations can be interrogated.

In *Beyond Good and Evil*, Friedrich Nietzsche argues for his conception of
a will to power using a modernized Ockham's razor: method, he writes, is a
matter of "economy of principles."[65] If we assume "that nothing is 'given' as
real other than the world of our desires and passions" and that "thinking is
only a relation of these drives to one another," then, he argues, it becomes
possible to understand "the so-called mechanistic (or 'material') world on
this basis as well."[66] According to Nietzsche, "the conscience of method"
therefore demands an attempt to explain everything that exists as an effect of
will. If such an epistemological experiment should succeed, he contends,
"the world viewed from within, the world defined and signified in relation to
its 'intelligible character' would be 'will to power' and nothing else." Foucault's "genealogies" all attempt to show that this kind of explanation is possible and indeed necessary. As he puts it in *Discipline and Punish*, "the subject who knows, the objects to be known and the modalities of knowledge
must be regarded as so many effects of these fundamental implications of
power-knowledge and their historical transformations" (27–28).

This philosophical stance is questionable on several counts. It is not simply that, like all attempts to establish first principles, the argument for the
will to power appears circular. More importantly, it is not in fact clear that
the best method for explaining human phenomena is to reduce complexity
by means of a monistic philosophical principle. Furthermore, in the particular case at hand, the historical links between the concept of a will to
power and the discourses Rabinbach analyzes suggest prima facie objections
to interpreting their historical significance using this concept. To analyze
subjectivity as an effect of power bears a family resemblance to evaluating
people in terms of their susceptibility and resistance to fatigue; to regard
"modalities of knowledge" associated with the science of work as effects of
power effectively elevates those modalities to timeless truths. In a word, the
explanatory power of the concept of the 'will to power' appears to be
grounded in discursive developments that are inseparable from the phenomena it purports to analyze.

To escape from what appears to be a vicious circle, it is necessary to shift
the focus from the purported metaphysical depths to the rhetorical surface.
From this perspective, the appeal of Nietzschean "transcendental materialism" is an historically specific effect of the disenchantment of the language of

---

[65] *Jenseits von Gut und Böse* (Nietzsche, *Sämtliche Werke* 5), section 13, 28.
[66] This quotation and the subsequent one: section 36, 54–55.

reflection on subjective experience in modernity. That knowledge and power appear to be essentially rather than historically interlinked is an effect of the triumph of Enlightenment modes of reasoning.[67] Ironically, Foucault's totalizing vision of the relations between knowledge, power, and modern subjectivity occludes the constitutive ambiguity of the materialist language of analysis on which its critical potential depends. Notions of 'will,' 'force,' 'fatigue,' and most of all 'power' are metaphors that exist in dialectical relationship to the historical reality in which they come to be applied to human experience. To proceed as if they are metaphysical realities is not simply to forget that they are metaphors—it is to treat the modern materialist rhetoric of reflection on subjective experience as though it were not another historically situated discourse but the *via regia* to absolute truth.

To put the point in simpler terms: a discourse analysis that takes the dynamics of power as its foundation cannot establish a critical relationship to the field in which the modern language of power emerged. It is not simply that Foucault's strategies—from his redescriptions of politics in terms of a "micro-physics" of power to his presentations of "the carceral" and "governmentality" as modes for "the fabrication of the disciplinary individual"—deploy the language of instrumental reason that they purport to criticize. His mode of discourse analysis, like Nietzsche's sometime elevation of the will to power to the ultimate explanatory principle, renders the historical particularity of that way of thinking invisible. The challenge is to develop a way of talking about the subjective effects of cultural modernization that is sensitive to the historical particularity of the materialist metaphysics—and metaphorics—that shape the way modern experience is described. To do so, I contend, it is necessary to construct an historical narrative centered not on alleged "fundamental implications of power-knowledge" but rather on the modern paradigm shift in the rhetoric of experience.

If Rabinbach's analysis of the discourse on fatigue is situated in the context of the global transformation of the rhetoric of reflection on subjective experience in the nineteenth century, it becomes apparent that the historical developments Foucault would take for evidence of a fundamental link between modernity and normalizing forms of domination are open to other interpretations. The science of work belongs to a broader cultural shift toward a materialist rhetoric of reflection on subjective experience propagated by the dual revolution—a shift that both reflects and fosters a disenchanted

---

[67] My objection is not that epistemic and ethical-political questions are inherently distinct but rather that the relationship between knowledge and power needs to be thought in its particularity in each historical instance.

attitude toward subjective malaise. By the mid-nineteenth century, 'fatigue' and its relative, 'boredom,' were appearing ever more frequently as ciphers for metaphysical, existential, or religious despair among members of all social classes. The language of rationalization was also a language of reflection—something more than an instrument of an "anatomo-politics of the human body" through which modern subjectivity was produced. If the "disciplinary individual" or, to use a more old-fashioned term, the bourgeois subject, was "exhausted" or "enervated," then not from factory labor but from the pointlessness of existence in a world where work—activity—had become an end in itself.[68]

From this perspective, the scientific study of fatigue can be seen to play a central role in the consolidation of a modern idiom of reflection on subjective experience. We have already noted the popularity of Brierre de Boismont's psychological analysis, which diagnosed an abstract need for a purpose to compensate for the loss of substantive ends in modern life.[69] The study of fatigue, in quantifying the somatic limitations to efficient industrial production, went even further toward radically disenchanting the discourse of reflection on subjective experience.[70] As Rabinbach shows, the science of work regarded fatigue as the body's contribution to the regulation of efficiency—for its proponents, fatigue "did not threaten modernity but defined the outer perimeter of excessive labor and energy expenditure" (178). However, the very techniques through which progressive scientists aspired to define and defend the function of normal, healthy fatigue soon came to be used to normal*ize* human labor. Rendering subjective discomfort accessible to regulation, study, and control by modern scientific methods represented a

---

[68]Seen in this context, the resonances of the notion of a body as machine with the much older history of automata and their threatening simulacra of human existence appear highly significant. See Kleist, "Über das Marionettentheater" and E. T. A. Hoffmann's "The Sandman" for two influential nineteenth-century literary instantiations.

[69]Within philosophical anthropology there is a distinct use of the concept of compensation to explain modernity's discontents. See Gehlen, *Der Mensch: Seine Natur und seine Stellung in der Welt*, Odo Marquard, "Inkompetenzkompensationskompetenz: Über Kompetenz und Inkompetenz der Philosophie" and "Kompensation: Überlegungen zu einer Verlaufsfigur geschichtlicher Prozeße."

[70]Jonathan Crary's work on the scientific study of attention illustrates that such quantification was not limited to the discourse on fatigue. In *Suspensions of Perception*, Crary argues that attention "became a decisively new kind of problem in the nineteenth century" (5). Like work on fatigue, the scientific study of attention took a recognition of the limitations of the human organism as a point of departure—"attention had limits beyond and below which productivity and social cohesion were threatened" (4). Here too, "the many, often conflicting efforts to explain attention empirically, and to render it manageable, were ultimately unsuccessful" (5). Nonetheless, both scientific efforts contributed not only to the emergence of modern industrial strategies for managing modern workers but also to the paradigm shift in the interpretation of subjective experience in this period.

great leap forward rhetorically, in that it altogether obviated the need to think about work in terms of subjective purposes, however abstract. Like psychology, sociology, and medicine, the science of work thus contributed to a discursive shift that shaped modern Western forms of identity. By quantifying fatigue, it helped to translate problems of meaning into a materialist vocabulary and thereby to establish the disenchanted language in which subjective malaise guarantees its legitimacy in modernity.

If the relations between the discourse on fatigue and the purposelessness and disaffection that plague modern subjects are emphasized, the science of work seems historically significant as much for its attempt to control and limit the effects of moral and epistemic uncertainty through a physiological rhetoric as for its endpoint in a Taylorist technology of industrial management. There was, as we have already seen, a productive ambiguity to the materialist language of reflection. While studies of fatigue doubtless contributed to the disciplining of work and workers necessary for modern industrial society to function efficiently, they also helped to open a potentially critical space for reflection within the regulatory regime. If fatigue and exhaustion applied to national populations as well as individuals, the moral, social, and even aesthetic problems of modern civilization could be reformulated in physiological terms. Modern cultural criticism from both the left and the right has drawn upon the notion, basic to the science of work, that the human body sets a natural limit to the progressively increasing demands of life in modern society.

Thus the vicissitudes of the science of work indeed point to a more complex relationship between knowledge and power than the Foucauldian vision of modernity can capture.[71] The gap between reformist intentions and disciplinary outcomes in the knowledge formations Rabinbach studies, a gap occluded when the will to power is elevated to the sole explanatory principle, is a function of a constitutive ambiguity in the materialist language these thinkers deployed. To speak of human beings as though they were machines made it possible to treat them as such. However, as a language of reflection, this thoroughly disenchanted account of subjective experience also transcends its own materialist presuppositions. As Foucault's own Nietzscheanism illustrates, it can redefine subjective experience in its own image. When the discursive relations between knowledge, power, and the "disciplinary in-

---

[71]It would be possible to construct a reading of the late Foucault's turn to bodies and their pleasures as an implicit response to some of the difficulties I have raised. The turn to issues of subjectivity and selfhood in the pre-modern world in the later volumes of the *History of Sexuality* would thus be an attempt to locate historical resources for conceptualizing human existence in a way that goes beyond the determinism of the power/knowledge paradigm.

dividual" are viewed historically, the materialist rhetoric of reflection reveals the dialectic in the process of Enlightenment.

As we continue our exploration of the relationship between historical transformations and the paradigm shift in reflection on subjective experience underway in the nineteenth century, it is important to keep the metaphoric quality of the materialist language of reflection on subjective experience in mind. As Rabinbach underlines, the topos of fatigue is located at the intersection between physical and psychic effects of modernization:

> A breakdown of body and mind, fatigue was increasingly identified as a "modern" disorder of overwhelming social and physical consequence. This perception appears frequently in the poetic literature of exhaustion, which arises almost simultaneously with the medical and scientific literature on fatigue. (40)

Such a "perception" can only be the consequence and not the cause of fundamental changes in how subjective malaise is conceptualized and experienced. The scientific study of fatigue and the broader literary and cultural discourse on ennui alike reflect these changes in the way they represent the mental and physical impact of modern life upon human beings. As Lamartine's example suggests, the metaphorics of 'ennui' play a central role in forging the possibility of such "perception" by providing the discursive link between the poetics of exhaustion, medical treatises on fatigue, and the physiological rhetoric of reflection on subjective malaise that was becoming increasingly hegemonic as the modern, populationist social sciences grew in importance.

Although the discourse on physical depletion may at first seem to locate the subjective effects of modernization in an entirely different register than the discourse on boredom, both in fact reflect the same evolution in the rhetoric of reflection on subjective experience. 'Fatigue' and 'boredom' are both paradoxical products of the industrial and political revolutions that were supposed to liberate human beings; they express the dialectical relationship to progress that characterizes modern subjectivity. Thus 'fatigue' and 'boredom' are frequently synonymous terms in nineteenth-century discourses on modernity and its discontents. In those realms where an overtly materialist, physiological discourse on subjective malaise reigns, as in safety studies of air traffic controllers or long-distance truckers, this identification persists.[72] On the whole, however, we have come to think of boredom in ways

---

[72]See Richard I. Thackray, "Boredom and Monotony as a Consequence of Automation: A Consideration of the Evidence Relating Boredom and Monotony to Stress." Thackray argues that although the evidence does not support the hypothesis that boredom (which he treats as synonymous with "monotony" and "understimulation" (2)), "per se produces the syndrome of stress," it

that make it surprising. Unlike the mute testimony of the exhausted body, legible without the cooperation of the subject, boredom exists first of all in language. It is a reflective experience, defined by its subjective interpretation rather than any objectively verifiable manifestations. Over time, it has thus come to be strongly associated with problems of meaning—the ennui of the decadent and satiated artist opposed to the fatigue of the factory worker. But this is simply to say that the tendency to separate problems of meaning from the material effects of modernization (and to map those differences along class lines) is inscribed in the historical development of the discourse of reflection on subjective experience.

As the contemporary sources attest, the distinctions were not nearly so clear at the time.[73] Modern subjectivity was still taking form, and the mid-nineteenth century discourse on boredom, with its admixture of idealist and materialist, religious and physiological perspectives, is a transitional phenomenon. In the multiple, conflicting, and often contradictory invocations of 'ennui' in this period, the instabilities of the modern rhetoric of reflection on subjective experience that was emerging alongside modern modes of knowing and ruling over populations become visible. Thus in the discourse on boredom, the tendency toward a medicalization of subjective malaise co-exists with a persistent religious interpretation of ennui as a revelation of the ontological dilemmas of human existence; the impulse to define boredom physiologically, as a manifestation of fatigue and exhausted nerves, vies with pessimistic philosophical visions of boredom as a symptom of the decline of civilization. The discourse on boredom brings the contradictions and complexities in modernity's impact on subjective experience to language.

Despite all these ambiguities, when it is viewed as an historically situated cultural phenomenon, the post-romantic discourse on boredom has a clear

---

does indicate that the "monotony coupled with a need to maintain high levels of alertness" characteristic of machine-paced work may do so. Other areas where such an approach shapes research on boredom include (cognitive and behavioral) psychology (where many studies similar to Thackeray's have been done using a "Boredom Proneness Scale" to investigate correlations between a tendency to boredom and other behaviors and health issues) and the intersection between psychiatry and neuro-physiology. See Carlo Maggini, MD, "The Psychobiology of Boredom" for a review of the issues in the latter literature. For a psychoanalytic perspective, see Martin Wanch, "Boredom in Psychoanalytic Perspective," and E. Mark Stern, ed., *Psychotherapy and the Bored Patient.*

[73]Consider the notion that doubt could itself be considered a form of insanity. According to Nordau, the "délire des négations" was first recognized as a "form of melancholia" by J. Cotard in 1891 (*Études sur les Maladies cérébrales et mentales*); in the following year, "The Third Congress of French Alienists ... devoted almost the whole of its conferences to the insanity of doubt" (Nordau, 397n).

evolutionary tendency. The examples of Brierre and Lamartine have confirmed what the discussion of etymology already made plain: that an emphasis on materialist explanation was reconfiguring the language of reflection on subjective experience even among the romantically or idealistically inclined. And yet, as a way of speaking about the fragmentation and dislocation lived by modern subjects, the discourse on boredom not only fosters but also resists the translation of subjective malaise into purely physiological terms. Indeed, because the experience itself raises questions of meaning, it indicates the limits of such translation. Thus even as the rhetoric of reflection on subjective experience as a whole moves toward a disenchanted, materialist vocabulary, boredom remains open to other, philosophical modes of interpretation.

I have argued, building on Koselleck, that in boredom the modern subject encounters the fatiguing temporality of progress in such a way that experience itself seems to disappear. The language that expresses such an historically unprecedented experience of the self in time is necessarily metaphorical, and the phenomenon of boredom is accordingly ambiguous. The discourse on boredom brings this perplexity of modern historicity to language by amalgamating a materialist perspective on subjective experience with philosophical and religious resonances of older experiences such as melancholy and acedia. In the metaphorics of boredom, the material effects of modernization refer to problems of meaning. As a consequence, 'boredom' retains its ambiguity long after enlightened modes of interpreting subjective malaise have triumphed in psychology as well as in industry. It is this ambiguity that undermines the intentions of those who would quantify ennui and reduce it to a physiological phenomenon. Or, to put the same point a little differently, the fact that the language of boredom is fundamentally metaphorical allows an idealist vision of the self to survive the eclipse of romantic aspirations in the momentous material and socio-political transformations of modernization. In emphasizing the evolution toward a materialist interpretation of subjective malaise, we have largely neglected the idealist aspect of the discourse on boredom. At this point, a detour through the emphatically anti-materialist interpretations of boredom equally characteristic of nineteenth-century post-romantic thought is called for. As will become clear, the discourse on boredom can only be understood as a reflective response to the democratization of skepticism in the modern world if both idealist and materialist interpretations of this "perception of modernity" are taken into account.

The Fate of Desire: Boredom as Negative Revelation

> Since boredom advances and boredom is the root of all evil, no
> wonder, then, that the world goes backwards, that evil spreads.
> This can be traced back to the very beginning of the world. The
> gods were bored; therefore, they created human beings. Adam
> was bored because he was alone; therefore, Eve was created. Since
> that moment, boredom entered the world and grew in quantity
> in exact proportion to the growth of population.
>
>   Søren Kierkegaard[74]

In Søren Kierkegaard's metaphysical apotheosis of boredom, the malaise
that plagued Werther and René appears as a necessary and universal feature
of the human condition.[75] "Boredom," he declares in the same text, "rests
upon the nothing that interlaces existence" (263). For Kierkegaard, far from
being a consequence of a "loss of cultural self-evidence" or a psychological
symptom of modernity's excess of stimulation, ennui is a philosophical response to an emptiness at the very heart of existence. The Danish philosopher was hardly alone with his despairing vision of human fate. From Novalis' longing for death to Büchner's grim resignation to the senseless of existence, from Jean Paul to Byron to St-Beuve, the victims of what came to be
called the *mal du siècle* had struggled to find meaning in the vacuity of a god-
forsaken world. Their ennui expressed the crisis of desire proper to the modern subject: in the absence of enduring values, there seemed to be no
grounds for action—in extreme cases, no reason to live.

In his "Reveries on the Primitive Nature of Man" (1809), Etienne Pivert de
Senancour (1770–1846) described the modern subject's crisis of meaning by
expanding upon Chateaubriand's "vague des désirs": "Ennui is born of the
opposition between what one imagines and what one experiences, between
the poverty of what is and the vastness of what one wants; it is born of the
diffuseness of desires and the indolence of action; of this state of suspension
and incertitude in which a hundred struggling affections mutually extinguish
themselves."[76] In a word, boredom is the fate of the desiring subject in the
aftermath of Enlightenment. Ennui arises through "the opposition between

---

[74] *Either/Or I*, 259. Unless otherwise indicated, subsequent citations of Kierkegaard refer to this
1842 text.

[75] But see Theodor Adorno's argument that Kierkegaard's melancholy interiority reflected
bourgeois alienation from nature and confinement in the interior space of the privatier's house
(Adorno 1979).

[76] *Rêveries*, IV, 196–201. Part of this passage is cited in Kuhn (226), whose translation I have
modified. Kuhn notes that Senancour uses Chateaubriand's phrase, which is here rendered 'the
diffuseness of desires.'

the unlimited sphere ... that we imagine and the narrow sphere ... where we find ourselves circumscribed.[77] And yet, so conceived, the malady contains the seeds of its own resolution. The gap between reality and imagination gives rise to an infinite longing, and it is through this longing that love or art or faith becomes possible; desire itself, in the romantic vision, strives to reunify the actual and the ideal, to recapture meaning and thus to overcome the discrepancy between self and world that is the source of ennui. In the fullness of romantic desire, then, dialectical triumph over skepticism.

As I have already argued, however, turning the sword of critical self-consciousness into the plowshare of self-cultivation leaves the skeptical legacy of Enlightenment intact. Thus, while the romantic impulse does not disappear, the genealogy of modern boredom leads in another direction—away from the life of the heart, into resignation to the permanency of unfulfilled desire. Post-romantic boredom no longer opens onto a voluptuous experience of the self sensing its own transcendence. Instead, in the recurrent struggle with ennui, the modern subject confronts the ultimate impossibility of realizing the strivings of the imagination. Such ennui constantly shadows that subject who, caught in an endless cycle of mundane longings and plagued by their futility, confronts the limitations of subjective freedom. In post-romantic thought, the crisis of desire becomes a crisis of self. However, the skeptical dialectic through which the romantics attempted to make longing itself the foundation of existence is susceptible to an ingenious elaboration.

The section of *Either/Or* already cited anticipates the homeopathic solution to the crisis of identity by which, from Barbey D'Aurevilly to Huysmans and into the twentieth century, the artistic embrace of boredom would result in a paradoxical intensification of subjectivity. Taking as its point of departure the notion that not idleness but boredom is the root of all evil, the text goes on to suggest a "method" for conquering ennui—the "Rotation of Crops." All too often, the narrator notes, "in an attempt to escape [boredom], one works one's way into it" (263). Since only a "spurious infinity" results from constantly changing the object of desire, it is better to change the subject (263). To remake oneself, he recommends forsaking the Promethean gift of hope, embracing the forgetfulness that erases the consciousness of loss, and distancing oneself from all emotions and all connections to other people, from all immediacy that is not absolutely arbitrary (265–66.). According to the narrator, the resulting "artistically achieved identity is the Archimedean point with which one lifts the whole world" (266).

---

[77] *Rêveries*, IV, 212–14.

The Kierkegaardian narrator is of course notoriously unreliable, and the author himself seems to have regarded such an aesthetic escape from boredom as ultimately insufficient. Early on, the narrator of *Either/Or* notes that the problem of boredom is deeply anchored in the self. He has longed, he confesses, for "a faithfulness that withstood every ordeal, an enthusiasm that endured everything . . . an idea that joined the finite and the infinite. But my soul's poisonous doubt consumes everything" (21). Only with the leap of faith in which subjective malaise is transformed once again into a religious category could this doubt be overcome. "What in certain cases we call 'spleen,' the mystics know under the name *tristitia* and the Middle Ages under the name *acedia*," Kierkegaard had written in his journal, "And it shows a deep knowledge of human nature that the old moralists should have included *tristitia* among the *septem vitia principalia*."[78] Like Pascal before him, Kierkegaard saw ennui in religious terms and regarded doubt and despair as perpetual problems of the isolated human self.

In 1848, Kierkegaard wrote of despair as "The Sickness Unto Death." Contrary to the "superficial view" that clings to the "appearances" of self-awareness and trusts that people know themselves, this text declares that despair "is quite universal."[79] In fact, it inheres in the quotidian existence that had so bored the narrator of "The Rotation of Crops." "The majority of men live without being thoroughly conscious that they are spiritual beings—and to this is referable all the security, contentment with life, etc., etc., which precisely is despair" (159). For Kierkegaard, then, the absence of malaise appears as the most sinister sign of the fallenness of bourgeois existence. As for Pascal, the flight from the self is flight from God. "Sin is: before God in despair not to will to be oneself, or before God in despair to will to be oneself" (212). By reestablishing the possibility of fulfillment on the foundation of radical skepticism about the things of the world, Kierkegaard paved the way for a renewal of Christian belief on epistemological grounds. If "sin is despair," this work concludes, "for the whole of Christianity it is one of the most decisive definitions that the opposite of sin is not virtue but faith" (213). As the flight into "artistically achieved identity" alleviates boredom but confirms despair by elevating doubt and self-doubt to a principle of existence, Kierkegaard reasons that the only genuine solution is to embrace despair and, through this embrace, to rediscover faith.

For Kierkegaard, boredom was very much the fate of the modern subject. In 1846, he had written: "Our age is essentially one of understanding and re-

[78] July 20, 1839; cited in Kuhn, 55.
[79] *The Sickness unto Death*, 155. All citations in this paragraph are to this text.

flection, without passion, momentarily bursting into enthusiasm, and shrewdly relapsing into repose."[80] The denizens of "The Present Age" of mechanization and excessive Enlightenment, paralyzed by "reflection" in doubt and universalized skepticism, are unable to construct anything of genuine, that is to say, spiritual, significance. From that perspective, the positive achievements of modernity are hollow and meaningless chimaerae, for they have rendered subjects into objects. Humanity has lost its way, and individuals are marooned in a senseless world without genuine values. Via the same ironic reversal that elevates boredom to a principle of creativity, Kierkegaard locates in the existential dilemma of the modern subject the dialectical resources for reversing and transcending the tendency of the age. For him, despair is the only source of hope. By experiencing radical indi-viduation and isolation, the subject may recognize the only possible route to freedom—throwing off the homogenizing shackles of rational reflection and plunging into creative action.

Kierkegaard connected the lived crisis of meaning characteristic of mod-ern existence with the material transformations of modernity, yet he ulti-mately interpreted boredom in metaphysical, rather than socio-historical, terms. For him, ennui was the fate of subjectivity as such. So, too, his con-temporary, Arthur Schopenhauer, who averred that every human life "is tossed to and fro, like a pendulum, between the pain and the boredom that are in fact its ultimate components."[81] For Schopenhauer, the life of the mind is merely a defense: just as walking is "merely an ever-interrupted falling" and the body's very life "merely a continuously interrupted dying," so too is the "liveliness of our spirit continuously delayed boredom."[82] For him, the dialectical consequence of such self-recognition is not faith in God but a re-lentless acceptance of the nihilistic will at the foundation of existence itself. Through artistic identification with that will, he writes, a "pure, true, and profound cognition of the essence of the world becomes an end in itself" that provides a temporary respite in which to recover the "force" (*Kraft*) to plunge once again into the senseless pendulum of existence.[83] For Kierke-gaard, the senselessness of a godless existence catapults the one who reflects in the direction of faith; for Schopenhauer, this utter futility itself becomes the stuff of transcendence, a means of overcoming the attachment to the illu-sion of self. What is modern about these thinkers—and what distinguishes

---

[80]"The Present Age" 33. A few pages later, he speaks of "sudden enthusiasms followed by apa-thy and indolence" (39).

[81]*Die Welt als Wille und Vorstellung*, Book 4, § 57, 390.

[82]*Die Welt als Wille und Vorstellung*, Book 4, § 57, 389–90.

[83]See *Die Welt als Wille und Vorstellung*, Book 3, § 52, 335.

their writings from their contemporaries' lamentations about the loss of meaning in modernity—is their embrace of purposelessness as the means of subjective equilibration. For both, negation is the path to freedom. They thereby dialectically rehabilitate the romantic project of rendering human life meaningful by stabilizing the anarchy of subjective desire.

While Schopenhauer's image of liberation through contemplative withdrawal from the world and Kierkegaard's plea for existential *engagement* appear diametrically opposed, both are idealistic and apolitical responses to the perceived meaninglessness of existence epitomized, for both, by the experience of boredom. Primarily concerned with the fate of the individual soul, neither Schopenhauer nor Kierkegaard really engages with the concrete historical situation that produces that experience in the first place. The antisubjective, nihilistic affirmation of life's meaninglessness by the former and the proto-existentialist embrace of individual uniqueness by the latter are complementary modes of withdrawal from the world into the fortress of the self. As we turn back to the project of locating the discourse on boredom within the broader historical context of the discourses on the subjective effects of modernization, we will see others who follow in the footsteps of these most prominent philosophies of boredom, integrating the romantic vision of subjective transcendence—albeit under a negative sign—into a post-romantic world view.

Ennui as Fatigue: Disenchantment in the Capital of the Nineteenth Century

> Le vieux Paris n'est plus (la forme d'une ville
> Change plus vite, hélas! que le coeur d'un mortel)
> Baudelaire, "Le Cygne"

The stagnation of which Lamartine had complained was soon to pass. In the period after the upheavals of 1848—themselves hardly boring—France embraced progress and movement, and urbanized, industrialized, and secularized with a rapidity that astounded contemporaries. During the Second Empire, the old Paris literally disappeared in a blur of activity, and the complaint that the city had become uninhabitable grew commonplace. Between 1851 and 1881, the population of Paris more than doubled[84]; railroads were under construction on a national scale for the first time, the *grands magasins* were appearing, and most importantly, Baron Haussmann's monumental modernization of Paris was underway. Beginning in 1859, the process of de-

---

[84]To 2.27 million—the previous doubling had taken more than fifty years.

struction, eviction, reconstruction and rearrangement of the urban surface on a scale never before seen was rapidly transforming a medieval into a modern city.[85]

Paradoxically, in the midst of all this innovation, complaints of boredom and fatigue multiplied. By mid-century, 'ennui' had become a generalized metaphor for the subjective effects of modernization, a process fatiguing, disorienting, and destabilizing at once. All of the changes associated with urbanization, industrialization, and the emergence of consumer society were linked in contemporary accounts to monotony, fatigue, melancholy, and boredom—an increase in precisely the sort of subjective malaise that Lamartine had associated with stagnation.[86] The backdrop against which that discourse took place is starkly depicted in Pierre-Joseph Proudhon's 1868 diatribe against modernized Paris:

> the new, monotonous, fatiguing city of M. Haussmann, with its rectilinear boulevards, with its gigantic official buildings, with its magnificent but deserted quais; with its grieving river that now carries only rocks and sand, with its railway stations which, replacing the gates of the ancient city, have destroyed their reason for existing, with its *squares*, its new theaters, its new barracks, its macadam, its legions of sweepers and its ghastly coal-dust.[87]

A melancholy cosmopolis with inhabitants but no dwellers, Proudhon's new urban space is hollow and banal—a dreary site of loss, exhaustion, and monotony. Industrialization has conquered the Seine; the modern state, with its bureaucratic apparatus and its army, has reshaped Paris in the image of inhuman needs. The destruction of the old *faubourgs* and the resulting mass displacement of population within the city combined with the massive influx of immigrants to create an atmosphere of desperation, loss, and homelessness. Paris had indeed become a modern city. It is these soulless streets which, in Baudelaire's poetry, become the paradigmatic space for a democratized experience of boredom.

Even as the perception that subjective malaise was taking on epidemic pro-

---

[85]For a nuanced discussion of the socio-political, economic, and symbolic dimensions of "Haussmannization," see T. J. Clark's *The Painting of Modern Life*, chapter 1, "The View from Notre-Dame."

[86]There is hardly a commentator on nineteenth-century life whose work could not be invoked as documentation of this link between modernization and malaise, which has its locus classicus in Walter Benjamin's elevation of melancholy to an historiographical principle in the *Passagen-Werk*. Of particular interest for my argument are Berman (on the modernist response to these subjective effects), Williams (on the emergence of the culture of consumption), Seigel (on the cultural dynamics of bourgeois society), and Schivelbusch (on the transformations of perception). For further references, see the bibliography.

[87]Proudhon, 124.

portions spread suspicion about progress itself, the culture-wide evolution away from idealist and toward materialist interpretations of such malaise extended the impetus of Enlightenment. Brierre's arguments notwithstanding, as time passed, boredom was increasingly viewed as a manifestation of nervous illness—though often as an illness "caused" by civilization. Conservative cultural critics were by no means alone in regarding modernity as a period of nervous degeneration, and yet it could be argued that the prestige associated with ennui passed to its medicalized descendant.[88] If in Naturalism the aspiration to create a scientific literature led leftist writers such as Zola to treat characters as specimens and biology as collective destiny, in fin-de-siècle Decadence, neurasthenia and even insanity would begin to compete with bored withdrawal as signs of spiritual distinction.[89] Thus a sense of boredom as a "philosophical" experience often persisted even among those who advocated a psychological interpretation of ennui as a nervous ailment.

In *A rebours* (1884), Joris-Karl Huysmans parted ways with Naturalism but not with its physiological determinism. In this archetype of the Decadent novel, Huysmans depicts ennui and the exclusive and aesthetic form of existence in which the last of the Des Esseintes line vainly attempts to flee it as simultaneously neurotic and transcendent. It is worth pausing to remark the conclusion of *Against the Grain*, for it illustrates how, even when boredom is assimilated to nervous illness, the discourse on the experience remains profoundly—philosophically—ambiguous. Des Esseintes, who has constructed an exquisite retreat at Fontenay, has been ordered by his physician to give up his solitude and return to Paris. He tries stoically to accept the medical necessity of abandoning his aesthetic consolations and "rejoining the depraved and servile rabble of this age" in order to preserve himself from insanity and death. Although his profound ennui overwhelms these efforts to regain equanimity, paradoxically, the rage and desperation into which it plunges him disclose a new, religious horizon. Contemplating the fallen state of the modern world—"there was nothing, nothing left, everything had been brought down" by the bourgeoisie—Des Esseintes longs for an apocalyptic proof of the existence of God in the form of a "rain of fire." The book closes with his imprecation for divine support to help him bear his expulsion from

---

[88] See Volker Roelcke, *Krankheit und Kulturkritik: Psychiatrische Gesellschaftsdeutungen im bürgerlichen Zeitalter (1790–1914)*. Although melancholy remained an important symptom, by the end of the nineteenth century, the medicalizing discourse on subjective malaise had been consolidated such that it no longer appeared as a specifically philosophical malady. Schiesari shows that the disappearance of this philosophical dimension maps onto the transformation of melancholy into a "feminine" ailment in modernity.

[89] For a naturalist depiction of ennui, see Zola's *Joie de vivre*.

his artificial paradise into the mediocrity of modern Paris: "'Lord, take pity on the Christian who doubts, on the unbeliever who longs to believe . . . who is setting sail alone, at night, under a sky no longer lit, now, by the consoling beacons of the ancient hope!'"[90] The way Huysmans ends *A rebours* suggests that at the limits of skepticism, the nervous ailment of ennui can be transmuted into a longing for religious deliverance—a resolution that both echoes Kierkegaard's ideas and anticipates the author's own biography.

Not everyone who regarded ennui as a nervous ailment shared Huysmans' religious proclivities. Nonetheless, he was not alone in thinking that the link between ennui and epistemological and moral skepticism entailed that a purely physiological interpretation of the experience was insufficient. A final example of the non-literary discourse on ennui will illustrate why it is significant that the ambiguity of the language of boredom persisted despite the cultural triumph of an enlightened, materialist rhetoric of reflection on subjective experience.

If Brierre de Boismont's 1850 "De L'Ennui" signals the infiltration of scientific materialism into a basically religious interpretation of subjective malaise, Émile Tardieu's 1903 treatise, L'Ennui, epitomizes the persistence of idealist assumptions within a disenchanted, scientific worldview. Tardieu was the student of the radical materialist philosopher-turned-clinician Théodule Ribot, a pioneer of modern experimental psychology and the author of an influential book on Schopenhauer. One of the key figures in the scientific study of fatigue, Ribot had argued in *Les maladies de la volonté* (1883), that ennui must be regarded as a secondary symptom of a diseased will.[91] According to Valentin Mandelkow, Tardieu, who was more influenced by Ribot's book on Schopenhauer than his "genuinely clinical work," represented the turning point "between the normatively oriented critique of 'ennui' that dominated before Ribot and the new medical approach, in the course of which . . . 'ennui' is subordinated to the phenomenon of 'action-inhibition'" (47). Thus Tardieu's *L'Ennui*, like Brierre de Boismont's, renders the contemporary paradigm shift in reflection upon subjective experience visible.

Subtitled "Étude psychologique," Tardieu's book offers a taxonomy of some of the "innumerable"[92] forms of ennui, which he defines as a "psycho-physiological complex of infinite variety" (1). For him, its "primary cause is an appreciable slowing of our vital movement"—that is, ennui is a manifestation of fatigue. However, he argues, ennui is experienced by the subject in a wide

---

[90] *Against Nature*, Mauldon's translations; all citations from 180–81.

[91] Mandelkow, 38–39.; see also Rabinbach, esp. 164–65.

[92] Emile Tardieu, *L'Ennui: Étude psychologique*, vii. Citations in parentheses refer to the French text.

variety of ways (e.g. as disgust, impotence, anger) and in its diversity may be traced to an equally wide variety of effective causes (e.g. monotony, satiation, spiritual poverty, age, etc.). Tardieu's system of classification thus assimilates the interpretive strategies of a materialist reductionism to a pessimistic philosophy of human experience. As we shall see, despite his emphasis on empirical variation, like Reinhard Kuhn's 'ennui,' Tardieu's 'fatigue' is the manifestation of an ontological reality that renders boredom virtually inevitable.

In his Preface, Tardieu announces philosophical principles that indicate his indebtedness to Schopenhauer:

> Life has no ground or purpose and pursues in vain a state of equilibrium and happiness . . . . every organism is born perishable and fatigues itself, exhausts itself and therefore suffers continuously. Ennui is the sentiment that results from our impotence and that shows the absurdity of the fate given us in a world where we are thrown without receiving sufficient explanations. (vii–viii)

On this account, ennui is the subjective expression of a fatigue grounded in existence itself, which is nothing but a cycle of meaningless suffering. Since there is no escape from this cycle, the experience is an inevitable feature of the human condition. Tardieu's pessimistic account universalizes a conspicuously modern notion of the purposelessness and absurd incomprehensibility of human life. As we shall see, these Schopenhauerian premises lead Tardieu to beg the question of the historical significance of the discourse on boredom in which his own book participates.

Most of the argument of *L'Ennui* is devoted to classifying the manifestations of ennui as discrete permutations of fatigue. However, in Chapter XIV, "L'Ennui moderne," Tardieu departs from his usual procedure to consider the phenomenon historically. Modern boredom, he contends, is distinct from the more universal malady in two ways: it "has become conscious, and continuously aggravates by reflection the woes that nourish it; second, its tendency to despair gives it over to intrigues" (255). That is, ennui has gained sway as a result of Enlightenment: it is the subjective expression of the disenchantment of human existence in modernity. Tardieu's argument seems to imply that the Schopenhauerian vision of boredom's ontological inevitability is an historically specific phenomenon. The "tendency to despair" and the resulting "intrigues" would then be the consequences of what his predecessor Brierre called the "abuse of reverie" through which the Enlightenment's legacy becomes visible in romanticism.

However, Tardieu does not draw this historicizing conclusion from his own argument. His explanation of the flourishing of ennui in modernity is paradigmatic for the discourse of fin-de-siècle conservative cultural criticism, which synthesizes a materialist account of human existence with a meta-physical account of Europe's historical progress toward universal decadence and cultural depletion. Identifying the "primary cause" of ennui as "an appreciable slowing of our vital movement" is only the first step in the analysis of this "psycho-physiological" phenomenon. The "general and profound causes" of modern boredom are to be found, Tardieu declares, "in the progress of the critical spirit; [ennui] is the product of the analysis that dissolves beneficent illusions; of a skepticism that reduces everything to dust" (255). The spirit of Enlightenment has had momentous moral effects: the "natural piety" of the past has been destroyed; God is dead.[93] Although ennui manifests itself as a physiological phenomenon, for Tardieu its significance can by no means be captured in materialist terms.

Like Spengler, Nordau, and many others at the fin-de-siècle, Tardieu mingles metaphysics and Darwin, linking the loss of religious belief to a fateful depletion of humanity's vital forces. Like Brierre, Tardieu contends that modern boredom was born "in the eighteenth century, at the moment when the dogmas gave way." The Revolution, which imagined that it could "make the heavens descend to the earth ... foundered, and the next century, which inherited its fever, proclaimed its bankruptcy" (258). In contrast to Lamartine's optimism about the principles of 1789, Tardieu represents a decisively, even cynically post-romantic point of view: he believes that the collapse of what Brierre called the "central pillars of France" has robbed humanity of the illusions that had made life bearable, plunging it into egoism and despair. For him, romanticism is truly dead. "Realism registers the death of the gods in heaven and the end of illusions on earth: it is disillusionment [*désabusement*]: it takes the form of ennui" (261). In 1839 Lamartine had regarded the national malaise as the expression of France's still-unfulfilled need for action; at the end of the century, Tardieu sees "a phenomenon of exhaustion, both moral and physical"[94] in which the imagination fatefully "submits to the control of reason" (259–60) as the historical result of the revolutionary era. By metaphorically extending the physiological definition of ennui as fatigue to national populations, he assimilates the historic loss of meaning to a state of collective enervation.

The tensions in Tardieu's position are considerable. He regards boredom as both philosophically justified and physiologically inevitable, given the cultural impact of Enlightenment. Nonetheless, he remains profoundly concerned about the moral and social transformations he says are caused by this

---

[93] Tardieu quotes the famous passage from Nietzsche's *Gay Science* at length.
[94] Here Tardieu refers his reader to Max Nordau's *Degeneration*.

symptom of civilizational decline and exhaustion. Like the romantic critics of capitalism, Tardieu complains that with the shattering of old ideals, society comes to be dominated by the pursuit of pleasure and personal gain. He holds ennui responsible for the turn to the pleasures of the body, the growth of prostitution, discontent among the lower classes, the pursuit of money as though it were an end in itself, and the increase in alcoholism and drug use (262–65). "By these multiple features, ennui reveals itself in the morés of the day. It may be sensed in our way of living exasperated, trembling, dissolute, distracted" (266). Here Tardieu is less psychologist than critic of boredom as a subjective symptom of modernization: ennui gives rise to restlessness and blaséness, to a relentless desire for new experiences that changes the face of society; everyone is skeptical, ironic, faithless.

Interpreting ennui as a symptom of exhaustion did not point Tardieu toward a solution to the problem of its prevalence in modernity. The difficulty is not simply that, given the state of neurophysiology, Tardieu could not go far enough in explaining boredom psychologically. It is, rather, precisely because he sees fatigue and disenchantment as ineluctable biological facts and views boredom as an expression of "realism" in the face of these facts that Tardieu can offer no real relief for the ennui of excess reflection. In his final chapter, "The Remedies for Ennui," he can suggest only "submitting to a duty, sacrificing oneself to an ideal" (290)—a strategy halfway between Brierre's injunction to conform to the social order and an existentialist attempt at self-realization. Tardieu recognizes that, unfortunately, his recommendation to follow the romantic poet Alfred de Vigny's remedy for this "malady of life" through love and will (*aimer et vouloir*) cannot be sufficient for those forms of boredom in which the reflective moment is highly developed. "The feeling of the nothingness of life is hard to bear when it is the feeling of our own nothingness" (294).[95]

Despite his materialist rhetoric, then, Tardieu ultimately regards boredom in philosophical terms. Although his point of departure is quite different, like Brierre before him, he ends by preaching resignation. However, while Brierre retains a weak hope for the return of faith, Tardieu embraces nihilism. When the pursuit of individual sensual gratification loses its charm, he thinks, an existential boredom must follow, and without any hope for a meaning that

---

[95] Walter Benjamin, who found *L'Ennui*, "a highly comical book" (*Passagen-Werk*, vol. I, 161), dismissed Tardieu's philosophizing in no uncertain terms. A description of his theses might lead one to expect "an impressive literary monument." However, "it is only the smug, petty science [*süffisante, mesquine Wissenschaft*] of a new Homais who debases everything great, the heroism of the hero and the ascesis of the saint into proofs for his unimaginative philistine distaste [*Mißvergnügen*]" (I, 157).

transcends the earthly, the bored subject can find succor only in the idea of its own annihilation. Ennui, he writes, is itself the refuge from the "vipers of thought," when "we are sure that life is vain, contemptible" (295–96). Avoiding the temptation of religious explanation, Tardieu's conclusion intertwines the physiological explanation of ennui with an affirmation of philosophical pessimism. "The ennui that results from disgust with life," although brought about in the final analysis by "the complete exhaustion [*usure*] of body and soul," finds completion, he writes, "in man's supreme consolation, the thought of death" (296). While the analyses in the body of the text appeal to a materialistic psychology, Tardieu's argument thus returns at the end to its ontological point of departure. This melancholy resumé is the pendant to his Schopenhauerian premise that boredom reveals the awful truth about the meaninglessness of human life. Fatigue, exhaustion, and boredom express the groundlessness of existence and the vanity of the search for happiness. In the final analysis, Tardieu's historical argument is but a footnote to this philosophical position, a mere elaboration of the sociological conditions that have made this timeless ailment so prevalent in modernity.

L'Ennui is a paradigmatic example of the fin-de-siècle discourse on boredom. Tardieu has renounced even the wish for what Des Esseintes called "the consoling beacons of the ancient hope" to help him face the awful realities of contemporary Paris. Unfortunately, his own argument implies that modern ennui is not, in fact, adequate to the task of protecting the sensitive subject adrift in the modern world. Tardieu's *L'Ennui* thereby betrays the dialectic of enlightenment at work in the disenchantment of subjective malaise.

Despite his avowed commitment to the rational, scientific analysis of the phenomenon and despite the connection he draws between the rise of skepticism and the spread of boredom, Tardieu's argument takes leave of the empirical. His *Étude psychologique* circles back to a mythical vision of ennui as the thinking man's ailment: as an experience outside of history, boredom reveals the truth of historical reality. This mythologization of ennui obscures the historicity of Tardieu's own materialist categories of analysis—of the very modern identification between skepticism, fatigue, and purposelessness that animates not only his work, but the late-nineteenth-century discourse on boredom more generally.

The concluding embrace of boredom as a refuge from life, though it appears to be a moment of critical distance from the reductive physiological rhetoric in which he has analyzed the forms of ennui, in fact exemplifies the deterioration of Enlightenment into mythology. Tardieu's analysis fails to achieve a reflective distance from the nihilistic dynamic of the experience itself, in which boredom seems to the sufferer to signify the meaninglessness of existence as such. Instead, his mythology of ennui hypostasizes this dynamic into a revelation of metaphysical truth, obscuring the historical specificity of boredom as a symptom of the loss of purpose that plagues modern identity. But as he himself has argued, boredom spreads as a consequence of the rationalization process. The malaise Tardieu describes cannot be understood in abstraction from its historically specific manifestations.

Contrary to Tardieu's intention, then, his work suggests that modern ennui cannot really be explained as an effect of fatigue. His own arguments underline that the experience reflects historic transformations in the ideological foundations of human society and gives rise to reflections that simply cannot be explained in physiological terms. Once again, the failure of a reductive method to account for the relationship between those transformations and the spread of boredom in modernity points us toward philosophical questions about the relationship between history and subjective experience. Even as Tardieu's *L'Ennui* collapses ontological and historical explanation in a fashion that underlines the limits of the "energeticist" rhetoric of reflection on subjective malaise, it illustrates how the discourse on boredom continues to pose the problem of the human being's interpretive relation to the historical process.

Boredom, Literary Culture, and the Democratization of Leisure

> Boredom is always counterrevolutionary.
>
> Situationist slogan

> Mais, dominant tout, noyant tout, son ennui devenait immense, un ennui d'homme déséquilibré, que l'idée toujours présente de la mort prochaine dégoûtait de l'action ... Il avait l'ennui sceptique de toute sa generation, non plus cet ennui romantique des Werther et des René, pleurant le regret des anciennes croyances, mais l'ennui des nouveaux héros du doute, des jeunes chimistes qui se fâchent et déclarent le monde impossible, parce qu'ils n'ont pas d'un coup trouvé la vie au fond de leurs cornues.
>
> Emile Zola[96]

The modern discourse on boredom began as a literary phenomenon. The nameless suffering of Werther and the "vague des désirs" of Chateaubriand's

---

[96]"But his ennui grew immense, dominating everything, suffusing everything, the ennui of a man fallen into disequilibrium, in whom the idea, always present, of impending death causes an aversion to action. . . . He had the skeptical ennui of his whole generation, no longer the romantic ennui of Werther and René, weeping with regret for bygone faith, but the ennui of the new heroes of doubt, the young chemists who get angry and declare the world impossible because they haven't in a single stroke found life at the bottom of their retorts" (Zola, *Joie de Vivre*, 1057).

René were the forerunners of the romantics' "mal du siècle." And as we have seen, even the most scientifically inclined nineteenth-century analysts draw a connection between romanticism and the malaise rampant in their own time. The second half of this chapter therefore turns from the science to the literature of ennui—from the rhetoric of the discourse on the experience to the representation of the experience itself. In the post-romantic literary discourse on boredom, not only are the 'idealist' and 'materialist' threads intertwined—they are woven into a metaphorics of ennui that links the ethical and epistemological dilemmas of modern existence to the historic transformation in the understanding of subjective malaise underway in the nineteenth century. The literary discourse on ennui, in other words, makes the question of the modernity of boredom more explicit. Literary representations of the experience allow a new set of questions to be raised. What is the structure of perception associated with boredom? How is its historical specificity to be understood? How does the experience of boredom fit into "modern" identity?

Thus far, I have emphasized how cultural modernization produces the conditions of possibility for boredom by democratizing skepticism. The literary discourse in which that skepticism is reflected must, however, also be situated in relation to the axis of cultural modernization I call the 'democratization of leisure.' Just as political liberties were extended in the course of the nineteenth century, so too did the more intimate freedom of disposable leisure time expand beyond the upper classes. New institutions and practices emerged or were democratized—the café-concert, outings to the countryside or to parks, department stores, industrial expositions, the cinema of spectacles . . . The list could go on. All belong to a world in which leisure is newly within the reach of the masses; such pastimes help define the new temporal regime of modern, urban life.[97] As we have seen, the scientific discourse on boredom centered on attempts to quantify and control an experience that kept evading conceptual determination. By contrast, the literary representation of the experience reflects on the complex relations between problems of meaning and material conditions that constitute subjective experience in modernity. By way of introduction, it will therefore be helpful to locate the literary discourse on boredom within the broader cultural, intellectual, and socio-historical context of the democratization of leisure.

One of the cultural consequences of Enlightenment was a much wider public for secular reading matter. By the end of the eighteenth century,

---

[97]On middle- and working-class culture in nineteenth-century France, see Charney and Schwartz, Clark, Gunning, Kracauer, Miller, Schwartz, Williams.

among a significant proportion of the middle class, novels had come to vie
with religious tracts as the source of sentimental education.[98] The proto-
romantic novellas "The Suffering of Young Werther" and "René" became the
bibles of fin-de-siècle youth.[99] As literary legend has it, these works inspired a
Europe-wide epidemic of malaise and a romantic rebellion colored equally
by narcissism and a longing for a higher reality.[100] To be sure, Goethe and
Chateaubriand each later complained that his critical stance toward his protagonist had been wrongly overlooked. Be that as it may, these brooding heroes, their creative individuality suffocated by social conventions, set the
tone for literary rebels from before 1789 through the post-Napoleonic era.
Significantly, neither Goethe nor Chateaubriand advocated a political solution for the malaise that their protagonists suffered in the face of the stultifying status quo. On the contrary: their paeans to the sensitive thinkers who
sacrificed all in the name of love presented the *mal du vivre* as a timeless
spiritual problem.[101] In showing the corruption that resulted when this vision
of human emotional life gripped that avid reader, the young Emma Bovary,
Flaubert commented on the democratization of such romanticism—and,
ipso facto, on its decline.

By the mid-nineteenth century, as we have seen, the ennui of romantic
melancholy was yielding to an emphatically un-aristocratic discourse in
which the experience of boredom was explicitly linked to the material effects

---

[98]See James van Horn Melton, *The Rise of the Public in Enlightenment Europe*, chapter 3,
"Reading Politics," for a recent synthesis of scholarship on the eighteen-century "reading revolution." Melton notes that novels were "the single most important growth industry in the eighteenth-century literary market" (94). Lending libraries "catered to the rising demand for fiction"
(108) among the broader public that could not (before the technological innovations that would
take place in the nineteenth century) afford to buy many books. The notion of a "reading revolution" is Rolf Engelsing's. See Melton's bibliography for more references to the scholarship on literary reading and reading publics. See also James Smith Allen 1991.

[99]In *Werther und Wertherwirkung*, Klaus Scherpe speaks of "a religious ersatz-function (97)
among the book's admirers. By contrast, however, for Werther's detractors, the "rationalist
dreamer, conscious visionary par excellence" (14) was according to Scherpe a threat to "bourgeois
ideas about value altogether" (15). But see Allen 1981 for an account of the socio-cultural field of
popular romanticism, which was focused on other works.

[100]One ought not to exaggerate the breadth of this movement, for despite the eloquence of its
partisans and their claims to speak for their generation as a whole, the readership in question was
limited to the upper echelons of society. Nonetheless, Flaschka estimates that 90,000 contemporaries read Goethe's book (243). The first (1774) edition of *Werther* went through thirty, the second (1787) through only slightly fewer editions in the author's lifetime (Zmegac, v. 1, 228).

[101]In a January 2, 1824 letter to Eckermann, Goethe wrote, "Thwarted happiness, inhibited action, unsatisfied desires are not the ailments of a specific era but of every single human being, and
it would be terrible, if everyone should not, once in life, have a period in which *Werther* seems to
have been written for him alone" (cited in Scherpe, 106).

of modernization. Although the boredom discourse as a whole retained the link to questions of meaning that defined its point of departure, as the experience grew ever more widespread, a much less flattering vision of subjective malaise gained sway. From a scientific point of view, ennui appeared to be a manifestation of fatigue and mental deterioration, a nervous response to the stresses of modern life. What amounted to a materialist deconstruction of the idealist interpretation of boredom already influenced the writers of the first post-romantic generation. Thus both Flaubert and Baudelaire have an ironic relationship to the very language of ennui which they deploy as a metaphor for the spiritual effects of modern life. Among the literati of their generation, ennui came to be valued as a reflected response to modernization rather than as a sign of spiritual sensitivity per se. It was the thinking man's answer to the ascendant ideology of progress and utilitarianism, to the jubilation over modernization that marked the industrial explosion of the second half of the century in France. If romantic melancholy had been nostalgic for lost wholeness, post-romantic boredom included an (often aestheticized) impulse toward social critique that explicitly renounced religious succor. By the mid-nineteenth century, 'ennui' had come to describe not suffering in the face of loss but resignation to the absence of what could not be found in the modern world.

A generation of artists arose who viewed themselves as hard-edged realists and merciless critics not only of romantic illusion but also of modern society itself. For most, rebellion remained squarely in the aesthetic sphere—the pursuit of art for art's sake simply carried the romantic critique of reality to a higher level. The self-understanding of those in Flaubert's generation was still shaped by the romantic ideal of the artist opposed to the tedium of ordinary life; however, while their predecessors had often been tempted by return to the Church, they embraced disenchantment. Flaubert was by no means alone in viewing boredom as his fate: "The opiate of boredom in which I was steeped in my youth will affect me to the end of my days. I hate life."[102] Cynicism, world-weariness, and disaffection to the point of violent revolt and hatred of existence itself afflicted the promising and well-placed youth of the generation that came of age during the Bourgeois Monarchy.

[102]Letter to Maxime du Camp of 21 October 1851. *Correspondance* II, 10. Compare the claim of Alfred de Musset's alter-ego, Octave, that he had been "attacked in early youth by an abominable moral malady" and Zola's plaint (in 1860, in a letter to Cezanne written when he was twenty): "Is not frightful ennui the malady with which all of us are afflicted, the wound of the century?" (Musset 1; subsequent citations in text follow the English edition). The letter is cited in Kuhn, 270.

Rejecting religious solace, yet unable to embrace the promises of Progress, they regarded boredom as the only realistic response to a secularized world in which existence was being robbed of meaning and beauty.[103]

According to the narrator of Alfred de Musset's 1836 *La Confession d'un Enfant du Siècle* (*Confession of a Child of the Century*), the problem was quite universal: "Napoleon dead, human and divine power were reestablished, but belief in them no longer existed" (9). "A feeling of extreme uneasiness began to ferment in all young hearts" (10). Like Lamartine, Musset joined materialist explanation to romantic ideals, declaring that the youth had been "condemned to inaction by the powers which governed the world, delivered to vulgar pedants of every kind, to idleness and to *ennui*." Those too poor to become libertines or to follow a profession "gave themselves up with cold enthusiasm to great thoughts" and "aimless effort" (11). Cynicism soon infected politics. "Upon returning home," Musset wrote, every participant in the dramatic struggles of the 1830's "bitterly realize[d] the emptiness of his life and the feebleness of his hands" (11). It was, according to George Steiner, the period of "the great ennui" that followed upon the upheavals of the Napoleonic era.[104]

Such rampant fatalism notwithstanding, among the literary intelligentsia, boredom was nonetheless deemed a sign of spiritual distinction; characteristically, the brothers Goncourt experienced this historically typical sentiment with sincerity and expressed it straightforwardly:

> There are moments when, faced with our lack of success, I wonder whether we are failures, proud but impotent. One thing reassures me as to our value: the boredom that afflicts us. It is the hall-mark of quality in modern men. . . . The essence of bourgeois talent is to be gay.[105]

[103] I include political aspirations under "the promises of progress"; in contrast to the romantic generation, which produced not only Hugo but also Lamartine and Chateaubriand, there are no significant political figures among the artists of Flaubert's generation. The temptations of the *sacrificio intellectualis*, as the example of Huysmans illustrated, would grow greater in the course of the nineteenth century. According to Schamber, art had a compensatory function for the aristocrats of the first romantic generation in France and was often abandoned when they were able to enter into politics. Members of the second generation, however, of whom a significant number were of bourgeois origins, tended to view their literary and artistic pursuits as ends in themselves. It is among this group (e.g. Gautier, Nerval, Berlioz, Delacroix) that the cultivation of boredom as an attitude leads to the rebellion against romanticism that finds its culmination in the ideology of art for art's sake.

[104] Steiner, *Bluebeard's Castle*. Although I will limit my discussion to French sources, this argument could be expanded to apply internationally to the period of reaction that followed upon the Peace of Vienna. Examples of important nineteenth-century writers in whose works the discourse on boredom plays a central role include Büchner, Turgenev, Ibsen, and Leopardi.

[105] July 30, 1861. Baldick 1984, 61.

According to the Goncourts, ennui distinguishes the true literary personage, for whom lack of popular success only confirms an inborn aversion to the modern world, from the hack who panders to his audience. The true artist, whatever his class origin, is bored by the bourgeois regime with its debased and materialistic standards of success.[106] Blasé indifference is the sign of opposition to modern mores. This attitude, which can be traced up to the present day, is epitomized in Baudelaire's vision of dandyism as "the last burst of heroism amidst decadence."[107] We shall turn shortly to the suffering artist of his own life, the direct descendant of the romantic heroes of Goethe, Byron, and Chateaubriand—or more precisely to his dissection by Baudelaire. First, however, it is necessary to stop to consider whether the Frères Goncourt were right to be so reassured by their ennui.

As a matter of fact, by the mid-nineteenth century, ennui was no longer an exclusive experience. The attempt by an artistic elite to claim boredom as a mark of spiritual distinction was paralleled by a democratic development of the very same symptoms of disaffection and metaphysical despair among those who supposedly lacked the sensitivity of the artists.[108] The pendant to the suffering artist is thus Emma Bovary, the paradigmatic bored housewife who is yet, as Kuhn averred, the victim of a "metaphysical malady." The bored poet was Parisian; Emma represents the arrival of ennui in the provinces.[109] Today, although boredom remains a key term in the languages of revolt, marginalization, and artistic upheaval, its elite connotations have faded even further. The strategy of the dandy and of art for art's sake—using boredom to create a new

[106] For a sociological perspective on artistic alienation, see César Graña's erudite *Modernity and Its Discontents*. For an eloquent defense of the bourgeoisie against the accumulated charges, see Peter Gay's five-volume cultural history, *The Bourgeois Experience,* especially the final volume, *The Pleasure Wars.* Gay examines the "modernist myth" of an artistic battle against "the dominant, hopelessly conventional middle class" (25) in a nuanced discussion of the bourgeoisie's complex relationship to nineteenth-century art. On the embarrassing fact that bohemia derived its most successful artistic denizens from that abominated class, see Jerrold Seigel, *Bohemian Paris.*

[107] OC II, 711. For a portrait of Byron's contemporary, the ur-dandy Beau Brummell, see Jules Barbey D'Aurevilly, *Dandyism.* (Barbey himself was allegedly the model for Huysmans' *Des Esseintes.*) For an historical perspective on dandyism, see Ellen Moers' classic *The Dandy: Brummell to Beerbohm.* Domna C. Stanton and Jessica R. Feldman offer more literary perspectives that expand the concept considerably.

[108] From a psychoanalytic point of view, the two may be related. Thus Gay suggests that Flaubert's maledictions against all that was 'bourgeois' indicates "that the cultural malaise he saw all around him might really be endemic in the class he so inexactly designated and so furiously denounced (32).

[109] It is worth noting that the conceptions of artistic and feminine identity at work in these figures are equally products of bourgeois society. See Thorsten Veblen on leisure and conspicuous consumption. The disoccupation of (artist) sons and (house)wives may, following Veblen, be labelled vicarious leisure.

hierarchy independent of the traditional social one—was vitiated as the phenomenon spread rapidly across class and status lines in the course of the
nineteenth century. To be sure, the attempts of successive avant-gardes to
turn their boredom into art would continue to animate bohemias well into
the next century and beyond, but the attitude of bored withdrawal had ceased
to be the possession of the creative few. By the end of the nineteenth century,
boredom would even have reached the masses who continued to be regarded
as its object.[110] To grasp the historical significance of this democratization
process, the problem of subjective malaise must be situated in relation to
cultural modernization as a whole in the period of the dual revolutions.

The same cultural and political processes of transformation that had undermined older, formerly stable strategies of social differentiation were still
proceeding. Urbanization and industrialization literally moved people out of
their old worlds into new ones, where identity was constructed in different
ways. We have already considered the problem of fatigue and tedium, with
their links to factory labor. But the new practices and institutions concerned
with leisure time are just as significant, for as leisure was democratized, so
too was boredom. The tendency of modern subjects to define themselves
through their uses of leisure, while not so marked as in the period since 1945,
was established during the nineteenth century. While the ennui cultivated by
the self-defined intellectual elite indeed resembled the older, aristocratic
form, it did so as much deliberately, even defensively, as spontaneously. The
emulation of aristocratic attitudes was a widespread characteristic of bourgeois cultural activity during this period, a characteristic that functioned
both to distinguish the rising classes from the masses and to establish the
propriety of their social and material successes.[111] Indeed, the "Bourgeois
Monarchy" was virtually defined by the general blurring of the criteria for
recognizing people of genuine culture. However, in the course of the nineteenth century, the bourgeoisie also adapted traditional elite practices to
form a culture of their own. As the new cultural history has demonstrated,
while the aristocracy had cultivated ennui in pastimes that emphasized their
freedom from practical responsibilities, the bourgeoisie developed strategies
for making leisure time, too, productive.

---

[110]This phenomenon is noted by writers on mass culture from Kracauer to Baudrillard. See
also Marcus, *Lipstick Traces.*

[111]This mode of self-identification and -differentiation, which was by no means limited to the
French bourgeoisie, was highly flexible. In presenting Emma's emulation of the aristocracy as de-
ranged mimicry, Flaubert distinguished himself and his reader from such petit-bourgeois folly via
their more truly "aristocratic" form of boredom. It is perhaps no accident that emphatically bour-
geois-hating bourgeoises like Flaubert and Kierkegaard were given to irony.

In *Leisure Settings: Bourgeois Culture, Medicine, and the Spa in Modern France*,[112] Douglas Peter MacKaman describes the "medicalized leisure" of nineteenth-century French spas as a locus of the production of bourgeois identity. At the spa, he argues, "hydrotherapeutics" constructed "a rational and ordered version of leisure practice" for those "with enough social aspirations and money to set out on vacation but lacking fully formed sensibilities regarding the links between leisure and social identity" (119). Unlike the old regime spas, which according to MacKaman had been known as sites of excess, the nineteenth-century spa offered a "regimented and medicalized vacation" that provided a "worthy and respectable" holiday for the bourgeoisie. Such medically supervised leisure, he argues, played a crucial role in the evolution of bourgeois culture by educating the newly monied in the art of consumption while providing them with the certainty of time (and money) well spent. The controlled setting of the spa hence helped to form bourgeois identity around a new ideal of pleasurable but not frivolous consumption. According to MacKaman, by the mid-1860's, those visiting spas without taking a cure outnumbered those who were, a change that reflected an increase in less well-to-do visitors (118). The latter came to be seen but also to watch, and thereby to learn "the cultural tactics necessary to live after a solidly bourgeois fashion," that is, to engage in "conspicuous but controlled consumption" (123). MacKaman argues that spas became a crucial site for the dissemination of bourgeois identity "because leisure—that hard-to-understand matrix of time, space, and status—was at their very essence" (153) and because they promised social mobility (and could deliver at least the temporary illusion of possibilities beyond one's reach at home). Like the bourgeois medicalized vacationers before them, the clerks and shop-girls hoping for something better came to the spas to make productive use of newfound leisure time.[113]

But the democratization of leisure in the course of the nineteenth century was by no means a univocal development. While it arguably marked an increase in quality of life for large portions of the population, it was inextricably linked to impoverishment for others, for the transformations with which it was associated brought massive socio-economic and cultural dislocation in their wake. Furthermore, and most importantly from our point of view, in the institutions and practices of modern leisure, subjectivity was literally being remade. The democratization of leisure is a sociological correlate of the democratization of skepticism. It was not simply that as the market in

---

[112] All citations in this paragraph are to this text.

[113] MacKaman notes that although the middle classes also traveled to other locales, "the vast growth of the spa industry in this period, more than anything else, testifies to the rise of the middle-class vacation" (123).

lowbrow versions of cultural and social practices like spa vacations burgeoned, bourgeois strategies of self-definition through the proper deployment of desire were undermined. As aesthetics, pleasure, and consumption—the occupations of the aristocracy and of artists—began to play a greater role in everyday bourgeois life, the limits of the productivist paradigm became apparent. And since the notion that time was to be used and not wasted was fundamental to bourgeois identity, disoccupation and leisure fed an increasingly widespread sense of the meaninglessness of existence.[114] The contradictions internal to the bourgeois conception of leisure became evident within the democratized discourse on boredom.

In *The Railway Journey*, Wolfgang Schivelbusch links boredom to the transformation of subjective experience wrought by "the industrialization of time and space" fostered by the railroad network built during the nineteenth century.[115] The railways speeded urbanization, facilitated industrialization by making production for distant markets efficient, and democratized travel.[116] The network of railway lines, Schivelbusch argues, materially instantiated the rationalized modern understanding of space that corresponded to the radically new experience of time which had been inaugurated by train travel. Adapting to a world rendered smaller yet far less safe by the speed of the new form of transportation also required a revolution in human perception that, he argues, amounted to a transformation of subjectivity as momentous as the external changes. *The Railway Journey* argues that the experience of train travel itself presented perceptual, social, and nervous challenges to the human organism. It shows that the standardization of time enforced by the exigencies of railroad technology had even wider-ranging effects on human existence.

Schivelbusch conceives of the human adaptation to train travel in Benjaminian terms, as a process of adjusting to a form of existence that amounts to a series of perceptual shocks. The phenomenological transformation associated with the nineteenth-century railway journey, epitomized by the refrain of passengers that they felt like packages, demonstrates for him how the punctual form of experience, Benjamin's "Erlebnis," has displaced historically articu-

---

[114]That bourgeois women, who were so to speak by occupation disoccupied, suffered en masse from nervous complaints in this period substantiates this observation—one must only keep in mind that complaints about the senselessness of such a life were not permitted them. For a stunning depiction of this circumstance, see Charlotte Perkins' 1899 story "The Yellow Wallpaper."

[115]*The Railway Journey: The Industrialization of Time and Space in the Nineteenth Century.* Citations in the paragraphs that follow refer to this text.

[116]In the first instance, democratization means the extension of travel beyond those who had means of their own or could afford to hire coaches. As MacKaman notes, a genuinely broad democratization of "travel and vacationing" did not occur "until the government of the Popular Front guaranteed holidays to French workers in 1936" (123).

lated "Erfahrung." For Benjamin, the continual nervous traumas to which the modern city dweller is subjected are not only exhausting but also produce anxiety and melancholy because they demand a level of generalized attention that can only be sustained at the cost of the perception of particulars.[117] Schivelbusch expands on this perspective, arguing that the "industrialization of space and time" in the nineteenth century produced the need for new forms of perception to accommodate the shock-structure of everyday life in a world where trauma had become the norm. This argument, while intriguing, accepts many of the premises of the medicalized discourse on subjective malaise, even as it attempts to construe their discursive connections to industrialization.[118] Schivelbusch explains the perceptual transformations associated with modernization in fundamentally materialist terms, yet within his account of the cultural effects of railway travel, the topos of boredom points to the insufficiency of reductive explanations of human malaise.[119]

Train travel, according to Schivelbusch, produced perceptual crises in those accustomed to the slower pace of the horse and buggy.[120] "Dullness and boredom resulted from attempts to carry the perceptual apparatus of traditional travel, with its intense appreciation of landscape, over to the railway" (58). Schivelbusch extends Dolf Sternberger's conception of panoramic vision[121] to explain this phenomenon. Industrialized travel, he argues, made it impossible to engage in the world through which one was moving by gazing at particular objects steadily over long periods of time. Those accustomed to

[117]See "Über einige Motive in Baudelaire," 103. Benjamin's conception can be traced to the essay by Georg Simmel that will be examined in Chapter 4.

[118]In particular, it depends on Freud's extremely influential account (in *Beyond the Pleasure Principle*) of the relations between anxiety, fear, and trauma. For a critical account of the concept of trauma, see Ruth Leys, *Trauma: A Genealogy*.

[119]For an examination of the industrial shaping of modern subjectivity that focuses not on shock and trauma but rather on the retooling of the perceptual apparatus around the maintenance of attention under the conditions of distraction proper to "modern disciplinary and spectacular culture," see Jonathan Crary's *Suspensions of Perception*. Crary argues that "the emergence of attention as a model of how a subject maintains a coherent and practical sense of the world" must be understood in relation to the requirements of modern "institutional power . . . that perception function in a way that insures a subject is productive, manageable, and predictable, and is able to be socially integrated and adaptive" (4). Unfortunately, Crary does not explore the relations between the late-nineteenth century discourse on attention and the problem of boredom. Indeed, his remark that "new technological forms of boredom" call for further investigations into "the question of how and whether creative modes of trance, inattention, daydream, and fixation can flourish within the interstices" of the technologically guided repetitions that dominate everyday modern life (78) implies that he regards boredom as an extra-discursive reality.

[120]According to Schivelbusch, the lower classes did not suffer from this difficulty in adjusting since they were "unencumbered by memories of previous forms of travel" (66).

[121]As developed in Sternberger's *Panoramen oder Ansichten vom 19. Jahrhundert*.

making such intensive observations while traveling[122] were often literally unable to see anything out the window of the train. To do so, according to
Schivelbusch, it was necessary for the traveler to "ignore . . . the portions of
the landscape that [were] closest to him, and to direct his gaze on the more
distant objects that seem[ed] to pass by more slowly" (56). To fail to adopt
this mode of abstraction was to court fatigue, since "the stimulus increase
produced by increased velocity is experienced as stressful" when travelers
"keep trying to grasp" the objects constantly being left behind (57). Those
who were unable to develop the "panoramic vision" required to transform
the experience of travel into one of an "intrinsically monotonous landscape
brought into an esthetically pleasing perspective by the railroad" (60) suffered from a sense that a journey had become an empty stretch of time to be
endured.[123] Boredom was the fate of those who could not modernize their
ways of seeing in the enforced idleness of the compartment (58).

According to Schivelbusch, entrepreneurs soon recognized a market opportunity in the boredom which arose as a result of this new form of leisure.
Railway libraries and bookshops were established—in the words of Louis
Hachette to facilitate "turning the enforced leisure and the boredom of a
long trip to the enjoyment and instruction of all."[124] The diversion of boredom through the consumption of books took on a life of its own. According
to Schivelbusch,

> Reading while traveling became almost obligatory. The dissolution of reality and
> its resurrection as panorama thus became agents for the total emancipation from
> the traversed landscape: the traveler's gaze could then move into an imaginary
> surrogate landscape, that of his book. (64)

Schivelbusch argues that reading became a substitute for sociality, for the
sheer speed of industrialized travel had eliminated the possibility of that

[122]For examples of such profound appreciation of landscape, see Goethe's *Reise nach Italien*, with its ample commentary on the geological as well as vegetal and human phenomena visible from the coach windows.

[123]Flaubert was among these. "Before a railway journey," according to Schivelbusch, "Flaubert stayed up all night in order to be able to sleep through the journey and not experience it at all" (58). He cites a letter that testifies to the intensity of Flaubert's aversion: "I get so bored on the train that I am about to howl with tedium after five minutes of it. One might think that it's a dog someone has forgotten in the compartment; not at all, it is M. Flaubert, groaning." ("Je me em-bête tellement en chemin de fer qu'au bout de cinq minutes je hurle d'ennui. On croit, dans le wagon, que c'est un chien oublié; pas du tout, c'est M. Flaubert qui soupire." Letter to Charles-Edmond Chojecki, 26 August 1873, *Correspondance IV*, 703.)

[124]Jean Mistler, *La Librairie Hachette de 1826 à nos jours*; cited in Schivelbusch, 66. Although English booksellers had established outposts in railway stations "in the late 1840's," the first such bookstalls opened in France in 1852 (65).

sustained conversational engagement which had characterized traditional travel.[125] The concrete link between the activity of reading and railway travel nicely illustrates how the alienating effects of modernization were correlated with the emergence of consumer society. The secularization and democratization of printed matter—the medium responsible for the first mass-produced commodity, the bible—would be decisive in disseminating mass-produced dreams of earthly happiness.

Hachette's vision of literature as consumer product through which the empty periods of time engendered by "enforced leisure" could be productively filled reflects the bourgeois conception of time, which must be 'used' rather than wasted. Thus while aristocratic ennui could be dissipated by "useless" pastimes whose function was simply to fill the hours, the boredom associated with train travel presented a market for travel books and better literature.[126] The imperative of overcoming ennui through a productive occupation marks the distance from the aristocratic understanding of such disaffection as the natural by-product of a life of leisure. In this case, mere distraction will not suffice, for the experience of boredom exposes as problematic a foundation of bourgeois self-understanding: the conception of time as a collection of inherently meaningless, empty moments whose unity must be constructed by a purposive activity. Not to pass time per se, but to forestall the confrontation with the limits of such an understanding of time, does the consumption of diversions come to play such a crucial role in the psychic economy of modern subjectivity. We shall return to the question of the structural relation between boredom and this conception of time—which, as I have already shown, can be traced to the Enlightenment vision of history—in Chapter 5. Here, our interest is primarily directed toward the legacy of romantic strategies for overcoming the experience of disaffection itself. Literary production and consumption alike involved the cultivation of dreamworlds through which the desire for meaning that arose through this emptying of temporality could be quenched, at least imaginatively.

The boredom of the railway compartment may be taken as a synecdoche for the broader effects of what Schivelbusch refers to as the industrialization of time and what we have already discussed under the aegis of the disappearance

---

[125] Here too he makes an exception for the lower classes, asserting that "[t]he primitive, spacious third- and fourth-class carriages into which the proletarian traveling public was crowded characteristically promoted continuous communication" (67).

[126] This would change, of course, but in France, it took more than ten years before newspaper sales overtook those of books. According to Schivelbusch, "in contrast to the supply of trashy mass literature in the regular bookstores," both English and French railway stalls offered "highly respectable" works (66).

of experience. The complex links between travel, reading, and boredom illustrate that it is no mere metaphor to speak of the democratization of boredom in this period. Ironically, the solution held out by the paperback industry to the rapidly expanding reading public ended by deepening the pervasive sense of the boredom and monotony of everyday life: by contrast with the dramatically eventful world of novels, real life can only appear banal. Furthermore, although reading may defer boredom by filling the time that cannot be used productively in the ordinary sense, because it is a contemplative activity, it cannot guarantee an escape. In fact, like travel, it may foster the most insidious sort of ennui, in which people begin to reflect on the senselessness of the ways they ordinarily spend their time. Where productive occupations are held to be the cure for boredom, where mere distraction will not suffice, the danger of falling prey to metaphysical pessimism looms. To succumb, it is by no means necessary to read texts that thematize this "philosophical" dimension of experience. Popular romances, as Madame Bovary's ennui attests, can also foster a longing for world-transforming meaning. These imagined worlds can generate further desires, desires that underline rather than ameliorate the boredom of ordinary existence. This dynamic, which is fundamental to mass culture, would only be exacerbated in the years to come.

As the reading public expanded, the romantic vocabulary of subjective malaise spread, bearing with it a new rhetoric of reflection in which the awareness of being modern became democratically accessible. The poor reputation of novels in the nineteenth century reflects the fact that literature was the vehicle of this contagion. If novels were held to have a pernicious effect on the morals of their (female) readers, then in part, at least, because even as the religious understanding of human existence lost its hegemony in the face of larger developments in modern culture, novel-reading helped to foster a new consciousness of self and of subjective individuation. This consciousness was then, in turn, articulated through the vocabulary developed in novels.[127] As the language of ennui was democratized in the course of the nineteenth century, so too was a way of thinking about the self that was recognizably modern.[128]

---

[127] Despite the questionable empirical value of the widespread allegations that Werther's suicide had spawned youthful imitators throughout Europe, they surely demonstrate that the characteristically romantic blurring between imagination and reality was not limited to literature. From an historical point of view, their sheer frequency attests to the paradigmatic status of literary representations in shaping subjective experience.

[128] James Smith Allen has shown that this statement holds for the lower classes as well. "Romanticism saw the beginning of a new literature, a new popular culture, and perhaps even a new mind-frame for many ordinary men and women, in Paris at least." As a consequence of romanticism, he writes, "the middling and lower classes shared values and attitudes far more in

Focusing on the discursive dimension of this paradigm shift has an historiographical advantage. If the dissemination of the discourse on boredom is emphasized, it becomes possible to speak about the historical efficacy of literature without appealing (à la Kuhn or his predecessor Brierre) to putative relationships between fictional representations of ennui and their creators' and readers' states of mind. In this period of rapid social change, uncertainty, anxiety, and disenchantment were understandably rampant. At the same time, the discourse of reflection upon subjective malaise was undergoing profound transformations. The dual revolution fostered a new consciousness about the relationship between subjective experience and cultural modernization and spurred the development of political, scientific, and secular explanations of the ennui that seemed the inevitable companion to progress. The preoccupations of romantic literature—the relation between the individual and society, between heart and mind, between self and the divine—corresponded to ongoing concerns in contemporary life and society. The role played by literary representations in contemporary accounts of the spread of ennui points to the crucial contribution made by literary language to the emergence of a modern idiom of reflection upon subjective experience.

A demeanor toward historical reality so pervasive as to constitute a form of life, the boredom that according to Walter Benjamin took on epidemic proportions in the 1840's was by no means exclusive to a spiritual elite. Boredom was becoming genuinely democratized, spreading to a far wider group during the Bourgeois Monarchy and virtually everyone under the Second Empire. Ironically, the very writers who proclaimed their blaséness as a hallmark of subjective distinction were often dependent upon this literary market for their livelihood. The architects of the modern discourse on boredom were acutely aware of this circumstance. Baudelaire's *Flowers of Evil* were proffered to his (male) readers with a strange and bitter gesture of identification. *Madame Bovary*—itself a great popular success in large part due to the scandal it caused as a purportedly immoral book—comments directly on the fact that the experience of boredom and the associated claim to spiritual distinction had trickled down to the lower middle classes in general and women in particular. Written after, but set in the years just before, 1848, Flaubert's novel depicts the boredom of the petit-bourgeois housewife whose role was defined by nonproductive consumption. In the figure of Léon, whose taste for adventure was eclipsed by the utilitarian demands of business

---

keeping [than their predecessors'—EG] with the self-assertion that made possible a new political and social system in the nineteenth century" (Allen 1981, 238).

life, it also illustrates the boredom that plagued the emerging class of white collar workers in attendance on the modern bureaucratic apparatus.

As I have already suggested, the spread of boredom to the lower classes during the second half of the nineteenth century is attested less by the increase in factory labor—though certainly tedious it was often too dangerous and always too exhausting really to be boring—than by the exponential growth of mass entertainments in this period. The modern forms of distraction that emerged during the Second Empire existed in relation to an experience of time radically different from the cyclical temporality of rural working class life.[129] As a paradoxical consequence of the industrial and bureaucratic regimentation of work in modern urban society, leisure time, too, had been democratized. And like reading, the diversions of the masses—Sunday outings, café concerts, the 'cinema of attractions'—should not be seen as simply compensating for the tedium of everyday occupations in a rationalized economy by canalizing it into consumption. These practices of leisure stood in complex relation to visions of alternative lives, so that here too, imagined worlds generated desires that underlined the boredom of ordinary existence. The democratization of leisure thus fostered the further diffusion of the new rhetoric of reflection on subjective experience: as modern mass culture emerged, the romantic ideal of individual self-realization spread throughout society.

Although 'ennui' had belonged to a secular language of interiority since at least the seventeenth century, it was this post-romantic development that definitively severed the experience from its religious overtones. As the etymological evidence considered at the beginning of this chapter attested, 'nothingness' and 'emptiness' had taken on new, more material meanings—and thereby become accessible to modernity's very material "solutions." Thus while the reading public continued to grow (particularly with the ascendance of affordable newspapers in the 1860's), romantic ennui threatened to become a cliché. The genre that provided the livelihood for the majority of nineteenth-century Parisian writers, the serialized novel, depended upon sensationalism to dispel the very material threat of readerly boredom.

The literary discourse on boredom had inherited the romantic project of establishing the spiritual superiority of an elite of sensitive souls who suffered from the meaninglessness of modern existence, who rejected progress and utilitarianism, and who could find succor only in Art. However, my discus-

---

[129]See Jacques LeGoff, E. P. Thompson, "Time, Work-Discipline, and Industrial Capitalism," and Moishe Postone, *Time, Labor, and Social Domination: A Reinterpretation of Marx's Critical Theory*. For a recent work that calls the Marxist account of temporal modernization into question, see Dohrn-van Rossum, *Die Geschichte der Stunde: Uhren und moderne Zeitordnungen* [*History of the Hour: Clocks and Modern Temporal Orders.*]

sions of Brierre, Lamartine, and Tardieu demonstrated that, its aristocratic origins notwithstanding, the language of ennui had been imbued with the very Enlightenment values such writers wanted to reject. Severed from the romantic longing for lost wholeness, avowals of boredom expressed a neo-Pyrrhonic resignation to the inalterable disenchantment of modern life. Attempts to make leisure productive fostered the very ennui they were meant to dispel. And by the mid-nineteenth century, literary boredom was an imitation confronted by the imitation of an imitation in the form of the petty bourgeois malaise of its readership. As Flaubert's own ironic depiction of the democratized version of such a retreat into aestheticism attested, ennui and romantic longings for meaning could too easily be transmuted into moral dissolution and mobilized for capitalist purposes. These bitter realities only exacerbated the philosophical pessimism to which the enlightened heirs of romanticism were prone anyway. For them, the pervasiveness of boredom in modern life signaled the ultimate ascendance of a materialist and irreligious vision of human being and the defeat of a vision of selfhood centered on genuineness of feeling. Thus in post-romantic thought, the nihilistic dynamic of the experience of boredom is elevated to a metanarrative about the inhuman consequences of historical progress itself.

In examining two authors whose writings epitomize this modern, post-romantic discourse on boredom, I shall focus on the historically specific ways in which they represent subjective malaise. Both Baudelaire and Flaubert's texts provide ample evidence of the broader discursive developments toward a disenchanted language of reflection in this period. However, my readings will concentrate not on the ways their strategies of representation are typical but rather on the ways in which literary language synthesizes new possibilities for reflection on modern experience. Although contextualization and historical analysis can demonstrate that literature has a privileged role in the discourse on boredom, only close reading can elaborate the nature of that role.[130] The peculiar status of romantic literary figures and the associated blurring of the line between fiction and reality is thematized in *Madame Bovary* as a phenomenon of both historical and philosophical interest. Similarly, Baudelaire evokes the fragmented world of modern Paris in ways that illuminate the oscillation between fantasy and despair, hope and nihilism proper to modern subjectivity. In exploring the temporal nature of the desiring self, the literature of boredom discloses entirely new possibilities for

---

[130] In *Dead Time: Temporal Disorders in the Wake of Modernity*, Elissa Marder subtly demonstrates how careful readings of Baudelaire and Flaubert can illuminate the temporal intricacies of modern experience from a psychoanalytically inflected perspective.

writing modern experience. Readings of literary representations of ennui can therefore disclose the intimate relation between the institution of literature and the modes of reflection on the self that constituted modern subjectivity.

Neither Gustave Flaubert nor Charles Baudelaire failed to perceive the urgency of the crisis of meaning that confronted the modern subject in the form of the experience of ennui. However, unlike Kierkegaard or Schopenhauer, these writers located the poetry of ennui firmly within the world. For them, affirming boredom as the ineluctable fate of the modern subject is the beginning of a critical appropriation of historical reality. In refusing to idealize boredom, they renounce not simply the hope of overcoming fragmentation in self-transcendent spirituality but the romantic structure of desire as such. Indeed, in their writings, the affirmation of boredom stands for a refusal to succumb to melancholic longings for meaning in a world disenchanted by reflection and modernization. For both Flaubert and Baudelaire, ennui reflects the skeptical dilemma of the modern subject; representations of the experience serve both formally and thematically to engage their readers in reflection on the problems of modern life and modern art. In *Madame Bovary* and in Baudelaire's poetry, 'ennui' thus becomes a synecdoche for the dilemma of the modern subject caught between the infinite, romantic longing for meaning and the sober reflection of disenchanted rationality.

Madame Bovary: Boredom and the Crisis of Romantic Self-Reflection

"What seems beautiful to me, what I should like to write, is a book about nothing." Thus did Gustave Flaubert, at the outset of what would become nearly five excruciating and laborious years immersed in imagining the inner life of a petit-bourgeois romantic, describe his artistic ideal in a letter to his lover. In such a book, "held together by the internal strength of its style . . . the subject would be almost invisible."[131] As the epic of modern boredom, *Madame Bovary* both succeeded and failed in realizing Flaubert's ideal. It succeeded insofar as he achieved his stylistic aim of giving to prose "the consistency of verse"[132] by fusing "the double abyss of lyricism and vulgarity . . . in analytic narrative."[133] It failed, however, insofar as the very act of writing

---

[131]Letter to Louise Colet, January 16, 1852 (*Correspondance II*, 31). According to Harry Levin, who sets the dramatic date as 1837–47, Flaubert worked on the novel from Fall 1851 to Spring 1856 (Levin, 260). Madame Bovary was published as a book in April 1857.

[132]Letter to Louise Colet, July 22, 1852; *Correspondance II*, 135.

[133]Letter to Louise Colet, March 20–21, 1852; *Correspondance II*, 57. (". . . dans une analyse narrative.")

elevated its deliberately insignificant subject out of nothingness. Emma Bovary—marooned in the provinces and longing for Paris, prone heart, soul, and body to the whims of fashion, full of virulent, unsatisfied desires, choked by petty despairs—became the prototypical bored subject. Or perhaps this was, indeed, success: a book about nothing. Not, however, as many of Flaubert's admirers have claimed, because Emma herself was really so insignificant but rather because *Madame Bovary* made the nothingness at the heart of desire into an object of knowledge—and thus turned "analytic narrative" into modern epic.

Madame Bovary relates how a romantic subject comes to grief. Emma's tragedy is brought on by her excessive faith in the power of desire to render life meaningful; she dies lonely and despairing, yet superior even in her anguish to those hardier and meaner beings who surround her and who she believes have made her life unlivable. If she suffers from delusions of grandeur, Emma's ennui is nonetheless a sign of her spiritual distinction: her longing for something greater makes the sheer ordinariness of her existence unbearable for her. However, *Madame Bovary* is narrated from a perspective that can by no means be called entirely sympathetic to her plight. Emma's most intimate thoughts and desires are related with an ironic disdain that renders her by turns poignant and ludicrous. Thus it is as the object as well as the subject of boredom that Flaubert's Emma Bovary epitomizes the dilemma of the modern subject, for whom desire has come unhinged from the narratives that once rendered life meaningful. Her tragedy exemplifies the fate of that subject, adrift in a world without God, without History, without hope.

In the crucible of an unprecedented stylistic purity, *Madame Bovary* transmutes quotidian suffering into exemplarity, rendering Emma's ennui at once absolutely historically specific and transcendently universal. For the reader capable of appreciating style as "an absolute manner of seeing,"[134] Flaubert's writing demonstrates how literature can embody the double consciousness of the enlightened subject. His sentences represent Emma's experience with absolute fidelity, even empathy, yet mercilessly dissect the terms in which she understands it. The result is a novel in which the heroine's ennui is at once hackneyed and significant, in which deeply felt romantic reveries are simultaneously laughable—a book torn between diffuse affection for its hapless subject and ruthless condemnation of her superficiality. *Madame Bovary* both illustrates and critiques the way the romantic language of reflection creates something—ennui—out of the nothingness of longing. In

---

[134]Letter to Louise Colet, January 16, 1852; *Correspondance II*, 31.

this sense, this work, which reflects on the cultural construction of an experience that is lived in ahistorical, metaphysical terms, is indeed a book about nothing.

My reading of this much-read novel draws upon opposing traditions of interpretation, treating *Madame Bovary* as at once modernist and realist. It brings close reading into conversation with discourse analysis by examining how the metaphorics of boredom both represent and construct subjective experience in the novel. Taking the historical specificity of the idiom in which Emma's malaise is expressed into account, I argue, brings the full complexity of the conception of the relation between language and experience, fiction and reality that constitutes *Madame Bovary* into focus. If this novel is, as Flaubert put it, "above all a work of criticism, or rather of anatomy,"[135] then because his stylistic strategies are imbricated with the very particular historical reality of the discourse on boredom. Emma's boredom is a literary construct both in the sense that it is an artifact of Flaubert's writing and in the sense that it comes into being through her attempt to live out the romantic narratives she consumes. Through the use of indirect free style, Flaubert makes Emma's boredom into an object of knowledge, evoking her malaise in a way that provokes reflection on how language constitutes interiority. By underlining the writtenness of Emma's experience, the novel also suggests the complexity of the relations between literature and life. But if the mode of narration directs the reader's attention to the discursive construction of subjective experience, the language of boredom emphasizes the historical specificity of that construction. *Madame Bovary* is, finally, "about nothing" because it anatomizes a world to which ennui seems to be the only adequate response—a world where love and hope refer only to the lack at the heart of the desiring subject, where the longing for meaning has been instrumentalized into fraudulence and hollow illusion.

In a stunning short chapter that critically illuminates the formation of her character, Flaubert sketches Emma's formation as a romantic subject. A daughter of the provinces, she had gone at puberty to be educated in a convent. In this setting, she was "far from being bored at first," for the convent not only provided intellectual stimulation but also provoked her sensuality and sentimental tendencies: "She was softly lulled by the mystic languor exhaled in the perfumes of the altar . . . she loved the sick lamb . . . or the poor Jesus sinking beneath the cross . . . When she went to confession, she invented little sins in order that she might stay there longer."[136] From the be-

---

[135]Letter to Louise Colet, January 2, 1854; *Correspondance II*, 497.

[136]I cite from the "substantially revised" version of Eleanor Marx Aveling's English translation

ginning, the narrator insinuates that Emma's spontaneous emotional responses are tinged with speciousness—that her romantic religiosity consists in artifice parading as impulse. Furthermore, despite her apparent piousness and affinity for the "sonorous lamentations of romantic melancholy" in Chateaubriand, Emma's distinctively bourgeois eroticism was already pronounced: "She had to gain some personal profit from things and she rejected as useless whatever did not contribute to the immediate satisfaction of her heart's desires" (63–64/26). At fifteen, she was thus ripe for introduction to the novels which would provide the secular components of her emotional vocabulary:

> love, lovers, sweethearts, persecuted ladies fainting in lonely pavilions . . . somber forests, heart-aches, vows, sobs, tears and kisses, little boatrides by moonlight, nightingales in shady groves, gentlemen brave as lions, gentle as lambs, virtuous as no one ever was, always well dressed and weeping like fountains. (64/26)

Her mother dies, and Emma responds in the mode of a romantic heroine, weeping for days on end and expressing her desire to be buried in the same grave. Although, as the narrator does not neglect to inform us, "Emma was secretly pleased that she had reached at a first attempt the rare ideal of delicate lives, never attained by mediocre hearts" (67/27), "she was soon bored but would not admit it." Having kept up the charade of romantic reverie out of "habit" and "vanity" until every shred of feeling had been consumed (67/28), Flaubert writes, her nature finally "rebelled against the mysteries of faith as it had rebelled against discipline, as something alien to her constitution," and Emma returned home. There, according to the narrator, she soon developed the conviction that she was "quite disillusioned, with nothing more to learn, and nothing more to feel" (68/28).

In emphasizing how Emma's malaise is constituted out of clichés, the enlightened voice of the narrator renders her romantic melancholy ludicrous. But Flaubert's mode of narration also makes his ironic portrait of the protagonist a more global indictment of modern habits of self-understanding. Not only, through the use of indirect free style to simultaneously depict and criticize the linguistic and particularly the literary construction of her experience, does the novel make Emma the vessel for an indictment of romanticism in general. Her story also becomes the basis for a dissection (in the words of the subtitle) of the "moeurs de province," for the terms in which

---

by Paul de Man (with Patricia K. de Man). Parenthetical references give the French text (Paris: Editions Gallimard, 1972) and then the English. Here: 63/25. I have occasionally made modifications to the translation; where these seemed significant, I have provided the original text in a footnote.

she is presented imply that the societal values of the Bourgeois Monarchy make it impossible to cultivate genuine interiority. In becoming clichés, the romantic ideals with which Flaubert himself ambivalently identified[137] come to signify the very thing they were meant to oppose—the artificiality of modern life as a whole. Although Madame Bovary indeed longs for greater things, her world has provided only a hackneyed and melodramatic vocabulary for her aspirations. In tracking the fate of this language through Emma's pursuit of religion, love, and the beautiful things she regards as the trappings of happiness, Flaubert shows how romantic subjectivity takes on the traits of a mass-produced, alienated identity. Narrated from a point of view at once imbricated in and critical of Emma's way of understanding the world, this account is at once historical analysis and philosophical critique of Emma's attempt to live a meaningful life.

Emma marries Charles Bovary in a misguided attempt to realize her ideal of romantic love and thereby overcome her disillusionment with her station in life. However, her husband is prosaic and unambitious; she finds him unworthy of her admiration. Despite his inchoate joy and adoring devotion to his lovely and elegant young wife, it is soon clear to the reader that all of his efforts to make her happy will be of no avail, for Charles' love eschews the vocabulary of romantic excess. Their marriage, lacking the atmosphere and trappings of her fictionally induced fantasies, inevitably disappoints her.

> Before marriage she thought herself in love; but since the happiness that should have followed failed to come, she must, she thought, have been mistaken. And Emma tried to find out what one meant exactly in life by the words *bliss, passion, ecstasy*, that had seemed to her so beautiful in books. (61/24)

Slyly thematizing the writtenness of *Madame Bovary*, Flaubert underlines the distance between literature and life while presenting his protagonist's emotional life as a sort of literary construct. As a fictional character whose every experience is mediated by a literary language of desire—a vocabulary whose metaphors may not refer to anything "exactly in life"—she is doubly written. Flaubert fosters ironic reflection on Emma's status as a romantic heroine by showering her with signs that life cannot live up to literature while underlining her passionate determination to make her experience conform to her

---

[137]The accomplishment of *Madame Bovary* may be gauged by the tension between the author's oracular pronouncements that "Emma, c'est moi" and his five agonizing years of labor on a novel in which "nothing in the book is drawn from myself" (Letter to Louise Colet, April 6, 1853; *Correspondance II*, 297). Perhaps it is true that Flaubert was 'assigned' the topic of provincial adultery by his friend Louis Bouillet in an attempt to quell his excessive romanticism with a tonic of realistic depiction. At any rate, his correspondence attests over and again that in writing *Madame Bovary*, Flaubert undertook to discipline the very tendencies he shared with Emma.

romantic vision of happiness. True to form, Emma will prefer renouncing reality to abandoning her ideals.

Bored and repulsed by the provincial world in which she is condemned to live, Emma loses herself in reveries that Flaubert represents from the intimate distance of indirect speech:

> the nearer things were the more her thoughts turned away from them. All her immediate surroundings, the wearisome [*ennuyeuse*] countryside, the petty-bourgeois stupidity, the mediocrity of existence seemed to her the exception, an exception in which she had been caught by a stroke of fate, while beyond stretched as far as eye could see an immense land of joys and passions. In her wistfulness [*désir*] she confused the sensuous pleasures of luxury with the delights of the heart, elegance of manners with delicacy of sentiment. Did not love, like Indian plants, need a special soil, a special temperature? (91/42)

Although her criticisms of her surround are well founded, Emma's unhappiness is premised on an unrealistic vision of life. Her dreams depend, the narrator implies, on a debased romanticism characterized by a confusion of material and ideal goods, of worldly success with higher things. Thus, barely concealing her disappointment with the reality of her life under a veneer of supercilious blaséness, Emma begins to withdraw into fantasy—or rather, from the narrator's point of view, into cliché. "Although she had no one to write to" she bought an elegant stationery set. "She longed to travel or to go back to her convent. She wanted to die, but she also wanted to live in Paris" (93/43).

Emma's misery at the uneventful nature of her provincial existence grows, and soon she seems to give up even her "waiting in her heart for something to happen" (95/44) and succumb to her fatalistic sense that the identical series of days "would keep following one another, always the same, immovable, and bringing nothing new" forever (96/45). As ennui overwhelms her, she gradually abandons her interests in music, books, and the household; she even neglects to cultivate her own beauty, spending "whole days without dressing" and "growing difficult, capricious" (99–100/47). Emma's second withdrawal from life into boredom and disenchantment is accompanied by a sort of moral decay: "She no longer concealed her contempt for anything or anybody and at times expressed singular opinions, finding fault with whatever others approved and approving things perverse and immoral" (100–101/48). Her secret desires grow ever more fervid—"she longed for lives of adventure . . . for masked balls, for shameless pleasures that were bound, she thought, to initiate her to ecstasies she had not yet experienced"—and she begins to develop the corresponding neurasthenic symptoms—fevers, torpors, palpitations (101/48). Charles dully but not inaccurately links her illness "to some local cause" and contemplates moving to another town; having heard this, Flaubert writes, "from that moment she drank vinegar to lose weight, contracted a sharp little cough, and lost all appetite" (101/48). Like so many real bourgeois housewives in the nineteenth century, Emma is soon diagnosed with "une maladie nerveuse" which her loving husband is advised to remedy with "a change of air" (101/48).

Upon moving not to Paris but to another, slightly larger, provincial town in the vicinity of Rouen, Emma meets a man after her own heart. Léon is a clerk whose ennui appears to her a sign of superiority. Their initial conversation, composed entirely of romantic clichés about travel, sunsets, music, and books, ends with a passage that anticipates the fate of what will turn out to be more than a friendship. Léon, who likes to cry over books, prefers poetry to prose, but Emma declares:

> 'But with time one tires of that. I have come to love stories that rush breathlessly along, that frighten one. I detest commonplace heroes and moderate feelings, as one finds them in nature.'
> 'You are right,' observed the clerk, 'since these works fail to touch the heart, they miss, it seems to me, the true end of art. It is so sweet, amid all the disenchantments of life, to be able to dwell in thought upon noble characters, pure affections, and pictures of happiness. For myself, living here far from the world, this is my one distraction. But there is so little to do in Yonville!' (122/59)

Léon's sentimentality already seems innocent by comparison with the grim intimation in Emma's words of a violent and unruly temperament satiated with romantic images of love and happiness—the temperament that, prone to ennui and desiring the stimulation of change at any cost, will bring Emma to grief.

Léon soon commences to love her from afar, without hope. "But by thus renouncing her, he made her ascend to extraordinary heights." The narrator, a Freudian *avant-le-lettre*, implies that romantic self-sacrifice is an alibi for narcissism. Transforming Emma into a "winged apotheosis," Léon's love for her, as the narrator acerbically remarks, "was one of those pure feelings that do not interfere with life, that are cultivated for their rarity, and whose loss would afflict more than their fulfillment rejoices" (151/76). Léon's romantic cultivation of sentiment is incipiently bourgeois, a mannered diversion from his bureaucratic career that he seems certain to outgrow when he moves to Paris. Emma, however, soon throws herself wholeheartedly into the drama of illicit and impossible love; growing thin and pensive, she cuts a romantic figure, enchanting the entire town with her ladylike bearing and beauty.

"But," the narrator declares, "she was eaten up with desires, with rage, with hate" (152/77). Emma is in open rebellion against her petit-bourgeois existence. The seeds have been sown for her fall from virtue, though at this point she finds solace in a similarly narcissistic fantasy of doomed and secret love that temporarily alleviates her ennui. This fantasy succeeds, so to speak, in turning boredom back into melancholy by reintroducing the longing for a lost love. But such romantic emotions are not, Flaubert suggests, compatible with real life interactions with the beloved. Emma "sought solitude that she might more easily delight in his image. His physical presence troubled the voluptuousness of this meditation" (152/77). Her own virtuousness in re-buffing Léon becomes a source of pride for her. Unfortunately, the consola-tion of "look[ing] at herself in the mirror striking resigned poses" is too slight. "Then," Flaubert writes, "the desires of the flesh, the longing for money, and the melancholy of passion all blended into one suffering, and in-stead of putting it out of her mind, she made her thoughts cling to it" (152/77). Everything annoys Emma and aggravates her nerves, and she culti-vates the state of dramatic agitation proper to a heroine condemned by fate to live in inappropriate circumstances.[138]

In Madame Bovary, romantic interiority emerges as a function of sensual, rather than spiritual, longings; her imagination, rather than rendering the in-effable more concrete, places ideals at the service of the body. If Léon's ro-manticism is a clerk's pretentious pastime that does not interfere with workaday bourgeois existence, Emma's is an ideology in the making, an imaginary compensation for all that life has failed to provide her in the way of meaning, pleasure, and adventure. Once Léon leaves for Paris, her fanta-sies intensify, but so does her frustration: "Her desires, increased by regret, became only the more acute. Henceforth the memory of Léon was at the center of her boredom" (172/88). His image becomes the counterpoint to her disaffection with the reality of her life; nonetheless, without her quite realiz-ing it is happening, his memory fades, the melancholic longing is effaced, and "the evil days of Tostes began again" (173/89). Her life is once again permeated by nameless malaise.

The narrator emphasizes how Emma, convinced that she has made tre-

---

[138]The outcome of what the narrator represents as Emma's narcissistic obsession with her own unhappiness is a scapegoating of her husband: "What exasperated her was that Charles did not seem to be aware of her torment. His conviction that he was making her happy looked to her a stupid insult. . . . [H]e became the butt of all the hatred resulting from her frustrations" (153/77). Her indignation and hatred would provide Emma with the excuse she needed to disregard her husband's devoted if inadequate love for her as she solipsistically pursued her idea of happiness.

mendous sacrifices, begins to indulge her every whim, spending money on gowns and trinkets, beginning to learn Italian, to make lace, to read history and philosophy and then dropping each occupation as quickly as she has begun it. Her ennui permeates everything, and her nervous symptoms worsen. At this juncture, she meets Rodolphe, a roguish pseudo-aristocrat who recognizes her vulnerability and sets out to exploit it. From the outset he comprehends her misery in the crudest of terms. Her husband must repel her. "How bored she gets! How she'd want to be in the city and go dancing every night! . . . She is gaping after love like a carp . . ." (180/93). Although he too speaks the longed-for language of books, there is none of Léon's naïveté in his words. When she laments that living in the countryside "nothing is worth while," he assents: "to think that not one of these people is capable of understanding even the cut of a coat" (190/99). For Rodolphe, all value is utilitarian, and romantic language is a mere means to an end. The desire for transcendence evident in Emma's lament is inaudible to him.

In the famous seduction scene at the agricultural fair, Rodolphe shamelessly exploits the romantic clichés dear to Emma's heart, avowing that he has only lacked someone who loves him to make him achieve something great. While the drama of mutual solipsism played out with Léon had assured that their flights of sentiment were confined to vague reveries of better things, Rodolphe aims directly at her sensuality. He attacks bourgeois respectability; passion is the source of everything that is fine in life. As the councilor recites his paean to the virtues of the rural population and their contributions to civilization, Rodolphe expolodes: "'Duty, duty!' ah! By Jove! as if one's real duty were not to feel what is great, cherish the beautiful, and not accept all the conventions of society with the hypocrisy it forces upon us" (197/104). Against Emma's pallid defense that one must "to some extent bow to the opinion of the world and accept its morality" he proclaims the superiority of another, "eternal" morality of nature. As M. Lieuvain drones on about "the uses of agriculture," Rodolphe draws closer, whispering in Emma's ear of the "conspiracy of society" in terms to which she is especially vulnerable.

> The noblest instincts, the purest feelings are persecuted, slandered; and if at length two poor souls do meet, all is organized in such a way as to keep them from becoming one. Yet they will try, they will call to each other. Not in vain . . . sooner or later . . . they will come together in love; for fate has decreed it, and they are born for each other. (199–200/105)

The narrator ironically underlines that Emma loses her head over these clichés not because she finds Rodolphe himself irresistible but because he reminds her of a Viscount with whom she once had waltzed, because she thinks of Léon. It is pleasant to have him near her, but the romantic platitudes he deploys gain their effect because the ground has already been prepared. The text continues: "The sweetness of this sensation revived her past desires," which stirred and swirled within her soul, and the seducer pushes his advantage, taking her hand and avowing that fate has brought them irresistibly together. Rodolphe's cynical manipulation of Emma—presenting her with the trappings of romantic passion to exploit what he sees as her need to escape from her boredom with her marriage—will succeed, but in a way that ironically implies her spiritual superiority over him.

After they make love for the first time, Emma finds her image in the mirror "transfigured" and delights at the "idea" that she has a lover, Flaubert writes, as in a "second puberty" (219/117). "So at last she was to know those joys of love, that fever of happiness of which she had despaired! She was entering upon a marvelous world where all would be passion, ecstasy, delirium." Despite the silliness of her vision of herself as romantic heroine, Emma is living for her ideal. While Rodolphe callously manipulates her emotions, she persists in viewing their affair as a way of living out her youthful dreams; for Emma, physical passion is a cipher for higher things. Her lover finds her sentimental, yet captivating:

> This love without debauchery was something new for him. . . . Although his bourgeois common sense disdained them, deep down in his heart, Emma's exaltations seemed charming, since they were directed his way. Then, sure of her love, he no longer made an effort, and insensibly his manner changed. (228–29/122)

Rodolphe soon ceases to speak to her and to caress her with the delicacy he had feigned to flatter Emma's idea of herself; revealing his coarseness and indifference, the narrator remarks, "he subjugated her" (229/123).

Emma is miserable anew; she attempts to free herself by transforming her husband into a worldly success and hence a worthy object of her love. When her scheme fails, Emma is furious with Charles for his very existence, which she blames for having ruined her life. The narrator is particularly cutting in describing the consequence:

> She repented of her past virtue as of a crime, and what still remained of it crumbled away beneath the furious blows of her pride. She reveled in all the evil ironies of triumphant adultery. The memory of her lover came back to her with irresistible, dizzying attractions; she threw her whole soul towards this image. (247–48/134)

Once again it is the image of her desire ("a lover") rather than the reality of Rodolphe's person that draws her toward him. Emma is in love with an idea that seems to render her life meaningful; in the narrator's dry words, "their love resumed its course."[139] Now Emma continually calls Rodolphe to her in order "to tell him again how bored she was, that her husband was odious, her existence dreadful" (249/134). Her romantic fantasies have become explicitly compensatory; "her tenderness ... grew daily as her repulsion toward her husband increased" (249/135). She begins to spin elaborate visions of escaping from Yonville with Rodolphe. At this point, her second, even more fateful, "seduction" commences. The draper Lhereux has her in his clutches, for he grants her credit, and "she abandoned herself to this easy way of satisfying all of her whims" (252/136), dressing herself like a courtesan and showering her lover with expensive gifts.

On the eve of their planned elopement, Rodolphe writes her a bathetic letter of regret in which he once again cynically invokes romantic tropes for selfish ends. They must not proceed into the "abyss"; despite his eternal "profound devotion" he is convinced that she would come to regret her decision; he cannot expose her to the persecution and insults of the world. "The mere idea of the grief that would come to you tortures me, Emma. Forget me! ... only fate is to blame!" (268/146). Emma is furious, suicidal, and finally despairing. She grows delirious; "brain fever" sets in, and she withdraws into herself, not speaking or listening, "as if both her body and her soul were resting after all their tribulations" (276/151). In the course of her slow recovery, Charles remains at her side, uncomprehending and unceasingly loyal.

As befits an invalid, Emma once again turns her romantic energies toward the heavens. Flaubert ironically underlines the hollowness of her religious strivings.

> Then a greater bliss existed than happiness, another love beyond all loves, without pause and without end, that would increase forever! ... She wanted to become a saint. She bought rosaries and wore holy medals; she wished to have in her room, by the side of her bed, a reliquary set in emeralds that she might kiss it every evening. (282–83/154)

The narrator accentuates the sensuality of Emma's religious aspirations, skewering her romantic fantasy of herself "seized with the most refined Catholic melancholy that an ethereal soul could conceive" while lying frustrated in bed (284/155). The idealization of her lover that had made his image the avowed center of meaning in her life persists even now. The memory of Rodolphe "locked away in the deepest recesses of her heart" exudes fragrances that,

> penetrating through everything, perfumed with tenderness the immaculate atmosphere in which she longed to live. When she knelt on her Gothic prie-Dieu,

---

[139]Literally, "they began again to love one another"—"Ils recommencèrent à s'aimer" (249/134).

she addressed to the Lord the same suave words that she had murmured formerly to her lover in the outpourings of adultery. It was to bring faith; but no delights ever descended from the heavens, and she arose with fatigued limbs and the vague feeling of an immense fraud. (284/155)

The vocabulary of romantic desire is, Flaubert implies, all too malleable. Enchanted by the phrases she learned from books, Emma is unable to distinguish the longing for God from corporeal desires. Her turn to religion is marred by the fleshliness of her ideals—thus Emma's piety is expressed in consumption, and her spiritual chagrin takes the form of nervous exhaustion. In representing the religious aspirations of a bourgeois temperament that needs "to gain some personal profit from things" (63–64/26), *Madame Bovary*'s "analytic narrative" makes the slippage between romanticism and materialism palpable.

When Emma fails to find what she is seeking in prayer, as she convalesces, her ennui, too, takes on religious form. While before her breakdown, she had fancied herself elevated above bourgeois morality, she now prides herself on her virtuousness, which the narrator insinuates fulfills precisely the same self-indulgent function as the worldly amusements she seems to have forsaken: "She gave herself up to excessive charity"; "it was a choice for resignation, a universal indulgence. Her language with regard to everything was full of idealized phrases" (284–85/155). The moral ambiguity palpable in the "saintly" version of her boredom is viewed within the diegesis as a symptom of her nervous illness, but it is represented to the reader as part of her romantic rebellion against the strictures of provincial existence in general. "[S]he now enveloped everything in such indifference, had such tender phrases and such haughty looks and such changeable ways that one could no longer distinguish egoism from charity, corruption from virtue" (286/156). Emma's romanticism permeates her piety; her entire existence is a pose constructed of mere words in which detachment is another form of prideful self-assertion rather than a humble acquiescence to the disappointments of earthly existence.

After the collapse of her love affair with Rodolphe, exalted boredom and the religious renunciation of happiness became Emma's refuge from a cruel world; her beautiful things, her virtuous reading, her elegant gestures are all means for passing time, for filling up the hours of what seems to her a meaningless and hopeless existence. Now, in her piously inflected indifference, Emma seems actually to live the disillusionment with life she had long affected yet continually belied by her actions. However, her emotional balance is tenuous; Flaubert implies that Catholicism has only provided a temporary guise for her sensuous desires. Emma's need to flee the boredom of her existence will soon reawaken and upset her listless virtuousness. A trip to the theater in Rouen leads to a reunion with Léon and then in rapid succession to Emma's moral degradation, financial ruin, self-abnegation, and suicide.

From this point on, *Madame Bovary* shows how the world draws the consequences of Emma's narcissistic fixation on her own desire by taking its revenge on her lifelong, heedless pursuit of happiness. We need not trace the process by which she and Léon romantically rewrite their pasts, excising their forgetfulness of one another and emphasizing their melancholy longings for higher things, nor detail how the mode in which their affair is narrated exposes the hollowness of their self-understandings as superior beings. What concerns us in *Madame Bovary* is not the progress of the plot but the way the novel represents ennui as the fate of the desiring subject in a world where ideals have no place. From the reader's perspective, that Emma's malaise takes a materialistic form appropriate to a provincial bourgeoise only underlines the generality of the problem of boredom in modernity. As we have seen, her attempts to find happiness began with a rejection of the traditional ends of feminine existence—family, Church, home. Since, all ironic distance from her ideas and behavior notwithstanding, Flaubert presents the world of provincial convention as truly intolerable, the reader has already been drawn toward a sympathetic relation to her fate. As Emma's illusions are stripped away and her aspirations for meaning trampled, her responses hint at inchoate philosophical depths, drawing the reader into reflection on the meaning of desire in a god-forsaken world.

During the third part of the novel, Emma's efforts to realize her romantic ideals grow ever more desperate and more heedless of reality. Ironically, the resulting pain and despair bring her ever closer to the quite unromantic insight that, as the narrator puts it, "speech [*la parole*] is like a rolling machine that always stretches the sentiment it expresses" (309/169) and hence into the proximity of self-reflection on the romantic illusions that have structured her life. In the moment when Emma realizes that her love for Léon is sustained only by habit, Flaubert ironically elevates her above the banal self-absorption that has heretofore characterized her pursuit of her passions. Sitting on a bench in front of her old convent, Emma "envied her first indefinable sentiments of love which she had tried to construct from the books she read." For a moment, Flaubert allows her to glimpse the lineaments of the illusion that has sustained her excesses—the bourgeois confusion between ideal and material goods that was sustained by her romantic conflation of literature and life. The icy irony with which the text usually narrates her paroxysms of despair seems to disappear. As she thinks back over the years, he writes, Léon suddenly seems "as distant from her as the others."

'Still, I love him,' she said to herself.

No matter! she was not happy, she had never been. But where did it come from, that insufficiency of life, that instantaneous rottenness of whatever she leaned upon?[140]

For once Emma does not retreat from the intimation of existential despair into romantic visions of substitute satisfactions. Or rather, she skeptically dismisses the visions that do arise, denying the romantic hope that she might meet a man with "a poet's soul in the form of an angel" in what is almost a philosophical rejection of her sensual idealism.

No, it would never happen! Besides, nothing was worth the trouble of seeking it; everything was a lie! Every smile hid a yawn of boredom, every joy a curse, every pleasure its own disgust; and the sweetest kisses left on your lips only an unattainable desire for a higher ecstasy. (368/206)

Despite the melodramatic form taken by her sentiments, Emma's disillusionment is profound. For the reader familiar with Flaubert's correspondence, this passage resonates with the author's own pronouncements about the impossibility of happiness in bourgeois society and the treachery of physical love. However, unlike her creator, she cannot console herself for life's failure to be as meaningful as literature by making literature into her life. Emma lacks both the inner and the outer resources to withdraw into the ironical renunciation of the world that Flaubert's critical distance from bourgeois values afforded him.[141] On the contrary, what defines her as a character makes her disillusionment both inevitable and inescapable: without the capacity to reflect on the language in which her joys and sorrows have been constructed, she can engage with others only through the lens of her fantasies. Her fate, as Flaubert continually underlines, demonstrates that romantic dreams cannot be transmuted into reality without destroying their ineffable essence. Emma's efforts to achieve happiness are doomed by the fleshliness of her ideals. But for this very reason, Madame Bovary's whole existence comes to symbolize the desolation and ennui of the modern subject whose "desire for a higher ecstasy" has lost its religious frame of reference.

After her epiphany of boredom, the novel depicts Emma's growing, if inchoate, awareness of a fundamental discrepancy between desire and reality. She and Léon are weary of one another but unable to part, and Emma's ro-

---

[140]"Et Léon lui parut soudain dans le même éloignement que les autres. —Je l'aime pourtant! Se disait-elle. N'importe! Elle n'était pas heureuse, ne l'avait jamais été. D'où venait donc cette insuffisance de la vie, cette pourriture instantanée des choses oú elle s'appuyait?" (368/206).

[141]This is put somewhat prejudicially, for Emma's predicament is framed by material, as much as spiritual poverty. Flaubert's fortune and the company of like-minded others tempered the austerity of his working life considerably.

manticism becomes ever more desperate. Flaubert underlines that imagination is her only refuge. She enters into a despairing lassitude, continuing to mount up debts despite her creditors' demands and living only for her "gala days" (374/210) with Léon. She withdraws entirely from her husband and begins to "stay up all night reading lurid novels full of orgiastic scenes and bloody deeds" (374/210). When composing the love letters which she continued to send to Léon "on the principle that a woman must always write to her lover," Flaubert writes, Emma

> saw another man, a phantom composed of her most ardent memories, of the most beautiful things she had read, of her strongest lusts. He finally become so real, so accessible, that she thrilled with amazement, even though she was never able to imagine him clearly, for he was lost like a god in the abundance of his attributes.[142]

From the reader's perspective, this dynamic of idealization has always structured Emma's relation to the world. However, it is only in the final, disillusioned phase of her affair with Léon that Emma herself gains something resembling a conscious relationship to the productivity of her own desire. An ironic image of Flaubert's own creative struggle, Emma at her desk feels the idol of her imagination draw near and then vanish. "Then she would fall back to earth, shattered, for these vague amorous transports fatigued her more than the greatest debaucheries."[143] The narrator underlines that all her efforts to sustain her love for Léon with artificial stimulants only exacerbate their mutual disaffection: "She was as sick of him as he was tired of her. Emma found again in adultery all the dullness [*platitudes*] of marriage" (376/211). In this final act of her sad story, what had begun as affected romantic melancholy attains the proportions of fate. Suffusing everything she does and atrophying her love from within, boredom now renders all positive action impossible. A degrading indifference, a submission to habit, takes the place of Emma's all-too-sensual ideals.

If in the end "everything was a lie"—the words that made passion more than bodily mere images without referents—the implication is that even Emma's ennui gave false promise of a better life. The despair in which she takes her life inchoately expresses this unhappy recognition. Perhaps Emma

---

[142]"en verue de cette idée qu'une femme doit toujours écrire à son amant. Mais, en écrivant, elle percevait un autre homme, un fantôme fait de ses plus ardents souvenirs, de ses lectures les plus belles, de ses convoitises les plus fortes; et il devenait à la fin si véritable, et accessible, qu'elle en palpitait émerveillée, sans pouvoir néamoins le nettement imaginer, tant il se perdait, comme un dieu, sous l'abondance de ses attributs" (376/251).

[143]"Ensuite elle retombait à plat, brisée; car ces élans d'amour vague la fatiguaient plus que de grandes débauches" (376–77/211).

had indeed been corrupted by her callous first lover, who had cynically ex-
ploited the very incongruency between the romantic ideal of love and its reality that now provokes her despair. For Rodolphe, love passes into boredom
by the eternal course of things: over time, tender gestures lose their meaning
and become mere repetitions, and the object of love is rendered abstract and
irrelevant.[144] Thus for him, the moment of disenchantment was a confirma-
tion, rather than a terrible revelation, of the vacuousness of desire. As the
narrator put it, after a time, predictably,

> the charm of novelty, falling away little by little like a garment, laid bare the eter-
> nal monotony of passion, which always has the same form and the same lan-
> guage. He, this man so full of experience, could not distinguish dissimilarities of
> feeling beneath equivalent expressions.[145]

For such a person, language is hollow; Rodolphe's cynical affirmation of
boredom is diametrically opposed to Emma's romantic faith in the ineffable
power of language to transform reality, to render physical passion a cipher
for something higher. However, this faith, which was permanently shaken by
the collapse of their affair, had always rested on shaky ground, since it was
based on the pursuit of ideas that had "seemed to her so beautiful in books."
Although her devotion to her lover had embodied aspirations that could by
no means be reduced to the "eternal monotony" of bodily desire, Emma's
sincerity of sentiment was mediated by an ideal of love that had cloaked their
sexual relations in the idiom of romantic fiction. Thus from the reader's
ironic perspective, that naïveté which blinded Emma to Rodolphe's callous-
ness had rendered her equally indifferent to his particularity. But even if she
had lived in a way that effectively undermined the distinction between her
vacuous idealism and his cynical materialism, her suffering still pointed to
subtleties of longing a Rodolphe could never discern.

Although Emma's desire for meaning remains almost unrecognizable under the burden of clichés, for the reader, her boredom with reality as she
knows it is nonetheless a sign of her spiritual superiority to those who surround her. The insight into the platitudinousness of her second love affair
that evokes Emma's sighs of acquiescence to the boredom of existence—
nothing worth seeking! everything a lie!—differs profoundly from Rodolphe's cynicism. Although her despair arises from the loss of what Flaubert

---

[144]Flaubert renders this result vividly in the passage when Rodolphe sets out to write his letter
of regret to Emma. Not only does her image fade from his mind once he has decided to end
things; he can no longer distinguish her from his other loves at all.

[145] "laissait voir à nu le'èternelle monotonie de la passion, qui a toujours les mêmes formes et
le même langage. Il ne distinguait pas, cet homme si plein de pratique, la dissemblance des sentiments sous la parité des expressions" (254/138).

presents as superficial ideals, her tragedy is real. Emma keeps going through the motions even though she and Léon are bored with one another because the drama of love and desire—the "affair"—is as close as she can come to the ineffable object of her youthful longings for a meaningful and beautiful life. Thus while Rodolphe's instrumental romanticism made him common and venal, Emma's world-shattering recognition that love cannot possibly render her existence meaningful ennobles her. If his pose of aristocratic ennui masked crude insensitivity, Emma's decadent indifference has a tragic aspect. The destruction of the link between sex and meaning which had animated her fantasy of love drains the atmosphere of her life of the beauty that once rendered the sensual transcendent. Despite the speciousness of the ideals that have organized her existence, Emma's final, quasi-existential boredom therefore harbors a deeper significance.

Hackneyed as her dreams may be, Emma's sincerity renders her extraordinary; her boredom is founded not on a cynical refusal passionately to engage with others but on an experience of the agonizing loneliness at the heart of desire. In this final phase, she almost enjoys the narrator's sympathy. Despite the apparent death of her love for Léon, he relates, "humiliated by the baseness of her satisfactions, she continued to cling to them out of habit or depravity; and every day she pursued them with greater determination, destroying all chance of happiness by insisting on too much of it."[146] Precisely this excessive, passionate desire for happiness distinguishes her from her lover, who is dismissed with the ringing phrase, "every notary bears within himself the remains of a poet."[147] For Léon, the narrator indicates, such romantic longings were a thing of youth.

> He was now bored whenever Emma suddenly burst out sobbing on his chest . . . his heart was lulled by indifference amid the tumult of a love whose more delicate nuances he could no longer distinguish.[148]

He who had once seemed to be a man after her own heart is indeed "as distant from her as the others"; he can neither understand her despair nor appreciate her heroic efforts to shatter the chains of habit. While Léon's reactions follow along the lines of Rodolphe's callous insensibility to the specificity of emotions, Emma grows more poetic, more passionate, more desperate as a result of the apathy which suffuses her heart as well. Although her

---

[146]"humiliée de la bassesse d'un tel bonheur, elle y tenait par habitude ou par corruption; et, chaque jour, elle s'y acharnait davantage, tarrisant toute félicité à la vouloir trop grande" (376/211).

[147]". . . chaque notaire porte en soi les débris d'un poète" (376/211).

[148]il s'ennuyait maintenant lorsque Emma, tout à coup, sanglotait sur sa poitrine; et son coeur . . . s'assoupissait d'indifférence au vacarme d'un amour dont il ne distinguait plus les délicatesses" (376/211).

disillusionment occurs in the cliché-ridden idiom of romantic love, it has a larger significance for the reader, who has come to recognize in Emma's insatiable desires a longing for meaning that transcends their physical form. Especially in this final phase, her boredom becomes a metaphor for the tragic fate of the romantic self in a world incapable of living up to the imagination.

Unable as she is to separate spiritual and sensual aspirations, Emma herself is not cut out for philosophical resignation to the inevitability of boredom. Through the strategy of indirect free style, however, the very limitations of her self-reflection and her naïve faith in the romantic narratives she consumes so avidly become the means by which *Madame Bovary* ironically transforms her fate into an object worthy of artistic contemplation. From the point of view of the novel, Emma's desires are a function of her profound need to escape the boredom of her provincial existence; their objects—lovers, beautiful things, even saintliness—are not ends in themselves but the symbolic trappings of what she understands as a significant life. Because none of these interchangeable objects of desire can modify the fundamental banality of her life, the novel proceeds inexorably to Madame Bovary's disenchantment—to her own confrontation with the eternal monotony of her passions in the form of the rediscovery in adultery of all the tedium of matrimony.

The novel makes clear that Emma's boredom has a deeper cause than she herself, in her naïve and unreflective way, can plumb. Her world—Flaubert's vision of nineteenth-century provincial bourgeois society—is marked by the absence of any meaningful understanding of the larger purpose of human life. In such a world, all action, and especially the ordinary activities that make up the repetitive immediacy of everyday existence, becomes problematic. There is no reason—or rather there are only venal and utilitarian reasons—for doing anything. The trajectory of Emma's boredom in Flaubert's novel poses the dilemma that arises from her historical situation in philosophical terms: where a religious guarantee of the correspondence of desire to a higher purpose for human existence is lacking, desire itself becomes a problem. Through the bitter lens of his irony, Flaubert shows that the secularization that has produced an emphasis on personal, earthly happiness leads to ever greater disillusionment—to a world where even a personage as limited as Emma Bovary can experience the terrors of ennui.

Language, Irony, and Artistic Transcendence

"Emma's dreams are destined, at the touch of reality, to wither into lies. Is that a critique of her or of reality?" Harry Levin's rhetorical question indicates an aporia. To understand her is to realize that this withering is the fate of all ideals, that "Madame Bovary c'est nous" (263). According to Levin, Flaubert is ironic because "irony dominates life"[149]; thus stupidity receives the cross of the Legion of Honor, true love goes unrecognized, and rakes prosper. On such a reading, by deploying a universalized irony that turns the contradictions of lived reality into objects of aesthetic contemplation, Flaubert differentiates his own philosophically inflected ennui from the unremitting tedium of the world he chronicles. *Madame Bovary*'s reader, empowered by his narrative strategy to understand the protagonist's boredom better than she understands it herself, can contemplate the ironic triumph of literary art over the tiresome predictability of existence.[150] But in emphasizing the modernist achievement of the novel, such a reading takes the nihilistic dynamic of the protagonist's represented experience—nothing worth seeking! everything a lie!—too much at face value. It thereby underplays the historical dimension in Flaubert's irony. That Emma's dreams wither at the touch of reality is a critique both of her superficial dreams and of the world that is too coarse to allow poetry to exist. The novel is an enlightened indictment of romanticism written from a perspective that cannot conceal its sympathy with her longing to find in real life the things that seem "so beautiful in books." As I have argued, Emma's ennui is grounded in a desire more profound than its romantic trappings: a longing to live a meaningful life. If the novel represents that as an impossibility, then not because such a desire is in itself ludicrous. *Madame Bovary* is a tragedy of fate—but in the universalist, post-Enlightenment register.

In *Flaubert: The Uses of Uncertainty*, Jonathan Culler calls the genre of the novel "an ironic form, born of the discrepancy between meaning and experience."[151] This discrepancy lies, he contends, at the heart of Flaubert's project as an artist, for "a desire not to understand, not to grasp the purposes that language, behavior, and objects serve in ordinary practical life, is one of the determining features of Flaubert's writing" (184). For Culler, it is this alienation from any recognizable communicative purpose and the associated displacement of understanding by the literary equivalent of reverie (184) that defines the specific modernity of that writing. Accordingly, on his view, the

---

[149] Levin's remark (269) takes as its point of departure a letter to Louise Colet of 8 May, 1852, in which Flaubert says as much ("L'ironie pourtant me semble dominer la vie" *Correspondance II*, 84).

[150] As Levin elaborates: "Hence the irony of ironies: a novel which is at once cautionary and exemplary, a warning against other novels and a model for other novelists, the classic demonstration of what literature gives and what literature takes" (269).

[151] Culler 1985, 24. Subsequent citations in text.

greatness of *Madame Bovary* "derives from those areas of maximum indeterminacy, if not irrelevance" for the plot (139). It lies in the way Flaubert
refuses his reader the consolation of any clear moral—or even a clear point
of view on his heroine—by shifting attention to the operations of language
and hence onto "the general problem of desire and its manifestations" (142).
As for Emma: "What she is as a character does not produce an inescapable
destiny . . . [Flaubert] chose indeterminacy at that level because the concept
of destiny is precisely one of those problematic novelistic constructs with
which we try to structure our lives and because the lack of a destiny is the
modern form of the tragic" (145). However, Culler argues, destiny is
"reinstated" in aesthetic form: Flaubert makes "style the source of fatality"
and thereby "poses the problem of the relationship between meaning and
experience in a particularly complex way" (145).

According to Culler, this thematic indeterminacy and the ironic mode in
which it is narrated create a new sort of reading experience; *Madame Bovary*
is a novel that critiques literary conventions. By contrast, the "one island of
certainty" in the book, the un-ironic "seriousness with which Emma's corruption is attributed to novels and romances" constitutes, on his view, the
novel's "greatest flaw" (146). What might appear as the author's "nascent sociological insight" (237) is for Culler a sign of Flaubert's uncharacteristically
uncritical acceptance of "the theory of the corrupting novel" (147). My
reading of *Madame Bovary* suggests, however, that the formal innovations of
the novel are integrally related to Flaubert's deployment of that "theory."

As I have shown, it is precisely as a novel about the perils of novel-reading
that *Madame Bovary* discloses a new, modern function for literature. In place
of sentimental education, Flaubert offers his enlightened readers a means of
cultivating a self-conscious relation to the language in which their own subjective experience is constructed. Culler is right to emphasize the uses of indeterminacy in the novel, but in abstracting these linguistic operations from
their historical context, he misses the historical point of Flaubert's critique of
romanticism as the source of the superficial, mass-produced modes of self-
understanding that dominate in modernity. On my reading, the fatality of
style is in the service of an ironic critique of an historically significant language of reflection. That is, where Culler reads Flaubert as an aesthete for
whom the only fatality is aesthetic, I emphasize his self-understanding as
moralist[152] and contend that the novel is constructed to foster readerly re-

[152] As Dominick LaCapra puts it in *"Madame Bovary" on Trial*, "Flaubert offered a critique of
bourgeois society which blended imperceptibly into an indictment of humanity and the human
condition in general" (LaCapra 1982, 67).

flection on the romantic construction of aesthetic fatality as an historical and linguistic phenomenon. To illustrate what is at stake in this objection to a reading that foregrounds Flaubert's aestheticism, it will be helpful to examine the remarks on boredom with which Culler frames *The Uses of Uncertainty*.

Culler regards ennui as a problem born of the aporetic relation between language and experience. Accordingly, he considers boredom "a literary category of the first importance; it is the background against which the action of reading takes place and which continually threatens to engulf it" (19). Indeed, for him, "criticism exists to make things interesting" (21)—that is, not to discover meaning or form but to fend off the menace of meaninglessness and the boredom implicated in all reading. These remarks, which occur in the introduction to *The Uses of Uncertainty*, are very revealing. Like so many of our nineteenth-century witnesses, Culler recognizes the historical particularity of this ahistorical understanding of boredom, yet interprets the phenomenon itself as existential fact.

In the first section of his first chapter, which is entitled "Precocious Boredom," Culler picks up a familiar trope. By the early nineteenth century, he claims, "reading and writing made disillusionment no longer the fruit of experience and possession of old age but something any child could acquire in idle hours in his father's library" (26). Thus, he asserts, ennui itself took on a "new temporal structure" (27) in Flaubert's generation. According to Culler, it was no longer true, as for the first romantic generation, that boredom and despair "implied nostalgia for a state that had actually been experienced and could be seen as a repository of values" (28). For the second generation, profound ennui was, rather, a universal, ahistorical given; the meaninglessness of the world was established. Under these circumstances, Culler writes, "all the Romantic themes are taken for granted as the modes of experience itself rather than as conclusions to be extracted from an experience" (29–30). Since there is no exit from disenchantment, it becomes the foundation of modern art. As his correspondence attests, Flaubert himself suffered endlessly from boredom, trapped between his skeptical inability to hold any ideals sacred and his longing for a life filled with meaning and beauty. His solution to the senselessness of living under such circumstances, to "look on the world as a spectacle and laugh at it,"[153] is a capitulation to ennui conditioned on a voluntary exit from history—in Culler's words a "neutralization of his own experience which seems the necessary correlate of his mature artistic posture" (36).

---

[153]*Correspondance I*, 30; cited in Culler, 33. See also the letter to Colet of 2 January, 1854, in which he cites Rabelais: "pour ce que le rire est le propre de l'homme" (*Correspondance II*, 498).

While Culler's notion that the distinction between romantic generations is linked to differing experiences of history is plausible, his account blurs the distinctions between history as *res gestae* and as *historia rerum gestarum*. Not only is his assumption that the first romantic generation had really experienced a state of wholeness highly questionable; he moves too quickly from the fact that disillusionment and despair were becoming universal in the nineteenth century to the assumption that existence really is boring and meaningless and in need of aesthetic relief. The fact that the dominant modes of narration were romantic does not prove their correctness. Similarly, that the ahistorical understanding of boredom which he attributes, not inaccurately, to Flaubert, becomes the basis of a new understanding of artistic endeavor does not demonstrate its truth. That Flaubert's generation of romantic artists saw "no need to explain and motivate disillusionment but only to explore its forms and consequences" (29) cannot, in itself, show that such explanation is unnecessary. Culler's account, like those of his predecessors Brierre and Tardieu, begs the question of the status of the historical transformations to which such a culture-wide shift in artistic practice attests.

On my reading, the fact that romanticism has in this way given rise to such forms and "modes of experience" is precisely what Flaubert is interrogating in *Madame Bovary*. Because he assumes the truth of Flaubert's philosophical position about the inevitability of boredom, Culler sees the historical critique of the institution of literature offered by the novel only as a flaw. However, Flaubert's modernism need not be so thoroughly severed from his realism. As I have shown, the indictment of literature as the source of skepticism was a commonplace in the mid-nineteenth century. Flaubert's vision of a scientific literature[154] is premised on a paradoxical embrace of this critique of literature's epistemic effects. Culler chides Flaubert for unironically accepting the notion that romantic literature corrupts its readers. Yet it is the way *Madame Bovary* represents that process of corruption that constitutes the linguistic indeterminacy he praises as its philosophical strength. The triumph of skepticism and indeterminacy Culler celebrates is inseparable from substantive as well as formal considerations, for Emma's sense of "the insufficiency of life" arises from the failure of a very particular language to render her experience meaningful.

In *Mimesis: The Representation of Reality in Western Literature*, Erich Auerbach argues that Flaubert's ideal of pure art is in the service of a recogniza-

---

[154]See, for instance, his remarks in the letter to Colet of August 14, 1853 regarding the relation between art and reality: "Poetry is as precise as geometry"; "My poor *Bovary* doubtlessly is suffering and weeping at this very moment in twenty French villages at once" (*Correspondance II*, 392).

bly realist social critique. Through the narrative strategy of indirect free style, Emma "is herself seen as one seeing, and is thus judged, simply through a plain description of her subjective life, out of her own feelings."[155] "Flaubert's artistic practice," he writes, depends on a "profound faith in the truth of language responsibly, candidly, and carefully employed" (486) to reveal the essence of what it represents. Auerbach discerns "a didactic purpose" in a strategy that the writer himself preferred to pass off as artistic disinterestedness. "The more one studies Flaubert, the clearer it becomes how much insight into the problematic nature and the hollowness of nineteenth-century bourgeois culture is contained in his realistic works" (490). Emma's ennui is an exemplary response to a very particular world.

> The essence of the happenings of ordinary contemporary life seemed to Flaubert to consist ... in the prolonged chronic state whose surface movement is mere empty bustle, while underneath it there is another movement, almost imperceptible but universal and unceasing, so that the political, economic, and social subsoil appears comparatively stable and at the same time intolerably charged with tension ... [T]he period is charged with its stupid issuelessness as with an explosive. (490–91)

But the historical import of Emma's chronic malaise is visible only to the reader. Despite her genuine longing for meaning, Emma never transcends this "world of illusions, habit, instincts, and slogans" (489) and is therefore not, for Auerbach, "a real tragic heroine" with whom the reader can identify (490).

On this point, Auerbach's realist reading of *Madame Bovary* converges with Culler's modernist interpretation. The reader, situated by the mode of narration in the position of the enlightened subject, regards Emma's shopworn romanticism with disdain. Through an emphasis on the material idiom of her longings, Flaubert makes it clear that Emma's very desire expresses the bourgeois milieu in which it was formed; born of a world where higher values have been rendered hollow, her strivings are easily turned toward the material satisfactions of consumption and physical desire. Because religion cannot provide her with immediate satisfactions, it too becomes a locus of her resignation to the unattainability of higher things. But is Flaubert's critique of romantic desire an indictment of a "foolish woman"[156] or of the world? On Auerbach's reading, too, it seems that irony fosters a more sophisticated resignation to the stupidity of the modern world in which things that seem so beautiful in books cannot survive.

---

[155]Auerbach, transl. Willard R. Trask, 485. Subsequent citations in text.

[156]In his Afterword to the second edition of *The Uses of Uncertainty*, Culler distances himself from the view of Emma put forward in his 1974 text. He traces the sexist "critical tradition" in which the "foolish woman" judgment was current to Percy Lubbock's *The Craft of Fiction*.

That both Culler's more philosophical and Auerbach's more sociological perspectives on the novel converge on the inevitability of boredom brings us back to Koselleck's theses about the disappearance of experience in modernity.[157] If the super-historical, enlightened perspective assumed by the Flaubertian narrator is interpreted historically, it appears as a means of expressing that the "essence" of modern life consists, as Auerbach puts it, "in the prolonged chronic state whose surface movement is mere empty bustle."[158] As we have seen, in the representation of Emma's ennui, the critique of historical reality is inseparable from a philosophical (retreat into) Art. Flaubert's novel is both a mode of reflecting *upon* social reality and a reflection *of* the reality it thematizes; Emma Bovary's story is related with an irony that makes a point both philosophical and historical. Here as elsewhere Flaubert is concerned with what Koselleck terms the "semantics of historical time." Emma's boredom, like Frédéric's in *Sentimental Education*, is both the product of a thoroughly inadequate and unrealistic understanding of life and a perfectly justifiable and adequate response to the world in which she lives. Indeed, from the ironic, enlightened perspective shared by the reader and the narrator, the boredom of Flaubert's protagonists is inescapable, for the discrepancy between their aspirations for meaning and the reality of their lives can never be overcome. To invoke Koselleck's language again: in a world dominated by the promises of "progress," such boredom is inevitable, for it is the locus in which the "abbreviation" or withdrawal of immediate experience in the all-encompassing anticipation of the future becomes tangible.

Flaubert's ironic dissection of romanticism exposes its illusions as enlightened myths. In an 1854 letter to Louise Colet, he wrote: "We are above all in an historical century. Thus it is necessary to recount everything honestly, but to recount it right down into the heart."[159] In *Madame Bovary*, the skepticism about the relation between meaning and experience fostered by literature is deliberately situated in relation to the historical shift in the meaning of the institution of literature in a secularized world. It is, as we have seen, the operation of romantic language that gives rise to the forms and modes of Emma Bovary's "experience" or, rather, to its absence. Since,

---

[157]To Koselleck and not to Benjamin, for at least on some readings, the latter regards the eclipse of historical *Erfahrung* by punctual *Erlebnis* in a fashion entirely coordinate with Culler's theses about the status of romantic "modes" of experience.

[158]Auerbach's phrase recalls Kierkegaard's already cited remark: "The majority of men live without being thoroughly conscious that they are spiritual beings—and to this is referable all the security, contentment with life, etc., etc., which precisely is despair" (*The Sickness unto Death*, 159).

[159]"Nous sommes avant tout dans un siècle historique. Aussi faut-il raconter tout bonnement, mais raconter jusque dans l'âme." April 22, 1854. *Correspondance II*, 556–57.

in Culler's wonderful phrase, "the lack of a destiny is the modern form of the tragic," Emma's fate ironically illustrates the utter exteriority of modern interiority. Doubly constituted in language, she embodies the lack that constitutes modern subjectivity, for in her, the discrepancy between meaning and experience that is indeed the central problem of the novel is figured as the consequence of the failure of the romantic construction of subjectivity. Style becomes "the source of fatality"; Flaubert's "absolute manner of seeing"[160] shows how the failure of romantic forms and modes of experience to render desire meaningful dooms Emma Bovary to ennui and despair. To refine the claim I have already made: from the reader's point of view, the protagonist's boredom signifies that the very desire to live a meaningful life has been rendered problematic in modernity.

The critique of romanticism that animates Flaubert's novel stands in the service of a philosophical indictment of historical reality. Emma Bovary may be too inarticulate and limited in her powers of self-reflection to recognize that she is the victim of an ideology that makes real life pale by contrast with the intoxication of literature. Yet her prosaic life becomes an exemplary fate because her boredom, though shaped in the crucible of a popularized literary imagination, expresses the universal malaise of modern existence in a world where the longing for meaning can never be fulfilled. The novel only partly blames her inability "to find out what one meant exactly in life by the words *bliss, passion, ecstasy,* that had seemed to her so beautiful in books" (61/24) on the unworthy provincial objects of her desires. At a deeper level, *Madame Bovary* represents this failure of life to live up to literature as a consequence of the insufficiency of language to capture the inchoate depths of human feeling.

From the enlightened perspective of Flaubert's analytic narrative, the failure of romanticism is symptomatic of a metaphysical truth. The boredom with life that results from the failure of romantic strategies, insofar as it opens up reflection on the linguistic construction of desire, is profound. It seems that an appeal to cliché is unavoidable. The most sincere "fullness of soul" must sometimes, Flaubert writes,

> overflow into the emptiest of metaphors, since no one, ever, can possibly express the exact measure of his needs, his conceptions or his sorrows, and human speech is like a cracked pot on which we beat out rhythms for bears to dance to when we are striving to make music that will wring tears from the stars.[161]

[160] Letter to Louise Colet, January 16, 1852; *Correspondance II,* 31

[161] "debordait . . . par les métaphors les plus vides, puisque personne, jamais, ne peut donner l'exacte mesure de ses besoins, ni de des conceptions, ni de ses douleurs, et que la parole humaine est comme un chaudron fêlé où nous batton des mélodies à faire danser les ours, quand on voudrait attendrir les étoiles." (254/138)

This passage, with its unusually direct address to the reader, speaks to the philosophical foundation of Flaubert's irony. It suggests that Henry James' complaint that Emma is "too small an affair," too weak a vessel for the significance she bears, betrays a misapprehension of *Madame Bovary*, for the novel itself demonstrates that even "the emptiest of metaphors" can hold transcendent significance. Rather than expressing, as James thought, a "defect of his mind,"[162] Flaubert's choice of pedestrian protagonists registers his commitment to creating a modern literature in which formal, technical perfection in the representation of historical reality provides the ironical foundation for a philosophical critique of that reality. However, the conflict between his commitment to an "absolute" style that would produce a timeless work of art elevated above the nothingness of its subject matter and his need to express his abhorrence for the bourgeois world makes *Madame Bovary* equivocate about the significance of its protagonist's suffering. Flaubert's impersonal mode of narration thus creates an ambivalent irony: it is precisely because Emma can appear to be "a stupid, vulgar and cruel woman"[163] who is only interesting as an object of analysis that her malaise can become paradigmatic.

Emma's persistent ennui is an experience at once literal and figurative. Because her malaise, though linked to a banal conception of happiness, embodies a profound human dilemma, *Madame Bovary* becomes an epic of the disaffected modern subject and an allegory for the sensitive, artistic temperament that founders on the banality of bourgeois existence. What is at stake is the status of that allegory. On the modernist reading, Flaubert's irony provides the reader with a place to stand. Art replaces religion—or more precisely, the devotion to pure literature rewrites the romantic aspiration of finding a spiritual principle with which to reorder the chaos of modern experience into a formalist practice. But since art is by its nature unable to remake real life in its own image, the outcome is a melancholy one: boredom inevitably returns, now transposed into the register of metaphysical necessity.

If we follow Culler's reading, the novel implies that the only way to escape the fate of the romantic subject is to follow along the path of the cynical man of the world—to renounce the desire for meaning and accede to the universality and necessity of boredom—but to turn this stoic renunciation into the matter of art rather than making it a justification for debauchery.[164] Such

---

[162] Cited in Flaubert 1965, 348.

[163] As Leo Bersani puts it in his introduction to Lowell Bair's 1981 translation of the novel (ix).

[164] This strategy was quite literally reflected in Flaubert's biography during this period. Although refusing for the most part to see her at all, he used his affair with Louise Colet to mine her

seems indeed to have been the foundation of Flaubert's quasi-religion of art, in which the romantic aspiration to remake life in the image of art gave way to a nihilistic desire to replace life with art, compensating for the lack of meaning by transmuting ennui into an ideal of impersonal beauty and total creative control. Postulating the metaphysical ineluctability of ennui as the fate of the sensitive subject in a godless world, such an attitude toward art justified the withdrawal from the world upon which it depended.[165] From this perspective, the real problem is the fatuousness of the romantic aspiration to render human life whole and meaningful. It follows that in exposing the futility of Emma's romantic idealism, Flaubert locates the inevitable failure of life to live up to the imagination as a consequence of the ontological inevitability of boredom.

The problem with this interpretation is that it rests on an ahistorical understanding of the forms of experience that Flaubert treats as historically specific. For Culler, disillusionment is literally correct: there is no need for experience once one has achieved philosophical insight into the ultimate meaninglessness of existence. Representing Emma Bovary's foolish attempts to render her life significant is but an allegorical mode for arriving at the aesthetic justification of existence. But this way of reading occludes what Flaubert has to say about the status of the modern way of narrating human life that guides Emma's misadventures. In emphasizing the philosophical resignation that suffuses Flaubert's mode of relating Madame Bovary's story, it underplays the tragic effect he achieves by depicting the fate of an insignificant provincial adulteress. To explain this effect—which follows, classically, upon the reader's cathartic identification with Emma's suffering—it is necessary to look beyond the formal thrill of Flaubert's prose and his unflappable handling of plot structure to ask about the historical dimensions of his approach to art.

I have argued that *Madame Bovary* thematizes the paradoxical relations

---

romantic fantasies for material during much of the period he was composing the novel. Indeed, he virtually advised Colet herself to follow his "practical dogma" for artists: "Divide existence into two parts: live like a bourgeois and think like a demigod" (August 21, 1853; *Correspondance II*, 402).

[165] But as I have already suggested, Flaubert's understanding of art as hard work that had more in common with the emergent societal values than he would have liked to admit. Art for art's sake replaced the deistic romantic faith in artistic creation with a secular commitment to a technology of production. In his correspondence, the production of literature has become an often tedious and self-sacrificing battle to wring beauty out of a utilitarian world. Flaubert's reverence for the literary and his wish to disappear into the work itself through the agency of a totally objective, scientific writing were ways of overcoming the boredom of reality that nevertheless conceded the inevitability of that boredom.

between life and literature in the form of reflection upon a democratized version of romanticism. The implied reader understands the poetic relentlessness of her fate better than she can herself, for from the point of view of the novel, the idealizations which Emma believes can compensate for the paltriness of bourgeois existence render the fundamental discrepancy between the language of desire and lived experience visible. Because Emma's boredom is at once a metaphysical destiny and a contingent mode of self-reflection fostered by a trickle-down romanticism, the fate of her ideals can become an allegory for the enlightened modern subject who is Flaubert's implied audience. The carefully constructed ironic effect through which the narrator's relationship to Emma Bovary creates the impression of a sovereign judgment upon the failure of romanticism and the ensuing ineluctability of boredom depends on a readerly perspective that recognizes boredom as an extra- as well as intra-diegetic problem. If Flaubert's skeptical mode of narrating Emma Bovary's story turns a melodrama of provincial mores into a philosophical meditation on the incongruity between language and desire, then because through the "empty metaphor" of her boredom, he underlines the aporiai of the modern language of reflection on subjective experience.

Madame Bovary presents Emma's predicament as at once the symptom of an historically constituted crisis of meaning and the result of the fundamental discrepancy between desire and reality—as the inevitable, yet inevitably crushing failure of meaning in an existence without a divine guarantee of their correspondence. Hers is the fate of a romantic sensibility that does not reflect upon the ineluctable limitations of the bourgeois framework in which it attempts to realize the longing for meaningful existence. The poverty of Madame Bovary's spiritual vocabulary only underlines the incongruity of her longing for higher things in the modern world. However, in the final analysis, the barrenness of that vocabulary is more a symptom than a cause of her fate. Through a narrative strategy that elevates the implied author to the status of God—"everywhere present and nowhere visible"[166]—in his text, Flaubert transforms Emma's persistent ennui into a metaphor for the crisis of meaning in modernity. The very irony with which her mass-produced aspirations are presented dignifies Emma's life by transforming it into an allegory for the fate of the skeptical modern subject.

Thus, even when Flaubert's disenchanted mode of narration seems to represent what happens from the perspective of metaphysical pessimism, a temporal critical interest is clearly at work. Running parallel to the absolute,

[166] Letter to Louise Colet, 9 December 1852; *Correspondance II*, 204.

philosophical resignation to what Culler calls indeterminacy, to the impossibility of making words mean, is a palpable moral and aesthetic outrage at the idiocy of the world in which Emma is condemned to live. Even as *Madame Bovary* represents the protagonist's longing to live a "meaningful" life as a mishmash of romantic clichés and vulgar materialism that together render her situation hopeless, her boredom irremediable, it implicitly links the metaphysical crisis of subjectivity to the process of cultural modernization. This is a world where even the priest is incapable of distinguishing spiritual from physical suffering, a world which has rendered the inherited understanding of human being objectively inadequate while offering only hollow materialism to replace it—a world that, from the narrator's point of view, is objectively boring. Emma Bovary comes to grief through a pride built on the illusions that shaped the everyday reality of bourgeois life under the July Monarchy. Her fate is simultaneously a social critique, one that takes place in and through language—through a form of writing that foregrounds the failure of the inherited vocabularies of reflection to signify.

With uncompromising realism, *Madame Bovary* anatomizes the provincial romanticism of its heroine, demonstrating how the literary language of reflection constructs something—ennui—out of the nothingness of her longing. In Flaubert's text, representation is simultaneously critique. Through the narrative device of indirect free style, *Madame Bovary* depicts Emma's consciousness being constituted by romantic clichés. By foregrounding her writtenness in this way, Flaubert invites his reader to reflect upon the historical status of that language of reflection. His mode of narration underlines how the vacuity of bourgeois ideals reinforces the way of thinking about herself as unique and different that Emma learned from books. And in emphasizing how a covert allegiance to those ideals shapes her existence, he critiques the very idea of a romantic "sentimental education." The resulting intimately ironic point of view emphasizes the double edge of the romantic rhetoric of reflection, which renders subjective malaise at once ineffable and easily imitated. This is, as many readers have noted, a critique from inside the romantic structure of desire. But if Emma's ennui is ultimately a literary construct, a means of redescribing a fundamental lack into a signifier of existence itself, then it is also a critique of that understanding of desire. Flaubert's mode of narration is not romantic but enlightened: resigned to the inevitability of suffering, deeply critical of the historical circumstances that have eviscerated hope for higher things, he strove to create a mode of writing that could make up for it all. A way of seeing absolutely. "Analytic narrative" as an ersatz for life.

Flaubert's project of dissecting romantic malaise from the perspective of a disenchanted, objective, and realistic art may be taken as paradigmatic for the rhetorical shift in the discourse of reflection on subjective experience in this period. In *Madame Bovary*, as in the broader discourse on boredom examined in the previous sections, although the vocabulary employed was often continuous with that of romanticism, a scientific impulse to explain the manifestations of malaise associated with modernization in materialistic terms is palpably gaining ascendance over more traditional religious and moral explanations. Flaubert does not endorse that materialist rhetoric of reflection, but he underlines the role it plays even in the provinces by mid-nineteenth century. Emma's malaise is attributed to nerves; religious strivings collapse into their material trappings; even Charles, "corrupted from beyond the grave" (438/250) by Emma's confusion of spiritual and material goods, turns to commodities to preserve his love for her. And like Brierre before him and Tardieu after him, Flaubert condemned the pernicious effects of materialism from a perspective itself indebted to the disenchanted effects of Enlightenment.

The inheritor of a romantic vision of literature as the refuge of spiritual strivings in a godless world, Flaubert was committed to a relentlessly disenchanted depiction of the world where such strivings had become inexpressible as a consequence of the literary abuse of the language of desire. In this work, ennui becomes the ambiguous sign of the desire for meaning and its disappearance. In representing such boredom as at once mass-produced and metaphysically significant, *Madame Bovary* affirms the very task of literature about which it seems to despair. This affirmation comes, however, at the cost of sacrificing the romantic desire for meaning on the altar of disenchantment that is the holy of holies in the cult of art for art's sake. Flaubert is at once moralist and pessimist. His form of resignation to ennui accordingly combines Brierre's injunction to work with Tardieu's recommendation to "sacrific[e] oneself to an ideal." In his oeuvre, as in their writings, ennui is the ineluctable fate of the thinking man—or woman—in modernity.[167]

---

[167]In a brief but noteworthy essay on *Madame Bovary* published in *L'Art romantique*, Charles Baudelaire argues that Emma Bovary is in fact a man—a "bizarre androgyne [who] has preserved all the seductions of a virile soul in a charming feminine body" (OC II, 81; English in Stromberg, *Realism, Naturalism, and Symbolism*, 42). On Baudelaire's view Emma combines the imaginative strengths of an "hysterical poet" with the qualities of a "man of action."

Refiguring Malaise: Baudelaire and
the Experience of Modernity

Society is now one polished horde,
Form'd of two mighty tribes, the Bores and Bored.
Byron[168]

Charles Baudelaire is the bard of ennui. As such, he is the prototypical poet of modernity. At once bohemian and dandy, romantic, melancholic lover of beauty and jaded, decadent aesthete, he chronicles the harrowing fate of desire in a world without God. The images in his beautiful, classically formed lyrics come from the stock of mythological tradition and from the gritty realities of everyday urban life, his adjectives from the vocabulary of love poetry and from the gutter. In reveries that take place against a landscape of destitution, a Paris populated by venal prostitutes, beggars, and lonely old people, the poet searches for meaning and beauty in fragments gathered up from the detritus of modern life. Baudelaire's central themes— love, beauty, sin, and redemption—emerge at the margins of the glittering world of upper-class nineteenth-century Parisian life, in a realm of loneliness and crowds. In his verses, the ennui that had been the prerogative of the idle rich is represented as having passed to all of those whose lives lack meaning in a world where time has become everyone's burden, where loss is ubiquitous, where love evokes contempt, beauty decay, the thought of God despair. The poet is their spokesman; his verses strain to capture the vagaries of longing in a world seemingly without hope. Baudelaire takes up the language of everyday life and transforms it into an instrument for registering the suffering and struggles of the modern soul, the unmoored self who inhabits the metropolis in which skepticism has been democratized.

The *Fleurs du Mal* trace a journey from the ideals of beauty that animate the artistic aspiration to create enduring meaning to the vagaries of carnal sin, moral devastation, and yearning for death. The path is haunted by ennui: from the indifference of the beloved to the torpor of the lover, from the spiritual despair that mourns beauty's passing to the celebration of Satan in which it issues, Baudelaire's world is one in which longing is suffused with despair. Like Flaubert, he deploys realistic depiction as a mode of critique. Upon closer examination, the flowers of evil that may at first glance may seem the bizarre visions of a febrile sensibility appear to rest on the most commonplace of perceptions. Indeed, according to Jules Laforgue, one of his

[168]Don Juan XIII, xlv, 1823.

poetic heirs, it was this feel for the quotidian realities of modern life that distinguished Baudelaire.

> He was the first to speak of Paris like any ordinary lost soul of the capital [*un damné quotidien de la capitale*], the street lamps tormented by the wind, "the prostitution which lights up the streets," the restaurants and their ventilators, the hospitals, gambling, the wood that is sawn into logs which echo on the paving-stones of courtyards, the chimney corner, cats, beds, women's stockings, modern makes of perfume . . .
>
> He is the first who is not triumphant, but accuses himself, reveals his wounds, his laziness, his bored uselessness in the midst of this hardworking, devoted century.
>
> The first who brought into literature the feeling of apathy in pleasure [*l'ennui dans la volupté*] and its bizarre decor . . . spleen and sickness (not poetical Consumption but neurasthenia) without once using the word.[169]

I have quoted this paean at length because it both illuminates Baudelaire's significance for the development of modern poetry and raises a key issue of interpretation.

Laforgue's catalog of the elements of Baudelaire's poetry elides the spiritual, even religious dimension of the poet's insistence on "his bored uselessness in the midst of this hard-working, devoted century." And by inserting a medical category, neurasthenia, it shifts the meaning of that "feeling of ennui in pleasure" entirely. Such a reading of Baudelaire's "spleen" as mental illness runs counter to the poet's own self-understanding. As we have already noted, 'neurasthenia' did not appear in the Larousse until 1888—three years before Laforgue published this text, but more than twenty years after his subject's death in 1867. However, the point is not simply that Baudelaire did not and from an etymological point of view could not have used the word. He surely would not spoken of "neurasthenia," even had the term been available. His analysis of the spiritual suffering of the modern subject deliberately invokes un-modern, indeed ancient vocabularies—the languages of melancholy, *taedium vitae*, and acedia.

Baudelaire's anatomy of ennui stands in critical relation to the medicalization of malaise that was proceeding apace in the nineteenth century. In two poems written after the initial *Flowers of Evil* were censored in 1857 for offending public morals, Baudelaire insisted on the spiritual significance of

[169]I cite Martin Turnell's translation (36–37) of selections from Laforgue's fragmentary remarks on Baudelaire. The collection *Mélanges posthumes*, edited by G. Jean-Aubry (Paris 1903), includes a selection under the title "Littérature"; the original text, "Notes inédites de Laforgue sur Baudelaire," was published in *Entretiens politiques et littéraires*, II (April 1891), 97–120. A more extensive English version of Laforgue's thoughts on Baudelaire may be found in William Jay Smith.

his 'spleen.' The first, a prose poem from *Paris Spleen* entitled "The Wicked Glazier ['Le mauvais Vitrier']," explicitly rejects the contemporary tendency to reinterpret spleen and melancholy in the terms of a thoroughly unpoetic and unreligious, medical understanding of desire. We shall return later to its dissection of "that humor, hysterical according to the doctors, satanic according to those who think a bit better than the doctors, that drives us unresistingly toward a multitude of dangerous or unseemly actions."[170] In a second poem, "Epigraph for a Condemned Book," the poet suggests that those who censored his work for immorality were among the former. Calling *The Flowers of Evil* a "saturnine book/Orgiastic and melancholic," the speaker advises the reader "If you have not learned your rhetoric/With Satan, that crafty elder,/Throw it away! You won't understand anything/Or will believe me hysterical."[171] But for the reader who does not fear the "plunge into the abyss," he continues, "Read me to learn to love me/Curious soul who suffers/and goes seeking your paradise,/Pity me . . . or I shall curse you!"[172]

Such curses would surely have been directed at Émile Tardieu, who called Baudelaire "prince of the impotent" and diagnosed his ennui as "intellectual sterility, mental disharmony, and all the convulsions of a failure who exhausts himself and does not succeed."[173] Tardieu's equation of failure and exhaustion indicates how right Laforgue was to praise the poet's revelatory self-accusation of "bored uselessness in the midst of this hardworking, devoted century" for blazing a new path. In his insistence on the moral dimension of experience, Baudelaire's evocation of the hopeless struggles of the metropolitan subject may succumb to Satanism, but never to such reductive materialism. His representations of ennui foreground the ethical and metaphysical significance of experiences Tardieu dismissed as the epiphenomena of physical and psychic exhaustion.

If such medicalizing interpretations of Baudelaire's 'ennui' must be re-

[170]OC I, 286. My attempts to provide literal renderings of Baudelaire's poems have come at the cost of poetic values better realized in the work of those who have been my guides—particularly William Crosby (Baudelaire 1991), William Aggeler (Baudelaire 1954), and Edward K. Kaplan (Baudelaire 1989b). I have also consulted the wonderful collective translation of the *Fleurs du Mal* by contemporary poets (Baudelaire 1989a).

[171]OC I, 137 ". . . ce livre saturnien,/orgiaque et mélancholique. //Si tu n'as fait ta rhétorique/Chez Satan, le rusé doyen,/Jette! tu n'y comprendrais rien,/Ou tu me croirais hystérique." According to Claude Pichois, this poem may either have been written for the 1861 edition and then withdrawn or composed for the third (1868) edition of *The Flowers of Evil*, where it was included for the first time (OC I, 1103–4). At any rate, Baudelaire published it in 1866 as the first of a group of *Nouvelle Fleurs du Mal* (op. cit. LIII).

[172]"Lis-moi pour apprendre à m'aimer; //Âme curieuse qui souffres/Et vas cherchant ton paradis,/Plains-moi! . . . Sinon, je te maudis!"

[173]Tardieu 58 and 56 respectively.

jected, so too must their counterpart, psychologization—the easy identification of the poet with the voices in his poems. The lyric subject who "accuses himself, reveals his wounds" and his "ennui in pleasure" does not speak for himself alone. Taking on a variety of personas, he describes the spiritual malaise of modernity. Compounded of moral lassitude and splenetic revolt against life, this 'ennui' leads sometimes to melancholy withdrawal, sometimes to an embrace of death, sometimes to creative despair, sometimes to criminal and violent acts. Baudelaire represents such ennui as the fate—or the vice—of modern subjects thrown back on themselves in the disillusionment and moral chaos that result from the passing of the old order.

In Baudelaire's world, ennui is universal, but it is by no means univocal. It leads to decadence, voluptuousness, and indifference to the fates of others; it provokes acts of senseless destruction and violent revolt against God. And yet, unlike Brierre de Boismont, whose essay on ennui he admired, Baudelaire did not dream that modern society might engage in "unanimous efforts . . . to reanimate religious faith" (584) and thereby to cure the problem at its source. As an acute analyst of life in the disenchanted modern world, Baudelaire ties these manifestations of vice to a broader historical vision of ennui as the fate of the modern subject. Resignation to the conditions of modern existence is the foundation of his art; his 'ennui' names the subjective response in which material and moral effects of modernization converge. In Martin Turnell's words, Baudelaire's poetry "is the anatomy of a highly complex mood which only crystallized in the last century and which must be identified with what he [CB] called 'the morality of the century' or 'the stamp which *time* imprints on our sensations'" (35). The modern poet's vocation is to register and express the very changes that he suffers as a modern person.

According to Turnell, Baudelaire was writing in and of radically new experiences: the very matter of human sensibility had been "modified by changes which had taken place in civilization. New feelings had emerged; old feelings had been broken up and had formed fresh combinations like the pieces in a kaleidoscope" (158). Since such an assertion is accessible only to indirect, linguistic proof, I have been suggesting that our attention is best directed not toward sensibility per se but toward the new rhetoric of reflection on subjective experience taking hold in the nineteenth century—a rhetoric centered on the body rather than the soul and in which material and psychological rather than ideal and moral modes of interpretation predominated. On my reading, Baudelaire's poetry represents a new mood, a new sensibility, in a way that interrogates the significance of that new way of talking and thinking about subjective experience.

Baudelaire's 'ennui' is compounded of elements of very different prove-
nance, and his poetry indeed reflects the historical and linguistic process in
which these elements combine kaleidescopically into novel forms. The term
is at the center of a modern vocabulary of reflection that Baudelaire forged
out of the fragments of the inherited languages of sensibility—languages that
had once linked human emotion to enduring realities—and the new idioms
of the enlightened and industrialized world. In Baudelaire's 'ennui,' I shall
show, not only do the moral and the metaphysical converge. The ambiguity
of the experience in his poetry reflects the multiple, often conflicting, vocabularies—religious, medical, psychological, and philosophical—that constitute ennui as both vice and fate of the modern subject. Through that ambiguity, Baudelaire raises very general questions about the nature of modern
experience and about the subjects who understand themselves and their lives
in this new idiom. My readings will therefore focus on how Baudelaire's representations of ennui evoke reflection on the historicity of experience—on
"the stamp which *time* imprints on our sensations."

I shall argue that Baudelaire's poetry simultaneously embodies and enacts
a refiguration of experience. Both in individual poems and at a more global
level, he forges a new rhetoric of experience out of the fragments of old and
new languages of reflection. This process is strikingly illustrated by the last of
the poems in the first section of the *Flowers of Evil*, "L'Horloge" (The Clock).
The poem begins with a summons: "Clock! sinister god, fearful and impas-
sive,/Whose finger threatens us and tells us 'remember.'"[174] Then the clock
begins to speak, using an idiom that mingles the ancient language of *taedium
vitae* with that of modern utilitarianism, biblical references with contemporary slang. "Vaporous pleasure flees to the horizon," it warns, "every instant
devours a morsel of the delights/granted to every man for his entire season."[175] In the fourth quatrain, the clock intones: "Remember! *Souviens-toi*,
prodigal one! *Esto memor!*/(My metal throat can speak all languages)," then
describes an experience of temporality that is stunningly modern: "Minutes,
blithesome mortal, are bits of ore/That you must not release without ex-
tracting the gold."[176] These lines, addressed by the clock to a "we" whose mediating function calls for examination, implicitly refer to the experience of

---

[174]"Horloge! dieu sinistre, effrayant, impassible,/Dont le doigt nous menace et nous dit:
'Souviens-toi!'"

[175]"Le Plaisir vaporeux fuira vers l'horizon . . ./Chaque instant te dévore un morceau du dé-
lice/A chaque homme accordé pour toute sa saison."

[176]"Remember! Souviens-toi, prodigue! Esto memor!/(Mon gosier de métal parle toutes les
langues.)/Les minutes, mortel folâtre, sont des gangues/Qu'il ne faut pas lâcher sans en extraire
l'or!"

ennui, which consists in such a failure to transform time into value. The poet who does not write or the reader who wastes time in transient pleasures experience an historically particular significance in the inevitable passage of time.

"The Clock" foregrounds the relationship between the utilitarian understanding of human activity that is ennui's negative condition of possibility and the historical transformation through which the rhythms of lived experience have been displaced by quantifiable, standardized clock time. But Baudelaire's sinister modern divinity also embodies a more ancient figure, "Time," that "avid gambler who wins without cheating every time."[177] In the penultimate stanza, the Clock warns that life's "daylight wanes" and uses its predecessor, the ancient water clock, as a symbol of death: "The abyss is always thirsty; the clepsydra drains."[178] In the final stanza, its speech integrates the vocabulary of modern utilitarianism with ancient and Christian figures. Here "Chance" "Virtue" and "Repentance" all cry out through its voice: "Die, old coward! It is too late!"[179] In this, the final poem of the section "Spleen and Ideal," the figure of the Clock links antique and theological senses of time's inescapability to the quantified rhythms of modern life. This poem subtly reflects Baudelaire's historical and critical vision of an experience of temporality that, as we have seen, many of his contemporaries understood to be the perpetual source of an ineffable, metaphysical ennui.

"The Clock" suggests the breadth and complexity of the thinking about time and temporality that underlies Baudelaire's conception of ennui as a specifically modern mode of encountering human mortality. Before turning to his representations of this experience, it will be helpful to examine the poet's ideas about art and modernity. Although Baudelaire dedicated *Les Fleurs du Mal* to Theophile Gautier, and at times spoke as a partisan of *l'art pour l'art*, it would be erroneous to regard him as an aesthete and dandy for whom historical and political realities were beneath serious concern. On the contrary, he was a moralist—though one hardly to the taste of the censors. This congruence of aestheticism and moralism seems less surprising if we recall the historical particularity of the ideas that underlay the slogan "art for art's sake." The notions that art ought to be pure of worldly engagement and the object of "disinterested" pleasure are products of the Enlightenment. Such a conception of art depends on the segregation of religious and intel-

---

[177]"Souviens-toi que le Temps est un joueur avide / Qui gagne sans tricher, à tout coup!"

[178]"Le jour décroît; la nuit augmente; souviens-toi! / Le gouffre a toujours soif; la clepsydre se vide."

[179]"Meurs, vieux lâche! Il est trop tard!" "Lâche" has the connotation of slothfulness.

lectual concerns from aesthetic ones.[180] In Baudelaire's case, this separation of spheres is turned to account: the invocation of aesthetic values forms part of a defense against those who objected to the apparent immorality of his themes. His devotion to art is in fact by no means tantamount to unworldliness, for it is precisely in the disenchanted modern world that the task of the poet becomes so pressing.

The complexity of Baudelaire's position is well illustrated by an essay written in 1859–60, "The Painter of Modern Life." In it, Baudelaire takes the work of a minor artist, Constantine Guys, as his point of departure for a series of reflections on "the painting of manners [*moeurs*] of the present"[181] that seem to have implications for his own work. According to Baudelaire's "rational and historical theory" (685/3), beauty is characterized by a fundamental duality. As "a fatal consequence of the duality of man" (685–86/3), he contends, beauty is composed of "an eternal, invariable element . . . and a relative, circumstantial element" (685/3)—soul and body, as it were. The transcendent dimension, "the eternal part of beauty" is simultaneously "veiled and expressed" according to the particularities of age and artist (685/3). Hence, Baudelaire reasons, the "sketch of manners" by one who—whether in images or words—is "the painter of the passing moment and of all that it suggests of eternity" (687/5) is eminently worthy of serious consideration.

Giving an innovative twist to the Aristotlean notion that, in its concern with universals, poetry is "more philosophical" than history (*Poetics*, 1451b), Baudelaire describes Guys' efforts to "extract [*dégager*] from fashion whatever element it may contain of the poetic within the historical, to distil the eternal from the transitory" as a pursuit of "modernity" (694/12). Unlike his classicizing predecessors, Baudelaire does not oppose 'modern' to 'ancient.' "'Modernity,'" he writes, is "the ephemeral [*transitoire*], the fugitive, the contingent, the half of art whose other half is the eternal and the immutable. Every old master has had his own modernity . . ." (695/12). Baudelaire's 'modernité' refers, then, not to the temporal concept of modernity, but to the temporality of art itself. Art must realize what Hegel would have called "concrete universality." The artist who neglects this fugitive element, he

---

[180] It is worth noting that Kant's original argument for the "disinterested" quality of aesthetic pleasure was made in the context of an attempt to reunify those spheres—to integrate practical and theoretical reasoning.

[181] "Le Peintre de la vie moderne," OC II, 683–724; English in *The Painter of Modern Life and Other Essays*, 1–40. The remark cited is on 684 in the French and 1 in the English text. Subsequent parenthetical citations give the French and then the English page numbers; I follow Mayne with modifications.

warns, must "tumble into the emptiness of an abstract and indeterminate beauty" (695/13). It is historical awareness, the "memory of the present" that makes an artist great, for "almost all our originality comes from the stamp which *time* imprints on our sensations" (696/14). Thus the "vestiges of barbarousness or naïveté" in the works of "Monsieur G." become for Baudelaire "fresh proofs of his faithfulness to the impression" and hence to "the fantastic reality of life" (697/15).

On Baudelaire's account, art's moral significance depends on such sensuous particularity, on its poetic, eternalizing relation to the phenomenal world in which it comes to be. The "painter of modern life" is distinguished by the bottomless curiosity of a "lover of universal life." "He is," Baudelaire writes, "an I [*moi*] insatiable for the *non-I* [*non-moi*]" (692/9). But it is not the depiction of the modern world per se that is important. The "value" of Guys' work, Baudelaire argues, lies in "the wealth of thoughts to which they give rise—thoughts however which are generally solemn and dark" (722/38). The painter's realism in depicting scenes of "moral fecundity" is thus the source of a "particular beauty" (722/38). Far from being salacious images put forward to stimulate the "unhealthy imagination," Baudelaire argues, the image of "inevitable vice" in Guys' depictions of prostitutes and courtesans is "nothing but pure art, that is to say, the particular beauty of evil, the beautiful amid the horrible" (722/38). Through their faithfulness to everyday phenomena, Guys' works represent modern life as a spectacle for reflection.[182]

While Baudelaire's "Flowers" also pursue *modernité* in the form of "the special beauty of evil," his own mode of evoking such reflection cannot simply be identified with Guy's. The poet's lyric voices comprise not only I's with an "insatiable appetite for the *non-I*" but also personas incapable of the immediate and unqualified embrace of modern life that defined the latter's art. Hence while "Monsieur G. has a horror of blasé people" (691/9), within Baudelaire's poetic project, the love of flânerie coexists with the capacity, despised by his Monsieur G., for being *"bored in the bosom of the multitude"* (692/10). There are certainly poems that describe pleasurable immersion in the crowd, but in Baudelaire's oeuvre, urban life is as likely to produce fits of spleen or heavy ennui as such ecstatic self-loss. Similarly, "The Painter of Modern Life" praises the marks of Guys' frenzied attempts to capture everything he has seen in his paintings (699/17) while the poet himself is more selective and by no means shared Guys' predilection for rapid, almost mass

[182]Thus Baudelaire emphasizes that Guys generally worked "from memory and not from the model" (698/16). Baudelaire's distinctive idealism echoes in this praise of a phenomenal representation of modern life based on the reflective images in an artist's mind.

production of images.[183] If, according to Baudelaire, its "modernity" made Guys' art significant, his own artistic ideal was rather different. He recognized the importance of the contingent—that "almost all our originality comes from the stamp which *time* imprints on our sensations" (696/14). However, Baudelaire was not content to be a painter of mores—to capture the changeable element of beauty—but attempted to realize its "eternal half" as well. Thus his poetry represents not only "the special beauty of evil" but also the "solemn and dark" thoughts that such modern beauty evokes. And since the problematic status of modern beauty raises epistemological as well as ethical questions, his poetry often thematizes the subjective process by which such beauty comes into being—by which the fragmentary impressions of the disenchanted modern world become the elements of artistic creation.

The novelty Laforgue praised should be underlined. Baudelaire fashions a new language for expressing modern experience by synthesizing modern words and sensations with the inherited vocabulary and rhetorical strategies of lyric poetry. Romantic gestures are imbued with the reflective consciousness of the enlightened subject; classical lyrical structures become the framework for an anatomy of modern identity and desire. As Laforgue's remarks indicate, 'ennui' plays a decisive role in this process. In accordance with his theory of art, in identifying ennui as the formal expression of an experience of temporality and desire that resonates into antiquity, Baudelaire grasps its specific modernity. The experience thus takes on a metaphorical function, enabling a certain reflective distance from the urban space that produces it. Baudelaire's 'ennui,' which is simultaneously dependent on the temporal and erotic disjunctions arising from the transformation of Paris in this period and a mode of transcending that historico-political context, thus becomes the cornerstone of a distinctively modern poetics, one that refigures contemporary cultural discourse to reflect historically on the subjective effects of modernization.

In Baudelaire's writing, the hunger for experience, the longing to see and appreciate the world, is paired with a despairing sense of meaninglessness and loss. It is this combination, rather than a faithfulness to the task of representing modern life per se, that makes his invocations of boredom historically and politically significant. Although there is the barest hint of the historic upheaval underway in the Paris of which he writes, fatigue, melancholy, and boredom suffuse his poetry, provoking fall after fall back from the heights of the ideal to the earth, to the body. For Baudelaire, 'ennui' distin-

---

[183]While Guys worked "on twenty drawings at a time" (700/18), Baudelaire's life's work fits into two fairly slim volumes.

guishes the poet and the "brothers" who will be his readers because it signals a specific relation to the modern urban world—one that defines an elite within the metropolitan crowd. For them, the material and moral effects of modernization converge in a form of suffering at once metaphysical and temporal, horrifyingly immediate and yet immaterial.

In describing modern life from the perspective not of Parnassus but of "an ordinary lost soul of the capital," Baudelaire brings boredom into a larger context that makes possible a new form of reflection on its significance. Rather than elevating boredom to a metaphysical inevitability, he places the absoluteness and universality that seem to characterize the experience into question. His 'ennui' describes a constellation of self and world that occurs *in* modernity as an experience *of* modernity, a mode in which the historical particularity of the perception and the perceiving subject is revealed. The "spleen" that gives rise to the despairing conviction that the universe is darkly meaningless is anatomized. The ennui of absolute futility and nihilism, of fatigue and exhaustion in the face of a world without divine succor, cannot simply be identified as a universal feature of the human condition. Many poems imply that the bored subject may be culpable for the collapse of longing into meaninglessness and the rejection of the world this entails. Boredom is not simply fate—it is also the vice of those who hunger for a fullness of experience under the conditions of its disappearance. As such, it points the way on the *via negativa* along which Baudelaire attempts to rekindle the romantic aspiration to render worldly existence meaningful in the very inferno of modern life: Paris.

Ennui as Vice and Fate

Plutôt la barbarie que l'ennui!
Théophile Gautier[184]

In the prefatory poem, "Au Lecteur," Baudelaire tenders his *Flowers of Evil* to a reader who inhabits the Paris into which we have peered—a world in which exhaustion and moral decay are the counterparts of civilization's progress, in which industrialization and modernization transmute the longing for meaning into a desperate search for new sensations. The poet addresses his reader as a fellow connoisseur of vice whose fits of remorse are but pretexts for more refined self-indulgence and exhorts him to recognize ennui as his most monstrous tendency. It is not simply, as the poem makes clear, that

---

[184]"Better barbarianism than ennui!" Gautier was the "master and friend" to whom *The Flowers of Evil* were dedicated (OC I, 3). Cited in Steiner 1971, 11.

boredom leads to ever greater transgressions. Ennui is itself the manifestation of an internal failure—a synecdoche for the spiritual crisis that the poet professes to share with his "hypocrite reader."

Baudelaire's lyrical voyage into modern life is addressed to an audience of inveterate sinners. "To the Reader" begins: "Stupidity, error, vice, and stinginess/Occupy our spirits and overwork our bodies,/And we feed our pleasant remorse/As mendicants nourish their vermin."[185] It would be incautious to identify Baudelaire with his (many) narrative voices. However, it is worth remarking that "Au Lecteur" invokes a "we" that reappears periodically throughout the work. This "we" rhetorically identifies the author of the book with the implied author of the poem, at once including Baudelaire within the crowd of modern sinners and marking his reflective distance from such an identification. It is a point of view that amalgamates irony, contempt, and despair: "Our sins are obstinate, our repentances lax"; despite consciousness of the debilitating effects of sin, the speaker observes, the most violent debaucheries are quickly forgotten. "We gaily reenter the filthy path/Believing our vile tears have washed away our blemishes."[186] With "the rich metal of our will" transmuted by Satanic alchemy, the implied author and his readers seek the allure of "repugnant objects"—"with every day we take a step toward Hell."[187] If "the banal canvas of our piteous destiny" has not been embellished by actual rape and murder, then because "our soul, alas! is not bold enough."[188] The "infamous menagerie" of vices that follows therefore culminates in "Ennui."

Because ennui affirms the indifference to life and death that colors the pursuit of crime and the pangs of remorse alike, Baudelaire writes, it is "more hideous, more evil, more unclean" than all the other vices. "Though he makes no great cry, no great display of trouble,/He'd eagerly demolish everything to rubble,/Gulp down the entire world in one convulsive yawn."[189] All-engulfing, all-consuming, ennui is more horrible than the other

---

[185]"La sottise, l'erreur, le péché, la lésine,/Occupent nos esprits et travaillent nos corps,/Et nous alimentons nos amiables remords,/Comme les mendiants nourrissent leur vermine."

[186]"Et nous rentrons gaiement dans le chemin bourbeux,/Croyant par de vils pleurs laver toutes nos taches."

[187]"Et le riche métal de notre volonté/Est tout vaporisé par ce savant chimiste . . . /Aux objets répugnants nous trouvons des appas;/Chaque jour vers l'Enfer nous descendons d'un pas . . ."

[188]"Si le viol, le poison, le poignard, l'incendie,/N'ont pas encor brodé de leurs plaisants dessins/Le canevas banal de nos piteux destins,/C'est que notre âme, hélas! n'est pas assez hardie."

[189]Crosby's translation. "Dans le ménagerie infâme de nos vices,/Il en est un plus laid, plus méchant, plus immonde!/Quoiqu'il ne pousse ni grands gestes ni grands cris,/Il ferait volontiers de la terre un débris /Et dans un bâillement avalerait le monde; //C'est l'Ennui!—L'oeil chargé d'un pleur involontaire,/Il rêve d'échafauds en fumant son houka./Tu le connais, lecteur, ce monstre délicat,/—Hypocrite lecteur,—mon semblable,—mon frère!"

vices because it embodies a nihilistic will to forget—smoking his hookah and dreaming of death, Ennui embraces evil wholeheartedly. "You know him, reader, this delicate monster,/—Hypocrite reader,—my double,—my brother!" However weak and self-indulgent the gestures of penitence mentioned at the outset of the poem may be, to succumb to ennui is to fail even to struggle against the "vaporization" of will wrought by Satan. Unlike the other vices, which feed on the self, ennui would willfully (*voluntiers*) devastate, then yawningly incorporate the entire objective world for its failure to gratify the insatiable subject and its debased desires.

It is important to emphasize that the knowledge of this "delicate monster" which makes "brothers" of Baudelaire and his readers is but a starting point. The work that follows challenges that reader to engage in reflection upon the longing to forget and upon the spectacularly destructive, vicious desire to destroy the evidence of disappointment that trails the defeated yearnings of the modern subject. In the context of the *Fleurs du Mal* as a whole, this image of world-engulfing orality is but a splenetic fantasy of the bored subject, whose adventures leave no impression upon his "piteous destiny."[190] Boredom renders the sufferer omniverous, yet impotent. Thus the affirmation of forgetfulness that initially seems to constitute ennui must be seen as a feint—as the distorted reflection of the very inability to escape the bonds of time that produces the longing for death. In Baudelaire's actual descriptions of the experience of ennui, the insufficiency of life dessicates the wellsprings of desire, flattening everything and leaving the sufferer stranded in a world that has become a meaningless desert. Ennui elongates time, and the remedies—love, gambling, narcotics—only worsen the disease.

In the closing poem of the second (1861) edition of *Les Fleurs du Mal*, "Le Voyage" (The Journey), ennui appears in this sense, not as vice but as fate. Childhood dreams of leading an adventurous life come to grief in the recognition of the monotonous sameness of past and future alike.[191]

> What bitter knowledge one gains from travel!
> The world, monotonous and small, today,

---

[190]Which is not to say that Baudelaire views this moment of destructiveness as insignificant for understanding ennui. On the contrary, consider "A une heure du matin" (in *Paris Spleen*) in which we overhear the speaker "alone at last," exclaiming "Horrible vie! Horrible ville!" and recounting his pointless deeds of malice. Or in the prose poem that precedes it, "Le Mauvais Vitrier," the sentiment of the narrator who in a sudden gust of will has dropped a flowerpot on an old glazier: "Mais qu'importe l'éternité de la damnation à qui a trouvé dans une seonde l'infini de la jouissance?"

[191]"Pour l'enfant, amoureux de cartes et d'estampes,/L'univers est égal à son vaste appétit./Ah! que le monde est grand à la clarté des lampes!/Aux yeux du souvenir que le monde est petit!"

> Yesterday, tomorrow, always, shows us our image:
> An oasis of horror in a desert of ennui![192]

The sole distinction of the self who is without hope in death or in life seems to be awareness of the dreadful meaninglessness of existence. "Curiosité," the striving after meaning and novelty that provokes the journey, can never be fulfilled: "Singular fortune where the goal moves about/And being nowhere can be anywhere."[193] Despite this tone of metaphysical renunciation, the language in which Baudelaire represents the voyagers' despair has pronounced theological resonances. There is nothing new under the sun:

> We have seen stars
> And waves; we have also seen sandy wastes;
> And in spite of many a shock and unforeseen
> Disaster, we were often bored, as we are here.

It would be too simple to say that the opulent cities and beautiful lands they have visited have disappointed the travelers' mortal vision. If they found more "mysterious attraction" in the fleeting images "chance made in clouds," then, they imply, because "desire always rendered us anxious [*soucieux*]." Baudelaire's implicitly allegorical framing of the voyage underlines the religious connotations of the apparently insoluble crisis of meaning suffered by the voyagers, for whom incessant longing distracts from every satisfaction, while every satisfaction renders desire more powerful.[194]

The image of those desires fed by pleasure as a source of anxiety resonates with the theological tradition according to which the idolatrous diversion of the longing for meaning into earthly pleasures ends in debauchery. Accordingly, even this degradation of their search fails to make a real impression on the voyagers: a nihilistic inability to distinguish qualitatively among pleasures makes the spectacle of life seem the same everywhere. And when they encounter the religious aspiration to ascend to the heavens, it, too, becomes a sign of the universality of their plight. "Saintliness," they report, is every-

---

[192]"Amer savoir, celui qu'on tire du voyage!/Le monde, monotone et petit, aujourd'hui,/Hier, demain, toujours, nous fait voir notre image:/Une oasis d'horreur dans un désert d'ennui!" Since the following stanza will be cited below, I include it here: "Faut-il partir? Rester? Si tu peux rester, reste;/Pars, s'il le faut. L'un court, et l'autre se tapit/Pour tromper l'ennemi vigilant et funeste,/Le Temps . . ."

[193]"Singulière fortune où le but se déplace,/Et, n'étant nulle part, peut être n'importe où!"

[194]"Nous avons vu des astres/Et des flots; nous avons vu des sables aussi;/Et, malgré bien des chocs et d'imprévus désastres,/Nous nous sommes souvent ennuyés, comme ici . . . //Les plus riches cités, les plus grands paysages,/Jamais ne contenaient l'attrait mystérieux/De ceux que le hasard fait avec les nuages./Et toujours le désir nous rendait soucieux! //—La jouissance ajoute au désir de la force." This quatrain goes on to depict desire as a tree nourished by pleasures and striving toward heaven.

where "seeking pleasure" in its pastimes—though not in the secular feather bed but rather in the hair shirt.

The voyagers recognize that the "bitter knowledge" embodied in their ineffable, universal ennui expresses an utter failure to escape the malaise that had compelled them to set sail. The longing for knowledge appears to be grounded in a vain desire to flee the human condition. Because time—"vigilant and deadly enemy"—is itself the source of woes, would-be voyagers could just as well stay at home; the real, the secret goal of travel is the pursuit not of knowledge but of the fruit of forgetfulness, figuratively represented by the lotus flower which they praise as the entryway into an eternal afternoon. Under its spell, what might have provoked ennui can become a source of infinite pleasure for a subject who no longer desires anything but the eternal return of the same.[195] Time—mortal existence—is the source of suffering, but Baudelaire's voyagers know no possibility of transcendence: their fantasy of escaping time is suffused by a longing for unvarying lassitude, for a state of desirelessness in which ennui is banished through a sort of homeopathy.

If throughout their travels, they have followed a "singular fortune" where the goal is always being displaced, at the end only oblivion seems to hold out any hope. Apparently they have stopped solely to disabuse their interlocutors—those who stayed home and long "to travel without steam or sail" through vicarious memories—of the delusion that life is different, more interesting, elsewhere. "Must one go? Stay? If you can stay, stay;/Go if it's necessary . . ." Having seen that human existence is but "an oasis of horror in a desert of ennui," they set no store by travel. Yet despite their hopelessness, the voyagers set sail again. In the final quatrain, they salute their "old captain Death," imploring him to impart his poison that they may "plunge into the depths of the abyss, Heaven or Hell, does it matter?/Into the depths of the Unknown to find something *new*."[196] Baudelaire's travelers are acutely aware that the curiosity that "torments" them cannot lead to knowledge, that the pursuit of pleasure cannot possibly quench their longing for meaning. An internal dynamic encloses them in a world "monotonous and small," a "desert of ennui." Whether fantasizing about eternal forgetfulness or calling for death, they are condemned to boredom, the burden of mortals whose de-

[195]"... Par ici! Vous qui voulez manger/Le Lotus parfumé! c'est ici qu'on vendange/Les fruits miraculeux dont votre cœur a faim;/Venez vous enivrer de la douceur étrange/De cette après-midi qui n'a jamais de fin?"

[196]"O Mort, vieux capitaine, il est temps! levons l'ancre./Ce pays nous ennuie, ô Mort! Appareillons! . . . /Verse-nous ton poison pour qu'il nous réconforte!/Nous voulons, tant ce feu nous brûle le cerveau,/Plonger au fond du gouffre, Enfer ou Ciel, qu'importe?/Au fond de l'Inconnu pour trouver du nouveau."

sire takes forms that make it impossible to fulfill. Only the final voyage out of time can, perhaps, offer an escape.

While the introductory poem treats ennui as vice, at the end of the *Flowers of Evil*, it has become a fate that may extend even beyond the grave. The longing for a timeless nirvana, for the pleasures of oblivion, may appear indistinguishable from the nihilistic impulse that provoked the initial fantasy of engulfing the whole world in ennui's vast yawn. To a thinker such as Schopenhauer, for whom the elimination of the will was a moral imperative, the two were indeed one. Here, however, the two forms of desire are distinct. For Baudelaire, ennui is both a vice for which people are culpable and a fate they suffer: the *Fleurs du Mal* relate the two dimensions of the experience in a vision of the modern subject adrift in a world where death itself is the image of life. Thus the poet may depict the lineaments of metaphysical despair with sardonic humor. (For example, in the "Dream of a Curious Man" who dreamt of dying. "Desire and horror mixed," but when "the cold truth was revealed," he found nothing had changed and exclaimed "what! is that all there is to it?"[197]) But his artistic vocation is not only to underline the horror of life in a world where salvation can no longer be imagined as anything more than possible release from senseless searching. For Baudelaire, it is the poet's obligation to interrogate, rather than to embrace, the metaphysical and moral dilemmas of modern existence, and he does so with an irony that underlines that the poet cannot be equated with the voyagers whose despairing vision of life he chronicles.[198] Baudelaire represents the poet as one who strives to render his experiences both salable and immortal—one thus on the front lines of humanity's confrontation with the spectre of temporal existence as a succession of empty moments in a life seemingly without transcendent meaning.

The four poems entitled "Spleen" meditate on the landscape of desire in which the modern subject's struggle to wrest meaning out of transiency takes place. Baudelaire adapts the metonymic English usage of spleen, according to which the organ thought to be the site of production of black bile (*melan kole*) stands for the melancholic effect that predominates in the saturnine, melancholic, character of the (implied) poet. In the first, January ("Pluvióse") "irritated with the whole city, / Pours . . . a gloomy cold / Over the pale inhabitants of the neighboring cemetery / And mortality upon the foggy

---

[197]"Eh quoi! n'est-ce donc que cela?" This poem immediately precedes *Le Voyage*.

[198]To do so is to commit the error of those who prosecuted this poet, whose finest hope was to evoke reflection on the meaning of modern moral decay, for immorality. Although she underplays his ironic distance from the discourses he invokes, Starkie offers an interesting reading of Baudelaire as misunderstood Catholic poet.

slums."[199] As the icy rain effaces the distinction between living and dead, the speaker has his fortune told. The sounds of the city—a clock, a bell, a dead poet's ghost—rattle senselessly and ominously around him.

In the second of the series, known by its first line, "I have more memories than if I had lived a thousand years,"[200] the voice becomes the landscape and the things, over-saturated with significance, that belong to it. Here unity with the surrounding world is anything but ecstatic. At once dispersed into the world and over-burdened with heavy memories, the lyric subject imagines his "sad brain" as a sepulchral vault (*caveau*) with "more corpses than the paupers' grave." He calls himself a "cemetery abhorred by the moon" and an "old boudoir" jammed with outdated dresses, withered roses, and faded rococo paintings.[201] As the contents of the "Chest of drawers encumbered with balance sheets/Verses, love letters, law-suits, romances,/With heavy locks rolled in receipts" with which this "I" compares his skull indicates, this is no pure romantic melancholy. In these images, the excess of memory is borne down to earth by the heavy weight of all-too-mortal concerns about money. But in the next stanza, the voice seems transferred outside this profusion of "bodies" into a distanced reflection on the whole highly "poetic" state of intermingling with evocative objects.

> Nothing is so long as those limping days,
> When under the heavy flakes of snowy years
> Ennui, the fruit of dismal incuriosity,
> Takes on the proportions of immortality.
> —Henceforth you are no more, O living matter!
> Than a block of granite surrounded by vague terrors,
> Dozing in the depths of a hazy Sahara[202]

When the distinction between self and world dissolves in the identification with the objects 'contained' in memory, the very possibility of experience is effaced. Days are endless; years a heavy blur. There is no hope for meaning,

[199]"Pluviôse, irrité contre la ville entière,/De son urne à grands flots verse un froid ténébreux/Aux pâles habitants du voisin cimetière/Et la mortalité sur les faubourgs brumeux."

[200]"J'ai plus de souvenirs que si j'avais mille ans."

[201]"Un gros meuble à tiroirs encombré de bilans,/De vers, de billets doux, de procès, de romances,/Avec de lourds cheveux roulés dans des quittances,/Cache moins de secrets que mon triste cerveau./C'est une pyramide, un immense caveau,/Qui contient plus de morts que la fosse commune./—Je suis un cimetière abhorré de la lune . . . /—Je suis un vieux boudoir plein de roses fanées./Où gît tout un fouillis de modes surannées,/Où les pastels plaintifs et les pâles Boucher,/Seuls, respirent l'odeur d'un flacon débouché."

[202]"Rien n'égale en longueur les boiteuses journées/Quand sous les lourds flocons des neigeuses années/L'ennui, fruit de la morne incuriosité,/Prend les proportions de l'immortalité/—Désormais tu n'es plus, ô matière vivante!/Qu'un granit entouré d'une vague épouvante,/Assoupi dans le fond d'un Saharah brumeux . . ."

and ennui "Takes on the proportions of immortality." In this experience, Baudelaire implies, the romantic subject's melancholy immersion in memory attains the status of fate: his apathy consumes all desire for knowledge, ossifying the speaker into a forgotten sphinx for whom the present world is but a murkily lapping threat. And this exile into the realm of things takes place not in the desert where hermits struggled against the demon of noontide but in a god-forsaken wasteland to which no Oedipus shall come.

In the third "Spleen," the lyric subject compares himself to "the king of a rainy [*pluvieux*] land, rich but impotent" who is incapable of enjoyment.[203] Like the prince in the prose poem "Une Mort Heroique" (OC I, 319–23) whose "faculties were greater than his States," such a man knows "but one dangerous enemy, ennui." Because nothing can excite his desire, he is driven to ever greater debaucheries. "The wise man who makes his gold could never / Extirpate the corrupt element from his being."[204] In his "insipid cadaver / Instead of blood, the green water of Lethe flows."[205] In this final image, the third "Spleen" allusively links melancholy and alienation from existence to the doctrine of the humors. Here the substance that explains this sickness of soul is not black bile, but rather the mythical water of forgetfulness that shades must drink upon entering the underworld.

While the previous poem identified 'spleen' with a surfeit of memory that ossifies living matter, here it is forgetfulness that turns the king corpse-like. Taken together, the poems delineate a complex vision of ennui as the bane of modern subjects, who liberate themselves from the icy hand of the past only to fall victim to the meaningless interchangeability of new experiences. Juxtaposing these diametrically opposed accounts of the wellsprings of ennui underlines the distinction between Baudelaire's point of view and that of his allegorical voyagers. As the ironic structure of "Le Voyage" itself suggests, the nihilistic longing for oblivion and the optimistic striving after the new that seem so opposed to them are, from a reflective perspective, identical. Memory and forgetfulness alike oppress the modern subject and turn him corpse-like. As "The Clock" reminds the reader, the utilitarian perspective on Time has not outsmarted death. Even as Baudelaire represents the experience of ennui as modern, he emphasizes that it is rooted in perennial features of the human condition.

The fourth poem entitled "Spleen" ("Quand le ciel bas et lourd pèse comme un couvercle") thematizes this historically specific experience of

---

[203]"Je suis comme le roi d'un pays pluvieux, / Riche, mais impuissant . . ."
[204]"Le savant qui lui fait de l'or n'a jamais pu / De son être extirper l'élément corrompu."
[205]". . . réchauffer ce cadavre hébété / Où coule au lieu de sang l'eau verte du Léthé."

transiency. It describes the spiritual existence of the modern subject who is weighed down by the heavens, who inhabits a world with no exit. The first three stanzas begin with "when," an anaphora that evokes not temporal specificity but a sense of unvarying sameness. This poem describes the timeless landscape of despair that surrounds those who suffer from spleen in a world where desire has no larger meaning.

> When the sky, low and heavy, weighs like a lid
> On the groaning spirit, prey to long ennuis,
> And from the all-encircling horizon
> Pours over us a black day sadder than the nights;
>
> When the earth is changed into a humid dungeon,
> Where Hope, like a bat
> Goes beating the walls with her timid wings
> And knocking her head against the rotten ceiling
>
> When the rain stretching out its immense train
> Imitates the bars of a vast prison . . .[206]

Baudelaire's use of the plural form, *longs ennuis*, in the second quatrain both expresses the unrelenting duration of imprisonment in this world and evokes the older sense of "ennui" as the pain and suffering that accompanies the loss of the beloved. Once again there is a romantic intermingling of interior and exterior, poet and world. However, as in "Spleen (II)," the loss of boundaries becomes painful and oppressive. The very possibility of sensory delight has been banished from this carceral existence. The earth is a dungeon—and one where the hope of escape—of transcendence—has been vanquished entirely.

In the final "Spleen," the audience is explicitly included in the experience. The horizon "pours over us a black day"; in the prison formed by the rain, spiders spin webs "in the depth of our brains."[207] The speaker's experience is neither unique nor collective but representative. In the penultimate quatrain, a furious roar goes up from the city's bells to the heavens, a "stubborn whimpering" like that of "wandering and stateless spirits."[208] The churches remain, but the divine music of bells no longer has the power to demarcate the structure of social time. Their tolling is experienced only as a violent

---

[206]"Quand le ciel bas et lourd pèse comme un couvercle / Sur l'esprit gémissant en proie aux longs ennuis, / Et que de l'horizon embrassant tout le cercle / Il nous verse un jour noir plus triste que le nuits / /Quand la terre est changée en un cachot humide, / Où l'Espérance, comme une chauve-souris, / S'en va battant les murs de son aile timide / Et se cognant la tête à des plafonds pourris."

[207]"au fond de nos cerveaux."

[208]"Des cloches tout à coup sautent avec furie / Et lancent vers le ciel un affreux hurlement, / Ainsi que des esprits errants et sans patrie / Qui se mettent à geindre opiniâtrement."

shock from outside, a brief and jarring interruption to melancholy reverie that quickly fades into oblivion. The final stanza evokes the splenetic subject's sense of reification even more horribly than the image of the abandoned block of granite:

> —And without drums or music, long hearses
> Pass by slowly in my soul; Hope,
> Vanquished, weeps, and Anguish atrocious, despotic
> On my bowed skull plants his black flag.[209]

In "I have more memories than if I had lived a thousand years," the speaker, occupied by memories, felt himself a cemetery; here the soul has become the city streets themselves, in which the dead parade silently by. In the former poem, ennui so assumed "the proportions of immortality" that the speaker imagined himself turned to stone, a lonely sphinx in a world made of memory alone. Here Baudelaire represents spleen with relation not to memory but to the eternal present of earthly suffering. Existence itself has become a prison that frustrates every hope; not loss but absence dominates. Hope is defeated, and the consciousness of mortality fills the soul with all-encompassing, "despotic," anguish. Time, unvarying, moves on, but without any human articulation. For one who is banished in a world without hope, where church bells merely screech into the emptiness of the heavens, temporality itself has become horrifying.

In the final "Spleen," the experience of ennui becomes a metaphor for the horrifying fate of the modern subject in a godless world. The victims of "long ennuis" groan beneath a sky that has become an oppressive prison because their isolation in empty, meaningless time precludes any communication with the heavens. Such spleen is no longer romantic melancholy, no longer the *taedium vitae* that seeks after fresh stimulations: it expresses the utter despair of the desolate modern subject whose world has become a nightmare of meaningless suffering. Hope bats in futility against the ceiling of the dungeon that the earth has become; even the bells tolling the hour from the church towers are exiled, ruminant spirits whose cries rise in impotent rage, then quickly fade into insignificance. Here spleen is far even from the voyagers' nihilistic affirmation of the meaninglessness of existence ("an oasis of horror in a desert of ennui"). Hope, having exhausted itself, lies defeated, and an immobilizing anguish tyrannizes the soul in which the death of God comes to consciousness.

---

[209]"—Et de longs corbillards, sans tambours ni musique, / Défilent lentement dans mon âme; l'Espoir, / Vaincu, pleure, et l'Angoisse atroce, despotique, / Sur mon crâne incliné plante son drapeau noir."

Such moments of despairing resignation to the fate of the poet and that of the "brothers" who make up his audience suffuse Baudelaire's work. And yet they invoke a religious dimension that distinguishes his perspective from that of the cynical voyagers who, having renounced their longing for meaning, simply roam the earth, by turns seeking new stimulations and longing for annihilation. Baudelaire suggests that the ennui that plagues him and his "hypocrite reader" is a manifestation of the mortal sin of sloth and, more profoundly, of acedia—the spiritual torpor in which God seems infinitely distant, all efforts to reach Him vain. Thus in one of the first poems in "Spleen and Ideal," "Le Mauvais Moine" (The Bad Monk), the speaker compares himself unfavorably to the good monks of days of old who "glorified death with simplicity," surrounded by the images of "holy Truth."

> —-My soul is a tomb where, bad cenobite,
> I wander and dwell eternally;
> Nothing adorns the walls of that loathsome cloister.

Here Baudelaire again describes an experience of self in which the distinction between inside and outside collapses horribly. Interred alive, trapped inside a soul that can no longer attain any connection to the divine, the lyric subject passes the empty hours without comfort, resigned to the impossibility of transcendence. His is not the prayer from the desert that faith may return; he aspires, rather, to gain the power to turn his ennui into art. The poem concludes:

> O lazy monk! When shall I learn to make
> Of the living spectacle of my bleak misery
> The labor of my hands and the love of my eyes?[210]

Such laziness can be alleviated not by the simple earthly labors recommended by the Church Fathers as a remedy against acedia but only by a form of work that an orthodox Catholic would have to condemn as a prideful apotheosis of the self. There is no escape from the dungeon the earth has become into the divine realm of pure ideas; Baudelaire turns rootedness in the modern world into an exemplum, an admonitory spectacle from which others may learn.

However, as the preceding poem, "The Venal Muse," makes clear, Baudelaire's morally ambivalent association of art with an escape from ennui is complicated by the actual conditions of production. To have "During the

---

[210]"—Mon âme est un tombeau que, mauvais cénobit,/Despuis l'éternité je parcours et j'habite;/Rien n'embellit les murs de ce cloître odieux. //O moine fainéant! quand saurai-je donc faire/Du spectacle vivant de ma triste misère/Le travail de mes mains et l'amour de mes yeux?"

black ennuis of snowy evenings / An ember to warm your two purple feet,"
the speaker warns his muse, it will be necessary to compromise the devotion
to beauty alone in a form of blasphemy:

> To earn your daily bread you are obliged,
> To swing the censer like an altar boy,
> And to sing *Te Deums* in which you hardly believe[211]

These verses underline Baudelaire's awareness of the tension within the religious rhetoric of experience he invokes. Because the old forms, whether
lyrical or spiritual, can no longer fulfill their purposes, the poet who depends
upon the traditional vocabulary of transcendence is entangled in contradiction. Both spiritual suffering and the desire for beauty have been democratized, and the poet who wants to survive in the modern world must turn "the
living spectacle of [his] bleak misery" into money-making distractions that
"drive away the spleen [*rate*] of the vulgar."[212] But the process of turning his
talents to satisfy such desires can only deepen the modern poet's despairing
conviction that his soul is as empty as the world he sings to, that he is a thing
among other things. Though he is by vocation unable to renounce the longing for meaning, a grimly nihilistic tendency inevitably gnaws at the foundation of his art. Herein lies one source of the profound ambiguity of Baudelaire's oeuvre. Ennui is at once an experience of metaphysical significance
and a show put on to effect the catharsis demanded by the "hypocrite readers" who pay his way.

   By inducing those readers to reflect both on the nature of their own experience and on the significance of the linguistic and social forms in which it
takes place, *The Flowers of Evil* achieve a certain distance from the poetry-
strangling temporality of modern existence. The tension, so crucial to
Baudelaire's poetic project, between *modernité* and the enduring realities of
human existence is beautifully illustrated by a poem he dedicated to the exiled romantic poet Victor Hugo, "The Swan." In it, the urban landscape becomes a melancholy allegory of loss through which "exiles, ridiculous and
sublime / And gnawed by ceaseless desire" wander aimlessly under a "sky
ironically and cruelly blue." The city demolished by Baron Haussmann becomes an enigmatic figure for the emptiness of the heavens. "The old Paris is

---

[211]"O muse de mon cœur, amante des palais, / Auras-tu, quand Janvier lâchera ses
Borées, / Durant les noirs ennuis des neigeuses soirées, / Un tison pour chauffer tes deux pieds
violets?. . . / / Il te faut, pour gagner ton pain de chaque soir, / Comme un enfant de chœur, jouer
de l'encensoir, / Chanter des Te Deum auxquels tu ne crois guère, . . ."
[212]"Pour faire épanouir la rate du vulgaire."

no more (the form of a city/Changes more rapidly, alas! Than the mortal heart)." But the material losses of modernization occasion a form of seeing that 'remembers' its poetic antecedents. What has been destroyed in the exterior world reappears in the interior. A fugitive swan evokes Andromache, exiled from Troy.

> Paris changes! but nothing in my melancholy
> Has budged! new palaces, scaffoldings, blocks,
> Old neighborhoods, for me all becomes allegory,
> And my precious memories are heavier than stones.[213]

Once again, the lyric subject is weighed down by memories, but in this case, melancholy leads beyond the grim defeats of the spleen poems. Here modern Paris "becomes allegory"—the ancient, the mythical echoes everywhere under the ironic sky where everyone is homeless. The resignation that suffuses this poem embodies a post-romantic melancholy. Doubly estranged from a world of universal exile, the lyric subject has found a sort of escape from the "ceaseless longing" that gnaws at the other inhabitants of the city. In the mode of perception through which "everything becomes allegory," the responsibility to memory has become an end in itself.

Representing Boredom: Spleen and Modernité

As my readings of the four poems entitled "Spleen" suggest, Baudelaire's strategy of poetic mediation between ancient and modern, ideal and material vocabularies of reflection on subjective experience operates globally in his use of that term. Playing on its ambiguities, he uses 'spleen' to link historically distinct rhetorics of reflection on subjective experience—to represent the kaleidoscope in which ancient elements such as melancholy, *taedium vitae*, and acedia are refracted through modern, materialist interpretations of subjective malaise to form modern ennui. The significance of Baudelaire's rhetorical strategy lies in its opposition to the global evolution in the rhetoric of reflection underway in this period. According to Bouillet's dictionary, we recall, spleen "consists in a state of consumption engendered by melancholy and characterized by the sadness of sickness, the distaste for life, a great apathy, and indifference toward everything." Such an understanding of spleen as a pathological state departs from the ancient doctrine of the humors: it be-

---

[213]"Paris change! mais rien dans ma mélancholie/N'a bougé! palais neufs, échafaudages, blocs,/Vieux faubourgs, tout pour moi devient allégorie,/Et mes chers souvenirs sont plus lourds que des rocs."

longs to the emerging discourse on modern nervous disease that I have discussed under the aegis of the medicalization of malaise. Indeed, Bouillet identified spleen as a "type of hypochondria."

Baudelaire had good reasons for rejecting such a medicalized vision of human malaise. His language of reflection blends the traditional and modern with a moral sense that integrates historical and aesthetic concerns. The modern poet's task of transforming into art the experience of an existence robbed of transcendent meaning takes as its point of departure an existential despair that incorporates ancient and modern elements into a new vocabulary of reflection. The concept of spleen, which appears in various, seemingly contradictory manifestations throughout Baudelaire's oeuvre, provides the medium in which all of these elements converge. As we have seen, "spleen" is linked to *taedium vitae* and to acedia; it is both a nervous response to modern life and a manifestation of the melancholy character linked since Aristotle to great men and their creativity. Thus the poet's evocations of spleen mediate the modern, materialistic language of fatigue and exhaustion with the ancient vocabulary in which acedia and melancholy lead to excessive reflection upon the sorrows of life and the inevitability of death. But there is a further complexity, for the modern register in Baudelaire's use of the term is not so much medical as cultural. An English import, the word 'spleen' resonated in a mediated way with the venerable vocabulary of human temperaments. It was tied for Baudelaire and his contemporaries to modern London, the home of the *maladie anglaise* and of Edgar Allen Poe's man of the crowd.[214] The reader who accepts Baudelaire's "we" must understand the foreign word as embodying allusions both contemporary and ancient.

Baudelaire underlines the importance of this concept for his reflections on modern existence in various ways. "Spleen" is not only the title of the four poems discussed above; paired evocatively with "Idéal," it also provides the subtitle for the first and longest section of the *Fleurs du Mal* in which they appear. In addition, the intended title of the collection of prose poems Baudelaire had been assembling in the decade before his death was *Le Spleen de Paris*.[215] The ambiguous genitive in this title alludes to an historical specificity of experience that (as in "The Swan") belies the supposed eternity of melancholy itself. It locates the dilemma of the ideal in modernity historically, as a function of the vain strivings for meaning that characterize modern

---

[214] Baudelaire, who translated Poe, invokes the figure of the man of the crowd in "The Painter of Modern Life."

[215] A number had been published under this title in 1864. According to Pichois, "Le Spleen de Paris est le seul titre attesté avec certitude durant les dernières années de la vie de Baudelaire." His discussion of the title question is to be found in OC I, 1298–1300.

existence. If *The Flowers of Evil* forge the fragments of inherited languages of reflection into a new idiom of reflection on modern existence, the prose poems of *Paris Spleen* delve into the world in which ennui has become universal.

In the modern urban landscape where these poems are set, 'spleen' not only provokes melancholic withdrawal from the world but also inspires venal and violent acts. In *Paris Spleen* we find the prototypes of the existentialist *actes gratuits* through which later sufferers of ennui sought to escape their despair, and much of Baudelaire's reputation for immorality rests on the unjustifiable assumption that the poet endorsed the acts of spleen he imagined. A poem touched on earlier, "The Bad Glazier," takes up spleen in this sense—as "a type of energy that springs from ennui and reverie" and which "the moralist and the doctor, who claim to know everything, cannot explain." In fact, when Brierre de Boismont wrote of the "abuse of reverie" associated with "ennui," he referred to the stultifying "predominance of thought over action." Baudelaire, equally concerned with another form of spleen in which that predominance is inverted, is closer to an Aristotelian vision of melancholy as an "anomalous capacity" for greatness. This poem describes how, under certain conditions, "contemplative natures" who are "completely unfit for action" suddenly start out of their disaffection and "discover the luxury of courage to commit the most absurd and often even the most dangerous acts." Perhaps, as the philosophical narrator of this poem, a confessed "victim of such crises and transports" suggests, these outbreaks justify a belief "that malicious demons insinuate themselves into us and make us carry out, unbeknownst to ourselves, their most absurd wishes." But the poem does not, finally, separate the religious and secular registers of explanation. Thus the "fortuitous inspiration" for such acts as the speaker himself "fatigued by idleness" claims to have committed, is said to come from "that humor, hysterical according to the doctors, satanic according to those who think a bit better than the doctors" which provokes a sudden ardor for "dangerous or unseemly actions."

One day, the speaker relates, he had awakened lethargic and sad, "impelled, it seemed to me, to do something great." In a fit of spleen directed against "the first person I noticed in the street," a glazier who had no colored panes to sell, he dropped a flowerpot onto him from the seventh floor, and "drunk with my folly," cried out repeatedly: "Make life beautiful!" Such a shocking affirmation of aesthetic values is an affront to traditional ideals of morality, and the speaker reflects that "such nervous pranks are not without peril." Although the poem ends on a note of demonic affirmation, the speaker has not entirely freed himself from concern for his immortal soul.

The final line—"what does an eternity of damnation matter to one who has found in a second an infinity of pleasure?"—echoes with consciousness of the profound ambiguity of such transgressive forms of greatness.

Sudden fits of lust or hatred notwithstanding, the properly poetic tendency, as illustrated by the four poems written in the first person and entitled "Spleen," is not destructive but despairing. In the absence of faith, a preoccupation with death turns the soul into a tomb, a microcosm of an exitless world. "Satanic" diversions can distract only for brief moments before being overwhelmed by the gnawing remorse alluded to in "Au Lecteur" as the inevitable fruit of sin.[216] Baudelaire is renovating the hallowed tradition that links melancholy and creativity. In his work, the poet figures as a paradigmatic modern subject burdened down by reflection. If the world is experienced as a prison, then his responsibility is, in the words of "The Bad Monk," to turn "the living spectacle" of suffering into art. In representing the experiences that are the implied foundation of the "we" with which he addresses his readers, Baudelaire is not revealing himself so much demonstrating how such fruitless longing can become an object of reflection. He is sketching, to recall Turnell's words, the "anatomy of a highly complex mood . . . which must be identified with what [CB] called 'the morality of the century' or 'the stamp which *time* imprints on our sensations.'" On one hand, Baudelaire identifies the moment of eternity in what he calls 'ennui' by illuminating its resonance with melancholy, acedia, and *taedium vitae*. On the other, he emphasizes its modernity by depicting this experience of the atrophy of experience as a response to the material conditions prevailing in urban Paris. Through this combination he renders lyrical the fragmentation and alienation that make up the daily stuff of modern life.

Ennui is amenable to allegory because as an experience of time, it links the transitory and the eternal. Indeed, it is beauty's other, for, poised between desire and despair, the bored subject is neither seduced by the ephemeral nor comforted by the transcendent. Hence in Baudelaire's poetry, to overcome ennui is to triumph over Time itself. But in his capacity as moralist, Baudelaire sets out for his readers the perils of this pursuit. For mortal beings in a world with no transcendence, no genuine escape from time is possible. Attempts to do so only lead back to ennui. Love proves but a temporary respite, for the transcendence bodily pleasure promises is illusory, tainted with death. In the end, it gives rise only to what the voyagers called "the boring spectacle of immortal sin." Only the diametrical opposite of ennui—a delirium in which reflection becomes impossible—can provide relief.

---

[216]To name but one example, see "L'Irréperable": "Can we suffocate implacable Remorse?"

In "Enivrez-vous" (Get Drunk), the speaker addresses this advice directly to the audience. "To not feel the horrible burden of time . . . it is necessary for you to be drunk without interruption . . . On wine, poetry, or virtue, whatever you like." All of nature and the clock, the speaker claims, will cry out in agreement that such ecstatic self-loss is the only way "to not be the martyred slaves of time."

Another prose poem, "La Chambre double" ("The Double Room"; OC I, 280–82), represents the form of such intoxication. The lyric subject evokes the transformation of his sordid surroundings into an artificial paradise through opium. But Baudelaire's reader is marked by the knowledge that, since delirium only masks the "horrible burden" of temporality, the diametrically opposed transformation, from empyrean to Satanic, is equally inevitable.

The poem begins with a description of a "truly *spiritual* room" in which "the soul bathes in indolence, scented with regret and desire." Everything is languid, indefinite, harmonious. The things around the speaker "live a somnabulent life" or speak the "mute language" of nature. In this romantic idyll, this "pure dream," the "unanalyzed impression" soars above all art. The evocation of "this supreme life" climaxes, then dissolves in the speaker's ecstatic sensation that "time has disappeared, it is Eternity that reigns, an eternity of delights!" But it is an artificial Eden: seemingly at the very mention of the word "time," there is a terrible knock at the door, and the narrator-poet is plunged from fantasy into nightmarish reality. The demands of reality—a "bailiff" asking for money, a "concubine" soliciting aid, a messenger demanding "the manuscript's next installment": it does not matter. The "paradisiacal room" is gone. "Horror! I remember . . . this abode of eternal ennui" with its unfinished manuscripts and "the calendar where the menacing dates are marked in pencil!" Only the sight of the laudanum bottle now provides any comfort.

"Time has reappeared" bringing "his demonic cortege of Memories, Regrets, Spasms, Fears, Anguish, Nightmares, Rages, and Neuroses." Every second, "solemnly accented," now cries out: "I am Life, intolerable, implacable Life!" The lyric subject is plunged back into the prison-world of the calendar; eternity is replaced by an infinite succession of moments, as the luxuriant stupor in which the speaker had been immersed in the pleasures of romantic desire gives way to the anxious anticipation of death—and to ennui. Once again, Baudelaire ruefully invokes the "we" he shares with his audience. "There is only one Second in human life that has the mission to announce good news, the *good news* that causes each of us an inexplicable fear." To be condemned to live under the "brutal dictatorship" of Time means to be shadowed by the memory and anticipation of the unknown moment of one's death.

Like love, opium is but a temporary expedient against Time; the only possibility of escape from ennui and from time itself is art. However, according to "Les Foules" (Crowds; OC I, 291–92), the impulses that make one a poet—"a craving for disguises and masks, hatred of home, and a passion for traveling"—also admit another form of rejuvenation, one that serves art above all. "What men call love," the speaker reflects, is insignificant by comparison with "that holy prostitution of the soul which gives itself entirely" to the rhythms of the urban street. In praising the practice of "taking a bath of multitude," this poem echoes Baudelaire's description of the "painter of modern life" as "an *I* insatiable for the *non-I*." In the urban mass, Baudelaire writes, the poet's skill at being "both himself and another" is called upon: for him there are no boundaries, and he "adopts as his all the professions, all the joys and all the miseries that circumstance presents to him."

Plunging into the crowd is the practice of despair, the ultimate expression of the ennui that arises, as Pascal had written, from not being able to sit quietly alone in one's room.[217] And yet, according to Baudelaire, by cultivating this solitary pleasure, in which loneliness is both affirmed and transcended, the alienated poetic subject can teach "the world's happy ones . . . that there are forms of happiness superior to theirs, more vast and more refined." Taking on the vitality of the masses, giving himself up "to the unexpected that appears, to the unknown that passes by" in an orgy of self-transcendence, the poet nonetheless remains himself. For if the bath in the crowd, the "singular intoxication of that universal communion," cleanses the poet of ennui, it does not rob him of his isolation. "Multitude, solitude: equal and interchangeable terms for the active and fertile poet." If, as Walter Benjamin argued, the urban mass is a silent presence in all of Baudelaire's poems,[218] then as the socio-historical space in which experience is dissolved. The crowd is the condition of possibility both of ecstatic self-loss and of the spleen that distinguishes the poet and his readers; immersion in the urban mass is the practice of skepticism.

In Baudelaire, ennui is both vice and fate—less an emotional response to the world than a reflective attitude about experience, a shaky equilibrium in an existence prone now to melancholic, now to ecstatic modes of self-dissolution. Another of the prose poems of *Paris Spleen*, "Le Joueur géné-

[217]In another prose poem, "Solitude," Baudelaire cites Pascal as witness against the error of seeking "happiness in movement" and in fraternity with others.
[218]According to Benjamin, the vitality of the crowd is the solitary poet's counterpart, his splenetic reveries the transmuted visions of revolutionary transformation.

reux" (The Generous Gambler; OC I, 325–28), attests to the explicit connection between boredom and modernity in Baudelaire's vision of human existence. In it, the speaker relates how he gambled his soul away to the devil in "a resplendent subterranean abode" where the atmosphere made him forget "all the tedious horrors of life." Like the speaker, for whom "the soul is such an impalpable thing, so often useless and sometimes even embarrassing" that he loses it "with heroic insouciance and frivolity," Baudelaire's prince of darkness is a suave man about town. Afterwards, the two of them drink, smoke cigars, and "chat about the universe, its creation and future destruction; about the great idea of the century, that is to say, about progress and perfectibility, and in general about every form of human infatuation." As they part, the devil magnanimously grants him, "in compensation for the irremediable loss of your soul" the stake against which he had gambled it: the ability "to alleviate and vanquish throughout your life that bizarre affection of Ennui, the source of all your maladies and all your wretched progress."

Other poems have attributed ennui to demonic causes; here Baudelaire's devil suggests that it is necessary to take a broader historical perspective on spiritual malaise. If ennui is the driving force behind modernity itself, the restless searching for meaning that began with the Enlightenment is worse than vain, for "wretched progress" only debilitates the spiritual resources of humanity. In short, Enlightenment frustrates the aspirations to which it gives rise and gives rise to aspirations that frustrate it. The imagined escape into the "pure dream," the "unanalyzed impression," must, as in "The Double Room," collapse into "eternal ennui." Disillusionment is but the other visage of Janus-faced modernity.

"The Generous Gambler's" description of what freedom from ennui entails illuminates why it is tempting to play cards with the devil. Not only will the lucky player be able to fulfill all of his material desires for fame and fortune and find those met which he does not imagine. The gift will also allow him to realize the metaphysical longing that underlies Baudelaire's ideal of the artist in "Crowds"—the magnanimous gambler grants him the ability to modify his identity at will: "You shall change your native land and country as often as your fantasies ordain it." Thus it is that the gift of freedom from ennui alleviates the peril through which pacts with the devil usually come to grief—the surfeit that comes of infinitely realized desire—making it possible, the prince of darkness tells him, for him to "gorge on sensual pleasures without satiety." The object of this fantasy of fulfillment without boredom is not simply material satisfaction, but rather the more spiritual (and hence potentially infinite) pleasure of enjoying one's desire.

This eroticized relation to self, here presented as the pendant to the relentless longing for progress which characterizes the era, recurs intermittently in Baudelaire's poetry. We find it also in *L'Invitation au voyage* (OC I, 301–3), where the speaker imagines a "true land of Cockaigne . . . where luxury takes pleasure in admiring itself in order," a place that satisfies poetic "nostalgia for an unknown land," a land of milk and honey from which ennui is banned. There the fantasy takes the form of a "China of Europe," where one can "breathe, dream, and extend the hours with an infinity of sensations . . . where the slower hours hold more thoughts, where the clocks chime out happiness with a more profound and significant solemnity." The orientalism that Baudelaire invokes is the romantic counter-dream to the Western vision of bringing progress and the efficient use of time to the East. However, this tale of correspondence is unusual, for, like "The Double Room," most of Baudelaire's poetic reveries devolve suddenly into nightmares, just as his love poems suddenly change into expressions of terror and hatred of women.

The sudden drastic reversal, the transformation of beauty into horror, ideal into spleen, is Baudelaire's poetic signature. As Benjamin demonstrated, this transformation is itself a correspondence, the poetic reflection of Baudelaire's perception of modernity. Ennui is the linchpin of the reversals that define the structure of modern experience as Baudelaire anatomizes it. While his writing does not accede to the ontological inevitability of boredom, it shows all attempts to overcome it—whether via opium, through immersion in the urban crowd, or by poetic flight into paradisiacal alternative worlds—dead-ending into the recognition of ennui's moral and historical inevitability. Because time is implacable, unless one really succeeds in selling one's soul to the devil, the dynamic of intoxication and despair represented by boredom in Baudelaire's poetry can only be eluded for brief lyrical moments. Ennui returns again and again in dark intimation of the ultimate senselessness of the journey on which all humanity is embarked. It seems that the same nihilistic dynamic that inflected Flaubert's account of modern ennui has reappeared in Baudelaire's. Once again, the perspective of reflection is unstable—the experience of meaninglessness seems to be a proof of the meaninglessness of existence itself. Art is a frail vessel on which escape from this dynamic may be impossible.

In the world of Baudelaire's poems, ennui is absolutely universal. There is, as in the first half of "The Double Room," a positive version of the experience: the opium-laden fantasy of annihilating time.[219] But the awareness of

---

[219] It echoes, too, in the voyagers' longing for the lotus, that "miraculous fruit" that promises escape from the fatiguing vice grip of memory in an eternal afternoon.

mortality—the ultimate source of melancholy—can only be fleetingly dimmed. Thus the speaker was soon recalled to himself, that is to say: to the memory of death that makes him a "slave" to time. As we have seen, in some poems this memory takes the form of melancholic regret about precious time wasted on unworthy or worthless ends. In other poems, 'ennui' has quite the opposite sense: it is the memory of mortality that renders every passing moment vain. In light of the annihilation that awaits at the end of life, the speakers are dominated by a nihilistic sense that all experience is but the eternal repetition of the same. In "The Double Room," this grim recognition of "life, implacable life" rather than the intrusion of the demands of the outside world per se, destroyed the speaker's illusion of timelessness and hence his freedom from ennui. Although it seems to be Satan rather than God who rules over Baudelaire's world, such universalized malaise bears a strong resemblance to the acedia of the desert fathers. As we have seen, the isolation in which Baudelaire's figures dwell is that of an absence born of internal failure—and if ennui is the "most monstrous" vice, then because, like acedia, it is a spiritual state that secretly wills the divine forgetfulness it laments.[220]

And yet such 'ennui' is represented neither as ahistorical vice nor as ahistorical fate. The perspective of reflection—the 'we' that differentiates Baudelaire and his readers from the figures who populate his poems—distinguishes the historical specificity of the underlying experience. Those poems trace the permutations of unhappy consciousness, the modern subject's vacillation between the anxious awareness of impending death and the nihilistic sense that life is but the eternal return of the same, between a longing for meaning and a despairing conviction that the world is fundamentally senseless, between romanticism and enlightenment. At a more mundane level, Baudelaire's 'ennui' also reflects the fatigue and disillusionment which ensue upon a too-enthusiastic embrace of sensual delights—a regimen that, as the paradigm of consumption overtook that of production during the nineteenth century, subtly displaced other sorts of ideals.[221]

Baudelaire's great achievement is to have forged a language that articulates the relations between the historically specific situation of the enlightened modern subject, the spiritualized understanding of ennui as vice, and the hallowed tradition linking melancholy and creativity that remain his

---

[220] On acedia see "La Solitude."

[221] This converges with the acedia dimension in Baudelaire's very Catholic approach to sex and beauty. Robbed of its transcendence and made accessible, Beauty turns vile—hence the monstrous visions of women. Consider also his strange, worshipful relation to Jeanne Duval, whom he seems often to have perceived as indifferent to him and especially to his writing.

most important frames of reference. As a consequence, his representations of boredom resist the interpretation of ennui as the inevitable fate of human beings condemned to a meaningless world. Even as they analyze the temptations of such despair in a world of democratized skepticism, they shift the reader's attention onto the language in which subjective experience is constructed.

Although the attitude of melancholic mournfulness about the lost city was no less common among writers than among other segments of the population, Baudelaire did not really share it.[222] For him, the transformation of Paris was a phenomenon to be confronted—as Benjamin has shown, its crowds, noise, traffic, and filth are all to be found embedded in his poems. In the gesture of acceptance and incorporation through which the realities of the city are taken up and lyrically transformed, Charles Baudelaire's poetics mimics the urban alchemy through which heterogeneous elements became aspects of Paris. Under the aegis of a boredom which can be reduced neither to exhaustion nor to melancholy, Baudelaire registers the significance of these transformations for the urban male subject. Merging the inherited religious and philosophical rhetoric of reflection on subjective experience with a modern, secularized vocabulary, Baudelaire created a language for representing modern experience that articulated the ideal and material, the eternal and historical dimensions of subjective malaise. While the religious resonances have grown less relevant to his twentieth-century readers, the power of Baudelaire's representation of ennui as the fate of the modern urban subject is unparalleled. If we take Baudelaire's understanding of beauty as a synthesis of the eternal and the temporal seriously, these "flowers of evil" allow us to discern both these moments in the distinctive experience of modern boredom.

Although within Baudelaire's oeuvre, 'ennui' represents an experience of time that typifies rather than transcends the ineffable circumstance of mortal existence, the poetic voice that vacillates between melancholic longing and splenetic outbursts nonetheless finds in it a temporary respite in which, however negatively, a sense of self can be found. Thus it is that the knowledge of 'Ennui' distinguishes the reader who will understand him—the

---

[222]Le Cygne, in which the famous lines "Le vieux Paris n'est plus (la forme d'une ville / change plus vite, hélas! que le coeur d'un mortel)" may be found, illustrates that his approach is diametrically opposed to such indulgence. Memory is oppressive, yet the melancholy it fosters is a means of stabilizing identity. "Paris change! mais rien dans ma mélancolie / N'a bougé! Palais neufs, échafaudages, blocs, / Vieux fauborgs, tout pour moi devient allégorie, / et mes chers souvenirs sont plus lourds que des rocs." For an interesting discussion of the political significance of the allegoresis in this poem, which Baudelaire dedicated to the exiled Victor Hugo, see Ross Chambers.

reader who, pursuing the imperishable ideal in secret pleasures of the modern city, understands why he is often overwhelmed by spleen. The "hypocrite lecteur" whom Baudelaire salutes as "my double, my brother" has lived through the upheavals of 1848 that shattered the dream of transcending modern utilitarianism by displacing the bourgeois king Louis-Philippe. Baudelaire's poetry, composed in the era of France's industrialization and Paris' transformation, is modern and post-romantic. Despite his occasional invocations of lost worlds, his lyrics are founded on an experience of resignation to the inevitability of the disappearance of the old world. It is this resignation that, as Walter Benjamin put it, allowed Baudelaire to give "the weight of an experience"—*einer Erfahrung*—to the fragmented form of perception—*Erlebnis*—that resulted from modernization.[223] Baudelaire's poetry suggests that a deeper attention to the historical complexity of the modern vocabulary of reflection may point the way beyond the nihilistic dialectic described by the experience of boredom, through which, as Georg Simmel would put it later, the devaluation of the external world ricochets against the modern self.

One might argue that however violent and destructive the desires it provoked, the ennui which bound Baudelaire to his readers was, in sociological terms, an expression of impotence. Unlike the melancholy which charged the romanticism of the eighteen-twenties and thirties with lustrous dreams of restoring royal pomp and provoked the effusions of Hugo and Lamartine, Baudelaire's ennui connotes a resignation that legitimates political retreat into the aesthetic realm. Of his brief enthusiasm for the revolution, Baudelaire commented in the autobiographical *Mon coeur mis à nus*—"My intoxication of 1848. What was the nature of this intoxication? Taste for vengeance. *Natural* pleasure in demolition. Literary intoxication—a souvenir of reading" (OC I, 679). In thus recuperating the failed attempt at direct political engagement into a narrative of surfeit and spleen, Baudelaire enacts the reversal that is his most characteristic poetic gesture. As we have seen, in the nineteenth century, "literary intoxication" was often put forward as an explanation of the consequences of romanticism. Baudelaire's distinctive reversal at once invokes and rejects this account of the relation between literature and life. Thus too his elevation of Ennui to the defining characteristic of the modern urban subject—"you know it, reader"—extends the very romantic discourse it criticizes. In Baudelaire, ennui is the fate of desire for the en-

---

[223] His poetry, according to Benjamin, "names the price at which the sensation of modernity is to be had: the annihilation of the aura in the shock-experience" (Benjamin, 1974, 149): "Er hat den Preis bezeichnet, um welchen die Sensation der Moderne zu haben ist: die Zertrümmerung der Aura im Chockerlebnis."

lightened subject, the consequence of the inescapable modern vice of reflection.

The question remains how to understand the historical significance of this all-engulfing, cosmic ennui, in which, in a most characteristic poetic gesture, Baudelaire reduces even his own engagement in the world to rubble. My contention is that this nihilistic impulse, forerunner of the *actes gratuits*, is inseparable from his other great legacy: the capacity to make poetry out of ordinary modern life. When he showed the way, in Laforgue's words, "to speak of Paris like any ordinary lost soul of the capital" by elevating boredom to the paradigmatic modern experience, Baudelaire established the aporiai that lie at the heart of our own language of reflection on subjective malaise. If we are to go beyond the drastic reversals of reverie and despair that define Baudelaire's boredom, it is necessary to attempt to sort out the philosophical and sociological dimensions of the experience from within a perspective that recognizes the historical specificity of the rhetoric of experience boredom represents. We turn, therefore, to an explicit consideration of the modern rhetoric of reflection on subjective experience, examining in Chapters 4 and 5 the efforts of Georg Simmel and Martin Heidegger to develop sophisticated sociological and philosophical accounts of the meaning of the form of experience Baudelaire and Flaubert depicted as both fate and vice of the modern subject.

PART II

The Rhetoric of Reflection

CHAPTER 4

Georg Simmel's Phenomenology of Modern Skepticism

——◆◆◆——

Es gibt vielleicht keine seelische Erscheinung, die so unbedingt der Großstadt vorbehalten wäre, wie die Blasiertheit.

Georg Simmel[1]

A Philosopher of Modernity

The sociologist and philosopher of modernity Georg Simmel was born in Berlin the year after the publication of "The Flowers of Evil" and came of age in a world gripped in transformations analogous to those Baudelaire remarked. According to Hans-Ulrich Wehler, while "the German industrial revolution began around 1845," the consciousness of this "historical turning point" did not become widespread until later in the century (26)—in the period of Simmel's maturity. It is worth stopping to reflect on some of the changes that fostered such a sense of living in a radically different world.

The city in which Simmel would spend nearly his entire life had, by mid-century, nearly a half-million inhabitants—a 150% increase since the turn of the century.[2] Developments in his lifetime were even more striking—though the population was "still just under a million in 1875," by 1907 it had exceeded two million, and it continued to grow.[3] The oft-lamented "belatedness" of German development brought technological advantages. By 1873, when the first phase of industrial revolution drew to a close,[4] Germany was a major economic and political force, the victor in wars against France and Austria and "the strongest state on the continent of Europe."[5]

[1] "There is perhaps no psychic phenomenon so exclusively restricted to the metropolis as blasé-ness" (GSG 7, 121/413).

[2] Wehler 1989, 22.

[3] Blackbourn, 352; see also 200 for a table of comparative data on other German cities that gives J. Reulecke's *Geschichte der Urbanisierung Deutschlands* (203) as the source. It should be noted that the figures for Berlin exclude Rixdorf (Neukölln) and Charlottenburg, both of which had populations numbered in the hundreds of thousands from at least the 1850's on.

[4] Wehler, op cit. 24.

[5] Palmer and Colton, 518. In this respect, of course, the situation in Berlin was not analogous to

Simmel was thirteen in 1871, when the German Reich was founded. The
son of a well-to-do merchant coming of age during the so-called *Gründer-
jahre*, the founders' era, he had first-hand experience of massive social and
cultural transformations, for in this period Berlin was becoming a modern
metropolis. The urban surface was undergoing rapid redefinition—railways
and industry had drawn city and countryside closer, though the boom in
construction had not kept up with population growth.[6] The economic life of
the new imperial capital depended on an extended urban transport network
made possible by the second (electricity and oil-fueled) phase of industrial
revolution.[7] Other technological innovations also had an enormous impact
on the texture of everyday life. The steadily increasing population of white-
collar workers, many of whom were now women, worked in offices outfitted
with typewriters and other new mechanical devices.[8] In a world made smaller
by the telegraph, particularly since the first transatlantic cable in 1866, there
was an exponential growth of newspapers. By the 1870's, the telephone (pat-
ented in 1876 and 77) made entirely new forms of communication possible.[9]

During Simmel's lifetime, the institutions and practices of modern mass
culture were also taking form in Berlin—as was the audience that his student
Siegfried Kracauer would dub the "homogenous metropolitan public."[10] Department stores, with their bureaucratized workforce, helped shape a modern regime of consumption.[11] Photography had become a popularly accessi-

---

that in Paris; as we have already remarked, among the vanquished of 1871, worries about inadequate rates of population growth ran rampant.

[6] According to David Blackbourn, "In Berlin, half of all dwellings had just one heatable room
in 1875 ... 20 per cent of the city's inhabitants lived five-to-a-room" (205). The construction
boom was from the 1840's to '70's (ibid., 202).

[7] Beginning in the 1860's, public transportation was made possible by the *Pferdebahn*, a precursor of today's streetcar in which horses pulled cars on metal tracks, busses, and horse-carriages
(both first- and second-class). An electric rapid train system was planned in the '80's; building began in 1896, and in 1902 the first underground train line opened (Schutte and Sprengel, 28).

[8] See Ute Frevert, "Vom Klavier zur Schreibmaschine—Weiblicher Arbeitsmarkt und Rollenzuweisung am Beispiel der weiblichen Angestellten in der Weimarer Republik." In *Frauen in der
Geschichte*, vol. I, 82–112. Simmel discusses the impact of the typewriter in GSG 6, 652.

[9] "Germans made 155 million phone calls in 1888 ... by 1904 the number reached a billion"
(Blackbourn 354).

[10] According to Kracauer, a new form of public came into being as a function of the technologically induced merging of an internally diverse population into the modern mass in the metropolis. See "Kult der Zerstreuung" in *Das Ornament der Masse*, 311–17.

[11] Although department stores had their origins in the 1840's, it was around 1900 that buildings
devoted purely to such commerce began to be built (Schutte and Sprengel, 28–29). Particularly
with the construction of the Kaufhaus des Westens in 1905, the area around Wittenberg Platz began to emerge as a center of fashion, a development accompanied by the same displacement of
poorer populations that had characterized the construction of fashionable boulevards in Haus-
mann's Paris (Schutte and Sprengel, 30).

ble medium, particularly with the introduction of George Eastman's afford-able box camera in 1888, and modern forms of amusement, including the precursors of cinema such as the *Kaiserspanorama*, were drawing crowds. As we shall see, it is worth keeping this cultural context in mind. Simmel's dis-tinctive philosophical attitude toward the phenomena of modernity—so un-like that of older contemporaries such as Schopenhauer or Nietzsche—incorporated something of the positive attitude toward progress characteris-tic of the Berlin bourgeoisie in this period. His writings are marked by ur-bane familiarity with the psychological and social realities of nineteenth century urban life and by his enthusiastic participation in the cultural efflo-rescence of Wilhelminian Berlin.[12]

I have argued that cultural modernization encompassed a paradigm shift in the rhetoric of reflection on human existence. Like the material transfor-mations of the modern metropolis, the ascendance of more materialist ways of thinking within the academic world had, on the whole, a stimulating effect on Simmel, and his attempts to come to terms with these modern ways of thinking, like his efforts to extend philosophical reflection to the everyday phenomena of modern life, remain highly significant, even if the conse-quences for his professional life were not always salutary. (His lectures were extremely popular, but Simmel was denied a regular professorship until the age of fifty-six, for this success was linked in the eyes of his critics both to his alleged "Jewishness"[13] and to his participation in an unproved discipline, so-ciology, that was understood to be subversive of the established values of state and church.[14])

---

[12]One particularly remarkable manifestation of this attitude was Simmel's serious engagement with the women's movement. His long friendship with Marianne Weber left its mark on her writings and his own. See, however, Inka Mülder-Bach. Both Köhnke and Lichtblau discuss Sim-mel's relation to new social movements in the period as a factor in interpreting his intellectual de-velopment.

[13]Simmel belonged to a family of assimilated bourgeois Jews; his wife was a Christian. Not only was he himself baptized, but his father had converted to Catholicism in the 1830's, and his mother had also been converted to Protestantism as a girl. During the First World War, he left the church, though not in order to return to Judaism. His decision, according to Michael Landmann, "was born solely of the need for intellectual independence [*weltanschaulicher Ungebundenheit*]" (Gassen and Landmann, 12). For a discussion of the impact of his alleged Judaism on Simmel's life, see Klaus-Christian Köhnke, Exkurs: "Georg Simmel als Jude" in Köhnke 122–48.

[14]A single example of Simmel's difficulties must suffice. In 1908, Simmel was second on the list for a professorship (after Rickert). Although the philosophy *Dekan* at Heidelberg wrote that Simmel "with his broad and many-faceted knowledge and the incisive energy of his thought, is called, if anyone is, to elevate sociology out of the state of empirical collection and general reflec-tions to the level of a truly philosophical investigation," Simmel did not receive the recommended *Berufung*. An openly anti-Semitic letter solicited from one of his detractors has been preserved. While the faculty praised Simmel's ability "to attract and captivate a large audience" despite the

During the period of Simmel's studies, from 1876 to 1884,[15] the intellectual consequences of the technological, cultural, and social changes that had taken place in the previous generation were making themselves felt in the university generally and in the philosophical faculty in particular. The idealist conception of *humanistische Bildung*—education as cultural "formation"—that had defined work there since the Berliner Universität was founded under Wilhelm von Humboldt in 1810 was being challenged by developments in the natural sciences, particularly biology and physics.[16] New disciplines were emerging out of unscientific pastimes[17]; empirical inquiry made inroads on topics once restricted to philosophical reflection. Simmel's writings, which can broadly be situated as part of the contemporary paradigm shift from the philosophy of spirit (*Geist*) to the philosophy of life in the late nineteenth century,[18] drew inspiration from a wide range of such sources—anthropology, psychology, linguistics, and post-Darwinian biology.

A few words of caution regarding the nature of my claims are perhaps in

---

"seriousness and difficulty" of his ideas, Dietrich Schäfer contended that the sort of public Simmel would attract would not benefit the university. Women and "the oriental world," he alleged, were much in evidence at Simmel's lectures. "His whole manner . . . corresponds to their taste. Not too much positive is taken away from the lectures; but one may accept with pleasure many a piquant allusion and transient mental pleasure." In general, Schäfer commented, intellectual "directions that are more dividing and negating than foundational and constructive have only a limited justification in a time that is inclined to bring everything into flux and not always only out of the desire for discovery but also out of a lust for sensations." Simmel's Jewish public and his suspicious disciplinary allegiances thus made him undesirable in such a period for a university of importance "for the State and the Empire." (All quotations from Dekan Hampe's and Dietrich Schäfer's letters to Minister Böhm are from Gassen and Landmann 25–27).

[15] After his first effort was rejected, Simmel's dissertation was accepted in January 1881; his Habilitation was finally accepted in 1884 after a second public lecture (the first, on "The Metaphysical Foundations of Cognition," having been judged insufficient, according to family legend, because Simmel "reacted gruffly and dismissively when [Prof.] Zeller asserted that the soul had its place in a certain cerebral lobe" (Gassen and Landmann 21).) For a detailed reconstruction of Simmel's early intellectual trajectory and its social context, see Köhnke 1996, chapter 1, "Studien," 30–166.

[16] Philosophically trained thinkers such as the physicist Hermann von Helmholz (1821–94), whose ideas influenced the science of work, and Rudolf Virchow (1821–1902), a pioneer in cell biology and epidemiology, argued that the discipline should take a more modest attitude and give the natural sciences their due. Both were students of Johannes Müller (1801–58), a physiologist who assumed a chair in philosophy in 1833 (Gerhardt et al., 104).

[17] See Suzanne L. Marchand, *Down from Olympus*.

[18] The transition to *Lebensphilosophie* is marked clearly in those writings that postdate his acquaintance with Bergson (1908), for instance in the remarkable essays on masculinity and femininity as cultural phenomena published in *Philosophische Kultur* (1911, reissued in a revised edition in November 1918, shortly after Simmel's death; now in GSG 14). The editors note that the second edition bears the inaccurate date of 1919 (Editorischer Bericht 480).

For an account of Simmel's real and imagined relations to Wilhelm Dilthey (1833–1911), who was professor in Berlin from 1882 to 1905 and was the most prominent proponent of *Lebensphilosophie*, see Köhnke 1996.

order. My concept of a rhetoric of reflection is importantly ambiguous. While it grows out of an historical analysis and is grounded in empirical evidence, the concept also engages philosophical issues about the conditions of possibility of experience. Insofar as it is not simply descriptive, the notion that there is a modern rhetoric of reflection embodies a distinctive way of thinking the relation between history and subjectivity. Thus far, I have focused on illustrating that this way of thinking is illuminating; it will be the task of Part II, "The Rhetoric of Reflection," as a whole to make the case that attending to this rhetoric allows us to talk about the relations between subjective experience and historical context without falling into the usual aporia. Having said this, I can, I hope, forestall a significant misunderstanding of my larger claims about Simmel's significance.

While the paradigm shift within the discipline of philosophy from *Geist* to *Leben* indeed helped foster the cultural hegemony of the modern materialist rhetoric of reflection, I am not equating the two orders of changes. It is not simply that developments within disciplines follow, at least to a certain extent, an internal logic born of their specific conceptual and methodological resources. More importantly, my contention that there has been a global shift within the rhetoric of reflection on subjective experience in modernity does not entail a claim that the shift has been either absolute or complete. On the contrary: it is precisely the ambiguity of the language of boredom that makes it a compelling object of investigation, given my larger thesis about the way linguistic resources for conceptualizing human experience have evolved since the Enlightenment. Thus while I have argued that there has been a general cultural evolution toward a "materialist" mode of conceptualizing of human life, I have also emphasized the incompleteness of that evolution and underlined the way idealist premises of all sorts continue to inflect thinking of the most disenchanted variety. As the discussion of Nietzsche and nineteenth-century "transcendental materialism" in Chapter 3 underlined, the paradigm shift toward a materialist rhetoric of reflection did not necessarily foster materialism *strictu sensu*. In Simmel's case, philosophy, psychology, and the study of society could not be entirely separated; thus, even at his most speculative, he retained a distinctively objective attitude toward his objects of analysis—an attitude that combined a Kantian critical awareness with empirical elan.

Simmel became a prominent intellectual figure in Wilhelminian Berlin, and his philosophical and historical significance has too often been underestimated since his death in 1918. A prolific writer[19] and a thinker of almost hy-

---

[19]Simmel published 25 books and over 300 articles. A fairly complete bibliography can be

perbolically synthetic bent, he was a pioneer of interdisciplinarity whose oeuvre brought the concerns of the German philosophical tradition into conversation with modern cultural reality. In the first part of his career, his distinctive combination of philosophical, psychological, and historical ideas and methods played a foundational role in efforts to systematize and institutionalize sociology.[20] While it is in this discipline that his achievements are best remembered, Simmel identified himself as a philosopher whose interests in sociology were only secondary.[21] As such, he was extraordinarily popular, lecturing on everything from aesthetics and social psychology to logic and ethics, from Kant and Fichte to Darwin and Schopenhauer before audiences that included much of fashionable Berlin.

---

found in Gassen and Landmann. The *Georg Simmel Gesamtausgabe*, which has been in preparation since 1989 and is nearing completion, will include not only essays that have never before been anthologized but also a substantial number of anonymously published essays (the latter in Volume 17: *Miszellen, Glossen, Stellungnahmen, Umfrageantworten, Leserbriefe, Diskussionsbeiträge 1889–1917. Anonyme und pseudonyme Veröffentlichungen 1888–1917. Beiträge aus der "Jugend" 1897–1916*).

Regarding the unsuccessful attempts of his wife to publish his widely dispersed writings after Simmel's death, see Landmann, "Bausteine." Recent publications in English include Frisby 2002, Leck 2000, Frisby and Featherstone 1997, Frisby 1994, Sellerberg 1994, Poggi 1993, Weinstein and Weinstein 1993.

[20] See Gassen and Landmann for attestations to Simmel's importance from a remarkable range of contemporary philosophical and cultural figures. Particularly in English, Simmel's reception has been remarkable for its extreme selectivity. Although certain essays played an important role in the formation of sociological theory in the early twentieth century, as many students of Simmel have lamented, a thorough-going confrontation with his oeuvre has not really taken place. This is true despite the efforts of a series of distinguished scholars who have often also become Simmel's translators, including Lewis Coser, David Frisby, Donald Levine, Harry Liebersohn, Guy Oakes, Robert Park, and Kurt Wolff. See Levine 1985, especially chapter 5, "Useful Confusions: Simmel's Stranger and his Followers," for an intriguing reading of Simmel's reception history as a source of productive misunderstandings. Frisby 1984 places Simmel's life and work in intellectual-historical context. See also Lepenies 1981 and 1985 (the latter is especially useful on his international contacts). Dahme and Rammstedt 1984 collects a number of crucial contributions to the literature. See also Rammstedt 1988 and Böhringer and Gründer 1976; for recent assessments of Simmel's importance in the German context, see *Berliner Journal für Soziologie*, Heft 2/1993.

[21] On 13 December, 1899, Simmel wrote a letter to the French sociologist Célestin Bouglé in which he expressed dismay "that I am known only as a sociologist abroad—while in fact I am a philosopher ... and pursue sociology only as a sideline." ("Es ist mir überhaupt einigermaßen schmerzlich, daß ich im Ausland nur als Soziologe gelte—während ich doch Philosoph bin, in der Philosophie meine Lebensaufgabe sehe u. die Soziologe eigentlich nur als Nebenfach treibe. Wenn ich erst einmal meine Verpflichtung gegen diese damit erfüllt haben werde, daß ich eine umfassende Soziologie publizire—werde ich wahrscheinlich nie mehr auf sie zurückkommen." Cited in GSG 11, 892; original in the Bibliothèque Nationale, Paris.). The problem would persist; in 1908 Simmel attributed his failure to receive professorships in Heidelberg and Greifswald to "the nonsense, that I am actually not a philosopher but a sociologist—in reality I only practice sociology 'on the side'" (Letter to Georg Jellinek, 20 March, 1908; cited in Köhnke 1996, 378; original in Bundesarchiv Koblenz).

Simmel's approach to the historical interpretation of subjective experience epitomizes his position between nineteenth-century philosophy and twentieth-century social thought. He reached intellectual maturity in a world structured by the oppositions between scientific and secular, materialist and idealist, world views. In his thinking, the skepticism with which the romantics and their successors struggled has become second nature. Indeed, Simmel argued that skepticism and the subjective disaffection associated with it were the inevitable consequences of what has come to be called modernization. Drawing upon the resources of the German philosophical tradition, he describes the historical genesis of the problems of meaning that plague modern subjects and relates them to larger socio-cultural transformations. In contrast to many of his philosophical and pseudo-philosophical contemporaries, though, he examined the cultural significance of the dilemmas of modern subjectivity not in order to condemn but in order to understand the world in which he lived. Through an innovative, modernist mode of reflection focused, as Ludwig Marcuse put it, upon "the significance of the insignificant,"[22] Simmel illuminated the fragmentation proper to modern existence.

By focusing not on society as an entity but on the forms of sociation (*Vergesellschaftung*) as such, Simmel defined a mode of inquiry that linked empirical interpretations to philosophical problems through the study of modern "forms of life." His 1900 magnum opus, *Philosophie des Geldes* (*Philosophy of Money*), examined the function of money in social life, creating a distinctive new perspective on the problem of value, on the process of objectification, and on a series of phenomena Simmel grouped under the rubric of "The Style of Life."[23] Neo-Kantian in his basic intellectual posture, Simmel had studied history, psychology, anthropology, and political economy as well as philosophy, and his writings evince a remarkable erudition. His purpose was never "sociological" in a narrow sense, for his descriptions of social forms were simultaneously interpretations of their significance.

Like Hegel and Nietzsche before him, Simmel saw human existence as historically shaped by the interaction of concerns about meaning and purpose with the quotidian realities of everyday existence. Indeed, his life's work

[22] Gassen and Landmann, 189.
[23] *Philosophie des Geldes*, GSG 6; see especially chapter 6, which bears this title, pages 591–655. In the letter to Bouglé cited above, Simmel remarks: "Im Lauf des nächsten Jahres kommt hoffentlich meine „Philosophie des Geldes" heraus—die eine Philosophie des ganzen geschichtlichen u. sozialen Lebens zu sein strebt." Simmel's way of thinking about the spiritual effects of the money economy was an important influence on Lukács and through him and Kracauer on the Frankfurt School.

may be understood as an attempt to reconcile his conflicting Hegelian and
Nietzschean impulses—toward totalizing, rational analysis on the one hand
and affirmation of life's irrational creativity on the other. His philosophy of
life combines Hegelian historicism with Nietzschean genealogy to arrive at
highly original interpretations of the "forms of life" that characterize modern
existence. These concrete analyses aim to rearticulate the relation between
individual and society in modernity using a synecdochic strategy that owes
much to Nietzsche, but which Hegel might have viewed as an illuminating
extension of his own vision of *Geist*.

For Simmel, a skeptical, enlightened attitude that recognized the "dissolution of everything substantial, absolute, eternal into the river of things" did
not preclude acknowledging the persistence in the modern world of the irrational need to abandon that skepticism. By reformulating questions about
the meaning and purpose of existence in terms that are neither reductively
psychologist nor abstractly subjectivist, Simmel's notion of form defines an
innovative strategy for thinking about the dilemmas of modern subjectivity
as cultural phenomena. In particular, as we shall see, it suggests a way of
thinking about boredom as a lived philosophical problem that will make an
important contribution to our attempt to go beyond the rhetoric of experience considered in Part I.[24]

Boredom and the Problem of Meaning in Modernity

David Frisby has argued that Georg Simmel's oeuvre should be understood as a sociology of modernity.[25] By focusing on the "fragments of modernity," he shows, Simmel developed a sociology of modern experience that
is valuable precisely for its failure to totalize the disparate aspects of existence
into a unified theory of their meaning. This reading should be extended, for
Simmel was not only a sociologist but also a philosopher of fragmentation.
His legacy, I contend, was a strategy of thought—one that disclosed a whole

[24]My phenomenological reading of Simmel, including the notion that modern forms of life
can be understood as lived philosophical problems, was first set forth in "'Eine specifisch moderne Begehrlichkeit': Fetischismus und George Simmels Phänomenologie der Moderne." An earlier version of the arguments about boredom presented in this chapter was published as "The
Modernization of Subjectivity: Boredom and Georg Simmel's Reading of Metropolitan Life." I
discuss Simmel's methodological and historical significance for contemporary work in the humanities in "Georg Simmels Phänomenologie der Kultur und der Paradigmenwechsel in den
Geisteswissenschaften" and in "Style as Substance: Georg Simmel's Phenomenology of Culture."
Many of the ideas touched on here are developed further in my work in progress, *Georg Simmel
and the Phenomenology of Culture*.
[25]See particularly 1985, 1992.

new range of concerns and questions to philosophical reflection for the first time. Put into historical, philosophical, and sociological perspectives, he tried to show, each "seemingly insignificant trait on the surface of life"[26] can be made to reveal a deeper meaning.[27] Simmel's texts, with their magisterial combination of symbolic and empirical analysis, remain fascinatingly up-to-date—and not only because he took up themes such as fashion and gender that have subsequently gained currency. His writings respond to epistemological dilemmas that, if anything, have grown more pressing since the *Philosophy of Money* was published in 1900. Furthermore, they demonstrate that it is possible to reconcile the profoundest skepticism about our powers of interpretation with a commitment to inquiry into the meaning of human existence.

This new way of thinking about cultural reality is Simmel's legacy as a modernist philosopher.[28] His work is remarkable not so much for its acknowledgment of the fragmentation of experience—a hundred years ago, as we have seen, fragmentation was already attested as a self-evident feature of occidental urban life—but for its demonstration that fragmentation can be captured reflectively as a mode of connection. Simmel was a modernist in the broadest sense; a marvelous stylist, he pursued intellectual interests that extended over the full range of cultural and social reality. In his essays, which embody the principle that the most everyday phenomena must be understood in relation to the dynamic whole of modern life, no interpretation is ever truly final.[29]

In the Preface to the *Philosophy of Money*, Simmel made explicit the philosophical ambition behind what I read as a performative rhetorical strategy. "The unity of these investigations," he declared, lay not in a positive claim of

[26] All translations from Simmel are my own, though where possible, I have also provided references to published translations. In parenthetical references, the first number is to the German critical edition, the *Georg Simmel Gesamtausgabe* (GSG), the second to the translation; I have omitted volume numbers when they are clear from the context. The above citation is GSG 7, 119/412.

[27] On my reading, this synecdochic strategy for illuminating the "insignificant" details of modern life constituted the unmarked currency through which, as Simmel himself predicted, his intellectual legacy would be diffused yet rendered unrecognizable. Perhaps his awareness of the power of his approach to the philosophical analysis of cultural phenomena can account for Simmel's remark "I know that I will die without spiritual heirs (and it is good so)" (Simmel 1923, 1). I argue this point more fully in "Georg Simmels Phänomenologie der Kultur und der Paradigmenwechsel in den Geisteswissenschaften."

[28] In "Style as Substance," I connect Simmel's relativism to his method of analysis to demonstrate the importance of reading him as a modernist philosopher.

[29] On essayism, see Lukács' Simmel-influenced *Die Seele und die Formen* and Adorno's "The Essay as Form."

any sort but rather in his aspiration to demonstrate through them "the possibility of finding in each of life's details the totality of its meaning."[30] Through analyses of particular, historically situated phenomena, Simmel conducts a neo-Kantian inquiry into forms of sociation (*Vergesellschaftung*) in which the concept of reciprocal action (*Wechselwirkung*, a category especially crucial for the third *Critique*) plays a key role. By relating these cultural "details" synecdochically to the cultural and historical macrocosms (*Sinneinheiten*) in which they are embedded, he reveals meanings that are ordinarily invisible. By linking the historical process of rationalization to the modes of experience it produces, this method, which I call Simmel's phenomenology of culture, fosters philosophical reflection upon socio-cultural conditions that seem to undermine the very possibility of reflection. On my reading, then, although Simmel's writings may appear fragmentary, they are methodologically unified. They consistently enact a phenomenological strategy of conceptualizing particular modes of sociation as "forms of life" that disclose the structure and meaning of the historical whole to which they belong. Precisely through an affirmation of relativism, of the historical particularity of cognition, Simmel's method attempts to bridge the chasm that had opened in the course of the nineteenth century between philosophical and socio-cultural interpretations of human existence.

The philosophical foundations of Simmel's approach to the analysis of modern culture are expressed with great clarity in a lecture of 1902.[31] In this text, entitled "Schopenhauer and Nietzsche and Their Place in Intellectual History," boredom appears as the link between the sociological transformations associated with modernization and the problems of meaning that plague modern subjects. Simmel's point of departure is the observation that "all higher culture" depends on lengthening and differentiating the processes by which human needs are fulfilled. By contrast with the relative immediacy of rural existence, he remarks, under urban conditions a long chain of social interactions and a high level of social organization is required simply for bread to reach the table. According to Simmel, this example reflects a more general, qualitative change brought about through the apparatus of advanced

---

[30] GSG 6, 12/55. Subsequent citations in text.

[31] According to a letter from Elisabeth Förster-Nietzsche of December 4, 1902 cited in the Editors' Report to the critical edition (GSG 10, 420), Simmel gave a series of lectures at the Victoria Lyceum in Berlin in 1902–3. These became the basis for the 1907 monograph, *Schopenhauer und Nietzsche: Ein Vortragszyklus* [*Schopenhauer and Nietzsche: A Cycle of Lectures*]. The following citations are from the introductory lecture (GSG 10, 176–91), the bulk of which was first published in 1906 under the title "Schopenhauer und Nietzsche" as an excerpt from the forthcoming book (GSG 8, 58–68).

civilization, one that has momentous consequences. When people are forced by the complexity of the world in which they live to focus on an endless succession of particular, localized means, they lose sight of their reasons for acting. "Life is made into a technical problem."

On Simmel's view, highly differentiated material circumstances thus quite literally become the basis for the spiritual problems that plague advanced civilizations.

> The technology [*Technik*], i.e. the sum of means for a cultivated existence, becomes the actual content of one's efforts and valuations until one is surrounded on all sides by ranks of undertakings and institutions intertwined in every direction but for which everywhere the definitive, valuable goals are lacking. It is only in this state of culture that the need of a final purpose for life arises at all. So long as life is filled by short series of goals, each satisfying in itself, that searching restlessness which must arise from reflection about being trapped in a network of mere means, detours, preliminaries, remains distant. Not until we understand countless activities and interests on which we concentrated as if on ultimate goals in their character as mere means does the anxious question about the meaning and purpose of the whole arise. (177)

Simmel's analysis initially takes the form of a sociological generalization: when people's lives are embedded in a social context that bestows tangible purposiveness on the activities of everyday existence, the question of the meaning and purpose of life as such does not arise. However, his claim about "higher cultures" is not simply descriptive. For Simmel, a subjective sense of meaninglessness is not just a consequence of the unfulfilled anthropological "besoin de faire quelque chose" discussed in Chapter 2. While the material complexity of advanced cultures may produce a sense of remoteness and dislocation, a careful reading of the passage just cited makes clear that on Simmel's view, a reflective change is necessary to transform such vague malaise into a philosophical problem. People must become aware that their attitude toward transient means is inappropriate before "the anxious question about the meaning and purpose of the whole" arises.

The discourse on boredom, as I argued in Part I, is an index of just such a change. To use my terms, the experiential transformation wrought by modernization gives rise to a transformation in the rhetoric of subjective experience. "Boredom" is a name for the state in which the lived discrepancy between the involvement with transient means and their value in a larger vision of existence enters subjective awareness. As an experience of dissociation from the series of instrumental ends that constitute the stuff of everyday existence in complex societies, boredom is symptomatic of an entire rhetoric of reflection in which the problem of "the meaning and purpose of the whole" appears. And as an experiential manifestation of the "searching restlessness" that results from reflection on "being trapped in a network of mere means," boredom may easily come to represent the meaninglessness of existence as such. A closer examination of Simmel's account of the genesis of the philosophical problems lived out in modern society will thus help to clarify why boredom spread in the nineteenth century. Though he does not use these terms, Simmel, too, sees boredom as a manifestation of the democratization of skepticism in modernity.

Although Simmel's point of departure is in sociological description, his argument has a strong historical component. The claims with which he begins are not, as it turns out, about modernity at all. It was "the culture of the Greco-Roman world," he writes, that "for the first time in world history . . . drove souls into this state" of general questioning about the meaning of life. Although this argument converges with Hegel's account of the origins of philosophy—i.e. in the departure from the immediacy of existence that had characterized the classical world before the subject/object split—Simmel's subsequent line of argument makes his debt to Nietzsche clear. Christianity, he claims, resolved the spiritual suffering of a humanity plunged into meaninglessness by the conflicts and complexities of advanced civilization.

> It gave life that absolute purpose . . . The salvation of the soul and the realm of God now presented itself to the masses as an unconditional value, as the definitive goal beyond everything particular, fragmentary, senseless in life. And they lived from this final purpose until, in the last centuries, Christianity lost its power over countless souls. (178)

Simmel's innovation lies in the way he develops the Nietzschean point that the desire for absolute meaning led through a devaluation of worldly existence to widespread nihilism. Linking his analysis to his sociological observations, Simmel ultimately integrates it into a very Hegelian argument about the "geistesgeschichtliche Stellung" of the two philosophers in his title (whose names are not actually mentioned until after he has concluded the present argument, three pages into the text).

The passage just cited continues:

> However, the need of a final purpose for life did not disappear simultaneously with Christianity's loss of power. On the contrary: since long satisfaction makes every need take root more firmly and deeply, life retained a profound longing for an absolute purpose even and precisely after the content that had effected the adaptation to this form of inner existence had withdrawn. This longing is the legacy of Christianity: it left behind the need for something definitive in the movements of life that continues to exist as an empty pressing toward a goal that has become unrealizable. (178)

Simmel's debt to Nietzschean genealogy is apparent: the human "need of a final purpose for life" must be viewed historically. In the actual "state of culture" to which Simmel addresses himself, it is not only on account of people's awareness of their imbrication in a differentiated web of "undertakings and institutions" that are not meaningful in themselves that life has become "a technical problem." "The masses" can become aware that their vague malaise indicates a deeper philosophical dilemma because the crisis of meaning is inscribed in the structure of individual subjectivity as well. After centuries of Christian institutional and cultural hegemony during which the meaning of life was defined in absolute terms, the need for a final purpose in life is so basic to human existence that its absence *per se* causes suffering and social dislocation. As beings with an historically developed need for an overarching purpose, people are bound to suffer from the apparent senselessness of their lives, even as they are unable to escape the grip of the very "technology of life" that robs them of immediate meaning. On Simmel's reading, then, both Schopenhauer's and Nietzsche's philosophies express the specifically modern spiritual dilemma that is "the legacy of Christianity." They are attempts to come to terms with the unrealizable yet indestructible desire for meaning that animates human existence in an era of radical disenchantment.

For Simmel, Schopenhauer's metaphysics of the will is "the absolute, philosophical expression of this inner state of the modern human being" (178). His philosophy "projects into a *Gesamtweltanschauung*" the contradictory circumstance in which the existence of a final purpose is held to be both necessary and impossible to attain and thereby "expresses the momentary state of culture, how it is filled with longing for a final purpose to life that it feels is illusory or forever lost" (179). Nietzsche, according to Simmel, begins from a recognition of this tragic tension. However, in place of Schopenhauer's horror at life as a manifestation of the senselessness of the will, he substitutes an affirmation of the life-process. On Simmel's reading, a Darwin-inspired conception of life as aiming at a quantitative increase of forces allows Nietzsche to shift the terms of the discussion definitively by comparison with his predecessor. Although his philosophy also takes its point of departure in a recognition of the spiritual conflict basic to enlightened consciousness, Nietzsche finds a philosophical solution. Through the concept of a drive to self-overcoming, according to Simmel, "*life itself can become the purpose of life*" (179; italics in original). When it is no longer viable to argue that human existence has a meaningful end, stoic resignation is not the only option: the function once served by the notion of a final purpose can be fulfilled by the concept of a global development of the human race.

"The radicality of the turn from Schopenhauer to Nietzsche" is revealed, according to Simmel, by the contrast between their understandings of boredom and its role in the life-process. For Schopenhauer, the "inner rhythm" of human existence is ineffably monotonous. With the loss of the externally imposed "absolute purpose" provided by a religious interpretation of everyday life, the world seems empty and the persistent longing for meaning gives rise to

> the torture of boredom, the indignation over the insipid dreariness of life's course, as the only appropriate emotional reaction. The fact of boredom proves to Schopenhauer the meaninglessness of life: for if we are occupied with nothing . . . then we feel, solely and purely, life itself—and that is what causes that unbearable state. (183)

On Simmel's reading, Nietzsche's concept of life enables a radical reinterpretation of this sense of purposelessness—a understanding of boredom that, as we saw in Chapter 3, was not limited to Schopenhauer. For Nietzsche, boredom is philosophically significant not because it offers proof of the meaninglessness of life but because it points to a need to reconceive questions of meaning. Thus the same denial of an external, transcendent purpose and source of value that was for Schopenhauer the basis for "the deepest degradation of the life-process" becomes for Nietzsche the source of its "triumph." For the former, boredom was a negative revelation: "Life, now empty and meaningless, appears to go in circles like a squirrel in a wheel." By reconceptualizing "life as development," Simmel claims, Nietzsche "takes the purposive character that has been torn away from outside back into life's most interior and individual essence" (183–84). The problem of boredom is overcome in the awareness of the significance of the eternal return of the same.

According to Simmel, Nietzsche sees the task of the modern human being to be transcending Schopenhauerian pessimism while facing the philosopher's substantial insight that the longing for a meaningful purpose for life is a means of self-deception that must be renounced. In affirming the historic loss of an ultimate purpose as the triumph of the life-process, Simmel thought, Nietzsche found a way to overcome Schopenhauer's nihilistic conclusions by sublating the emptiness of an existence without external goals into an end in itself. For Simmel, this philosophical strategy has world-historical significance.

> That life according to its ownmost meaning and in its innermost energies possesses the possibility, striving, security to go forward to more perfect forms, to something greater than itself beyond every Now—this is surely the great comfort . . . of the modern spirit, which through Nietzsche became the illumination of the

whole mental landscape. This fundamental motif ... appears in contrast to Schopenhauer as the much more adequate expression of the contemporary feeling for life. (188)

Simmel's Nietzsche is not at all untimely—he is, on the contrary, an avatar of nineteenth-century progressivism! If Schopenhauer had counseled divesting oneself of the fetters of individuality and embracing boredom as philosophical truth, Nietzsche advocated a self-overcoming of boredom that transmuted identity in the name of an activist vision of history. Making life itself the final purpose of life resituates the problem of meaning in terms more amenable to the materialism that dominates the era; it suggests a practical attitude toward the malaise that arises in the face of the complex technologies of modern existence. Thus on Simmel's view, while Schopenhauer's metaphysical pessimism is a philosophically more profound response to the dilemma of the modern subject, Nietzsche's philosophy better captures "the contemporary feeling for life."[32]

Even before his explicit turn to metaphysics, Simmel's own writings enact this basic Nietzschean conceptual strategy of affirming life in all its conflicts. At the same time, his debt to Hegel also becomes apparent in his attempts to incorporate historico-philosophical self-awareness into his interpretations of the subjective effects of modernization. Just as the lectures on Schopenhauer and Nietzsche underline the historical importance of the philosophical problems that defined them as thinkers, Simmel's studies of forms of sociation consistently pose the problem of the historical significance of the particular "forms of life" he analyzes. If "Schopenhauer and Nietzsche" defines the philosophers' contributions in relation to a *Zeitgeist* indelibly marked by the unsatisfiable longing for meaning, Simmel's readings of diverse manifestations of what he calls "objective spirit" demonstrate that modern existence is thoroughly permeated by that longing.[33] For Simmel, the study of outstanding historical figures complements the fine-grained investigation of

---

[32] On the multifarious influence of Nietzsche on contemporary thought in this period, see Steven E. Aschheim, *The Nietzsche Legacy in Germany, 1890–1990*.

[33] The concept of *objectiver Geist*, which has its locus classicus in Hegel, underwent an important development in the course of the nineteenth century. In a series of programmatic essays that laid the groundwork for both cultural anthropology and the philosophy of culture, Simmel's teacher, Moritz Lazarus (sometimes writing with his brother-in-law, Heymann Steinthal) developed the notion of objective spirit into a tool for examining concrete cultural manifestations largely ignored within the idealist tradition. These writings, which mostly appeared in the *Zeitschrift für Völkerpsychologie und Sprachwissenschaft* edited by Lazarus and Steinthal in the 1860's, have recently been issued with a helpful introduction by Klaus Christian Köhnke (Lazarus 2003). See also Eckardt and Belke. Köhnke 1996 (337–55) and Lessing, "Bemerkungen zum Begriff des 'objectiven Geistes' bei Hegel, Lazarus und Dilthey" offer illuminating readings of the intellectual and historical context of this conceptual development.

quotidian forms of life. Not only is philosophy "its time, grasped in thought"; the social forms of temporal existence are lived philosophical problems.

Rationalizing the Self: The Forms of Subjective Experience in Modernity

In what is probably his most famous essay, Georg Simmel reformulates the question of the significance of boredom in a highly original fashion—one that elaborates the analysis of purposelessness just examined in a fashion that supports my larger claims about the experience without qualities. "Die Großstädte und das Geistesleben" (Metropolises and Mental Life) defines the mental attitude associated with the experience of boredom in relation to the historical and cultural circumstances of urban existence.[34] In this essay, a broader investigation into the relations between subjective experience and cultural modernization, Simmel's point of departure is the assertion that "the most profound problems of modern life have their source in the claim of the individual to preserve the autonomy and individuality of his existence in the face of overwhelming forces of society, of the historical heritage, of external culture and the technology of life." On one hand, Simmel's conception of *Geistesleben* is Nietzschean: the struggle for subjective integrity, he writes, is the "latest metamorphosis of the battle with nature which the primitive human being had to wage for his *bodily* existence." On the other, it is Hegelian: the Kantian conflict between freedom and determination manifests itself in the constitutive dilemma of the modern subject, who must resist "being homogenized and used up by a social-technological mechanism." In this essay, which presents the central argument of the *Philosophy of Money* in highly compact form, Simmel analyzes "modes of adaptation" through which individuals maintain their psychic integrity despite the fragmenting effects of modern metropolitan technologies of life on subjective existence. These analyses proceed phenomenologically, in line with the hermeneutic principle laid out in the introduction to the longer work, to seek "in each of life's details the totality of its meaning."

---

[34]"Die Großstädte und das Geistesleben" was originally a lecture given at Dresden in the winter of 1902/1903 in connection with what was probably the first exhibition on metropolitan life in Germany. Although the translations are my own, I have provided citations both to the original and to the published translation—the first number refers to GSG 7, the second to Wolff 1950. All citations in this paragraph are to 116/409; all italics in original. It should be emphasized that "Geistesleben" refers not to "mental life" in the narrow sense but to all of the phenomena of human spiritual, intellectual, and psychological existence—to subjective experience in general.

By placing the nervousness and fatigue generated by modern urban conditions in relation to Simmel's analysis of the philosophical consequences of
the modernization process for modern subjects, "Metropolises and Mental
Life" establishes a new perspective on the phenomena thematized in the discourse on boredom, one that avoids the aporiai which had come to characterize that discourse by the early twentieth century. Simmel neither views the
phenomena associated with boredom à la Schopenhauer, as signs of the
meaninglessness of life as such, nor simply reduces them to sociological effects of the modernization process. By showing that the characteristic "blasé"
attitude of the bored subject represents an historically significant adaptation
to modern life, his cultural phenomenology relocates the philosophical
questions associated with boredom in a way that provokes reflection on the
human significance of cultural modernization.

After the introductory passage just cited, which presents the problem of
individuation from the metaphysical perspective of the philosophy of life,
Simmel detours through a psychological interpretation of metropolitan
subjectivity before arriving at the sociological analyses that anchor his philosophical argument historically.

> The *intensification of nervous activity* [*des Nervenlebens*] that proceeds from the
> rapid and uninterrupted succession of external and internal impressions is the
> psychological foundation upon which the type of metropolitan individuality
> arises. (116/409–10)

This statement situates Simmel's approach within the tradition of materialist
reflection on the subjective effects of modernization. It would become the
point of departure for Walter Benjamin's influential interpretation of the
shock-structure of modern existence as the cause of a fundamental transformation of experience—the eclipse of historical *Erfahrung* by punctual *Erlebnis.*[35]

Simmel accepts the psychological thesis that in modernity the unpredict-
ability and sheer rapidity with which sense impressions alter makes it impossible to respond consciously to each or even most of them. However, unlike
his contemporary Émile Tardieu, who viewed such conditions as leading via
organic fatigue to metaphysical despair, he emphasizes how human beings
adapt to life in a milieu characterized by permanent nervous overstimulation. The tempo and variety of urban existence, Simmel argues, provide the
"sensual foundation" for the "intellectualizing character of metropolitan

---

[35]Both in "Das Paris des Second Empire bei Baudelaire" (Benjamin 1974, 35) and in "Einige
Motive von Baudelaire" (Benjamin 1974, 146), he explicitly acknowledges the importance of Simmel's ideas.

psychic life," which stands in "profound opposition" to the emotional orientation of provincial and rural life, with its "slower, more habitual and more regularly flowing rhythm." Without a dampening of immediate emotional response, the relentless pulse of nervous stimulation in the city would produce "convulsions and inner upheavals"; "the metropolitan type," he writes, develops the intellect (*Verstand*) as "a protective organ against the uprooting threatened by the currents and discrepancies of his external milieu." The resulting skeptical attitude is adaptive. "The intensification of consciousness" gives priority to intellectual over emotional response and thereby "transfers the reaction to these phenomena into the least sensitive psychic organ, the one furthest from the depths of the personality" (117/410). In other words, reacting rationally rather than emotionally is the condition of psychic survival in the modern city.

However, for Simmel, the visceral effects of nervous stimulation cannot explain the spiritual significance of modern metropolitan life. The meaning of rationality cannot be grasped reductively: it is necessary to go beyond the psychological-somatic—to regard people not as bodies but as social beings.[36] "Metropolises and Mental Life" therefore links this topology of urban subjectivity to a sociological analysis of the relationship between rationality and rationalization in the urban milieu, connecting the materialist account of the subjective effects of modernization back to a philosophical interpretation of the relationship between progress and individuation. To relate subjective experience to the larger wholes that define people as beings in time, the argument must enter into the ambiguous terrain governed by the logic of *Wechselwirkung*, reciprocal causation.

According to Simmel, the tempo of nervous stimulation in the modern city exacerbates a long-established tendency to rationality, the source of which has been lost in the mists of time. Because the metropolis has always been "the seat of the money economy," which "stands in the profoundest connection to the hegemony of the intellect [*Verstandesherrschaft*]," it is not possible to determine which is the ultimate cause of the objectifying attitude that characterizes city dwellers.

[36]Simmel's approach should be contrasted with that of Sigmund Freud, who uses a similar topological description of such a "protective organ" in *Das Ich und das Es* as the basis of an account of the formation of subjectivity as such. Although Freud could not entirely correlate the physiological account of ego formation with the explanation of subjectivity (personality) as a function of the Oedipus conflict, he always maintained faith that such an articulation of the bodily and social dimensions would one day become possible. In contrast to Freud's commitment, at least in principle, to reductivist explanation, Simmel's thought posits a fundamental distinction between socio-historical reality and the visceral level of bodily experience as basic to human existence.

> The purely intellectual [*rein verstandesmäßige*] human being is indifferent to every-
> thing genuinely individual because it gives rise to relations and reactions that can-
> not be exhausted with the logical intellect—just as the individuality of phenomena
> does not enter into the pecuniary principle. (118/411)

Simmel interprets the rationalism of modern urban subjects in relation to
the historical whole in which they are situated. He emphasizes that, unlike
commodity production for the anonymous market, which calls for an objectifying and calculating attitude that treats others more like things than human individuals, "more primitive" economies involve ways of life that depend upon knowledge of and interaction with particular others. Because the
"reciprocal action" between rationalism and the money economy is so complete

> no one really can say whether the psychic, intellectualizing state pushed toward
> the money economy or whether the latter was the determinative factor for the
> former. What is certain is only that the form of metropolitan life is the most fer-
> tile ground for this reciprocal action. (119/412)

By conceptualizing phenomena characteristic of modern subjectivity as historically significant instances of such reciprocal action, Simmel's cultural
analyses articulate the interplay between cultural rationalization and subjective rationality that fosters the democratization of skepticism in modernity.
Before proceeding to his concrete analyses of the forms of metropolitan life,
it will therefore be helpful to consider more closely the arguments about
money that provide their sociological and philosophical foundation.

The *Philosophy of Money*, written in opposition to the Marxian claim that
modern cultural developments must ultimately be explained in terms of
economic processes, is a gargantuan attempt to interpret the historico-
philosophical significance of psychic and social phenomena associated with
the development of the money economy. From a "methodological perspective," Simmel wrote in the Preface, his "fundamental intention" could be expressed as an attempt

> to construct a further story beneath historical materialism such that the ex-
> planatory value of the incorporation of economic life into the causes of spiritual
> [*geistige*] culture is preserved, while these economic forms themselves are recog-
> nized as the result of more profound valuations and currents, of psychological or
> even metaphysical prerequisites. (13/56)

Linked in this way to a broader analysis of modernization, the study of the
development of the money economy places the philosophical problems of
modern existence into the context of an analysis of cultural evolution as
such. In chapters on individual freedom, the evolution of values, and "The

Style of Life," Simmel examines "the historical phenomenon of money . . . in
its effects upon the inner world—upon the vitality of individuals, upon the
linkage of their fates, upon culture in general" (10/54). As we have already
noted, the stated purpose of the *Philosophy of Money* was to demonstrate "the
possibility of finding in each of life's details the totality of its meaning"
(12/55), and thereby to illustrate the fruitfulness of the principle of reciprocal
causality for a philosophical approach to culture.

On Simmel's view, money is the motor of modernization—a process he
presents in a way that combines the Hegelian language of increasing objectification and spiritualization with a Nietzschean interpretation of modernity
as the locus of subjective fragmentation and alienation. He argues that as the
universal mediator of value, money facilitates the rationalization of existence
through which historically specific, substantive socioeconomic relations are
displaced by abstract functions of exchange. On one hand, by promoting exchange relations over great distances, money fosters the division of labor and
specialization and thereby frees individuals to develop their particular talents. On the other, Simmel observes, anonymity, impersonality, and objectification also increase in proportion to the increase in economic complexity.
As a result of the *Wechselwirkung* between subjective and collective reality,
rationality and objectivity become the medium of existence and interaction
in the increasingly complex, highly mediated culture that the growing money
economy brings about.

Because money is the principle of abstraction par excellence, this cultural
transformation impoverishes subjective life. Since under the highly differentiated modern mode of production, the individual creates only part of an
object, the products of labor gain "objective independence" (633/457) and
begin to appear to their producers as autonomous things—i.e. as commodities. Furthermore, human interactions are themselves objectified in a money
economy: "Subjectivity must be fragmented and transposed into cool reserve
and anonymous objectivity once so many intermediate stages are introduced
between the producer and the customer that they lose sight of one another"
(634/457). When human interactions are always mediated through objects
and money, the self too becomes thing-like.[37]

As the source of reification and of alienation, then, the money economy
provides the concrete foundation for the lived loss of meaning and purpose
that, as we have already seen, Simmel identified as underlying the paradigm

[37]Simmel's way of describing the subjective effects of modernization had a significant, as yet
unwritten, history of effects. These ideas may be traced, for example, in the writings of his student
Georg Lukács, who called him "the most important and interesting transitional phenomenon in
all of modern philosophy" (Gassen and Landmann 171).

shift in modern philosophy. A remarkable talk published in 1896, "Money in Modern Culture," anticipated the future development of his ideas by forging a theoretical link between Simmel's interpretation of money and his analysis of the disintegration of teleological frameworks in modernity.[38] Even as "the technique of all aspects of life . . . the system of mere means and tools" through which human beings both gain power over nature and regulate their collective lives increases in complexity and power, he argues here, the goals and purposes those technologies of living originally served fall away, so that means and techniques increasingly appear as "final purposes satisfying in themselves." Simmel calls the resulting "hypertrophy of means over ends" one of the "main problems of every higher culture" (189).

This argument provides the groundwork for an analysis of modern desire that makes the evolutionist notion that customs or mores (*Sitten*) live on long after their purpose has been forgotten into the basis of an intriguing interpretation of subjective malaise.[39] Simmel contends that the complexity of modern life has speeded up the process in which ends are converted into means, giving rise to the widespread feeling that "the definitive thing, the genuine meaning and central point of life and of things" has yet to be revealed (189). This feeling, a sense of restless anticipation that yields easily to boredom, is what Reinhart Koselleck described as "the present with-draw[ing] into inexperienceablity." Fostered by the increasing autonomy of the money economy, which entails that "a mere means of getting other goods" comes to be "felt as an independent good" (188), it is the psychic expression of what Horkheimer and Adorno would call the dialectic of enlightenment. Living in a world in which the internal dynamic of scientific and technological advancement has become an end in itself renders people ever less able to comprehend the technology of living in which they are embedded—let alone to ask about its ultimate value. The rationalization process that disenchants the world by dissolving all substantive, inherited values makes people dependent upon a way of life whose meaningfulness they cannot contemplate.

By interpreting money as the principle of symbolic conversion par excellence, Simmel is able to link questions of meaning to material socio-cultural transformations—to construct a new story about, if not beneath, historical materialism. In a passage reminiscent of the *Communist Manifesto*, Simmel describes the restless process of modern life.

---

[38] Georg Simmel: "Das Geld in der modernen Cultur." In: GSG 5, 178–96.

[39] For a fuller interpretation of the theoretical implications of Simmel's model of desire, see Goodstein 1996.

> With the money economy, the same transition from stability to lability which characterizes the entire modern vision of the world has gripped the economic cosmos as well, the fates of which, because they constitute a part of that movement, both symbolize and mirror the whole. (195)

The spiritual significance of money—or, more precisely, the reciprocal action between its objective and subjective significance—can therefore be made visible by focusing on particular moments or historical locations that reveal the synecdochic relationship between the money economy and cultural modernization as a whole. Because the forms of life that arise in the money economy both symbolize and mirror the historical whole, it is possible "to find in each of life's details the totality of its meaning."

We can now turn back to "Metropolises and Mental Life." Here Simmel anchors his philosophical interpretation of cultural modernization in analyses of concrete "forms of life" in which the modern "hypertrophy of means over ends" inflects subjective experience. As we have already noted, he argues that "the intellectualistic character of metropolitan inner life" in which immediate emotional reactions are suppressed and consciousness heightened to protect the organism against the "uprooting threatened by the currents and discrepancies of its external milieu" (117/410) stands in a relationship of reciprocal causation to the money economy. The essay goes on to examine a series of "apparently insignificant traits on the surface of life" through which the complex relationship between subjective experience and the "technology of living" that constitutes modern life becomes visible. These traits are the synecdochic parts that illuminate the whole of modern existence.

The first of these phenomenological nexuses of reciprocal action between subjective experience and the money economy is epitomized by "the universal diffusion of pocket watches." "The modern spirit," according to Simmel, is "calculative." Not only does the rationalistic "ideal of natural science . . . correspond to the calculative exactness of practical life which the money economy has brought about"; in the modern city, people's actual lives are filled with "weighing, measuring, counting" and otherwise "reducing qualitative values to quantitative ones" (119/412). Simmel's object is not to reject this quantitative focus in the name of a Nietzschean rediscovery of creative valuation but, in a Hegelian fashion, to grasp the phenomenon as a manifestation of a higher order of meaning.

Viewed from the perspective of historical sociology, the omnipresence of pocket watches expresses a mode of subjective adaptation to the rationalized form of modern life that itself has a larger significance.[40] According to the

---

[40]According to Köhnke, the importance of phenomena such as "pocket watches, weekly mar-

principle of reciprocal causation, the conditions of metropolitan existence are both cause and effect of the precision that dominates modern life.[41] For Simmel, that each individual human being carries a time-piece synecdochi-cally expresses that a temporal technology defines the whole of modern existence.

> The relationships and affairs of the typical metropolitan dweller usually are so varied and complex that without the strictest punctuality in promises and services the whole structure would break down into an inextricable chaos . . . . The technology of metropolitan life is unimaginable without the most punctual integration of all activities and mutual relations into a stable and super-subjective temporal schema. (119–20/412)

The pocket watch symbolizes subjective adaptation to the highly rationalized form of metropolitan life. Its "universal diffusion" both represents and facilitates the domination of an objectified temporal schema over individual, bodily needs and desires in determining the rhythms of daily life. Since to participate meaningfully in the social order defined by the modern money economy, it is necessary to mediate one's relations to the larger social world through the objectivity it embodies, the personal time piece is, quite literally, a condition of possibility for metropolitan subjectivity.

This example thus illustrates the methodological principle that underlies Simmel's phenomenological mode of cultural analysis. Indeed, having presented his interpretation, he makes a remark that echoes his programmatic statements in the Preface to the *Philosophy of Money*. "But here we see what it can only be the whole task of these reflections to show: that from every point on the surface of existence . . . it is possible to send a plummet into the depths of the soul, that all the most banal externalities are ultimately bound up . . . with final decisions about the meaning and style of life" (120/412). Showing that subjective life is thoroughly permeated by the effects of the money economy is a means of illuminating the philosophical implications of cultural modernization. Thus "the punctuality, calculability, exactitude that are forced upon metropolitan life by its complications and extension" not only mirror the intellectualism of the money economy in which the technology of modern life is rooted. They also take on a symbolic function. The effects of temporal technology extend into the interior depths of the self to

> color the contents of life and to favor the exclusion of those irrational, instinctive,

---

kets and postal delivery" was already recognized by Aron Bernstein, whose work Lazarus read in Berthold "Auerbach's Volkskalender auf das Jahr 1861" (Köhnke 1996, 352).

[41]"Es sind aber die Bedingungen der Großstadt, die für diesen Wesenszug so Ursache wie Wirkung sind" (119/412).

sovereign traits and impulses that want to determine the form of life from themselves instead of receiving a universal, schematically precise form from outside. (120/412)

The very quality of human subjectivity is reshaped in the image of rationality by modern circumstances. Thus, Simmel remarks, "natures like Ruskin and Nietzsche have a passionate hatred for the metropolis," for it seems to threaten to destroy all individuality. From his point of view, however, it would be more accurate to say that through the *Wechselwirkung* between subjective experience and cultural modernization, the philosophical problems of identity take concrete form.

Simmel's phenomenological analysis of the second "point on the surface" of urban existence links psychological and historical interpretation to examine one of these lived philosophical problems. The same socio-historical factors "that have coalesced into a formation of the highest impersonality in the exactitude and minute precision of this form of life," he writes, also make their effects felt in a "highly personal" way. "There is probably no psychic phenomenon so exclusively restricted to the metropolis as blaséness [*Blasiertheit*]" (121/413). On Simmel's account, physiological and historical factors converge to constitute this distinctively metropolitan subjective state. His interpretation articulates the materialist rhetoric of reflection on subjective experience into a philosophical account of the significance of blaséness as a reflection of larger historical processes.

Simmel initially explains the subjective attitude of permanently bored withdrawal in terms of modernity's most material effects, as the adaptation of a nervous system overtaxed by the frequency and intensity of stimulation in the modern city. The "essence" (*Wesen*) of blaséness, he writes, is a "blunting" (*Abstumpfung*) of sensitivity such that "the significance and the value of the differences among things and thus of the things themselves is felt to be insubstantial [*nichtig*]" (121–22/414). As such, blaséness is "the faithful subjective reflex of the fully established money economy," with its quantitative leveling of qualitative differences among things. Here Simmel picks up his argument linking money to alienation and reification in a passage that echoes with the critiques of modern society familiar from Chapter 3—one with no trace of Des Esseintes' "consoling beacons of the ancient hope." Under urban conditions, "money, with its colorlessness and indifference" becomes "the common denominator of all values." Everything is leveled into interchangeable commodities hollowed of "specific value" and "incomparability" (121/414). Simmel's analysis suggests that there is a contradiction at the heart of Des Esseintes' original retreat from the world: a dandyish cult of beautiful objects simply underlines the hollowness of the self, for it reinscribes the loss of inherent value suffered by everything that enters the money economy. On such a reading, boredom is neither, as the Goncourts claimed, a sign of subjective distinction nor, as Schopenhauer thought, a universal "fact" that "proves ... the meaninglessness of life" but rather an historically specific symptom of the loss of meaning that conditions all subjective experience in a highly developed money economy.

Simmel's analysis of metropolitan life describes the experiential conditions of possibility for boredom in a way that articulates very material historical analysis with philosophical interpretation. As we have seen, the omnipresence of pocket watches exposes the "supersubjective temporal schema" that makes subjective existence viable in the modern city. The "highly personal" correlate of the same form of life, the characteristic blasé demeanor of the urban dweller, reveals how deeply the rationalization process has formed the intimate dimensions of subjective experience itself. It is a way of living with the fragmentation of inherited systems of value that subjectively reproduces the global evacuation of meaning in modernity: the blasé subject has adapted to the objectification of the lifeworld by becoming object-like.

Simmel's analysis thus suggests a way to integrate the materialist and idealist paradigms for interpreting boredom. Metropolitan subjectivity, he argues, depends on blaséness, a "distinctive adaptive phenomenon" (*eigentümliche Anpassungserscheinung*) that is both product and symptom of the rationalization process—the embodiment of the *Wechselwirkung* between the material and spiritual effects of modern urban life. However, "the nerves find in the refusal to react the last possibility of accommodating to the contents and form of metropolitan life ... at the price of devaluing the entire objective world, which in the end unavoidably draws the personality itself down into the same feeling of devaluation(122/415). The modern subject's habitual insensitivity to qualitative distinctions, whether it finds expression in bored withdrawal or in a restless search for new forms of stimulation, thus becomes, in my terms, a lived metaphor for the hypertrophy of means over ends in modernity. In the permanently bored attitude of blaséness, the loss of meaning that permeates modern life forms appears as indifference to meaning itself.

However, "Metropolises and Mental Life" is not concerned with subjective experience per se but rather with the historical and philosophical significance of the forms of life that are the (objective and subjective) effects of urbanization. Just as the ubiquity of timepieces represented the integration of individuals into the "super-subjective temporal schema" of the metropolis, the psychological adaptation of blaséness gains its significance in relation to another more general sociological phenomenon: the urban crowd. The "self-

preservation" of the subject is not achieved merely by the psychological adaptation of blaséness; to sustain agency under metropolitan conditions requires an equally "negative" form of social behavior: reserve (*Reserviertheit*).
Anyone who tried to respond to the endless stream of others encountered in
the urban crowd as human beings, Simmel writes, would "fully atomize
themselves internally and end up in an entirely unimaginable psychic state"
(122–23/415). At the same time, "the sphere of indifference is not so great as it
appears superficially": at a physiological level, people inevitably respond to
the presence of others, so that there is a constant flux of impressions below
the level of consciousness (123/416). Beneath the apparent indifference and
restraint of the city dweller's equanimity, then, he discerns "antipathy, the
latent and preliminary stage of practical antagonism which brings about the
distances and aversions without which this type of life could not be led at
all." Blaséness and reserve are complementary modes of subjective adaptation to metropolitan life; these negative forms of psychological self-assertion
facilitate the functional integration of the subject into the larger historical
whole of the metropolis, in which a rational attitude toward things and persons is indispensable.

Simmel has arrived at the heart of his argument. This self-defensive form
of sociality epitomizes the world-historical significance he sought to identify
through his examination of metropolitan life: through it, the modern subject
struggles "to preserve the autonomy and individuality of his existence in the
face of overwhelming forces of society, of the historical heritage, of external
culture and the technology of life" (116/409). For Simmel, the "indivisible
whole of metropolitan life-formation [*Lebensgestaltung*]" includes not only
unifying elements—the money economy, rationalism, and the temporal
schema in which they converge—but also the negative modes in which individual subjects accommodate to the global circumstances of modern existence. "What appears to be dissociation is in reality only one of its elemen-
tary forms of sociation" (123/416). If people were not protected by a defensive
attitude, their spontaneous, irrational impulses toward others would overwhelm them and render them unable to function within the rationalistic
framework of modern existence. Just as "the universal diffusion of pocket
watches" assures that subjective experience is rationalized into line with "a
super-subjective temporal schema" and the blasé attitude guarantees that the
indifference to all qualitative distinctions required for the smooth functioning of the money economy is internalized, the survival of society as a whole
requires that people relate to one another with reserve.

This analysis marks Simmel's approach as a decisive departure from both
"idealist" and "materialist" interpretations of subjective experience that

shape the discourse on boredom. Focusing on the ways modern subjects adapt to metropolitan life by intensifying rational and minimizing emotional responses, he places subjective experience in the context of cultural evolution, neither abstracting it from its historical context nor reducing it to an epiphenomenon of physiological or sociological realities. Although these modern forms of experience have their origins in the development of the money economy, as the bearers of the problem of the meaning to which that development gives rise, they provide a synecdochic site for reflection on the larger—*geistige*—significance of cultural evolution itself. Moving from the "details on the surface" of urban existence—the subjective "adaptations" that are both product and symptom of the modernization process—to the historical totality, Simmel develops his argument about the world-historical significance of the subjective effects of cultural modernization. The defensive form of subjectivity manifested in blaséness and extended into the social sphere as reserve is, he argues, the condition of possibility for modern individuality and personal freedom as such.

> This reserve with the overtone of hidden aversion appears simultaneously to be the form or cloak of a much more universal spiritual essence [*Geisteswesen*] of the metropolis. Namely, it guarantees the individual a sort and measure of personal freedom for which there is not even an analogy under other [social] conditions. (123–24/416)

Here Simmel's account of the modern "form" of subjectivity resonates with the philosophical understanding of boredom as, in its very negativity, a mode of subjective transcendence. However, for him it is the historical rather than the existential truth of human being that is revealed.

Simmel argues that the isolated individuality he has interpreted as the subjective adaptation par excellence to urban life has its origins in "one of the great developmental tendencies of social life itself" (124/416). Viewed as a site of the global *Wechselwirkung* between collective and individual life that for him constitutes the historical process of cultural evolution, the distancing mode of sociation that defines the metropolitan form of life illuminates the metaphysical significance of the modernization process it exemplifies. To elaborate this point, he turns from phenomenological description of the urban form of subjectivity to a consideration of its socio-historical genesis.

Simmel traces the emergence of subjectivity in the modern sense to the elaboration of the division of labor that occurs as social groups increase in size. In particular, the growth of cities meant ever-greater specialization both of production and of consumption (needs being reciprocally related to the services and goods on offer). Increasing personal differentiation within the urban public resulted, "and this led to the more narrowly speaking spiritual [*geistige*] individuation of psychic qualities, to which the city gives rise in proportion to its size" (128/420). However, the same historical process gives rise to diametrically opposed phenomena. As we have already seen, physiological and spiritual threats to subjective integrity are intrinsic to the conditions of modern metropolitan life, and blaséness and reserve are double-edged phenomena. According to Simmel, this ambiguity reflects a basic feature of cultural evolution.

It thus brings him back to the question of the historico-philosophical significance of the tension between the individual and the "technology of living" invoked at the outset of "Metropolises and Mental Life." Because "subjective" culture cannot keep pace with the historical process through which the collective world or "objective" culture becomes richer and fuller, modern individuals experience the intersubjective context in which they are supposed to find meaning and fulfillment in ever more partial and fragmentary ways. In the terms he would adopt later on, it is "the tragedy of culture" that "subjective" culture atrophies as "objective" culture develops. Steeped in the romantic and idealist philosophical traditions which saw culture as the quasi-organic, historical process through which "humanity" developed, Simmel was also profoundly influenced by the Schopenhauerian and Nietzschean critique of those traditions. In his late writings, the philosophical conception of a "tragedy of culture" emphasized the ambiguity of an historical process in which scientific and technological progress come at the cost of human wholeness. Here, he does not yet focus on the alienating experience of modern culture as a locus of such fragmentation. Instead, Simmel emphasizes the reciprocal relations between spiritual and material historical forces in the forms of sociation to theorize the historical significance of modern individuality itself.

Modern life, he argues, makes visible the disproportion between the speed with which "objective spirit" develops and the individual subject's ability to assimilate that increase. The historical consequence is "the atrophy of individual through the hypertrophy of objective culture" (130/422). In the modern metropolis, according to Simmel, the individual grows ever more insignificant in the face of "a monstrous organization of things and powers, which take all progress, spirituality, values . . . and transfer them out of the form of a subjective life into that of a purely objective one" (129–30/421–22). This perspective marks the distance between Simmel's phenomenology of culture and Hegel's *Phenomenology of Spirit*. While the latter had envisioned a modern subject who could assimilate this objectification into a higher form of rational self-reflection, for Simmel, the modern subject is sustained negatively, through an intellectualizing skepticism about the value of the external world that, as we have seen, takes the form of blaséness.

The form of urban existence thus reveals the historical operation of the dialectic of enlightenment. The very historical process that gives rise to individuation comes to threaten subjective particularity; the distinctive problems of modern subjectivity follow on what from the perspective of society as a whole is rationalization. However, Simmel is not interested in lamenting the loss of meaning experienced as a consequence of the "hypertrophy of means over ends." He focuses on the significance of the correlative structures of experience from the perspective of a larger, metaphysical framework of reflection on the evolution of cultural complexity. It is from the latter point of view that he proposes to interpret the internal conflicts that are constitutive of modern subjectivity.

The final move in Simmel's argument is to situate the two "forms of individualism which are nourished by the quantitative conditions of the metropolis: individual autonomy and the elaboration of personal particularity" in historical context, whereby, he declares, the metropolis "gains an entirely new value in the world history of spirit" (130/423). According to Simmel, the ideal of individual freedom and equality that emerged in the eighteenth century constitutes the basis of modern, democratized social forms, yet the nineteenth-century ideal of unique individuality which arose on the basis of romantic critiques of the enlightened version of the self is equally basic to the self-understanding of the modern subject.[42] The "struggle" between these alternative visions of "the role [of] the subject within the totality," he writes, constitutes "the external as well as the internal history of our time" (131/423). Through the forms of modern urban life, the tensions between individual and society, uniqueness and equality are inscribed in the self. From the perspective of Simmel's philosophy of culture, because "it is the function of the metropolises to deliver the location for the battle and for the attempts at unification" of these alternative conceptions of human being, cities have a crucial "place in the evolution of psychic existence." However, as historical formations in which the contradictions and complexities that comprise life itself come to light, he writes, they fall "entirely outside the sphere where it is appropriate for us to bring the attitude of a judge . . . our task is not to accuse or to forgive, but only to understand" (131/423–24). The movement from the "details on the surface" to the depths of life is hermeneutic, not critical.

---

[42]See also his *Grundfragen der Soziologie,* chapter IV, "Individuum und Gesellschaft in den Lebensanschauungen des 18. und 19. Jahrhunderts" (GSG 16, 122–49).

Simmel interprets modern subjectivity as the locus of historically significant tensions. "Blaséness" is both a form in which individuals can assert their unique individuality and a consequence of the leveling effect of rationalization on subjective experience as such; reserve is a form of self-protection and a condition of social survival. An indispensable adaptation to modern conditions, the defensive form of subjectivity Simmel describes is a site of historically significant *Wechselwirkung* in which the problem of meaning is lived. However, in the final analysis, "Metropolises and Mental Life" does not really address "the deepest problems of modern existence" that "flow from the claim of the individual to preserve the autonomy and individuality of his existence in the face of overwhelming forces of society, of the historical heritage of external culture and technology of life." Disregarding his own interpretation of the money economy, which emphasizes the concrete relationship between modern forms of life and the destruction of teleological metanarratives, Simmel comes down on the side of a longing for meaning that he knows is historically obsolete.

Simmel sublates the tensions that define spiritual life in the modern metropolis into a neo-Hegelian interpretation of cultural evolution as a whole at the cost of the insights that follow from the Nietzschean critique of the Enlightenment notion of rational progress. In particular, interpreting the defensive form of modern subjectivity as a synecdoche for the differentiation and individuation that characterizes cultural evolution effectively recuperates the modern metropolitan subject's experience of fragmentation and anomie, conflating the atomization of experience and the reification of the self into the historically achieved radical freedom of modernity's unique individual subject. While Simmel's account of the subjective adaptations to the modern metropolitan form of life elegantly links skepticism to the material effects of cultural modernization, in moving to the next level of abstraction, his analysis combines the weaknesses of less philosophically sophisticated sociological analyses with those of universalizing philosophical interpretations of subjective malaise. He locates the negative form of modern subjectivity in its historical context only to reduce it to a manifestation of extra-personal forces and realities; furthermore, in attaining this objectifying point of view, he seems to lose his reflective perspective on the phenomena that formed his point of departure. The blaséness that, on his analysis, is tantamount to an indifference to meaning reappears in his skeptical conclusion, which takes a philosophically distanced perspective on the subjective phenomena it considers.

These difficulties may all be traced to the fact that "Metropolises and Mental Life" pronounces on the significance of modern experience without engaging with the actual discourses in which modern subjects reflect upon their lives. For Simmel, "the urban subject" is an object of analysis whose "blaséness," like Emma Bovary's boredom, is a significant symptom of a larger reality that subject cannot understand. From the perspective of a model that relegates the actual discourse on boredom in which reflection on subjective experience takes place to the level of historical epiphenomenon, significant reflection can take place only at the level of historico-philosophical metanarrative.

Nonetheless, Simmel's synecdochic strategy for articulating the relationship between the fragmentary "details" of subjective experience and the historical "whole" of cultural modernization suggests an illuminating perspective on the metaphorics of boredom. In his argument, the subjective attitude of blaséness is at once an immediate response to the most material effects of modernization—the relentless nervous stimulation of the urban environment—and the "highly personal" counterpart of the temporal and social technologies that make metropolitan life cohere. The negative form of subjectivity it epitomizes exemplifies the psychic effects of the rational attitude toward things and persons demanded by the highly differentiated mode of existence proper to the modern money economy. To the blasé subject, all "ultimate goals" appear "in their character as mere means." If this global analysis of urban subjectivity is resituated in discursive terms, Simmel's approach can be seen to articulate the way the philosophical questions raised within the discourse on boredom are linked to the historical realities that conditioned the emergence of that discourse. Complementing his phenomenological approach with rhetorical analysis helps illuminate why "boredom" is a form in which "the anxious question about the meaning and purpose of the whole" enters modern life.

The experience of boredom is not simply a symptom of the hypertrophy of the complex "technologies" of modern life over the capacity of the individual to assimilate and make sense of them. The bored subject invokes a very particular language of reflection, one in which these very material effects of cultural modernization appear as grounds for a universalized skepticism. In boredom, as we have already noted, skepticism about the value of particular possible ends easily extends to dubiousness about the very possibility of purposive action as such. But indifference to meaning is a double-edged sword. Thus the negative form of reflection through which modern subjects attempt to cope rationally with the overload of irrational stimulation leads to the nihilistic dynamic Simmel described, which proceeds from a physiological "refusal to react" via the "devaluing of the entire objective world" to the evacuation of the self and metaphysical despair about the meaning of life.

"Boredom" names the eclipse of subjective experience itself in the face of the global flowering of objective culture in modernity; thus it becomes a lived metaphor for the problem of meaning that defines modern subjectivity. Even though Simmel's phenomenology of blaséness abstracts the subjective attitude of the bored subject from the discourse of reflection in which it is situated, his analysis of the synecdochic relationship between the defensive rationality that is the subjective adaptation par excellence to modern life and the irrational whole constituted by the hypertrophic technology of modern life illuminates why modern skepticism is democratized in the form of this particular language of reflection.

On Simmel's view, as on Marx's, modernization effects a rationalization of the human world while giving "objective independence" to the products of labor. As we have noted, Simmel characterized his work in this period as an effort to "construct a further story beneath historical materialism" by investigating the spiritual effects of the growth of the money economy. His investigations of the urban "form of life" suggest that it is precisely because the self is rendered thing-like that people can become aware of the problem of meaning that permeates modern existence. The discourse on boredom that has flourished since the mid-nineteenth century is a form in which that reflection takes place; the experience of self and world to which it refers is a democratized form of skepticism. Simmel's phenomenology of culture, which links the philosophical dilemmas of modern subjectivity to the actual conditions of life in the modern metropolis, thus provides an important corrective to the very different phenomenology we shall take up in the next chapter. Martin Heidegger's fine-grained analysis of the experience of boredom provides a rich field for reflection upon the philosophical questions it raises, but at the cost of effacing the historical and discursive context in which those problems become acute in the name of a renewal of metaphysics.

CHAPTER 5

Martin Heidegger's Existential
Grammar of Boredom

————•◆•◆◆————

Die Langeweile entspringt aus der Zeitlichkeit des Daseins
Martin Heidegger[1]

For Georg Simmel, blaséness was the psychological condition of possibility for metropolitan subjectivity. Like the orientation to standardized clock time, this "distinctive adaptive phenomenon" facilitated the individual's integration into the chaotic conditions of modern metropolitan existence. But if blaséness was the "subjective reflex of the fully established money economy," with its tendency to level things and people into interchangeable commodities, it also seemed to him more than a sociological symptom. The blasé attitude was a means of spiritual self-protection, a bulwark against the stimulations and stresses of modern existence that literally threatened the subject with dissolution. Thus in and through the defensive form of subjectivity it represented, the decisive tension between conflicting modern understandings of identity was experienced—between the equality and freedom paradigmatically expressed by blending into the urban crowd and the uniqueness of the self paradigmatically expressed through dressing and acting in ways that rendered one visible in that crowd. Simmel's analysis confirmed and extended my argument about the connections between the democratization of boredom and the process of modernization. His phenomenology of culture allowed me to elaborate the links between boredom, understood as a concretization of the modern subject's adaptive attitude, and modernization as a process that has rationalized and commodified the conditions of human existence. Finally, his philosophy of culture placed subjective disaffection into a global perspective that I suggested could be combined with an emphasis on the discursive construction of experience to conceptualize the historical constitution of boredom in a more rigorous way.

---

[1]"Boredom arises from the temporality of Dasein" (Martin Heidegger, *Gesamtausgabe* V, 29/30, 191; subsequent references in text).

This chapter focuses on the very different phenomenology of boredom Martin Heidegger developed in lectures at Freiburg in 1929–30. In contrast to Simmel's philosophical phenomenology of culture, which underlines the relationship between cultural complexity and questions of meaning, Heidegger's phenomenological regrounding of philosophy brackets the historical and material conditions of existence. Simmel had analyzed indifference to and detachment from a world seemingly without inherent value as the condition of possibility of urban subjectivity. Although he calls boredom the "fundamental mood," the *Grundstimmung,* of modernity, Heidegger does not associate this configuration of subjective experience with the culturally specific surround of the modern metropolis at all. For him, the philosophical significance of boredom is to be sought not by situating it in world-historical context but rather by demonstrating how it reveals the existential lack that characterizes modern subjectivity. Where Simmel's cultural phenomenology examines the way the money economy and the material conditions of modern existence foster a disinterested, even apathetic attitude toward the world and therewith the tendency to boredom, Heidegger focuses on the experience itself as a lived symptom of modern nihilism. If for Simmel the global, sociological framework is decisive in defining the significance of the negative form of subjectivity epitomized by blaséness, for Heidegger, it is the relation to individual mortality that renders the experience of boredom philosophically significant.

However, even if he regards the significance of boredom in ahistorical terms, Heidegger's point of departure is boredom as an historical phenomenon, and he is concerned both implicitly and explicitly with the question of the relation between this form of subjective malaise and the historicity of human existence. As we have seen, Simmel articulates the relationship between subjective experience and cultural modernization as a problem of reflection rather than of material determination and thus overcomes the reductivism of the sociological interpretations considered in Part I. Heidegger, for his part, relates the reflective experience of boredom to the historical context in which it arises and thereby similarly outstrips the idealist and ahistorical tendency of the other, "philosophical," branch of the scholarly literature examined there. By elucidating what I call an "existential grammar of mood," Heidegger's phenomenology of boredom makes his claim that the experience reveals the structure of human existence as such plausible in a way that arguments which assume that the experience is a transhistorical universal cannot. Nonetheless, the notion that boredom is the "fundamental mood" of the time remains abstract. Heidegger reflects neither on the historical specificity of the particular cases of boredom he discusses nor on the discursive position he occupies in analyzing them. As we have seen, in failing to examine the linguistic construction of the phenomena he interprets, Simmel situates reflection outside the realm of lived experience. Heidegger ostensibly focuses on the lived experience of boredom as a universally accessible entry into philosophy, yet he ends by reinscribing the elitist distinction between the mundane boredom of everyday existence and the deep boredom that leads to metaphysical questions. Here, too, I shall show, the philosophical limitations of the approach are grounded in a failure to reflect on the historical and discursive specificity of the experiences being analyzed.

This chapter centers on Heidegger's most extensive discussion of boredom, which took place in a lecture course held in the Winter Semester of 1929–30, the year after he returned to Freiburg to assume the chair of his former teacher, Edmund Husserl. These lectures, entitled *The Fundamental Concepts of Metaphysics: World—Finitude—Solitude (Die Grundbegriffe der Metaphysik: Welt—Endlichkeit—Einsamkeit)*, formed an introduction to Heidegger's innovative mode of philosophizing. As the subtitle indicates, he was far from promulgating the traditional conceptual apparatus of metaphysics. Instead, he aimed to bring his listeners to an understanding of the existential significance of metaphysical questions and thereby to revitalize philosophy. Approximately the first half of the semester was devoted to a detailed analysis of boredom. In these lectures, Heidegger develops the notion that boredom (*Langeweile*) is the *Grundstimmung* of the modern era and argues that "awakening" this "fundamental mood" is a necessary propaedeutic for the renewal of philosophy. Contemporary boredom both attests to the urgency of such a renewal and epitomizes the challenges involved in achieving it—the challenges, as Heidegger understood them, of philosophizing in modernity. His strategy of argumentation is both part of the broader discourse on boredom and, implicitly, a mode of reflection on that discourse. However, despite his intricate attention to language, Heidegger fails to reflect on the discursive and historical construction of the experience of boredom. My reading of the lectures will therefore provide an historical and philosophical critique of Heidegger even as it demonstrates the significance of this neglected text on boredom.[2]

---

[2] Although Heidegger regarded these lectures as highly significant for the development of his thought (See the Editor's afterword, 541), relatively little commentary has been written on them. A translation of the lectures was published (Heidegger 1995) after the original version of the present text was completed, but with few exceptions, this neglect has persisted. For a more sympathetic reading than my own, see Parvis Emad, "Boredom as Limit and Disposition." Tom Rockmore in *On Heidegger's Nazism and Philosophy* and Michel Haar in "Attunement and Thinking" argue from quite different perspectives for the centrality of the lectures to the development of Heideg-

The Fundamental Concepts of Metaphysics is a linguistically dense and internally complex text, and the ideas advanced in it are at the heart of Heidegger's early thought. The lectures put forward a vision of the historico-political task of philosophy in the modern world that is particularly significant given the persistent question of the meaning of the philosopher's relation to National Socialism. The reversals in Heidegger's thinking on boredom during the 1920's trace the evolution of his vision of philosophy. He first took up the question of the meaning of boredom in "The Concept of Time" (1924), as his conception of his philosophical mission was taking form. The changes that his interpretation of the experience had undergone by 1929 register the philosophical breakthrough to the understanding of historicity and everydayness of *Being and Time* (1927) and indicate lines of development for the future. Despite the undeniable originality of his approach to philosophizing, these texts attest that Heidegger's critique of everyday life in modernity is consonant with the romantic anti-capitalism that fueled the Nazi cultural revolution. Since his interpretation of boredom evolves in relation to that critical understanding of everydayness, placing it in this larger discursive context reveals how his understanding of the experience reflects the political and historical realities of inter-war Germany.[3] Seen in this light, I argue, the lectures of 1929–30 illuminate Heidegger's passage from *Being and Time* in 1927 to the Rectorate in 1933.

This consideration of the historical significance of Heidegger's conception of historicity and everydayness will form the horizon for my close reading of the phenomenology of boredom through which, in the lectures of 1929–30, he attempted to "awaken" his audience's understanding of philosophical questions. Heidegger's interpretation of boredom is suffused with the same attitude toward the modern world that defined the modernist discourse on ennui as a form of subjective distinction. Like Kierkegaard and Schopenhauer before him, he invoked the commonplaces of the discourse on boredom in the name of a new understanding of human existence. In Heidegger's case, however, the political costs of what Adorno called the "jargon of

---

ger's thought. See also Miguel Beistegui, "'Boredom: Between Existence and History': On Heidegger's Pivotal *The Fundamental Concepts of Metaphysics*," Klaus Held "Fundamental Moods and Heidegger's Critique of Contemporary Culture," and Jean Paumen "Ennui et Nostalgie chez Heidegger."

[3] See Hugo Ott, *Martin Heidegger: Unterwegs zu seiner Biographie*, Michael E. Zimmerman, *Heidegger's Confrontation with Modernity: Technology, Politics, and Art*, Richard Wolin, *The Politics of Being: The Political Thought of Martin Heidegger*, George Leaman, *Heidegger im Kontext, Gesamtüberblick zum NS-Engagement der Universitätsphilosophen*, Hans Sluga, *Heidegger's Crisis: Philosophy and Politics in Nazi Germany*, and Rüdiger Safranski, *Ein Meister aus Deutschland: Heidegger und seine Zeit* on the wider cultural context of Heidegger's political engagement.

authenticity" become apparent. The rhetoric of boredom supports a form of reflection that—in sharp contrast to Georg Simmel's approach—abstracts subjective identity from its cultural context and formulates questions of meaning in individualistic terms. Heidegger's existential grammar of boredom is paradigmatic for the way the modern rhetoric of reflection occludes the historicity of the discourse on subjective experience in which it is embedded. Read against the grain, however, it reveals the historical specificity of the gesture of reflection that rejects the modern world in the name of a neo-Christian elevation of individual existence.

Boredom and the Search for Philosophical Renewal

Heidegger's phenomenology of boredom must be understood in the context of the rhetorical strategy of *The Fundamental Concepts of Metaphysics*. Because the declared objective of these lectures is nothing less than a renewal of philosophy itself,[4] substance and method are intertwined. Heidegger undertakes his analysis of boredom in order to evoke in his listeners an encounter with the most fundamental questions of human existence and thereby to initiate them into his new mode of philosophizing, a transformation of Husserlian phenomenology that aspires to move beyond the limits of Cartesian rationality to a more primordial form of thinking. If Simmel was an impressionist, Heidegger was an expressionist. Here the relationship of particular to universal is not grasped in the external reflection on the relation between detail and whole, but rather in the immanent shift from temporal to ontological awareness. His very distinctive rhetorical stance—less professorial than oracular—seems to confirm Rüdiger Safranksi's claim that Heidegger understood himself as a "philosophical charismatic."[5]

Philosophy, he tells his students in the opening lecture, is "neither science nor the proclamation of world views" (3); it must be experienced—all the more so since, on Heidegger's view, modern subjectivity is epitomized by indifference to the essential dimension of existence in which it moves.[6] Heidegger therefore unfolds his ideas in the form of a phenomenological journey through the foreign, yet uncannily familiar terrain of metaphysical reflection. An introductory discussion guided by Novalis' identification of

---

[4] After his appointment as Husserl's successor, Heidegger wrote to Karl Jaspers: "Freiburg will again be the test for me whether there is still something to philosophy or whether everything dissolves into learnedness (24.11.28, *Briefwechsel* 104).

[5] Safranski, 219.

[6] Heidegger's phrase is "weder 'Wissenschaft' noch Weltanschauungsverkündigung." This conception of philosophy should be read in the context of the contemporary debate about method and value in the social sciences. Compare Max Weber's views in "Science as a Vocation."

philosophy with homesickness (*Heimweh*) brings him to "the first and genuinely fundamental task of our lectures and the beginning of a truly animated [*lebendigen*] philosophizing": the task of "awakening a fundamental mood" and thereby raising metaphysical questions "in their necessity and possibility" (87). Part I, in which Heidegger analyzes boredom (*Langeweile*) as the fundamental mood (*Grundstimmung*) of the day, delineates the relationship between quotidian experience and metaphysical questioning; Part II poses the fundamental question: "What is world?" that arises from this discussion of boredom. Thus the lectures move from "ordinary everydayness" to the "question of being," and by rendering in more accessible form the major lessons of *Being and Time* extend the practical-philosophical aim of that work.[7]

Heidegger augments Husserl's call for a "return to the things themselves" with what he sees as an historic confrontation with the philosophical tradition. Or more precisely, his "return" to the question of being transforms what it means to have a tradition; it enables him to reinterpret the entire history of Western thought. Thus his lectures on the "fundamental concepts" of metaphysics redefine what it means to ask a metaphysical question. The "world-problem," Heidegger tells his students, "has gone unrecognized as such" in philosophy. It is this failure to think how human existence includes the relation to "being as a whole"—the world (8)—that has, he contends, resulted in the remoteness of philosophy from the vital problems of existence.

Toward the end of the lectures, Heidegger explicitly advocates making philosophy practical again through a critical appropriation of the past very much in the spirit of Nietzsche.[8]

> We only learn from the past when we first of all and simultaneously awaken it. That we are unable to learn anything more from the past means only that we ourselves have been left without history. No era has known such a flood [*Zustrom*] of tradition and none was so poor in genuine inheritance. Logos, ratio, reason [*Vernunft*], spirit [*Geist*] are all obscurantist [*verdeckende*] titles for the world-problem. (508)

[7]This reading clarifies the special importance Heidegger accorded to the lectures (which were first published in German in 1983). In the early sixties he applied for a stipend from the Deutsche Forschungsgemeinschaft to finance Ute Guzzoni's production of a typescript from his 94-page folio (Nachwort des Herausgebers; Heidegger 1983, 538). According to the editor, Friedrich-Wilhelm von Hermann, during the meetings in which they were preparing the way for the publication of his collected works, Heidegger "repeatedly directed the conversation . . . toward these lectures, emphasizing alongside their significance for the concept of world [*Weltbegriff*] the detailed analysis of boredom" (540–41).

[8]The lectures conclude with the citation of the "trunkne Lied" from *Thus Spoke Zarathustra*, in which, Heidegger says, "the last great philosopher" allows us "to experience what the world is" (532).

Like Nietzsche, who saw the "overgrowth of history" as choking life, Heidegger advocates a sort of genealogical therapy—a critical examination of the philosophical tradition that uncovers and recovers the primordial problem of the human being's relation to the world. His introduction to metaphysics therefore follows a twofold strategy. While in the first part of the lecture series Heidegger reformulates the task of philosophy phenomenologically, in the second part he demonstrates conceptually that the link between logic and metaphysics that has defined the philosophical tradition conceals the world problem in a definite way. For him, this is the sense in which "we have been left without history" (*wir selbst sind geschichtslos geworden*) (508). Through the connection to the tradition, the problem of boredom provides the point of entry for a mode of thinking that grasps human historicity anew.

Although the rudiments of what Heidegger would later formulate as the history of the forgetting of being are thus apparent in these lectures on "The Fundamental Concepts of Metaphysics," the emphasis still falls, as in *Being and Time*, on the thematics of "Dasein"—on human existence and on the human being as inquirer.[9] Heidegger's critical appropriation of the tradition is explicitly in the service of existential renewal; his critiques of the contemporary understanding of history remain focused on the way that individuals grasp their relation to the world. As the forty-year-old philosopher saw it, his task was to find a way to "transform the human being and therewith received metaphysics into a more primordial Dasein [*ursprünglicheres Dasein*] in order to allow the old fundamental questions to arise anew" (508). The crucial issue from our point of view is why and how a phenomenological investigation of boredom could, on Heidegger's view, enable such a renewal of philosophy. Before beginning to clarify these questions by examining the evolution of his thinking on boredom, however, it will be helpful to consider the testimony of a star witness to his distinctive pedagogy.

Hannah Arendt's recollections of her experiences as Heidegger's student, published in 1969, bear out his exalted vision of existential transformation from the podium. In addition, her remarks confirm the appropriateness of Heidegger's decision to focus on this particular fundamental mood in introducing Freiburg students to his new mode of philosophizing. "After the First

[9]Since the English edition of *Being and Time* provides page references to the German, I have simply cited the latter; subsequent references (in text) are marked by SZ. I have not capitalized 'Being' (*Sein*) because the convention of doing so seems to me to foster a philosophical misunderstanding (that Being is an entity somehow separable from beings). I have generally preferred to attempt literal renderings; however, with some trepidation I follow the standard usage that leaves 'Dasein,' Heidegger's word for the human mode of being, untranslated in an effort to retain the existential emphasis implicit in this term—literally, 'being-there.'

World War," she wrote, there was "a widely disseminated malaise [*Unbe-hagen*]" with the academic status quo "among all the students for whom their course of study meant more than preparation for a career."[10]

> The university generally offered [the philosophy students] either schools—the neo-Kantians, neo-Hegelians, neo-Platonists, etc.—or the familiar school-discipline, in which philosophy, neatly divided into subdivisions ... was not so much communicated as executed [*erledigt*] through endless boredom. (894)

Heidegger transformed Husserlian phenomenology by returning to the classical philosophical tradition in a way that renewed it. In his hands, according to Arendt, the teachings of the past took on the role of the things themselves: "Plato was not discussed and his doctrine of ideas represented, but rather a dialogue [was read closely] ... until there was no more thousand-year-old teaching but only a highly contemporary problematic" (894–95). Arendt vouches for Heidegger's ability to "transform" his students by awakening thought to its own mystery and power in this way. Even before the publication of *Being and Time*, she recalls, his "name traveled through all of Germany like the rumor of the secret king" (893). Word spread that "thinking is that "thinking is alive again, the supposedly dead cultural treasures of the past are being brought to speak ... There is a teacher; one could perhaps learn to think" (895). According to Arendt, Heidegger's "*passionate* thinking" was not goal-directed in any instrumental sense. It was, rather "pure activity" (896)—a radical break with the boredom of the inherited discipline and at the same time a reawakening of Aristotle, of Hegel, of the tradition itself.

As Arendt notes, Heidegger's renewal of philosophy not only transformed his German audiences, but also set the course for much of twentieth-century thought. The return to the texts themselves, which would be carried to the new world by students as diverse as Leo Strauss and Herbert Marcuse, effected a "destruction" of traditional ontology.[11] By radically refiguring philosophical questions, Heidegger provoked a new sort of reflection on the foundations of thought, even if his claim to have returned philosophy to the things themselves came to seem questionable. Thus from the perspective of a hearer such as Arendt, the connection Heidegger saw between transforming his hearers and transforming metaphysics itself seemed plausible.[12] As we

---

[10] Arendt, 1969, 893–94. Subsequent citations in text.

[11] On Heidegger's conception of the "destruction of the history of ontology" as a "critique" of the present through a rediscovery of the unrecognized resources of the past, see *Being and Time*, § 6.

[12] Their affair seems to have continued until 1929 (Young-Bruehl 69). However, after her year in Marburg (1924–25, the period in which Heidegger was thinking through what would become *Being and Time*), Arendt had left for Freiburg to study with Husserl, then gone on to Heidelberg

shall see, however, the role boredom plays in the lectures of 1929–39 attests to Heidegger's own sense of the difficulty of awakening authentic reflection on the dilemmas of modern existence.

The Emergence of the Problem of Boredom

The importance of the conception of boredom developed in the lectures on "The Fundamental Concepts of Metaphysics" for an understanding of Heidegger's early thought only becomes apparent when it is situated in the context of the evolution of his ideas about this phenomenon between 1924 and 1935. Since that evolution reflects the unfolding of his fundamental ideas about historicity, mortality, and everydayness in this period, a reading of three key references to boredom in other early works will demonstrate the historical and philosophical significance of his choice to focus on this particular mood—as opposed, for example, to angst—in the 1929 lectures. In addition, since these lectures perform rather than argue for this new mode of philosophizing, identifying some of Heidegger's fundamental points of departure as articulated in earlier texts will help orient my discussion.

The most recent and most famous of these passages encapsulates Heidegger's mature view of the significance of boredom. It appears at the very beginning of the 1935 lectures, *Introduction to Metaphysics*, under the heading "The Fundamental Question of Metaphysics."[13]

> The question is there in a certain boredom in which we are equally removed from despair and rejoicing, and in which the stubborn ordinariness of what is diffuses a tedium in which it appears to us a matter of indifference whether what is, is or is not—with this the question "Why are there beings at all and not instead nothing?" is evoked in a singular form. (1)

As an experience of absolute blaséness and disaffection, such boredom is a form of alienation from the everyday world and its ordinariness so complete that the sufferer is rendered indifferent to its very being. Paradoxically, according to Heidegger, in this state of apathy, one comes unawares upon the fundamental question of metaphysics. Or rather the fundamental question— why are there beings at all rather than nothing?—comes to us, as it also may

---

to write her dissertation under Jaspers before Heidegger was offered a professorship at Freiburg. See Ettinger for more on Arendt's continuing relationship with Heidegger.

[13]Though *Einführung in die Metaphysik* (Heidegger, *Gesamtausgabe* 40; citations in text) was first published in 1953, the lectures were held in the summer semester of 1935, that is, the year after Heidegger resigned from the rectorate but during the period when he was still hopeful about the possibilities of philosophy under the National Socialist regime. See Lacoue-Labarthe 1990 on the controversy over Heidegger's (disavowed) editorial changes to this text.

when we are entirely immersed in the world—in moments "of great despair" or of "rejoicing" (1).

However, Heidegger did not always view boredom as a mode of access to the fundamental question of metaphysics. The conviction expressed in the 1935 lectures that the experience was philosophically significant, though consonant with the understanding of boredom articulated in the lectures of 1929, in fact represents a total reversal from Heidegger's earliest thinking on boredom. Eleven years before delivering the first version of the *Introduction to Metaphysics*, Heidegger had taken up the problem of boredom for the first time, in a talk entitled "The Concept of Time" ("Der Begriff der Zeit") held before the Marburg Theological Society in July 1924.[14] At this point, Heidegger was far from viewing boredom as giving access to the question of being. Instead, he understood it as a mode of lived indifference to the finitude of one's own existence—like Kierkegaard, he regarded it as a sign of human being mired in inauthenticity.

"The Concept of Time" is recognized as a significant precursor to *Being and Time* because in it Heidegger anticipates both the language and many of the conceptual moves of his 1927 magnum opus. However, the gap between his interpretation of boredom in this talk and his mature view of its significance underlines the distance he still had to travel. Here boredom arises not from the ordinariness of being itself but rather from the prosaic way it is experienced. It is born of a form of temporality that is, in itself, alienated and alienating—a reading appropriate to his theological audience, but one that lacks the subtlety of the interpretation he would develop using the conception of mood as a constitutive aspect of Dasein developed in *Being and Time*.

In "The Concept of Time," Heidegger situates boredom within a form of living called *Alltäglichkeit*—everydayness. When human beings are absorbed in the everyday world, he contends, their existence is de-individuated, their agency displaced by habitual submission to "what one does." For Heidegger, what Simmel characterized more positively as the "super-subjective temporal schema" of modern life epitomizes inauthenticity. The temporality of everydayness is the temporality of the clock, which distracts Dasein from what he calls the "how" of existence. In everydayness, attention is turned toward present things, absorbed in the succession of "what" fills up time. Such absorp-

---

[14]*Der Begriff der Zeit* will appear as Volume 64 of the *Gesamtausgabe*. My references follow the bilingual English edition. Where I have altered the translations, no E is given after the page number. In light of the importance of the religious tradition of reflection on boredom and kindred experiences, it is interesting to note that he first takes up this issue before a theological audience (he was there at Bultmann's invitation).

tion occludes the indeterminacy that constitutes human temporality: the indeterminate certitude of individual mortality (14). This is the "how" of human being, which Heidegger names "the being-over-with" (*das Vorbei*). For him, mortality is not just a perpetual possibility for human beings—it is the possibility par excellence: "indeed the authentic 'how' of my Dasein" is at every moment my unique potential for ceasing to exist (12E).[15] According to Heidegger, to exist authentically is to live in the proper relation to one's mortality, not to dwell upon the instability and groundlessness of existence but rather constantly to return to the genuine "futurity" of remembering that one will have died. Dasein must be its singular future "in such a way that in this being futural it comes back to its past and present. Dasein, conceived in its most extreme possibility of being, *is time itself*, not *in* time" (13E–14E). This movement of return to futurity, Heidegger declares, "can never become what one calls boring, that which uses itself up and becomes worn out" (14E). Boredom, then, is inherently a sign of inauthenticity.

We are not far from the biblical imprecation to keep mortality in mind, "that we may become wise."[16] Heidegger contends that it is the forgetful mode of living by the clock, of focusing on 'what' rather than 'how' one is, that leads to this lengthening of hours, to boredom. Immersed in everydayness, Dasein

> grows weary [*überdrüssig*] in the 'what,' weary to fill up the day. Time suddenly becomes long for Dasein as being-present . . . . Time becomes empty because Dasein, in asking about the 'how much,' has in advance made time long, whereas its continual returning in running ahead towards the being-over-with never becomes boring. (16)

Living by the clock brings forth boredom by turning time into a series of present moments which must be filled up. Heidegger sees boredom as an ex-

---

[15] In *Being and Time*, Heidegger speaks in terms of existential awareness of Dasein's ownmost possibility of being (299). In the 1924 talk, he paves the way for this more differentiated analysis, for instance in his explication of what it means to "have" rather than merely to "know" one's death. "Es ist ein Vorlaufen des Daseins zu seinem Vorbei als einer in Gewißheit und völliger Umbestimmtheit bevorstehenden äußersten Möglichkeit seiner selbst. Dasein als menschliches Leben 'ist primär Möglichsein,' das Sein der Möglichkeit des gewissen und dabei unbestimmten Vorbei" (12). In *Being and Time*, the difficulty of sorting out the way in which "one" has interpreted mortality looms much larger; he speaks of freedom towards death as an authentic potentiality-for-being which must first extract itself from the common illusions of human existence.

[16] In this context it is worth noting that Luther's rendering of Psalm 90:12—"laß uns gedenken, daß wir sterben müssen, worauf wir klug werden" ("let us reflect that we shall die, that we may become wise)—varies significantly from the English version: "Teach us to number our days, that we may become wise."

perience of time in which the ordinary, objectifying mode of existing becomes a problem, but in such a way that the "how" of temporality still remains effaced by the "what" of presence.

Like the conception of everydayness in which it is embedded, this idea of
boredom is transitional. In it, Dasein remains entangled in everydayness because the experience reflects the ordinary understanding of time. The idea
that boredom can reveal to the sufferer the existential structure of temporality depends on the central thesis of *Being and Time* that "the question of being" is "nothing other than the radicalizing of a tendency of being that belongs essentially to Dasein itself, of the pre-ontological understanding of
being" that inheres in such everydayness (SZ, 15).

Nonetheless, although Heidegger does not yet see boredom as itself
evoking the question of being, in "The Concept of Time," the ideas that
would lead to this reversal in his understanding of the experience are taking
shape. First, the temporality of everydayness, in which "Dasein would like
constantly to encounter new things in its own present" is understood as a
shared mode of being in the world under the dominant interpretation that
Dasein gives of itself (16E). In describing this way of being, Heidegger emphasizes the role of the impersonal third person in a way that prefigures the
analysis of *das Man* in *Being and Time*.[17]

> In everydayness Dasein is not that Being that *I* am. Rather the everydayness of
> Dasein is that Being that *one* is. And Dasein, accordingly, is the time in which *one*
> is with another: 'one's' time. The clock that *one* has, every clock, shows the time
> of being-with-one-another-in-the-world. (17E)

Although he here condemns everyday being as such as inauthenticity, Heidegger describes the mode of temporality in which boredom arises in a
fashion that emphasizes its status as common understanding. In *Being and
Time,* such being-with-one-another-in-the-world will be reinterpreted in
such a way that the shared understanding of existence inherent in everyday
temporality becomes the foundation of genuine existence. There, "one" (*das
Man*) is not simply the "*who* of everyday Dasein" (SZ, 128). Since the impersonal form of self-understanding defines everyday being-together, Heidegger
writes, "*authentic being-a-self* does not rest on a state of exception of the
subject disconnected from one *but is rather an existential modification of one
as of an essential existentiale*" (SZ, 130). The mature conception of mood that
forms the basis of the argument for boredom's ontological significance in the

---

[17]In that work, see especially § 27, "Everyday Being-One's-Self and the 'They.'" The "who" of
everyday existence in being with others "is not this one, not that one, not oneself [*man selbst*],
and not the sum of them all. The 'who' is the neuter, the *'they'* [*das Man*]" (126).

1929–30 lectures turns on this reinterpretation of everydayness as a shared mode of being-in-the-world.

In "The Concept of Time," Heidegger goes on to make several remarks on human historicity. These constitute the second way in which the 1924 talk paves the way for subsequent development of his thought. For those who live by the clock, he writes, "history" becomes an alibi for the absence of existential authenticity. Failing to live in relation to its own "most extreme possibility" (i.e., its mortality), Dasein "is so little ready to admit that it has stolen away from authentic futurity that it says it has seized upon the future out of care for the development of mankind, culture, etc." (16E). Heidegger dismisses the notion of progress that authorizes a whole range of political stances as an excuse for existential inadequacy.

Genuine historicity, he contends, must begin with a radical focus on one's own individuation; the existential failure to "have" one's death has consequences for Dasein's relation to the past as well as to the future. In conceiving of time as a series of homogeneous present moments, spatializing it into a phenomenon irreversibly proceeding along a line, Dasein instead makes history into a series of occurrences. Heidegger calls this the failure of Dasein to be historical. Rather than recognizing existence in time as the foundation of a relation to the past, Dasein clings to an understanding of temporality which shuts off the possibility of experiencing "authentic historicity" (19E). And far from achieving a critical perspective on the falsity of the contemporary mode of understanding history, Dasein "moans about historicism" and seeks a *Weltanschauung* "on the fantastical path to supra-historicity" (20E). In these passages, Heidegger distinguishes himself both from those who, embracing Enlightenment, speak in vague terms of the future of humanity, and from romantic critics of modernity who desire to escape from history by overcoming the rationalism and relativism of modern *Gesellschaft* in a putative renewal of *Gemeinschaft* or organic community.

Heidegger's radically individualized view of historicity places him in implicit opposition to both (contemporary left-wing) ideologies of progress and (contemporary right-wing) strivings for mythical reunification. Although before the theological audience, he emphasizes the methodological, rather than the political, consequences of his philosophical views, these methodological consequences do, of course, turn out to have profound political implications.[18] In particular, the focus on individual mortality entails

---

[18] Heidegger's political naïveté in assuming that the Nazi cultural revolution could be mobilized for a rejuvenation of philosophy is prefigured in his emphasis on individuals' interpretation of their historicity at the expense of the cultural and historical contexts in which such interpretations are located.

for Heidegger the priority of philosophy over other realms of inquiry (and more generally, the *Geisteswissenschaften* over the natural sciences)[19] that was a primary motivation in his acceptance of the Freiburg Rektorat in 1933. As we shall see, in his treatment of boredom in the 1929 lectures, Heidegger begins to draw the political consequences of his views on history and historicity. Since the problem of boredom is inseparable from the temporality of everydayness, its interpretation is at the center of the resulting critique of modernity. Understood as the "fundamental mood" of modernity, boredom provides the crucial link between the inauthentic understanding of temporality that must be overcome in existential reflection and the conception of history in which it is embedded. Furthermore, the declared objective of the 1929–30 lectures—"to transform the human being and therewith received metaphysics into a more primordial Dasein" via a rethinking of human historicity—prefigures Heidegger's hopes that the National Socialist reorganization of the universities would lead to a philosophical revolution in the understanding of human existence.[20]

In "The Concept of Time," Heidegger invokes *Unheimlichkeit*, uncanniness, three times.[21] Because these rather different uses of the term implicitly link his emergent interpretation of the temporality of everydayness to his critique of modern historicity, they point the way toward the development of his thought in *Being and Time*. Placed in this context, I argue, his remarks on uncanniness illuminate how the problem of boredom becomes linked for Heidegger to the question of historicity; they thus foreshadow the transformation in his understanding of boredom from a mere reflection of "living by the clock" into a mode of confrontation with the question of being itself.

We begin with the final passage, which occurs in the context of the critique of modern historicity just considered. In it, Heidegger calls the desire to escape history altogether via the creation of a new *Weltanschauung* "the uncanniness [*Unheimlichkeit*] that constitutes the time of the present" (20E).

---

[19]Heidegger also developed this point in his inaugural speech at Freiburg, "Was ist Metaphysik?" ("What is Metaphysics?"), a text that indicated the point of departure for the lectures of the following year.

[20]As we know, by the late 1930's, Heidegger was dismayed both by the pro-modern, technological tendencies of National Socialism and by its anti-philosophical bent. Although he understood himself to be opposing both aspects in his later, "anti-humanist" work, Heidegger's profound opposition to the Enlightenment and his deployment of irrationalist rhetoric have led many to see him as advocating a suprahistorical *Weltanschauung*. See Adorno, Habermas, and Wolin for examples of this view and Lacoue-Labarthe for a spirited defense of Heidegger.

[21]'Unheimlichkeit' is, literally, un-homelikeness. However, 'heimlich' also means 'secret' or 'secretive'; for Heidegger, the word implies both coming out of hiddenness and alienating unfamiliarity. See Freud 1924 for a now-classic discussion of this notion. See Freud's 1924 "Das Unheimliche" for a now-classic discussion of this notion.

Because human existence in modernity is so given over to the clock (that is, to the punctual temporality that on his 1924 understanding produces boredom), Dasein is driven down the "fantastical path to supra-historicity" (20E). What Heidegger here calls "uncanny" is the historically constituted longing to renew existence by eliminating the very possibility of genuine temporality, which on his view can be given only in the recognition of individual historicity. Thus, a few pages earlier, Heidegger identifies the same dynamic in the understanding of time through which individual mortality is forgotten: "losing time and acquiring a clock for the purpose! Does not the uncanniness of Dasein irrupt [*aufbrechen*] here?" (15E).

Heidegger's repeated use of the term *unheimlich* to refer to the way time is understood in modernity is worth remarking because *Unheimlichkeit* plays a crucial role in the existential analytic of *Being and Time*.[22] There he writes: "This uncanniness constantly follows Dasein and threatens, if inexplicitly, Dasein's everyday immersion in the one [*das Man*]" (SZ, 189). The first reference to uncanniness in "The Concept of Time" (15E) is consonant with this more positive usage of the term: *Unheimlichkeit*—literally, the sense of not being at home—is an effect of Dasein's confrontation with mortality, with the possibility of "being over."[23] That possibility, Heidegger says, "is able to place Dasein, amid the glory of its everydayness, into uncanniness" (13). How can this positive usage be reconciled with the negative uncanniness associated later in the text with living by the clock and with the search for an ahistorical *Weltanschauung*? Is it not a contradiction to say that the temporality based on the refusal to recognize mortality has the same effect as taking cognizance of the possibility of dying? Reconsidering Heidegger's interpretation of boredom in "The Concept of Time" will help to clarify the relation between his critique of the modern way of understanding time and history as somehow *unheimlich* and the notion that the awareness of mortality can uncannily displace Dasein out of immersion in the everyday world.

In "The Concept of Time," boredom appears as a consequence of the absence of profound, existential uncanniness: it is a sign of Dasein's immersion in the everyday.[24] The initial symbolic submission to the time of the "*Man*"

[22]There it is linked to the problem of anxiety. See §40, especially 189, where Heidegger argues that anxiety is more primordial than its absence. "That kind of Being-in-the-world which is tranquilized and familiar is a mode of Dasein's uncanniness, not the reverse."

[23]I use "being over" to translate "das Vorbei," which Heidegger uses only to refer to Dasein's possibility of death. (McNeill renders both "das Vorbei" and "die Vergangenheit" (the historical past) with "past."

[24]Similarly, in *Being and Time* it is the *absence* of anxiety which signals fallenness into the world of "what one does."

in the form of "living by the clock," which Heidegger calls uncanny, establishes the general condition for boredom. But he also says that the apparently opposed longing for a *Weltanschauung*, via which Dasein attempts to flee that everydayness into a superhistorical world flooded with meaning, is "uncanny." For Heidegger, the understanding of time which ineluctably gives rise to boredom and the yearning to interpret history in a way that circumvents or supersedes that understanding are equally uncanny. However, these negative modes of uncanniness cannot be understood as simply *opposed to* the existential transformation of everydayness by the intrusion of mortality. These are, rather, the symptoms through which Dasein's failure to recognize the nature of everydayness is exposed. It is for this reason that, from the perspective of philosophical reflection, they reveal the very quality of uncanniness that Dasein seeks to flee in forgetfulness of mortality. Read in this way, these invocations of *Unheimlichkeit* prefigure the development of Heidegger's thought.[25]

From the outset, the trajectories of *Langeweile* and *Unheimlichkeit* are intertwined; as modes of experiencing historicity and everydayness, both are linked to the problem of temporality. In 1924, boredom appeared to Heidegger a brute symptom of the temporality of everydayness rather than an experience that could lead to distinctive forms of reflection upon the world which gives rise to it, and he did not go beyond the aporetic recognition of two apparently unrelated registers of uncanniness. Thus in "The Concept of Time" boredom is linked to the forgetfulness rather than the awareness of mortality, to the negative form of uncanniness. *Being and Time* resolves the apparent contradiction between these senses of uncanniness by underlining the ambiguity within everydayness itself. In that work, Heidegger depicts the ambiguous presence-absence of mortality as an aspect of *Alltäglichkeit* as such; it appears under the aegis of Dasein's "fallenness" into the world.[26] Authentic existence, he argues, is only accessible through a transformation of ordinary everydayness that recognizes Dasein's forgetfulness of mortality as a particularly uncanny manifestation of finitude. In the 1927 text, of course, it was anxiety rather than boredom that gave rise to the reflection on uncanniness that promised to lead Dasein out of fallenness in the time of *das Man* and toward authentic existence. Nonetheless, the strategy by which *Being and Time* reads everyday, negative uncanniness as a manifestation of a deeper,

---

[25] However, it should be emphasized that Heidegger did not make these connections explicitly: rather, the ambiguity of "uncanniness," which functions as a sign both of the presence and the absence of mortality for Dasein, appears as a marginal paradox within his account of the concept of time.

[26] See SZ §38, "Das Verfallen und die Geworfenheit."

existential uncanniness suggests the way Heidegger's thinking on the problem of boredom would evolve.

As we shall see, the 1929/30 lectures make the insight into the existential ambiguity of Dasein the basis of an ambitious rhetorical strategy. Through it, Heidegger will extend the conceptual apparatus developed in *Being and Time* to interpret boredom as a "fundamental mood" of modernity and to historicize and particularize the existential analytic of that work in the service of a renewal of philosophy. In this text, boredom no longer appears as an external, affective symptom of modern life and its inauthentic temporality. Instead, Heidegger attempts to bring his audience to philosophize through a defamiliarizing strategy of reflection upon the phenomenon of boredom that confronts his hearers with the uncanniness of their everyday understanding of time. He shows that the historically specific understanding of temporality and worldliness experienced in boredom entails a certain relation to mortality, one that he argues must be "awakened" by relating boredom to the metaphysical problems of world, finitude, and solitude. This strategy grasps the uncanny ambiguity of everyday existence from the perspective of philosophical reflection; it identifies Dasein's potential for a genuine encounter with metaphysical questions in the very symptoms of inauthenticity that constitute everyday life.

I close these preliminary remarks by considering the sole reference to boredom in "What is Metaphysics?," the lecture with which Heidegger inaugurated his tenure at Freiburg in July, 1929. This passage may be viewed as the turning point between his earlier view of boredom as an experience which epitomizes the inauthentic experience of time and the diametrically opposed view that boredom, in its very everydayness, reveals the question of being—the view espoused, as we have already noted, in 1935, at the beginning of the *Introduction to Metaphysics*. This text brings the relationship between everydayness and the question of being as it was interpreted in *Being and Time* together with the distinction that would guide Heidegger's argument in the lectures he would begin to give a few months later. It is therefore worth quoting at length.

> As fragmented [*aufgesplittert*] as the everyday appears, it still keeps what is as a whole together, if in a shadowy fashion. Even and especially when we are not actually [*eigens*] occupied by things and our selves, we are overcome by this 'on the whole,' for example in genuine boredom. This boredom is still distant when this book or that play, this occupation or that pastime simply bores us. It irrupts [*bricht auf*] when "it is boring." Profound boredom, moving back and forth in the abysses of existence like a silent fog, conflates all things, people, and oneself with them in a remarkable indifference. This boredom reveals what is as a whole. (Heidegger 1930, 14–15)

In the lectures on "The Fundamental Concepts of Metaphysics," Heidegger develops an interpretation of boredom that combines the critique of everyday "living by the clock" which informs the references to boredom in "The Concept of Time" with the insight expressed here, that boredom with "what one is" may itself point the way out of the fragmentation of everyday life toward the question of the whole that is being. The interpretation of boredom put forward in these lectures thus amounts to an anatomy of the philosophical rhetoric of experience considered in Chapter 1. What I call Heidegger's existential grammar of mood achieves an unparalleled subtlety in the interpretation of the experience, yet it simultaneously makes the limitations of an approach that disregards its own relation to the historically constituted discourse on boredom acutely apparent. A reading of these lectures will therefore also help to clarify the constructive task of this book.

Mood and the Rhetoric of Reflection

While other moods could have replaced boredom as a point of entry into "The Fundamental Concepts of Metaphysics,"[27] given the history of the discourse of reflection on boredom, Heidegger's selection of this experience as the starting point for the project of "awakening" his listeners to philosophy in the lectures of 1929/30 is noteworthy. Indeed, both the path by which he arrives at the determination of boredom as the fundamental mood of the era and the phenomenology of boredom itself are strewn with elements and strategies familiar from the nineteenth-century discourse on the experience. In examining the arguments by which Heidegger advances his interpretation of boredom as a means of access to perennial philosophical questions, we shall therefore reflect upon the ways that discursive context inflects his analysis. To do so, it must be emphasized, is to read against the grain of his conception of mood as a means of access to the foundations of individual existence, for despite his initial emphasis on the cultural actuality of boredom, Heidegger's phenomenology abstracts from the worldly context in which boredom becomes a problem. To situate his interpretation of boredom discursively is thus to identify the analytic limits of Heidegger's nuanced interpretation of the existential significance of the experience.

In the lectures on "The Fundamental Concepts of Metaphysics," Heidegger sets himself no less a task than bringing his listeners to philosophize. There is, he contends, no short cut, no other way to introduce them to phi-

---

[27] Anxiety plays an analogous role in *Being and Time* and "What is Metaphysics"; besides these two, other moods are also potential starting points, as the Hölderlin lectures illustrate. See Michel Haar's essay, "Attunement and Thinking" in Dreyfus and Hall, 1992.

losophy. *"Philosophy is philosophizing"* (6). But how is he to bring them to experience as "our own, human action" what seems so remote? (6), The first step, according to Heidegger, is to overcome the prevailing interpretations of philosophy as science (*Wissenschaft*) or as *Weltanschauung* and to grasp it as an activity grounded in the fundamental possibility of Dasein, of human existence.

> Metaphysics is an asking in which we ask our way into the whole of what is [*in das Ganze das Seinden hineinfragen*] and ask in such a way that we ourselves, the questioners, are at the same time put into the question, are put in question. (13)

The proof that metaphysical questioning is by nature both directed toward the whole and transformative of human existence can only be performative: Heidegger must draw his audience and himself into the activity of philosophizing. In doing so, he will be neither proselytizing for a worldview (*Weltanschauung*) nor treating metaphysical questions scientifically, as objects of disinterested inquiry.

In these lectures, Heidegger's guiding task is therefore to demonstrate that metaphysical questioning is an essential occupation of human beings, one grounded in existence as such.[28] As he puts it, with a rhetorical flourish: "But what is the human being that he philosophizes in the ground of his being, and what is this philosophizing?" (7). Using Novalis' definition of philosophy as "homesickness, as the drive to be at home everywhere"[29] as his point of departure, Heidegger develops the three questions of his subtitle: "what is world?," "what is finitude?," "what is solitude?" Taken together, he argues, these questions circumscribe the fundamental, metaphysical dilemma of human existence, the dilemma that defines being-human. On Heidegger's view, the human longing for wholeness can never be fulfilled because our belonging to the world is radically limited by our mortality, which isolates us. The three questions close a circle, for it is this very isolation which produces the experience of the world, of being "as a whole" opposed to our individual selves.

The appeal to Novalis suggests the beginning of a significant transformation in the way Heidegger frames the question of the meaning of being, one that would ultimately lead away from the early emphasis on individual existence altogether in his mature idea of the history of being. "We ask: *What is*

---

[28]To the extent that Heidegger's problem of beginning recapitulates Hegel's in the *Phenomenology of Spirit,* the movement discussed here, which illustrates how the "double tack" of these lectures places existential and conceptual strategies in a relation of supplementarity, may be seen as a reinscription of Hegelian phenomenology.

[29]Heidegger (7) gives a reference to the 1923 Jena edition of Novalis's writings: vol. 2, 179, Fragment 21.

that—world? We are driven to it, to being as a whole, by our homesickness. Our being is this being-driven [*Getriebenheit*]" (8). This rhetoric resonates with the romantic melancholy of the poet whom he invokes as authority: a lack in our existence points us toward philosophy; we can never really arrive "home," yet we are always, essentially, "underway." Indeed, for Heidegger, "the *fundamental way* [*Grundart*] *of our being*," finitude,

> *is* only in true being-finite [*Verendlichung*, a play on '*verenden*,' to perish and *Endlichkeit*, 'finitude'—EG]. Herein, however, the isolation [*Vereinzelung*] of every human being with his Dasein is fulfilled . . . [I]n that *becoming-lonely* [*Vereinsamung*] every human being first attains proximity to what is essential to all things, to the world . . . (8)

Here, as in *Being and Time*, it is the individual's confrontation with mortality that defines authentic human being. At the same time, however, both the thematics and the argumentative strategy of the lectures anticipate Heidegger's movement toward worldly engagement and exemplify his activist understanding of his place in the university.

Beginning with Novalis' definition, Heidegger has reached an initial determination of the project of philosophy which, however rich, remains exoteric. If the lectures are to be truly philosophical in his sense, that is, if they are to bring his listeners to genuine engagement with the meaning of their existence, then the questions of world, finitude, and solitude can no more be invoked on the authority of Novalis than they may be understood scientifically. Indeed, Heidegger tells his audience, questions that articulate metaphysical concepts must be lived to be understood.

> We will never have grasped [*begriffen*] these concepts [*Begriffe*] and their conceptual rigor [*begriffliche Strenge*] if we are not first *gripped* [*ergriffen*] by what they are supposed to grasp [*begreifen*]. The fundamental endeavor of philosophizing is to awaken and sow this being-seized [*Ergriffenheit*]. But all being-seized comes from and remains in a mood [*Stimmung*]. (9)[30]

It would be pointless, he tells them, to attempt to move from the questions themselves to the appropriate mood. "Then we would only have theoretical explanations (science), which we then, afterwards, made fruitful 'for a worldview'" (87). Philosophy would not thereby have overcome its "externality" to the human being. To put his listeners "into the question," he must find a way to awaken their lived sense for the concepts of world, finitude, and

---

[30]This passage traces a distinctive slippage between "Frage" and "Begriff" which must, I think, be understood as a manifestation of Heidegger's debt to Hegel. The concept is a movement that can be understood both as a response to and as a resolution of a lived question of human existence.

solitude, and thereby get the students to put themselves "in question." The same procedure that is to renew philosophy will, he contends, awaken them, for "only philosophizing is wakeful Dasein" (34).

In other words, authentic understanding of metaphysical concepts must be grounded in his listeners' existential experience. Otherwise, Heidegger says, the three key questions "appear arbitrary," and "even if we will allow that they are metaphysical ... they leave *us* indifferent, do not touch *us* at bottom, let alone grip *us*" (87). To awaken his audience to metaphysics, he must therefore find a way to make the questions of world, finitude, and solitude seize his hearers. After an extensive introductory discussion of the history and status of metaphysics, Heidegger has arrived at the necessity of phenomenology. "We must first of all allow these questions to emerge in their necessity and possibility *out of a fundamental mood*. ... Thus we actually fulfill this questioning when we set ourselves to awakening a fundamental mood of our philosophizing" (87). This, the "the first and genuinely fundamental task of our lectures and the beginning of a truly animated [*lebendigen*] philosophizing" is to be achieved through an interpretation of a mood that, once awakened, is to provide the existential link between the abstract questions of world, finitude, and solitude.

But how to locate the fundamental mood through which the need for philosophy can be awakened and hence from which genuine philosophizing can begin? Although Heidegger proceeds phenomenologically, his procedure is entirely different from that used in *Being and Time* to examine the relations among anxiety, individual mortality, and the question of being. The project of renewing philosophy is shared with his audience. Thus, rather than beginning from the existential analytic of Dasein as such, he sets out to identify the mood that needs to be awakened "for *us, today.*" To do so, Heidegger says, it is necessary to "know *our* state [*Lage*] itself well enough in order to gather from it by what fundamental mood we are dominated" (104). In *Being and Time,* philosophical investigation began from Dasein's everyday mode of existence as *das Man*; here, not 'what one is' but what "we" are forms the point of departure. Heidegger asserts that the work of defining this "we"—"the challenge of identifying our state" comprehensively—has already been met by contemporary *Kulturphilosophie* (104). According to him, the (post-Nietzschean) 'philosophy of culture' can therefore provide a means of locating the shared "fundamental mood" that is to define his phenomenal point of departure.

By treating the philosophy of culture as a sign of the times, Heidegger underlines how his own project of awakening his listeners to philosophy differs from what he regards as efforts to invoke science to advance pronouncements of worldviews.[31] He presents the theories of Spengler, Klages, Scheler, and Ziegler extremely schematically (devoting only a brief paragraph to each [105–6]) as a "summary and formulaic indication" of "what one knows today." These ideas provide, he asserts, matter for casual conversation, which "permeates the higher journalism of our era and creates the spiritual space [*geistiger Raum*]—if one may speak in this way—in which we circulate" (106).[32] That is, Heidegger's interest lies not in these theories of culture as such, but rather in articulating the everyday understanding of modern existence they all share. He therefore reduces all the thinkers to a common denominator: "The essential thing that concerns us is the fundamental trait of all these interpretations or rather the perspective in which they all view our contemporary situation. That is, to put it formally again, the relation between life and spirit [*Leben und Geist*]" (106–7). In focusing on this relation, Heidegger argues, the philosophers of culture and philosophical anthropologists prove themselves epigones of Nietzsche, for the terms of their discourse, *Geist* and *Leben* (or *Seele*, soul) are derived from the latter's distinction between Apollonian and Dionysian.[33]

Heidegger subjects the rhetoric of cultural reflection that defines the philosophy of culture to a sort of phenomenological reduction. Entirely failing to grasp human existence in a metaphysically adequate fashion, he argues, these thinkers wrongly understand culture as the "expression" of humanity, an expression (*Ausdruck*) that represents (*darstellt*) humanity as playing a role in the drama of the cosmos. In this very failure to seize Dasein's historicity in a philosophically adequate fashion, the philosophy of culture reflects 'what one thinks.' It therefore provides him with a point of attack for the project of fostering genuine philosophizing. The issue, he contends, is not whether "these interpretations of our state" are accurate, although "[i]n such cases the greater part is always correct" (111). It is, rather, why such "world-historical position-finding," the "cultural diagnoses and prognoses" in which the philosophy of culture finds expression, leaves its readers unmoved (112). In the conception of culture as "the expression of our soul"

---

[31] See 16 passim.

[32] Heidegger's characterization of the philosophy of culture is overtly polemical and arguably inaccurate. Compare, for example, Simmel's writings or those of Heidegger's unmentioned opponent, Ernst Cassirer. See also Zimmerman on Heidegger's debt to Spengler.

[33] However, Heidegger denies that these thinkers proceed from a genuinely viable interpretation of Nietzsche. He devotes a few pages to problematizing their Nietzsche-interpretation with citations from the Nachlaß (i.e. the 1920 Musarion *Wille zur Macht*), but does not yet draw out the interpretation he would develop in the series of lectures on Nietzsche he would offer beginning in 1936.

consisting of symbolic forms[34] that "carry a significance in themselves and on the basis of this significance give the Dasein that expresses itself a meaning," Heidegger says, "nearly everything is right except that which is essential" (113). Human historicity is misunderstood if human beings are interpreted in light of their accomplishments. The philosophy of culture thus not only fails to "grasp" modern existence,[35] but indeed "disengages us from ourselves by conferring on us a role in world history" (115). However, the fact that such an understanding of Dasein has come to embody 'what one thinks' suggests to Heidegger a way to identify the fundamental mood which he hopes to awaken in his audience.

In a phenomenological transmutation of the cultural-critical attitude that characterizes a Spengler, Heidegger interprets the philosophy of culture as the expression of a fundamentally flawed modern understanding of human historicity. Echoing Nietzsche's reflections on historicism, he wonders, "have we become so *insignificant* for ourselves that we need a role?" Why, he asks, even as "world trade, technology, the economy, seize hold of and hold the human being in motion," does everything seem so indifferent?

> Must we make ourselves interesting to ourselves again? Why *must* we do so? Perhaps because we have ourselves, for ourselves, become *boring*? . . . *Is it finally thus with us, that a profound boredom moves back and forth in the abysses of Dasein like a silent fog?* (115)

Understood phenomenologically in this sense, the philosophy of culture appears as a response to a deep lack in modern existence, as a symptom of the "absence of distress" Heidegger will subsequently identify as the existential predicament of modern life. In this way, he contends, it reveals the *Grundstimmung*, the fundamental mood, that defines 'what one is' at present: the "state" of contemporary Dasein is defined by this profound malaise. Renewing philosophy will thus entail thinking through the metaphysical significance of the deep boredom indirectly revealed by the very existence of such a philosophy of culture. According to Heidegger, "awakening" that "profound boredom" is a necessary first step toward setting aside the search for roles in favor of a more authentic form of historicity—and of philosophizing.

Rather than engaging in the sort of metaphysical speculation that anchored the analyses of a Spengler or a Klages in a global narrative about hu-

---

[34]Heidegger refers to *Symbol* und *Gestalten*—the language of his unacknowledged adversary, Ernst Cassirer. It should be recalled that the Davos debate had taken place earlier in 1929. See John Michael Krois, "Aufklärung und Metaphysik: Zur Philosophie Cassirers und der Davoser Debatte mit Heidegger."

[35]It "at most represents the actuality of our state [*das Heutige unserer Lage*] but does not grasp *us*" (115).

manity, Heidegger aims to reawaken metaphysical questions beginning from the phenomenological perspective of individual existence as such. He proposes to begin from boredom as it is usually lived, an experience which he says barely enters our awareness since "we are always [*jederzeit*], whether consciously or unconsciously, occupied with whiling away the time" (118). Through his lectures, he promises, "this *superficial boredom* shall reveal itself as the *profound* [*tiefe*] one, resonating [*durchstimmen*] in the foundations of our Dasein" (122). Heidegger proposes to trace a movement not into the putative interiority of the subject but through the phenomenon of boredom as it is lived into the essence of human existence as being (in) time. In the course of the lectures, the existential grammar of the mood itself is to unfold the metaphysical questions of world, finitude, and solitude in a way consonant with the rethinking of human being as Dasein.

Although Heidegger explicitly rejects the stance of those who offer *Kulturdiagnosen*, he shares many precepts with both cultural conservatives and those who have been called "reactionary modernists."[36] By basing his analyses on an indirect, phenomenologically mediated approach to the ideas they share, Heidegger attempts to establish his own philosophical diagnosis on higher metaphysical ground. The quasi-phenomenological 'reduction' of the philosophy of culture that provides his starting point is crucial. By identifying boredom as the fundamental mood of modernity through a symptomatic reading of this intellectual tradition, he appears to free his own thought from the objections to which Spengler et al. are vulnerable: that their analyses are founded on extrinsic rather than intrinsic analyses of modern existence.

However, Heidegger's introductory strategy of establishing philosophical distance from the culturally dominant rhetoric on the dilemmas of contemporary life cannot really establish a foundation for his own analyses outside the broader common discourse. Contrary to what he seems to believe, the boredom that Heidegger identifies as a fundamental phenomenon is by no means free of historical content; the ordinary language he uses to develop his phenomenology of the experience resonates with the same critique of modern life found in the philosophy of culture he scorned. Although he puts forward his interpretation of boredom as fundamental mood as a rethinking of the "everyday understanding" of modern existence exemplified by thinkers such as Spengler and Klages, Heidegger's way of pursuing his philosophical objectives thus remains constitutively linked to its origins in the anti-

---

[36] Jeffrey Herf, *Reactionary Modernism: Technology, Culture, and Politics in Weimar and the Third Reich.*

modern discourse of cultural conservatism. The philosophical power of his analysis of boredom as a "fundamental mood" of modern human beings is continuous with the polemical project of indicting modern existence which he, too, inherited from Nietzsche.

The Rhetoric of Mood and the Renewal of Philosophy

Let us return to the passage in "The Fundamental Concepts of Metaphysics" in which Heidegger articulates his goal of transforming his listeners and with them metaphysics itself into a "more primordial" state. Appearing toward the end of the course, when the discussion of boredom conducted during the first part of the semester has presumably faded from his listeners' memories, this passage goes on to provide an especially clear account of Heidegger's strategy for fostering this renewal of philosophy. The lectures, he explains, have taken a dual tack (*doppelten Ansatz*):

> [F]irst, without orienting toward a definite metaphysical question, through *awakening a fundamental mood* [or "attunement": *Grundstimmung*] *of our Dasein*, that is to say, to transform the humanity of us humans in each case into the being-there [*Da-sein*] of our self. Then we tried inversely, without constant express reference [*Bezugnahme*] to the fundamental mood but nonetheless in silent recollection, to unfold a metaphysical question under the title of *the world-problem* . . . [The] interpretation of the thesis: the human being is world-making [*weltbildend*] . . . became a return [*Rückgang*] into a primordial dimension, into a fundamental occurrence, of which we now claim that world-formation [*Weltbildung*] occurs in it. (509).

Heidegger understands the first move ("awakening a fundamental mood") to be the metamorphosis of humanity into existence because to grasp boredom as a mode of being related to the world as a whole is to recognize how the question of being arises in ordinary existence. Boredom is not privileged in the sense that it is the only possible mode of existential access to metaphysical questions; on the contrary, the strategy of "awakening" boredom builds upon the insight developed in *Being and Time* that having-a-mood is one of the fundamental characteristics of Dasein.[37]

Heidegger's second, "inverse," move ("unfold[ing] a metaphysical ques-

---

[37] In the 1929–30 lectures, Heidegger elaborates on this point in a section which the editor christened "Preliminary Circumscription of the World-concept." "In a mood one *is* in such and such a way . . . the mood reveals precisely *what is as a whole* and we ourselves as finding ourself amidst it . . . Having a mood and the mood is in no sense a cognition of psychic states but rather the *being-carried-out* into the always specific openness of what is as a whole, that is: into the openness of existence as such, thus, as it finds itself in the midst of this whole in each case" (410). "Grundstimmung sind ausgezeichnete Möglichkeiten solcher Offenbarkeit" (411).

tion under the title of 'the world-problem'") corresponds to the task of establishing a new relationship to the tradition via the creative "destruction" of
traditional ontology. The renewal of philosophy he envisions could only be
accomplished if his listeners had in fact followed his readings in "silent rec-
ollection" of the immediacy of the question of being disclosed in the first
half of the lectures. To *experience* the phenomenological interpretation of the
world-problem as a more primordial mode of philosophizing, each listener
would have to have linked the personal "awakening" of his or her boredom
to the deepest and oldest questions about the "fundamental occurrence" of
being itself. As Heidegger puts it: *"Liberation from the tradition is ever-new-
appropriation [Immerneuaneignung] of its rediscovered [wiedererkannten]
powers"* (511). As the lectures draw to a close, he says, *"both paths"*—the
"path of awakening of a fundamental mood" and that "of the treatment of a
concrete problem without reference to the fundamental mood"—therefore
"run together" (512).

It may be helpful to reformulate this point in terms of the larger argumentative development of the lectures. Heidegger has just finished linking an
extended discussion of Aristotle's theory of propositions to a phenomenological analysis of the fundamental possibility of assertion altogether. He is
about to articulate what he sees as an intimate connection between the
structure of worldhood and the question of being itself. In stopping to reflect
on the lectures as a whole, Heidegger underlines his return to the problematics of existence raised in the first half of the lectures. He also prepares the
way for the concluding argument by which he will connect the ontological
difference to the definition of human existence as *Entwurf,* projection. However, the full significance of this rhetorical strategy will not become clear until the very end of the lectures, where Heidegger grounds his approach in a
distinctive understanding of the relation between philosophy and historicity
centered on the notion of projection as "the primordial structure of world-
formation" (530). His remarks at that point bear citing at length.

> Neither possibility nor reality is the object of the projection [*Entwurf*]—it has no
> object at all but is the *opening-oneself for the making-possible.* In the latter, the
> primordial relatedness [*Bezogenheit*] of possible and real, possibility and reality
> altogether are revealed as such.
>   *Projection* as this *revealing* [disclosure; *Entbergen*] *of making-possible* is the
> genuine *happening of the difference between being and beings.* ... It first makes
> possible the differentiated in its differentiability. The projection *unveils the being
> of beings.* (529)

The ontological difference is not a substance but a process; for Heidegger,
human existence is fundamentally historical because it reveals the difference

between being and beings. Human being-in-the-world delimits, interpretively demarcates, the boundaries of the world in every case: finitude and isolation spring out of the fundamental projective activity of Dasein, which discloses beings, and in disclosing them also discloses the ontological difference that makes them possible.

The movement of Heidegger's lectures from "the awakening of the fundamental mood" via a reappropriation of the metaphysical tradition into the "primordial dimension" where world-formation (*Weltbildung*) occurs has been, in other words, a propaedeutic to a lived recognition of the ontological difference—to an embrace of what he understands as genuine historicity. However, he emphasizes that the "philosophizing entry and return [*Ein- und Rückgang*] of the human being into the Dasein in himself [*in das Dasein in ihm*] can only be prepared, not caused" (510).[38] The function of philosophy is limited to awakening the sense for the mystery of being as a whole through which it then becomes possible "to ask about it conceptually [*begreifend*]" (510). Philosophy is reflection on the possibility of philosophy.

These strictures dictate a complicated rhetorical strategy. It is not enough simply to evoke the problem of being—as one might argue he had done in "The Concept of Time" or "What is Metaphysics?" And on Heidegger's view, conceptual analysis could do no more than prepare the way for the transformation of existence that was a necessary condition of the philosophical revolution he sought to foster. The organization of the lectures therefore underlines the ineluctability of phenomenological reflection for awakening anew the question of the meaning of being. With all this in mind, it is unsurprising that Part I—nearly a quarter of the lectures—is devoted to the phenomenology of boredom. *Langeweile* functions on one hand as an example of a fundamental mood that demonstrates that having-a-mood or attunement is foundational for human being, and on the other—for the silently remembering listener—as a point of entry into the renewal of metaphysical questions Heidegger attempts in the second half of the lectures. It is worth stopping to reflect on the fact that boredom in particular became the point of departure for Heidegger's attempt to foster existential renewal in his Freiburg lecture hall.

As in the earlier texts, the analysis of boredom serves to elicit reflection on the temporality of human existence. By moving from the familiar experience of *Langeweile* to the existential grammar that underlies this "fundamental mood," Heidegger's discussion of boredom particularizes the existential

---

[38]Thus, as we have already noted, from the outset Heidegger opposes philosophy to the dissemination of worldviews (cf. 1–2, 15–16).

analytic articulated in *Being and Time*. Mood, he tells his listeners, is a "*fundamental way*" of being "*how Dasein is as Dasein*. . . . Because the mood is the primordial how, in which each Dasein is, as it is, [mood] is . . . that which gives to Dasein from the beginning *grounding* [*Bestand*] *and possibility*" (101). Recalling the analysis of the 'how' in "The Concept of Time," we may elaborate: mood is by its very nature a mode of temporality and thus a way of being related or unrelated to one's own future non-existence. The existential grammar of mood therefore entails Dasein's historicity in Heidegger's specific sense of the term.

However, if having-a-mood is one of the fundamental characteristics of Dasein, boredom is by no means the only possible mode of existential access to metaphysical questions. In fact, these "must be capable of being unfolded *out of* Dasein's *every* fundamental mood" (269).[39] Heidegger's choice of boredom cannot for that reason be understood as indifferent. On the contrary: his point of departure for the attempted renewal of philosophy is indeed what Arendt attested was a "widely disseminated malaise" among his audience. As we saw, in identifying boredom as the "fundamental mood" to be awakened through phenomenological reflection, Heidegger grasped this malaise as a super-individual phenomenon—as a symptom of the collective spiritual "state" (*Lage*, 104) of the era. This conception of mood thus represents a significant step beyond the existential analytic of *Being and Time* toward his mature notion of the history of being.[40]

Heidegger's choice to "awaken" this particular mood also has profound political implications. He argues that being is obscured in a distinctive way by the emptiness lived in profound boredom. This emptiness corresponds, he says, to "the absence of distress [*Bedrängnis*], the lack of mystery in our Dasein" (254)—to the nihilism that characterizes modern existence. The emptiness that marks over-civilized modern life, which according to Heidegger lacks "mystery" and therefore "the inner terror . . . that gives Dasein its

[39]The idea that diverse moods could lead to metaphysical questions is already established in *Being and Time* (1927). The shift is not "from" anxiety "to" boredom, but rather from a narrow focus on awareness of mortality per se to an emphasis on unfolding the possibilities of everydayness through existential reflection. I am not arguing that the crucial evolution of Heidegger's thought in the thirties, his "turn" from individual existence to collective destinies, is the product of a focus on different moods than before. What is striking, rather, is how much of his mandarin rejection of ordinary everydayness remains intact through the changes his thinking undergoes.

[40]The previous year, Heidegger had already written to Karl Jaspers, "ich denke schon gar nicht mehr daran, daß ich vor kurzem ein sogennantes Buch geschrieben habe," 24.9.28; *Briefwechsel* 103. In "'Boredom: Between Existence and History': On Heidegger's Pivotal *The Fundamental Concepts of Metaphysics*," Miguel Beistegui argues that this turn toward the history of being manifests itself in the implicit overcoming of the concept of metaphysics in these lectures.

greatness" (244) corresponds to what he had once called the *Unheimlichkeit* of Dasein. It is this emptiness that must be awakened to renew metaphysics. By explicating the existential crisis of modern existence in such a way that it is articulated with the fundamental questions of the philosophical tradition, Heidegger clearly hopes for a renewal that goes beyond the lecture hall, an aspiration that, like his rather ominous language, uncannily prefigures his objectives in taking over the Freiburg Rectorate in 1933.

To awaken boredom is to awaken his listeners to the way this collective historico-philosophical situation is reflected in individual experience. On Heidegger's view, precisely because boredom reflects the inauthentic mode of existing that dominates everyday life in the modern world, grasping it as one's own fundamental mood can reveal the possibility of overcoming the attitude that makes life itself a matter of indifference.

> Corresponding to the absence of distress on the whole . . . [is] the necessity of the most extreme demand upon the human being [*Menschen*] that he must once again, expressly and individually, take over, shoulder, his Dasein. (254)

The significance of Heidegger's focus on boredom is clear. Because for him, it expresses the absence of such existential engagement, it is an appropriate locus for reflection for a teacher who hopes to prepare "the readiness for this distress" through the "*liberation of Dasein in the human being* [*Befreiung des Daseins im Menschen*]" (254f).

The lectures must appeal to each person as an individual: to take up the challenge of existence, Heidegger admonishes his audience, means neither "to withdraw from today's reality . . . [nor] to take, as it were, emergency measures for the threatened culture" (255). However, he is less concerned to argue against withdrawal from the modern world than to criticize the latter, liberal misunderstanding of historicity, which clings to the notion of historical progress. He continues:

> In understanding this challenge [*Forderung*] that the human being today must again himself take over his Dasein, we must from the outset avoid misunderstanding it to mean that this could occur through a universal fraternity in the inessential that would somehow finally bring us nearer to the essential. The challenge is rather this, that each Dasein must grasp this necessity for himself out of the foundation of his own essence. (255)

According to Heidegger, this individual task takes priority because only "in this basis and in this dimension" can it again become possible for a human being "to encounter something like the mystery of his Dasein" (255). Existential awareness of individual historicity is the prerequisite for "being touched" by the "mystery" of being. Cultural renewal cannot take place from within the everyday modern world because that world is constituted in such a way that Dasein, immersed in the average understanding of *das Man*, is unable to recognize its essence. The task of philosophy is to awaken the individual's sense of mortality in order to make possible participation in something larger, something by definition categorically distinct from liberal political action. The latter is necessarily "a universal fraternity in the inessential" because it takes place in the sphere of what *Being and Time* called "publicness" (*Öffentlichkeit*), the sphere of *das Man*. Authentic historicity cannot be realized in this realm of conventionality and conformity.

The rhetoric of this passage escalates uncannily into the Blut-und-Boden register of right-wing revolutionaries. For Heidegger, what he proclaims from the rostrum seems to have world-historical significance: "We," he tells his students, must expect that "today's normal human being and philistine [*Biedermann*] will be frightened" and "cling even more fervently to his idols" as a result of the challenge to renew philosophy in this way. This is only the beginning. He exhorts his audience:

> We must first once again summon up what is capable of awakening terror in our Dasein [*unserem Dasein einen Schrecken einzujagen vermag*]. For how does it stand with our Dasein if such an event as the World War passed us by essentially without leaving a trace? Is that not a sign that perhaps no event, be it ever so great, can fulfill this task if the human being has not first prepared himself to awaken? If it is awake, this fundamental mood of profound boredom *can* reveal to us the *absence* of this distress . . ." (255–56)

The presence of boredom reveals not simply individuals' lack of awareness of mortality but a general, yet unrecognized malaise—what Robert Musil would call the "mysterious disease of the time" and trace to the time before World War I. It must be emphasized that Heidegger does not understand boredom as a political problem in any conventional sense. His point is that fundamental philosophical questions are not theoretical problems but rather "questions posed by the essential need of Dasein itself" to "become transparent to itself again in order to allow itself to be touched by another" (255). This 'other' is being; the negativity of boredom reveals the profound alienation of modern existence.

Nonetheless, as Heidegger's invocations of terror and fateful tasks attest, the Freiburg lectures on "The Fundamental Concepts of Metaphysics" provide a crucial link between *Being and Time* and the rectoral address of 1933. Against the background of violent political unrest and general discontent that characterized the final years of the Weimar Republic, Heidegger called for existential responsibility as a propadeutic to reawakening the mystery of being. Placed in its historical context, his stated aim in these lectures to "transform the human being and therewith received metaphysics into a more primordial Dasein" acquires disturbing political overtones. Indeed, not only does the language of these lectures anticipate the vocabulary of Heidegger's engagement in the 1930's; their argumentative strategy illuminates why the philosopher would come to place his thought, however briefly, at the service of National Socialism.

Heidegger's politically resonant language has a structural correlate in his analysis of Dasein's being in the everyday world. As a number of scholars have shown, quite concrete commitments, including an aversion to both political and economic dimensions of modernity, colored the purportedly suprahistorical phenomenological analysis of the world into which Dasein "falls" in *Being and Time*. Not everydayness as such but everyday modern existence—life under the highly mediated conditions of advanced culture— is inauthentic. The condemnation of quotidian life in modernity, which becomes even more explicit in the 1929/30 lectures, marks Heidegger's work as part of the wider "conservative revolution" of the 1920's.[41] As my rhetorical analysis has underlined, in his attempt to awaken his audience to the historic significance of boredom, political and philosophical objectives are intertwined. Indeed, on Heidegger's understanding, a transformation in the way historicity is understood is the conditio sine qua non of the philosophical renewal for which he strives.

The lectures on "The Fundamental Concepts of Metaphysics" employ a different, more complicated rhetorical strategy for putting forward this critique of everyday life than his 1927 masterwork. Much is at stake in shifting the focus from the individual's relation to the world as such as revealed in angst to the purportedly pervasive mood of boredom. The Freiburg lectures do not simply aspire to persuade readers that they are capable of transcending their immersion in "what one does" to ask anew the question of the meaning of being. Here, Heidegger aims explicitly to move an audience, to awaken his listeners to the historico-existential dilemma which he believes occludes the modern human being's apprehension of metaphysical questions. The premise of the lectures is that it is only on the basis of such an awakening that the question of the meaning of being can be posed at all. As a

---

[41] See Breuer, *Anatomie der Konservativen Revolution* for a critical account of this concept. On Heidegger and modernity, see especially Zimmerman. Jacques Derrida's subtle response to the controversy launched by Victor Farías remains a landmark ("Heidegger, l'enfer des philosophes," 1987). On the politics of *Being and Time* in particular, see Johannes Fritsche, *Historical Destiny and National Socialism in Heidegger's "Being and Time"* and Mark Blitz, *Heidegger's Being and Time and the Possibility of Political Philosophy*.

consequence, the slippage between a suprahistorical perspective on historicity and historically specific analyses that was already apparent in the analysis of everydayness in *Being and Time* becomes even more overt.

Paradoxically, these levels collapse because Heidegger sees historicity in terms of individual mortality. Just as in the earlier work, where the description of everydayness and being-with (*Mitsein*) shift reflection from the concrete manifestations of historicity to their existential significance, in these lectures, philosophical reflection "awakens" boredom not through reflection on the historical and political specificity of this "fundamental mood" but through an interpretation of its meaning for the individual attempting to establish a relation to the question of being. The task of philosophy is *"not to describe human consciousness but to summon up [beschwören] the Dasein in the human being"* (258). Although it is "historical," for Heidegger the question of being is not cultural or political. It is at the level of the individual listener that his lectures on boredom aim to transform human existence. Thus it is precisely in their philosophical ambition—and naïveté—that his lectures on the "Fundamental Concepts of Metaphysics" prefigure the philosopher's turn to National Socialism. Nonetheless, Heidegger's philosophical claims about the significance of boredom in modernity deserve to be taken seriously. To do so while rejecting the rhetoric of "awakening" entails developing a more differentiated account of the cultural and historical construction both of this "fundamental mood" and of the process of reflecting upon it.

The Phenomenology of Boredom

We turn now to the intricate argument by which Heidegger sets out to demonstrate that the experience of boredom can reveal the metaphysical dilemmas of human existence as they lie hidden in the everyday modern world. This phenomenology of boredom is philosophically central to the development of his ideas about subjective experience and historical reality. However, these ideas cannot be treated in abstraction from their rhetorical deployment in the lectures. Heidegger is not simply developing an account of "The Fundamental Concepts of Metaphysics"; he is engaged in an attempt to renew philosophy. Only by considering the way philosophical and rhetorical considerations converge in his arguments can we truly make sense of his claim that, even as it goes unrecognized—remains "unawakened"—boredom is the "fundamental mood" (*Grundstimmung*) of modernity. And, conversely, the fact that Heidegger's interpretation of boredom has a practical philosophical purpose has profound consequences for the evaluation of his claims about the experience.

Heidegger's notion of boredom appears to be, in the broadest sense, a political one—boredom reflects the emptiness which results from the "absence of distress" that characterizes over-civilized modern life, with its lack of "mystery" and therefore of "the inner terror . . . which gives Dasein its greatness" (244). But it is necessary to "awaken" boredom to bring his listeners to the point where this interpretation of the "fundamental mood" can achieve its philosophical-existential impact. Heidegger thus sets out first to provoke those listeners to reflect on how their blaséness is a symptom and an expression of their embeddedness in the realm of "what one does," in that unthinking everyday existence where the fundamental questions of metaphysics fail to arise. Second, he attempts to show that as a fundamental mood, boredom points beyond this realm—that the very emptiness it embodies implies a philosophically significant lack in ordinary existence. In these depths of boredom, Heidegger discovers not the nihilism of the self but the inexplicable entry/presence of being—and thereby, ideally, brings his audience to the questions of world, finitude, and solitude. In this section, I trace how the phenomenology of boredom through which Heidegger sets out to move his listeners discloses the existential grammar of the mood and thereby points the way toward the metaphysical questions he contends are suppressed by everyday existence in modernity.

At the beginning of the discussion, Heidegger lays out three "forms" of boredom, or more precisely, three ways in which boredom may be understood. The first, most familiar form is "being bored by something" (*gelangweilt werden von etwas*); his example is a book. He demonstrates that the ordinary understanding expressed in the claim "this book is boring" is inadequate to the experience of boredom. The grammatical structure "this is boring" implies that "the boring" (*das Langweilige*) is an objective quality with causal efficacy. However, the existential grammar of the experience calls into question our ordinary understanding of causality; it cannot be understood as the effect of an object on a subject, since in our very boredom we recognize that others—or we ourselves at other times—may in fact not be bored by the book in question. What is important is the *relation* of subject to object: "What bores us, the boring, is what holds itself out yet leaves [us] empty" (130). Here Heidegger describes the quotidian boredom of consumption: for example, the novels Emma Bovary reads, in their very promise of a better life, seem to empty out her actual existence.

The first, so to speak naïve description of boredom is inadequate. Because it is a *Stimmung*, a mood or an attunement, boredom cannot be adequately grasped in the causal terms implied by the grammar of the subject-predicate structure.[42] Heidegger says that it is, like all moods, a *Zwitterwesen*, a "hybrid, partly objective, partly subjective" (132). The existential grammar of boredom will thus point toward the limits of the language we use to speak about experience more generally. His argument will proceed by exploiting the tension between subjectivity and objectivity inscribed in the experience itself.

Heidegger's phenomenological method begins before grammar in the ordinary sense in an attempt to capture the existential grammar of the experience—the structure of boredom as it is lived. The point is to avoid the errors of traditional philosophical and psychological approaches to the analysis of subjectivity, which begin, quasi-scientifically, by setting out what he calls an orderly "region of experiences." Heidegger admonishes his listeners to focus not on theories of consciousness but on the thing itself—to put their methodological efforts into "obtaining [*erhalten*] and retaining [*festhalten*] the immediacy of everyday Dasein" with "the *composure* [*Gelassenheit*] *of the everyday, free gaze*" of pre-philosophical, pre-theoretical thought (137). If they do so, he promises, phenomenological reflection on boredom can reveal an experiential complexity that cannot be resolved into 'objective' and 'subjective' dimensions of the experience.

With this methodological goal in mind, the goal can be further specified: the "task is now not the interpretation of the boring thing [*des Langweiligen*] as such, but the being-bored-by . . . [*das Gelangweiltwerden von . . .*] and being-bored-with . . . [*das Sichlangweilen bei . . .*]" (138). With this experiential distinction comes a new understanding of boredom: although the second, reflexive form, "being-bored-with . . ." implies an object, such boredom is no longer causally linked to the object. It is "almost as though the boredom came from us and as if boredom spun itself forth without needing to be caused by or bound to the boring thing." Rather than "being concentrated" on the book which bores us, such boredom "emanates out over the other things . . . everything becomes boring" (138–39). Here Heidegger describes what I have called the "nihilistic dynamic" of boredom, through which the modern subject's quotidian discontents spiral into negative revelations of the meaninglessness of existence. From the perspective disclosed by such boredom, there can be no reflection on the philosophical significance of the experience that does not simply affirm its universality. Heidegger will argue that the way such boredom comes to permeate our existence points to yet a third

---

[42] Here Heidegger's affinities with Nietzsche are especially evident. This problematic is developed further in his reinterpretation of propositional logic in Part II, chapter 6. See especially the discussion of Aristotle, §72.

aspect of boredom, one in which the subjective and objective dimensions are melded. In the form of experience captured in the phrase "it is boring," he will claim, the otherness of being manifests itself.[43] Here Heidegger reinterprets the relationship between mortality and boredom that runs through the philosophical discourse on the experience from Kierkegaard to Kuhn.

However, before pursuing the nature and origin of these distinctions within the mood, the question of what the diverse, subjective and objective, aspects of boredom have in common must be clarified—in my terms, its existential grammar explicated. To do so, Heidegger examines concrete instances of boredom. In their particularity, as we shall see, these introduce an historical specificity supposedly excluded from phenomenological reflection. Both his examples and the analytic terms he uses to interpret them resonate with the discourse on boredom established in the previous century as a mode of reflection on the subjective effects of modernization. A close reading of these passages will therefore illustrate how Heidegger's phenomenological "awakening" of his audience's understanding of boredom appeals to a rhetoric of reflection on subjective experience that his phenomenological method (and the existential analytic) allegedly transcend.

In Heidegger's example for the first form of boredom, the temporality of modern existence appears in a far less abstract form than in his discussion thus far. Being bored by something (*gelangweilt werden von etwas*) manifests itself not "in itself" but in the *Zeitvertreib*, the pastime through which we attempt to overcome it. When we are bored by something, we are not genuinely at leisure, for time seems to us a thing that must be used up or endured. The *Zeitvertreib* is that with which we kill time (in the German, literally "what drives away time"). Heidegger's example expands on the case of the boring book:

> We sit for example in a small tasteless train station of a remote minor railway. The next train will not arrive for four hours. The region is without charm. We do have a book in the knapsack—to read, then? No. Or think through a question, a problem? It is impossible. We read the train schedule or study the index of various distances between this station and other places equally unknown to us. We look at the clock—only a quarter hour has passed. Out then onto the road. We walk back and forth, just to do something. But it doesn't help. We count the trees along the highway, look again at the clock—just five minutes since we checked it. (140)

All of these activities are futile attempts to banish boredom. The constant "looking at the clock" (or watch—the German is ambiguous, and Heidegger

---

[43] In the German "es ist einem langweilig," Heidegger's point that this experience of otherness is constitutive of the self is clearer.

may be referring to a personal time-piece rather than the station clock) reveals the existential structure of the experience. In this being-bored-by, he says, "we" are held up, delayed—*hingehalten*—through the peculiar temporal structure produced in the train station where we must wait out the time between arrival and departure. The station forces us, in the most insidious fashion, to live by the clock.

Heidegger's example is particularly appropriate, for the "tasteless" train station represents the historical locus of the mechanization and standardization of time. As we have seen, boredom understood as a consequence of pure temporal duration first arises with the modern experience of temporality based not on lived but on clock time. Perhaps, following Schivelbusch, one might also argue that such hypothetical travelers, encountering the world in the mode fostered by modern, industrialized travel as a grid of interchangeable destinations, find the landscape which surrounds the station charmless because it is no longer anything but an obstacle which must be surmounted on the way to their goals. However, Heidegger does not treat being bored by the train station as an experience that exemplifies a peculiarly modern way of being in the world. His analysis ignores the historical associations between rail travel and the objectification of subjective experience in modernity. For Heidegger, this example does not link the experience of boredom to the historical process by which the world had been reified and commodified, time itself rationalized and industrialized, but rather opens onto a very general set of questions about the relation between time and things, questions about the structure of everyday existence as such, which he does not identify as historically specific.[44]

Focusing on the temporal structure—"the hesitating passage of time" that envelops and delays—while disregarding the context that produces it, Heidegger elaborates on the boredom of the train station: "Being bored is a distinctive *numbing perplexity* [*Betroffenheit*] *from the hesitating passage of time and time altogether*, a perplexity that distresses [*bedrängt*] us in its way" (148). On his reading, it is this, historically speaking, abstract distress that provokes the attempts he catalogs to find a pastime—and thereby to transform the temporal structure which defines confinement in the train station, "to overcome the *hesitating* passage of time . . . which distresses us" (151). It is no accident that this analysis fails to take into account the historical specificity of the relation between subject and world expressed in "driving away"

---

[44]Even when "thinking technology" became central for Heidegger, he did not engage in reflection on the historical specificity of technological changes but remained focused on the level of ontological generality.

time in such a fashion. In opposing the boredom produced by the enforced leisure of the train station to pleasurable immersion in activities like reading and strolling that characterize genuine leisure, Heidegger is attempting to disclose the dimension of authentic Dasein through which metaphysical questioning can take place. Such an analysis occludes the possibility that "genuine" leisure is unattainable and even anachronistic in the context of the train station, the literal site of the clock by which modernity lives.

Indeed, for Heidegger it is precisely this ahistorical, abstract quality that makes the boredom of the delayed traveler disclosive of the structure of everyday existence. One who is held up in the train station, he maintains, is thrown into the search for occupation as such. But the experience of "being left empty," which the pastimes of walking up and down, counting trees, etc., futilely attempt to alleviate, cannot really be said to be caused by the tastelessness or lack of interest in the train station as such. For Heidegger, it is not really "caused" by anything at all in the usual sense. Such emptiness is, rather, a consequence of the things around us inappropriately becoming (in the terms of *Being and Time*) present-at-hand (*vorhanden*). Understood properly, the boredom of the train station reveals something about Dasein's being-in-the-world.

Even as Heidegger emphasizes the particular temporality of the train station, he defines it in ahistorical terms. If the objects around us loom large, and "we" are unable to find a diverting way of filling the time, he argues, then because the time we are delayed in the train station is no longer imperceptible "between-time." The temporality of boredom is a consequence of the train station itself being inappropriately brought into our awareness. For in entering a train station, Heidegger says, we expect

> to be able to use it as a train station, that is, that we can immediately board and travel forth as quickly as possible. It is a proper train station precisely when it does not force us to tarry. The present-at-hand train station denies itself to us as train station and leaves us empty because the train which belongs to it is not yet arriving, making the time until it does so long, so hesitating. (155)

This temporal structure is, Heidegger says, the ultimate source of "our being left empty by things" in the boredom that permeates our stay in the station (157). Our enforced leisure—or *désœuvrement*—reveals our surroundings to be meaningless for us, forcing us to become aware of things in a disconnected manner. The world loses its power to hold us, and when we seek to occupy our time, we fail practically of necessity, for we are moved not to act but to fill up our emptiness. The situation in the train station that becomes present to us through the failure of its proper, transitional temporality is thus paradigmatic for Heidegger's first form of boredom, "being bored by some-thing," which he defines as a particular modality of experiencing time, an "essential being-delayed in a being left empty."[45]

The abstracted phenomenological "essence" of the first form of boredom evokes reflections on the temporality of everydayness in general.

> In order for the station not to bore us through this specific form of boredom, we must encounter it in its *specific* time, which in a certain way is the ideal time [*Idealzeit*] of the train station: that is, before the departure of the train . . . . Bore-dom is only possible altogether because each thing, as we say, has *its* time. (159)

Human beings normally experience objects integrated in a temporal context. In boredom, however, objects become inappropriately evident—*vorhand-en*—because that context has been ruptured. Heidegger remarks that his the-sis that each thing has its time "must be explicated" by extending and deep-ening "the interpretation of these distinctively joined fundamental moments of being-bored: delayedness and being-left-empty" (159).

The rupture in the temporal structure of everyday existence that Heideg-ger calls "delayedness" produces an experience of emptiness familiar from the analyses of *Being and Time*. Like anxiety, boredom initially appears as a modification of being-in-the-world, in which things are no longer prereflex-ively ready-to-hand. We cannot just change trains; the time is not "ideal"; we are forced out of immersion in the world. The irritating presence of what surrounds us as we wait must be understood, Heidegger contends, as a mode in which time manifests itself. The puzzle of how delayedness is related to being-left-empty in boredom thus leads him to the philosophical question of "*what time itself is*, that it can have such a relation to things, and furthermore that out of such a relation something like boredom as a *mood* that resonates *through us* [*die uns durch-stimmt*] is possible" (158). Because mood has its source in Dasein's temporality, it can disclose fundamental structures of human existence. In my terms, the grammar of "being bored by" the train station points to a more basic, existential grammar of mood.

For Heidegger, this example exposes something about the constitution of everyday temporality as such. Thus, although within the discourse on bore-dom, both the train station itself and what he calls present-at-handness—the experience of things alienated from their contexts—are linked to the histori-cal process of rationalization and instrumentalization, the example leads him away from the specificities of modern existence. Emulating Husserl's phe-nomenology, he aims to reduce the particulars of experience to fundamental

---

[45]"*Die Zeit für sich, der bloße Ablauf, ist auch nicht langweilend, sondern das Gelangweiltwerden ist dieses 'wesentliche Hingehaltensein im Leergelassenwerden'*" (159).

structures that cannot be understood historically. The next step is to move
below the level of everydayness toward a more profound interpretation of
the basic relation between time and things that he has begun to uncover.
Heidegger turns, therefore, to a *"deeper"* and "more deadly" form of boredom, one that "seizes more at the roots of our existence" (162).

The phenomenology of this experience, "being-bored-with," also uses the
"structural moments" of delayedness and being-left-empty to move from the
grammatical form of the experience—in this case, its reflexivity—to the existential grammar of mood as such.[46] In introducing his second example, Heidegger calls it "an emphatic and extreme, relatively extreme, counter-example
to the first form of boredom" but nonetheless a "truly everyday and universally accessible, practically inconspicuous case." Once again, he tells a story.

> We are invited somewhere in the evening. We do not have to go. But we were
> busy [*angespannt*] all day, and we have time in the evening. So we go. There is the
> usual food with the usual table-talk; everything is not only quite pleasant but also
> tasteful. One sits afterwards, as one says, animatedly together, perhaps listens to
> some music, chats; it is witty and amusing. Already it is time to leave. The ladies
> attest . . . it was really very nice . . . . In fact. There is absolutely nothing about this
> evening which could have been boring, neither the conversation nor the people
> nor the accommodations. One thus comes home quite satisfied. Takes a quick
> look at his interrupted work in the evening, makes an estimate and preview for
> the next day—and then it comes: Actually I was bored [*Ich habe mich eigentlich
> doch gelangweilt*] this evening, during [*bei*] this engagement. (165)

Heidegger invokes a rhetoric of shared experience with his audience which
must be followed in order to trace his argument. While "we"[47] could take no
pleasure in the enforced idleness of the train station, in the chosen leisure of
the dinner party, "we" enjoy ourselves. On his account, the dinner party is
no escape from the temporality of everydayness; it is not a rupturing
"between time" but a leisurely interlude that seamlessly encompasses a variety of purposeless occupations (chatting, smoking, etc.). Still, Heidegger
emphasizes that while the time of the train station imposes itself upon us—it
bored us—we were not bored *by* the party. On the contrary, time passed
quickly, and boredom with the whole evening was recognizable only retrospectively, from outside of the situation itself. As Heidegger puts it, in the

---

[46]The distinction between being-bored-by and being-bored-with is made more emphatically
in German because the first is grammatically passive, the second a reflexive (hence middle) form.
As we shall see, the third form "es ist einem langweilig" is impersonal.

[47]Heidegger's use of pronouns is worthy of note. On the whole, his imaginary protagonist
seems to combine features of the 'royal we' with the impersonal 'one' of 'das Man.' However, in
the final passage, where a look at his abandoned desk prompts an abrupt reinterpretation of the
evening, there is an equally abrupt shift to the third and then to the first person.

second example, "killing time" has assumed a different form than in the train station. The particular activities that constituted the evening were neither boring in themselves nor were they expressions of boredom (like reading the schedule or walking back and forth in front of the station). Rather, the whole evening, the engagement itself, was a pastime, one that could suddenly seem pointless when seen in comparison with the genuine work lying ahead and behind.

In this second form of boredom, the emphasis shifts from the objective to the subjective. It is no longer simply that boredom reveals the structure of everyday temporality in which "we" are usually immersed. There was nothing wrong or boring about the party itself, yet a retroactive revelation has rendered our very enjoyment suspect. It does not matter, Heidegger asserts, if this could only happen "to a quite blasé person, who is used to seeing everything in advance in this distinctive light of a fundamental being-bored" (166). The example of being bored with the party must be interpreted "in itself and out of itself" (166). In this way, it reveals a crucial aspect of the existential grammar of mood. As "we" reflect, "the boredom concentrates itself more and more upon us, upon our situation as such, so that the particularities of the situation are unimportant; it is only coincidentally that *with* which *we* are bored [*bei dem wir uns langweilen*] not *that which* bores us [*was uns langweilt*]" (170). On Heidegger's reading, the retrospective confrontation with the boredom of apparently pleasurable immersion in the party reveals the dilemma of subjectivity itself.

From his phenomenological perspective, the fact that being-bored-with is independent of the situation to which it refers marks this experience as a "deeper" boredom than being-bored-by. In being-bored-with, the structural moments of 'being delayed' and 'being left empty' have been transformed—they are lived as a malaise that is, implicitly, the question of our existence. "We don't know what bores us. Or more precisely: we know quite clearly, that is, what bores us is just this 'I know not what,' this uncertain, unknown thing" (179). Heidegger's phenomenological interpretation of this form of boredom reinscribes the analysis of anxiety in *Being and Time*. It is we ourselves who bore ourselves in pursuing such pastimes. Such is immersion in *das Man*. The oppressive being-left-empty no longer appears as an imposition from outside, for it clearly comes from our having given ourselves over to a situation which does not, cannot, "fill out the *decisiveness of our whole Dasein*." Our "being or nonbeing" does not, cannot "depend on such things," for no matter how much such an evening engages and amuses us, according to Heidegger, it "does not correspond to that which we, without knowing it clearly, actually seek" (179–80).

The reflexive grammatical structure of the verb for the second form of boredom, *sich langweilen,* thus reflects an existential grammar of mediation: the temporally indeterminate boredom with the dinner party reflects Dasein's inadequate relation to the world. When, in looking back, "we" confront the existential limitations of the situation, it retroactively alienates us from what had seemed to be "our" enjoyment of the pastime. Participating in what Heidegger represents as a perfect dinner party requires absolute absorption into the everyday mode of being 'what one is.' The retrospective 'actually, I was bored the whole time' is spoken from another point of view, that of the authentically existing Dasein for whom everyday fallenness into being "what one is" constitutes a loss of self—to wit, the form of boredom "defined by this forming [*Sichbilden*] of an emptiness in the apparently fulfilled going along with what is happening" (180).

The second form of boredom thus exposes the existential grammar of Dasein's everyday relation to the world as a whole. When we are bored by the train station, it appears to be an effect of the experience of time *it* produces. However, being-bored-with is a different sort of experience of time, one that may be revealed first in retrospect.[48] The second form of boredom is thus "deeper" in the sense that the situation to which we give ourselves over, hoping to find amusement and occupation, becomes the occasion for self-reflection on constitution of everyday being-in-the-world. If being-bored-by reveals the structure of things made present-at-hand through the breakdown of the temporal nexus that ordinarily renders them invisible, being-bored-with reveals that our ordinary way of being is itself the source of this invisibility. Thus Heidegger argues that the emptiness one recognizes in retrospect as having lurked beneath such an engagement phenomenologically reveals the deep reflexivity of this form of the experience: in being-bored-with, *sich langweilen,* we are literally bored with ourselves. "This emptiness is the being-left-behind of our authentic self. This emptiness which arises is the 'I know not what'" that is the source of distress (180). Such boredom thereby discloses the intimate relation between everydayness and inauthenticity.

From the point of view of authentic Dasein, the whole relation to time expressed in the pastime of the party leaves one empty. Just as the train station became paradigmatic for a certain experience of the world, boredom with the dinner party functions as a symptomatic example of the meaninglessness that permeates the apparent satisfactions of everyday life (at least in-

---

[48] Although this does not seem to be logically necessary, it does seem likely that any experience of boredom which captured the dissonance between one's existence as "das Man" and the perspective of authenticity would have to do so from the sort of reflective distance that ordinarily arises after the fact.

sofar as his listeners can find themselves in his "we"). Once again Heidegger has reduced the experience of boredom to an existential grammar of temporality that disregards the way his analysis participates in an historically specific discourse on boredom. The mandarin who loses himself in the feminized pleasures of the dinner party, only to pull himself up short when he catches sight of his abandoned desk, enacts the ubiquitous strategy of establishing a sovereign distance from the threatening pleasures of the modern world by proclaiming oneself bored with everything. Indeed, as Heidegger's denial inadvertently attests, this is the experience of someone "who is used to seeing everything in advance in this distinctive light of a fundamental being-bored" (166). As for Kierkegaard, everyday pastimes are diversions from authentic existence, pleasures for those who cannot recognize the emptiness of the social self.

Although his phenomenological approach renders the inherited rhetoric of reflection almost unrecognizable, Heidegger's interpretation belongs to the idealizing tradition that depicts boredom as a timeless form of spiritual discontent with everyday existence. What I have called his existential grammar centers philosophical questions on the self in a highly innovative, modern way even as it occludes the historical specificity of the mood it thematizes. For Heidegger, the "oppressiveness," the often imperceptible "distress" of being-bored-with signals Dasein's avoidance of an authentic confrontation with the question of being or nonbeing—with individual mortality. The retrospective epiphany of the second form of boredom discloses that the structural moments of *Hingehaltenheit*, delayedness and *Leergelassenheit*, being-left-empty, are grounded in the self that has fled more authentic ways of spending time, for, as Heidegger explains, in taking time for the engagement, we have cut ourselves off from "our *ownmost past* [*Gewesenheit*] and our *ownmost future*," thus "dissolving" our temporality "in mere presence" (187–88).

Heidegger can now clarify the fundamental existential structure of boredom: it is a modification of temporality that brings time to a halt in a present which, since it is cut off from past and future, "expands." In experiencing this "now," which has been retrospectively revealed as "our own, but abandoned and empty self," we realize that we were bored the whole evening (189). The "structural unity" of the moments of being-delayed and being-left-empty is grounded in human being-in-the-world as the source of time. "*Boredom arises from* [*entspringt*] *the temporality of Dasein*. . . . It emerges out of a very definite way in which our temporality *matures* [literally, temporizes: *sich zeitigt*—EG]" (191). We are, in other words, the source of our own boredom. The retrospective temporality that characterizes the example of being bored with the party serves to underline how boredom reveals a whole way of being in the world; Heidegger's analysis belongs to the long tradition that sees boredom as exposing the truth about the inauthenticity of modern life from the perspective of the superior individual.

As we have seen, the first two forms of boredom embody quite different relations to time. Since for Heidegger, human temporality provides the point of entry into reflection on existence as such, the contrast between these modes of boredom is to point his listeners on the way toward philosophy. In the context of the lectures as a whole, the phenomenological analysis of the relation between boredom and time prepares the way for a radical critique of the understanding of temporality that constitutes the foundation of modern, i.e. Cartesian, subjectivity. Before moving to the third form of boredom, Heidegger sums up what has been established, juxtaposing the case of the party, for which we "allow ourselves time," with the enforced leisure of the train station, for which we "have no time."

Initially, he notes, it seemed that we were bored by the train station on account of an earnest engagement with life that could not endure wasting any time. However, the second example has revealed the limitations of such an understanding. In attributing boredom to external causes such as the train station, we obscure the fact that we ourselves are the source of the emptiness of time which leads us to pursue occupations for their own sake. Thus, Heidegger concludes, "the 'not having any time' which looks like the most rigorous earnestness is perhaps the most thorough being-lost in the banalities of Dasein" (195). The interpretation of boredom has by no means reached an end. Even though the second form, being-bored-with, points to ourselves as the source of the boredom, it still remains tied to a situational understanding of time and does not, therefore, open onto the metaphysical questions that are the object of his lectures. At the end of this section, which apparently marks the beginning of the winter holidays,[49] Heidegger reminds his listeners: "It is not a matter of your carrying a definition of boredom home with you but of your learning to understand how to move in the profundity of Dasein" (198).

As I have emphasized, not the historical specificity of boredom but its basic structure—its existential grammar—makes it a *Grundstimmung*, a fun-

---

[49]This assumption is based on evidence internal to the text. The editors of Heidegger's works have restricted themselves to brief reports about the manuscript basis and prehistory of the texts they are publishing. In the prospectus from Klostermann (Stand März 2000), they explain that "in accordance with Heidegger's own wishes, his collected works are not a critical edition [*historisch-kritische Ausgabe*] but a final revised edition [*Ausgabe letzter Hand*]. This means that the volumes of the collected works are published fundamentally in the way that the philosopher himself made them accessible: without a philological apparatus and without indices."

damental mood. In Heidegger's phenomenology, historically determinate aspects of boredom are important only insofar as they indicate the existential structure of experience as such—like the philosophy of culture, they serve as symptoms of a lack that is not fundamentally historical. In the course of his analyses, the philosophical purpose of interpreting boredom to reveal the basic relation between Dasein and time becomes ever more evident. Even if, in a sense, the analyses of being-bored-by and being-bored-with have merely spun out the consequences of the ambiguity in his very first example—the boring book that attested to boredom's ambiguous subjectivity-objectivity— Heidegger has made clear to his audience that to proceed with the conceptual clarification of boredom requires deeper reflection about time and human temporality. These reflections will ultimately bring the discussion to individual historicity—to what in *Being and Time* is called Dasein's ownmost possibility of being. Although Heidegger's interpretation of boredom has evolved considerably since "The Concept of Time," he has by no means abandoned the notion that "history" in the more conventional sense serves as an alibi for the absence of existential authenticity, for Dasein's failure to grasp time in relation to that most individual possibility of not-being.

He now approaches the overall objective of the first part of the lecture series, the "awakening" of boredom in a fashion that will reveal to his audience the mood's imbrication with metaphysical questions. Heidegger declares that he "must *first* call into question the *essence* of consciousness and the *essence* of subjectivity" phenomenologically if he is to use reflection on boredom to awaken his audience to the "primordial time" of human temporality (201). He therefore proceeds to explore a "deeper" form of boredom, one that both reflects the temporal structure of Dasein and provides a perspective for reflecting on the philosophical significance of the mood's existential ambiguity. But does his phenomenology of boredom thereby establish the genuine distance from the modern rhetoric of reflection on subjective experience that has eluded him thus far?

At the outset of the lectures, Heidegger had announced his intention to ground philosophy and human existence in a more primordial fashion. The phenomenology of boredom, I have argued, is the means by which he attempts to achieve this goal. The grammar of the experience as it had been revealed up to this point in the lectures is supposed already to have led his audience to a deeper questioning about the phenomenon of boredom and prepared his turn to the third form of being-bored, in which, he contends, "*the profundity of the essence of boredom reveals itself*" (202). In my terms, the third form of boredom is to reveal the existential structure of mood as such.

This time, Heidegger needs no anecdote: his example consists of a grammatical construction alone: besides being bored by something or with something, we are at times simply bored.[50] "When we say, or better, when we silently know: it is boring [*es ist einem langweilig*]" (203), according to Heidegger, we point beyond the idea that something boring "causes" boredom to indicate the limits of the subject-object distinction itself—a distinction, as we have seen, still embedded in the situational understanding of being-bored-with.

> *It is boring*. What 'it'? That 'it' that we mean when we say . . . it's thundering, it's raining. It—that is the title of the indeterminate, unknown. But we do know it and know it as belonging to the deeper form of boredom: the boring [*das Lang-weilende*] . . . . It—one—not for me as me, not for you as you, not for us as us, but *for one* [*einem*]. Name, status, occupation, role, age, and fate as mine and yours falls [sic] away from us. More clearly, precisely this 'it is boring for one' lets all this fall away . . . . In this way we become an indifferent no one. (203)[51]

In Heidegger's account of the third form of boredom, the "we" gives way to the indefinite third person: "one" is bored—a one that is, as *Being and Time* already argued, "no one," *Niemand*. While in being-bored-with, we retrospectively grasp that we have neglected the fundamental questions of existence in our absorption in the "one" of *das Man*, here the impersonality of the experience has its origins in the fact that we are *not* absorbed in the everyday.[52] The third form of boredom is an experience of time that takes us out of time. The impersonal form "it is boring" thus reflects the deep, existential grammar of mood: one simply feels a given way, for mood comes to us from an indeterminate 'there.' This third form of boredom is not caused by *something* boring, nor is it a mode of reflection on our everyday being in the world; it is, in the most palpable form, a way of being into which we are thrown. As a fundamental mood, it does not determine us as subjects, as individuals with identities in the everyday world, but rather exposes us as beings faced with the problem of the meaning of our transient being.

[50] Since this form of boredom "is not related to a particular situation and particular causes and the like," "no example can be found" that would correspond to those given for the first two forms. Interestingly, he does offer an illustration that "may have happened to one or the other" of his listeners: "'Es ist einem langweilig,' wenn man an einem Sonntagnachmittag durch die Straßen einer Großstadt geht." Unfortunately, Heidegger does not elaborate (203–4).

[51] In this passage and in the citation from 205 cited on the following page, I have translated "einem" as "one," which I generally use for Heidegger's technical term "Man." However, in the body of the text, I have used the colloquial phrase "it is boring" rather than the awkward literal translation "it is boring for one."

[52] It must be emphasized that Heidegger profits from the fact that German has two different forms for rendering impersonal constructions. Although I have retained the conventional translations, the significance of his distinction might sometimes be better captured by translating *man* as "you" rather than "one." (Thanks to Dave Blake for this suggestion.)

Heidegger had already argued in *Being and Time* that mood has a quasi-transcendental function of articulating the way in which things appear to us. Like understanding (*Verstehen*) and language (*Sprache*), being-in-a-mood (*Gestimmtsein*, also called *Befindlichkeit*, state-of-mind) belongs to what he had analyzed as the existential constitution of the "there" in human being-there (Da-sein); it is a dimension of human being-in-the-world that discloses the world as a whole.[53] At this point, his students should be ready to grasp that the "understanding of boredom" expressed in the impersonal construction 'it is boring' reflects this fundamental, existential nature of mood. Boredom, Heidegger reminds them, has been approached not through external, psychological observation but via phenomenological illumination. The third form, with its impersonal grammatical structure, attests that boredom itself "has precisely in itself *the* character that it *reveals how it is with us*. This mood brings us into the possibility of a *distinctive understanding* (205)." Because for the most part, he continues, we confuse it with "the usual superficial" boredom, we fail to recognize the sense that "in and through this being-in-a-mood something is being 'said'" (205).[54] However, he indicates that if his listeners focus on the phenomenon itself in this, its third form, they will find that the uncanny impersonality of such boredom can move them to engagement with fundamental metaphysical questions. Indeed, the German "es ist einem langweilig" literalizes what the phenomenon of mood as such "says": that Dasein is a worldly being-in-time.

Living boredom in this third way, Heidegger argues, we are forced to attend to our existence itself. To grasp boredom as an impersonal phenomenon is to experience the emptying that characterized the other modes in a new register. With the third form, "we are not merely *removed from the everyday personality*, somehow distant and foreign, but at the same time also elevated [*in eins damit hinausgehoben*] above the actual particular situation. ... The whole situation and we ourselves as this individual subject are indifferent in it"; it makes "*everything mean equally much and equally little*" (207). Such boredom may arise through the structure of everydayness, yet it is not simply a manifestation of the nihilistic dynamic by which every *thing* becomes boring. Understood in its deep existential structure, boredom represents a rupture in our ordinary immersion in the world which comes to frui-

---

[53] See *Being and Time*, §29, 134f.

[54] This passage, which makes extensive use of the dative and of the multiple impersonal constructions available in German, is particularly untranslatable. The final sentence reads: "Genauer, in dieser Stimmung ist es einem so, daß wir wissen, es soll einem in und durch diese Gestimmtsein etwas 'gesagt' werden"—literally: "More precisely, in this mood it seems to one that we know that one is supposed to be being 'told' something in and through this being-in-a-mood."

tion in the absolute crisis of meaning embodied in the third form. "The in-difference of what is as a whole reveals itself. . . . Through this boredom, the Dasein finds itself placed directly before what is as a whole insofar as in this boredom, the being [that which is, *das Seiende*] which surrounds us offers no possibility of doing and no possibility of letting happen anymore" (210).

If the first form of boredom corresponds to the proto-philosophical expe-rience of things becoming present-at-hand and the second to the recognition that Dasein itself is the structure of temporality which makes possible the ordinary invisibility of things in the world, the third form reveals how hu-man being in the world discloses the structure of being as such—albeit in a negative form. Here being-left-empty is *"Dasein's being delivered over to the being that refuses itself as a whole [an das sich im Ganzen versagende Seiende]"* (210). At the same time, through the other "structural moment" of boredom, being-delayed, the very emptiness of this refusal becomes an *"indicating of the possibilities that lie fallow"* for Dasein (212).[55] In grasping the phenome-nology of the third form of boredom, his audience can therefore gain a sense for what it means to abandon the certitude of everyday existence and allow metaphysical questions to arise.

The third form completes Heidegger's interpretation of boredom, which by bringing his listeners to recognize the question of the meaning of being as an essential issue for Dasein as a temporal being is to prepare them for phi-losophizing in a new way. Although the form of boredom that discloses the indifference of being as a whole initially appears to be timeless, he argues that it actually reveals the fundamental structure of being-in-time itself. Such boredom is distant "from every use of the clock," yet in it, according to Hei-degger, we "move . . . in the essence of time" (217). In this impersonal third form of boredom, which paradigmatically reflects the existential grammar of mood, the structure of temporality as such is revealed—time is "in each case *the Dasein itself as a whole*" (221). It is neither a "particular now" nor "an ex-tended now" in which we are bored: this boredom discloses the "un-articulated unity" of our temporal "horizon" as such in all its "simplicity." "The whole time of Dasein is there and not at all specially articulated and demarcated into past and future" (222). In such boredom, the problem of being itself is implicit.

The full significance of this "deep" boredom only becomes clear when Heidegger turns to the interpretation of the second structural moment. In delaying Dasein, such impersonal boredom reveals the possibilities that have thus far gone unrealized; what time, experienced in this way, discloses "is

[55] It "speaks"; Heidegger puns on *versagen* and *sagen*.

nothing less than the *freedom of Dasein* as such" (223). This freedom comes, according to Heidegger, through the "self-liberation" that occurs when Dasein "*decides for itself*, i.e., discloses itself for itself as Da-sein" (223).[56] Following Kierkegaard, he declares that this decision "in the midst of beings always to be" oneself constitutes "the moment" [*der Augenblick*]. Indeed, "the moment is nothing other than the *look* [*Blick*] of resolve in which the full situation of an acting opens and remains open" (224). The moment in this sense should not, Heidegger says, be confused with "the punctual now"; it is, rather, "Dasein's look [*Blick*] . . . into present, future, and past" (226). Boredom indirectly fosters the recognition of the moment "as the fundamental possibility of Dasein's authentic existence" (224), for delayedness discloses the possibilities for being that lie fallow in the everyday experience of temporality. In boredom, Heidegger says, and "most especially" in its third form, time becomes long—literally a *lange Weile*—and indeterminate. The moment loses its "sharpness"; yet even as it empties out, "the *moment* intrudes . . . as the authentic possibility of that which makes the existence of Dasein possible" (229). By thus moving the one who is bored out of the everyday experience of clock time, this boredom reveals Dasein's fundamental, existential temporality—the way Dasein "temporizes" [*sich zeitigt*] (230).

When, at the conclusion of this discussion, Heidegger puts forward a "definition" of boredom (§ 34), he warns his listeners that his interpretation is not to be understood as "knowledge" that can be applied to boredom but rather as "a preparation . . . for asking about a *definite* boredom *of our* Dasein" (233). In the first instance, he is calling for self-reflection; only if he has succeeded in phenomenologically awakening his hearers' experience of boredom will he have brought them to philosophize. I have argued that in moving from superficial to profound boredom, these lectures enact an existential rather than a simply logical development, for while "we" are embedded in ordinary existence in the first two forms, the third form has revealed the structure of being in time itself and disclosed "the moment as the fundamental possibility of Dasein's authentic existence" (224). Boredom in this deeper sense is not alienation but authenticity, for on Heidegger's understanding, the third form reveals the existential structure of temporality as such.

The grammar of the third form of boredom directly reflects the deep existential grammar of mood: as an experience of subjects without objects, it

---

[56]"Das Sichbefreien des Daseins geschieht aber je nur, wenn es sich *zu sich selbst entschließt*, d.h. für sich als das Da-sein sich erschließt."

captures the impersonality of the encounter with being as an event that is constitutive of Dasein in every moment. According to Heidegger, all the phenomena of boredom must therefore be grasped as fundamentally unified: the third form, he now reveals, is the "condition of possibility" of the other two—an existential unity underlies the 'subjective' and 'objective' formations of the mood. "*Only because this 'it is boring' lurks as a constant possibility in the depths of Dasein can the human being experience boredom [sich langweilen] or be bored by the things and people around him*" (235). However, on his view the everyday way we understand ourselves obscures the fact that "*every* form of boredom rises up *out of this depth* of Dasein"; because we misapprehend and ignore the profundity of human being "it appears as though boredom had no origin at all" (235).

The phenomenology through which Heidegger has grasped boredom as a "fundamental mood" is simultaneously a critique of the inherited understanding of the relation between self and world. The grammar of the experience he has uncovered by moving from 'superficial' to 'profound' boredom therefore reveals what he sees as the deeper ambiguity of Dasein itself, which is constantly drawn away from authentic existence into the banal understanding of itself as a subject in a world of objects. From this perspective, even as the boredom of the train station and that of the party evade the fundamental experience of boredom, which reveals the sufferer's meaningless suspension in a moment being lived inauthentically, they point to their existential foundation. What bores us, Heidegger says, is "*temporality in a specific mode of its temporizing*" (237), we ourselves as beings in time who are in a particular relation to time. Since temporality is the condition of possibility of subjects and objects "in such a way that *the essence of subjects* consists precisely in *having Dasein*—i.e. a priori always already to have circumscribed being as a whole" (237)—his phenomenology of boredom constitutes the first step in revolutionizing his audience's understanding of human existence. By contrast, the "vulgar" interpretation of boredom, because it rests on a fundamental "*misunderstanding of the essence of mood altogether*," actually "*suppresses profound boredom*" and thus, by fostering its appearance in the superficial forms that reflect inauthentic Dasein, obscures the true nature of human being in time (238).

The argument has come full circle: to the question of what boredom as the contemporary fundamental mood reveals about "what is happening *today* in our Dasein" and to the task of grasping boredom not anthropologically or culturally or psychologically, but in a genuinely philosophical way (236). In "awakening" his listeners' boredom—or at least fostering a greater "receptiveness" (239) for recognizing and hearkening to what, in an existential sense, it "says"—Heidegger understands himself to be engaged in a task of historic import. For him, everything about contemporary life that seems to testify against the idea that a deep boredom is the fundamental mood of modernity in fact attests to its invisible hegemony. Incessant activity and movement manifest Dasein's fallenness to the everyday temporality of clock-time. The superficial forms of boredom fostered by modern life project the source of the emptiness outside the self, but phenomenological analysis shows that such a misapprehension of the mood merely serves to suppress awareness of existential emptiness. From a philosophical point of view, the apparent absence of the profound form of boredom is an illusion. On the contrary, for Heidegger, its omnipresence is attested by fact that a failure to grasp the temporality of Dasein defines the everyday way of being in the world.

The purpose of "awakening" boredom thus goes beyond the objective of bringing his individual listeners to philosophize. The historic task of his lectures is to expose the way boredom upholds the ultimately inauthentic understanding of human being that defines modern life. "*Our question*—has the human being today become boring for himself?—can only mean: *In the end, is the Dasein in today's human being as such bored?*" (242). There is not, Heidegger concedes, any lack of "convulsions, crises, catastrophes, emergencies" (243)—he speaks, after all, in Germany in early 1930. However, he contends, the "emptiness in the whole" is not the sum of social, political, scientific, artistic, philosophical, and religious problems.

> The absence of an essential distress of Dasein is the *emptiness of the whole,* so that no one stands with another and no community with another stands in the rooted unity of essential acting . . . The *mystery* is lacking in our Dasein, and thus the inner terror is missing . . . that gives greatness to the Dasein. The absence of the distress is . . . the *at bottom boring emptiness.* (244)

If there is a collective lack, then because individuals have failed to grasp the imperative of temporal, that is to say mortal, existence. The evidence that boredom is the fundamental contemporary mood is not simply that the modern human being turns away from the urgency of the moment, confusing "the hurriedness of his reactions" and "the suddenness of his programs" with resolution (248). If "we cannot identify that deep boredom in the Dasein of the contemporary human being," Heidegger believes, the question becomes "whether the contemporary human being does not suppress that profound boredom precisely in and through all of his contemporary humannesses, and that means, whether he does not conceal his Dasein as such"

(248). As he sees it, the philosophical task is thus to "liberate the Dasein in the human being" (248) by pursuing the question raised by the fundamental mood itself—the question of finitude.

Although the problem is collective, authenticity is, for Heidegger, a matter for individuals. Nonetheless, the critiques of humanist ideals, of liberal politics, of modern ways of life that suffuse the text of these lectures illuminate the trajectory of his thought in the years to come. As we have already noted, Heidegger's beliefs that the "greatness" of Dasein depends on existential "distress" and that the modern human being is plagued by a lack of "mystery" and "inner terror" portend his susceptibility to a politics aimed at using precisely those means to bring forth a new and better form of human being. In terms of the phenomenology of boredom itself, however, the issue is rather different. Heidegger has produced an existential analytic that abstracts the experience from its historical context and eternalizes the understanding of time manifested in boredom by defining it in relation to everydayness as such. Through the phenomenological 'reduction' to what I have called the existential grammar of mood, Heidegger arrives at an interpretation of boredom that assimilates it to other fundamental world-disclosing experiences such as terror and anxiety. Perhaps these are moods that may be legitimately considered in abstraction from their worldly context; however, as we have seen in examining his examples, the discursive situatedness and historical specificity of his interpretation of boredom are undeniable.

The movement from "superficial" to "profound" through which Heidegger aims to "awaken" the boredom of his listeners is effected through a rhetorical strategy that decontextualizes familiar examples. I have shown how he mobilizes a discourse on boredom with roots in nineteenth-century critiques of modernization to develop a philosophical perspective that supposedly transcends historical specificity. Furthermore, I have argued, the discourse in which the experience of boredom he analyzes is embedded shapes his very account of metaphysical questions. The bored self in lonely confrontation with the moment in which mortality is revealed as the foundation of meaning is familiar to us from the writings of more than one of Heidegger's predecessors, as is the unacknowledged historical particularity of the experience he presents as the route to philosophy.

Heidegger's attempt to establish a more primordial understanding of metaphysics fails to take into account the historical specificity of the understanding of time that, as his own examples attest, structures the experience of boredom. His avowedly Kierkegaardian conception of "the moment" in which Dasein's authentic possibilities may be revealed is parasitic on the clock time to which it is opposed. And even if the concepts through which

Heidegger develops his notion of human being in time are undeniably directed toward overcoming the subject-object division that he sees as the great error of modernity, his attention to individual as opposed to collective existence, to mood as opposed to character, to mortality as opposed to eternity, all embody an emphatically modern conception of human being. Therefore, although his demonstration that boredom raises "the question of being" articulates with unparalleled clarity why boredom is significant from a philosophical perspective, his approach to the experience ultimately exhibits the same failings that characterized Reinhard Kuhn's universalizing account of ennui as a transhistorical *idée force* in Western civilization. It is not simply that the boredom he describes is a modern experience. The claims that he makes for it, like Kuhn's notion that the confrontation with nothingness is the universal foundation of creativity, are unthinkable outside the historical context of modern thought. The lacunae in his argument therefore indicate a crucial failing of the philosophical rhetoric of reflection on the experience—the lack of historical self-reflection already encountered in Chapter 1.

Heidegger argues that the third, impersonal form of boredom reveals the existential structure of human temporality as such. It is, he claims, the condition of possibility for the appearance of other forms of boredom, just as that being-in-time is the condition of possibility for the appearance of subjects and objects. By severing the question of the meaning of the experience from the analysis of its relation to everydayness, this final argument for the philosophical significance of boredom thus legitimates Heidegger's failure to reflect on the historical specificity of the everyday understanding of time that provides the context for both the seemingly objective boredom of the train station and the apparently subjective boredom of the dinner party. If boredom's importance must be grounded in its deep existential structure, in its relation to mortality as such, then there is no need to reflect on the specific forms of everyday existence which give rise to specific forms of boredom. In an analysis centered on the way boredom gives rise to the question of being, it suffices to speak of everydayness as such—and thus of the genderless, classless "ones" who are immersed in it. The philosophical discourse on boredom reinscribes the gesture by which boredom effaces its own historicity, elevating the nihilistic dynamic that takes this experience without qualities as a sign of the meaninglessness of existence as such to a universal truth.

However, as Heidegger's own point of departure in *Kulturphilosophie* attests, calling boredom the "fundamental mood" of modernity implies more than that it is a privileged form in which human beings can recognize the limits of their subjectivity. In his own terms, boredom is not simply a form of individual existential distress; it is the symptom of a malaise of historic proportions. Heidegger's existential phenomenology simply lacks a means of mediating historically between boredom as an individual experience and the cultural phenomenon of boredom as modernity's *Grundstimmung*. In developing an existential grammar of mood out of his interpretation of boredom, Heidegger abstracts from the historically embedded language of reflection that forms his point of departure, substituting a philosophical account of human being-in-time for specific reflection on the historically particular temporal structure of that modern experience of boredom. My discussion of Heidegger's subsequent argumentative strategy in his lectures on "The Fundamental Concepts of Metaphysics" demonstrated the decisiveness of his failure to articulate the historical significance of the temporal structure revealed by boredom. By emphasizing boredom's uncanniness as an experience of the limits of human existence, he uncannily develops an account of human historical being that effaces all concrete evidence of historicity. Heidegger's phenomenological reduction of boredom to its existential grammar not only fails to grasp the symbolic significance of the experience but also encourages the fateful tendency to view individual philosophical awakenings as tantamount to historical revolutions.

CHAPTER 6

Being without Qualities: Robert Musil and the Self-Overcoming of Skepticism

Es ist sehr anmaßend: ich bitte mich zweimal zu lesen, im Teil und im Ganzen.

Dieses Buch ist religiös unter den Voraussetzungen der Ungläubigen.

Robert Musil[1]

The Man without Qualities is an unwieldy giant of a novel: by turns philosophizing, lyrical, acerbically insightful and cynically dismissive, with a vast cast of characters intertwined via intricate subplots into a portrait of bourgeois life in the Austro-Hungarian capital before the First World War, it places bitter irony and vivid psychological realism alike at the service of a reflective project that can fairly be called metaphysical in nature. Explicitly through the meditations of its eponymous protagonist, but also through the adventures which befall him, *The Man without Qualities* poses the question of what sort of relationship to one's own experiences is possible in modernity. While the absence of qualities and the loss of meaning go hand in hand, Robert Musil also unfolds—or began to unfold, for the novel is unfinished—a new language for expressing and reflecting upon the vicissitudes of subjective experience, a vocabulary at once scientific and mystical. Intertwining critical analysis with this constructive, utopian moment, Musil's novel attempts an ironic transformation of the modern rhetoric of experience that has larger implications for reflection on modern life. Although nothing much happens in this novel of ideas and their vicissitudes, the sense of groundlessness and meaninglessness that pervades both individual and collective experience in modernity is thought through: *The Man without Qualities* diagnoses the human condition in an age of democratized skepticism.

Musil identified his own boredom as a significant obstacle to the book's

---

[1] "It is very presumptuous: I ask to be read twice, in the part and in the whole"; "This book is religious with the presuppositions of the unbeliever" *Gesammelte Werke* [GW] 5, 1941 and 1940 respectively.

composition.[2] However, the term is almost never mentioned in the novel[3]: the protagonist's malaise and disaffection with his life go unnamed, as does the "mysterious disease of the time" that is said to have infected the early twentieth century. And yet the problem of boredom, with its literal and figurative relations to the process of cultural modernization, permeates *The Man without Qualities*. All the elements of the discourse on boredom are present—whether in the form of existential signs (characters are fatigued, withdrawn, morally indifferent, cynical, decadent) or as societal symptoms (they lament the decay of traditional meanings, the loss of a sense of purpose, the eclipse of soul by the spirit of science)—and they are represented as responses to the epistemic groundlessness of modern existence. Every idea has its counter-idea, and a corrosive doubt infiltrates everyone in the novel as soon as they begin to think over what they believe, who they are, what they should do. In the world of *The Man without Qualities*, identity, whether of the individual or of the nation or of an event, has become radically uncertain, and the elements of the discourse on boredom are placed in explicit relation to this historical circumstance. Musil's novel thus configures those elements as adaptive responses to the modern landscape of universalized skepticism in which people are adrift, bereft of epistemic certainty, of moral conviction, and even of a sense of their own genuine presence as actors.

My seemingly paradoxical claim is that it is through eschewing the language of boredom that Musil gains purchase on the historical and philosophical significance of the modalities of experience to which it referred. By representing the dilemmas of modern existence without defining their meaning in the terms of any singular vocabulary, *The Man without Qualities* establishes a perspective for reflection that avoids the aporiai of the boredom discourse as it had developed since Flaubert and Baudelaire. Because these difficulties themselves exemplify more general features of the modern rhetoric of reflection on subjective experience, it is not a matter of arguing that Musil's achievement depended on his consciously avoiding the term 'Langeweile,' though in fact the word is practically never used. It is, rather, that his effort to develop new

---

[2] In 1929 difficulties in completing Volume I moved Musil to consult a psychotherapist, Hugo Lukács, who recommended that he keep a record of his efforts. A page from the posthumous papers with the title "Technik sub specie Lukács" (Mappe VI/3; in *Tagebücher* [TB] II, 1182) refers to the "boredom" brought about by the clash of incommensurable alternatives as the key factor in his writing block. (See also the diary entry to which this paper is appended: TB I, 715.) Interestingly, it was also "boredom"—with life as an engineer—that had motivated Musil's turn to literature in the first place (See Berghahn 1991, 40).

[3] This is not true of Musil's earlier work. The most significant example is young Törless, whose boredom provokes a descent into sadistic excess that threatens to become a way of life (though without eradicating its cause) GW 6, 7–140.

ways of talking about subjective malaise effectively avoids both the Scylla of sociological reduction and the Charybdis of ahistorical philosophizing that characterize not only the discourse on boredom but also the modern rhetoric of reflection on subjective experience more generally.

I read Musil's ironic strategy for representing the dilemmas of the modern subject in *The Man without Qualities* as an attempt to develop a reflective idiom that can renew the poetic project originally associated with the bore-dom discourse—a project that had been eclipsed by the actual historical de-velopment of that discourse. That is, the novel is structured so as to move its audience to think historically about experiences that seem to be located in the interior, private realm of subjectivity—in my terms, to recognize the ethical and epistemic dilemmas that plague them as products of the democ-ratization of skepticism in modernity. What Musil avoids in eschewing the language of boredom—or more precisely, by refiguring the established mod-ern vocabularies of reflection on subjective experience—can be seen by re-calling the relationship between the historical evolution of the discourse on boredom and the rhetoric of reflection on subjective experience.

Well before Robert Musil began writing his novel, the language of bore-dom, which originally thematized the relation between historical and cul-tural transformations and subjective malaise, had lost its critical edge. While Flaubert and Baudelaire's use of the term explicitly raised questions about the meaning of history for the subject in a godless world, by the fin-de-siècle, the literary discourse on boredom functioned to obscure its own historical origins as a mode of reflection on the epistemic and ethical dilemmas con-stitutive of modern subjectivity. In the course of time, the experience of boredom had been naturalized. As a consequence, the language of boredom was robbed of the metaphoric force through which representations of the experience had so compellingly figured the relation between historical and cultural transformations and problems of meaning.

Ironically, this occlusion was the consequence, at least in part, of social changes that actually democratized the *experience* of boredom. Urbanization and industrialization had thoroughly transformed the temporality of every-day life, integrating people into modern orders of work and consumption that depended on the highly rationalized temporal framework of "living by the clock." As I showed in Chapter 3, the newly distinct spheres of work and leisure were equally structured by an experience of time as a series of empty moments. In this mode of experience, grounded in what Koselleck charac-terized as the historical semantics of progress, "the present withdraws into in-experienceablity." The language of boredom democratized in this period, I argued, names the disappearance of experience in the historical horizon de-

fined by all-encompassing anticipation of the future—by the idea that, as Brierre put it, humanity is *"marching toward the unknown."* However, insofar as
the notion that history was defined by infinite linear progress toward an unknown future gained acceptance, the language of boredom ceased to function
as a critical vocabulary for describing the failure of modern experience to cohere into meaningful constellations. The fragmented modern mode of experiencing time was naturalized, and the assumption that boredom was in fact
an eternal feature of the human condition grew ever more plausible. In retrospect, it is easy to see that the potential for de-historicization is inscribed in
the very metaphorics of "boredom," which function discursively to represent
what are both literally and figuratively consequences of cultural modernization as an individual, subjective response to the world.

My reading of *The Man without Qualities* situates the novel as a response
to these central dilemmas within the rhetoric of reflection on subjective experience in modernity. As many commentators have noted, the tensions
between "precision" and "soul," between objective, "scientific" explanation
and introspective accounts of subjective experience are both thematically
and formally central to Musil's work.[4] Whether or not his novel, if completed,[5] could in principle have succeeded in resolving these tensions by creating a new idiom of human self-understanding, Musil's narrative strategy
engages the reader in reflection upon the dilemmas brought about by the
conflict between modern, scientifically inflected and traditional, religiously
grounded modes of interpreting subjective experience. By foregrounding the
limits of established languages of reflection, Musil attempts to open the possibility of new, historically situated ways of thinking about the dilemmas of

[4]Within the vast literature on Musil, these problems are often treated in terms of the way Musil's thought incorporates the philosophical impulses behind Ernst Mach's critique of experience.
See for example Arvon, von Allesch, von Heydebrand, and Ryan.

[5]*The Man without Qualities* is radically unfinished. Musil died suddenly, leaving many papers
and notebooks with chapters and chapter-drafts in more or less fragmentary forms. In the *Gesammelte Werke*, although Volumes 1–5 are devoted to the novel, only Volumes 1–3 contain texts
Musil published during his lifetime. The novel in this sense is 1041 pages long, but Volumes 4 and
5 include 991 pages of additional material from Musil, material that in its internal complexity and
contradictoriness leaves the directions the novel could have taken quite open to interpretive
speculation. Volume 4 includes twenty chapters that had been intended as the continuation of
Book 2 (Volume 3 in the GW), typeset for publication and then withdrawn by Musil in 1937–38
(the "Druckfahnen-Kapiteln"); variant versions of six of those chapters; other drafts and attempts
to continue the novel beyond the "Druckfahnen-Kapiteln"; and a wide variety of sketches, notes,
and experiments of all sorts. In Volume 5 the material becomes even more fragmentary. Adolph
Frisé has, thankfully, included a remarkable editorial apparatus. The five volumes devoted to the
Mann ohne Eigenschaften are numbered consecutively, and where only a single number is given as
a reference, it refers to these volumes.

subjective experience in modernity. On my reading, a specifically rhetorical concern with forging a language of reflection adequate to the historical circumstance of modern human "being without qualities" shapes both thematic and formal dimensions of the novel.

Chapter 28, which is entitled "A Chapter that Can Be Skipped by Anyone Who Has No Special Opinion of the Occupation with Thoughts," thematizes the task of representing thinking in a disenchanted era. The protagonist is at his desk; ostensibly, he is working, but his thoughts have strayed. In an uncharacteristically direct fashion, the narrator interrupts the flow of description to soliloquize upon the problem that "unfortunately, nothing is so difficult to render in belles lettres as a thinking person." First of all, "unexpected ideas" do not come about spontaneously but rather as a result of tenaciously pursuing them. "How boring such persistence would have to be!" he confides to the reader. But the deeper problem is apparent to everyone from his or her own experience: the moment in which a problem is solved retains something ineffable. Something, the narrator says,

> is there all of a sudden; and one can quite distinctly perceive in oneself a faintly disconcerted feeling that one's thoughts have created themselves instead of waiting for their originator. This disconcerted feeling refers to something that many people nowadays call intuition, while formerly it used also to be called inspiration, and they think they must see something suprapersonal in it; but it is only something impersonal, namely the affinity and kinship of the things themselves that meet inside a head. ... [W]hen [thinking] is complete it no longer has the form of thought in which one experienced it, but has already taken on the form of the thing thought, and this unfortunately is an impersonal one, for the thought is then turned outwards and prepared for communication to the world.[6]

Despite the narrator's matter-of-fact endorsement of a "scientific," impersonal description of the activity of thinking, the literary difficulty in

---

[6]There are two English translations (Musil 1979 and 1995). I have consulted both, and while I sometimes follow Wilkins and Kaiser, whose renderings are more faithful to the letter, if not the music, of Musil's remarkable German, I have found it necessary to retranslate most passages. I have provided citations to both this older and the more recent English edition. While the German and 1995 English editions are continuously numbered, the 1979 English version is not. Thus it has been necessary to indicate volume numbers for that edition. Where no roman numeral appears, the passages indicated are in Volume 1. The passage just cited is chapter 28; 111–12 (German edition)/128–29 (English 1979)/115–16 (1995). Subsequent citations to the text of the novel will follow this order but omit the indication of editions.

In the 1995 English edition, Sophie Wilkins and Burton Pike rendered selections from the posthumous material (including a number of unpublished but substantially completed chapters omitted from the earlier English edition), but much of the very fragmentary material is still available only in German. Where possible I have given references to these translations when quoting from the posthumous material; where two numbers appear, the second refers to the 1995 edition.

representing the process remains. If religiously derived categories for describing the apparent lack of subjective control over the process of thinking are unsatisfyingly irrationalist, the consequence of the breakdown of conventional explanations has been a dearth of reflection altogether. Because the activity of thought, "the moment between the personal and the impersonal" cannot be captured in language, the narrator concludes, "thinking is such an embarassment for writers that they like to avoid it." The arch ambiguity of this phrase hearkens back to the title of the chapter. Musil's implied readers must be willing to think about thinking—and in particular to reflect upon the formal strategies through which *The Man without Qualities* represents thought as attempts to gain a more effective grip on the thinker's "disconcerted feeling" than do the old, discredited languages of reflection.

"However," the narrator continues, gradually ceasing to speak in his own voice and returning to the project of representing consciousness, "the man without qualities was now reflecting, and one may draw the conclusion that it was at least partly not a personal matter. What is it then? The world going in and out, aspects of the world forming shapes inside a head." A stream of associations about water under its geographical, mythological, religious, and scientific aspects follows, at the end of which the man without qualities reaches the conclusion that

> in the whole wide world there were only a few dozen people who thought alike about even so simple a thing as water; all the rest talked about it in languages that were at home somewhere between today and several thousands of years ago. So one must admit that a person who reflects even a little bit gets, so to speak, into pretty disorderly company! (28; 113/130/117)

Turning in this way from the particular example of water toward the general problem of thought, the protagonist's stream of consciousness underlines the peculiar modernity of the narrator's quandary, which is conditioned by the same skepticism that throws his characters' reflections into such disarray. The thinking of the man without qualities is exemplary. And because the world "going in and out" and "forming shapes" or failing to preoccupies him both as a personal and as an impersonal occurrence, his wide-ranging reflections directly engage the reader in thinking about thinking. Through his chronicle of the struggles of the man without qualities to find an adequate vocabulary for self-reflection on his life from a perspective "not so much godless as God-free" (1092/1187), Musil probes the limits of the established rhetoric of reflection on subjective experience. *The Man without Qualities* is critical of both the subjectivism and the reductionist materialism that structure that rhetoric.[7] His protagonist is in search of a new way of thinking about thinking that transcends the limitations of both modern and inherited idioms of self-reflection.

These passages directly illustrate Musil's concern with what I call the rhetoric of reflection and attest to the importance of the medium of language in his vision of the epistemological and ethical dilemmas of modern existence. While the protagonist, in his pursuit of an "impersonal" mode of living, could toy with affirming the perspective of the few dozen scientifically minded types who could agree on the determination of water, as the narrator's struggles attest, the novelist could not extricate himself from the mixture of old and new vocabularies of experience by such fiat. Rather than creating a new language out of whole cloth, Musil exploits the discursive possibilities of the contemporary melange of languages "at home somewhere between today and several thousands of years ago." Through the medium of free indirect style, he represents the thought of each of his characters as an intermingling of individual perspective and cultural accretions. The reader's attention is thus directed toward distinguishing the operation of historically constituted idioms within the medium of language that constitutes the novel.[8] Everyone in *The Man without Qualities* confronts the skeptical impasse symbolized by the problem of defining water from a different perspective, and thus the reader encounters the problem of the insufficiency of language to express experience not as an artistic dilemma but as a crisis of meaning lived by everyone in the world it depicts—the world of pre-war Viennese society.

The artful way in which Musil interweaves the representation of particular characters' perspectives with a satirical commentary on the larger discourse on the subjective effects of modernization in the period is illustrated by a passage presenting the reflections of Ermelinda Tuzzi, the cousin of the man without qualities. Nicknamed "Diotima" for her combination of intellect

---

[7]Musil, who had written a dissertation entitled "Beitrag zur Beurteilung der Lehren Machs," was particularly concerned to synthesize these elements.

[8]In a striking notebook entry from the late 1920's (GW 5, 1820) Musil reminds himself that this is

A means of representation (*Darstellungsart*) that should be used often. Put together a person but with all the cards on the table! Out of the fixed ideas and a couple of unavoidable connections between them[. . .]In this way all spiritual people . . . Arnh., D., and so on . . .

    Events
    Descriptions*
       are the sole bearers of the narration.
    Conversations
    Digressions

    * of the essence of changes of the physical and moral landscape.

and beauty, she becomes the de facto leader of the "parallel action" that provides the mise-en-scène for the novel's panoramic representation of life at the end of the Hapsburg empire. Diotima experiences the incommensurability of vocabularies of reflection from the perspective of a society hostess: under the vexed spiritual circumstances of modern bourgeois marriage, the fulfillment of her youthful dream of participating in her beloved "old Austrian culture [*Kultur*]" had been rendered "not merely monotonous but also strenuous and even hopeless."

> When one was on such close terms with culture [*Bildung*] as Diotima was, it became apparent that what was insuperable was not the depth but the breadth of it. Even questions so close to the human being as the noble simplicity of Greece or the meaning of the prophets dissolved, when one spoke with experts, into an incomprehensible variety of doubts and possibilities. Diotima learned from experience that during her evenings, even her famous guests always talked in twos, for already at that time a human being could only talk rationally and to the point with at the most one other human being, and she could not really do it with anyone. Thereby, however, Diotima had discovered in herself the well-known affliction of the contemporary human being that is called civilization [*Zivilisation*]. It is a frustrating circumstance, full of soap, wireless waves, the arrogant symbolic language of mathematical and chemical formulae, national economics, experimental research and the human inability to live in simple but sublime community . . . [C]ivilization thus meant everything that her mind [*Geist*] could not cope with. (24; 102–3/116–17/105)

In this passage Musil deftly shows how Diotima's failure to "harmonize" the conflicting voices and draw them out of dyads into more general concourse conditions her embrace of the commonplaces of contemporary cultural criticism, with its allegation that modernization was destroying Germanic culture. "Civilization" has brought specialization and a division of intellectual labor that itself produces more fragmentation: from Diotima's drawing room perspective, the problem is not the historical accretion of incommensurable languages of reflection but the proliferation of life-destroying and internally conflicted rationality, the enemy of holistic traditional culture.

The narrative strategy that relativizes Diotima's idealist views as a product of her particular social situation is crucial to Musil's project of promoting readerly self-reflection. Such satirical representations of characters' intellectual motivations assure that in scenes where characters interact whose different experiences and interests appear to converge in shared vocabularies of reflection, the reader's attention is directed toward interpreting the systematic significance of this convergence for the intellectual project of the novel. By continually emphasizing that the same words mean different things to different people, Musil demands that the reader confront the epistemic and ethical dilemmas basic to the modern rhetoric of reflection on subjective experience. Nothing can be taken at face value, no point of view is privileged, and the meaning of the novel resides not in the story but in the reflection it aims to promote about the fact that, in Musil's own words, "the story of this novel comes down to the fact that the story which is supposed to be told in it is not told" (GW 5, 1937).

Because the man without qualities is unable to experience anything without skeptically distancing himself from the process, his perspective often converges with the narrator's reflections on the global circumstance of thought in the modern world. This feature of the novel has often led commentators to identify Musil himself with the man without qualities. However, such a privileging of the ideas of the man without qualities runs the risk of forgetting that he is a character whose raison-d'être must be found in the project of the novel as a whole: the reader is meant to reflect on the character's reflections rather than to adopt them or to identify directly with him.

This having been said, let us consider a passage from a later chapter to which we shall have occasion to return. In it, Musil seems to use his protagonist's reflections on the way modernization has transformed intellectual life to comment directly on the meaning and value of thought after the industrial revolution. Sitting in a streetcar, the man without qualities muses: "A thought that does not have a practical purpose is surely a not quite decent secret occupation." Times have changed since "Schiller's day." Rather than looking up to one who has

> noble and exalted questions in his breast ... nowadays, the prevailing feeling is that there is something not right with such a person, if it does not happen to be his profession and his source of income. Obviously, one has divided the thing up a different way. One has taken certain questions out of the human heart. One has set up for the breeding of high-flying thoughts a kind of poultry-farm known as philosophy, theology, or literature, where in their own way they multiply beyond counting; and that is quite good, for in the face of such expansion nobody needs to reproach himself anymore with not being able to concern himself with them personally. (83; 358–59/II66/389)

With its satirical opposition to the ban on "impractical" thinking, this passage signals Musil's allegiance to the Schillerian vision of literature as serious play engaging the basic questions of human existence. He demands a reader adequate to the man without qualities, who "in his respect for professionalness and specialization" attempted to affirm this division of intellectual labor, yet "still permitted himself to think, although he was no professional philosopher" (83; 359/II66/389).

Even more lucidly than his cousin Diotima, the protagonist recognizes that the growth of specialized knowledge and expertise has isolated individuals and rendered them unable to communicate. Within the diegesis, the global breakdown of the common languages that once gave orientation to action shapes the ineffective collective attempt to find a "great idea" around which to unify the "parallel action"—but it is also crucial for what happens to the man without qualities himself, who is in search of a way of living that can engage his unrealized potentials. Thus Musil's novel poses the question: What does it mean to think—to live—in a world that "has taken certain questions out of the human heart"? By representing the effects of the democratization of skepticism in the consciousness of his stable of characters, Musil's novel fosters reflection on the dilemmas of the modern subject: his narrative strategy forces the reader to "reproach himself . . . with not being able to concern himself with such questions" and thus to think about thinking historically.

As a response to dilemmas that are constitutive of the modern rhetoric of reflection on subjective experience, Musil's literary project can be situated in relation to my critique of the way boredom has been theorized. As the "fundamental mood" of the modern subject, the attitude toward existence that results from the rationalization of experience and the fragmentation of reflection in modernity, boredom both expresses and occludes the individual's disconnection from the fundamental questions of human existence. The literature on boredom (unlike the literature of boredom) fails to link these "sociological" and "philosophical" dimensions to gain purchase on the relationship between the experience of boredom and the historical construction of this reflective category. Even the thinkers considered in Part II, who recognized the exemplarity of boredom as an historically constituted mode of experience, failed to examine the language in which the experience is represented as a cultural and historical phenomenon. I have been arguing that such a self-reflexive illumination of the modern rhetoric of reflection on subjective malaise and thereby of boredom's historical and philosophical significance is a necessary propadeutic to the emergence of viable new languages of reflection. By representing the world of democratized skepticism as a world of being without qualities, Musil establishes a perspective that can illuminate the relationship between lived experience and the historical development of the discourse of reflection in which it is embedded. However, unfortunately, it turns out that this effort to develop a new language for expressing the vicissitudes of subjective experience in modernity is tantamount to an analysis of why such a project cannot succeed. It is no historical accident that Musil's novel remains incomplete.

Beyond Boredom: Life as Experiment

The Man without Qualities is set just before World War I in the imperial
capital of "Kakania,"[9] a city that the narrator playfully introduces as a refuge
from modernity. It was a place entirely unlike the "socially compelled vision"
of the ideal modern metropolis, a "super-American city where, stop-watch in
hand, everyone rushes about or stands still," where "each person has nothing
but quite definite tasks," where "tension and relaxation, activity and love are
kept meticulously separate in time and are weighed out according to formu-
lae arrived at in extensive laboratory work." In this other, real, city "in the
good old days when there was still an Imperial Austria," one could escape the
"unceasing motion" in which "we are borne along" with a speed entirely out
of human control toward such a super-rationalized existence. When gripped
by "homesickness for being kept at a standstill, not evolving, being stuck,
turning back to a point that lies before the wrong fork" one could in those
days escape the relentless tempo of transformations constituting modern life,
"leave the train of time [*der Zug der Zeit*], climb into an ordinary train of an
ordinary railway and travel back home" (8; 31–32/30–31/26–27).[10] This elegy to
the uniqueness of good old Vienna stands in marked contrast to the narrator's remarks in the third paragraph of the novel:

> Like all big cities, it consisted of irregularity, change, sliding forward . . . of a great
> rhythmic pulse and the perpetual discord and dislocation of all its contending
> rhythms, and on the whole resembled a bubble boiling in a vessel consisting of the
> durable matter of buildings, laws, regulations, and historical traditions. (1; 10/4/4)

The satiric force of the narrator's paean to the distinctiveness of what had
initially appeared as a city without qualities becomes clearer if we consider
how the images in the passage resonate with the discourse on boredom as it
emerged in the nineteenth century.

[9]Musil's scatological nickname plays on the abbreviation for the dual monarchy: as both an
empire and a kingdom, as *kaiserlich und königlich*, the state was Ka-Ka-nia.

[10]This passage resonates with the tradition that regards the final years of the Austro-Hungarian Empire as a prime locus for indulging this sort of melancholic longing. As we shall see,
Musil's efforts to establish an alternative perspective on the modern phenomena that so often
produced pessimism and resignation among his contemporaries are of particular note. On Musil
in his historical context, see Luft. On Austrian modernity see Beller, Janik and Toulmin, Le Rider,
and Schorske. Johnston offers a broader intellectual and social history of Austro-Hungarian developments from 1848 to 1938. Russell Berman's essay, "The Vienna Fascination" (Berman 1989,
204–41) raises important issues about the contemporary cultural status of the fascination with fin-
de-siècle Viennese culture. Two recent publications on the wider Austro-Hungarian cultural space
are worthy of note: Péter Hanák, *The Garden and the Workshop*, and Scott Spector, *Prague Territories*.

As we saw in Chapter 3, the experience of boredom had literalized the metonymic identification between progress and a speeding train which, though debased to a cliché, is still with us. Boredom was experienced as a product both of the perception-blurring speed and of the totally regulated temporal framework of rail travel. Although by the early twentieth century, trains themselves had long been an accustomed part of the landscape, the metaphoric force of the identification remained, and so did the dual link to subjective disaffection. In this passage, the time-train that rushes society ineluctably along toward that inhuman ideal, the Americanized city of the future, produces "homesickness," a longing for a world of stable meanings. Such a world is opposed to the monotonous, hyper-rationalized and etymologically inspired society that is perhaps to come, where "a genial whole" can be constructed out of "a sum of reduced individuals." Musil's narrator represents the melancholic desire for simpler forms of life as a response to the threat to subjectivity posed by this vision, at once nightmare and prophecy, of an existence so busy that even love must be regulated scientifically—a world in which boredom is universal.

While recognizing the melancholic desire to escape the conditions of modern existence that theorists of boredom often subtly substituted for the resignation that characterizes the experience itself, Musil by no means endorses this homesick longing for stasis. Surface appearances to the contrary, Imperial Vienna was not in fact a safe refuge from the speeding train of history. As he remarked in a diary entry from 1920 that we will consider in more detail later on, "this grotesque Austria is nothing other than an especially clear case of the modern world" (TB 353–54). The description of Kakania as refuge must therefore be read with an ironic grain of salt. If throughout the novel both narrator and protagonist attempt to keep an open mind about the quality of life in the totally regulated society of the future, it is because Musil saw quite clearly how the malaise of modernity already permeated the enforced standstill that was Austrian prewar culture, with its discourse on the loss of meaning, with its famous crisis of subjectivity and decline of traditional morality, with its spectacularly senseless politics. By 1913 it was already too late to step off the train of time, even if central Europeans had not yet recognized the fact.

One who, like the protagonist, actually did go home to this city would necessarily be disappointed in his desire to escape into a contemplative standstill. In the opinion of the narrator, it was not backwardness but a sort of philosophically moderate modernity ("there was speed [*Tempo*], but not too much speed") that made Kakania "in so many things, without recognition, a model" (8; 32/31/28). Most importantly, it was in the ferment of nationalities that made up the dual monarchy that the characteristically modern instability of identity first gained political significance.

> In that state, every human being's dislike of every other human being's attempts to get ahead—a dislike in which today we are all agreed—crystallized early and, so to speak, assumed the form of a sublimated ceremonial that could have had enormous consequences had its evolution not been prematurely cut short by a catastrophe. (8; 34/33/30)

The "sublimated ceremonial" of mutual dislike corresponds to Simmel's account of metropolitan blaséness as an affective response to excessive nervous stimulation in general and excessive proximity to anonymous others in particular. As we have seen, for Simmel this attitude masked the hostility provoked in people by these defining psychological circumstances of modern existence.[11] Although Musil's depiction of Kakanian society abounds in actual streetcars as well as metaphoric trains, his central image of the "sublimated ceremonial" of mutual hostility and feigned indifference is the "Parallel Action." In it, feudal and religious ideals intermingle with the most modern social tendencies, and the whole moves forward toward an end that remains uncertain to the participants. The final meeting at the close of Part 3[12] ends when a nominally pacifist resolution—"Anyone should be prepared to be killed for his own ideas, but one who induces men to die for ideas not their own is a murderer" (Part 3, 38; 1035/III438/1124)—brings on a social cataclysm that ominously portends the coming war.[13]

In Simmel's account, the metropolis's historic contribution to spiritual life was to be the site of the modern individual's self-assertion of uniqueness in the face of the levelling tendencies of collective life. Thus Simmel's theory of metropolitan life sublated the mutual hostility at the basis of modern social organization into a neo-romantic understanding of the subject whose very individuality was forged in response to the conditions of everyday life under high capitalism. Publishing after Freud's major works on civilization, Musil

---

[11] This attitude had its sensory correlate in an adaptation necessary for mass transportation. In his *Sociology*, Simmel remarks that "before the development of busses, trains and streetcars in the nineteenth century, people were actually unable to tolerate" having to see others "without being able to speak with them." This circumstance, he says, surely contributes to the problematic of the modern feeling for life, to the feeling of disorientation in the collective life, to isolation . . ." (GSG 11, 727). Interestingly, Blaise Pascal was the founder (with Herzog von Roannez) of an omnibus-line (*carosses à cinques sols*)—the "first urban transport enterprise" (Mittelstraß, *Encyclopaedie Philosophie und Wissenschaftsgeschichte*, 67).

[12] That is, at the end of the portion of the novel Musil actually published during his lifetime.

[13] Compare also Part 2, chapter 120, where the confusing politics of the Parallel Action leads to nationalist demonstrations and Ulrich is mistaken for the political figure behind the curtains.

interprets the problem of modern identity in a far less romantic fashion.[14] Feelings of mutual hostility are not the condition for individual self-transcendence but form the foundation of the modern state. The passage continues:

> For not only was aversion toward one's fellow-citizens intensified there into a feeling of community [*Gemeinschaftsgefühl*]; even mistrust toward one's own person and destiny assumed the character of profound self-certainty.[15] In this land one always acted—sometimes indeed to the most extreme degrees of passion and its consequences—differently from how one thought, or thought differently than one acted. (8; 34/33–34/30)

Kakania, far from being the utopian *Gemeinschaft* that was the object of melancholic desire, was an archetypically modern place, where identity was based on fragmentation. The problem of meaning and its correlate, the problem of political legitimacy, were reflected in the "sublimated ceremonial" of the internally conflicted Kakanian state. There modern bureaucracy, bourgeois parliamentarism, and feudal privilege coexisted without coalescing and were superimposed on the national conflicts that would ultimately lead to World War I.

Thus although Musil's narrator is clearly post-Freudian, his account of the internal conflicts of modern identity is grounded not in unconscious motives but in socio-historical circumstances.[16] In a society where skepticism

---

[14]My point is that this context is important for examining the psychologically inflected analysis of modernity Musil incorporates into his work, his hostility to the Freudian conception of the unconscious notwithstanding. For examples of the latter, see "Der bedrohte Oedipus" in GW 7, 528–30 and the posthumously published remarks in his planned collection of aphorisms entitled "Aus einem Rapial" (GW 7, 824–25). See also Part 3, chapter 38 (from the posthumous publications), "Agathe stößt zu ihrem Mißvergnügen auf einen geschichtlichen Abriß der Gefühlspsychologie" (GW 4, 1138–46) and the note from 1938 "Zu den Kapiteln über Gefuhlspsychologie: das ist nicht Psychologie (in der Endabsicht), sondern Weltbeschreibung" (GW 5, 1941).

[15]A diary entry from the late thirties extends this analysis into contemporary politics: "What prospects hate (e.g. anti-semitism) has can best be seen in the fact that even self-hate, pessimism, can enchant the world" (TB , 974).

[16]In a resumé from the twenties reproduced in Frisé's meticulously documented edition of his diaries, Musil sketches out his view of the historical background to the spiritual circumstance described in the passage just cited (TB II, 1147–48).

> . . . In 1870 a vast European organism constituted itself. Until 1890 it lived off of [*aufzehren*] the received basis of ideas [*Ideenfond*]: was virtuously in battle against speculative mania [*Gründertum*], post-war intoxication and so on, until all the ideas were empty. Then around 1890 came the spiritual crisis, lamentation of one's own soul. This attempt miscarried. The idea of a saviour that emerged around 1910 was already resignation, similarly the turn to religion and soul. The synthesis soul-ratio miscarried.
>
> That leads in a direct line to war.
>
> German history as paradigm of world history.
>
> Germany as model for the world, as world-savior [*Weltheiland*].
>
> Must therefore in all irony be written with a certain sympathy.

is a way of life, the fragmented individual is the mirror of the state. Further on in the chapter the narrator makes this even more explicit. Kakania

> was the state that was somehow only going along with itself, in it one was nega-tively free, constantly sensing the insufficient grounds of one's existence and lapped by the great fantasy of what had not happened, or at least not yet irrevo-cably happened. . . . (8; 35/34–35/33–34)

The man without qualities, in whom "the sense of possibility" predominates over "the sense of reality," epitomizes the radical skepticism that character-izes this land of negative freedom. For him, thought and action diverge as a matter of course. Like the country itself, he is so permeated with boredom and disaffection that his malaise has been refined into a philosophical atti-tude toward life as something that "just happens."

Like the land of which he is a native, Musil's protagonist is both exem-plary and unusual; his extra-ordinariness consists most of all in his relentless (or perhaps reckless) self-reflection upon the state of his own existence as a modern human being. That is, it is Ulrich's consciousness of being a man without qualities, not his being without qualities *per se,* that distinguishes him from his fellows—as Musil remarks in a notebook, "of course they are all without qualities but in Ulrich it is somehow visible" (1831/1729). On the protagonist's considered view, his state expresses the historical dilemma of the modern subject—being without qualities is a consequence of the Coper-nican revolution having arrived at the self, which henceforth appears to be not an essence or center but only a negative, reactive formation.[17] Nonethe-less, the recognition that he is a man without qualities has produced a crisis in his own life.

At thirty-two he has already been an officer, an engineer, and a mathema-tician without ever being able truly to identify himself with any of these pro-fessions. We encounter him not long after an unceremonious departure from the university, a flight that occurred in the wake of the following sud-

---

[17]We shall return to Ulrich's reflections on identity later on. In chapter 8, the narrator articu-lates the same view through an elaborate warning to the reader not to interpret the peculiarities of collective life in Kakania as expressions either of "charm" or "weakness" proper to the Austrian character. "For the inhabitant of a country has at least nine characters—a professional, a national, a civic, a class, a geographical, a gender, a conscious, an unconscious, and perhaps even a private character [*Charakter*]; he unifies them in himself, but they dissolve him, and he is actually noth-ing but a small basin washed out by all these trickling streams, a basin into which they trickle and which they desert again to join with other little streams to fill another basin. Thus every inhabi-tant of the earth also has a tenth character, and this is nothing other than the passive fantasy of spaces unfilled; it permits the person everything, with one exception: he may not take seriously what his at least nine other characters do and what happens to them; in other words, the very thing that ought to be the filling of him" (8; 34/34/30).

den and disheartening revelation: "With wonderful clarity he saw in himself all the abilities and qualities favored by his time—with the exception of moneymaking, which he didn't need—but the possibility of their application had escaped him" (13; 47/49/44). It is August 1913, and he is taking a "year's holiday from his life" to devote himself to reckoning and exploration. He is an outsider, but one of a particular sort: with a logician's faith in scientific methods ironically tempered by his visceral awareness of the limitations of reason, Ulrich[18] embodies the dilemma of the modern "enlightened" subject faced with the disenchanted world. The self-imposed task of his vacation from life is to come to terms with the purpose of his existence as a denizen of that world, "to seek an appropriate application for his abilities" under conditions where action seems inherently futile (13; 47/49/44).

He is hampered in this effort by his alienation from himself and from the world in which he lives—a habit of feeling which is basic to his being a man without qualities. Nonetheless, he sees himself as possessing "fragments of a new way of thinking and feeling" (13; 47/49/44) based on the extension of scientific principles into life as a whole.

> It was his opinion that in this century, together with everything human, one was on an expedition, which required as a matter of pride that one oppose all useless questions with a 'not yet,' and lead life with provisional principles [*Interimsgrundsätzen*], but in consciousness of a goal that will be reached by those who come later. (13; 46/48/43)

While his experimentalism can be seen as an expression of his boredom and disaffection with the state of the world, it is equally an attempt to locate new human potentials within the process of modernization.

Ulrich's youthful sense of himself as a means toward some higher future end had translated thus far mainly into the ironic and negating attitude toward life which he had maintained throughout his three attempts "to become a man of significance." A deep affinity between the discourse on boredom and his experimentalist affirmation of disenchantment is expressed in the protagonist's Nietzschean tendency to "live against himself": "With the pride of a person who is called to action, he led the life of another person who has made of his inclinations and abilities more or less ordinary, practical and social use" despite his lack of respect for all this meant (40; 151–52/176/160–61). However, the realization that his naïve sense of purpose was fading with immersion in regular bourgeois existence had prompted Ulrich to drop everything and move back home to Vienna. Through a vacation from life that affirmed his boredom with the process of becoming a man of

---

[18] In early drafts Musil's protagonist was called "Anders," literally: "Other."

socially recognizable importance, the man without qualities was seeking a
meaningful way of living, one that would allow him to escape his disaffection
by fostering the utopian dimension of his experimentalism.

Musil's protagonist is in pursuit of a mode of relating to his experience
appropriate to a world where the traditional bases of meaning have dissolved.
As a figure, he conjoins the impulses of Enlightenment and romanticism.
The man without qualities is in search of a new understanding of the human
soul that can make the fragmentation and impersonality of the modern self
the basis for a new, self-consciously modern, yet spiritually integrated form
of existence. In the first two parts of the novel, his efforts to maintain an experimental attitude toward life lead him further and further into the detached and cynical indifference of one who refuses to act. However, in Part 3,
after the death of his father, the same experimentalism moves him away from
idle intellectual, sexual, and social games into the cultivation of a terrestrial
mysticism that is linked to his attempt to forge a spiritual union with his
(formerly) "lost sister." At the same time, he is still plagued by the radical
skepticism that emerges out of the rationalistic attitude he turns upon self
and world alike. Its consequence is a disaffection so pervasive that, asked at
one point what he would do if he were put in charge of the world, he responds: "Abolish reality" (69; 289/343/312).

Ulrich thus resembles the radically bored, decadent figures who populated the novels and the streets at the fin-de-siècle. Yet the man without
qualities is philosophically opposed to what Charles Baudelaire called the
dandy's aesthetic "religion" of "elegance and originality" and to his blasé attitude toward life. Baudelaire's hero of modern life, who cultivates the air of
an "unemployed Hercules," deliberately withdrawing from the hectic pace of
modern life and surrounding himself with the "symbols of his aristocratic
superiority of mind,"[19] maintains an anachronistic attitude toward both self
and world. The man without qualities wants to "eliminate reality" not via
flight into personal eccentricity but by embracing a scientific relation to the
world. Rather than retreating into interiority, he wants to reform his life in
accord with the spirit of modern science, which constantly transforms all
stable "realities," including the supposedly inherent "qualities" of the self, in
new and unexpected ways.

This aspiration embodies the legacy of one of the dandy's arch-enemies,
the man of science:

> He was less scientifically than humanly in love with science. He saw that, in all the
> problems where science considered itself responsible, it thought differently from

---

[19] Baudelaire, OC II 710–12; English: Baudelaire 1964, 27–29.

ordinary people. If for 'scientific attitude' [*wissenschaftliche Anschauung*] one were to read 'attitude to life' [*Lebensanschauung*], for 'hypothesis' 'attempt' and for 'truth' 'action,' then there would be no respected natural scientist or mathematician whose life's work did not in courage and revolutionary power far outmatch the greatest deeds in history . . . . And Ulrich felt: 'People simply don't know this; they have no glimmer how one can already think. If one could teach them to think in a new way, they would also live differently. (11; 40–41/41/37)

Ulrich's notion that "reality" should be abolished is based on the intuition that human attachment to the here and now constitutes an obstacle to the realization of the world's possibilities. While Baudelaire's dandy clings to the supposedly timeless "aristocratic" value of personal originality, Musil's protagonist advocates not being, but becoming. Through affirming his hypothetical state of being a man without qualities and attempting to live as a harbinger of new ways of existing that have yet to take form, he hopes to achieve a renewal of meaning.

An argument could be made that boredom was the cause not just of Ulrich's disillusionment with each of his "attempts at becoming a man of importance" but more generally of the disaffection with life that makes him a man without qualities. On this reading, Musil's *Man without Qualities* is a philosophical novel situated in the existentialist tradition identified by Reinhard Kuhn, a tradition in which ennui distinguishes the genuine protagonist of modern life who wrests his individuality from the confusion and inauthenticity of modern existence. Such a reading would emphasize the relationship between boredom and the "other condition" of thoroughgoing significance which Ulrich comes to pursue in the third part of the novel in concert with his even more disaffected sister, Agathe. Having "discovered" one another upon the death of their father, the siblings who have each existed as bystanders in their own lives attempt to transform this detachment from self into its positive counterpart—the Other Condition—and with each other's help to transcend their ontological solitude through a mutual existence in love.[20]

However, the quasi-existentialist transcendence of the "Other Condition" remains tenuous and unstable, and Ulrich, with his contempt for mere writers, explicitly opposes the idea that he should turn his energies toward a literary or artistic self-overcoming of his disaffection with his life. The man without qualities is no romantic individualist who longs to escape from the arid fields of science into the timeless groves of philosophical experience. In-

---

[20] For a differentiated account of the "epic function" of love in the novel, see Freese, "Verinnerte Wirklichkeit." Zingel explores the connections between this theme and Musil's critical agenda regarding "the world of its like happens."

stead, the novel chronicles his efforts during what is only meant to be a vacation from life to locate the possibility of a new form of *historical* existence, one that can make the destructive impulse of ennui—which, as Baudelaire wrote, longed "to engulf the world with a yawn"—into a constructive principle. However justly the *Man without Qualities* can be placed in the religious and philosophical tradition that sees boredom as a perpetual point of transit between the banality of ordinary life and the bliss of eternal meaning, Musil is a profoundly historical thinker who emphasized the cultural context of the emotional and intellectual phenomena about which he wrote.

From the point of view of the artistic project of the novel, it would thus perhaps be more accurate to argue along sociological lines that boredom was the effect, rather than the cause, of Ulrich's being a man without qualities. As an enlightened subject faced with a disenchanted world, his tendency to boredom rendered him not unique but typical. For Musil, "being without qualities" was a symptom of the fragmentation of the world, a metaphorical expression for the circumstance of the modern subject. Thus it seems in the spirit of Simmel's tragedy of culture that Ulrich muses: "Every advance [of spirit] is a gain in the particular and a separation on the whole; that is, an increase in power leads to a progressive increase in impotence, and one can't let up" (40; 154/179/163). On this reading, what distinguishes Musil's project from the aestheticist and existentialist invocations of the discourse on boredom is his focus on humanity's not being able to stop: his is a world where the resources of critique must be rethought in accord with the inevitably fragmented nature of modern experience.

However, rather than condemning the modern subject to anomie, blaséness, and impotence as a result of the overwhelming nature of "objective culture," Musil's novel presents the process of depersonalization that characterizes modern life as opening up the possibility of a new, experimental attitude toward one's own existence that affirms the ineluctable transformations of modernization. Like Nietzsche, he holds it necessary to embrace the disenchantment that is inseparable from the progress of spirit, and like Hegel, he conceives not of an integral individuality but of a conceptual universality as the reference point for modern experience. By representing the state of "being without qualities" as an historically determined phenomenon that nonetheless has transformative spiritual potential, Musil synthesizes philosophical and sociological perspectives on modern existence.

The chorus of voices raised against the life-destroying effects of scientific progress and in favor of irrationalism echo ever-louder in the later parts of the novel. Ulrich's skeptical detachment and cool analysis embody the positive potential of the dialectic of enlightenment, which lies in an ability to recognize the constructedness of one's own identity without thereby coming to see it as transcended. Ironically, it seems to be the man without qualities who knows who he "is"; his bored attitude toward his life appears as a permutation of philosophical skepticism. That is not to say that Musil intended to offer Ulrich's mode of skeptical distance from his own identity as a viable solution to the dilemmas of modern existence. His notebooks reveal that the protagonist's attempts to synthesize science with mysticism, to discover new forms of experience that can satisfy both the emotional and intellectual craving for meaning that characterizes the disaffection of the modern subject, are doomed to fail.

The philosophical object of the novel cannot therefore be located immanently but must be identified in its rhetorical strategy. *The Man without Qualities* is a work addressed to an audience struggling with the same issues that define Ulrich's quest for a meaningful modern way of life, an audience filled with malaise at the present and anxiety about the future, an audience for whom boredom is a quotidian rather than an heroic experience. In creating a protagonist whose character was defined as being without qualities, Musil thematized the dissolution of the self under the pressures of modern urban existence. At the same time, *The Man without Qualities* identifies the fate of the modern subject as a locus of possibilities for the transformation and renewal of human existence. By making Ulrich a mystically inclined rationalist who wanted to live his life as an experiment, Musil turned the impersonality of human personality in modernity into an occasion for innovative reflection on the alienation between self and world upon which the boredom discourse is predicated. The next section examines the strategy of representation by which Musil's novel escaped the impasse inscribed in the discourse on boredom, transforming the modern rhetoric of reflection on subjective experience to interpret the malaise of the modern subject both historically and philosophically.

"An Immanent Depiction of the Time": Musil's Historical Irony

The Man without Qualities begins on "a beautiful day in August in the year 1913" (1; 1/9/3)—that is, just one year before the outbreak of World War I. The plot, such as it is, centers on the struggle to define the theme of the "Parallel Action," a civic and cultural campaign of which Ulrich becomes the General Secretary. The idea is to make "the whole of the year 1918 into a jubilee year" celebrating the seventy-year reign of the Austrian "Emperor of Peace" and thereby to outdo the Germans, who are planning to celebrate the thirtieth anniversary of Kaiser Wilhem II's acession to the throne on the fifteenth of July, 1918. The source of this paralyzingly vague idea of "a great patriotic action" is Count Leinsdorf, an aristocrat who is blessed with "a complete absence of doubts" about the rectitude of his paternalistic view of modern politics.

> [T]he peoples [*Völker*] of Europe were all whirling along in the vortex of a materialistic democracy, and what hovered before him was a sublime symbol that would be to them at once an admonition and a sign to return to the fold. It was clear to him that something must be done that would put Austria at the head of all, so that this 'splendid demonstration of the Austrian spirit' should become a 'milestone' for the whole world and thereby help it to find the way back to its true nature. (21; 88–89/100/89–90)

A diffuse patriotic fervor notwithstanding, those who engage themselves as members of the committee whose task, in the words of Diotima, is to "create an organization to prepare the way for the formation of suggestions leading towards this goal" (42; 171–72/201/182) are entirely unable to agree upon any concrete form to express the great idea of the "true Austria." Their plots and meetings produce the endless stream of indeterminate talk about the spiritual crisis of modernity that, in its intersection with the protagonist's philosophical reflections on modern life, forms the novel's true object of interest.

From the reader's perspective, the chaotic doldrums of Robert Musil's Kakania appear as the preliminaries of war. However, obsessed with cultural decline and the moral and intellectual predicament of modern existence, none of the characters involved in the "Parallel Action" see it coming. Musil's ironic representation of Viennese high society in 1913 underlines that politicians, diplomats, and imperial army officers were as incapable as poets and society ladies of recognizing the impending catastrophe. Only the reader, conscious of the dramatic date, forges the inevitable link between the serio-comic search for a unifying "great idea" that can give form to Austria's cultural mission and the silently approaching debacle. Historical irony is a principle of construction for Musil, who plays implicitly and explicitly on the reader's awareness that the innocent earnestness of this world will soon be eclipsed in an explosion of archaic passions. Indeed, the anonymity of death in the no man's land between the trenches would give rise to another sort of Man without Qualities, the "Unknown Soldier" who would be commemorated for the first time after the Great War.[21]

---

[21] A series of notes under the heading "Schlußteil" (Conclusion) begins: "Umfassendes Problem: Krieg/Seinesgleichen führt zum Krieg!/Krieg als: Wie ein großes Ereignis entsteht. Alle Linien münden in den Krieg. Jeder begrüßt ihn auf seine Weise./Das religiöse Element im Kriegsausbruch./Tat, Gefühl, und andere Zustand fallen in eins./Jemand bemerkt: das war es, was die

Musil's ironic mode of narration entails that the reader cannot infer a stable point of view on the characters and events that comprise the story, but this uncertainty is not, as in Flaubert, an artistic end in itself. *Madame Bovary* uses irony to expose the fatuousness of Emma's strivings to make her life meaningful and exciting in the terms of dime-novel narratives. Dissecting the modern "moeurs du province" from the perspective of a disenchanted skepticism, Flaubert's irony turns banality into an aesthetic object while rigorously refusing to provide the reader with any positive alternative to Emma's ennui. *The Man without Qualities* invites the reader to engage with the narrator in historical reflection upon their common implication in the circumstances that produce the protagonist's skeptical retreat from reality and make the idea of "living life as literature" a conscious temptation for him. For Musil, irony is a method for developing sympathetic comprehension of the spiritual crisis that led to the First World War.[22] He turns the discrepancy of historical consciousness between audience and characters to account through a narrator who narrates as the reader reads, from a time after the war.

Although he is generally far from obtrusive, functioning as a nearly transparent presence in the novel, Musil's narrator occasionally speaks in his own voice to remind the reader of the coming war, thereby casting a strange light on the act of reading itself.[23] Not only do remarks such as "the time was on the move. . . . One just didn't know what it was moving towards" (2; 13/8/7) or a casual reference to "those national struggles that justifiably aroused Europe's curiosity and are today completely misrepresented" (8; 34/33/29–30) redouble the reader's awareness of the historical futility of the Parallel Action. By shifting the focus onto the fictional nature of the narrative, such comments tend to undermine the reader's unreflective involvement in the

Parallelaktion immer gesucht hat. Es ist die gefundene große Idee." (GW V, 1902; I have spelled out Musil's abbreviations). I cite this passage in English on page 384.

[22]The shift from the romantic irony of self-reflection to a more historically engaged use of the trope in this period is of course not limited to Musil alone. See especially Fussell.

[23]A significant portion of the secondary literature tends to equate the narrator's voice with that of the author. This assumption finds support in a notebook entry from the nineteen-twenties in which Musil reflects on his mode of narrating "the story of my friend": "I narrate. This I is however not a fictitious person, but the novelist. A informed, bitter, disillusioned human being. Me. . . . This I can't experience anything and endures everything. . . . without acting, incapable of coming to a clear insight and to an activity, corresponding to today's diffuse, incomprehensible situation. With reflection from my point of view. As told by a last, wise, bitter, resigned survivor from the catacombs" (TB 579). While this passage stems from an earlier stage in the genesis of his novel, Musil's narrative technique in the published work seems consistent with this characterization. However, our interest will be focused primarily on the linguistic texture of Musil's mode of narration, and I will treat the vexed question of his relationship to Ulrich at that level.

story of this attempt to create a meaningful manifestation of "true Austri-anness." The reader's attention is directed toward the vicissitudes of the tell-ing: not only does nothing much happen in this novel of ideas, but the ironic awareness that the Parallel Action is doomed to end in the horrors of war underlines the allegorical nature of the plot.

For Musil, the issue was how to realize what he saw as literature's utopian potential of providing "partial solutions" to the ultimately insoluble dilem-mas of human existence (1837). In the *Man without Qualities*, the intermit-tent, ironic shift of emphasis from *histoire* to *discours* serves a constructive purpose that points beyond the sphere of the text itself. As Musil wrote in a notebook, "The immanent depiction of the time that led to the catastrophe must be the real substance of the story, the context to which it can always retreat as well as the thought that is implicit in everything" (1855/1748). Al-though what happened in fact led to the war, historical inevitability is a far cry from logical or metaphysical necessity: Musil's "immanent depiction" serves to emphasize ambiguities and thus to reveal alternative, unrealized possibilities in the material of history. He by no means underestimated the diffiulty of this task: Musil planned to end his novel, like Thomas Mann's *The Magic Mountain,* with his protagonist marching off to war. This conclu-sion was to be the equivalent of Ulrich's suicide, an expression of the failure of the man without qualities to turn his intermittent personal synthesis of rationality and mysticism into an intersubjectively sustainable way of living.[24]

This projected conclusion and the pervasive futility of the Parallel Action notwithstanding, the narrative does not reinforce a generalized cynicism about the blurry idealism that had animated Europe's plunge into the Great War. Instead, *The Man without Qualities* attempts to awaken a sense that something else could have happened, that the cultural foment of the prewar era had multiple possibilities. However, it does so not by directly represent-ing a possible alternative but rather by the indirect method of depicting the unsuccessful struggles of a modern man without qualities to find a mean-ingful way of living when he has "lost his grip on the primitive epical" form (122; 650/II436/709) that makes it possible to weave one's life into a mean-ingful narrative. On my reading, then, the "utopian" dimension of the novel does not reside in the shift from the public realm of the Parallel Action in the first two parts into the private pursuit of a mystical "other condition" in the third.[25] Musil's notes make clear that he also planned to show the foundering

---

[24]There are numerous references to this thematic nexus in Musil's notebooks. See for example 1904, 1831.

[25]As Hösle puts it, "The wish for synthesis that finds expression in the relationship between Ulrich and Agathe also throws a light on Musil's irony, which wants not so much to destroy as to

of Ulrich's attempt to invent a way of living with his sister that expressed their sense of having a single soul in two bodies, of being each other's lost "other halves."[26] He was not so politically naïve as to believe that the collective crisis of meaning could be resolved in the private realm of subjective experience, through a revival of mysticism, incestuous sexuality, or some combination of the two. As the volumes unfold, the rhetorical structure of the novel, in which nothing really happens even as the cry for action ("something must happen") grows ever shriller, serves to exacerbate the reader's sense of irony.

By frustrating the reader's desire to engage with a story, both the pointlessness of the Parallel Action in Part 2 and the oddly insubstantial efforts by Ulrich and his sister in Part 3 underline that the protagonist's dilemma is the result of a loss that cannot be considered personal. As we have already noted, for Musil "the story of this novel comes down to the fact that the story which is supposed to be told in it is not told" (GW V, 1937). Through its counterfactual mode, *The Man without Qualities* illustrates that the passage into industrialized destruction was the de facto response to a crisis of meaning that was ultimately ethical and epistemological as well as political in nature. Musil's novel aims to awaken a perspective for reflection that locates utopian potential in the historical dilemma of the modern subject—within the world in which skepticism has been democratized.

For Musil, irony is more than a stylistic device, for it makes possible a relation to the world that is at once empathetic and clear-sighted and a mode of writing that is at once descriptive and analytical. In a word, Musil's irony is a mode of critique; *The Man without Qualities* aspires to represent the world it portrays so thoroughly that the inner truth of the time gives itself up to the reader's understanding. Thus for Musil, irony is by no means equivalent to setting himself up in judgment over the world.

> Irony is: representing a cleric in such a way that along with him you have also captured a Bolshevist. Presenting a blockhead so that the author suddenly feels: that's partly me too. This kind of irony, constructive irony, is fairly unknown in Germany today. It is the connectedness among things from which it emerges naked. One thinks of irony as ridicule and jeering. (1939/1764)

In what Musil calls the "constructive" form of irony, author and audience alike are not raised above what occurs but rather are self-reflexively impli-

---

direct away from the surface of things and thereby open the way to a side of them that is usually neglected . . . he regards ironic behavior only as a provisional but insufficient solution, since the world itself is not yet ripe for seriousness" (90).

[26] One part of the fragmentary *Nachlaß* has their idyll disintegrating on a trip to Italy in a paroxysm of boredom.

cated in it through a sympathy for what is depicted. This sympathy is established through strategies of representation that underline how the figures in the novel, like the reader and the author, are struggling with a common historical situation. A thoroughgoing irony reveals the lineaments of the time; it allows Musil to make "the thought that is implicit in everything" the immanent connection between what is represented and the impending "catastrophe."

For Musil, the representation of "Kakania" is the ironic gesture through which his reflections on the state of Europe before the First World War become constructive. In 1920, a lengthy diary entry begins: "The time: everything that revealed itself in the war and after the war was already there beforehand. . . . The time just decomposed like an abscess. In the prewar novel one must show everything already below the surface." Musil goes on to mention key elements of what would become the world of his novel ("Parliamentarism and Court-Aristo-Bureaucracy"; "The insane book- and newspaper-production"; "A utopian, who perhaps really does have the recipe. To whom no one listens"; "The officers"; "This city Vienna, that only in appearance did the duties of an imperial city") and concludes with the sentence quoted earlier: "But this grotesque Austria is nothing other than an especially clear case of the modern world" (TB 353–54). In representing the lost empire as an archetypically modern state, he eschewed expressionism, naturalism, and realism alike, although elements of each are present in his work. For Musil, the crucial stylistic device was the mode of narration: irony becomes constructive by establishing a perspective for the reader to grasp through the "connectedness among things" the deeper historical significance of what is represented. Musil's ironic depiction of how "its like happens" (*Seinesgleichen geschieht*) to and around a "man without qualities" thus incorporates a critical, self-reflexive perspective on its own representation of the world of democratized skepticism.

Because Flaubert, too, deployed an ironic style as a critical tool, contrasting his use of irony with Musil's will help define the distinctiveness of the latter's artistic project. For Flaubert, irony is a means of authorial self-assertion. While his anti-Bildungsromanen demonstrate the failure of experience to educate the modern subject, they use the ironic depiction of figures who personify the clichéed traits of modern subjectivity to emphasize how literary technique can turn the meaninglessness of modern existence to account. If Frédéric and Emma fail to learn anything, the same cannot be said for the reader, who is able to appreciate literature's supple transformation of the detritus of everyday life into art. Seduced by the operation of the text into complicity with the author, Flaubert's reader is rendered superior to the characters whose fate he witnesses. Irony is the privilege of those outside the text; Emma achieves, at most, a melodramatic sentimentality that recognizes the tedium of existence while refusing to reflect on its meaning.[27] Although the mechanisms of his impeccably orchestrated *style indirect libré* are de-signed to sever Flaubert from his creation and to render her transparent to the reader, the power of the novel derives in large part from the way this de-vice allows him to represent ennui as inescapable. "The author in his work" as he put it in a letter to Louise Colet, "must be like God in the universe, eve-rywhere present and nowhere visible . . . one must feel in every atom, on every surface, a concealed and infinite indifference."[28] Flaubert's is the tech-nique of absolutized ennui: art not merely as the means of transforming the petty drama of provincial mores into a modern tragedy but art as the sub-stitute for life itself.

By contrast, Musil's relation to the skeptical landscape of modernity is not omniscient. On the contrary: his deliberate extension of irony and un-certainty into the narration itself expresses his self-reflexive ideal of impli-cating himself in the "constructive" irony he deploys. If Flaubert's ideal reader will appreciate the spectacle of his artistic achievement with a shiver at his icily professional, more-bored-than-thou dissection of Emma's fate, Mu-sil's has no such option. In *The Man without Qualities* irony arises from the connection between things rather than out of the tension between narration and object; Musil's novel draws the reader in and forces an intellectual and emotional confrontation with the author's vision of modern life.

If Flaubert left the clichéed vocabulary of Emma's experience intact in or-der to expose its insuperable banality, Musil deploys a narrative strategy that shows how modernity is rendering the very rhetoric of reflection on subjec-tive experience obsolete. Rather than aligning himself with the ideal of an omniscient, "scientific" literature, Musil is interested in depicting the process by which the vocabulary of interiority and soul is undermined, leaving peo-ple without the means to reflect upon what is happening to them, with no words for their feelings. In the world of the man without qualities, the loss of cultural self-evidence has left people without any orientation for action—a circumstance that takes symbolic form in the inability of the forces of "Besitz

---

[27]An even more emphatic example of this foreclosure of genuine reflection within the narra-tion is the scene at the end of *A Sentimental Education* when Frédéric and Deslaurier, the com-panion of his youth, reminisce about their past. What passes for irony between them expresses no more real insight than Bouvard and Pecouchet's return to copying at the end of their search for more meaningful occupations. Only the reader, in sly alliance with the author, can fully appreciate the nihilistic point of their life stories.

[28]Letter to Louise Colet, 9 December 1852; *Correspondance II*, 204.

und Bildung" (Property and Culture) to find any focus for the Parallel Action through which to distinguish the greatness of "the true Austria" from Germany's rationalistic and mechanistic achievements. As we have noted, the collective search for a "great idea" combining interiority and modernity, soul and intelligence, which leads even the most unreflective characters explicitly to confront the divergence between public language and private experience, ends in a chaos that prefigures the impending outbreak of war. In *The Man without Qualities*, nothing can be taken literally. As the title of Part 2 proclaims, "Its Like Happens": both the plot and the extreme perspectivism of the novel foster endless conflicting interpretations and proffer little by way of assurance that one is on the right track. Musil demonstrates his ironic conviction that there is no stable position outside the spiritual crisis of modernity by showing that the various modes in which his characters respond to the radical skepticism into which they have been thrown are all expressions of being without qualities.

Musil's achievement thus stands in the tradition of the literature of ennui, but marks either its end or, perhaps, the beginning of a new phase. Unlike *Madame Bovary* or the *Fleurs du Mal*, *The Man without Qualities* does not hold out the possibility of an aesthetic retreat from the hectic banality of modern existence. On the contrary, Musil embraces and turns to literary account aspects of modernization that Flaubert found abhorrent. And while for Baudelaire the atomization of the self and its dispersal into a field of influences and determinants that accompanied the disappearance of faith in the eternal soul was threatening, for Musil this circumstance constitutes the condition of possibility of modern subjectivity. Furthermore, although the malaise that suffuses Musil's Kakania in 1913 may resemble the *mal du siècle*, the poetic haze of ennui which still hung over the mid-nineteenth century, he precludes our identifying the two by positioning the narrator in the postwar world. My contention is that Musil inherits the critical project linked since Flaubert and Baudelaire with the artistic deployment of the boredom discourse—the task of representing the link between the material and subjective effects of modernization. However, Musil presents the problem of meaning in a new way, inventing narrative strategies that allow him to establish a critical perspective both on modernity and on the rhetoric of reflection in which the epistemic and ethical crisis of modern existence has been expressed.

Baudelaire's poetry, I argued, made visible how the language of boredom crystallized out of the fragments of inherited and modern vocabularies of experience into a powerful mode of reflecting on the subjective effects of modernization. However, as we have seen, because 'boredom' referred to a subjective experience, in the course of time, the malaise it named came increasingly to be understood individualistically and ahistorically. By the nineteen-twenties, when Musil began writing *The Man without Qualities*, ennui had long since become a cliché. In the prewar world he depicted, Schopenhaurian pessimism and Nietzschean resignation were already giving way to the irrationalism and decisionism that would accompany many of the best and the brightest of Europe on their way to the appalling boredom of the trenches.

On my reading, Musil's novel attempts to reestablish the metaphoric function that had originally charged the literary representations of that experience in new sites. This effort to rejuvenate the rhetoric of reflection on modern subjectivity through "constructive irony" operates by transferring the metaphoric function of the boredom discourse—linking the subjective and objective effects of modernization—onto the intertwined metaphors of "being without qualities" and "its like happens." Foregrounding his mode of narration through rhetorical devices centered on temporality (particularly anachronism), this constructive use of irony establishes a distinctive relation to the reader and allows Musil to represent modern experience as an object of critical reflection. As I shall show, the metaphors he uses to redefine the dilemmas of modern subjectivity operate in his text in a fashion not unlike the appeal to a common experience of ennui with which Baudelaire proffered the *Fleurs du Mal* to his readers.

The task of the *Man without Qualities* as Musil conceived it was to mirror the spiritual dilemma of its time so accurately that its architecture and mode of narration would literally draw the reader into reflection upon modern life. The artistic key was the impersonal precision through which the epoch was represented, rather than the story itself. As Musil put this "principle" in one of his posthumously published notes: "It does not matter what, but how, one depicts" (1941/1766). In a projected retrospective foreword explaining why he has published before the novel was completed, he proclaims this principle once more: "Today the structure of a work of literature [*einer Dichtung*] is more important than its action" (1937/1761). However, Musil's fidelity to the dictum that form is prior to content in modern art should not be understood to mean that he was a formalist in any ordinary sense. His self-professed aim was to produce a *Gestalt* in which thought and feeling merged, in which "the richness of ideas is part of the richness of feelings" (1942/1769). Like Proust, his subject is experience itself.

However, while the Proustian work of art could also be said to have aimed at a self-sufficient gestalt of thought and feeling, it retained a fundamentally introspective and subjective relation to the past. Musil's novel, by contrast, represents an analysis of the fundamental problems of the era in intuitively accessible form, appealing rhetorically to the contemporary reader's actual historical locatedness to elicit reflection on the collective past. For him, the question of the significance of the experience of the modern subject must be posed historically, in terms of the spiritual dilemmas of the era. Thus while Musil's novel and *À la recherche du temps perdu* are both invoked as illustrations of the world lost in the European conflagration of the Great War, Proust's project has appealed more to literary theorists and philosophers than to sociologists and historians. But if Proust's work illuminated individual subjectivity through an exploration of the vicissitudes of memory and language, Musil's *Gestalt* aimed to effect no less than a rethinking of modern identity itself. The prodigious ambition of *The Man without Qualities* is to achieve what Musil early identified as the task of *Dichtung*: to express what cannot be accounted for scientifically but only through "emotional connections [*Gefühlszusammenhänge*], sequences of events, vague relations, for which there is still no system."[29] Proust sought to link the scientifically inaccessible aspects of human experience via a narrative recapitulation and artistic transformation of the durée as experienced by a single subject. Musil eschewed such a narrowing of perspective and attempted, through means as much philosophical as literary, to create a taxonomy of the unclassifiable. His diagnosis of modern human being without qualities extended reflection on the experience of time to the problem of the historicity of the individual subject.

In a series of notes for a preface he was considering writing, probably in early 1930,[30] Musil connected his ideas about *Dichtung* directly to the philosophical project of his novel.

> A depiction of a time? [*Zeitschilderung*] Yes and no. A representation of constitutive relations. Not current; rather a level further down. Not skin, but joints. . . . The fundamental thing is the spiritual [*geistige*] constitution of a time. Here the opposition between empirical thinking and emotional thinking [*Gefühlsdenken*]. (1938/1761)

For the reader who experiences the novel as gestalt, these two dimensions of thought and feeling are linked in reflection that is both historical and personal. Musil's notion of the "spiritual constitution" of a time should not be

---

[29] Draft of a letter to Franz Blei, 1917/18, *Briefe*, 133. "There are things in the human being that cannot be ordered into scientific connections at all, but only into emotional connections, sequences of events, vague relations, for which there is still no system . . . These are the object of literature [*Dichtung*]."

[30] Although these notes are undated, there is a reference to the Prussian Kulturminister Adolph Grimme's February 15, 1930 lecture, which makes it possible that he intended to place this "nachgestellte Vorrede" either at the end of Volume I (which he finished correcting for publication in March 1930) or before the first part of Volume II, which at that time he expected to publish expeditiously, though it did not actually appear until the end of 1932.

understood in purely philosophical terms, for in another passage he admonishes himself to remember: "Behind the problems of the day the constitutive ones, which are not the so-called eternal ones" (1937/1761). Musil's reflective project is centered not on abstract questions about the meaning of human life, but on an effort to articulate the historically specific dilemmas of modern subjects as embedded in the forms of everyday (bourgeois, Austrian) life.

As these reflections make clear, literature has an analytical task for Musil: modernity's spiritual constitution is to be anatomized through a representational gestalt in which the empirical and emotional dimensions of thought converge. The task of his novel lies neither in character nor in plot development nor in meta-reflection upon the failure of the two. Rather, by joining philosophical reflection and realistic representation, *The Man without Qualities* aims to provide the reader with resources for reflection upon lived historical experience.

> Some will ask: What standpoint does the author take and what is his conclusion? I cannot give a satisfactory account of myself. I take the matter neither from all sides (which is impossible in a novel), nor from a single side; rather from various interconnected sides. One may not, however, confuse the incompleteness of a thing with authorial skepticism. I carry my task forward even if I know that it is only part of the truth and I would do so even if I knew that it were false, because certain errors are stations of the truth. I do as much as possible in a definite task. (1937/1760)

The principle of constructive irony, which reveals the interconnection among things, is reflected in Musil's perspectivist philosophy of composition, which demands that the reader actively engage in the search for meaning in history. A few entries further on, immediately after drawing the distinction between "constitutive" and "eternal" problems, Musil adds: "This is not a skeptic speaking but a person who considers the problem difficult and who has the impression that it is being worked at unmethodically" (1937/1761). By metaphoric transformation of the modern rhetoric of reflection on subjective experience, *The Man without Qualities* was to proceed systematically to a gestalt that illuminated the fundamental dilemmas of existence in a world where skepticism had been democratized.[31]

---

[31] Musil's methods of composition are of considerable interest; he not only wrote and rewrote chapters but also followed out multiple possible trajectories for the novel as a whole, all of which he meticulously documented through a system of abbreviations and cross-references that kept the various possibilities for weaving the story together simultaneously accessible for reflection. The work is therefore not simply unfinished but radically uncertain in its incompleteness. Musil died suddenly of a stroke on April 15, 1942, and the question of how he would have proceeded, had he been able to continue writing (as he had expected) for many more years has given rise to a vast secondary literature. For a synthetic perspective on Musil's life and work, see Corino.

Disenchantment and Reflection: The Man without
Qualities as a Man of His Times

The reader first encounters the protagonist engaged in what appears to be an attempt to overcome his boredom through scientific analysis. Although he is standing at the window, watching the city go by, the man without qualities is no flaneur. He is poised with watch in hand, counting what comes into view and "estimating the speeds, the angles, the living forces of masses being propelled past," each of which compels an infinitesimal period of attention before being overpowered by the next impression. However, he soon abandons this attempt to analyze the objective circumstance that corresponds to the subjective impression of ceaseless activity, concluding that it has been a senseless waste of time ("daß er Unsinn getrieben habe"), because the energy in play is sheerly incalculable.

> If all those leaps of attention, flexings of eye muscles, fluctuations of the psyche, if all the effort it takes for a man just to hold himself upright within the flow of traffic on a busy street could be measured, he thought—as he toyed with calculating the impossible—the grand total would surely dwarf the energy needed by Atlas to hold up the world, and one could then appreciate what a tremendous achievement it is nowadays for a person even to do nothing at all. (2; 12/7/7)

At this point, the narrator interrupts with the remark, "For the man without qualities was just now such a person." Marked by a paragraph break, this intervention shifts the reader's attention abruptly onto the *discours*, thereby producing a critical perspective on the protagonist's parodic experiment. Perhaps Ulrich's attempt to "calculate the impossible" is no idle pastime but an effort to justify his own inertia. The narrator's intervention may be read as an ironic commentary on how the familiar imagery of the discourse on the subjective effects of modernization—nervous overstimulation, psychic stress, and physical fatigue—serves the symbolic function of legitimating indolence and withdrawal.

However, the protagonist himself stands in an ironic relation to his own *désœuvrement*; the relationship between his reflections and the narrator's (thus doubly ironic) commentary upon his reflective pastimes will form the foundation of Musil's transformation of the discourse on subjective malaise. The man without qualities is no dandy, ranged above modernity in the guise either of heroic artist or bored decadent. Stopwatch in hand, he is engaged in a scientific attempt to comprehend the subjective effects of modernization. As we have already noted, Musil did not, like Simmel, identify the blasé attitude that resulted from the excess of nervous stimulation provided by the modern city as a means for subjective transcendence. The thoughts of the man without qualities flow in quite the opposite direction, toward the idea that the telos of modernity may be the elimination of subjective particularity altogether in a fully functionalized social order. "Perhaps it is precisely the philistine [*Spießbürger*] who has the first intuition of the beginning of a collosal new, collective, antlike heroism? One will call it rationalized heroism and find it very beautiful. Who can know today?!"

The reader perceives the irony that pervades the protagonist's thoughts, but what happens next indicates that their content must be taken seriously nonetheless. At this point, the indirect free style breaks off abruptly, and without any change in punctuation the narrator begins to address the reader directly:

> In those days there were hundreds of such unanswered questions of great importance. They lay in the air, they burned under the feet. The time was on the move. People who were not yet alive then will not want to believe it, but in those days time was already moving as fast as a cavalry camel. One just didn't know what it was moving towards. Nor could one properly distinguish what was up and down, what was going forward and backward. (2; 8/13/7)

Once again Musil's doubling of irony directs the reader's attention toward the historical significance of the discourse on the subjective effects of modernization operating in the narrative itself. This intervention has taken us outside of the protagonist's consciousness, and the narration now returns to the security of the third person with a direct citation, "'one can do what one likes, said the man without qualities to himself with a shrug, 'in this tangle of forces it doesn't make any difference.'" The protagonist's apparent cynicism notwithstanding, what happens next implies that he cannot really shrug off the tension associated with the historical circumstance of being catapulted along by a time "on the move" without knowing whence or wherefore. Ulrich "turned away like a person who had learned renunciation, almost like a sick person who shrinks from every intensive contact," yet as he left the room where we have observed him, the narrator informs us, he jabbed a punching-ball he passed with more force than is "usual in moods of resignation or conditions of weakness" (2; 8/13/7–8).

At first glance, the man without qualities is the archetypical bored subject, a bystander to modern life who vacillates between "doing nothing" and reminding himself that he can do whatever he likes, since nothing is of any consequence. However, his idle pastime of objectively analyzing the quotidian reveals a genuine respect for the "tremendous achievement" of ordinary modern life. As a man of science, he considers himself obligated to take seriously the possibility that humanity will be better off in the "ant-like" world of "rationalized heroism" where individual achievements are no longer of any importance. Or rather, to be more precise, his tentative embrace of such a personally dismaying result in the name of science is a consequence of the same crisis that brought about his decision to take a vacation from his life. *The Man without Qualities* locates the protagonist's crisis of meaning in a larger historical context; the narrator's reflections on the philosophical dilemmas of the era are interpolated in this passage in a way that exemplifies Musil's strategy for provoking his reader to reflect on the symbolic significance of Ulrich's withdrawal from the world of action.

Chapter 13, "A Genial Racehorse Fosters the Awareness of Being a Man without Qualities," recounts Ulrich's disillusionment with his idea of himself as "a young man of promise." The passage cited earlier, which describes his conviction that one must live life as an expedition, with only "provisional principles," goes on to describe how his view of science became de-idealized.

> The truth is that science has developed a conception of hard, sober, intellectual strength that makes the old metaphysical and moral ideas of the human race simply intolerable, even though all it can put in their place is the hope that a distant day will come when a race of spiritual conquerors will descend into the valleys of soulful fruitfulness.
>
>   But that works well only so long as one is not forced to direct one's gaze out of the visionary distance onto the nearness of the present and made to read the sentence that in the meanwhile a race-horse has attained to genius. (13; 46/48/43)

Reading that sentence elicits in the protagonist the recognition that his "fragments of a new way of thinking and of feeling" were being drowned through immersion in the humdrum routine of everyday life: "'Surely I can never have intended to spend my whole life as a mathematician?'" (13; 47/49/44).

The violent recoil that punctuates his musings at the end of Chapter 2 does not express the mood of resignation or condition of weakness that accompanies ennui, but rather embodies a rebellion against the nihilistic implications of the idea that "in this tangle of forces it doesn't make any difference" what one does. The man without qualities is in search of a way of bringing the modern faith in "hard, sober, intellectual strength" in touch with the heart, a way of living meaningfully that can "save his uniqueness" through providing "an appropriate application for his abilities" (13; 47/49/44). As the strivings of a man of science to find meaning without renouncing the achievements of modern thought, his efforts symbolize the project of locating positive historical possibilities in the disenchanted world.

Ulrich's vacation from life is thus not a withdrawal into boredom and resignation but rather an attempt to overcome his tentative and disaffected attitude toward his existence. Unfortunately, turning his attention away from his work exacerbates his alienation, for he comes to understand that attitude as a configuration of historical significance. For the reader, Ulrich's story has this significance from the outset, for it is ironically saturated by the narrator's interventions, which inform one, for example, that "unanswered questions" permeated the atmosphere in 1913. These interventions not only place Ulrich's immobility in the context of historical events but also situate the personal crisis that leads him to search for a meaningful way of living in the broader philosophical context of reflection upon the relationship between historical change and the experience of modern identity.

Ulrich, the narrator tells us, had been young in the time "shortly after the last turn of the century, when many people imagined that the century too was young," a time in which suddenly there had occurred "a small surge of soul. . . . No one know exactly what was coming; no one could say, whether it was a new art, a new human being, a new morality or perhaps a regrouping of society. Thus everyone said about it what suited him. But everywhere people stood up to fight against the old" (15; 54–55/58–59/52–53). In the chapter entitled "A Mysterious Disease of the Time," the protagonist contemplates how his own estrangement from his youthful dreams corresponds to a larger historical development away from that surge of energy. "It seemed to Ulrich that at the beginning of his adult life he had found himself in a general slackening which, in spite of occasional quickly disappearing eddies, ran itself down into an every more listless, erratic pulse-beat. It was hard to say wherein the change lay." It was not that there had been no progress, he thought. Nowadays

> the whole world visits both the crystal palaces and the Secession and even the Secession of the Secession. What then had been lost? [*Was ist also abhanden gekommen?*]
> Something imponderable. A prognostic. An illusion. . . . The sharp boundaries had everywhere blurred, and a new, indescribable capacity to enter into hitherto unheard-of relationships elevated new people and ideas. These were not bad, certainly not; no, it was just that the good was adulterated with a bit too much of the bad, the truth with error, meaning with accommodation. . . . There is as much a lack of everything as of nothing; it is as though the blood or the air had changed; a mysterious disease had consumed the previous era's slight disposition to geniality, but everything sparkles with novelty, and in the end one doesn't know if the world has really grown worse or one has oneself simply grown older. At this point a new time has definitively arrived. (16; 57–58/62–63/55–56)

The final sentence shifts us out of Ulrich's consciousness into the perspective of the narrator, who goes on to say that the time had changed "without waiting for Ulrich," who "retaliates" by blaming the mysterious, genius-consuming disease of his time on a "thoroughly prosaic stupidity." However, since stupidity "has something extraordinarily winning and natural" about it—"a good platitude always has more humanity in it than a new discovery"—this effort at revenge ironically underlines the tenacity of the problem (16; 58–59/63/56–57). While Flaubert could use the diagnosis of *bêtise* to accuse his era from a perspective of moral superiority, this option is no longer open to Musil, who wants to show how the adulterated hopes of modernity catapulted the world into the utter stupidity of trench warfare. His protagonist reflects upon rather than exemplifies the irony that the modern rhetoric of experience forecloses original thought, and his actions are located in an historical rather than an aesthetic whole.

In *The Man without Qualities*, irony operates constructively to establish an historical perspective for reflection on the dilemma of the modern subject. What Helmut Arntzen calls Musil's satirical style reveals an inner connection between Ulrich and his time both at the level of the symbolic articulation of the novel as a whole and in the particularities of the language in which his own crisis of self is narrated. The "new time" that has "definitively arrived" is, as a symptom of how originality becomes absorbed by the historical process, not new at all. Musil uses the same verbal phrase, "abhanden kommen," to refer to what the time has lost as he did to describe Ulrich's insight upon reading of the genial race-horse: "With wonderful clarity he saw in himself all the abilities and qualities favored by his time . . . but the possibility of their application had escaped him [*war ihm abhandengekommen*]" (13; 47/49/44). But what has escaped Ulrich is precisely what his era has gained in losing the imponderable of its youth: the ability to put everything to use. As we have already remarked, the man without qualities understands his propensity for impractical thought to be at odds with the modern commitment to efficiency and the division of labor. His disaffection is a response to the "mysterious disease of the time" that has made life somehow shallow and stupid. What he has lost in losing the ability to apply his talents is his sense of belonging to his world, and this loss, not the stupidity of what he rejects, is the real source of his malaise.

> 'One cannot be mad at one's time without injuring oneself,' Ulrich felt. He was indeed ready at any time to love all these [modern] life-formations. What he never succeeded in doing was simply to love them without reserve, as the feeling of social well-being demands; for a long time there had been a haze of disinclination lying over everything that he did and experienced, a shadow of impotence and loneliness, a universal disinclination to which he could not find the complementary inclination. (16; 59–60/64–65/58–59)

We have already noted the narrator's claim that a "sublimated ceremonial" of mutual "aversion" defined Kakanian society, which had forged this negativity into "a feeling of community [*Gemeinschaftsgefühl*]" (8; 34/33–34/30). While Ulrich experiences this social tendency as a highly personal problematic, his disaffection marks him as a paradigmatic modern subject. No one is identical with their social role, and in his skeptical distance from the world he cannot embrace unquestioningly, the man without qualities suffers with special acuteness from the isolation and powerlessness this circumstance produces. Because he lacks the "complementary inclination" that drives people into conformity, however, he cannot participate even in the social feeling based on sublimated animosity.

From the perspective of the novel as a whole, the protagonist's ideal of "living hypothetically" is less significant as a reflection of his commitment to science than as a metaphor for his attempt to turn "disinclination," negativity, and indifference to account by locating the positive possibilities of being "without qualities." In this way, Ulrich's struggle to find a meaningful way of living when he cannot bring "narrative order" into his life comes to represent a more general modern problem. The man without qualities knows he has "lost his grip on the primitive epical [*daß ihm dieses primitiv epische abhanden gekommen sei*]," on the narrative sense that allows other people to weave their private lives into a coherent story despite the global circumstance that "publicly everything has already become unnarratable [*unerzählerisch*] and no longer follows a 'thread' but spreads itself out in an infinitely woven surface" (122; 650/II436/709). The "connectedness among things" that Musil's constructive irony strives to represent inheres, paradoxically, in the fact that this story cannot be told, in the way the protagonist's loss of "the primitive epical" reflects the "spiritual constitution of a time." The problem of how to tell the story of the man without qualities converges with the problem of how to live a life in modernity.

It's Like Being without Qualities: Musil's Ironic Metaphorics of Modernity

The satirical intent of the novel is most clearly revealed in Musil's deployment of the central metaphor of being without qualities. Although the narrator refers to the man without qualities from the outset by his epithet, the concept first enters into the narrative through the contemptuous efforts of another character to describe what is amiss with Ulrich.

> 'He is a man without qualities!' ... There are millions of them nowadays. ... When he's angry, something in him laughs. When he's sad, there's something brewing. When he is moved by something, he rejects it. Every bad act will appear

good to him in some respect. For him it's only a possible connection that finally decides what he takes a thing to be. Nothing is stable for him . . . Thus each of his answers is a partial answer, each of his feelings only an opinion.' . . . When he was finished, he had recognized that Ulrich expressed nothing other than the dissolved essence of all phenomena today. (17; 64–65/70–71/62–63)

While this diatribe against Ulrich has a particular function in the story, it is its systematic significance for the novel as a whole that concerns us. According to the narrator's report (in the first subjunctive) the speaker comes to think of the protagonist as an object whose existence metaphorically 'expresses' the insubstantiality of modern identity.[32] Although the narrator ironically relativizes the value of this judgment, it is indeed as a symptom of modern "being without qualities" that Ulrich is the subject of Musil's novel.[33]

The "man without qualities" is not simply one of the "millions" whose most basic responses to the world have been permeated by a radical skepticism; he is a person in whom this circumstance has become an object of reflection. The romantic critique of Ulrich as an exemplar of modern fragmentation has its global analogue in the explicit object of Musil's satire—the search by the participants in the Parallel Action for a unifying idea to save the dissolving phenomena. The meetings and discussions that constitute this "action" provide a foil for the protagonist's skepticism: while Ulrich nominally participates in them throughout the first two volumes of the novel, his dubiousness about their prospects underlines the futility of the project. Explicitly opposing romantic aspirations to reinvest the world with substantial meaning, Ulrich sets out to make his own state of fragmentation into the basis of a specifically modern morality. While he indeed experiences the remoteness from life emphasized in the speaker's negatively slanted description as an enormous burden, as the story of his attempt to affirm his state of being without qualities unfolds, the links between protagonist and historical context highlight the allegorical significance of Ulrich's efforts.

His being "without qualities" metaphorizes the dilemma of the radically skeptical modern subject. By depicting the protagonist's efforts to under-

---

[32] The final sentence of the passage just cited reads: "Als er fertig war, hatte er erkannt, daß Ulrich nichts ausdrücke als dieses aufgelöste Wesen, das alle Erscheinungen heute haben." Here "ausdrücke" refers not to any statement or action of Ulrich's, but to the image of him created by the speaker.

[33] The sentence just quoted is preceded by the narrator's remark that translating personal animosity toward the protagonist into a diatribe has had the effect on the speaker (his boyhood friend, Walter) that "in seinem Inneren löste sich dabei etwas auf, das ihm nicht bewußt wurde." Thus Musil underlines that the speaker's "objectification" of Ulrich as synecdoche for modernity's dissolved essence itself expresses something more than he is himself aware.

stand and come to terms with the historically situated crisis of meaning embodied in his unstable identity, Musil's satire pursues the constructive purpose of provoking a new mode of reflection in his readers. From the perspective of the narrator, the man without qualities is trying to recognize the
positive potential involved in being a person whose life is dominated not by
the "sense of reality" but by the "sense of possibility." A person possessing
this sense

> does not say, for example: Here this or that happened, will happen, must happen;
> rather he invents: Here could, should or must happen; and if someone explains to
> him that something is the way it is, then thinks: Well, it could probably also be
> different. Thus the sense of possibility might be defined outright as the capacity to
> think of everything that just as well could be and not to take what is more seri-
> ously as what is not. It will be seen that the consequences of such a creative dis-
> position can be remarkable, and regrettably they not infrequently make that
> which people admire appear wrong and that which they forbid appear permitted
> or even make both appear a matter of indifference. (4; 16/12/11)

From the narrator's perspective, then, the protagonist's thoroughgoing skepticism is more than a symptom of the "dissolved essence common to all
phenomena" in modernity. Because "the possible comprises not only the
dreams of neurasthenic people, but also the as yet unawakened intentions of
God" (4; 12/16/11), Ulrich's state of being has a utopian tendency as well.
Skeptical detachment from reality is also what makes it possible for the man
without qualities periodically to achieve the "other condition," an "utterly
changed form of life" in which one drifts "into the heart of the world" so that
"everything that generally goes to make up ordinary life [is] imbued with
transforming significance" (32; 125–26/144–45/131). A diary entry of Musil's
makes this connection explicit: "The sense of possibility—*that which the
sense of possibility could hold onto* would be the other condition. The world
has no goal for Ulrich. Universal disinclination, to which there is apparently
no inclination—the missing complement in such people is the other condition" (1831).

Since as I have emphasized the novel holds out the lineaments of a possible solution only to disavow them, what concerns us is not the "other condition" but Musil's diagnosis of the problem of universalized skepticism. This
diagnosis operates first of all through the protagonist's self-reflection on the
historical significance of his personal crisis of meaning. Depending on his
mood, the fact that for him no values are absolute and everything gains its
meaning only from its context may be either a source of pride or a cause of
dismay. However, he comes to recognize his ambivalent sense of himself as
either superman or decadent as an historical phenomenon. Being without

qualities is the fate of the modern subject: it is not just that the modernization process has robbed individuality of "character"; skepticism about personal identity is the logical extension of the radical uncertainty about events and their meanings that characterizes modern life.

"In earlier times, one had an easier conscience about being a person than one does today," Ulrich muses. "Being without qualities" is a result of the same process that has disenchanted the world and robbed history of its narrative continuity. In modernity

> responsibility has its center of gravity not in people but in the connections among things. Has one not noticed that experiences [*Erlebnisse*] have made themselves independent of people? They have gone on the stage, into books, into reports of research institutes and explorers ... so far as experiences are not part of work, they are up in the air; who can say today that his anger is really his anger, when so many people interrupt and know better than he?! A world of qualities without a man has arisen, of experiences without the person who experiences them, and it almost looks as though ideally a person won't experience anything at all privately and that the friendly gravity of personal responsibility is to dissolve into a system of formulas of possible meanings. Probably the dissolution of the anthropocentric point of view ... has finally arrived at the "I" itself, for the belief that the most important thing about experience is that one experiences it or of action that one does it, is beginning to strike most people as naïve. (39; 150/174–75/158–59)

Although the man without qualities affects an ironic and objectifying air, this is a serious matter. The "world of qualities without a man," where even one's own anger is not safe from the proliferating scientific discourses that have severed subjects from their objects, is a world without either individual identity or historical meaning. While Ulrich attempts to assess the situation coolly, the reader will not have overlooked the distressing implications of "most people" finding an attachment to the particularity of their feelings and actions "naïve." The dissociation between identity and experience described here as a result of the progressive disenchantment of the world mirrors the fragmentation of human activity into an endless series of nervous fluctuations whose only purpose is to prevent one's being run down in traffic on a typical modern street. For Musil, the question of meaning takes a particularly acute form for modern subjects, for how can one ask how one should live one's life in a fully rationalized world of "experiences without the person who experiences them"?

Ulrich's ideal of experimental living embraces this fundamental paradox of modernist subjectivity. Because even when throwing himself into action, "his attitude was at once passionate and detached," he had developed the conviction that his life and his qualities "belonged more to each other than to him" (39; 148/172–73/156–57). The sardonic endorsement of the split between identity and experience is part of Ulrich's attempt to make his disenchanted understanding of the circumstance of the modern subject the foundation of a new morality.

> He did not doubt that this distinction between having one's own experiences and qualities and their remaining foreign was only a difference in attitude. . . . To put it quite simply, one can behave toward the things that happen to one or that one does in a more universal or more personal fashion. . . . (39; 149/173/157)

Musil represents his protagonist's "partial solution" of embracing the idea of being a man without qualities who consciously lives out the historical situation of the modern subject as a point of departure from which to rethink the relation between history and identity.

The first step is Ulrich's recognition of his alienation as the fundamental condition of selfhood. His indifference has just provoked a break with his lover when, in Chapter 34, "A Hot Ray and Walls Grown Cold," "he didn't feel like working any more" (34; 128/148/134). Gazing around his home, he suddenly finds everything senseless, superfluous, hideous. "Fundamentally, there wasn't much to it: a veneer had flaked off, a suggestion had lost its hold, a chain of habit, expectation, and tension had snapped, a flowing secret equilibrium between feeling and world had for an instant been upset" (34; 128/148/134). What Sartre would call 'nausea,' an existential malaise, fills him, for Ulrich has become conscious of what must remain unconscious if thought and feeling are to continue flowing successfully "in the direction of life." However, "it occurred to Ulrich that all the moments that had meant something decisive in his life had left him the same feeling as this" (34; 128/148/134).

When he goes out into the street in an attempt to give himself up to the crowd, it only makes matters worse. While feeling the "happiness of flowing in the same direction" as their fellows, the narrator remarks, people ordinarily find the "thought that the life they lead—and are led by—does not concern them much, not inwardly" remote. However, for Ulrich the experience of the crowd intensifies his sense of estrangement and reawakens his youthful mistrust of the existing world. He remembers the "unsettling feeling" that had accompanied him while walking in this way a decade earlier, "a nagging suspicion that in this world, the untrue, careless, and personally insignificant expressions have a more powerful resonance than the most personal and authentic ones" (34; 129/149/135). Unable to be refreshed by taking a Baudelairean "bath in multitude" and deliberately experiencing the dispersion of his self, the man without qualities is overwhelmed by the social reality of mass society represented by the urban crowd.

The alienation Ulrich experiences as a result of being borne along by the mass is mirrored in the discursive structure of Musil's text. The narration shifts first from the indirect discourse of interior monologue into the third person configuration of reported speech and then into a questioning of indeterminate origin which voices the suspicion that what "one" experiences as reality is not "the real reality" at all. Finally comes a sentence that the reader cannot with confidence locate even as an unconscious response by the protagonist. It must be the narrator, commenting on the phenomena of historical life, who says: "What is so palpable to one's mistrust are the established arrangements and forms of life, the "its like" (*das Seinesgleichen*), this preformation by the generations, the ready-made language not only of the tongue but also of sensations and feelings" (34; 129/149–50/135).[34] Because the very language of subjective experience has come to seem mass-produced, the dispersal of self in the crowd can no longer—as for Baudelaire, as in the protagonist's youth—be experienced ecstatically. It has become a lived metaphor not for poetic freedom but for the rudderless existence he is living, for his failure to find a truly original language to renew his experience.

The narration's shifting perspective[35] is significant not only as a formal representation of Musil's concern with the way thinking bears one along via "the affinity and kinship of the things themselves that meet inside a head" toward "impersonal" insights that have lost the "form of thought" as it is experienced. Significantly, the impersonally formulated reflection upon impersonality just cited is the first occurrence within the text proper of Musil's opaque but crucial notion of *Seinesgleichen*, "its like," which provides the title of the second part of *The Man without Qualities*, "Seinesgleichen Geschieht," "its like happens." The floating point of view represents the dimension of impersonal occurrence, the "something happening" felt within thought, as an object of thematic significance. It does so both discursively and performatively, for this passage creates an experience of the text through

[34] The awkwardness which arises from my attempt at a literal rendering of this passage is also present in the original. The crucial phrase, "das Seinesgleichen, dieses von Geschlechtern schon Vorgebildete" is translated by Wilkins and Kaiser as "the ever-recurring sameness of it, the preformations passed down by generation after generation" and by S. Wilkins as "semblances of reality, the molds set by earlier generations." Neither of these choices is entirely consistent with their translations of "Seinesgleichen Geschieht," the title of this section of the novel. While the first translation uses the more literal "The Like of It Now Happens," the more recent one ventures "Pseudoreality Prevails." The latter has been much praised by reviewers of the new translation (Steiner, Bernstein). However, it is not only less faithful than the older rendering but decisively tilts interpretation toward a philosophical problematics of truth and appearance alien to Musil's project.

[35] For more on Musil's "hovering" narrator, see Peters.

which the attentive reader "can quite distinctly perceive . . . a faintly disconcerted feeling" that Ulrich's thoughts have not "wait[ed] for their origina-
tor."

By introducing a concept crucial to the novel as a whole in such an
oblique fashion, Musil accentuates the writtenness of the passage and provokes the reader to engage with the philosophical project of *The Man without
Qualities*. As I have already argued, his narrative strategy demands that the
reader who wants to untangle what is happening think about thinking. Doing
so entails reflecting both upon the way the story deploys the "ready-made
language" of experience to reveal the constructedness of structures of
thought and feeling and also upon the conceptual apparatus that provides
the framework for Musil's constructively ironic transformation of that language. By emphasizing the narrative perspective in the passage where he introduces the structural metaphor of *seinesgleichen* into the *discours*, Musil
stresses that it is the historical significance of Ulrich's desire for personal
originality, rather than his plight as a romantically conceived individual, that
should concern the reader.

The man without qualities is an exemplary figure whose own modes of
thought, like those of the other characters, must be seen as the expressions of
historically constituted discursive formations. By deploying a shifting point
of view, Musil provokes reflection on the historical significance of the represented thoughts that constitute the primary matter of *The Man without
Qualities*. Although the novel might thus be said to be narrated from a position of skepticism about its own meaning, the mode of narration nonetheless
allows Musil to guide the reader's developing reflection on the historical and
philosophical significance of the ideas expressed in the *histoire*. His object of
creating an "immanent depiction of the time that led to the catastrophe" requires that the reader contemplate and articulate the relations among the
interpenetrating themes. The same ideas look different from different angles,
when represented in the service of different interests, and for the attentive
reader these undergo a process of mutual correction that distills their historical signficance as the novel proceeds. Thus, for example, the narrator's notion that youth instinctively rebels against all inherited forms resituates what
the protagonist had called the "mysterious disease" of the time. While Ulrich
lamented that a "slight disposition to geniality" had been squandered, the
narrator's point of view radically relativizes this idea.[36] After all, the process

---

[36] A few lines further on, we find the following pronouncement: "And this transition from
finding the world old to finding it beautiful is about the same as that from young people's outlook
to the higher morality of adults, which remains a laughable bit of didacticism until one day, suddenly, one has it oneself" (34; 130/150/136).

of accommodation inherent to human life inevitably produces the sense of banality and lost promise, and one must view disillusionment with one's era as part of the process of growing up.

However, the "ready-made language" of experience in question also corresponds to the "established arrangements and forms of life" of a world that is already gripped in dissolution. As we have already noted, the new time that "has definitively arrived" at the point when "one doesn't know if the world has really grown worse or one has oneself simply grown older" is not new at all. In the context of the novel as a whole, the notion that only "its like" happens refers not to the phenomenon of aging but to the very structure of historical experience in modernity.

Narrating Dissolution: The Attempt to Make History Possible

In an *Exposé* of the second volume of *The Man without Qualities*, Musil reflects upon the critiques garnered by the first. Reviewers had asked

> what probably or actually will happen in Volume II. The answer to this is simple: Nothing or the beginning of the World War. One should note the title of the main part of the first volume: *Seinesgleichen geschieht* [its like happens]. That means: Today the personal here and there of a happening is probably determinate, but its universal or its meaning indeterminate, faded, equivocally and unintelligibly repeating itself. The person who is awakened to consciousness of contemporary circumstances has the feeling that the same things are always happening to him, without there being a light to lead him out of this disorderly circle. . . . [In this central idea] lies the continuity which makes it possible to grasp the present time already in the past, and the technical problem of the book may also be characterized as the attempt to make a history possible in the first place. (1844)[37]

Seinesgleichen geschieht is a concept directed toward the peculiarly modern constellation of experience characterized by the severing of the subjective and objective, the particular and the universal. As such, it is central to the novel's project of developing a mode of reflection that will make it possible to escape the "disorderly circle" of uncomprehended repetition that characterizes the modern subject's emotional reality. Such escape is the condition

---

[37]This text is probably from 1930. I reproduce the most crucial passages in German: "Seinesgleichen geschieht. Das heißt, daß heute wohl das persönliche Hier und Dort des Geschehens ein bestimmtes ist, das Allgemeine daran aber oder seine Bedeutung unbestimmt ist, verwaschen, äquivok und unübersichtlich sich wiederholend . . . .[D]as technische Problem des Buches ließe sich so bezeichnen als den Versuch eine Geschichte überhaupt erst möglich zu machen."

of possibility for having a history, for without it, the incomprehensible return of the same makes it impossible for people to establish any determinate meaning for what is happening to them. Thus although "nothing" will "actually" happen—even if Volume II had reached the beginning of the Great War, it could hardly have satisfied critics seeking narrative closure— Musil sees himself as making history itself possible! The German "eine Geschichte" can also mean simply "a story." The task of understanding the novel and the worldly tasks of modern subjects converge: "The story of this novel comes down to the fact that the story which is supposed to be told in it is not told" (GW 5, 1937). That is, the fact that nothing "happens" is to bring the reader to understand the importance of the conception that "its like happens" for reflection on existence in a world "of experiences without the person who experiences them." Through it, the historical significance of Musil's satirical representation of prewar Vienna is linked to the more general issue of the conditions of possibility for having a history—eine *Geschichte*, a narrative framework—at all.

On my reading, Musil uses "being without qualities" and its historical counterpart, "its like happens" as structural metaphors to rearticulate the relationship between subjective and objective phenomena of modernization in a fashion that avoids the aporiai of the boredom discourse. By linking reflection on the meaning of history to a disenchanted conception of modern subjectivity, *The Man without Qualities* brings what I have called "sociological" and "philosophical" rhetorics of reflection on subjective experience into conversation. The crisis of meaning experienced by the man without qualities is at once personal and historical—but rather than withdrawing into the state of boredom that symbolically represents the impasse of the modern subject, he rebels against resignation and attempts a rethinking of the relationship between subjectivity and history, identity and experience that embraces skepticism and science without abandoning the desire to find a spiritually meaningful form of life. An ironic perspective on the historical whole is encapsulated in the rubric of "Seinesgleichen Geschieht," and as the novel unfolds, this topos directs the reader's attention to the figurative relations between Ulrich's personal crisis and the Parallel Action. While other characters lament modernity's purported "soullessness" and indulge in pseudopolitical longings for a great and unifying idea to facilitate genuine and direct expressions of the heart, the metaphoric framework created by the topoi of being without qualities and its like happens underlines the novel's occupation with the rhetoric of experience embedded in these historical discourses.

Let us return to the protagonist's struggle with existential malaise in the chapter that Musil's notebooks repeatedly identify as the exemplar of *seinesgleichen.* Having been rendered even more isolated by walking in the crowd, Ulrich stops to contemplate the facade of a church, only to rediscover the indifference to beauty that had driven him away from home in the first place. Though he stops only briefly, the full force of youthful revolt against the prefabricated language of emotional response flares up at the "obligation of admiring" the aged building before him. The seconds "grew down into the depths and oppressed his heart with the whole primeval resistance that one originally has against this world petrified into a million tons of stone" (34; 130/150/136). Located securely outside the protagonist, whose heart is laid open to our understanding, the reader sees the elongation of time into existential ennui as a phenomenon of historical significance. This time the remark that follows can be attributed to the narrator with greater certainty:

> It may be that for most people it is an amenity and a relief to find the world ready-made [*fertig*] except for a few small personal details; yet although there is no reason at all to doubt that what persists as a whole is not only conservative but also the basis of all progress and revolution, mention must be made too of a deep, shadowy malaise [*Unbehagen*] that it causes in people living by their own lights. The thought forced itself on Ulrich . . . that one could just as easily eat people as build such monuments [*Sehenswürdigkeiten*] or let them stand. (34; 130/150/136)

In the novel as a whole, Ulrich's malaise in response to the completely "ready-made" world of "its like" suggests transformative possibilities. However, the hidden historical potential of "what persists as a whole" is not really apparent to Ulrich: the shadowy isolation of his malaise admits only the first, still ambiguous glimmers of a broader vision of experience. Still, his radically skeptical equation of cannibalism and cathedrals leads Ulrich's thoughts further away from their beginnings in his existential experience of ennui. Although "at this moment he wished to be a man without qualities," the passage which follows places this experience in a sociological category. The wish is not so unusual at all:

> by the middle of their lives few people know anymore how they actually came to themselves, to their amusements, their world-view, their wife, their character, occupation, and their successes, but they have the feeling that not much can change any longer. It could even be asserted that they have been cheated, for one can nowhere discover a sufficient reason for the fact that everything came about as it did; it could also have come out differently. The events have, after all, only to the least degree originated in themselves . . . . [A]nd yet when noon comes there is all at once something that may justly claim to be their life now . . . . But what is still stranger is that most people don't notice this at all; they adopt the man who has come to them, whose life has merged into their own lives, his experiences appear to them now as the expression of their qualities, his fate as their reward or misfortune. (34, 130–31/151/136)

Ulrich's rebellion against the solidity of the world expresses his discomfort with the muddled way one gets along in a world ruled by the principle of "its like." All of life—morality, character, experience—seems to be a result of random, indifferent experiences that bear no relation to one's inner being. This impersonal vision of human personality passes into reflection on what constitutes human historicity if everything "could also have come out differently"; the whole passage seems to have been laid out from the narrator's perspective.

But what comes next implies that Ulrich's own thoughts have slipped into the third person—that the view of history encapsulated in the phrase "its like happens" has infiltrated his consciousness. After a series of ruminations upon how the petrification of identity ironically results from the impetuousity of youth, which indiscriminately appropriates the contents of life so that "personally insignificant" formations drown out the delicate tendrils of individuality, the same paragraph arrives at the following remark. "This then is the sole basis—thought Ulrich, and naturally all of this touched him personally as well . . . of the everlasting phenomenon which one calls new generations, fathers and sons, intellectual revolution, change of style, development, fashion, and revival" (34; 132/152/138). Change is only apparent, for all attempts to make something truly new are undermined by the fact that youthful enthusiasm exercises itself on socially produced forms. And since identity is formed through the appropriation of forms that do not foster individual uniqueness, vitality and the yearning for the new all too soon give way to the stultification characteristic of the accumulated achievements of the past. "What makes the striving for the renovation of existence into a perpetuum mobile," reads the next sentence,

> is nothing other than the trouble that between one's own misty I and one's predecessor's, which has already become an alien shell, is inserted only a pseudo-I, a group soul that fits only approximately. And if one pays just a bit of attention, one can probably always recognize in the latest future, which has only just arrived, the old days to come. (34; 132/152–53/138)

Once again Musil's mode of narration renders the reader uncomfortably uncertain about the origin of these ideas. It seems to be the narrator's pessimism about historical change that is expressed, yet the sentences may be enunciated from the perspective of the protagonist as well. This ironic strategy serves to direct attention to the structural significance of the ideas expressed—the pseudo-I of convention, the pseudo-novelty of historical innovation—as elements in a gestalt representing the fragmentation of experience as a phenomenon of historic significance.[38] Though Ulrich's skepticism about history is presented as a consequence of reflection on his own uncertain identity, the ambiguity of the narrative perspective simultaneously locates his ideas as manifestations of the historical circumstance captured by the notion that "its like happens." The man without qualities can maintain his individuality only by refusing to "adopt the man who has come to him." By identifying himself as a man without qualities, then, he rejects the ordinary course of historical existence in which a human life turns out to be constituted by nothing but the eternal return of the same.

As we saw at the outset, the crisis of meaning that had prompted Ulrich to take a year's vacation from life centered on his loss of faith that scientific progress would bring about the cultural revolution that had seemed imminent during his youth. Chapter 83, "Its Like Happens or Why Does One Not Invent History?," underlines the historical significance of the protagonist's malaise. Challenged to distinguish his "active passivism" from the pernicious noninterference in the world that is allowing it to "increase into the void," Ulrich attempts to give an account of why he "does nothing." Once again, the responses of the man without qualities both resonate with the discourse on boredom and distinguish his matter-of-fact attitude from any aestheticist position. Ulrich's thoughts move from mysticism to mathematics:

> God does not mean the world literally at all; it is an image, an analogy, a figure of speech . . . we may not take him at his word, we must ourselves figure out the sum that he sets us . . . What one calls an age . . . , this wide, unregulated flow of circumstances would then mean about as much as a desultory succession of unsatisfactory and (when taken singly) false attempts at a solution out of which the correct and total solution could issue, if only humanity understood how to unite them. (83; 357–58/II65–66/388)

Ulrich's sense of impropriety at thinking such thoughts in the streetcar occasions the narrator's excursus, considered at the outset of the chapter, on the way thinking without "a practical goal" has become a matter for philosophical specialists since modernization has "taken certain questions out of the human heart." Once again, Ulrich tries and fails to affirm an insect-like social order, a "bee-state" lying at the end of the rationalization and specialization of the life-world. Perhaps, he thinks, his interest in the life of the mind is only a "prejudice." To "divert himself" from these questions, "he contemplated his face in the pane of glass opposite his seat," but suddenly it blurred and "demanded some sort of complement."

---

[38]They are formulated in a language ironically resonant with contemporary cultural criticism ("den Augenblick des Seins," "geistige Umwälzung," "Renovierungssucht des Daseins").

The narration implies that such a complement is to be found in a turn to history. A new paragraph begins here with the ominous words, "Was there actually war in the Balkans or not?" A series of facts arrayed in the fashion of newspaper headlines follows, interspersed with reflections that could be attributed either to the narrator or to Ulrich himself.

> In a word, a great deal was happening, these were stirring times [*es war eine bewegte Zeit*], around the end of 1913 and the beginning of 1914. But the times two or five years earlier had also been stirring, each day had had its excitements, and nonetheless it was possible to remember only faintly or not at all what had actually been going on at the time. (83; 359/II67/390)

Although this passage seems to represent the stream of Ulrich's thoughts, once again Musil shifts perspectives, and in a long and crucial passage come sentences written in the third person that both thematically and performatively direct the reader's attention to the writtenness of the discourse. Once again the topic is the disconcerting relationship between identity and experience that characterizes modern existence.

> What a strange affair history is! It is possible to assert with certainty that this or that event had already found its place in history or definitely would do so, but whether this event had taken place at all, that was not certain. For it is proper to the occurrence of a thing that it take place in a definite year and not in another or even not at all; and it is proper to it that it take place itself and not in the final analysis merely something similar or its like [*seinesgleichen*]. But that is exactly what no person can assert about history, unless he has written it down, as the newspapers do, or it is a matter of professional and pecuniary affairs ... in such connections even wars can become memorable occurrences. (83; 359–60/II68/390)

Like the sentence in which the term *seinesgleichen* was first introduced, this passage is doubly ironic. Though these reflections on history—which probably must be attributed to the narrator—may initially seem improbable, they must be taken earnestly. Only what is written down, or what otherwise enters into a narrative, can become a matter of certainty. Human experience and especially memory is so permeated by indefiniteness, by conflicting interpretations that ordinarily one is left only with "something similar or its like" instead of the definitiveness of an event. Though it resembles recollected experience, "History" is by no means what anyone remembers; *seinesgleichen* names the discrepancy between lived experience and what turns out actually to have occurred, once the dust settles.

> This history of ours looks pretty unsafe and messy ... and then in the end, strangely enough, a path runs across it after all, that very 'path of history' of which no one knows whence it came. This being the material of history was

something that made Ulrich indignant. The luminous, swaying box in which he rode seemed to him like a machine in which a few hundred kilograms of human being were being shaken back and forth in order to make the future out of them. A hundred years ago they had sat in a mail-coach with similar looks on their faces. (83; 360/II68/390)

A hundred years in the future it would be the same story, though with new "future-machines."

> He was furious at this defenseless submission to changes and conditions, at this helpless contemporaneity, this desultory, acquiescent conformity to the centuries quite unworthy of human beings. (83; 360/II68/390)

So Ulrich descends from the train of time, and "in that larger human container of the city . . . his malaise composed itself back into cheerfulness" (83; 360/II68/390).

By combining ironic contextualization of Ulrich's thoughts with direct reflection on the circumstance of being a man without qualities, Musil establishes a complex critical perspective on this historical malaise. The end point of this particular trail of ideas will turn out to be Ulrich's response to the question of why he does not act—his proclamation that one should live life as literature by living "the history of ideas instead of the history of the world." The difference "would lie less in what happened than in the significance one attached to it" (84; 364/II73/395). The problem is that people live their lives on the basis of established narratives and hackneyed emotions. Even what count as great political events are all too predictable: they

> bore on account of their lack of imagination [*Geist*] and novelty but thereby bring us into that unresisting sleepy condition in which we will put up with anything if only it is a change. Seen in this way, history arises out of the routine of ideas and the ideally indifferent [*aus der ideelen Routine und aus der ideelen Gleichgültigkeit*], and reality arises principally because nothing happens for the sake of ideas. (84; 364/II74/395)

The boring repetition of plagiarized plots and unoriginal personalities makes up the stuff of history, which, since it is not made but suffered, diverts humanity with an impression of change without making individual lives significant except as "matter" strewn along the path of history. The man without qualities is in a highly particular form of rebellion against this circumstance. Because he acknowledges the momentous powers of repetition and inertia and does not grasp his own situation in political terms at all, he can offer only the whimsical idea that one should live for the sake of possibilities instead of realities—live the history of ideas.

Musil's concept of *seinesgleichen* redefines the sense of depletion and meaninglessness, the malaise that arises in those who do not find it "an amenity and a relief" that the world is largely finished when one arrives in it—in a word, boredom—both historically and philosophically. Taken positively, the precept that "its like happens" becomes the basis for a reawakening of religious sensibility: "God does not mean the world literally," and human life is a process of infinite interpretation. However, the resulting skepticism can be overwhelming, especially since the upheaval proper to a "stirring time" renders it impossible to trust one's own thoughts and memories when attempting to unravel the significance even of events of which one seems to have immediate knowledge. In the end, the religious dimension of Ulrich's withdrawal from the world defines the lineaments of his unhappiness, for modernity is structured ironically, as a metaphor, rather than allegorically, as a lesson to be patiently unraveled.

Thus the perception that "its like happens" is also responsible for Ulrich's indignance at "being the material of history," his revulsion at subjectivity being transformed into packets of objectivity on the train of time. For him, the sheer contemporaneity that places people at the mercy of history is "unworthy of human beings"—all the more so in modernity because the sheer acceleration of change entails that there is no hope of gaining control over the process or of finding the necessary leisure to decipher the hidden significance of one's existence. In the context of the novel, this philosophical dilemma has a very particular historical significance.

The chapter entitled "From a Country that Perished on Account of a Linguistic Error," in which the fact that "something was continually occurring" is linked explicitly to the impending dissolution of Kakania into war, begins:

> The train of time is a train unrolling its rails before itself. The river of time is a river that sweeps its banks along with it. Traveling with it, one moves about on a solid floor between solid walls; but walls and floor are being moved along too, imperceptibly and yet in the most lively fashion, by the travelers' movements. (98; 445/II174/484)

The truth that "its like happens," that history proceeds in a way that prevents those who make it up from understanding the significance of what is going on, is the source of both possibility and despair. This ambiguity, which defines the dual critical and diagnostic project of Musil's novel, is reflected in the slippage of narrative perspectives characteristic of his prose. The reader is not permitted to remain a passive witness to these pleasantly vivid musings on the nature of history, but must engage explicitly in reflection on the historical circumstance thematized by the novel. A few pages further on, there is a series of references to military and political events of the day (Italy in

Libya; England and the Baghdad question; Kakania in Serbia). The narrator remarks,

> there was a great deal going on, and one knew it . . . The particulars every school-boy could understand, but on the whole no one really knew what was actually taking place, except for a few people, and they were not certain whether they knew. Some time later it all might just as well have happened in a different or inverse order, and one wouldn't have noticed any difference, with the exception of certain changes that incomprehensibly endure in the course of time and form the slime trail left by the snail of history. (98; 449/II178–79/488–89)

Musil himself seems to have been overwhelmed by the difficulty of distinguishing between indifferent possibilities and those which might indeed, properly grasped, have made a difference in the inexorable movement toward catastrophe that provides the background narrative of his novel. The central metaphors of his novel are also the bearers of this ambiguity. As Musil put it in notes for the conclusion of *The Man without Qualities* written in June, 1936:

> Comprehensive problem: War
> Its like [*Seinesgleichen*] leads to war The Parallelaktion leads to war!
> War as: How a great event comes into being.
> All lines flow into the war. Everyone greets it in his own way.
> The religious element in the outbreak of war.
> Act, emotion, and other condition collapse into one.
> Someone remarks: that was it, what the Parallel Action always sought. It is the great idea discovered. (1902)

This is Musil at his grimmest: all of the vague aspirations for spiritual regeneration that characterized prewar Austria—the diverse tendencies that constitute the "substance" of the Parallel Action the novel depicts—appear as the harbingers of destruction. "Its like happens": in 1936, the idealistic hopes of rejuvenating Austrian culture collapse into the dark premonition of the inevitable return of barbarism.

Nonetheless, from the perspective of the novel as a whole, Ulrich's affirmation of his state of being without qualities has a utopian potential, for it is the sense of possibility, not the sense of reality, that can identify the fact that in history only "its like happens" as a source of hope for the future. What appears as Ulrich's boredom and indifference to the existing world is a philosophical effort to grasp the historical significance of his own radical skepticism and thereby to locate transformative potential within the malaise evoked in him by the ready-made character of the modern world. In a chapter with very pronounced slippage between the protagonist's and narrator's perspectives, Musil advances the notion of a "utopia of essayism."

He intuits that this order of things is not as solid as it pretends to be; no thing, no I, no form, no principle is certain, everything is gripped in invisible but never-ceasing transformation ... and the present is nothing but a hypothesis that one has not yet gotten beyond. What better can he do than hold aloof from the world in that good sense [of scientific skepticism] .... This is why he hesitates to make something of himself. (62; 250/296–97/269)

For such a person, any "definite mode of existence" is a harbinger of death. "Being without qualities" is thus an affirmation of the loss of self that accompanies the radical boredom of a world ruled by the principle of "its like"; it is a metaphor for a Nietzschean state of flux in which the meaning of anything can only be deciphered by reference to its historical significance as a symbol of other possible realities. Ulrich's affirmation of his lack of identity and his skepticism about the renewal of Austrian culture yield a different perspective on the circumstance that, taken literally as the cause of war, tends to provoke a global skepticism.

Although the man without qualities is in rebellion against the (false) "utopia of exact living" represented by the ideals of science, he is repulsed by the anti-intellectualism of his age, with its enthusiasm for vagueness and soul. "Ulrich could not abandon himself to vague intimations ... but neither could he conceal from himself that in all those years of pure exactitude he had merely been living against himself" (62; 256/304/276). In the world of qualities without a man, the landscape of totally democratized skepticism, there are no longer any genuine grounds for action, and Ulrich's life is guided by a radically perspectivist affirmation of the moral relativism that results when the process of disenchantment arrives at the self. For the man without qualities,

all moral events took place in a field of forces whose constellation charged them with meaning, and they contained good and evil just as an atom contains the potentialities of chemical combination. They were, so to speak, what they became .... In this manner an infinite system of connections arose in which there was no longer any such thing as independent meanings, such as those ordinary life, in a crude first approach, ascribes to actions and qualities; in it the apparently solid became a permeable pretext for many other meanings; what was happening became the symbol of something that was perhaps not happening but was felt through the medium of the first; and the human being as the quintessence of his possibilities, the potential human being, the unwritten poem of his existence confronted the human being as transcription, as reality and character ... For Ulrich morality in the usual sense was no more than the aged form of a system of forces that may not be mistaken for morality without a loss of ethical force. (62; 250–51/297–98/270–71)

Ulrich's philosophy of life affirms Nietzschean flux, but rather than (as Simmel put it), turning life itself into the purpose of life and simply affirming the circumstance that "its like" is all that happens, he attempts to turn the radical uncertainty of modern existence into a forest of symbols. Rejecting the tautologies of "ordinary life" and reducing the inherited vision of how one should live to the reflection of a regime of power without historical currency, Ulrich legitimates his refusal to "adopt the person who had come to him" metaphysically.

As I have shown, the narrator's perspective on Ulrich's state of being without qualities recognizes and emphasizes the (historical) possibilities that flow from this attitude toward self and world. However, Musil's ironic mode of narration also embodies a critical perspective on Ulrich's own understanding of the problem, a critique that finds expression as well in the projected failure of the protagonist's efforts to turn this mystically reconceived experience of fragmentation into the basis of a new way of living. The reader is invited to wonder whether Ulrich's ruminations on "the unwritten poem of his own existence" are not rationalizations of his own inactivity. While "he waited behind" the persona with which he could not identify, "the silent despair dammed up behind it rose higher every day." From the perspective of the novel as a whole, the attitude that Ulrich understands as an expression of his critical perspective on the problem of modern identity is symptomatic of the historical circumstance of the modern subject; the idea that "what was happening became the symbol of something that was perhaps not happening but was felt through the medium of the first" may be ironically applied to the impending war. "*Seinesgleichen* leads to war."

Boredom, the Other Condition, and the Return of History

In the later part of the novel, including the chapters that Musil prepared for publication and then withdrew again in 1937–38, the man without qualities has withdrawn from the Parallel Action to devote himself to his search for a way of living meaningfully. He has a series of "holy conversations" with his sister on the topic of morality. Ulrich is attempting to revivify mysticism without abandoning his scientific attitude, that is, to think about ultimate meanings from a disenchanted perspective, one "not so much godless as god-free" (1092/1187). This search for the "other condition" seems the natural outgrowth of the philosophical project of affirming his state of being without qualities, for morality forms the point at which one's most intimately individual convictions intersect with socially imposed orders of meaning. However, according to the narrator, while a preoccupation with morality is proper to "young people whose will to live is still entirely unblunted, . . .

[w]hen Ulrich spoke of morality it signified . . . a profound disorder" of the soul (Part 3, 11; 746/III94/811). Having failed to immerse himself in a form of life that would free him from reflection on the question of how he should live, the man without qualities was exposed to the "paralyzing effect" of theories that refused to go into practice. This effect, according to the narrator, can be "characterized at the most general level" by the fact that

> every principle of European morality leads to such a point, where it deadends; so that a person taking stock of himself at first appears to be wading in the shallows as long as he feels solid convictions under himself, but then, when he goes a bit further, suddenly gesticulates like one drowning horribly, as though the foundation of life dropped immediately from the shallows to an entirely uncertain abyss. (Part 3, 11; 747/III94/811)

The inability of the man without qualities to treat his own existence as a given is not a matter of personal decadence but a manifestation of a more general cultural crisis. His solution, too, bears the marks of the collective impasse that for Musil characterized modern society.

It would perhaps not be wrong to see it as the ultimate instance of Musil's constructive irony that Ulrich's critique of modern forms of life leads him toward the study of the mystical tradition. The man without qualities is searching for the positive potential to be found in the depths of total uncertainty. For him, the stultification of morality is ultimately the result of perceptions and experiences that have "no nouns or verbs" being pressed into a language of "subjects and objects" (Part 3, 12; 754/III103/819). Through such linguistic closure, ineffable experiences are subordinated to religious institutions that bore and oppress people by closing off the question of the profoundly figurative character of experience that opens onto the "as yet unawakened intentions of God" (4; 12/16/11). The goal of the "journey to the farthest limits of the possible" he undertakes with his sister is a transformation of experience that saturates every moment of ordinary life with meaning. Ulrich defines this aspiration in relation to what I have called the bifurcation in the modern rhetoric of reflection on subjective experience: "Today the truth is that the human being has two states of existence, of consciousness, and of thought [the calculating-rational and the moral-aesthetic] and only protects himself against the deadly terror this would have to awaken in him because he takes one to be a vacation from the other. . . . Mysticism on the other hand would be connected with the intention of going permanently on holiday" (Part 3, 12; 767/III118–19/833).

That is to say, he is in pursuit of a reinvigoration of leisure in the most ancient sense. But Ulrich and Agathe's attempt to withdraw into a temporality of their own founders. As I have argued, modern leisure is thoroughly structured by the temporality of the world it pretends to escape, by notions of productivity and personal improvement—ultimately by the modern "semantics of historical time" that, as Koselleck wrote, "abbreviates the dimensions of experience [*Erfahrungsräume*]" so radically that "even the present withdraws into inexperienceablity [*Unerfahrbarkeit*]." Just as the political and historical realities of the world outside cannot be held at bay indefinitely, this temporality shapes the privacy of contemplative retreat. The attempt to turn a "vacation from life" into a "permanent holiday" leads back to boredom.

In an uncharacteristically direct series of pronouncements, Ulrich reveals his despair about ever finding the "other meaning glimmering behind" the inherited morality whose ordinances are but a collection of "concessions to a society of savages" (Part 3, 12; 769/III121/835–36). True, an inborn "other morality" makes him "indifferent" to the conventional definitions of what makes something good or beautiful: whatever arguments are offered, "I shall take my bearings solely by the sign of whether its proximity elevates or diminishes me. Whether it rouses me to life or not." However, his Nietzschean affirmation of a radical moral perspectivism is, in itself, far from being a solution to the problem of defining the right way to live. He himself recognizes his being without qualities as an ambiguous circumstance: "I can't prove anything either. And I'm even convinced that a person who surrenders to this [play of forces] is lost. He sinks into twilight. Into fog and nonsense. Into unarticulated boredom" (Part 3, 12; 770/III122/836). Life, he continues, depends on "the unequivocal." As much as he hopes that humanity is moving toward a new morality that merges mysticism with exactitude, Ulrich recognizes that he cannot transcend his dependence on the strictures arising from antiquated orders of meaning and simply affirm his individual responses as perceptions of moral value. "Gliederlose Langeweile," unarticulated boredom, arises when one gives oneself up to a life without any external determinations; it imperils anyone who wants to live "permanently on holiday" by embracing the indeterminacy of historical existence. It is, in other words, an inevitable byproduct of the attempt to transform historical existence into an "other condition." Romantic strivings to reinvest existence with meaning collapse, as ever, into the enlightened precepts that gave rise to them.

Musil's representation of Kakania and the Parallel Action illustrates the depth of the modern crisis of meaning; the man without qualities is both a symptom and a symbol of that crisis. Plagued by boredom, moral fatigue and emotional malaise, Ulrich is determined to turn his radically skeptical indifference to inherited ideals into a critical appropriation of the world. Unfortunately, the project of living his life as an experiment in which particular events are understood impersonally is doomed to fail. By beginning his novel in August 1913, Musil has assured that his readers cannot forget that circumstances beyond the protagonist's control are already looming down at the moment he decides for a vacation from life. It is crucial to keep this historical dimension in mind, for although he suggests that being without qualities is the ineluctable fate of modern subjects, Musil's objective was not to provide material for a cynical affirmation of the bored attitude that "pseudo-reality prevails." On the contrary, through constructive irony, he aimed to engage the reader's sympathetic understanding in reflection on the dilemmas of life in a world where history and identity are no longer interwoven in a fabric of collective meaning but are instead subordinated to the infinite, impersonal system of connections that constitutes history. By telling a story whose point lay in the non-telling, Musil was analyzing the spiritual origins of the cataclysm that was the First World War.

Musil is unrelenting in his insistence on reflecting on the problems that concern him from every possible angle; the reader, subjected to these endless recapitulations of historically significant discourses, may be driven to boredom and long for distraction from the serious intent of the novel. Nonetheless, this failure to tell a story is perhaps his most subtle ironic strategy. By forcing his reader to forsake immersion in the narrative and always to think about why the story is being told as it is—to make the conceptual connections to the vexing notions of "being without qualities" and "its like happens"—Musil invites reflection on the relationship between the impending historical "catastrophe" and the confrontation with possibilities that for him is the foundation of historical experience. His story of a man without qualities, who had "lost touch with the primitive epical," in which "its like" is all that happens, must be read for the sake of the historical importance of its ideas and their vicissitudes.

The task of the novel that became identical with that of Musil's life was to make the Great War comprehensible as the consequence of the spiritual crisis of the fin-de-siècle. He wrote neither as cynic nor as skeptic, but as one who found cynicism and skepticism, historically speaking, inevitable. His objective of creating a gestalt merging thought and feeling was a response to this dilemma. Exposing the fundamental features of modern thought was to awaken the reader to the necessity of non-materialist forms of explanation—of ways of thinking about what the forms of subjective experience signify. *The Man without Qualities* suggests that impotent responses of rebellion against emptiness and the denial of rationality had been as responsible as the foment of nationalism and the trail of broken treaties for the debacle of the trenches. The structural metaphors of "being without qualities" and "its like happens" give form to Musil's *Gestalt*; together, they circumscribe the condition of the modern subject adrift in a world where history and identity are equally uncertain, a world drifting toward "catastrophe."

Musil's ambition to represent, ironically yet realistically, the inner truth of the times, to merge scientific and artistic methods into a novel that would renounce aestheticism without allowing formal values to be displaced by didactic ends, proved formidable to realize. In 1931, more than a year before the publication of the second volume, he wrote in a letter: "The main difficulty turned out to be formally incorporating the growing stock of ideas [*Ideenmaterial*] which in the course of working, as lies in the nature of thinking, diverged from one another."[39] This is not a formal, philosophical problem but a profoundly historical one. To fulfill the demand for precision of feeling as well as of thought, Musil's *Gestalt* would have to integrate this *Ideenmaterial* into a representation of the world that, as his notes repeatedly emphasize, would end in war. For the reader who grasped the ironic "connection among things," the whole of the novel would illuminate the fragmentation of the modern subject, whose "being without qualities" was at its thematic center, from the "social side" as well.[40]

The fact that his project was directed at an historically situated audience also meant, however, that Musil's project was at the mercy of time, and his intentions grew more complex and more difficult to realize as the years passed. In 1938, admonishing himself not to let his philosophical interests overwhelm his focus on the mode of representation, Musil wrote: "Quietly, in the course of working, this book has become an historical novel: it takes place 25 years ago! It was always a novel about the present [*Gegenwartsroman*] developed out of the past, and now the range and tension are very great, but what lies under the surface, which has always been one of its main objects of representation, does not need to be put even deeper still" (GW 5, 1941). On one hand, he was convinced that he could "stick with [his] old examples" despite the intervening enhancement of the tendency toward "the democracy of the spirit" they thematized. "I believe that the investigation of

[39]This letter was published in "Die Literatur" along with a picture of Musil and a facsimile of a manuscript page in Heft 7, April 1931. Briefe I, 510–11. Cf. GW 5, 1910, 1940. Compare a diary entry from 13. August, 1910 in which Musil comments on his way of working on his novellas: "What matters to me is the passionate energy of thought. Where I can't work out some specific thought, the work immediately becomes too boring for me; this is true of practically every paragraph" (TB, 214).

[40]In the "Studienblatt Soziale Fragestellung" dated 1926, Musil remarks that in working over his papers he recognized the necessity of "including the social side of the problematic. That is the same as the fundamental idea of the depiction of the time" (1861).

these examples must have the same result. (I deprive myself of effect but gain in anatomy or some such)."[41] On the other hand, however, with the passage of time, the resonance of the examples and hence his task in drawing out their possibilities had changed along with the perspective of his readers.

Since Musil could no longer count on his readers' sharing memories of the world he was satirizing, the task of achieving a formally satisfactory means of presenting the "level further down," at which the spiritual joints of the prewar era could be revealed, grew ever more arduous. Although the Great War was always intended to remain outside the novel itself as part of the reader's framework of reflection, the meaning of its exclusion from the *histoire* changed over time.[42] I have cited a number of diary entries that define the *Problemaufbau* of Volume II in terms of the objective of precisely depicting the spiritual constitution of the time before the war. For Musil, it was not a matter of documenting a lost world but of displaying the movement within that world toward the fundamentally transformed Europe of the postwar period. Thus as the years wore on and the remnants of his canvas dissolved into barbarism, the project of reflection upon history grew ever more urgent, the demands he placed upon the novel ever greater. No longer convinced of the viability of his aspiration to "partial solutions," Musil came to see his task as a writer in even more explicitly historical terms.[43]

Particularly after 1933, when the National Socialist accession to power prompted Musil and his wife to leave Berlin and return to Vienna, the notebooks take an increasing interest in politics—or more precisely, in the cultural meanings manifested by political transformations. A key passage links the historical significance of the war to the ideological transformation of Germany after 1933.

> Actually Germany's enthusiasm for the Nazis is a stunning proof for the correctness of my claim that nothing is so important to people as a stable spiritual stance, an Archimedean point, and so forth. The people want an active good conscience. The war was the first attempt.[44]

[41]GW 5, 1938; probably circa 1930.

[42]So much so that today it is necessary to emphasize how large a shadow the coming debacle cast over the novel, lest the reader focus on what is still modern in the story of the man without qualities and thereby abstract the import of the work into a more or less ahistorical framework of reflection.

[43]In 1932 he wrote in his notebook: "The notion of life as a partial solution and so forth as untimely. Comes from the pre-war era, where the whole appeared relatively stable even to one who didn't believe in it. Today existence as a whole has been thrown into disorder . . ." (1856, abbreviations spelled out). See Luft 1980 on Musil's engagement during the ensuing years.

[44]TB II, 749 (also 1862). This sentiment recurs repeatedly in Musil's notes. At what appears to be its first occurrence, Musil adds a remark a few lines later that may be interpreted either as a critique or as an endorsement of the bourgeois-liberal "Vernunftrepublikaner," whose half-

A stable spiritual stance (*feste Geisteshaltung*) was of course the diametric opposite of the protagonist's experimental mode of being. Under modern conditions, the novel implied, it could only be achieved artificially, by suppressing the evidence of fragmentation and inherent instability—of being without qualities. Nonetheless, Musil recognized the depth and breadth of the longing for stable identity and saw its historic appeal foreshadowed in the semi-comic aspiration of the Parallel Action to reinvest modern life with enduring meaning.

As the Nazi response to the epistemic and ethical crisis of modern subjectivity took shape, Musil sought to interpret the concept of *Gleichschaltung*,[45] with its uncanny resonance with the notion that "its like happens," into the thematics of *The Man without Qualities*.[46] These efforts underline the tensions in Musil's struggle to establish a perspective for historical reflection that integrates the poles of social diagnosis ("anatomy") and philosophical critique. The rebellion against the social determination of identity that animates Ulrich's desire to understand himself as a man without qualities and conditions his embrace of a correlative vision of history as a process where "its like happens" would have to be situated more critically if Musil's use of these concepts were to evoke the historical self-reflection he set out to provoke, for in the meanwhile the "coming catastrophe" that had provided the orientation for his novel had come to seem the portent of an even deeper movement from science to myth in modern society.

In June, 1936 Musil made another attempt to synthesize the problematic of *The Man without Qualities*, underlining in his diary his conviction that the war had meant more than the end of a particular era:

> collapse of culture (and of the idea of culture). That is in fact what the summer of 1914 introduced.
>   Now it is clear that that was the great idea the Parallel Action had sought, and what happens is the unfathomable flight from culture. (1904)

For Musil, the return to barbarism, first in the war and then in the National Socialist attempt to remythologize modern existence, was a response to the phe-

---

hearted participation in the Weimar Republic helped spell its doom. "The error of the democracy was the lack of any deductive foundation; it was an induction that did not correspond to the fundamental spiritual attitude" of the age (1860).

[45] The Nazi term for the deliberate coordination of all forms of social and political organization along party lines may perhaps best be translated "forcing into line."

[46] In his notebooks, Musil repeatedly links the Nazi concept to chapter 34, where "Seinesgleichen" first appears in the novel in the context of Ulrich's reflections on the significance of the fact that one's life "might just as well have turned out differently." See particularly 1864–65, which belong to the pages headed "Studienblatt Soziale Fragestellung."

nomenon I have called the democratization of skepticism. The Nazi alternative to Ulrich's cultivation of possibility over reality shrewdly addressed the fact that, as another notebook entry has it, "The collective needs a stable spiritual stance" (1902). While Musil envisioned his protagonist as an "individualist with the consciousness of the impossibility of this standpoint" (1902), in having him pursue intellectual solutions or at most the mystical reinterpretation of the everyday in "the other condition," he had provided no historically viable way beyond what would have to remain an elitist perspective. The rise of the National Socialists' alternative vision of history and identity thus underlined the limitations of the critique of Ulrich embodied in the novel. In the face of such effective mobilization of elemental strivings for the immediate unification of feeling and action, the attempt to provoke in the reader a reflective recognition that it was impossible to live one's life in an "other condition"—that this idea was a utopian dream—appeared woefully inadequate.

In the end, Musil's optimism about his protagonist's pursuit of a way of life based on "possibilities" rather than realities was overshadowed by the very cultural and historical tendencies he had tried to criticize. However, his own awareness of the limitations of *The Man without Qualities* only underlines the complexity of the novel's attempt to develop a new vocabulary for reflection on the dilemmas of modern existence. I have argued that the interlocking structural metaphors of 'being without qualities' and 'its like happens' allow Musil's work to combine concrete, differentiated socio-cultural observation with philosophical and historical reflection on the problems of modern identity in a fashion that overcomes the conceptual limitations of the inherited discourse on boredom. By refiguring key elements of that discourse so as to bring material and ideal explanations of subjective experience into conversation, Musil's novel fosters reflection on modernity itself as a world of experience without qualities. In *The Man without Qualities*, fragmentation and alienation, the transformation of temporality via industrialization and urbanization, the widespread metaphysical despair of subjects condemned to existence in a world robbed of higher meaning all combine in a satirical representation of the Austrian capital as "an especially clear case of the modern world"—as a landscape of boredom and the staging ground of a desperate search for meaning—even when it was still ostensibly a destination off the main lines of the train of time.

My reading of the novel has emphasized not Ulrich's doomed efforts to transcend historical reality by achieving an alternative existence in the mystical "other condition" but Musil's project of provoking his readers to reflect historically on the subjective dilemmas that had shaped the discourse on boredom. He writes of modernity as "a world of qualities without a man . . . of experiences without the person who experiences them" in which the collective ideal seems to be helping "the friendly gravity of personal responsibility . . . dissolve into a system of formulas of possible meanings." Through an "immanent depiction" of this world, in which, as in the reader's own experience, "the personal here and there of a happening is probably determinate, but its universal or its meaning indeterminate, faded, equivocally and unintelligibly repeating itself," Musil linked the lived experience of being without qualities to the problem of the meaning or possibility of history altogether. In the Kakania he evokes, action is without purpose; every idea has its counter-idea, every perspective its diametrical opposite. In the course of the futile search for a unifying "great idea" to define the Parallel Action and thereby mobilize the nation in cultural renewal, all of the characters confront the problem that the inherited frameworks of meaning have grown too unstable to support such efforts.

The concepts of 'being without qualities' and 'its like happens' anchor Musil's strategy for elucidating the "spiritual constitution" of the time so as to expose "behind the problems of the day the constitutive ones, which are not the so-called eternal ones." These concepts operate synecdochically in the novel to link the fragmentary parts of subjective experience to the whole of cultural modernization in a way that provides a new framework for reflection on the historical origins of the catastrophe of world war. Through narrative strategies for representing subjective experience that articulate the dilemmas of modern identity with philosophical and historical circumstances, *The Man without Qualities* establishes a perspective for reflection on modern existence that overcomes the bifurcation between "sociological" and "philosophical" modes of explanation that characterizes the modern rhetoric of reflection on subjective experience as a whole.

As in Ulrich's morality, "an infinite system of connections" arises where there are no "independent meanings" and "what was happening became the symbol of something that was perhaps not happening but was felt" through what was. By locating the philosophical problems of identity at once historically and metaphorically, Musil's concepts of 'being without qualities' and 'its like happens' intertwine to form a framework for reflection on the very phenomena that brought the discourse on boredom into being. *The Man without Qualities* uses these interlocking metaphoric registers of the individual and the historical to locate the experiences of emptiness and malaise that plague modern subjects not as existential but as historical phenomena and thereby to engage the reader in reflection on the discursive construction of apparently unique, individual experiences.

For Musil, skepticism is an indissoluble feature of modern life. The strategy he suggests for overcoming the boredom that permeates the world he depicts, in which neither public nor personal reality can any longer be integrated in narrative wholes, is not Hegelian sublation but an historicist reinterpretation of the Nietzschean eternal return of the same. 'Its like happens,' and one is what one has become: by finding a way to interpret this historical circumstance impersonally, he hoped, we might become able to recognize the possibilities that reside in modern 'being without qualities.' The full affirmation of this state may only be intermittent, for the "other condition," if it can be achieved, cannot be sustained. However, the conception of modern existence as a being without qualities in which the spread of skepticism has rendered even the I an anthropocentric fiction suggests the possibility of metaphorically overcoming the impasse represented by the problem of boredom. Unfortunately, this possibility remained a utopian dream. It would be eclipsed by historical developments in which the romantic desire for reunification was placed most horribly at the service of rationality. In the face of what amounted to a National Socialist resignification of *Seinesgleichen geschieht* into *Gleichschaltung*, the potential for "being without qualities" to be appropriated for mythical rather than mystical purposes became evident. Musil's struggles to adapt his conceptual apparatus to these historic transformations could not compensate for the fact that under such circumstances, there was no refuge in a language of reflection. But this development should not for that reason be regarded as extrinsic to the rhetoric of reflection on subjective experience.

I have argued that the discourse on boredom came into being as a metaphoric mode of articulating the material realities of modern life with the philosophical problems of modern subjectivity. Over time, the specific historicity of boredom was forgotten, obscured by the ubiquity of that very mode of temporality—the experience of time as a series of empty, meaningless moments—that defines boredom itself. The historical evolution of the discourse on boredom thus exemplifies the dialectic of enlightenment by which the effects of the rationalization process are naturalized. Although boredom is a product of modernization, the nihilistic dynamic of the experience itself effaces this historical dimension, so that the problems of meaning associated with it come to seem eternal features of human existence itself. The rhetoric of the experience thus embodies the very philosophical mythology of radically isolated subjectivity that helped to provoke the Nazi mythologization of history—its instrumentalization as a means of integrating such subjects into the putatively ahistorical totality of the nation.

Despite the historical fate that rendered it not only unfinished but probably unfinishable, Musil's novel reinterprets the problematics of boredom in a fashion that does, perhaps, suggest a viable approach to reflection upon subjective malaise in modernity. If we recognize that it is our enlightened skepticism that makes even our own selves seem empty, it suggests, we may avoid the danger of treating the problems of meaning that plague modern existence ahistorically—and thereby supersede not only the nihilistic tendency of the bored subject but also the temptation to remythologization that hypostasizes historically specific modes of experience into ahistorical features of the human condition. In the anti-mythological affirmation of skepticism represented by the formula "its like happens," the philosophical and historical goals of *The Man without Qualities* converge. From the perspective of the discourse on boredom, the fact that "its like happens" functions only as an affirmation of the meaninglessness of life itself. If, however, we are convinced that "experience without qualities" is the historical fate of a subject no longer stably integrated in metanarrative wholes, then Musil's approach to the philosophical dilemmas of modern subjectivity may provide the foundation for a skeptical rethinking of modern experience. In the context of the present work, we may thus gauge the achievement of Musil's ambition to "make history possible at all" more modestly, by his success at linking the malaise of senseless repetition in which "its like happens" to modern "being without qualities" and thereby conceptualizing the philosophical dilemmas of modern subjectivity historically.

Conclusion: Boredom and the Rhetoric of Reflection on Modernity

———◆◆———

Es sind die fertigen Einteilungen und Formen des Lebens, was sich dem Mißtrauen so spürbar macht . . . die fertige Sprache nicht nur der Zunge, sondern auch der Empfindungen und Gefühle.

Robert Musil[1]

The Critique of Experience

In *The Critique of Cynical Reason,* Peter Sloterdijk redefines the starting point of Critical Theory. If, as Walter Benjamin argued, "'impartiality,' the 'unbiased perspective,' have become lies"[2] in modernity, then not, as the members of the Frankfurt School thought, because the process of enlightenment had destroyed the subjective position from which critique must take place. In fact, as their own work had demonstrated, neither such a "dispersion of the ego" (*Ich-Zerstreuung*) nor the "decline of critique" predicted by Benjamin had taken place; on the contrary, according to Sloterdijk, "the most important renaissance of critique in the twentieth century is connected with the name of Walter Benjamin" (18–19/xxxiii). Riffing on Nietzsche, Sloterdijk locates the foundation of the "provisional ego of critique" not in distance but in "a stance of extreme closeness" based on "a priori pain" (19/xxxiii). "Critical Theory was based on the assumption that in '*Weltschmerz,*' we know this world a priori. . . . Critical Theory thereby makes the ever 'elitist' assumption of an intact sensibility"(20/xxxiii). Indeed, ac-

---

[1]"What is so palpable to one's mistrust are the established arrangements and forms of life…the ready-made language not only of the tongue but also of sensations and feelings"(34;129/149–150/135). This passage is quoted in full in Chapter 6, page 374.

[2]Walter Benjamin, *Einbahnstraße:* "Narren, die den Verfall der Kritik beklagen. Denn deren Stunde ist längst abgelaufen…. Die 'Unbefangenheit', der 'freie Blick' sind Lüge…," in Benjamin 1996, 121; cited in *Kritik der Zynischen Vernunft,* I, 18 (xxxii in the translation). Subsequent citations to Sloterdijk in text give German and then English page references; I follow Eldred with modifications.

cording to Sloterdijk, for Theodor Adorno, "to remain sensitive was, as it were, a utopian stance" (21/xxxiv). But this vision of human existence is anachronistic. It is, he writes, "time for a new critique of temperaments. Where enlightenment appears as a 'melancholy science,' it unintentionally furthers melancholic stagnation" (26/xxxvii).

My own project has an obvious affinity with Sloterdijk's effort to affirm the fragmentation of modern existence. As I have shown, the rise of the discourse on boredom is a symptom of the dissolution of the "intact sensibility" in modernity. If the rhetoric of melancholy comprised a romantic longing for the reunification of the world—a longing often overt in Benjamin and still palpable under the veneer of renunciation in Adorno's writings—then resignation to the inexorable disenchantment of the world defines the rhetoric of boredom. The historical development of the discourse of reflection on subjective experience has rendered melancholy as anachronistic as its religious ancestor, acedia. It has effectively become an elite privilege, the distinguishing malaise of those who understand themselves and their experience in the terms of a literary and philosophical tradition that has long since lost its actuality. Attempts to identify boredom with melancholy or acedia thus efface the distinctive modernity of the experience without qualities, in which the definitiveness of the loss of traditional frameworks of meaning registers in a hollow emptiness of self. In the boredom that is so ubiquitous in modern society, the melancholic hopefulness of *Weltschmerz* has been burned out by nihilistic resignation.

Boredom, I have argued, is at the center of a distinctively modern rhetoric of reflection on subjective malaise. Similarly, for Sloterdijk, "discontent in our culture [*das Unbehagen in der Kultur*] has assumed a new quality: It appears as a universal, diffuse cynicism" (33/3). For him too, the decisive change lies in a new, disenchanted mode of experiencing self and world: "Cynicism is *enlightened false consciousness*. It is that modernized, unhappy consciousness on which enlightenment has labored both successfully and in vain" (37/5). Cynicism is not far from boredom. However, Sloterdijk's description of the operations of such consciousness is grounded in the medicalized materialist discourse on subjective experience that I have demonstrated is inadequate to describe the dialectical effects of enlightenment:

> Psychologically, present-day cynics can be understood as borderline melancholics, who can keep their depressive symptoms under control and remain more or less able to work . . . Their psychic [*seelisch*] apparatus has meanwhile itself become elastic enough to incorporate as a survival factor a permanent doubt about their own activities. They know what they are doing, but they do it because the force of circumstances and the instinct for self-preservation are speaking the same language. (36–37/5)

As we have seen, boredom turns habitual skepticism into a "survival factor." From Sloterdijk's point of view, then, it would appear to be the symptom of a psychic structure that forecloses genuine reflection, the reflex of an ideology that takes the form "they know very well what they are doing, but still they are doing it."[3] However, there is reason to resist the equation of boredom with such cynicism. I have argued that it is a form of reflective consciousness, but it is so in a quite different sense than Sloterdijk's cynicism.

The difference can best be seen by considering the alternative, "kynical" form of critique Sloterdijk advocates, which "discovers the living body as a sensor of the world [*Weltfühler*]" and thereby allegedly "secures a realistic foundation for philosophical knowledge of the world" (20/xxxiii). It is not simply that this attempt to embrace a Nietzschean elevation of life to the purpose of life appears to depend on a pre-critical epistemology according to which we can gain access to a pre-linguistic, preconceptual bodily experience of the world. According to Sloterdijk, since traditional forms of thought are helpless in the war against cynicism, which turns those weapons against its opponent in guerilla-like appropriations of rationality,

> Kynical reason culminates in the knowledge—decried as nihilism—that we must snub the grand goals. In this regard, we cannot be nihilistic enough . . . . Cynicism can only be stemmed by kynicism, not by morality. Only a joyful kynicism of ends is never tempted to forget that life has nothing to lose but itself. (367/194)

Seen in light of my analysis of the discursive evolution toward a disenchanted, materialist rhetoric of reflection on subjective experience, Sloterdijk's attempt to escape the dialectic of enlightenment appears to have fallen prey to its most sophisticated, modern incarnation. Such a romantic affirmation of purposelessness as purpose is the mirror image of the insistence that there is a human "besoin de faire quelche chose." It echoes not only with the melancholic decisionism of Kierkegaard and Schopenhauer but also with the crude psychologism of a Tardieu, who saw universal fatigue as the source of malaise. Cynicism is the exhaustion of thinking, kynicism its celebration.

A "critique of temperaments" is indeed called for. But such a critique cannot neglect the historical analysis of the language in which bodily phenomena are shaped into reflective experience. The language of boredom is therefore a better point of departure for reflection on the way subjective experience is constructed in modernity than the cynical attitude to which it so often gives rise.[4] In examining the vicissitudes of the language of reflection

---

[3] In Slavoj Zizek's Althusserian formulation (Zizek 1989, 29); see his writings on ideology for an intriguing, psychoanalytically informed elaboration on this position.

[4] For Sloterdijk, the explosion of cynicism and widespread malaise in the aftermath of the First

on subjective experience rather than seeking entry into a putatively non-linguistic realm, I have argued, we further the historical task of coming to terms with the fragmentation of subjective experience in the face of the dissolution of metanarratives that is the legacy of Enlightenment.

Significantly, the language of boredom began as a literary language, one that represented subjective malaise as configured by very material effects of modernization. In the metaphorics of boredom, the fundamental poetic task of forging a way of speaking about human experience—or, to use a more old-fashioned vocabulary, of mimesis—takes a modern form. I have argued that what is at stake in theorizing boredom is developing an historically and philosophically adequate account of the operations of this metaphorics, through which a form of reflective distance—what Flaubert called the experience of oneself as "thinking phantom"—anchors modern subjectivity in a new attitude toward experience altogether. According to Aristotle, artistic imitations even of painful objects call forth delight because "to be learning something is the greatest of pleasures" and in seeing such representations, "one is at the same time learning—gathering the meaning of things."[5] Since boredom is not a universal feature of the human condition, it is by placing this metaphorics in cultural and historical context that the philosophical significance of this modern mode of representing subjective malaise can be made visible.

Thus Benjamin read Charles Baudelaire as a witness to the ways "experience has changed its structure"[6] in response to the distinctive psychological

World War makes Weimar Germany one of the best places to "study how the modernization of a society has to be paid for" (702/385). Commentators (including Andreas Huyssen in the introduction to the English edition) have noted that Sloterdijk's account of that accounting disregards questions of gender even as it advocates a "kynicism" rooted in bodiliness. More recently, Helmut Lethen has linked the "coldness" cultivated as part of Weimar's "new sobriety" (*neue Sachlichkeit*) to masculine strategies of survival in modernity. In "World Weariness, Weimar Women, and Visual Culture," Patrice Petro demonstrates that, in contrast to the cynical (and often violently misogynist) representations that dominated the work of many male artists, women like Hannah Höch often responded to the failed promises of Weimar culture with a critical attitude that was "perhaps merely cool rather than cold, not cynical but only bored" (Petro 2002, 123). Such boredom, she suggests, may be read as a mode of active waiting for the sort of cultural and political transformation that would fulfill the promises of modernity, one that simultaneously resisted the siren calls of remythologization to which Germany would soon fall prey. Emphasizing the gendering of cynical and bored modes of experiencing modernity, Petro suggests, allows us to see distinctions among critical attitudes toward the effects of modernization—and thereby to identify the unfulfilled historical and theoretical potential of what I have called the democratization of skepticism in modernity.

[5] Poetics 1148b 10–20; Bywater's rendering.

[6] Walter Benjamin, "Über einige Motive bei Baudelaire" in *Charles Baudelaire: Ein Lyriker im Zeitalter des Hochkapitalismus*, 104. Citations in the next two paragraphs also refer to this text.

and socio-historical circumstances of modern life. Speculatively extending Freud's late model of trauma by merging it with Georg Simmel's description of metropolitan mental life, he took as his point of departure the thesis that in Baudelaire's world, shock had become the norm.[7] The urban dweller was constantly subject to fragmentary, punctual stimulations that flooded the sensorium and made integration impossible. Under such conditions, sustained, narrative connection to a collective past and future was impossible—in Benjamin's terms, "experience" in the traditional sense of *Erfahrung* had been obliterated and replaced by an endless series of momentary perceptual events—*Erlebnisse*—that could not be integrated into a unified whole. On Benjamin's account, Baudelaire's greatest accomplishment is "to have given the weight of an experience [*Erfahrung*]" to this lived fragmentation. "He designated the price at which the sensation of modernity is available: the disintegration of the aura in the shock-experience [*Chockerlebnis*]. Consent to this disintegration cost him dearly. But it is the law of his poetry" (149).

The discourse on boredom, I have argued, is a symptom of what Benjamin called "the growing atrophy of experience" in modernity (107). But as the poetry that expressed Baudelaire's "consent to disintegration" demonstrates, it also embodies a new way of understanding experience. In Baudelaire's lyrics, boredom appears less the inevitable fate of human beings condemned to a meaningless world than the fundamental expression of a temptation to despair woven into the skeptical, post-Enlightenment rhetoric of reflection. Baudelaire gives to modern fragmentation "the weight of experience" through representations of 'spleen' and 'ennui' that mark out the parameters of a specifically modern mode of reflection on time and identity, one that delineates the historical specificity of an experience of malaise it evokes as though it were eternal.

Baudelaire's 'ennui,' I argued, describes the slippage between material and psychic effects of modernization as the foundation of the nihilistic tendency—the "goût du néant"—of the modern subject. It signifies a destructive, even apocalyptic, indifference to existence itself, which arises for Baudelaire out of a malaise at once timeless and historically induced. Instantiat-

---

[7]110. Benjamin makes his debt to Simmel much clearer in the first version of his essay, "Das Paris des Second Empire bei Baudelaire." Intended for publication in Horkheimer's *Zeitschrift für Sozialforschung,* this essay was adamantly critiqued by Theodor Adorno for its "allegorical" reading of the poet. "Über einige Motive bei Baudelaire" was the result. (For a sensitive reading of what was at stake in Adorno's objections to Benjamin's methods, see Buck-Morss 1989). *Charles Baudelaire: Ein Lyriker im Zeitalter des Hochkapitalismus* contains, besides these essays on Baudelaire (both drawn from Benjamin's vast *Passagen-Werk*), "Zentralpark," a collection of theoretical aphorisms taken from Konvolut J of the *Passagen-Werk* devoted to Baudelaire.

ing his concept of *modernité*, this ennui combines the moments of eternity and contemporaneity, universality and subjectivity. At once a studied pose and a profound experience of groundlessness in a world without God, a crisis of desire and identity and a mode of recognizing the ineffability of time, Baudelaire's boredom is a synecdoche for the modern subject's malaise, a fragmentary moment that signifies the whole of modern experience. His evocations of ennui anatomize the fundamental structure of modern subjectivity, exposing the relations between desire and finitude that are its incommensurable components.

On my reading, Baudelaire's poetry embodies and enacts a refiguration of experience that at once represents and critiques the constitution of the modern, disenchanted rhetoric of reflection on subjective experience underway in the nineteenth century. In making visible how a new, modern vocabulary of reflection comes into being out of the fragments of inherited languages of sensibility and the rationalized vocabularies of the industrialized metropolis, Baudelaire called for reflection on the nature of modern experience and the subjects who understood themselves and their lives in this new idiom. His oeuvre is therefore a crucial point of departure for the analysis of the modern "consent to disintegration" through which permanent doubt becomes a strategy for subjective survival. However, as I demonstrated in Chapter 3, such reflection on the constitution of modern subjectivity cannot stop with literary representations of fragmentation. Only by situating the metaphorics of boredom in the historical context of cultural modernization does it become possible to counteract the problematic tendency, inscribed in the nihilistic dynamic of the experience itself, to interpret boredom as a universal feature of the human condition.

The Genealogy of Boredom:
Discourse, Temporality, History

Part I, "The Rhetoric of Experience," examined the constitution of the modern discourse on boredom and traced its diffusion and evolution in the course of the nineteenth century. The metaphorics of boredom, I argued, exemplify a new mode of reflection on subjective experience—a rhetoric centered on the individual, embodied subject struggling with the meaning and purpose of existence in a world increasingly bereft of both religious and worldly certainties. In contrast to more traditional vocabularies for expressing subjective malaise, that language does not situate the suffering individual in a spiritual or psychological context distinct from the physical environment. Unlike 'melancholy,' 'acedia,' or *taedium vitae*, it refers malaise to the world rather than to the nature of the self. The rhetoric of boredom thus implies that the experience is an objective response to external realities. Since the bored subject seems to reflect in an enlightened and unemotional way upon the senselessness of life, ennui comes to be regarded as a philosophically or spiritually significant mark of distinction.

Part I argued that as it was constituted, the discourse on boredom referred to both material and spiritual effects of modernization. At its romantic origin, the painful longing of ennui was associated with a lost sense of belonging and wholeness, of integration into a larger divine order. The romantic experience of subjective individuation was inseparable from such a sense of loss—which is not to say that there really was a golden age of undifferentiated belonging. In fact, romantic ideas about the self, nature, love took shape around the very experience of isolated differentiation they attempted to overcome. Romantic images of reunification—in nature, in a utopian past, in a renewed Christianity—were reflections of the social fragmentation already lamented by Schiller as the cause of a diminution of human existence in modernity. The language of ennui in which, from Chateaubriand to Emma Bovary, this sense of subjective isolation was reflected did not explicitly thematize the historic origins of the malaise. Nonetheless, the emptiness and meaninglessness the victims of ennui longed to overcome were demonstrably linked to the transformations associated with the dual revolution. And as romantic hopes for reintegration faded to the margins, the discourse on boredom came to express resignation to the disenchanted world and to the subjective malaise it fostered.

In the post-romantic discourse on boredom, I showed, the spiritual effects of modernization were ever more explicitly linked to the material transformations associated with urbanization and industrialization. As the monotonous temporality of city and factory brought the experience of ennui to the masses, it came to seem less a sign of subjective distinction than the mark of modernity on individual experience. The religious and moral conception of emptiness was yielding to a materialist notion of lack, and boredom, as the etymological evidence underlined, was increasingly thought of as a function of nervous fatigue. Among those who reflected on its philosophical implications, resignation trumped longing, and the modern discourse on boredom, in which the experience appears to be an objective response to a meaningless world, emerged. By the fin-de-siècle, the absence of historical and religious metanarrative frameworks for interpreting subjective experience no longer even needed to be problematized. Psychologists and philosophers attributed the once-nameless malaise to exhaustion brought on by the purposelessness of existence.

Part I thus constructed a genealogy of an experience we tend to assume is a universal feature of the human condition. The condition of possibility for boredom, I argued, was a peculiarly modern experience of temporality as a linear progression through an infinitely extending uniform succession of identical moments. For the great Enlightenment thinker Immanuel Kant, such temporality, like the corresponding conception of three dimensions of infinitely extending space, was by no means historically specific. This concept of time was, rather, a "form of sensory intuition" [*eine reine Form der sinnlichen Anschauung*] coeval with subjectivity in the sense that it made it possible to experience anything at all.[8] In boredom, these interrelated forms of temporality and subjectivity are experienced as problematic—the conditions of possibility of experience as conditions for its disappearance.[9] Thus was the awareness of subjective individuality and uniqueness associated with romanticism paired with malaise.

In the course of the nineteenth century, the skeptical attitude toward self and world upon which scientific investigation depended (that is, the conception of the conditions of knowledge set out in the *Critique of Pure Reason*) was being democratized—and with enlightenment came ennui. Via urbanization and industrialization, the abstract conception of time as an homogeneous succession of empty moments penetrated further into everyday life, making the conditions for boredom increasingly prevalent. However, as a response to an ahistorical conception of the self in time, boredom did not, in itself, foster reflection on its own historical specificity—that is, on the historically specific form of temporality that made it possible. From the perspective of analysis, the discourse on boredom indeed articulated spiritual and material effects of modernization. But the organization of the modern rhetoric of experience around a universalist conception of identity and the global evolution toward materialist explanations of subjective malaise made that linkage increasingly invisible to contemporaries. Thus although bore-

---

[8]In technical terms, Kant held "daß alles Mannigfaltige der Anschauung unter Bedingungen der ursprünglich-synthetischen Einheit der Apperzeption stehe"—"that the whole manifold of intuition stands under the conditions of the primordial-synthetic unity of apperception" (*Kritik der reinen Vernunft:* B 136).

[9]Thus romantic ennui posited the unique temporality of the desiring subject, and romanticism was historicist, directed not only against the rationalist understanding of subjectivity but also against the view of time as homogeneous succession devoid of substantial, cultural context. As I showed in Chapter 1, the idea of boredom plays a crucial role in the great critique of Kant's *Critique of Pure Reason*, G. W. F. Hegel's *Phenomenology of Spirit*. My argument follows Hegel's demonstration that the romantic cultivation of individuality and subjectivity ultimately consolidated the hegemony of rational thought—though not his interpretation that this triumph is evidence for the progress of reason through history.

dom itself registers the limits of the enlightened conception of the subject in
time, the reflective discourse on the experience occluded the historical significance of the epistemological and moral crisis associated with this experience without qualities.

Kant, it will be recalled, still regarded the lack of a natural end for human
existence as a practical problem and advised avoiding boredom through
"fill[ing] out the time with progressively ordered occupations that have a
great purpose in mind as their consequence." One should, he advised, "learn
to love work" and, through deferring pleasures, assure oneself "of a capital of
satisfaction that is independent of accidents or natural laws." The enlightened individual, in other words, should use the notion of rational progress to
structure both his inner and his outer life. Kant, whose conception of boredom is still the ancient *taedium vitae*, did not recognize that the modern
subject was in danger of satiation not with pleasure but with time itself. As it
turned out, embracing the temporality of progress was anything but a cure
for that subject's struggle against the boredom in and through which the
skeptical notion that human existence was purposeless was democratized.
Indeed, this was the very "semantics of historical time" through which, on
Koselleck's description, subjective experience would be "abbreviated" into
oblivion. In modern boredom, I argued, those conditions of possibility of
experience appear as the conditions for its disappearance; the enlightened
and rational approach to human life, the source of its meaninglessness.

As I have shown, the discourse on boredom evolved in such a way as to
efface the historical specificity of this way of conceiving of subjective malaise.
By the late nineteenth century, there were two predominant modes of interpreting the experience—as a primarily subjective or fundamentally objective
problem. I have argued that these should be understood as constitutive,
complementary dimensions of the discourse as a whole. Thus the enlightened skepticism that is boredom's historical condition of possibility is the
common ground of both the existentialist interpretation of boredom as an
encounter with the ultimate senselessness of existence and the anthropological notion that boredom signifies an unfulfilled need for purposive activity.
However, neither philosophical nor social scientific approaches incorporate
methodological awareness of their positions in the discourse on boredom.
Instead, they generate circular self-justifications: ennui is a universal feature
of the human condition because the encounter with nothingness is the enabling moment of human creativity; boredom is a socio-cultural phenomenon because it appears when subjects lack purposes that integrate them into
the social fabric. Neither of these modes of interpretation can, therefore, reflect adequately on the historical particularity with which the language of

boredom expresses subjective malaise—the way it relates socio-historical circumstances to problems of meaning.

My contention is that what manifests itself as a methodological impasse is
better understood as a bifurcated rhetoric of experience. Not only do sociological and philosophical perspectives both illuminate the phenomenon of
boredom itself; the opposing models of interpretation have themselves been
generated through the very historical development that has made this apparently timeless experience of meaninglessness so pervasive in modern society.
The divergence between subjectively and objectively oriented interpretations
of boredom ultimately reflects the aporetic relation between idealist and
materialist perspectives that characterizes the modern discourse of reflection
on subjective experience as a whole. From a philosophical point of view, that
aporetic relation is itself a manifestation of the metaphysical ambiguity of
modern skepticism—according to which, as the third Kantian antinomy of
reason has it, human existence must be understood as both free (ideal) and
determined (material).

In Chapter 3, I showed how historically grounded and philosophically articulated rhetorical analysis can mediate between these seemingly incommensurable approaches to reflection on subjective experience. Although the
discourse on boredom evolved within the context of the post-Enlightenment
paradigm shift toward materialist interpretations of subjective malaise,
"boredom" remained ambiguous—a form of disaffection implicated at once
in problems of meaning and in the material conditions of experience. Thus, I
argued, the discourse on boredom illustrates the complexities and contradictions of the modern discourse of reflection on subjective experience more
generally. Seen in this light, the disjunction between humanistic and scientific rhetorics of explanation appears less as aporia than as complementarity.

If the metaphoricity of boredom and the metaphoric operation of the discourse on boredom are emphasized, the idioms of socio-historical causation
and moral-epistemological significance no longer appear to be fundamentally incommensurable modes of explaining its historical significance. As I
showed, the discourse on boredom spread through nineteenth-century
European society as a function of transformations in collective and individual experience that were both spiritually and materially highly significant; the
experience—or more precisely: the new way of conceiving of subjective malaise—spread as part of a modern language of reflection in which the skeptical attitude toward self and world that accompanied those changes was democratized. From a rhetorical point of view, then, both of these perspectives
must be situated in relation to the process I call democratization of skepticism in modernity.

Boredom and the Modern Rhetoric of Reflection
on Subjective Experience

My overall claim is not that boredom as such is the key to theorizing modernity, but rather that the problems of theorizing boredom are the problems of theorizing modern experience more generally. Using this example, I have developed a philosophically reflexive mode of rhetorical analysis that steps outside the modern rhetoric of experience that forms its point of departure while attending to the historical specificity of the discursive and conceptual transformations associated with modernization. Part I described the bifurcated rhetoric of reflection that gives rise to competing, mutually contradictory, and singly unsatisfying rhetorics of experience. Part II developed a conception of boredom as a metaphor for the experiential predicament of the modern subject and thereby negotiated the aporia embedded in the divergent models of explanation. Just as boredom itself mediates between the subjective and objective, spiritual and material, consequences of modernization, so too does the notion that boredom is a linguistically constructed experience of the limits of subjective experience in modernity mediate between subjectively and objectively oriented explanations of its significance.

Part II, "The Rhetoric of Reflection," treated texts that begin from an awareness of the historical specificity of the modern experience of self and world exemplified by boredom. Through readings of Georg Simmel, Martin Heidegger, and Robert Musil that illuminated the rhetorical construction (in various senses) of subjective experience in modernity, I established a perspective for reflection on the operation of the modern rhetoric of experience through which boredom effaces its own historicity and thereby seemingly confirms the universality and necessity of the enlightened conception of time as an empty continuum of identical moments. Thus while "The Rhetoric of Experience" focused on analyzing the conceptual structure of the discourse on boredom as an historical phenomenon, "The Rhetoric of Reflection" emphasized the philosophical importance of the experience itself as a mode in which questions about the meaning and purpose of human existence arise in modernity.

Part I treated texts that took the phenomenon of boredom as a given and concentrated on interpreting its significance; the texts examined in Part II ask how subjective experience is constituted in modernity such that the phenomenon of boredom becomes possible at all. All, however, attest to the convergence of the modern conception of history as rational progress with widespread subjective disaffection. This concrete manifestation of the dialectic of enlightenment, I have argued, underlines the need to interpret the seeming ubiquity of boredom in modernity in a way that joins socio-historical and philosophical perspectives—in my terms, as a function of the modern rhetoric of reflection on subjective experience as such. Read in this light, these sources demonstrate that the problems that arise in the attempt to conceptualize boredom as a specifically modern experience instantiate more general theoretical issues about reflection on modern subjectivity.

The experience of boredom as we know it came into being in the aftermath of Enlightenment, as a product of the struggle to express how modern subjects lived problems of meaning in a world without God. The language of boredom originally linked the spiritual crisis of modern subjectivity to a critical perspective on the socio-historical conditions of modern existence. However, as a name for the experience of time lived as a fragmented eternal present filled with indifferent objects, boredom quickly became a metaphor for the meaninglessness of history as such. Due to a powerful nihilistic dynamic internal to the experience itself, boredom tends to evoke the fatalistic generalization that life itself is a senseless series of momentary encounters with irrelevant objects. This dynamic, through which the spiritual or epistemological aspect of boredom eclipses the socio-critical dimension of the discourse, underpins what I have called the normalization of anomie through which boredom has come to seem an eternal feature of the human condition. My objective has been to establish a perspective for reflection on this circumstance by examining how the discourse on boredom gradually lost its specificity as a language of reflection on *modern* existence in the course of the historical period in which, to use Claessens' term, the "loss of cultural self-evidence" ceased to be an extraordinary feature of human existence.

While the efforts of Reinhard Kuhn and Wolf Lepenies clearly fail to gain a purchase on the problem of boredom because they remain within the frameworks of idealist and materialist thought, the attempts of Simmel and Heidegger to place sociological and philosophical explanation of the experience on more secure ground by recognizing the historical specificity of boredom fail in more complicated ways. Neither is able adequately to grasp this historicity as a metaphorical relation between the "ideal," or subjective and "material" or objective effects of modernization, for neither treats the experience of boredom in the context of the discursive construction of modern experience. Because each takes the experience "literally" within the terms of a sociological or philosophical rhetoric of reflection, Simmel and Heidegger's very different phenomenologies of boredom reinscribe the aporia discussed in Part I. By way of entry into a consideration of the larger implications of this study's strategy for shifting the emphasis onto the figurative dimension of experience—onto the modern rhetoric of reflection on subjective experience as such—it is worth briefly reviewing the outcome of those discussions.

Simmel carries the sociological interpretation of boredom to another level when he argues that a blasé attitude of being, so to speak, always already bored with everything that impinges on consciousness is the condition of possibility for modern subjectivity. From this perspective, the very structures of metropolitan existence that de-differentiate objects and reduce sensory impressions to a minimum make possible a subjective sense of radical freedom. However, Simmel denies—à la Kant—that it is possible to explain the "ultimate significance" of this circumstance. For him, the philosophical questions basic to modern subjectivity—in particular, the problem of freedom and determination—are undecidable. Eschewing a neo-Hegelian (in particular, a Marxian) attempt to link the subjective phenomena associated with modernization to a philosophy of history via a theory of alienation, Simmel turns to a sociological description of consciousness.

Blaséness is the key subjective adaptation to the conditions of modern metropolitan existence not because people think of themselves as blasé but because, according to Simmel, they *are* blasé. As a state of being that results from the very process of rationalization that produces the modern individual, blaséness is for him a form of life in which the unresolvable problem of meaning is lived. Although Simmel powerfully connects the philosophical dilemmas of the modern subject to the historical process of modernization, he does not do so in a way that locates reflective potential within the experience of that subject. It is from the point of view of sociological reflection that the blasé attitude can be recognized as a condition of possibility for modern existence. Because the rhetoric of reflection proper to sociological analysis disregards the actual languages in which "the" metropolitan subject interprets experience, Simmel obscures the reflective potential within boredom. By flattening its various manifestations into an allegedly universal attitude of blaséness, Simmel reduces boredom to an epiphenomenon of historical processes that can be understood sociologically.

If the rhetoric of sociology proceeds outside of subjective experience in search of its extra-subjective determination, philosophical rhetoric probes into experience in pursuit of extra-historical significance. Thus while Simmel sought a systematic historical and sociological explanation of the genesis of the blasé attitude that would situate it historically as the condition of possibility of modern individuality, Heidegger's argument moved in the opposite direction. For him, the question becomes what the language of blaséness reveals—what does it mean to be bored by something? with oneself? as such?

By delving into what I have called the grammar of the experience to generate an existential analytic of boredom, Heidegger developed a philosophical interpretation of boredom that stood in a very different relation to the modern rhetoric of reflection than Simmel's sociologically grounded analysis of the same phenomenon.

While the observation that blaséness is the defining feature of modern metropolitan subjectivity leads Simmel from individual experience to the sociological interpretation of modernity, Heidegger's notion that boredom is the fundamental mood of modernity moves him in the opposite direction. For him, the modalities of being bored point beyond the epistemological dilemmas that mark the limits of the inherited philosophical rhetoric of subjectivity and objectivity. From the point of view of his existential analytic of mood, the "grammar" of boredom provides an entrée into the fundamental problems of human existence. Thus Heidegger's existential analysis purportedly reveals in the experience not the historically specific conditions of possibility for modern subjectivity but the ontological structure of human existence as such.

As part of a venerable tradition of interpreting boredom as belonging to the basic repertoire of human emotional response, Martin Heidegger's meditations on the experience as the "fundamental mood" of modernity actually occlude reflection on the historical specificity of the experience. The strength of his exposition lies in the clarity with which he articulates how this "mood," precisely *because* it expresses the relation between human being and time in modernity, constitutes an aspect of being-in-the-world as such. From this ontological perspective, the argument for the historical significance of the discourse on boredom that comes into such prominence in the nineteenth century is moot. The etymological and historical evidence that differentiates the modern experiences of boredom, ennui, and *Langeweile* from their more ancient cousins such as acedia, melancholy, and *taedium vitae* is an insufficient rejoinder to Heidegger's reinscription of the philosophical claim that boredom by whatever name is an eternal feature of the human condition, for his philosophical interpretation of boredom rests on premises about the nature of experience that are incompatible with historicist argument as such. Although he clearly shifts these questions onto different ground, the early Heidegger shares with Kierkegaard (and Reinhard Kuhn) a basic assumption that the epistemological and ethical problems related to boredom must be understood as rooted in the human condition as such.

While from an historical perspective, the boredom discourse is clearly "about" the subjective effects of cultural modernization, the force of Heidegger's point of view is buttressed by the fact that sociological approaches to boredom, melancholy, etc., cannot give a satisfactory account of the relation between these phenomena and philosophical problems. As an experience of time, boredom indeed seems to be linked to dilemmas of subjectivity that transcend the historical specificity of the language in which they are phrased. Conversely, however, in interpreting boredom as the "fundamental mood" of modernity, Heidegger raised questions about the relation between individual and collective experience that could not be resolved within the individualizing, existentialist framework he developed. This difficulty is manifested in the ways Heidegger's own argument for the philosophical significance of boredom depends on an (unacknowledged) appeal to historically specific features of modern existence.

As the genealogy of boredom developed in Part I demonstrated, the temporality of the train station and the bifurcation between work and leisure that play crucial roles in his analysis belong not to an ahistorical grammar of mood but to a broader cultural rhetoric of reflection that links subjective experience to the rationalization of time in modernity. That Heidegger's argument turns on a series of examples that describe the experience of the isolated and radically individuated subject of modernity has implications for his claim that philosophical reflection on the grammar of *Langeweile* leads beyond the particularities of the experience to disclose the structure of human being in the world as being in time.[10] Though Heideggerean philosophy points the way beyond the conventional modern understanding of subjectivity, it does so in a way that evades the question of the historical and political significance of boredom and of the rhetoric of experience in which it is embedded. His highly abstract, philosophical understanding of human historicity as being in time collapses the question of the concrete historical construction of experience into ontological considerations. Attending to the way a particular metaphorics inflects Heidegger's attempt to locate an opening for the fundamental questions of philosophy in boredom is therefore crucial for developing a more differentiated account of what it means to call boredom the "fundamental mood" of modernity.

From a perspective that emphasizes the discursive construction of subjective experience, the structural limitations of materialist interpretation condition Simmel's historicizing failure to take the reflective perspective of the modern subject seriously, just as those of idealistic reflection color Heidegger's attempted circumvention of the historical operations of the boredom

---

[10]Similar historicizing arguments could perhaps be made for Angst and the other "fundamental moods" analyzed by the early Heidegger as disclosing the structure of the world as such. (See Haar).

discourse through existential grammar. Only by theorizing the contributions
of both modes of thought to the modern rhetoric of reflection does it become possible to develop a critical and historical conception of boredom.
Neither the "philosophical" approach to boredom as an individual "mood"
or subjective mode of relating to the world nor the "sociological" understanding of boredom as a culturally and historically constituted mode of response to the conditions of modern existence could transcend its own, disciplinarily specific rhetoric of reflection in this way. However, once the two
contrasting approaches are seen as exemplifying two different aspects of the
dominant contemporary rhetoric of experience, the aporia that arises from
the complementary failures of these interpretive models to theorize boredom
adequately can be grasped as paradigmatic for a more general problem in
theorizing the relation between discourse and experience. From a rhetorical
perspective, the failure of both subject-centered and society-centered approaches to explain the meaning of boredom points to a need to theorize the
convergence of language and experience in the historically constituted metaphorics of boredom. The conclusion to be drawn from the failure of each of
these incommensurable arguments to account for the insights of the other is
that the problem of the meaning of boredom must be posed from a rhetorical perspective, in relation to an account of the discursive formation of subjective experience in modernity.

Boredom and the Democratization of
Skepticism in Modernity

The emergence and dissemination of the discourse on boredom must be
understood, I have argued, in relation to the processes of cultural and historical transformation by which skepticism was democratized. To approach
boredom in this way is to articulate idealistic and materialistic perspectives by
situating the epistemic and ethical dilemmas associated with the experience
without qualities in the context of the larger discourse of reflection on subjective experience in modernity. Emphasizing how the rhetoric of boredom
exemplifies more general features of the modern discourse on subjective experience escapes the aporia represented by the opposition between sociological reduction and philosophical interpretation by defining boredom as an
historically constituted experience of the philosophical problem of the
meaning of human agency. However, describing it in this way does not in itself transcend the rhetoric of experience proper to the discourse on boredom.

It is necessary to take the rhetorical line of argument a step further to pose
the question of the symbolic significance of the discourse on boredom for

modern life. Experientially, the bored subject is cut off from the world and from history in what appears to be a profound experience of meaninglessness. However, as my reading of Heidegger's analysis underlined, the grammar of the experience, which renders its historicity invisible and naturalizes boredom's relation to language, is the product of specific sociological transformations. Linking modernization to the spread of skepticism provides a framework for conceptualizing the relationship between language and experience historically that can articulate the insights of Simmel and Heidegger's methodologically opposed attempts to theorize boredom as the fundamental mood of modernity.

My concept of the democratization of skepticism in modernity describes the rhetorical transformation of the commonly available categories of reflection in the historical context of modernization. Like Weber's "disenchantment of the world," it is both a descriptive and an analytic concept: my claim is that epistemological and ethical skepticism color modern experience and differentiate it from traditional modes of understanding and dwelling in the world. However, unlike the sociological category of disenchantment, which is linked via a thesis about the secularization of experience in modernity to a melancholy metanarrative of loss, the notion of the democratization of skepticism leaves open the question of the epistemological significance of modernization. By emphasizing that the pervasiveness of the skeptical dilemma is an historically constituted feature of the modern rhetoric of reflection on subjective experience, my account sheds a new light on the historical and philosophical significance of an experience that is generally lived as a "mood" devoid of such larger meaning.

By accounting for the naturalization of the ahistorical rhetoric of reflection on experience that gives rise to that occlusion of historicity, the concept of the democratization of skepticism thus provides a means of answering the question raised at the outset: How can we understand why boredom "began to be felt on an epidemic scale" in the mid-nineteenth century? From a sociological perspective, the transformations of subjective experience in modernity are symptomatic of the loss of meaning, the fragmentation of traditional social order, and the undermining of inherited standards of value that accompany the "disenchantment" of the world through the ascendance of scientific thought. While Weber focuses on the sociological and political consequences of the ultimate groundlessness of modern existence, my approach aims to foster reflection on the philosophical and historical possibilities that result from the process of disenchantment as it affects individual experience. Rather than creating a global narrative, my account aims to relate boredom to the historical process of the democratization of skepticism in a

way that identifies the potential for reflection on the process of modernization within the very experiences that are symptomatic of the transformations
it has wrought. Boredom, I contend, should be seen not only as a symptom
of the breakdown of older ways of being in the world but also as a locus of
new possibilities. The nihilistic "battle of the gods" that seems inevitable at
the level of broad historical generalization is configured quite differently
from the perspective of the bored subject, once that subject is seen as a
bearer and not just a symptom of modern skepticism.

As we have seen, the language of boredom that emerges in the West after
the Enlightenment represents the dilemma of the modern subject whose existence is no longer meaningfully embedded in traditional religious and social narratives. In the mid-nineteenth century, the boredom discourse took
form as a metaphoric articulation of the subjective effects of modernization
with the material changes that constituted the process. Although the epistemic and ethical dilemma of the bored subject, for whom all objects are indifferent and all actions equally meaningless, appears to express a timeless
experience of the futility of human existence, as I have shown, this experience is in fact the dialectical expression of an historical situation. 'Boredom'
(*ennui*, *Langeweile*) names a crisis of meaning lived by the modern subject
whose most fundamental relation to the world has become problematic.
However, the historical development of the discourse toward an aesthetici-
zation of the experience obscures the linkage between the philosophical
problems associated with boredom and the sociologically constituted form
of the experience without qualities.

This development is reflected in the bifurcation of reflection on boredom
into sociological and philosophical literatures and continues to structure
Simmel and Heidegger's more sophisticated attempts to think subjective experience historically. Because neither recognized the significance of the historical specificity of the discourse on boredom for his account of the modern
rhetoric of experience, both Simmel's sociohistorical account of the blasé attitude and Heidegger's existential grammar of boredom abstract experience
from its discursive construction. In taking boredom too literally, whether in
sociological or in philosophical terms, their accounts failed to link the sociological question of why boredom is so pervasive in modernity to the
philosophical dilemmas raised by the experience. While Simmel's analysis
fails to recognize the importance of the language in which the modern subject reflects on the effects of rationalization and fragmentation of the life-
world, Heidegger's focus on the structure of reflection revealed by the
grammar of boredom abstracts the questions of meaning to which it leads
from the modernization process.

The interpretation of boredom as a symptom of the democratization of skepticism in modernity articulates these two dimensions by reading the rhetoric of experience inscribed in the boredom discourse historically and thereby revealing the metaphoric function of the experience as a form in which the dilemmas of the modern subject are lived. However, such an interpretation overcomes the aporetic confrontation between sociological and philosophical interpretations of the experience and incorporates both perspectives into an historical conception of it only by establishing a perspective outside the metaphorics of boredom itself. Because the nihilistic dynamic by which punctual disaffection becomes a universalized sense of meaninglessness structures the lived experience of boredom, such an interpretation cannot overcome the occlusion of historical reflection inscribed in the experience itself.

As we have seen, neither sociological nor philosophical approaches to boredom can come to terms with this dynamic, which epitomizes the way the modern rhetoric of reflection individualizes, subjectivizes, and dehistoricizes lived experience. In a sense, locating the problem of boredom within a philosophical interpretation of the democratization of skepticism in modernity only underlines the deeper problem represented by the aporetic structure of the modern discourse of reflection on subjective experience—the way the rhetoric of boredom forecloses reflection on its own historicity to become the basis both of cynicism and of exuberantly nihilistic kynicism. As a thesis about the rhetoric of reflection, my approach can explain why neither idealist nor materialist accounts can give an adequate account of boredom, but it cannot refigure the experience itself.

I have argued that Robert Musil's strategy for representing the dilemmas of modern existence was an attempt to overcome the aporetic impasse in the modern rhetoric of reflection on subjective experience in a more figurative way. By focusing the reader's attention on the metaphoric dimension of experience itself through a novel whose story "comes down to the fact that the story which is supposed to be told in it is not told," he pursues the possibility of developing a critical, reflective perspective on the nature of experience under modern conditions of democratized skepticism. Thus Musil's man without qualities not only recognizes his blaséness, ethical indifference, and epistemological relativism as a response to the depersonalization and reification wrought by modernization; he reflects on his own state of being "without qualities" as a phenomenon of philosophical as well as historical significance. *The Man without Qualities* poses the question of what sort of relation to one's own experience is possible in modernity.

In Chapter 3 we saw how 'boredom' emerged out of the broader discourse on the subjective effects of modernization to become a privileged metaphor for epistemic and ethical dilemmas of the modern subject. From the beginning, the discourse on boredom served to isolate those dilemmas from the social conditions that evoked them, and, in contrast to the more political languages of reification and alienation, to figure them as problems proper to the individual subject. Synthesizing medical and religious elements into a language of reflection, the discourse on boredom fostered the perspective of interiority over that of historical analysis. While social thinkers tended to emphasize the material foundations of the "crisis of subjectivity" as it took form in the nineteenth century, the rhetoric of reflection embedded in the language of boredom gained force. Although there were always demonstrable links between boredom and capitalism—from the beginning, the experience was linked to industrialization, urbanization, and commodification—as the "epidemic" spread and consumer society emerged, 'boredom' came to stand for a retreat from all of that. Especially in the wake of Nietzsche's call to re-define authentic selfhood in non-religious terms, the phenomenon of boredom came to represent a neo-aristocratic distance from the leveling forces of modern society. In the process, the historically constituted metaphor of boredom became naturalized as a mood that bore no necessary connection to the conditions of modern existence. If it expressed alienation, it was alienation from and not of society: 'boredom' became a key term in a rhetoric of reflection centered on the subject as an isolated individual whose malaise was existential rather than social.

By the time Musil was writing the *The Man without Qualities*, the critical perspective on modern existence originally inscribed in the boredom discourse had thus lost its socio-historical edge. The literary and cultural permutations of boredom in late nineteenth- and early twentieth-century Europe resonated more with Kierkegaard's melancholy and subjectivist rebellion against "The Present Age" than with the critical vision of modern life formulated in Haussmann's Paris. While Flaubert and Baudelaire had used the representation of ennui to establish a critical distance from which to dissect the romantic melancholy of the *mal du siècle*, by the next fin-de-siècle, the discourse on boredom they helped to frame had loosed itself from history. The romantic project of cultivating the self was resumed in an aestheticist discourse that associated ennui with escaping from rather than realistically representing modern reality. Within Musil's milieu, many saw nihilism as the logical consequence of their disaffection with modern existence. However, decadence and seduction are but the dark side of the leap into faith that so often served as a cure for ennui.

In transforming literary language into an instrument for representing the enigmatic realities of modern existence, Musil establishes a perspective that should be seen as the legacy of both Flaubert and Baudelaire. By ironically reworking the rhetorics of reflection on modern life embedded in the literary tradition and the natural sciences alike, *The Man without Qualities* establishes a critical, reflective perspective on the dilemmas of modern subjectivity that neither abstracts experience from history nor neglects its philosophical dimension. Indeed, Musil's novel forthrightly affirms skepticism as the fundamental modern condition and then attempts to develop a utopian vision on this basis.[11] In trying to imagine what it would mean to live for the sake of possibilities rather than realities, Musil's novel strives to reconnect the philosophical and social-critical rhetorics of experience that were originally conjoined in the discourse on boredom.

Musil's novel thus establishes a perspective outside the rhetoric of reflection that bifurcates the world in which skepticism has been democratized. Because it represents the dilemmas of modern existence as the lived problems of an historically situated protagonist, it avoids Heidegger's abstraction of philosophical questions from their discursive contexts, yet does not render an account of that context prior to the questions themselves, as Simmel did. The "man without qualities" lives in a world in which history has become as unreliable as identity. Although he belongs to the genre of the "bored subject," his very existence exemplifying the operation of the rhetoric of experience in which the conditions of modern life produce a pervasive sense of alienation, isolation, and indifference to things and people, Musil's protagonist is only rarely referred to as "bored." Instead, the focus is on developing a vocabulary of reflection that combines idealist and materialist rhetorics of experience to establish a critical perspective on the historically constituted dilemma of the modern subject—a perspective that, by the early twentieth century, could no longer be achieved through the metaphorics of boredom.

Through the method he called "constructive irony," Musil compels his reader to confront this vision of modern life both intellectually and emotionally. Rather than commenting on the dilemmas of the modern subject, *The Man without Qualities* builds on their ambiguity. By representing the effects of disenchantment not as conclusions but as potential beginnings, as possible sources of spiritual renewal, Musil establishes a distinctive perspective on the subjective effects of modernization. Turning the modern rhetoric

---

[10] For a reading that attempts from a different perspective to articulate Musil's innovative idea of subjectivity as the basis of the utopian dimension of the novel, see Jonsson, *Subject without Nation.*

of reflection on subjective experience against itself through an ironic representation of existence under the conditions of universalized skepticism, *The Man without Qualities* articulates the spiritual and socio-critical dimensions of reflection on experience that had been severed in the literature of reflection on boredom through the bifurcation into existential-philosophical analysis and sociological symptomology. Through the structural metaphors of "being without qualities" and "Seinesgleichen geschieht," "its like happens," his representation of the dilemmas of modern existence moves toward an overcoming of the aporia manifested in the historical development of the boredom discourse. Unfortunately, the tropes in and through which this articulation took place did not attain the immediacy of the language of boredom. Musil (and his readers) may see proof of the accuracy of his analysis everywhere, but Musil's notion that it is a world of "being without qualities" remains extrinsic. In the end, the failure of his novel to refigure experience attests to what may be viewed as the historical legacy of the boredom discourse: the evacuation of reflection on subjective experience itself in modernity.

I have argued that the metaphorics of boredom were at the center of a new language of reflection forged out of the fragments of inherited and modern vocabularies of experience. Musil's novel confronts a world in which this synthesis no longer holds together at all—a world so rationalized and so dominated by a materialist rhetoric that "one has taken certain questions out of the human heart." Such disenchantment cannot be reversed. It is not simply that since the inherited language of reflection fails to capture the subjective experience of modern existence, a new vocabulary is called for. Modernity has undermined the very conditions of possibility of reflection, of experience in the sense of Benjamin's *Erfahrung.* Thus *The Man without Qualities* takes as its point of departure the notion that "the dissolution of the anthropocentric point of view . . . has finally arrived at the "I" itself." It poses, implicitly but also quite explicitly, the problem of how to generate an objective form of reflection on subjectivity, one appropriate to "a world of qualities without a man" and "experiences without the person who experiences them." Musil's inability singlehandedly to forge a language that could mediate, as the boredom discourse once had, between the subjective and objective affects of modernization reflects not an artistic but an historical fate. The links he forges between the experience of history in which only "its like happens" and modern "being without qualities" are better viewed as a diagnosis of modern existence in an age of democratized skepticism than as a means of giving to modern fragmentation "the weight of experience." Nonetheless, the great achievement of this gargantuan fragment of a novel is to have grappled directly with the problem to which the metaphorics of boredom appeared for a brief time to be an answer: the absence of a language of reflection adequate to the subjective experience of modernity.

In a world where "its like" is all that happens, a world in which resignation has turned to cynicism and amusement to obsession, we increasingly lack the most basic language for reflection on subjective experience. In a sense, the problem is not new: Georg Simmel was contemplating the significance of Nietzsche and Schopenhauer when, in 1902, he wrote of the persistence of a "longing for an absolute purpose" that "continues to exist as an empty pressing toward a goal that has become unrealizable" in the aftermath of the decline of religious metanarratives. Simmel's view that it is the complex technology of modern life that calls forth such an awareness of purposelessness in the first place is seconded by Sigmund Freud in *Das Unbehagen in der Kultur* (*Civilization and Its Discontents*), where he suggests that the malaise pervasive in modern Western culture reflects an inchoate awareness of the potential for absolute destruction embodied in technological and scientific progress. However, as a consequence of intellectual developments that may be traced in part to these founding fathers of materialist strategies of reflection, our ability to see the dilemmas of subjective existence in relation to their historical conditions of possibility has grown ever more limited.

In the late twentieth century, the medicalization of malaise entered an entirely new phase: today, problems of meaning appear increasingly obsolete in the face of advances in neurophysiology and pharmacology. Happiness itself is subject to quantitative measures.[12] Depression is rampant in modern society, but it is no longer linked via the ancient language of melancholy to perennial questions about the ends of human existence. Instead, we have the language of boredom, in which the refusal or inability to feel becomes a stable configuration of the self. With its nihilistic ineffability, the experience without qualities comes to express the historic foreclosure of reflection of which it is a symptom.

Boredom is a crucial mode of experience for modern subjects—whether at work, in school, in prison, or at leisure—but one that conceals its own historicity. Such effacement need not operate as explicitly as in the philosophical discourse on boredom. Even those who recognize their malaise as historically specific are likely to fit Musil's description: "The person who is awakened to consciousness of contemporary circumstances has the feeling that the same things are always happening to him, without there being a light to lead him out of this disorderly circle." Its like happens: we no longer share

---

[11] See Veerhoven et al., *World Database of Happiness.*

modes of understanding the significance of human life that "make a history possible" by weaving individual existence into larger temporal frameworks. And without a language of reflection capable of illuminating the experience of modernity, the sense of being inescapably caught in cycles of meaningless repetition grows ever more pervasive.

While the discourse on boredom has largely lost its critical force, boredom itself can thus be seen to function as a lived metaphor for the dilemma of the modern subject: the experience without qualities is the existential reflection of the rationalized modern world in which the present has been abbreviated into oblivion—in which experience itself has atrophied. That is to say, however, that the internal dynamic of boredom encloses the foreclosure of reflection of which it is a symptom. The evacuation of the language of reflection on subjective experience in modernity has rendered boredom mute: a dead metaphor whose metaphoricity has been forgotten.

The historical irony of the discourse on boredom is that a phenomenon so deeply tied to modernization has come to seem a negative revelation of the nihilistic truth of human existence as such. But the mythological foreclosure of reflection that naturalizes the experience without qualities is itself a symptom of the problematic legacy of Enlightenment. That boredom "takes on the proportions of immortality" expresses the failure of reflection to come to terms with the embodied, historical experience of modernity—and the often inchoate striving to live meaningfully in a world whose complexity surpasses understanding.

REFERENCE MATTER

Bibliography

Abrams, M. H. *Natural Supernaturalism*. New York: Norton, 1971.

Adorno, Theodor. *Jargon der Eigentlichkeit: zur deutschen Ideologie*. Frankfurt am Main: Suhrkamp Verlag, 1964.

———. "Der Essay als Form." In Rolf Tiedemann, ed., *Gesammelte Schriften*, vol. 11, 9–33. Frankfurt am Main: Suhrkamp Verlag, 1974.

———. *Kierkegaard: Konstruktion des Ästhetischen*. Frankfurt am Main: Suhrkamp Verlag, 1979.

Allen, James Smith. *Popular French Romanticism: Authors, Readers, and Books in the Nineteenth Century*. Syracuse: Syracuse University Press, 1981.

———. *In the Public Eye: A History of Reading in Modern France, 1800–1940*. Princeton: Princeton University Press, 1991.

Allesch, Johannes von. "Robert Musil in der geistigen Bewegung seiner Zeit." In Karl Dinklage, ed., *Robert Musil: Leben-Werk-Wirkung*. Vienna: Almathea-Verlag, 1960.

Arendt, Hannah. *The Human Condition*. Chicago: University of Chicago Press, 1958.

———. "Martin Heidegger ist achtzig Jahre alt." *Merkur* 23 (1969): 893–902. (Trans. by Albert Hofstadter as "Martin Heidegger at Eighty," *The New York Review of Books*, 1971; reprinted in Michael Murray, ed., *Heidegger and Modern Philosophy*, 293–303 [New Haven: Yale University Press, 1978].)

Aristotle. *The Complete Works of Aristotle: Revised Oxford Translation*. Ed. J. Barnes. Princeton: Princeton University Press, 1984.

———. *Opera*. Berlin: W. de Gruyter, 1960–.

———. *The Rhetoric and the Poetics*. Trans. W. Rhys Roberts, Ingram Bywater. New York: Random House, 1984.

Arntzen, Helmut. *Musil-Kommentar: zu dem Roman 'Der Mann ohne Eigenschaften.'* Munich: Winkler, 1982.

———. "Satirischer Stil: Zur Satire Robert Musils im 'Mann ohne Eigenschaften.'" *Abhandlungen zur Kunst- Musik- und Literaturwissenschaft 9*. Bonn: Bouvier, 1960.

Arvon, Henri. "Robert Musil und der Positivismus." In Karl Dinklage, Elisabeth Albertsen, and Karl Corino, eds., *Robert Musil: Studien zu seinem Werk*, 200–213. Reinbek bei Hamburg: Rowohlt, 1970.

Aschheim, Steven E. *The Nietzsche Legacy in Germany, 1890–1990*. Berkeley: University of California Press, 1992.

Asendorf, Christoph. *Batteries of Life: On the History of Things and Their Perception in Modernity*. Trans. Don Reneau. Berkeley: University of California Press, 1993.

Auerbach, Erich. *Mimesis: Dargestellte Wirklichkeit in der abendländischen Literatur* Berne: Francke, 1946. (Trans. by Willard R. Trask as *Mimesis: The Representation of Reality in Western Literature* [Princeton: Princeton University Press, 1953].)

Aulinger, Barbara. *Die Gesellschaft als Kunstwerk: Fiktion und Methode bei Georg Simmel*. Vienna: Passagen Verlag, 1999.

Augustine. *Confessions*. Trans. John K. Ryan. New York: Doubleday, 1960.

Baldick, Robert, ed. *Pages from the Goncourt Journal*. Singapore: Penguin, 1984.

Ballard, Bruce W. *The Role of Mood in Heidegger's Ontology*. Lanham, Md.: University Press of America, 1991.

Banfield, Ann. *Unspeakable Sentences: Representation and Narration in the Language of Fiction*. New York: Routledge, 1982.

Bann, Stephen. *Romanticism and the Rise of History: Studies in Intellectual and Cultural History*. New York: Twayne, 1995.

Barbalet, J. M. "Boredom and Social Meaning." *British Journal of Sociology* 50 (1999): 631–46.

Barbey D'Aurevilly, Jules. *Dandyism*. Trans. Douglas Ainslie. New York: PAJ, 1988.

Barrett, William. "Leibniz's Garden: Some Philosophical Observations on Boredom." *Social Research* 42 (1975): 551–55.

Barrows, Susanna. *Distorting Mirrors: Visions of the Crowd in Late Nineteenth-Century France*. New Haven: Yale University Press, 1981.

Barthes, Roland. *Le degré zéro de l'écriture*. Paris: Seuil, 1953.

———. *Le plaisir du texte*. Paris: Seuil, 1973.

Baudelaire, Charles. *The Flowers of Evil and Paris Spleen: Poems*. Trans. William H. Crosby. Brockport, N.Y.: BOA Editions, 1991.

———. *The Flowers of Evil*. Ed. Marthiel Mathews and Jackson Mathews. New York: New Directions, 1989.

———. *The Flowers of Evil*. Trans. William Aggeler. Fresno, Calif.: Academic Library Guild, 1954.

———. *Intimate Journals*. Trans. Christopher Isherwood. Reprint of 1957 ed. New York: Howard Fertig, 1977.

———. *Œuvres completes* [OC]. Ed. Claude Pichois with Jean Ziegler. 2 vols. Paris: Gallimard, 1975–76.

———. *The Painter of Modern Life*. Trans. and ed. Jonathan Mayne. New York: Phaidon, 1964.

———. *The Parisian Prowler: Le Spleen de Paris, Petits Poèmes en prose*. Trans. Edward K. Kaplan. Athens: University of Georgia Press, 1989.

Baudrillard, Jean. *Selected Writings*. Ed. Mark Poster. Stanford: Stanford University Press, 1988.

———. *Simulacra and Simulation*. Trans. Sheila Faria Glaser. Ann Arbor: Michigan University Press, 1994.

———. *The Mirror of Production*. Trans. Mark Poster. St. Louis: Telos, 1975.

Beard, George. *A Practical Treatise on Nervous Exhaustion (Neurasthenia)* [1870]. New York: E. B. Treat, 1905.

Beckett, Samuel. *Waiting for Godot*. New York: Grove, 1954.

Beistegui, Miguel. "'Boredom: Between Existence and History': On Heidegger's Pivotal *The Fundamental Concepts of Metaphysics.*" *Journal of the British Society for Phenomenology* 31, no. 2 (May 2000): 145–58.

Belke, Ingrid, ed. *Moritz Lazarus und Heymann Steinthal: Die Begründer der Völker-psychologie in ihren Briefen.* Tübingen: Mohr, 1971.

Bell, Carolyn Shaw. "The Value of Time." *Social Research* 42 (1975): 556–63.

Bell-Villada, Gene H. *Art for Art's Sake and Literary Life: How Politics and Markets Helped Shape the Ideology and Culture of Aestheticism 1790–1990.* Lincoln: University of Nebraska Press, 1998.

Bellebaum, Alfred. *Langeweile: Überdruss und Lebenssinn—Eine geistesgeschichtliche und kultursoziologische Untersuchung.* Opladen: Westdeutscher Verlag, 1990.

Beller, Steven. *Vienna and the Jews, 1867–1938: A Cultural History.* Cambridge: Cambridge University Press, 1989.

———, ed. *Rethinking Vienna 1900.* Austrian History, Culture, and Society 3. New York: Berghahn Books, 2001.

Bender, John, and David E. Wellbery, eds. *Chronotypes: The Construction of Time.* Stanford: Stanford University Press, 1991.

Benhabib, Seyla. *Critique, Norm, and Utopia.* New York: Columbia University Press, 1986.

Benjamin, Walter. *Charles Baudelaire: Ein Lyriker im Zeitalter des Hochkapitalismus.* Ed. Rolf Tiedemann. Frankfurt am Main: Suhrkamp Verlag, 1974. (Trans. by Harry Zohn as *Charles Baudelaire: A Lyric Poet in the Era of High Capitalism* [London: New Left Books, 1973].)

———. *Walter Benjamin: Ein Lesebuch.* Ed. Michael Opitz. Leipzig: Suhrkamp Verlag, 1996.

———. *Gesammelte Schriften.* Ed. Rolf Tiedeman and Hermann Schweppenhäuser with the assistance of Gershom Scholem and Theodor W. Adorno. 7 vols. Frankfurt am Main: Suhrkamp Verlag, 1972–89.

———. *Das Passagen-Werk.* 2 vols. Frankfurt am Main: Suhrkamp Verlag, 1983.

Berger, Peter, Brigitte Berger, and Hansfried Keller. *The Homeless Mind: Modernization and Consciousness.* New York: Vintage, 1974.

Berghahn, Wilfried. *Robert Musil: Mit Selbstzeugnissen und Bilddokumenten.* Reinbek bei Hamburg: Rowohlt, 1963.

Bergson, Henri. *Matière et mémoire.* Paris: F. Alcan, 1896.

Berman, Marshall. *All That Is Solid Melts into Air.* 2d ed. New York, 1988.

Berman, Nina. *Orientalismus, Kolonialismus und Moderne: Zum Bild des Orients in der deutschsprachigen Kultur um 1900.* Stuttgart: M & P, Verlag für Wissenschaft und Forschung, 1997.

Berman, Russell. *Modern Culture and Critical Theory: Art, Politics, and the Legacy of the Frankfurt School.* Madison: University of Wisconsin Press, 1989.

Bernstein, J. M. *Adorno: Disenchantment and Ethics.* Cambridge: Cambridge University Press, 2001.

———. *The Fate of Art: Aesthetic Alienation from Kant to Derrida and Adorno.* University Park: Pennsylvania State University Press, 1992.

———. *The Philosophy of the Novel: Lukács, Marxism and the Dialectics of Form.* Brighton: Harvester Press, 1984.

Bernstein, Michael Andre. "Precision and Soul: The Unbounded Vision of Robert Musil." *The New Republic*, May 29, 1995, 27–36.

Bersani, Leo. *Baudelaire and Freud.* Berkeley: University of California Press, 1977.

———. *The Culture of Redemption.* Cambridge, Mass.: Harvard University Press, 1990.

Bescherelle, Ainé, ed. *Dictionnaire Nationale ou Dictionnaire Universel de la langue française.* 4th ed. Paris: Garnier Frères, 1874.

Besnard, P. *L'anomie: Ses usages et ses fonctions dans le discipline sociologique depuis Durkheim.* Paris: Presses Universitaires de France, 1987.

Biemel, Walter. *Martin Heidegger in Selbstzeugnissen und Bilddokumenten.* Reinbek bei Hamburg: Rowohlt, 1973.

Bilz, Rudolph. "Langeweile: Versuch einer systematischen Darstelung." In Bilz, *Paläo-anthropologie: Der neue Mensch in der Sicht der Verhaltensforschung.* Frankfurt am Main: Suhrkamp Verlag, 1971, 241–76.

Blackbourn, David. *The Long Nineteenth Century: A History of Germany, 1780–1918.* New York: Oxford, 1998.

Blackbourn, David, and Geoff Eley. *The Peculiarities of German History: Bourgeois Society and Politics in Nineteenth Century Germany.* Revised and expanded. Oxford: Oxford University Press, 1984.

Blanchot, Maurice. *L'Entretien Infini.* Paris: Gallimard, 1969.

———. *L'espace littéraire.* Paris: Gallimard, 1955.

———. *L'attente l'oubli.* Paris: Gallimard, 1962.

Blattner, William D. "Existential Temporality in Being and Time (Why Heidegger Is Not a Pragmatist)." In Hubert L. Dreyfus and Harrison Hall, eds., *Heidegger: A Critical Reader,* 99–129. Cambridge: Basil Blackwell, 1992.

Blitz, Mark. *Heidegger's Being and Time and the Possibility of Political Philosophy.* Ithaca: Cornell University Press, 1981.

Bloomfield, Morton. *The Seven Deadly Sins.* East Lansing: Michigan State College Press, 1952.

Blumenberg, Hans. *Die Legitimität der Neuzeit.* Rev. ed. 2 vols. Frankfurt am Main: Suhrkamp Verlag, 1973. (Trans. by Robert M. Wallace as *The Legitimacy of the Modern Age* [Cambridge, Mass.: MIT University Press, 1983].)

———. "Geld oder Leben. Eine metaphorologische Studie zur Konsistenz der Philosophie Georg Simmels." In Hannes Böhringer and Karl Gründer, eds., *Ästhetik und Soziologie um die Jahrhundertwende: Georg Simmel.* Frankfurt am Main: Vittorio Klostermann, 1976.

Bogner, Artur. *Zivilisation und Rationalisierung: Die Zivilisationstheorien Max Webers, Norbert Elias' und der Frankfurter Schule im Vergleich.* Opladen: Westdeutscher Verlag, 1989.

Böhringer, Hannes, and Karlfried Gründer, eds. *Ästhetik und Soziologie um die Jahrhundertwende: Georg Simmel.* Frankfurt am Main: Klostermann, 1976.

Bouillet, M-N., ed. *Dictionnaire Universel des Sciences, des Lettres et des Arts.* 7th ed. Paris: Libraire de L. Hachette et Cie, 1864.

Booth, Wayne. *A Rhetoric of Irony.* Chicago: University of Chicago Press, 1974.

Bouchez, Madeleine. *L'ennui: De Sénèque à Moravia.* Paris: Edition Bordas, 1973.

Bourdieu, Pierre. *The Rules of Art: Genesis and Structure of the Literary Field.* Trans. Susan Emanuel. Stanford: Stanford University Press, 1996.

Böhme, Hartmut. "Die 'Zeit ohne Eigenschaften' und die 'Neue Unübersichtlichkeit': Robert Musil und die Posthistoire." In Josef Strutz, ed., *Kunst, Wissenschaft und Politik von Robert Musil bis Ingeborg Bachmann.* Musil-Studien 14. Munich: Wilhelm Fink, 1986.

Böhringer, Hannes, and Karl Gründer, eds. *Ästhetik und Soziologie um die Jahrhundertwende: Georg Simmel.* Frankfurt am Main: Vittorio Klostermann, 1976.

Bouillet, M-N. *Dictionnaire Universel des Sciences, des Lettres et des Arts.* 7th ed. Paris: Librairie de L. Hachette et Cie, 1864.

Brenner, Michael, Vicki Caron, and Uri R. Kaufmann, eds. *Jewish Emancipation Reconsidered: The French and German Models.* Tübingen: Mohr Siebeck, 2003.

Breuer, Stefan. *Anatomie der Konservativen Revolution.* Darmstadt: Wissenschaftliche Buchgesellschaft, 1993.

Brierre de Boismont, Alexandre. "*De l'ennui.*" *Annales médico-psychologiques* 2 (1850): 565–85.

———. *Du suicide et de la folie suicide, considérés dans leurs rapports avec la médecine, la statistique, et la philosophie.* Paris: Librairie Médicale, Creimer Baillière, 1856.

Brombert, Victor. *The Novels of Flaubert: A Study of Themes and Techniques.* Princeton: Princeton University Press, 1966.

Brown, Peter. *The Body and Society.* New York: Columbia University Press, 1988.

Brunner, Otto, Werner Conze, and Reinhart Koselleck, eds. *Geschichtliche Grundbegriffe: Historisches Lexikon zur politisch-sozialen Sprache in Deutschland.* Stuttgart: E. Klett, 1972–97.

Büchner, Georg. *Sämtliche Werke in Zwei Bänden.* Ed. Henri and Rosemarie Poschmann. Frankfurt am Main: Deutscher Klassiker Verlag, 1999.

Buck-Morss, Susan. *The Dialectics of Seeing: Walter Benjamin and the Arcades Project.* Cambridge, Mass.: MIT Press, 1989.

———."The Flaneur, the Sandwichman and the Whore: The Politics of Loitering." *New German Critique*, 39 (1986): 99–140.

———. *The Origin of Negative Dialectics: Theodor W. Adorno, Walter Benjamin, and the Frankfurt Institute.* New York: MacMillan Free Press, 1977.

Bürger, Peter. "Der Ursprung der ästhetischen Moderne aus dem *ennui.*" In Ludger Heidbrink, ed., *Entzauberte Zeit: Der Melancholische Geist der Moderne,* 101–19. Munich: Hanser, 1997.

Burgin, Victor, James Donald, and Cora Kaplan, eds. *Formations of Fantasy.* London: Methuen, 1986.

Burke, Kenneth. *A Rhetoric of Motives.* Berkeley: University of California Press, 1969.

Butler, E. M. *The Tyranny of Greece over Germany.* Cambridge: Cambridge University Press, 1935. (Reprinted, Boston: Beacon, 1958.)

Butler, Judith. *Bodies That Matter: On the Discursive Limits of "Sex."* New York: Routledge, 1993.

———. *The Psychic Life of Power: Theories in Subjection.* Stanford, Calif.: Stanford University Press, 1997.

———. *Subjects of Desire: Hegelian Reflections in Twentieth-Century France.* New York: Columbia University Press, 1987.

Calinescu, Matei. *Five Faces of Modernity.* Durham: Duke University Press, 1987.

Canetti, Elias. *Masse und Macht.* Düsseldorf: Claasen, 1960.

Chambers, Ross. *The Writing of Melancholy: Modes of Opposition in Early French Modernism.* Trans. Mary Seidman Trouille. Chicago: University of Chicago Press, 1993.

Charney, Leo, and Vanessa R. Schwartz. *Cinema and the Invention of Modern Life.* Berkeley: University of California Press, 1995.

Chateaubriand, François-René, Vicomte de. *Atala, Réné, les Aventures du dernier Abencerage.* Rev. ed. Paris: Flammarion, n.d.

———. *Atala and René.* Ed. Colin Smethurst. London: Grant & Cutler, 1995.

Christian, Petra. *Einheit und Zwiespalt: Zum hegelianisierenden Denken in der Philosophie und Soziologie Georg Simmels.* Berlin: Duncker und Humblot, 1978. (Ph.D. diss. Heidelberg, 1977.)

Chytry, Josef. *The Aesthetic State: A Quest in Modern German Thought.* Berkeley: University of California Press, 1989.

Claessens, Dieter. "Rationalität, revidiert" [1965]. Reprinted in *Freude an soziologischem Denken: Die Entdeckung zweier Wirklichkeiten*, Sociologische Schriften, 58. Berlin: Dunker and Humblot, 1993.

Clark, P. "Suicide, Societé, et Sociologie: De Durkheim à Balzac." *Nineteenth-Century French Studies* 3 (1975): 200–212.

Clark, T. J. *The Painting of Modern Life.* Princeton: Princeton University Press, 1984.

Corbin, Alain. *Le temps, le désir et l'horreur: essais sur le dix-neuvième siècle.* Paris: Aubier, 1991.

———. *L'avènement des loisirs, 1850–1960,* with Julia Csergo et al. Paris: Aubier, 1995.

Corino, Karl. *Robert Musil: Eine Biographie.* Reinbek bei Hamburg: Rowohlt, 2003.

Coser, Lewis, ed. *Georg Simmel.* New Jersey: Englewood Cliffs, 1965.

Cotard, J. *Études sur les Maladies cérébrales et mentales.* Paris: J. B. Baillière et fils, 1891.

Crary, Jonathan. *Suspensions of Perception.* Cambridge, Mass.: MIT, 1999.

———. *Techniques of the Observer: On Vision and Modernity in the Nineteenth Century.* Cambridge, Mass.: MIT Press, 1990.

Crothers, Charles. *Robert K. Merton.* Key Sociologists series. New York: Tavistock Publications and Methuen Inc., 1987.

Csikszentmihalyi, Mihaly. *Beyond Boredom and Anxiety.* 2d ed. San Francisco: Jossey-Bass, 2000 [1975].

Culler, Jonathan. *Flaubert: The Uses of Uncertainty.* Rev. ed. New York: Cornell, 1985.

———. *Structuralist Poetics: Structuralism, Linguistics, and the Study of Literature.* Ithaca: Cornell University Press, 1975.

Dahme, Heinz-Jurgen, and Ottheim Rammstedt. *Georg Simmel und die Moderne: Neue Interpretationen und Materialien.* Frankfurt am Main: Suhrkamp Verlag, 1984.

Daniel, Ute. *Compendium Kulturgeschichte: Theorien, Praxis, Schlüsselwörter.* Frankfurt am Main: Suhrkamp Verlag, 2001.

de Certeau, Michel. *The Practice of Everyday Life.* Trans. Steven Rendall. Berkeley: University of California Press, 1984.

de Grazia, Sebastian. *Of Time, Work, and Leisure.* New York: Anchor, 1964.

de Jaucourt, M. le Chevalier. "Ennui." In Denis Diderot, ed., *Encyclopédie, ou Dictionnaire-Raisonné des Sciences, des Arts et des Métiers*, XII. Lausanne: Sociétés Typographiques, 1782: 467–69.

de Man, Paul. *Allegories of Reading.* New Haven: Yale, 1979.

———. *Blindness and Insight: Essays in the Rhetoric of Contemporary Criticism.* Rev. 2d ed. Theory and History of Literature 7. Minneapolis: University of Minnesota Press, 1983.

de Rougemont, Denis. *Love in the Western World.* Rev. and augmented ed., trans. Montgomery Belgion. New York: Pantheon, 1956.

Debord, Guy. *La Société du spectacle.* Paris: Buchet/Chastel, 1967.

Decher, Friedhelm. *Besuch vom Mittagsdämon: Philosophie der Langeweile.* Lüneburg: zu Klampen, 2000.

Deleuze, Giles, and Felix Guattarri. *L'Anti-Oedipe.* Paris: Minuit, 1972.

Deleuze, Giles. *Différance et Répétition.* Paris: Presses Universitaires de France, 1968.

———. *Nietzsche et la philosophie.* Paris: Presses Universitaires de France, 1963.

Derrida, Jacques. *Marges de la philosophie.* Paris: Minuit, 1972.

———. *Writing and Difference.* Trans. Alan Bass. Chicago: University of Chicago Press, 1978.

———. "Heidegger, l'enfer des philosophes."*Le Nouvel Observateur,* November 6–12, 1987, p. 173.

Dijkstra, Bram. *Idols of Perversity: Fantasies of Feminine Evil in Turn-of-the-Century Culture.* New York: Oxford University Press, 1986.

Dinklage, Karl, ed. *Robert Musil: Leben-Werk-Wirkung.* Vienna: Almathea-Verlag, 1960.

Dinklage, Karl, Elisabeth Albertsen, and Karl Corino, eds. *Robert Musil: Studien zu seinem Werk.* Reinbek bei Hamburg: Rowohlt, 1970.

Dinklage, Karl. "Musils Definition des Mannes ohne Eigenschaften und das Ende seines Romans." In Karl Dinklage, Elisabeth Albertsen, and K. Corino, eds., *Robert Musil: Studien zu seinem Werk,* 112–23. Vienna: Almathea-Verlag, 1960.

Doehlemann, Martin. *Langeweile? Deutung eines verbreiteten Phaenomens.* Frankfurt am Main: Suhrkamp Verlag, 1991.

Dohrn-van Rossum, Gerhard. *Die Geschichte der Stunde: Uhren und moderne Zeitordnungen.* München: Carl Hanser Verlag, 1992. (Trans. by Thomas Dunlap as *History of the Hour: Clocks and Modern Temporal Orders* [Chicago: University of Chicago Press, 1996].)

Dörr-Backes, Felicitas, and Ludwig Nieder, eds. *Georg Simmel zwischen Moderne und Postmoderne.* Würzburg: Königshausen & Neumann, 1995.

Dresler-Brumme, Charlotte. *Nietzsche's Philosophie in Musils Roman 'Der Mann ohne Eigenschaften': Eine vergleichende Betrachtung als Beitrag zum Verständnis.* Literature in der Geschichte Geschichte der Literatur 13. Frankfurt am Main: Athenäum, 1987.

Dreyfus, Hubert L., and Harrison Hall, eds. *Heidegger: A Critical Reader.* Cambridge, Mass.: Basil Blackwell, 1992.

Durkheim, Emile, et al. *Essays on Sociology and Philosophy.* Ed. Kurt H. Wolff. New York: Harper, 1964.

———. *Le Suicide: Étude de Sociologie* [1897]. Paris: Presses Universitaires de France, 1990. (Trans. by John A. Spaulding and George Simpson as *Suicide: A Study in Sociology* [New York: Free Press, 1951].)

———. *The Division of Labor in Society.* New York: Free Press, 1933.

Ebeling, Hans, ed. *Subjektivität und Selbsterhaltung: Beiträge zur Diagnose der Moderne.* Frankfurt am Main: Suhrkamp Verlag, 1976.

Eckardt, Georg. *Völkerpsychologie—Versuch einer Neuentdeckung: Texte von Lazarus, Steinthal und Wundt.* Munich: Beltz, 1997.

Egan, Rose Frances. "The Genesis of the Theory of 'Art for Art's Sake' in Germany and in England." *Smith College Studies in Modern Langugages* 2, no. 4 (July 1921).

Eksteins, Modris. *Rites of Spring: The Great War and the Birth of the Modern Age.* New York: Anchor, 1989.

Elias, Nobert. *Gesammelte Schriften.* Nördlingen: Suhrkamp Verlag, 1997–.

———. *Studien über die Deutschen. Machtkämpfe und Habitusentwicklung im 19. und 20. Jarhhundert.* Frankfurt am Main: Suhrkamp Verlag, 1989. (Trans. by Eric Dunning and Stephen Mennell as *The Germans: Power Struggles and the Development of Habitus in the Nineteenth and Twentieth Centuries*, ed. Michael Schröter [New York: Columbia University Press, 1996].)

———. *Über den Prozeß der Zivilization: Soziogenetische und Psychogenetische Untersuchungen* [1939]. 2 vols. Bern: Francke, 1969. In *Gesammelte Schriften*, vol. 3.1, 3.2. (Trans. by Edmund Jephcott as *The Civilizing Process: The History of Manners* [Oxford: Basil Blackwell, 1978].)

Eliot, George. *Daniel Deronda.* New York: Knopf, 2000.

Emad, Parvis. "Boredom as Limit and Disposition." *Heidegger Studies* 1 (1985): 63–78.

Enders, Josef. *Angst und Langeweile: Hilfen und Hindernisse im sittlich-religiösen Leben.* Europäische Hochschulschriften, Reihe 20, Philosophie 101. Frankfurt am Main: Lang, 1983.

Engelsing, Rolf. "Die Perioden der Lesergeschichte in der Neuzeit." *Archiv für Geschichte des Buchwesens* 10 (1970).

Ettinger, Elzbieta. *Hannah Arendt Martin Heidegger.* New Haven, Yale University Press, 1995.

Evans, Richard. *Social Romanticism in France, 1830–1848.* New York: Octagon, 1969.

Fanta, Walter. *Die Entstehungsgeschichte des "Mann ohne Eigenschaften" von Robert Musil.* Vienna/Cologne/Weimar: Böhlau, 2000.

Farmer, Richard, and Norman D. Sundberg. "Boredom Proneness—The Development and Correlates of a New Scale." *Journal of Personality Assessment* 50, no. 1 (1986): 4–17.

Feldman, Jessica R. *Gender on the Divide: The Dandy in Modernist Literature.* Ithaca: Cornell University Press, 1993.

Felski, Rita. *The Gender of Modernity.* Cambridge, Mass.: Harvard University Press, 1995.

Fenichel, Otto. "Zur Psychologie der Langeweile." *Imago* 20 (1934): 270–81.

Flaschka, Horst. *Goethe's "Werther": Werkkontektuelle Deskription und Analyse.* Munich: Fink, 1987.

Flaubert, Gustave. *Correspondance.* Ed. Jean Bruneau. 4 vols. Paris: Gallimard, 1973.

———. *Madame Bovary: Moers de province.* Paris: Gallimard, 1972.

———. *Madame Bovary.* Trans. Lowell Blair, ed. Leo Bersani. New York: Bantam, 1981.

———. *Madame Bovary: Backgrounds and Sources, Essays in Criticism.* Edited and with a "substantially revised" version of Eleanor Marx Aveling's trans. by Paul de Man. New York: Norton, 1965.

Fortescue, William. *Alphonse de Lamartine: A Political Biography.* London: Croom Helm, 1983.

Foucault, Michel. *Folie et déraison: histoire de la folie à l'âge classique.* Paris: Plon, 1961.

———. *L'Archéologie du savoir.* Paris: Gallimard, 1969.

———. *L'ordre du discours.* Paris: Gallimard, 1971.

———. *Surveiller et punir: naissance de la prison.* Paris: Gallimard, 1975. (Trans. by Alan Sheridan as *Discipline and Punish,* 2d ed. [New York: Vintage, 1995].)

———. *The History of Sexuality,* vol. I: *An Introduction.* Trans. Robert Hurley. New York: Vintage, 1980.

———. *Language, Counter-memory, Practice: Selected Essays and Interviews.* Ed. Donald F. Bouchard, trans. Donald F. Bouchard and Sherry Simon. Ithaca, N.Y.: Cornell University Press, 1977.

Fouillée, Alfred. *L'evolutionnisme des Idées-forces.* Paris: F. Alcan, 1890.

———. *La psychologie des Idées-forces.* Paris: F. Alcan, 1893.

———. *Morale des idées-forces.* 2d ed. Paris: F. Alcan, 1908.

Fournier, Xavier de la. *Lamartine.* Paris: Perrin, 1990.

Freese, Wolfgang. "Verinnerte Wirklichkeit: Zur epischen Funktion der Liebe im 'Mann ohne Eigenschaften.'" In Karl Dinklage, Elisabeth Albertsen, and Karl Corino, eds., *Robert Musil: Studien zu seinem Werk.* Reinbek bei Hamburg: Rowohlt, 1970.

———. "Zur neueren Musil-Forschung. Ausgaben und Gesamtdarstellungen." *Text und Kritik 21/22: Robert Musil.* Munich: Edition Text und Kritik, 1985.

Freud, Sigmund. "Das Ich und das Es." In Anna Freud, E. Bibring, W. Hoffer, and E. Kris, eds., *Gesammelte Werke* 13, 235–90. London: Imago, 1940.

———. "Jenseits des Lustprinzips." In Anna Freud, E. Bibring, W. Hoffer, and E. Kris, eds., *Gesammelte Werke* 13, 1–70. London: Imago, 1940.

———. "Massenpsychologie und Ich-Analyse." In Anna Freud, E. Bibring, W. Hoffer, and E. Kris, eds., *Gesammelte Werke* 13, 71–162. London: Imago, 1940.

———. "Trauer und Melancholie." In Anna Freud, E. Bibring, W. Hoffer, and E. Kris, eds., *Gesammelte Werke* 10, 428–46. London: Imago, 1949.

———. *Das Unbehagen in der Kultur.* In Anna Freud, E. Bibring, W. Hoffer, and E. Kris, eds., *Gesammelte Werke,* 14, 421–506. London: Imago, 1955.

———. "Das Unheimliche." In Anna Freud, E. Bibring, W. Hoffer, and E. Kris, eds., *Gesammelte Werke* 12, 229–68. London: Imago, 1947.

Frevert, Ute. "Vom Klavier zur Schreibmaschine—Weiblicher Arbeitsmarkt und Rollenzuweisung am Beispiel der weiblichen Angestellten in der Weimarer Republik." In Annette Kuhn and Gerhard Schneider, eds., *Frauen in der Geschichte.* Geschichtsdidaktik: Studien, Materialien 6. Düsseldorf, 1979. Vol. I, 82–112.

Friedan, Betty. *The Feminine Mystique.* New York: Dell, 1963.

Frisby, David. *Fragments of Modernity: Theories of Modernity in the Work of Simmel, Kracauer, and Benjamin.* Cambridge: Polity, 1985.

———. *Georg Simmel.* 2d, rev. ed. Key Sociologists. London: Routledge, 2002.

———. *Simmel and Since: Essays on Georg Simmel's Social Theory.* London: Routledge, 1992.

———. *Sociological Impressionism: A Reassessment of Georg Simmel's Social Theory.* London: Heinemann, 1981.

———. *The Alienated Mind: The Sociology of Knowledge in Germany, 1918–33.* New Jersey: Humanities University Press, 1983.

————, ed. *Georg Simmel: Critical Assessments*. London: Routledge, 1994.

Frisby, David, and Mike Featherstone, eds. *Simmel on Culture: Selected Writings*. London: Sage, 1997.

Fritsche, Johannes. *Historical Destiny and National Socialism in Heidegger's "Being and Time."* Berkeley: University of California Press, 1999.

Fussell, Paul. *The Great War and Modern Memory*. London: Oxford, 1975.

Gadamer, Hans-Georg. *Gesammelte Werke*, vol. 1: *Neuere Philosophie*. Tübingen: Mohr, 1987.

Gassen, Kurt, and Michael Landmann, eds. *Buch des Dankes an Georg Simmel: Briefe, Erinnerungen, Bibliographie* [1958]. Berlin: Duncker und Humblot, 1993.

Gay, Peter. *The Bourgeois Experience*. 5 vols. New York: Norton, 1998.

Gehlen, Arnold. *Der Mensch: Seine Natur und seine Stellung in der Welt* [1940]. Edition Wiesbaden: Aula, 1986.

Gellner, Ernst. *Reason and Culture: The Historic Role of Rationality and Rationalism*. Oxford: Blackwell, 1992.

Genette, Gerard. *Figures of Literary Discourse*. Trans. Alan Sheridan. New York: Columbia University Press, 1982.

Gephart, Werner. "Georg Simmels Bild der Moderne." *Berliner Journal für Soziologie* 2 (1993): 183–92.

Gerhardt, Volker, Reinhard Mehring, and Jana Rindert. *Berliner Geist: Eine Geschichte der Berliner Universitätsphilosophie*. Berlin: Akademie Verlag, 1999.

Gerth, H. H., and C. Wright Mills. *From Max Weber: Essays in Sociology*. New York: Oxford University Press, 1946.

Geßner, Wilfried. "Geld als symbolische Form." *Simmel Studies* [=*Simmel Newsletter*] 6 (1996): S. 1–30.

————. *Der Schatz im Acker: Georg Simmels Philosophie der Kultur*. Weilerswist: Velbrück Wissenschaft, 2003.

Geuss, Raymond. *The Idea of a Critical Theory*. New York: Cambridge University Press, 1981.

Gilman, Charlotte Perkins. "The Yellow Wallpaper" [1899]. Ed. Dale M. Bauer. Boston: Bedford Books, 1998.

Gillespie, Michael Allen. *Nihilism before Nietzsche*. Chicago: University of Chicago Press, 1995.

Glasser, Richard. *Time in French Life and Thought*. Trans. C. G. Pearson. Manchester: Manchester University Press, 1972.

Gnüg, Hiltrud. *Kult der Kälte: Der klassische Dandy im Spiegel der Weltliteratur*. Stuttgart: Metzler, 1988.

Goldmann, Lucien. *Method in the Sociology of Literature*. Trans. and ed. William Q. Boelhower. Oxford: Basil Blackwell, 1981.

Goncharov, Ivan A. *Oblomov*. New York: Knopf, 1992.

Goethe, Johann Wolfgang von. *Die Leiden des jungen Werthers* [1774]. Weimar: Lichtenstein, 1922. (Trans. by Martin Swales as *The Sorrows of Young Werther* [Cambridge: Cambridge University Press, 1987].)

Goodstein, Elizabeth S. "Getrennte Liebe." In *Weibliche Ängste: Ansätze feministischer Vernunftkritik*, 120–45. Tübingen: Edition Diskord, 1989.

————. "Das Begehren des Begehrens: Ödipus und die Metamorphose zur Weiblichkeit." *Die Philosophin* 6 (October 1992): 8–17.

————. "'Eine specifisch moderne Begehrlichkeit': Fetischismus und George Simmels Phänomenologie der Moderne." *Die Philosophin* 13 (May 1996): 10–30.

————. "The Modernization of Subjectivity: Boredom and Georg Simmel's Reading
of Metropolitan Life." *Simmel Studies* [formerly *Simmel Newsletter*] 8, no. 2
(1998): 94–106.

————. "Georg Simmels Phänomenologie der Kultur und der Paradigmenwechsel in
den Geisteswissenschaften." In Willfried Geßner and Rüdiger Kramme, eds., *As-
pekte der Geldkultur: Neue Studien zu Georg Simmels Philosophie des Geldes*, 25–59.
Berlin: Edition Humboldt, 2002.

————. "Langeweile und die Demokratisierung der Skepsis in der Moderne." In
Bernd Hüppauf and Klaus Vieweg, eds., *Skepsis und literarische Imagination*, 123–
38. Munich: Wilhelm Fink Verlag, 2003.

————. "Style as Substance: Georg Simmel's Phenomenology of Culture." *Cultural
Critique*, special issue on "Everyday Life," 52 (Fall 2002): 209–34.

Graña, Cesar. *Modernity and Its Discontents*. New York: Torchbook, 1967. (Originally
published as *Bohemian Versus Bourgeois* by Basic Books in 1964.)

Grande Larousse de la langue française. 7 vols. Paris: Larousse, 1971–78.

Green, Bryan S. *Literary Methods and Sociological Theory: Case Studies of Simmel and
Weber*. Chicago: University of Chicago Press, 1988.

Großheim, Michael. *Von Georg Simmel zu Martin Heidegger: Philosophie zwischen Leben und Existenz*. Bonn: Bouvier, 1991.

Guignon, Charles. "History and Commitment in the Early Heidegger." In Hubert L.
Dreyfus and Harrison Hall, eds., *Heidegger: A Critical Reader*, 130–42. Cambridge,
Mass.: Basil Blackwell, 1992.

Gunning, Tom. "The Cinema of Attraction: Early Film, Its Spectator and the Avant-
Garde." *Wide Angle—A Quarterly Journal of Film History Theory & Criticism* 8,
nos. 3–4 (1986): 63–70.

Guyau, Augustin. *La Philosophie et la sociologie de Alfred Fouillée*. Paris: Alcan, 1913.

Haar, Michael. "Attunement and Thinking." In Hubert L. Dreyfus and Harrison
Hall, eds., *Heidegger: A Critical Reader*, 159–72. Cambridge, Mass.: Basil Blackwell,
1992.

Habermas, Jürgen. *Der philosophische Diskurs der Moderne*. Frankfurt am Main: Suhrkamp Verlag, 1985.

————. *Strukturwandel der Öffentlichkeit: Untersuchungen zur Kategorie der bürgerlichen Gesellschaft*. Berlin: Luchterhand, 1965.

Hanák, Péter. *The Garden and the Workshop: Essays on the Cultural History of Prague
and Budapest*. Princeton: Princeton University Press, 1998.

Hansen, Miriam. "Early Silent Cinema: Whose Public Sphere?" *New German Critique*, no. 29 (Spring-Summer 1983): 147–84.

Healy, Sean Desmond. *Boredom, Self, and Culture*. Cranbury, London: Associated
University Presses, 1984.

Heftrich, Eckhard. *Musil: Eine Einführung*. Munich: Artemis, 1986.

Hegel, G. W. F. *Werke in zwanzig Bänden*. Frankfurt am Main: Suhrkamp Verlag,
1970.

Heidegger, Martin. *Der Begriff der Zeit: Vortrag vor der marburger Theologenschaft,
Juli 1924*. Ed. Hartmut Tietjen. Tübingen: Niemeyer, 1984. (Trans. by William
McNeill as *The Concept of Time*, bilingual edition [Oxford: Blackwell, 1992].)

————. "Einführung in die Metaphysik." In Petra Jaeger, ed., *Gesamtausgabe* 40. Frankfurt am Main: Klostermann, 1983. Reprint of Heidegger's *Vorlesungen in Sommersemester 1935 in Freiburg*; original publication Tübingen: Niemeyer, 1953. (Trans. by Ralph Manheim as *An Introduction to Metaphysics* [New Haven: Yale University Press, 1959].)

————. *Die Frage nach dem Ding* [1962]. Tübingen: Max Niemeyer, 1975.

————. *Die Grundbegriffe der Metaphysik: Welt—Endlichkeit—Einsamkeit.* In Friedrich-Wilhelm Herrmann, ed., *Gesamtausgabe, Band 29/30.* Frankfurt am Main: Klostermann, 1983. (Trans. by William McNeill and Nicholas Walker as *The Fundamental Concepts of Metaphysics: World, Finitude, Solitude* [Bloomington: Indiana University Press, 1995].)

————. *Gesamtausgabe.* Frankfurt am Main, Klostermann, 1975–.

————. *Nietzsche.* 2 vols. Pfullingen: Neske, 1961.

————. *Sein und Zeit.* Rev. ed. Tübingen: Niemeyer, 1979.

————. *The Concept of Time.* Bilingual edition. Trans. William McNeill. Oxford: Blackwell, 1992.

————. "Was ist Metaphysik?" Antrittsvorlesung, 24 July 1929. Freiburg. Bonn: Friedrich Cohen, 1929.

Heidegger, Martin, and Karl Jaspers. *Briefwechsel, 1920–1963.* Ed. Walter Biemel and Hans Saner. Frankfurt am Main: Klostermann, 1990.

Heidbrink, Ludger, ed. *Entzauberte Zeit: Der Melancholische Geist der Moderne.* Munich: Hanser, 1997.

Hein, Peter Ulrich, ed. *Georg Simmel.* Frankfurt am Main: Lang, 1990.

Held, Klaus. "Fundamental Moods and Heidegger's Critique of Contemporary Culture." In J. Sallis, ed., *Reading Heidegger: Commemorations*, 286–303. Bloomington: Indiana University Press, 1993.

Helle, Horst Jürgen. *Soziologie und Erkenntnistheorie bei Georg Simmel.* Erträge der Forschung 259. Darmstadt: Wissenschaftliche Buchgesellschaft, 1988.

Herf, Jeffrey. *Reactionary Modernism: Technology, Culture, and Politics in Weimar and the Third Reich.* Cambridge: Cambridge University Press, 1984.

Herwig, Dagmar. *Der Mensch in der Entfremdung: Studien zur Entfremdungsproblematik anhand des Werkes von Robert Musil.* Schriftenreihe zur Politik und Geschichte. Munich: Paul List, 1972.

Heydebrand, Renate von. *Die Reflexionen Ulrichs in Robert Musils Roman 'Der Mann ohne Eigenschaften': Ihr Zusammenhang mit dem zeitgenössischen Denken.* Münster: Aschendorff, 1966.

Hickman, Hannah. *Robert Musil and the Culture of Vienna.* London: Croom Helm, 1984.

Hobsbawm, Eric. *The Age of Revolution 1789–1898* [1962]. New York: Vintage, 1996.

Hochstätter, Dietrich. *Sprache des Möglichen: Stilistischer Perspektivismus in Robert Musils 'Mann ohne Eigenschaften.'* Frankfurt am Main: Athenäum, 1972.

Hoffmann, E. T. A. *Werke.* Ed. Herbert Kraft and Manfred Wacker. Frankfurt am Main: Insel Verlag, 1967.

Hoffmeister, Gerhart. *Deutsche und Europäische Romantik.* 2d ed. Stuttgart: Metzler, 1990.

Hogen, Hildegard. *Die Modernisierung des Ich: Individualitätskonzepte bei Siegfried Kracauer, Robert Musil und Elias Canetti.* Würzburg: Königshausen & Neumann, 2000.

Honneth, Axel. "Pathologies of the Social: The Past and Present of Social Theory." In David M. Rasmussen, ed., *The Handbook of Critical Theory*, 369–96. Oxford: Blackwell, 1996.

———. *The Fragmented World of the Social: Essays in Social and Political Philosophy.* Ed. Charles W. Wright. Albany: SUNY Press, 1995.

Horkheimer, Max, and Theodor Adorno. *Dialektik der Aufklärung* [1947]. Frankfurt am Main: Fischer, 1969.

Hösle, Johannes. "Wirklichkeit und Utopie in Robert Musils 'Mann ohne Eigenschaften.'" In Karl Dinklage, Elisabeth Albertsen, and Karl Corino, eds., *Robert Musil: Studien zu seinem Werk*, 82–93. Reinbek bei Hamburg: Rowohlt, 1970.

Hughes, H. Stuart. *Consciousness and Society: The Reorientation of European Social Thought.* New York: Knopf, 1958.

Huguet, Michele. *L'ennui et ses discours.* Paris: Presses Universitaires de France, 1984.

Hunt, Lynn, ed. *The New Cultural History.* Berkeley: University of California Press, 1989.

Hunt, Lynn, and Victoria E. Bonnell, eds. *Beyond the Cultural Turn: New Directions in the Study of Society and Culture.* Berkeley: University of California Press, 1999.

Hüppauf, Bernd. *Von sozialer Utopie zur Mystik: zu Robert Musils 'Der Mann ohne Eigenschaften.'* Munich: W. Fink, 1971.

———. "Von Wien durch den Krieg nach Nirgendwo: Nation und utopisches Denken bei Musil und im Austromarxismus." *Text und Kritik 21/22.* Munich: Edition Text und Kritik, 1985.

Hurst, Charles E. *Living Theory: The Application of Classical Social Theory to Contemporary Life.* Boston: Allyn and Bacon, 2000.

Huysmans, Joris-Karl. *Against Nature.* Trans. Margaret Mauldon. Oxford: Oxford University Press, 1998.

Huyssen, Andreas. Foreword to English edition of *Kritik der Zynischen Vernunft* by Peter Sloterdijk, ix–xxv. Minneapolis: University of Minnesota Press, 1987.

———. "Mass Culture as Woman: Modernism's Other." In Tania Modleski, ed., *Studies in Entertainment: Critical Approaches to Mass Culture*, 188–207. Bloomington: Indiana University Press, 1986.

———. *After the Great Divide: Modernism, Mass Culture, Postmodernism.* Bloomington: Indiana University Press, 1986.

Iggers, G. G. *Geschichtswissenschaft im 20. Jahrhundert.* Göttingen: Vandenhoeck & Ruprecht, 1996 [2d ed.].

Irigaray, Luce. *Speculum de l'autre femme.* Paris: Minuit, 1974.

Jameson, Frederic. "The Vanishing Mediator; or, Max Weber as Storyteller" [1973]. Reprinted as "The Syntax of History," in *The Ideologies of Theory: Essays 1971–1986*, vol. 2. Theory and History of Literature 49. Minneapolis: University of Minnesota Press, 1988.

Janik, Allan, and Stephen Toulmin. *Wittgenstein's Vienna.* New York: Touchstone, 1973.

Jankélévitch, Vladimir. *L'aventure, l'ennui, le sérieux.* Paris: Aubier, 1963.

Jarausch, Konrad, and Michael Geyer. *Shattered Past: Reconstructing German Histories.* Princeton, N.J.: Princeton University Press, 2003.

Jauss, Hans Robert. *Toward an Aesthetic of Reception.* Trans. Timothy Bahti. Minneapolis: University of Minnesota Press, 1982.

————. *Literaturgeschichte als Provokation*. Frankfurt am Main: Suhrkamp Verlag, 1970.

Jay, Martin. *Marxism and Totality*. Berkeley: University of California Press, 1984.

————. *The Dialectical Imagination*. Boston: Little, Brown, 1973.

————. "Experience without a Subject: Walter Benjamin and the Novel." In Michael S. Roth, ed., *Rediscovering History: Culture, Politics, and the Psyche*, 121–33. Stanford: Stanford University Press, 1994.

Jenkyns, Richard. *The Victorians and Ancient Greece*. Cambridge, Mass.: Harvard University Press, 1980.

Johnston, William M. *The Austrian Mind: An Intellectual and Social History, 1848–1938*. Berkeley: University of California Press, 1972.

Jonard, Norbert. *L'Ennui dans la Littérature Européenne: Des origines à l'aube du xxe siècle*. Paris: Honoré Champion, 1998.

Jonsson, Stefan. *Subject without Nation: Robert Musil and the History of Modern Identity*. Durham: Duke University Press, 2000.

Kadi, Ulrike, Brigitta Keintzel, and Helmuth Vetter, eds. *Traum, Logik, Geld: Freud, Husserl und Simmel zum Denken der Moderne*. Tübingen: edition diskord, 2001.

Kaern, Michael, Bernard S. Phillips, and Robert S. Cohen, eds. *Georg Simmel and Contemporary Sociology*. Boston Studies in the Philosophy of Science. Boston: Dordrecht und Kluwer, 1990.

Kant, Immanuel. *Werke in 10 Bänden*. Darmstadt: Wissenschaftliche Buchgesellschaft, 1983.

————*Anthropologie in Pragmatischer Hinsicht*. In *Werke*, vol. 10.

————*Kritik der reinen Vernunft*. Hamburg: Meiner, 1998.

Kaplan, Alice, and Kristin Ross, eds. "Everyday Life." *Yale French Studies* 73 (1987).

Kaufmann, Doris. *Aufklärung, bürgerliche Selbsterfahrung und die 'Erfindung' der Psychiatrie in Deutschland, 1770–1850*. Göttingen: Vandenhoeck & Ruprecht, 1995.

Kern, Stephen. *The Culture of Space and Time 1880–1918*. Cambridge, Mass.: Harvard University Press, 1983.

Kessel, Martina. *Langeweile: Zum Umgang mit Zeit und Gefühlen in Deutschland vom späten 18. bis zum frühen 20. Jahrhundert*. Göttingen: Wallstein, 2001.

————. "Balance der Gefühle. Langeweile im 19. Jahrhundert." *Historische Anthropologie* 4 (1996): 234–55.

Kierkegaard, Søren. *Either/Or*. Ed. and trans. Howard V. Hong and Edna H. Hong. Princeton: Princeton University Press, 1987.

————. *The Point of View for My Work as an Author*. Trans. W. Lowrie. New York: Oxford University Press, 1962.

————. *Fear and Trembling: and the Sickness unto Death*. Trans. Walter Lowrie. Princeton, N.J.: Princeton University Press, 1970.

————. *The Present Age*. New York: Harper Torchbook, 1962. (Reprint of Alexander Dru translation from *The Present Age and Two Minor Ethico-religious Treatises* [London: Oxford University Press, 1940].)

Kisiel, Theodore J. *The Genesis of Heidegger's Being and Time*. Berkeley: University of California Press, 1993.

Klapp, Orrin. *Overload and Boredom: Essays on the Quality of Life in the Information Society*. New York: Greenwood, 1986.

Kleist, Heinrich von. "Über das Marionettentheater." In *Werke in einem Band*, 802–7. Munich: Carl Hanser Verlag, 1966.

Klibansky, Raymond, Erwin Panofsky, and Fritz Saxl. *Saturn und Melancholie*. Trans. Christa Buschendorf. Frankfurt am Main: Suhrkamp Verlag, 1990.

Köhnke, Klaus Christian. *Der junge Simmel—in Theoriebeziehungen und sozialen Bewegungen*. Frankfurt am Main: Suhrkamp Verlag, 1996.

———. "Georg Simmel als Jude." *Simmel Studies* [= *Simmel Newsletter*] 5 (1995): 53–72.

Kolb, David. *The Critique of Pure Modernity: Hegel, Heidegger, and After*. Chicago: University of Chicago Press, 1986.

Koselleck, Reinhart. *Vergangene Zukunft: Zur Semantik geschichtlicher Zeiten*. Frankfurt am Main: Suhrkamp Verlag, 1979.

Kracauer, Siegfried. *Die Angestellten: Aus dem neuesten Deutschland* [1929]. In Karsten Witte, ed., *Schriften* I. Frankfurt am Main: Suhrkamp Verlag, 1971.

———. "Georg Simmel." *Logos* 9 (1920/21). Reprinted [1971] in *Das Ornament der Masse*. Frankfurt am Main: Suhrkamp Verlag, 1977.

———. *Jacques Offenbach und das Paris seiner Zeit* (originally entitled *Pariser Leben*). Amsterdam: A. de Lange, 1937.

———. "Kult der Zerstreuung." In *Das Ornament der Masse*, 311–17. Frankfurt am Main: Suhrkamp Verlag, 1977.

———. *Das Ornament der Masse*. Frankfurt am Main: Suhrkamp Verlag, 1977. (Trans. by Thomas Y. Levin as *The Mass Ornament: Weimar Essays* [Cambridge, Mass.: Harvard University Press, 1995]).

———. *Schriften*. Ed. Karsten Witte. Frankfurt am Main: Suhrkamp Verlag, 1971–.

Krieger, Leonard. *The German Idea of Freedom: History of a Political Tradition*. Boston: Beacon, 1957.

Kristeva, Julia. *Soleil Noir: Dépression et mélancolie*. Paris: Gallimard, 1987.

Krois, John Michael. "Aufklärung und Metaphysik: Zur Philosophie Cassirers und der Davoser Debatte mit Heidegger." *Internationale Zeitschrift für Philosophie* 2 (1992), 273–89.

Kuhn, Reinhard. *The Demon of Noontide: Ennui in Western Literature*. Princeton: Princeton University Press, 1976.

Lacan, Jacques. *Écrits*. Paris: Seuil, 1966.

LaCapra, Dominick. *'Madame Bovary' on Trial*. Ithaca: Cornell University Press, 1982.

———. *Rethinking Intellectual History: Texts, Contexts, Language*. Ithaca: Cornell University Press, 1983.

Laclau, Ernesto, and Chantal Mouffe. *Hegemony and Socialist Strategy*. London: Verso, 1985.

Lacoue-Labarthe, Phillipe. *Heidegger, Art, and Politics: The Fiction of the Political*. Oxford: Blackwell, 1990.

Lacoue-Labarthe, Philippe, and Jean-Luc Nancy. *The Literary Absolute: The Theory of Literature in German Romanticism*. Albany: SUNY University Press, 1988.

Laermann, Klaus. *Eigenschaftslosigkeit: Reflexionen zu Musils 'Der Mann ohne Eigenschaften.'* Stuttgart, 1970.

Lafargue, Paul. *The Right to be Lazy*. Trans. Charles H. Kerr. Chicago: Kerr, 1989.

Laforgue, Jules. *Mélanges posthumes*. Ed. G. Jean-Aubry. Paris, 1903.

———. "Notes inédites de Laforgue sur Baudelaire." *Entretiens politiques et littéraires* II (April 1891): 97–120.

Lamartine, Alphonse de. *Des Destinées de la Poésie.* Paris: Librairie de Charles Gosselin, Librairie de Furne, 1834.

———. "Sur La Discusssion de L' Adresse en Réponse a M. Thiers." In *La France Parlementaire (1834–1851): Oeuvres Oratoires et Écrits Politiques,* vol. 2. Paris: Librairie Internationale, 1864.

La Rochefoucauld. *Œuvres Complètes.* Paris: Bibliothèque de la Pléiade, Paris, 1957.

Lazarus, Moritz. *Grundzüge der Völkerpsychologie und Kulturwissenschaft.* Ed. Klaus Christian Koehnke. Hamburg: Meiner, 2003.

Leaman, George. *Heidegger im Kontext, Gesamtüberblick zum NS-Engagement der Universitätsphilosophen.* Hamburg: Argument, 1993.

Leck, Ralph. *Georg Simmel and Avant-garde Sociology: The Birth of Modernity, 1880–1920.* Amherst, N.Y.: Humanity Books, 2000.

Le Rider, Jacques. *Modernité viennoise et crises de l'identité.* Paris: Presses Universitaires de France, 1990. (Trans. by Rosemary Morris as *Modernity and Crises of Identity: Culture and Society in Fin-de-siècle Vienna* [New York: Continuum, 1993].)

Leconte, Frantz Antoine. *La Tradition de L'Ennui Splénétique en France de Christine De Pisan à Baudelaire.* New York: Peter Lang, 1998.

Lefebvre, Henri. *Critique de la vie quotidienne.* Rev. ed. Paris: L'Arche, 1958.

LeGoff, Jacques. *Time, Work, and Culture in the Middle Ages.* Trans. Arthur Goldhammer. Chicago: University of Chicago Press, 1980.

Lemaire, Michel. *Le Dandysme de Baudrillard à Mallarmé.* Montreal: University of Montreal Press, 1978.

Lepenies, Wolf. *Die Drei Kulturen: Soziologie zwischen Literatur und Wissenschaft.* Munich: Carl Hanser Verlag, 1985.

———, ed. *Geschichte der Soziologie: Studien zur kognitiven, sozialen und historischen Identität einer Disziplin.* 4 vols. Frankfurt am Main: Suhrkamp Verlag, 1981.

———. *Melancholie und Gesellschaft* [1969]. Frankfurt am Main: Suhrkamp Verlag, 1998. (Trans. by J. Gaines and D. Jones as *Melancholy and Society* [Cambridge, Mass.: Harvard University Press, 1992].)

———. *Soziologische Anthropologie.* Munich: Carl Hanser Verlag, 1971.

———. *Sainte-Beuve: auf der Schwelle zur Moderne.* Munich: Carl Hanser Verlag, 1997.

Lessing, Hans-Ulrich. "Bemerkungen zum Begriff des 'objectiven Geistes' bei Hegel, Lazarus und Dilthey. *Reports on Philosophy* 9 (1985): 49–62.

Lethen, Helmut. *Verhaltenslehre der Kälte: Lebensversuche zwischen den Kriegen.* Frankfurt am Main: Suhrkamp Verlag, 1994.

Levin, Harry. *The Gates of Horn: A Study of Five French Realists.* New York: Oxford University Press, 1963.

Levine, Donald N. *Simmel and Parsons: Two Approaches to the Study of Society.* New York: Arno Press, 1980.

———. *The Flight from Ambiguity: Essays in Social and Cultural Theory.* Chicago: University of Chicago Press, 1985.

———. *Visions of the Sociological Tradition.* Chicago: University of Chicago Press, 1995.

———, ed. *On Individuality and Social Forms: Selected Writings.* Chicago: University of Chicago Press, 1971.

Leys, Ruth. *Trauma: A Genealogy*. Chicago: University of Chicago Press, 2000.

Lichtblau, Klaus. *Kulturkrise und Soziologie um die Jahrhundertwende: Zur Genealogie der Kultursoziologie in Deutschland*. Frankfurt am Main: Suhrkamp Verlag, 1996.

Liebersohn, Harry. *Fate and Utopia in German Sociology*. Cambridge, Mass.: MIT University Press, 1988.

Littré, Emile, ed. *Dictionnaire de la langue française*. Paris: Gallimard et Hachette, 1860.

Lohmann, Georg. "Die Anpassung des individuellen Lebens an die innere Unendlichkeit der Großstädte: Formen der Individualisierung bei Simmel." *Berliner Journal für Soziologie* 2 (1993): 153–60.

Lough, John, and Muriel Lough. *An Introduction to Nineteenth-century France*. London: Longman, 1978.

Löwith, Karl. *Vom Hegel zu Nietzsche*. 2d ed. Stuttgart: Kohlhammer, 1950.

Lubbock, Percy. *The Craft of Fiction*. London: J. Craft: 1921.

Luft, David S. *Eros and Inwardness in Vienna: Weininger, Musil, Doderer*. Chicago: University of Chicago Press, 2003.

———. *Robert Musil and the Crisis of European Culture 1880–1942*. Berkeley: University of California Press, 1980.

Luhmann, Niklas. *Soziale Systeme: Grundriß einer allgemeinen Theorie*. Frankfurt am Main: Suhrkamp Verlag, 1984.

Lukács, Georg. *Die Seele und die Formen*. Berlin, 1911.

———. *Geschichte und Klassenbewusstsein*. Berlin: Luchterhand, 1968.

Lukes, Stephen. *Emile Durkheim: His Life and Work*. New York: Harper and Row, 1973.

Lunn, Eugene. *Marxism and Modernism: An Historical Study of Lukács, Brecht, Benjamin, and Adorno*. Berkeley: University of California Press, 1982.

Lyotard, Jean-François. *The Postmodern Condition: A Report on Knowledge*. Trans. Geoff Bennington and Brian Massumi. Theory and History of Literature 10. Minneapolis: University of Minnesota Press, 1984.

MacIntyre, Alasdair. *After Virtue*. 2d ed. Notre Dame: Notre Dame University Press, 1984.

MacKaman, Douglas Peter. *Leisure Settings: Bourgeois Culture, Medicine, and the Spa in Modern France*. Chicago: University of Chicago Press, 1998.

Mae, Michiko, and Jurgen C. Thöming. "Auswahlbibliographie zu Robert Musil." In *Text und Kritik 21/22: Robert Musil*. Munich: Edition Text und Kritik, 1985.

Maggini, Carlo. "The Psychobiology of Boredom." *CNS Spectrums* 5, no. 8 (2000): 24–27.

Makropoulos, Michael. *Modernität als ontologischer Ausnahmezustand? Walter Benjamins Theorie der Moderne*. Munich: Fink, 1989.

Mandelkow, Valentin. *Der Prozeß um den "ennui" in der französischen Literatur und Literaturkritik*. Würzburg: Königshausen & Neumann, 1999.

Mannheim, Karl. *Ideology and Utopia*. Rev. English ed. Trans. Louis Wirth and Edward Shils. New York: Harcourt, 1936.

Marchand, Suzanne L. *Down from Olympus: Archaeology and Philhellenism in Germany, 1750–1970*. Princeton: Princeton University Press, 1996.

Marcus, Greil. *Lipstick Traces: A Secret History of the Twentieth Century*. Cambridge, Mass.: Harvard University Press, 1989.

Marder, Elissa. *Dead Time: Temporal Disorders in the Wake of Modernity (Baudelaire and Flaubert)*. Stanford: Stanford University Press, 2001.

Marquard, Odo. "Inkompetenzkompensationskompetenz: Über Kompetenz und Inkompetenz der Philosophie." *Gießner Universitätsblätter* VII (1974): 89–99.

———. "Kompensation: Überlegungen zu einer Verlaufsfigur geschichtlicher Prozeße." In K. G. Faber and Chr. Meier, *Historische Prozeße*, 330–62. Munich: DTV, 1978.

Maurina, Zenta. *Die Langeweile und der gehetzte Mensch.* Memmingen: Maximilian Dietrich, 1962.

McGann, Jerome. *The Romantic Ideology: A Critical Investigation.* Chicago: University of Chicago Press, 1983.

Meja, Volker, Dieter Misgeld, and Nico Stehr, eds. *Modern German Sociology.* New York: Columbia University Press, 1987.

Melton, James van Horn. *The Rise of the Public in Enlightenment Europe.* Cambridge: Cambridge University Press, 2001.

Merton, Robert K. *A Life of Learning.* Charles Homer Haskin Lecture. American Council of Learned Societies Occasional Paper no. 25. New York: ACLS, 1994.

———. "Social Structure and Anomie." In Robert K. Merton, *Social Theory and Social Structure*, 2d ed., 185–214. New York: Free Press, 1968. (Originally published in *American Sociological Review* 3 [1938]: 672–82.)

———. *Social Theory and Social Structure.* Enlarged 2d ed. New York: Free Press, 1968.

Mestrovic, Stjepan. *The Coming Fin de Siècle.* London: Routledge, 1991.

———. "The Theme of Civilization and Its Discontents in Durkheim's Division of Labor." *Journal for the Theory of Social Behavior* 19 (1989): 443–56.

Mestrovic, Stjepan, and H. M. Brown. "Durkheim's Concept of Anomie as Dérèglement." *Social Problems* 33 (1985): 81–99.

Miller, Michael. *The Bon Marché: Bourgeois Culture and the Department Store, 1869–1920.* Princeton: Princeton University Press, 1981.

Mistler, Jean. *La Librairie Hachette de 1826 à nos jours.* Paris: Hachette, 1964.

Mittelstraß, Jürgen, with Siegfried Blasche et al. *Encyclopaedie Philosophie und Wissenschaftstheorie.* Stuttgart: J. B. Metzler, 1995.

Moers, Ellen. *The Dandy: Brummell to Beerbohm.* New York: Viking, 1960.

Mülder, Inka. *Siegfried Kracauer—Grenzgänger zwischen Theorie und Literatur: Seine frühen Schriften 1913–1933.* Stuttgart, Metzler, 1985.

Mülder-Bach, Inka. "'Weibliche Kultur' und 'stahlhartes Gehäuse': Zur Thematisierung des Geschlechterverhältnisses in den Soziologien Georg Simmels und Max Webers." In Sigrun Anselm and Barbara Beck, eds., *Triumph und Scheitern in der Metropole: zur Rolle der Weiblichkeit in der Geschichte Berlins*, 115–40. Berlin: Dietrich Riemer Verlag, 1987.

Murray, Michael, ed. *Heidegger and Modern Philosophy.* New Haven, Yale University Press, 1978.

Musil, Robert. *Briefe 1901–1942.* Ed. Adolph Frisé with Murray G. Hall. Reinbek bei Hamburg: Rowohlt, 1981.

———. *Gesammelte Werke.* Ed. Adolph Frisé. 9 vols. Reinbek bei Hamburg: Rowohlt, 1978.

———. *Tagebücher.* Ed. Adolph Frisé. 2 vols. Reinbek bei Hamburg: Rowohlt, 1976.

———. *The Man without Qualities.* Trans. Eithne Wilkins and Ernst. Kaiser. London: Picador, 1979.

———. *The Man without Qualities.* Trans. Sophie Wilkins and Burton Pike. New York: Knopf, 1995.

Musset, Alfred de. *Confession of a Child of the Century* [1836]. New York: H. Fertig, 1977.

Nagl-Docekal, Herta, and Cornelia Klinger, eds. *Continental Philosophy in Feminist Perspective: Re-reading the Canon in German*. University Park: Pennsylvania State University Press, 2000.

Nietzsche, Friedrich. *Sämtliche Werke: Kritische Studienausgabe*. Ed. Giorgio Colli and Mazzino Montinari. 15 vols. Munich, Berlin: Deutsche Taschenbuchverlag de Gruyter, 1967–77.

Nipperdey, Thomas. *Wie das Bürgertum die Moderne fand*. Berlin: W. J. Siedler, 1988.

Novalis, *Schriften*, ed. J. Minor. Jena: Diederichs, 1923.

Nordau, Max. *Entartung*. 2d ed. Berlin: C. Duncker, 1893. (Anonymous English translation, *Degeneration* [Lincoln: University of Nebraska Press, 1968], reprint of 1895 translation.)

Nowotny, Helga. *Eigenzeit: Entstehung und Strukturierung eines Zeitgefühls*. Frankfurt am Main: Suhrkamp Verlag, 1989.

Nye, Robert A. *Crime, Madness, and Politics in Modern France: The Medical Concept of National Decline*. Princeton: Princeton University Press, 1984.

"On Boredom." Special issue, *Documents* 1, nos. 1–2 (1993).

Oppenheim, Janet. *"Shattered Nerves": Doctors, Patients, and Depression in Victorian England*. New York: Oxford University Press, 1991.

Orru, M. *Anomie: History and Meanings*. London, Allen and Unwin, 1987.

Ott, Hugo. *Martin Heidegger: Unterwegs zu seiner Biographie*. Frankfurt am Main, New York: Campus, 1988.

Palmer, Robert R., and Joel Colton. *A History of the Modern World*. 5th ed. New York: Knopf, 1978.

Parsons, Talcott. *Essays in Sociological Theory*. Rev. ed. New York: Free Press, 1954.

Pascal, Blaise. *Pensées*. Paris: Seuil, 1962.

Pateman, Carole. *The Sexual Contract*. Stanford: Stanford University Press, 1988.

Paumen, Jean. "Ennui et Nostalgie chez Heidegger." *Revue Internationale de Philosophie* 43 (1989): 103–30.

Peters, Edward. "Notes toward an Archaeology of Boredom." *Social Research* 42 (1975): 493–511.

Peters, Frederick. *Robert Musil: Master of the Hovering Life*. New York: Columbia University Press, 1978.

Petro, Patrice. "After Shock/Between Boredom and History." *Discourse* 16 no. 2 (Fall 1993–Spring 1994): 77–99.

———. *Aftershocks of the New: Feminism and Film History*. New Brunswick: Rutgers University Press, 2002.

———. *Joyless Streets: Women and Melodramatic Representation in Weimar Germany*. Princeton: Princeton University Press, 1989.

Phillips, Adam. *On Kissing, Tickling, and Being Bored: Psychoanalytic Essays on the Unexamined Life*. Cambridge, Mass.: Harvard University Press, 1993.

Pikulik, Lothar. *Romantik als Ungenügen an der Normalität: Am Beispiel Tiecks, Hoffmanns, Eichendorffs*. Frankfurt am Main: Suhrkamp Verlag, 1979.

———. *Warten, Erwartung: Eine Lebensform in End- und Übergangszeiten*. Göttingen: Vandenhoeck & Ruprecht, 1997.

Pinkard, Terry. *German Philosophy 1760–1860: The Legacy of Idealism*. Cambridge: Cambridge University Press, 2002.

Pippin, Robert B. *Hegel's Idealism*. Cambridge: Cambridge University Press, 1989.

──────. *Modernism as a Philosophical Problem: On the Dissatisfactions of European High Culture*. Oxford: Blackwell, 1991.

Poggi, Gianfranco. *Money and the Modern Mind: George Simmel's Philosophy of Money*. Berkeley: University of California Press, 1993.

Postone, Moishe. *Time, Labor, and Social Domination: A Reinterpretation of Marx's Critical Theory*. Cambridge: Cambridge University Press, 1993.

Praz, Mario. *The Romantic Agony*. 2d ed. Trans. Angus Davidson. London: Oxford University Press, 1970.

Prendergast, Christopher. *Paris and the Nineteenth Century*. Cambridge, Mass.: Blackwell, 1992.

Prevost, John C. *Le Dandysme en France 1817–1839*. Paris: Minard, 1957.

Proudhon, Pierre-Joseph. *De la Capacité politique des classes ouvrières*. Paris: Libraire internationale, 1868.

Puppe, Heinrich. *Muße und Müßiggang in Robert Musils Roman 'Der Mann ohne Eigenschaften.'* Beiträge zur Robert-Musil-Forschung und zur neueren österreichischen Literatur 1. St. Ingbert: Röhring, 1991.

Rabinbach, Anson. *The Human Motor: Energy, Fatigue, and the Origins of Modernity*. New York: Basic Books, 1990.

Radkau, Joachim. *Das Zeitalter der Nervosität: Deutschland zwischen Bismark und Hitler*. Munich: Prophyläen Taschenbuch, 1998.

──────. "Die wilhelminische Ära als 'nervöses Zeitalter,' oder: Die Nerven als Netzwerk zwischen Tempo- und Körpergeschichte." *Geschichte und Gesellschaft*, 20. Jahrgang, vol. 2, April–June 1994, 211–41.

Rammstedt, Otthein, ed. *Simmel und die frühen Soziologen: Nähe und Distanz zu Durkheim, Tönnies und Max Weber*. Frankfurt am Main: Suhrkamp Verlag, 1988.

Raposa, Michael L. *Boredom and the Religious Imagination*. Charlottesville: University Press of Virginia, 1999.

Ray, Larry, ed. *Formal Sociology: The Sociology of Georg Simmel*. Schools of Thought in Sociology. Aldershot: Elgar, 1991.

Rehm, Walter. *Gonscharow und Jacobsen; oder, Langeweile und Schwermut*. Göttingen: Vandenhoek & Ruprecht, 1963.

Rémy, Jean, ed. *Georg Simmel: Ville et Modernité*. Paris: L'Harmattan, 1995.

Reulecke, J. *Geschichte der Urbanisierung Deutschlands*. Frankfurt am Main: Suhrkamp Verlag, 1985.

Revers, Wilhelm Josef. *Die Psychologie der Langeweile*. Meisenheim am Galn: Westkulturverlag A. Hain, 1949.

Ricoeur, Paul. *De L'interprétation: Essai sur Freud*. Paris: Seuil, 1965. (Trans. by Denis Savage as *Freud and Philosophy* [New Haven: Yale University Press, 1980].)

──────. *La métaphor vive*. Paris: Seuil, 1975. (Trans. by Robert Czerny as *The Rule of Metaphor: Multidisciplinary Studies of the Creation of Meaning in Language* [Toronto: University of Toronto Press, 1977].)

──────. *Lectures on Ideology and Utopia*. Ed. George H. Taylor. New York: Columbia University Press, 1986.

Ringer, Fritz. *Fields of Knowledge: French Academic Culture in Comparative Perspective, 1890–1920*. Cambridge: Cambridge University Press, 1992.

Bibliography   443

————. *The Decline of the German Mandarins: German Academic Culture, 1890–1933.* Cambridge, Mass.: Harvard University Press, 1969.

Ritter, Joachim, and Karlfried Gründer, eds. *Historisches Wörterbuch der Philosophie.* Basel: Schwabe, 1971–. (Fully revised edition of Rudolf Eisler, *Wörterbuch der philosophischen Begriffe.*)

Rockmore, Tom. *On Heidegger's Nazism and Philosophy.* Berkeley: University of California Press, 1992.

Roelcke, Volker. *Krankheit und Kulturkritik: Psychiatrische Gesellschaftsdeutungen im bürgerlichen Zeitalter, 1790–1914.* Frankfurt am Main: Campus, 1999.

Rogowski, Christian. *Distinguished Outsider: Robert Musil and His Critics.* Columbia: Camden House, 1994.

Ronell, Avital. *Crack Wars: Literature Addiction Mania.* Lincoln: University of Nebraska Press, 1992.

Ross, Dorothy. *The Origins of American Social Science.* Cambridge: Cambridge University Press, 1991.

————, ed. *Modernist Impulses in the Human Sciences 1870–1930.* Baltimore: Johns Hopkins University Press, 1994.

Rose, Gillian. *Hegel contra Sociology.* London: Athlone, 1981.

Roth, Michael S. "Dying of the Past: Medical Studies of Nostalgia in Nineteenth-Century France." *History and Memory* 3, no. 1 (1991): 5–29.

Roth, Michael S., ed. *Rediscovering History: Culture, Politics, and the Psyche.* Stanford: Stanford University Press, 1994.

Rothe, Wolfgange. "'Seinesgleichen geschieht': Musil und die moderne Erzähltradition." In Karl Dinklage, Elisabeth Albertsen, and Karl Corino, eds., *Robert Musil: Studien zu seinem Werk,* 131–69. Reinbek bei Hamburg: Rowohlt, 1970.

Ryan, Judith. *The Vanishing Subject: Early Psychology and Literary Modernism.* Chicago: University of Chicago Press, 1991.

Safranksi, Rüdiger. *Ein Meister aus Deutschland: Heidegger und seine Zeit.* Frankfurt am Main: Fischer, 1998.

Sagnes, Guy. *L'Ennui dans la littérature française de Flaubert a Laforgue (1848–1884).* Paris: Armand Colin, 1969.

Sartre, Jean-Paul. *Baudelaire.* Trans. Martin Turnell. New York: New Directions, 1950.

Scaff, Lawrence. *Fleeing the Iron Cage: Culture, Politics, and Modernity in the Thought of Max Weber.* Berkeley: University of California Press, 1989.

Schamber, Ellie Nower. *The Artist as Politician: The Relationship Between the Art and the Politics of the French Romantics.* New York: Lanham, 1984.

Schenk, H. G. *The Mind of the European Romantics.* London: Constable, 1966.

Scherpe, Klaus. *Werther und Wertherwirkung.* Bad Homburg v.d.H.: Gehlen, 1970.

Schiesari, Julia. *The Gendering of Melancholia: Feminism, Psychoanalysis, and the Symbolics of Loss in Renaissance Culture.* Ithaca: Cornell University Press, 1992.

Schiller, Friedrich. *Über die ästhetische Erziehung des Menschen in einer Reihe von Briefen.* In *Schillers Werke, Nationalausgabe,* vol. 20, 309–412. Weimar: Hermann Böhlaus Nachfolger, 1962.

————. *Über naïve und sentimentalische Dichtung.* In *Schillers Werke Nationalausgabe,* vol. 20, 413–503. Weimar: Hermann Böhlaus Nachfolger, 1962.

Schivelbusch, Wolfgang. *Geschichte der Eisenbahnreise.* Munich: Carl Hanser Verlag,

1977. (Trans. by author as *The Railway Journey: The Industrialization of Time and Space in the 19th Century* [Berkeley: University of California Press, 1986].)

———. *Lichtblicke: Zur Geschichte der künstlichen Helligkeit im 19. Jahrhundert.* Munich: Carl Hanser Verlag, 1983.

———. *Das Paradies, der Geschmack und die Vernunft: Eine Geschichte der Genußmittel.* Frankfurt am Main: Fischer, 1990.

Schopenhauer, Arthur. *Die Welt als Wille und Vorstellung.* 2 vols. Zürich: Diogenes, 1977.

Schorske, Carl E. *Fin-de-Siècle Vienna: Politics and Culture.* New York: Vintage, 1981.

Schutte, Jürgen, and Peter Sprengel, eds. *Die Berliner Moderne: 1885–1914.* Stuttgart: Reklam, 1987.

Schwarz, Christopher. *Langeweile und Identität: Eine Studie zur Entstehung und Krise des romantischen Selbstgefühls.* Frankfurter Beiträge zur Germanistik 25. Heidelberg: Universitätsverlag C. Winter, 1993.

Schwartz, Vanessa R. *Spectacular Realities: Early Mass Culture in Fin-de-Siècle Paris.* Berkeley: University of California Press, 1998.

Scott, Joan Wallach. *Gender and the Politics of History.* New York: Columbia University Press, 1988.

Seigel, Jerrold. *Bohemian Paris: Culture, Politics, and the Boundaries of Bourgeois Life, 1830–1930.* New York: Penguin, 1987.

Sellerberg, Ann-Mari. *A Blend of Contradictions: Georg Simmel in Theory and Practice.* New Brunswick, N.J.: Transaction Publishers, 1994.

Senancour, Etienne Pivert de. *Rêveries sur la nature primitive de l'homme.* E. de Senancour Edition Critique, ed. Joachim Merlant, vol I. Paris: Librairie Droz, 1939.

———. *Obermann.* Ed. G. Michaut. Paris: E. Droz, 1931.

Seyhan, Azade. *Representation and Its Discontents: The Critical Legacy of German Romanticism.* Berkeley: University of California Press, 1992.

Shorter, Edward. *From Paralysis to Fatigue: A History of Psychosomatic Illness in the Modern Era.* New York: Free Press, 1992.

Sigmund, Steffen. "Georg Simmel in Berlin." *Berliner Journal für Soziologie* 2 (1993): 161–82.

Simmel, Georg. *Georg Simmel Gesamtausgabe* [GSG], ed. Otthein Rammstedt. Frankfurt am Main: Suhrkamp Verlag, 1989–.

———. *Georg Simmel Gesamtausgabe*, vol. 5: *Aufsätze und Abhandlungen 1894–1900.* Ed. Heinz-Jürgen Dahme and David P. Frisby. Frankfurt am Main: Suhrkamp Verlag, 1992.

———. *Georg Simmel Gesamtausgabe*, vol. 6.: *Die Philosophie des Geldes.* Ed. David P. Frisby and Klaus Christian Köhnke. Frankfurt am Main: Suhrkamp Verlag, 1989. (Trans. by Thomas Bottomore and David Frisby as *The Philosophy of Money* [Boston: Routledge, 1978].)

———. *Georg Simmel Gesamtausgabe*, vol. 7: *Aufsätze und Abhandlungen 1901–1908*, v. I. Ed. Rüdiger Kramme, Angela Rammstedt, and Ottheim Rammstedt. Frankfurt am Main: Suhrkamp Verlag, 1993.

———. *Georg Simmel Gesamtausgabe*, vol. 8: *Aufsätze und Abhandlungen 1901–1908*, v. II. Ed. Alessandro Cavalli and Volkhard Krech. Frankfurt am Main: Suhrkamp Verlag, 1993.

———. *Georg Simmel Gesamtausgabe*, vol. 10: *Philosophie der Mode, Die Religion,*

Kant und Goethe, Schopenhauer and Nietzsche. Ed. Michael Behr, Volkhard Krech, and Gert Schmidt. Frankfurt am Main: Suhrkamp Verlag, 1995.

———. *Georg Simmel Gesamtausgabe*, vol. 11: *Soziologie: Untersuchungen über die Formen der Vergesellschaftung*. Ed. Otthein Rammstedt. Frankfurt am Main: Suhrkamp Verlag, 1992.

———. *Georg Simmel Gesamtausgabe*, vol. 14: *Hauptprobleme der Philosophie, Philosophische Kultur*. Ed. Rüdiger Kramme and Otthein Rammstedt. Frankfurt am Main: Suhrkamp Verlag, 1996.

———. "Aus Georg Simmels Nachgelassenem Tagebuch." *Logos* 8 (1919/20): 121–51. (Reprinted in Gertrud Kantorowicz, ed., *Fragmente und Aufsätze aus dem Nachlaß und Veröffentlichungen der letzten Jahren* (Munich: Drei Masken, 1923).

———. "Die Bedeutung des Geldes für das Tempo des Lebens." In *Georg Simmel Gesamtausgabe*, vol. 5, 215–34.

———. *Brücke und Tür: Essays des Philosophen zur Geschichte, Religion, Kunst, und Gesellschaft*. Ed. Michael Landmann with Margarete Susman. Stuttgart: Koehler, 1957.

———. *The Conflict in Modern Culture and Other Essays*. Trans. K. Peter Etzkorn. New York: Teacher's College, 1968.

———. *Fragmente und Aufsätze aus dem Nachlaß und Veröffentlichungen der letzten Jahren*. Ed. Gertrud Kantorowicz. Munich: Drei Masken, 1923.

———. "Das Geld in der modernen Cultur." In *Georg Simmel Gesamtausgabe*, vol. 5, 178–96.

———. "Die Großstädte und das Geistesleben." In *Georg Simmel Gesamtausgabe*, vol. 7, 116–31. (Originally published in *Die Großstadt: Vorträge und Aufsätze zur Städteausstellung, Jahrbuch der Gehestiftung* 9 (1903): 185–206; trans. by H. H. Gerth with C. Wright Mills as "The Metropolis and Mental Life," in Kurt H. Wolff, ed., *The Sociology of Georg Simmel*, 409–24 [Glencoe: Free Press, 1950].)

———. *Grundfragen der Soziologie (Individuum und Gesellschaft)*. Berlin and Leipzig: Göschen, 1917.

———. *Das Individuum und die Freiheit, Essais*. New edition of *Brücke und Tür*, ed. Michael Landmann. Berlin: Wagenbach, 1984.

———. "Der Konflikt der modernen Kultur." 2d ed. Munich: Duncker and Humblot, 1921.

———. *Lebensanschauungen: Vier Metaphysischen Kapitel*. Munich and Leipzig: Duncker und Humblot, 1918.

———. *Philosophische Kultur: Über das Abenteuer, die Geschlechter und die Krise der Moderne*. Berlin: Wagenbach, 1986.

———. "Schopenhauer und Nietzsche." In *Georg Simmel Gesamtausgabe*, vol. 8. Original publication March 2, 1906. *Vossische Zeitung*, no. 102, morning ed, Feuilletonteil, Berlin.

———. *Schopenhauer und Nietzsche: Ein Vortragszyklus*. In *Georg Simmel Gesamtausgabe*, vol. 10, 167–408. (Trans. by Helmut Loiskandl, Deena Weinstein, and Michael Weinstein as *Schopenhauer and Nietzsche* [Amherst: University of Massachusetts Press, 1986].)

Sloterdijk, Peter. *Kritik der zynischen Vernunft*. 2 vols. Frankfurt am Main: Suhrkamp Verlag, 1983. (Trans. by Michael Eldred as *Critique of Cynical Reason* [Minneapolis: University of Minnesota Press, 1987].)

Sluga, Hans. *Heidegger's Crisis: Philosophy and Politics in Nazi Germany*. Cambridge, Mass.: Harvard University Press, 1993.

Smith, William Jay. *Selected Writings of Jules Laforgue*. New York: Grove, 1956.

Snow, C. P. *The Two Cultures; and, A Second Look: an expanded version of "The Two Cultures and the Scientific Revolution."* London: Cambridge University Press, 1965.

Spacks, Patricia Meyer. *Boredom: The Literary History of a State of Mind*. Chicago: University of Chicago Press, 1995.

Spector, Scott. *Prague Territories: National Conflict and Cultural Innovation in Franz Kafka's fin de siècle*. Berkeley: University of California Press, 2000.

Stanton, Domna C. *The Aristocrat as Art: A Study of the Honnête Homme and the Dandy in Seventeenth- and Nineteenth-Century French Literature*. New York: Columbia University Press, 1980.

Starkie, Enid. *Baudelaire*. London: Faber and Faber, 1957.

Steegmuller, Francis. *Flaubert and Madame Bovary: A Double Portrait*. Rev. ed. New York: Farrar, Straus and Giroux, 1968.

Steiner, Georg. *In Bluebeard's Castle*. New Haven: Yale University Press, 1971.

———. Review of *The Man without Qualities*, trans. Burton Pike and Sophie Wilkins. *The New Yorker* 17, no. 8 (17 April 1995): 101.

Stern, E. Mark, ed. *Psychotherapy and the Bored Patient*. New York: Haworth Press, 1988. (Previously *The Psychotherapy Patient*, vol. 3, nos. 3/4 [Spring/Summer 1987].)

Sternberger, Dolf. *Panorama oder Ansichten vom 19. Jahrhundert*. Hamburg: H. Goverts, 1938. (Trans. by Joachim Neugroschel as *Panoramas of the Nineteenth Century* [New York: Urizen, 1977].)

Stewart, Susan. *On Longing: Narratives of the Miniature, the Gigantic, the Souvenir, the Collection*. Baltimore: Johns Hopkins University Press, 1984.

Stromberg, Roland N., ed. *Realism, Naturalism, and Symbolism*. New York: Harper and Row, 1968.

Strutz, Josef, ed. *Kunst, Wissenschaft und Politik von Robert Musil bis Ingeborg Bachmann*. Musil-Studien 14. Munich: Wilhelm Fink, 1986.

Tardieu, Émile. *L'Ennui: Étude psychologique*. Paris: Alcan, 1903.

Taylor, Mark. C. *Journeys to Selfhood: Hegel and Kierkegaard*. Berkeley: University of California Press, 1980.

Terdiman, Richard. *Discourse/Counter-discourse: The Theory and Practice of Symbolic Resistance in Nineteenth-Century France*. Ithaca: Cornell University Press, 1985.

Thackray, Richard I. "Boredom and Monotony as a Consequence of Automation: A Consideration of the Evidence Relating Boredom and Monotony to Stress." U.S. Department of Transportation, Federal Aviation Administration, Office of Aviation Administration, February 1980.

Theory, Culture, and Society: Special Issue on Georg Simmel, vol. 8, no. 3. London: Sage Publications, 1991.

Thompson, E. P. "Time, Work-Discipline, and Industrial Capitalism." *Past and Present* 38 (1967): 56–97.

Le Tresor de la Langue francaise: Dictionnaire de la Langue du XIX et du XXe Siècle. Paris: Centre Nationale de la Recherche Scientifique, 1979.

Tucker, Robert C., ed. *The Marx-Engels Reader*. 2d ed. New York: Norton, 1978.

Turnell, Martin. *Baudelaire: A Study of His Poetry*. New York: New Directions, 1972.

Unger, Roberto Mangabeira. *Passion: An Essay on Personality*. New York: Free Press, 1984.

Veblen, Thorstein. *The Theory of the Leisure Class*. New York: Mentor, 1953.

Veenhoven, Ruut, et al. *World Database of Happiness: Correlates of Happiness: 7838 Findings from 603 Studies in 69 Nations, 1991–1994*. Rotterdam, Netherlands: RISBO, Erasmus University, Rotterdam, 1994.

Venturelli, Aldo. *Robert Musil und das Projekt der Moderne*. Europäische Hochschulschriften. Reihe 1, Deutsche Sprache und Literatur 1039. Frankfurt am Main: Lang, 1988.

Vogt, Guntram. "Robert Musil: Politik als Methode: Zum Kontext von Kunst, Wissenschaft, Politik." In Josef Strutz, ed., *Kunst, Wissenschaft und Politik von Robert Musil bis Ingeborg Bachmann*. Musil-Studien 14. Munich: Wilhelm Fink, 1986.

Völker, Ludwig. *Langeweile: Untersuchungen zur Vorgeschichte eines literarischen Motivs*. Munich: Fink, 1975.

Wanch, Martin. "Boredom in Psychoanalytic Perspective." *Social Research* 42 (1975): 538–50.

Wagner-Egelhaaf, Martina. *Die melancholie der Literatur: Diskursgeschichte und Textfiguration*. Stuttgart: Metzler, 1997.

Watier, Patrick, ed. *Georg Simmel: La Sociologie et l'expérience du monde moderne*. Paris: Meridiens, 1986.

Watt, John, and Stephen Vodanovich. "Boredom Proneness and Psychosocial Growth." *Journal of Psychology* 133 (1999): 303–14.

Weber, Max. "Politik als Beruf." *Geistige Arbeit als Beruf 2*. Munich: Duncker und Humblot, 1919. (Trans. as "Politics as a Vocation," in H. H. Gerth and C. Wright Mills, *From Max Weber: Essays in Sociology*, 77–128 [New York: Oxford University Press, 1946].)

———. *Die Protestantische Ethik und der 'Geist' des Kapitalismus*. Ed. Johannes Winckelmann. Gütersloh: Gütersloher Verlagshaus Mohn, 1991–95.

———. "Wissenschaft als Beruf" [1919]. In Michael Sukale, ed., *Schriften zur Wissenschaftslehre*, 237–73. Stuttgart: Reklam, 1991. (Trans. as "Science as a Vocation," in H. H. Gerth and C. Wright Mills, *From Max Weber: Essays in Sociology*, 129–56 [New York: Oxford University Press, 1946].)

Wehler, Hans-Ulrich. *Modernisierungstheorie und Geschichte*. Göttingen: Vandenhoeck & Ruprecht, 1975.

———. *Deutsche Gesellschaftsgeschichte*, vol. II: *Von der Reform Ära bis zur industriellen und politischen 'Deutschen Doppelrevolution' 1815–1845/49*. Munich: Beck, 1989 [2d ed.].

———. *Die Herausforderung der Kulturgeschichte*. Munich: C. H. Beck, 1998.

Weinstein, Deena and Michael A. *PostModern(ized) Simmel*. London: Routledge, 1993.

Wenzel, Siegfried. *The Sin of Sloth: Acedia in Medieval Thought and Literature*. Chapel Hill: University of North Carolina Press, 1967.

White, Hayden. *Metahistory: The Historical Imagination in Nineteenth-Century Europe*. Baltimore: Johns Hopkins University Press, 1973.

———. *Tropics of Discourse*. Baltimore: Johns Hopkins University Press, 1978.

Williams, Raymond. *Culture and Society 1780–1950*. New York: Harper, 1958.

———. *Problems in Materialism and Culture*. London: Verso, 1980.

Williams, Roger L. *The Horror of Life*. Chicago: University of Chicago Press, 1980.

Williams, Rosalind H. *Dream Worlds: Mass Consumption in Late Nineteenth-Century France*. Berkeley: University of California Press, 1982.

Wilson, Elizabeth. *Adorned in Dreams: Fashion and Modernity*. London: Virago, 1985.

Wolff, Janet. *Feminine Sentences: Essays on Women and Culture*. Berkeley: University of California Press, 1990.

———. *Resident Alien: Feminist Cultural Criticism*. New Haven: Yale University Press, 1995.

Wolff, Kurt H., ed. *The Sociology of Georg Simmel*. Glencoe: Free Press, 1950.

Wolin, Richard, ed. *The Heidegger Controversy: A Critical Reader*. Rev. ed. Cambridge, Mass.: MIT, 1993.

———. *The Politics of Being: The Political Thought of Martin Heidegger*. New York: Columbia University Press, 1990.

Wordsworth, William. *Selected Poetry of William Wordsworth*. Ed. Mark van Doren. New York: Random House, 2002.

Young-Bruehl, Elisabeth. *Hannah Arendt: For Love of the World*. New Haven: Yale University Press, 1982.

Zimmerman, Michael E. *Heidegger's Confrontation with Modernity: Technology, Politics, and Art*. Bloomington: Indiana University Press, 1990.

Zingel, Astrid. *Ulrich und Agathe: Das Thema Geschwisterliebe in Robert Musils Romanprojekt 'Der Mann ohne Eigenschaften.'* St. Ingbert: Röhrig, 1999.

Žižek, Slavoj. *The Sublime Object of Ideology*. Trans. Jon Barnes. London: Verso, 1989.

Žmegač, Viktor, ed. *Geschichte der deutschen Literatur vom 18. Jahrhundert bis zur Gegenwart*. 3 vols. Königstein: Athenäum-Verlag, 1978.

Zola, Emile. *Joie de Vivre*. In Armand Lanoux and Henri Mitterand, eds., *Les Rougon-Macquart, histoire naturelle et sociale d'une famille sous le Second Empire*, vol. 3, 807–1130. Paris: Gallimard, 1970.

Index

In this index an "f" after a number indicates a separate reference on the next page, and an "ff" indicates separate references on the next two pages. A continuous discussion over two or more pages is indicated by a span of page numbers, e.g., "57–59."

Acedia, 4, 21, 33, 35–37, 39–40, 134, 155; in Baudelaire, 215, 233, 235–6, 238, 243; distinguished from boredom, 45, 64, 110, 398, 402–3; identified with boredom, 53, 99, 111, 113, 158, 410

Action-inhibition, 65, 79–80, 84–86, 88f, 92, 94, 131, 163

Adaptation(s) to modern life, 71–74, 176, 260, 264–65, 270–75, 278, 280, 346n, 409

Adorno, Theodor Wiesengrund, 156n, 257n, 269, 284–85, 294n, 398, 401n

Allen, James Smith, 170n, 180–81n

Anomie, 61–63, 68–78, 86–87, 97, 118, 278, 352, 408; in Durkheim, 62, 69–70, 72–73, 118; in Kuhn, 53, 55–56, 61–63, 66; in Lepenies, 66–69, 72, 73–78, 79, 84–86; normalization of, 61–63, 86, 97, 408. *See also* Anthropological view of subjective malaise

Anthropological view of subjective malaise, 28, 74–80, 84–85, 88, 93, 97, 329; and need to do something meaningful, 80, 85, 118, 131, 259, 405. *See also* Anomie; *Besoin de faire quelque chose*; Purpose(s); Purposelessness

Anthropology, 62, 252, 255, 263; philosophical, 90–92, 151n, 302. *See also* Philosophy of culture

Aquinas, St. Thomas, 36, 36n; *Summa Theologica*, 36

Arendt, Hannah, 89n, 299, 288, 289n

Aristocrats, aristocracy, 19, 81–83, 85, 92, 172n, 176, 350f, 354; aristocratic boredom, 68, 79, 81–85, 88–94, 95–96, 112, 174, 179. *See also* Boredom, and class; Bourgeoisie; Leisure

Aristotle, 9, 38–39, 91, 288, 306, 314n, 400; Aristotelianism, 53, 116, 220, 236–37; *Problems*, 38, 116. *See also* Melancholy

Art, 8–9, 49, 361; for art's sake, 171–74, 213, 219; Baudelaire's conception of, 219–23, 233, 236, 240, 242; Flaubert's conception of, 202, 205–6, 209–10, 213, 359. *See also* Literature

Aschheim, Steven, 263n

Auerbach, Erich, 48n, 205–7, 271n

Austria, 250, 341, 344–48, 353–54, 356, 358, 360, 384–85. *See also* Vienna

Barbey, D'Aurevilly, 157, 173n

Barrows, Susanne, 143n

Barthes, Roland, 1

Baudelaire, Charles, 6, 106–7, 120, 133n, 173, 213n, 214–46, 350ff; and boredom, 100, 128, 161, 171, 181, 183–84, 335–36, 360–61, 416–17; Flowers of Evil [*Fleurs*

45714080R00281

Made in the USA
Middletown, DE
19 May 2019